EARLY INTERACTIONS BETWI
SOUTH AND SOUTHEAST A:

Nalanda-Sriwijaya Series

General Editors: Tansen Sen and Geoff Wade

The Nalanda-Sriwijaya Series, established under the publications program of the Institute of Southeast Asian Studies, Singapore, has been created as a publications avenue for the Nalanda-Sriwijaya Centre. The Centre focusses on the ways in which Asian polities and societies have interacted over time. To this end, the series invites submissions which engage with Asian historical connectivities. Such works might examine political relations between states; the trading, financial and other networks which connected regions; cultural, linguistic and intellectual interactions between societies; or religious links across and between large parts of Asia.

1. *Nagapattinam to Suvarnadwipa: Reflections on the Chola Naval Expeditions to Southeast Asia*, edited by Hermann Kulke, K. Kesavapany and Vijay Sakhuja
2. *Early Interactions between South and Southeast Asia: Reflections on Cross-Cultural Exchange*, edited by Pierre-Yves Manguin, A. Mani and Geoff Wade

The **Institute of Southeast Asia Studies (ISEAS)** was established as an autonomous organisation in 1968. It is a regional centre dedicated to the study of socio-political, security and economic trends and developments in Southeast Asia and its wider geostrategic and economic environment. The Institute's research programmes are the Regional Economic Studies (RES, including ASEAN and APEC), Regional Strategic and Political Studies (RSPS), and Regional Social and Cultural Studies (RSCS).

ISEAS Publishing, an established academic press, has issued more than 2,000 books and journals. It is the largest scholarly publisher of research about Southeast Asia from within the region. ISEAS Publishing works with many other academic and trade publishers and distributors to disseminate important research and analyses from and about Southeast Asia to the rest of the world.

Early Interactions between South and Southeast Asia

Reflections on Cross-Cultural Exchange

Edited by

PIERRE-YVES MANGUIN
A. MANI
GEOFF WADE

INSTITUTE OF SOUTHEAST ASIAN STUDIES
Singapore

MANOHAR
India

First published in Singapore in 2011 by
ISEAS Publishing
Institute of Southeast Asian Studies
30 Heng Mui Keng Terrace
Pasir Panjang, Singapore 119614

Co-published for distribution in South Asia only by
Manohar Publishers & Distributors
4753/23 Ansari Road, Daryaganj,
New Delhi 110 002
India

Manohar ISBN 978-81-7304-895-1

ISEAS Library Cataloguing-in-Publication Data

Early interactions between South and Southeast Asia: reflections on cross-cultural exchange /
    Pierre-Yves Manguin, A. Mani and Geoff Wade
    Papers originally presented at a Conference on Early Indian Influences in Southeast Asia:
    Reflections on Cross-cultural Movements, 21-23 November 2007, organized by the
    Institute of Southeast Asian Studies, Singapore
    1.   Southeast Asia—Civilization—Indic influences—Congresses.
    2.   India—Relations— Southeast Asia—Congresses.
    3.   Southeast Asia—Relations—India—Congresses.
    I.   Manguin, Pierre-Yves.
    II.   Mani, A.
    III. Wade, Geoff
    IV.   Institute of Southeast Asian Studies.
    V.   Conference on Early Indian Influences in Southeast Asia: Reflections on
          Cross-Cultural Movements (2007: Singapore)
DS523.2 E13   2011

ISBN 978-981-4345-10-1 (soft cover)
ISBN 978-981-4311-16-8 (hard cover)
ISBN 978-981-4311-17-5 (e-book PDF)

Cover photo of Candi Senar and Candi Arjuna on the Dieng Plateau, Java,
courtesy of Julie Romain

Printed by Salasar Imaging Systems, Delhi 110 035, India.

Contents

Foreword

In late 2006, the National Library Board (NLB), in the person of Mrs Pushpa Latha Devi Naidu, approached ISEAS with a proposal for a 'Conference on Early Indian Influences in Southeast Asia'. The conference was to be held in conjunction with an exhibition that NLB was organising. Professors Mani and Ramasamy were asked to coordinate the conference with funding contributions from the NLB, Institute of South Asian Studies (ISAS), Asia Research Institute (ARI), and the Chola Mandalam Group in Tamil Nadu. ISEAS on its part provided the logistical support and coordination for the conference with additional funding support. It is important to note the help that Professors Hermann Kulke and Pierre-Yves Manguin, visiting scholars at ARI rendered to the conceptualisation of the conference. A total of 52 regional and international experts presented papers on various aspects of early Indian Influence in Southeast Asia at the three-day conference from 21 to 23 November 2007. The themes of the conference included 'naval expeditions of the Cholas', 'archaeological and inscriptional evidence of early Indian influence', 'ancient and medieval commercial activities' and 'regional cultures and localization'.

The papers are being published as two separate volumes under the auspices of the Nalanda-Sriwijaya Centre at ISEAS. Hermann Kulke, K. Kesavapany and Vijay Sakhuja edited the volume on *Nagapattinam to Suvarnadwipa: Reflections on the Chola Naval Expeditions to Southeast Asia*, while Pierre-Yves Manguin, A. Mani and Geoff Wade edited this volume on *Early Interactions between South and Southeast Asia: Reflections on Cross-Cultural Exchange*. The papers in both volumes present the reflections of scholars on this important historical period of Southeast Asia and its relations with South Asia.

I wish to thank all the co-sponsors of the project, namely the Directors of NLB, ISAS and ARI for their generous support. I also wish to thank Mr Subbiah of the Chola Mandalam Group in Tamil Nadu for the interest he showed by his active participation in the three-day conference. Finally I extend my appreciation to Professor Manguin, Professor Mani and Dr Wade for their editorial contributions in successfully completing the editing of this large volume.

K. Kesavapany
Director
Institute of Southeast Asian Studies
Singapore

Preface

This volume brings together twenty-three papers contributed by twenty-seven authors who have carried out research on the interactions between Southeast Asia and South Asia in the period between 500 BCE and CE 1500. Though there has been much debate on the nature of these interactions, the volume begins with an introduction to the question of whether Southeast Asia was 'Indianised' before 'Indianisation'. As recent archaeological findings have pushed back the period of 'Indianisation' prior to the Common Era, the introductory paper provides an overview to the rest of the volume.

Beyond the introductory chapter by Manguin, the remaining chapters of the volume are divided into two large sections. The ten papers in Part I relate to the new archaeological evidence from South Asia and Southeast Asia. The papers draw on archaeological evidence that has been unearthed on both sides of the Bay of Bengal in recent years. Part II, consisting of thirteen papers, addresses the issue of localisation of South Asian cultures in Southeast Asia.

While more research remains to be done in this area of interactions across the Bay of Bengal, we hope that this volume is able to bring together the ongoing research and reflections in this area of study. We extend our thanks for the cooperation of all the contributors to the volume and at the same time we wish to thank Ms. Betty Tan, who helped coordinate the correspondence with all the authors. Ms Kay Lyons created the excellent index.

PIERRE-YVES MANGUIN, A. MANI AND GEOFF WADE
Editors

Introduction

Pierre-Yves Manguin

Southeast Asia is today among the most exciting areas for research in historical archaeology.

HENRY T. WRIGHT (1998: 343)

The present book is the final product of a conference convened in Singapore in November 2007. The title given to this conference was 'Early Indian Influences in Southeast Asia', a concept with a 'well-established pedigree', which 'has rightly left an indelible mark on the field of Southeast Asian studies' (in the words of Daud Ali in his essay for the present volume). Organisers first sent invitations to a broad community, encouraging papers on the Chola expeditions to Southeast Asia. The many positive answers – too numerous for financial and practical reasons – were filtered down to accommodate some fifty participants, and their presentations were then divided into panels and plenary sessions. Presentations that were related to the Chola expeditions and their context were gathered into one panel, and subsequently published in a separate volume (*Nagapattinam to Suvarnadwipa: Reflections on the Chola Naval Expeditions to Southeast Asia*, edited by H. Kulke, K. Kesavapany and Vijay Sakhuja). The other, much larger group of papers was reorganised for publication in the present book, which is the result of a further selection, needed to reduce its size as well as to give it more coherence. As a broad rule, the editors retained only those papers which presented recent data and innovative or renewed approaches. Archaeology *lato sensu* ended up occupying a large proportion of the book. For reasons explained below, the discipline has thrived in the past years, and its place in this volume is a reflection of its present-day situation in Southeast Asian studies.

Chapters presenting and discussing relevant empirical data, mainly derived from recent excavation programmes in both South and Southeast Asia were regrouped in Part I of the book. Some papers on art and architecture, because they presented, rather than empirical data, more of an investigation into the processes at work for the transmission of Indian culture to Southeast Asia, were regrouped with textual studies and history of religions into Part II of this book.

This introduction is no place to discuss all the fine points of the long-standing, rich debate on the Indianisation of Southeast Asia. Others have done so more than once over the past century, from Bosch and Cœdès for the last truly orientalist generation, to Mus, Mabbett, de Casparis, and Wolters for the following generations of historians with a more open view of the dynamics of ancient Southeast Asian societies. More recently, Hermann Kulke and Sheldon Pollock have brought new light to the subject as, in spite of their different approaches, they share an invaluable experience acquired while researching cultures on both sides of the Bay of Bengal, all of them peripheral in regard of the sources of Indianity and Sanskritisation in northern India.[1]

'Indianisation' has never been a standardised paradigm; definitions have evolved with the passage of time and as the concept became entwined in multiple historicities, each one with its own different cultural background. The case of the historical narratives popularised by the scholars of the Greater India Society is one prominent example of such competing historicities. Their narratives were widely held in the 1930s, with all their underlying political claims; and such views keep re-emerging to this day in India, where we have, as elsewhere, a classical debate between histories and identities that remain nationally, or regionally focused and a truly trans-cultural, holistic historiography (as suggested in Selvakumar's essay and which the various chapters in this volume will no doubt reinforce).

Considering the fact that the initial study of the Indianisation process, for broad chronological reasons, fell within the realm of the first specialists of ancient Southeast Asia, most of them trained Indologists, the debate was for long kept in the hands of philologists (mostly epigraphers) and historians of art and architecture. Archaeologists dealing with the historical periods (many of them architects by training) restricted their endeavours to the study of monumental remains, most of them religious buildings, rarely venturing into urban or settlement excavations, and when doing so, paying little attention to those parts of the archaeological assemblages that would have taught them more mundane aspects of Southeast Asian societies. As inscriptions and stone or brick temples and associated statues only appeared in Southeast Asia after the first few centuries of the Common Era, the erudite quest of these scholars, therefore, left us with no information on the transition between what they perceived as simple, 'uncivilised' societies, best studied by prehistorians, and those 'Indianised', newly 'civilised' people who produced remains worthy of their attention. R.C. Majumdar, the most vocal promoter of the Greater India Society paradigm summed up these views in unambiguous terms: 'The Hindu colonists brought with them the whole framework of their culture and civilisation and this was transplanted in its entirety among the people who had not yet emerged from their primitive barbarism.'[2] As late as 1968, however, George Cœdès put it in gentler but unambiguous terms in the last edition of his otherwise remarkable synthesis of the achievements of the orientalist school: 'In most cases, we pass without transition from the late Neolithic to the first Indian remains (...). So we can say, without great exaggeration that the people of Further India were still in the middle of a late Neolithic civilisation when the Brahmano-Buddhist culture of India came into contact with them.'[3] With no transition, quiescent, passive societies entangled in a prehistoric morass would then have found themselves enlightened by the imposition of a great civilisation from overseas. This was of course a current paradigm of colonial times, when greater civilisations were said to be there to help lesser ones in their path to progress. The Greater India enlightenment paradigm and the corollary 'colonisation' of Southeast Asia, whether cultural or even military and migratory as then often claimed against all evidence, was largely a transposition into an imagined past of a contemporary state of affairs.

After the crucial papers by Harry Benda and John Smail – both published in the early 1960s – significantly, in the Singapore-based *Journal of Southeast Asian History* – two generations of historians, with a variety of approaches, have worked hard at 'decolonising' Southeast Asian history.[4] Scholars of various origins and schools have since then contributed to the production of an autonomous history for this region of the world that earlier on had carried such unpromising names as Further India, Greater India, East Indies, Indo-China or Indonesia before it became known as Southeast Asia. This shift in historiographic trends also affected those scholars interested in the period during which the first complex polities of our region appeared on the world scene, producing a generation of 'autonomist' historians and archaeologists. A variety of rationalisations were produced in between the two opposite trends, the Orientalist tradition (best illustrated in Georges Cœdès' seminal work), and the 'indigenists' with a more anthropological approach (the 'sociologists', as they were still termed by Cœdès and his peers until the 1960s).[5]

Art historians and epigraphers did succeed in reappraising and redefining the process of Indianisation to better fit the new paradigms and allow more room for Southeast Asian agency in the process. However, the scarcity of additional iconographic or written source material, the all too frequent uncoupling between this material and the original archaeological sites, and the mere fact that such data did not appear in Southeast Asia before the third or fourth century CE, made it difficult for these scholars to build up a radically new paradigm.

Social scientists who wanted to reappraise those centuries during which Southeast Asian societies entered the world economic scene were thus confronted with a millennium-long historiographic no-man's land. On the one hand, Southeast Asian societies that thrived between the fifth century BCE and the fifth century CE were for long treated, at best, as prehistoric communities that were increasingly complex, but remained cut off from economic transformations and developments in world economy happening elsewhere in Asia. On the other hand, we had the far more sophisticated polities who had adopted and adapted – or 'localised' to use Oliver Wolters' handy concept[6] – a set of cultural values imported from India: political and religious ideologies, a broad spectrum of architectural and iconographic agendas, together with a distinguished language, Sanskrit, and scripts soon adapted to transcribe their own languages. In the still currently accepted meaning of the term, these Southeast Asian polities, starting around the third or fourth century CE, had then become 'Indianised'. In the absence of written sources and monuments, philology and art history were unable to fill in the gap between these two opposed phases of Southeast Asian history. Much of the research carried out in the past few decades, however, as shown in the chapters of Part I of this book, has been focused on this historiographic gap, which for convenience sake most historians now designate as the proto-history of Southeast Asia. It is now perceived as a millennium-long phase of exchange between the two shores of the Bay of Bengal leading, among other processes, to the Indianisation of those parts of the region that straddled the main routes of exchange between the Indian Ocean and the South China Sea.

WAS SOUTHEAST ASIA INDIANISED
BEFORE INDIANISATION?

The bridging of this gap is very much the result of archaeological research. In Southeast Asia like in other parts of the world, modern archaeological techniques, with controlled, stratigraphic excavations, were by and large developed by prehistorians and for prehistorians. For periods when written sources were available, archaeological excavations were for long considered superfluous, or redundant, and excavation techniques remained crude. With few exceptions (Mortimer Wheeler's pioneering work in India should be mentioned here), only religious monuments were explored, cleared and eventually restored, their statues sent to museums, and their inscriptions to epigraphers. In other areas of the world where written sources were available, historical archaeology has similarly come of age only recently, with excavations now used on a par with textual studies, and no longer as a mere producer of data and illustrations for the historians, in terms of temples, statues, and inscriptions. The recent, troubled history of much of Southeast Asia only allowed the deployment of large-scale, systematic fieldwork and the adoption of new methodologies after the 1980s (some areas in the region remain, even today, out of reach for archaeologists). Despite this relatively late start, recent archaeological research in the transition period that leads from late prehistory to early history, with its resolutely inter-disciplinary approach, is inducing a significant heuristic revolution in the assessment of the history of Early Southeast Asia.[7] It has also created a renewed knowledge basis for this fertile proto-historic period upon which we can reassess the trans-cultural, mutual processes that took place within complex sets of networks, in terms of chronology, of directionality, of quality and of intensity, within what Sunil Gupta rightly names the 'Bay of Bengal Interaction Sphere'.[8]

Ian Glover, following his excavation in the 1980s on the late prehistoric site of Ban Don Ta Phet, in West Central Thailand, pioneered this new line of enquiry. The results obtained by the excavators were the first to reveal early contacts with India, much earlier than the Indianisation period as it was then still envisioned. Ian Glover drew out the first conclusions from these finds in his programmatic booklet *Early Trade between India and Southeast Asia: A Link in the Development of a World Trading System* in 1989. The archaeology of proto-historical and early historical sites in Southeast Asia has, since then, flourished, finally bringing to light sites that provide a more comprehensive view of the societies under study during the crucial, formative millennium (approximately fifth century BCE to fifth century CE). New sets of data gathered from older burial sites and from early urban or proto-urban settlements allowed archaeologists to scrutinize ancient Southeast Asian societies not only through the limited prisms of their religious or political activities, and through the monumental buildings these produced, but also through their more mundane conducts: daily life, settlement patterns, and economic activities (production and exchange). The western façade of Southeast Asia being situated at the crossroads between the two massive economic blocs of India and China, exchange and organised trade have by necessity been major components of local economies. Much has been written since then on the role of trade in the development of complex polities in early Southeast Asia.[9] Recent archaeological excavation programmes have devoted much research to artefacts that suggest long distance exchange of goods, to the technologies used to produce them and, as a corollary, to the agency of artisans proficient in such techniques.

Contributions published in this book (by Lam Thi My Dzung, Glover with

Bellina, Bouvet, Boonyarit Chaisuwan, and Manguin with Agustijanto) offer much detail on some relevant archaeological sites and artefacts from Thailand, Vietnam or Indonesia, starting roughly in the fifth or fourth centuries BCE. Other contributions reveal new sites or reconsider sites and exchange patterns based on excavations and surveys carried out in India (Rajan, Selvakumar, and Sundaresh with Gaur); the first two take into consideration technological influences in the ceramic or shipbuilding domains that would have travelled East to West – a novel approach in Indian archaeology. Research work carried out in the field of nautical archaeology in Southeast Asia, referred to by Selvakumar, did not find its way into this book for lack of space. The prominence of Southeast Asian shipbuilding techniques (as documented in local sites and now growingly in India and in the Maldives, as well as in the early spread of Austronesian nautical vocabulary in many Indian Ocean languages) and the large size of first millennium CE seagoing ships built in Southeast Asia (as revealed by recent archaeological finds), also raise the question of the identity of the agents of maritime exchange and trade across the Bay of Bengal. Whatever the role of Indian ships and shippers (not confirmed as yet by nautical archaeology), it is by now clear that their Southeast Asian counterparts must have also held an outstanding position during this formative period.[10]

Other proto-historic sites recently excavated in Southeast Asia have not been presented in the chapters of this book. Research at those sites does, however, confirm or qualify the arguments developed in these pages. The pioneering work on the Northern Bali coastal sites of Pacung and Sembiran should be mentioned here, as this was the first to reveal exchange with India in the form of ceramics found during systematic excavations of local burials. It is also the site situated furthest East, along the maritime route leading to Eastern Indonesia and its spices and aromatic woods, thus confirming the role of trade in the dispersal of Indian material culture.[11] Funan sites (referred to by Lê Thi Liên and Anna Ślączka in this book only for their Hindu imagery and consecration rituals) have also been thoroughly investigated in recent years, in both Cambodia (Angkor Borei) and Vietnam (Oc Eo).[12] Angkor Borei shows signs of early occupation by a complex society before developing, early in the first millennium CE, into a large urban, Indianised site, possibly a capital of Funan. Oc Eo appears to have been occupied only at the turn of the first millennium; the people there not only soon adopted some Indian material culture for daily use (new pottery styles, tiles), they also almost immediately (second-third century CE) show clear signs of having developed what must have been a pioneering urban pattern, no doubt after contact with India and its culture. Other recently discovered third-fourth century CE coastal sites in South Sumatra, downstream from Palembang where the capital of Srivijaya was to be founded three centuries later, appear to have been in contact with other similar sites of Southeast Asia, and to present distinct proto-urban patterns.[13]

All such Southeast Asian proto-historic sites, as revealed by the arch-aeological work carried out in the past years, therefore show signs of having been occupied by societies of growing complexity in terms of indigenous settlement patterns and practising distinctly local burial rituals (of the kind observed in much of Southeast Asia). All such sites, however, also bring proof that, in their earlier phases, exchange and possibly trade networks linked, directly or indirectly, most of these people together, and with peoples further north in the South China Sea and further West in the Indian Ocean. Sites such as Khao Sam Kaeo and Phu Khao Thong (in Peninsular Thailand) turned out to be importing from India and locally producing, in remarkable quantities, glass and precious stone beads as early as the fourth century BCE, no doubt for growing Southeast Asian markets.[14] Textiles and both imported Indian or locally produced 'Indianised' pottery bring to light the role of artisans and of technological transfers from India to Southeast Asia.[15]

These pioneering contributions on artefacts that are considered as 'markers' of exchange activities point up the need for more studies on the dissemination of technical knowledge. We should not limit ourselves to the study of the transmission of intangible concepts and cultural behaviours. It will take a few more years for all this ongoing work to produce enough results and bring analyses to fruition. What is at stake here is not only the material aspects of this artefact production (their study, however, provides the foundations for further interpretations): the social environment of the voyaging objects also needs to be considered, and the hesitant relationship between the inherited and the assigned meaning of objects, their reinterpretations according to local systems of values, and the subsequent creating of new meanings in a new economic and social context. This also introduces into the historical scene the creators of these objects, the artisans. They constitute a social group whose share in the Indianisation process has been much neglected, since older narratives only considered the Indian trilogy of Brahmins, warriors, and the merchant class. Artisans now appear prominently in recent archaeological discourse on protohistoric sites, and we can no longer neglect their agency.[16]

It is, therefore, only after centuries of intense contact that peoples active at such sites became progressively 'Indianised', as conceived within the earlier Indianisation paradigm. They did this in diverse ways, following different chronologies, depending on geographical situation, on the relative importance of growing political systems, and on the intensity of their involvement in trading networks.

On the basis of the chapters grouped in the first part of this book (and of comparable articles published elsewhere), it is necessary to conclude that by the time Indian-inspired temples, statues and epigraphy appeared in Southeast

Asia, sometime between the third and the fifth century CE, the relationship between Southeast Asian and Indian societies had already come a very long way. We are now far removed from the tenets of the Greater India Society and the imagined vision of a sudden imposition of Indian culture, as a *deus ex machina*. In other words, one is entitled to raise the question as to whether Southeast Asia was Indianised before 'Indianisation?'

It all depends of course on what is meant by 'Indianisation'. Some will prefer to use this term in its literal sense, now including both phases of the process under the same designation. Others, as I personally do, if only for convenience sake, will prefer to keep employing the term 'Indianisation' for the second phase of cultural exchange between South and Southeast Asia, as used until now: that is, to denote the profound socio-political modifications brought about by the adoption, at least by the ruling elites, of state concepts, broad based, universalist religions and their props (temples and statues), and writing in Sanskrit (the language of power, as demonstrated by Pollock).[17] The preceding period, would then only be considered as a contact and exchange phase with South Asia, allowing for a variety of comparable but variable processes to be seen at play, depending on the place or the social background of the agents, as well as other factors, before a clear acceleration of cross-cultural exchange brings about a remarkable uniformity into the process, between the fourth-fifth and the seventh-eighth centuries CE.

DRIFT, EXCHANGE OR TRADE?

Proponents of the trade-generated model of state formation in littoral Southeast Asia have always been keen on identifying trade networks and trade goods linking China or India to Southeast Asia, and the agents at work in such commercial processes. For many years, after work by historians such as Oliver Wolters (1967) and Jan Wisseman Christie (1990, 1992, 1995) and that of the archaeologist Ian Glover (1989) one has been aware that there was a distinct possibility that exchange between the shores of the Bay of Bengal and the South China Sea was one crucial component of the process of state generation for late prehistoric to early historical times.[18] One may disagree with Glover's views of the early developments of global, 'world' economies but he did nevertheless raise the question we are now squarely confronted with, which is the scope of long-distance exchange in those littoral societies that were then growing in complexity.[19] As made obvious in the chapters of this book, we may eliminate the possibility of a simple 'drift' to Southeast Asia of rare goods, resulting from occasional overseas contacts. The technological transfers and movement of artisans in the glass and stone bead industry – to take the best-documented example from late prehistory – can only be explained in broader economic terms: only the emergence in

Southeast Asia of new markets for such artefacts can explain the systematic appearance in archaeological context of evidence for early mass production. Data on other identified items of material culture is far more questionable, at least in economic terms. Research on exchange of ceramic technologies and productions between the two sides of the Bay of Bengal is still in progress and it may be too soon to draw conclusions (see, in this volume, Phaedra Bouvet's essay on Indian wares in Southeast Asia and remarks in Rajan's and Selvakumar's essays about possible technological transfers of ceramic decoration from Southeast Asia to India). The term 'trade' is often used to qualify the circulation of Indian ceramic wares in the Indian Ocean, as evidenced by their usage in Southeast Asian proto-historic sites. However, one may argue that the very small amount of 'rouletted wares' brought to light in such sites cannot offer proof of systematic, organised exchange that would qualify as trade (less common Indian ceramic wares often appear as a single shard on a given site): all in all, this best-known family of wares, frequently used as a marker for such exchange patterns by archaeologists since it was first noticed in the 1960s, must have produced in all Southeast Asian sites, for some four centuries of exchange activities, enough whole dishes to set tables for only five dozen people, hardly a major 'trade' item.[20]

This remark provides a good illustration of the difficulties encountered when using the small amount of data presently available to historians, and the resulting ambiguities in the usage of terms such as 'trade' or 'exchange' to explain the circulation of sets of material culture. The fact that we have no data at all on prices of such goods in Southeast Asian harbours during proto-historic times does not facilitate sound reasoning on such matters. The figures quoted above do show that, if Indian ceramic wares had any strictly economic value, it could only have been within a 'prestige goods' paradigm, a somehow overworked concept. The exchange of such ceramic wares could hardly have generated enough economic surpluses, in a nascent market economy, to be seriously taken into account. Other artefacts such as high tin content bronze bowls would fare even worse in such accounts. On the other hand, gold, tin, textiles and spices are goods that may be assumed to have been traded in much larger, or more valuable quantities and thus to have driven exchanges between South and Southeast Asia. This, however, is inferred on the basis of textual sources exceedingly poor on economic data (only isolated archaeological data are available on textiles or spices, some as yet unverified). Spices, textiles and gold are artefacts extremely difficult to document in archaeological contexts: precious metals were immediately melted; while organic materials only survived over centuries by accident. Tin, one major production of Southeast Asia in later times, may well have been exported in our period: it is not, however, documented in archaeological sites as a trade good (only in alloys of manufactured objects). These trade goods are, therefore, either conspicuously absent from all relevant archaeological sites or preserved there in such small quantities that one can only speculate about their economic value. Such inescapable gaps leave little room for sound analysis by economic historians.

Archaeology, until recently, had not been too good at producing evidence on the agents of the exchanges that accompanied the developments witnessed in Indian and Southeast Asian sites. Artisans, as we have seen, have become one significant element in the equation; in the early historical period of Southeast Asian history, we have proof that religious networks, Buddhist or Vaishnavite, were also active factors of change, through the agency of merchants, adventurers or itinerant religious entrepreneurs.[21] When, in the 680s, the South Sumatran inscriptions written in Malay produce a first vernacular representation of the newly-founded Srivijaya polity, merchants and shipmasters figure among the props of the polity: the former carry a Sanskrit name (*vanyaga*), the latter a Malay name (*puhawang*).[22] This would seem to indicate a sharing of roles: to the Indians the itinerant merchant role, to the Malays the agency for ship ownership and entrepreneurship (the latter would receive confirmation from the fact that large, locally-built ships have been found in Southeast Asian waters). This is one flimsy indication of an exchange organisation, with specialised agents, hence of the existence of institutionalised trade.

The question of the impact of trade and trade-related economic development on South and Southeast Asian societies may be tackled from another angle. If comparisons are made with India in the few centuries preceding the Common Era, we have so far no evidence in Southeast Asia for a hierarchy of settlements crowned with urban centres that should normally be associated with organised trade networks (in other words, we have no comparable developments to those taking place at the same time in India).[23] Is this because we have not yet found these early urban sites? There are so far only flimsy indications of proto-urban settlements in the Thai-Malay peninsula or in South Sumatra, as noted above. This does not mean that others are not there waiting to be brought to light by archaeologists. After all, it is only in recent times that later, much larger and more conspicuous urban settlements like the Srivijaya capital at Palembang or the Funan cities of Oc Eo, Go Thap or Angkor Borei have been clearly revealed by archaeologists.

CULTURAL ASYMMETRIES?

One more necessary question regarding the relationship between India and Southeast Asia in the period under consideration needs to be raised in this introduction. I have alluded to the shifts in historiographic trends during the past decades among historians of Southeast Asia, between the Indo-centric and the autonomist or 'indigenist' traditions. The latter group always felt uncomfortable with the obvious – not to say inescapable – asymmetry of overall exchanges between India and Southeast Asia. Historians who were educated during the coming of age of what is now a Southeast Asian identity (among which I count myself), worked as Southeast-Asianists within the tenets set up by 'indigenists', and were always confronted with this previously over-emphasised and potentially threatening asymmetry. However, trying to leave aside the historical circumstances in which this generation carried out research in and on Southeast Asia, it is useful to consider that such cultural asymmetries are more than common in world history and have more than once resulted in controversial narratives. Asymmetrical exchange of ideas and of goods between Mediterranean Europe and Western Asia accompanied profound socio-cultural transformations, linked to patterns of interaction between societies during the Greek, the Roman and the Byzantine periods. Historians of Southeast Asia should keep in mind the fact that increasingly complex societies in the Atlantic façade and the north of Europe, contemporary to those of Southeast Asia's proto-history, were then undergoing comparable transformations, and adapting to a modernity introduced from distant Mediterranean shores (admittedly under military pressure, which is not obviously the case in Southeast Asia). It is no surprise then to be witness to the adoption in Southeast Asia of a broad set of cultural traits, comprising religious and administrative practices, monumental buildings and art forms, and even new forms of finer tableware. After all, no historian – as far as I know – has ever contested the asymmetry of the process when Chinese stoneware and porcelain, in the early ninth century CE, ruthlessly and forever eliminated a whole variety of local pottery forms previously in daily usage in the urban sites of the Southeast Asian region, no doubt a change in production patterns that permanently affected Southeast Asian village level economies.

In the field of material culture, new research, as mentioned above, has given some scope to Southeast Asian contributions, as in nautical or ceramic technologies. When immaterial exchange is considered, useful concepts such as 'lasting relationship' (de Casparis), 'localisation' (Wolters), or even Goethe's 'elective affinities' (Kulke), to name only a few, have been called upon over the years to tone down the earlier paradigms. Southeast Asian societies have regained in the process an entrepreneurial role in the adoption and adaptation of Indian concepts and constructions to pre-existing social and economic patterns, from scripts and learned languages to literary genres and motifs, from religious texts and discourses to associated art and architectural forms, and to state and urbanisation models.

The recent publication of Indologist Sheldon Pollock's *magnum opus* on Sanskrit, culture, and power in pre-modern India (2006) has prompted three authors to reflect on some of his arguments in this book, which allows itself extensive forays into Indianised cultures of Southeast Asia and argues for strong continuities in the cultural and social development of South and Southeast Asia. Johannes Bronkhorst and Daud Ali question the relevance of some of Pollock's analyses and confront them with Southeast Asian inscriptional sources. Julie Romain, for her part, writes about one aspect of Pollock's 'Sanskrit cosmopolis' that was neglected in his book, bringing to the fore plausible connections between the spread of Indian literary texts and the architectural culture in Java.

Recent researches in the history of religions, based on a much improved knowledge of texts, contest the often assumed mono-directionality of cultural movement: Peter Skilling, in this volume, raises 'the possibility of cross-cultural and trans-regional exchange, of dialogue, or of interaction' and complains that Buddhist studies in Southeast Asia lag behind, remaining under the shadow of outdated theories of 'Indianisation', when 'early categories in the field of Indian (as well as Tibetan and East Asian) Buddhism have since been, refined, revised, or rejected'.

Most of the papers in the second part of this book deal, in one way or another, with the 'localising' process, in a variety of domains. In the light of progress in South and Southeast Asian field and textual studies, art historians re-consider analyses advanced by previous generations, to modify and improve them (Robert Brown, Julie Romain), and always to better understand the borrowing processes at work and the usage that was locally made of the newly adopted intellectual and artistic constructs. By making use of computer-driven methodologies, Martin Polkinghorne, after confirming earlier, structural approaches, shows how his fine-grained analysis brings to the fore individual artists and discrete workshops. Two other papers in the second part of this volume (by Le Thi Lien and Anna Ślączka) have in common the approach confronting Southeast Asian archaeological data and Indian texts, whether these describe religious pantheons or temple consecration rituals: they show the difficulties encountered when bridging the divide between (Indian) texts and (Southeast Asian) terrain, between canon and practice.

One single essay by Kyaw Minn Htin presents us with new inscriptional data from the neglected Buddhist surroundings of Arakan in Myanmar. Had the Singapore conference been convened a couple of years later, epigraphy, now also thriving anew in Southeast Asian studies, would no doubt have been better represented in this volume.

Some societies of the western façade of Southeast Asia underwent major transformations at the turn of the second millennium, driven by the growing impact of Tamil merchants of Chola times. Edwards McKinnon, Daniel Perret with Heddy Surachman, and John Guy, in papers bridging the first and second parts of this book, consider changes in trade patterns, the building of the only true (if short-lived) pre-modern Indian settlements in Southeast Asia, and interactions, in North Sumatra, with societies that had not been Indianised in earlier phases of exchange with South Asia.

To complete this impressionistic overview of 'Indian influences in Southeast Asia', one author ventures into the rarely-visited field of musicology (Arsenio Nicolas). Anthropologist Boreth Ly follows the process into the second millennium, showing how a recent globalism shapes notions of ritual authority among itinerant Tamil Nadu 'Brahmins', whose practices legitimate the political scene of modern nations, even when this is done under the guise of an Angkorian ancestry. In the same vein, Sachchidanand Sahai demonstrates how, on the basis of the classic Indian *Ramayana*, Laotian writers, story-tellers and painters use the legend to produce their own social space, and express the cultural ethos of Buddhist communities along the Mekong, even after the fall of the monarchy and the installation of a Communist regime.

* * *

This book does not provide, by far, a full review of progress made in the past decades, or of all pending questions regarding early cultural exchange between South and Southeast Asia. Because of the initial unfocused scope of the conference, the choice of papers kept for final publication remains, by force, impressionist. Any expectations on exhaustivity regarding the Sisyphean task of reappraising the Indianisation of Southeast Asia would have anyway been downright unrealistic. The editors' more modest ambition was to take stock of the results of two to three decades of intensive archaeological research in the region carried out in parallel, or in combination with renewed approaches of textual sources and of art history.

Almost twenty years after Ian Glover raised the question of the linkage – therefore of the relevance – of Southeast Asian exchange patterns into a world economy, it appears that considerable progress has been made. However, do we have enough data to confirm that the overall economic activities in which India was involved were substantial enough to generate significant surpluses (in strictly economic terms), to help generate state formation and urbanisation in Southeast Asia? Can we now better measure the relative impact of exchange of material goods or intangible concepts on Southeast Asian societies of protohistoric and early-historic times? We have a better comprehension today of the agents of these processes; but can we precisely define the relative share of Southeast Asian and Indian participants in this newly redefined long-term process? The answers to such questions, unfortunately, remain elusive. In the absence of indigenous written sources for most of this period, archaeological excavation programmes bear most of the burden. There will always be too few of these considering the immensity of the task at hand; and field archaeology, moreover, despite remarkable methodological progress, is far from being able to answer all pending questions. In the face of such difficulties, many hypotheses will therefore remain within the realm of speculation.

More than anything else, the present volume shows that to improve our understanding of the trans-cultural process referred to as Indianisation, we need to get specialists of both India and Southeast Asia to work together, to confront in an inter-disciplinary state of mind the experience acquired in each other's field of study, the methodologies, and the models. In other words, there is a need for a truly trans-cultural historiography. To conclude this Introduction, and to make this point even more obvious, let me harness the help of two prominent authors who have made similar remarks in very recent times. Sheldon Pollock justly remarked (2006: 16): '… in the first millennium, it makes hardly more sense to distinguish between South and Southeast Asia than between north India and south India. (…) Everywhere similar processes of cosmopolitan transculturation were under way, with the source and target of change always shifting, since there was no single point of production for cosmopolitan culture.' Hiram Woodward (2007), when discussing esoteric Buddhism as practiced in Sumatra and Java, and its possible influence upon subsequent developments in India, thought 'a good argument can be made for treating Indonesia and India as an integral unit well into the ninth century'.

NOTES

1. Bosch 1961; Cœdès 1968, chap. II *sq.*; Mus 1975; Mabbett 1977; Casparis 1983; Wolters 1999; Kulke 1990; Pollock 1996, 2006. These references are only the more prominent in a long list of works dealing with Indianisation in a way or another, by the same authors or by a large array of other scholars. Possibly the best summary of Southeast Asian historiography will be found in John Legge's introduction to the first volume of the *Cambridge History of Southeast Asia* (Legge 1992).
2. Majumdar 1941.
3. Cœdès 1968: 7-8. Cœdès' views on the Indianisation process were in essence left unchanged after the 1948 edition of his *Etats hindouisés d'Indochine et d'Indonésie* (the first edition was published in 1944 under a different title). The 1968 English edition, the last one to appear, is a very slightly revised translation of the last French edition (1964), approved by the author.
4. Smail 1961, Benda 1962.
5. On this debate between Orientalists and 'sociologists', which started in the 1930s within the Ecole française d'Extrême-Orient (EFEO), see Manguin 2006. See also the article by the anthropologist Bernard Formoso (2006), for an analysis of conflicting approaches in the Western perceptions of Southeast Asia.
6. Wolters 1999 (1st edn. 1982), where he discusses at length his 'localisation' concept.
7. A first attempt by archaeologists Peter Bellwood and Ian Glover at producing a textbook encompassing this crucial period (*Southeast Asia: From Prehistory to*

History) came only in 2004 (Bellwood and Glover 2004). On the new approaches in historical archaeology, as practised in Southeast Asia, see also Stark and Allen 1998, Stark 1998, Wright 1998 and the other papers collected by these editors in the same issue of the *International Journal of Historical Archaeology*.

8. Gupta 2005.
9. See among many other studies Christie 1990, 1992, 1995, Manguin 1991, 2004.
10. Manguin 1996.
11. Ardika 2003; Ardika and Bellwood 1991, 1993.
12. Stark 1998, 2004; Stark and Bong Sovath 2001; Bourdonneau 2003; Manguin and Vo Si Khai 2000; Manguin 2004: 289-93, 2009.
13. Soeroso 1998, Tri Marhaeni 2002, Manguin 2004: 286-87.
14. See the chapters by Boonyarit Chaisuwan and Glover with Bellina in this book, and, in more detail, some of their recent contributions published elsewhere: Boonyarit Chaisuwan and Rarai Naiyawat 2009, Bellina-Pryce and Praon Silapanth 2006; see also Pryce, Bellina-Pryce and Bennett 2006, Lankton, Dussubieux and Gratuze 2006.
15. On Indian and 'Indianised' pottery, see Bouvet 2006, her chapter in this book, and the chapter by Manguin and Agustijanto, also in this book. On textiles, see Judith Cameron (2007).
16. Bérénice Bellina's pioneering dissertation on stone ornaments found in archaeological sites on both sides of the Bay of Bengal and on related technological transfers led her to significant conclusions on the role of artisans in the transmission of Indian culture to Southeast Asia (Bellina 2006).
17. One should also take into consideration the analogy with a later process of major cross-cultural exchange in Southeast Asia: 'Islamisation' of parts of Southeast Asia became effective, starting in the thirteenth century, only after centuries of post-Hijrah (and earlier) exchange with the Middle East.
18. See also Manguin 1991 for a study of the relationship between trade and political power in the myths of Southeast Asian coastal polities.
19. 'World history' is an active – and much discussed – school of thought (publishing mainly in the *Journal of World History*). Among other considerations, it reflects on the early, pre-modern 'globalisation' of economies. The results of the past years of archaeological work on proto-historic Southeast Asia is only now finding its way into publications of 'world historians': see, for instance, Beaujard 2006; and Beaujard, Berger and Norel 2009. Lockard attempts to link early Southeast Asia to world systems, but still bases his study on outdated paradigms about Indianisation (Lockard 2007, 2009). For an earlier, distanced reflection on 'world history' and the study of Asian economies, see Zurndorfer 1998.
20. Less than 3,000 shards (as counted in 2007), hence some 60 dishes only, counting fine and coarse 'rouletted' wares together; far less still if only fine paste, true 'rouletted' wares are taken into consideration. As a basis for comparison, the same number of shards of Chinese export wares, bridging four centuries of Srivijaya trade, were found in one single sector in Palembang, in only one month of excavations by the present author.
21. On Buddhism and trade, see the major work by Himanshu Ray (1989); on the role of Vaishnava networks, see Dalsheimer and Manguin 1998.
22. One thorough analysis of political representations in Malay inscriptions is that of Kulke 1993. On a recent, critical view of Kulke's and others' hermeneutic approach, see Zakharov 2007, 2009. On the role of the 'overseas' merchants, see Manguin 1991.

23. On the relationship between urban development in India and trade patterns, see Ray 1997.

REFERENCES

Ardika, I. Wayan, 2003, 'Archaeological Excavations at Pacung, Northeastern Bali, Indonesia', in Anna Karlström and Anna Källén (eds.), *Fishbones and Glittering Emblems: Southeast Asia Archaeology 2002*. Stockholm: Museum of Far Eastern Antiquities, pp. 207-11.

Ardika, I. Wayan and Peter Bellwood, 1991, 'Sembiran: The beginnings of Indian Contact with Bali', *Antiquity*, 65, pp. 221-32.

Ardika, I. Wayan, Peter Bellwood, I. Made Sutaba et al., 1993, 'Sembiran and the First Indian Contacts with Bali: An Update', *Antiquity*, 71, pp. 193-95.

Beaujard, Philippe, 2005, 'The Indian Ocean in Eurasian and African World-Systems before the Sixteenth Century', *Journal of World History*, 16(4), pp. 411-65.

Beaujard, Philippe, Laurent Berger and Philippe Norel (eds.), 2009, *Histoire globale, mondialisations et capitalisme*. Paris: La Découverte.

Bellina, Bérénice, 2006, *Cultural Exchange between India and Southeast Asia: Production and Distribution of Hard Stone Ornaments (VI c BC-VI c AD) / Echanges culturels entre l'Inde et l'Asie du Sud-Est: Production et distribution des parures en roches dures du VIe siècle avant notre ère au VIe siècle de notre ère*. Paris: Editions de la Maison des Sciences de l'Homme / Editions Epistèmes.

Bellina-Pryce, Bérénice and Praon Silapanth, 2006, 'Weaving Cultural Identities on Trans-Asiatic Networks: Upper Thai-Malay Peninsula – An Early Socio-Political Landscape', *Bulletin de l'Ecole française d'Extrême-Orient*, 93, pp. 257-93.

Bellwood, Peter and Ian C. Glover (eds.), 2004, *Southeast Asia: From Prehistory to History*. London: RoutledgeCurzon.

Benda, Harry J., 1962, 'The Structure of Southeast Asian History: Some Preliminary Observations', *Journal of Southeast Asian History*, 3(1), pp. 103-38.

Boonyarit, Chaisuwan and Rarai, Naiyawat, 2009, *Thung Tuk: A Settlement Linking together the Maritime Silk Road*. Songkhla: Trio Creation.

Bosch, Frederik D.K., 1961, 'The Problem of Hindu Colonisation of Indonesia (Inaugural address delivered at the University of Leiden on March 15th, 1946)', in *Selected Studies in Indonesian Archaeology*. The Hague: Martinus Nijhoff, pp. 23-46.

Bourdonneau, Eric, 2003, 'The Ancient Canal System of the Mekong Delta – Preliminary Report', in Anna Karlström and Anna Källén (eds.), *Fishbones and Glittering Emblems: Southeast Asia Archaeology 2002*. Stockholm: Museum of Far Eastern Antiquities, pp. 257-70.

Bouvet, Phaedra, 2006, 'Étude préliminaire de céramiques indiennes et "indianisantes" du site de Khao Sam Kaeo IVe-IIe siècles av. J.-C.', *Bulletin de l'Ecole française d'Extrême-Orient*, 93, pp. 353-93.

Cameron, Judith, 2007, 'New Research into Dongson Cloth from Waterlogged Sites in Vietnam', in Elizabeth Bacus and Ian C. Glover (eds.), *Uncovering Southeast Asia's Past: Selected Papers from the Tenth Biennial Conference of the European Association of Southeast Asian Archaeologists*. Singapore: NUS Press, pp. 196-203.

Casparis, Johannes G. de, 1983, *India and Maritime South East Asia: A Lasting Relationship*. Kuala Lumpur, University of Malaya [Third Sri Lanka Endowment Fund Lecture].

Cœdès, George, 1964, *Les Etats hindouisés d'Indochine et d'Indonésie*. Paris: de Boccard.

————, 1968, *The Indianized States of Southeast Asia* (ed. W.F. Wella, tran. S.B. Cowing). Kuala Lumpur/Honolulu: University of Malaya Press / University of Hawaii Press.

Christie, Jan Wisseman, 1990, 'Trade and State Formation in the Malay Peninsula and Sumatra, 300 BC – AD 700', in J. Kathirithamby-Wells and John Villiers (eds.), *The Southeast Asian Port and Polity: Rise and Demise*. Singapore: Singapore University Press, pp. 39-60.

————, 1992, 'Trade and Settlement in Early Java: Integrating the Epigraphic and Archaeological Data', in Ian C. Glover, Pornchai Suchitta and John Villiers (eds.), *Early Metallurgy, Trade and Urban Centres in Thailand and Southeast Asia*. Bangkok: White Lotus, pp. 181-97.

————, 1995, 'State Formation in Early Maritime Southeast Asia: A Consideration of the Theories and the Data', *Bijdragen van het Koninklijk Instituut voor Taal-, Land- en Volkenkunde*, 151(2), pp. 235-88.

Dalsheimer, Nadine and Manguin, Pierre-Yves, 1998, 'Visnu mitrés et réseaux marchands en Asie du Sud-Est: nouvelle données archéologiques sur le Ier millénaire apr. J.C.', *Bulletin de l'Ecole française d'Extrême-Orient*, 85, pp. 87-123.

Formoso, Bernard, 2006, 'L'Indochine vue de l'Ouest', *Gradhiva*, 4, pp. 35-51.

Glover, Ian C., 1989, *Early Trade between India and Southeast Asia: A link in the Development of a World Trading System*. Hull, University of Hull, Centre for Southeast Asian Studies (Occasional paper, no. 16).

Gupta, Sunil, 2005, 'The Bay of Bengal Interaction Sphere (1000 BC – AD 500)', *Bulletin of the Indo-Pacific Prehistory Association*, 25, pp. 21-30.

Kulke, Hermann, 1990, 'Indian Colonies, Indianisation or Cultural Convergence? Reflections on the Changing Image of India's Role in South-East Asia', in H. Schulte Nordholt, *Onderzoek in Zuidoost-Azie: Agenda's voor de jaren negentig*. Leiden: Rijksuniversiteit te Leiden (Semaian 3): 8-32.

————, 1993, ' "Kadatuan Srivijaya"– Empire or Kraton of Srivijaya? A Reassessment of the Epigraphical Evidence', *Bulletin de l'Ecole française d'Extrême-Orient*, 80, pp. 159-81.

Lankton, James W., Laure Dussubieux and Bernard Gratuze, 2006, 'Glass from Khao Sam Kaeo: Transferred Technology for an Early Southeast Asian Exchange Network', *Bulletin de l'Ecole française d'Extrême-Orient*, 93, pp. 317-51.

Legge, John D., 1992, 'The Writing of Southeast Asian History', in N. Tarling, *The Cambridge History of Southeast Asia*, vol. I. Cambridge: Cambridge University Press, pp. 1-50.

Lockard, Craig A., 2007, 'Southeast Asia in World History', *World History Connected*, 5(1), http://www.historycooperative.org/journals/whc/5.1/lockard.html (accessed Dec. 2009)

————, 2009, *Southeast Asia in World History*. Oxford: Oxford University Press.

Mabbett, Ian W., 1977, 'The "Indianisation" of Southeast Asia: Reflections on the Prehistoric Sources / The 'Indianisation' of Southeast Asia: Reflections on Historical Sources', *Journal of Southeast Asian Studies*, 8(1, 2), pp. 1-14, 143-61.

Majumdar, Ramesh Chandra, 1941, *Greater India (Sain Das Foundation Lectures, 1940)*. Bombay: Dayanand College Book Depot.

Manguin, Pierre-Yves, 1991, 'The Merchant and the King: Political Myths of Southeast Asian Coastal Polities', *Indonesia*, 52, pp. 41-54.

————, 1996, 'Southeast Asian Shipping in the Indian Ocean during the 1st Millennium AD', in H.P. Ray and J.-F. Salles (eds.), *Tradition and Archaeology: Early Maritime Contacts in the Indian Ocean*. Lyon/New Delhi: Manohar/Maison de l'Orient méditerranéen/NISTADS, pp. 181-98.

————, 2004, 'The Archaeology of the Early Maritime Polities of Southeast Asia', in P. Bellwood and I.C. Glover (eds.), _Southeast Asia: From Prehistory to History_. London: RoutledgeCurzon, pp. 282-313.

————, 2006, 'Un "sociologue" parmi les orientalistes: Paul Mus à l'École française d'Extrême-Orient (1927-1937)', in C. Goscha and D. Chandler (eds.), _L'espace d'un regard: Paul Mus et l'Asie (1902-1969)_. Lyon, Paris: Institut d'Asie Orientale, Les Indes savantes, pp. 109-16.

————, 2009, 'The Archaeology of Funan in the Mekong River Delta: The Oc Eo Culture of Vietnam', in Nancy Tingley (ed.), _Arts of Ancient Vietnam: From River Plain to Open Sea_. New York: Houston: Asian Society Museum of Fine Arts, pp. 100-18.

Manguin, Pierre-Yves and Vo Si Khai, 2000, 'Excavations at the Ba Thê / Oc Eo Complex (Viêt Nam): A Preliminary Report on the 1998 Campaign', in Wibke Lobo and Stefanie Reimann (eds.), _Southeast Asian Archaeology 1998: Proceedings of the 7th International Conference of the European Association of Southeast Asian Archaeologists, Berlin 1998_. Hull / Berlin: Centre for Southeast Asian Studies, University of Hull / Ethnologisches Museum, Staatlich Museen zu Berlin, pp. 107-22.

Mus, Paul, 1975 [1933], _India Seen from the East: Indian and Indigenous Cults in Champa_ [tr. I. Mabbett & D. Chandler]. Clayton: Monash University (Monash Papers on Southeast Asia 3).

Pollock, Sheldon, 1996, 'The Sanskrit Cosmopolis, 300-1300: Transculturation, Vernacularisation, and the Question of Ideology', in J.E.M. Houben (ed.), _Ideology and Status of Sanskrit: Contributions to the History of the Sanskrit Language_. Leiden: E.J. Brill, Brill's Indological Library.

————, 2006, _The Language of the Gods in the World of Men: Sanskrit, Culture, and Power in Premodern India_. Berkeley: University of California Press.

Pryce, Thomas Oliver, Bérénice Bellina-Pryce, and Anna T.N. Bennett, 2006, 'The Development of Metal Technologies in the Upper Thai-Malay Peninsula: Initial Interpretation of the Archaeometallurgical Evidence from Khao Sam Kaeo', _Bulletin de l'Ecole française d'Extrême-Orient_, 93, pp. 295-315.

Ray, Himanshu Prabha, 1994, _The Winds of Change: Buddhism and the Maritime Links of Early South Asia_. New Delhi: Oxford University Press.

————, 1997, 'The Emergence of Urban Centres in Bengal: Implications for the Late Prehistory of Southeast Asia', _Bulletin of the Indo-Pacific Prehistory Association (The Chiang Mai Papers, vol. III)_, 16, pp. 43-48.

Smail, John R.W., 1961, 'On the Possibility of an Autonomous History of Modern Southeast Asia', _Journal of Southeast Asian History_, 2(2), pp. 72-102.

Soeroso, 1998, 'Bangka sebelum Sriwijaya', _Sangkhakala_, 2, pp. 18-33.

Stark, Miriam T., 1998, 'The Transition to History in the Mekong Delta: A View from Cambodia', _International Journal of Historical Archaeology_, 2(3), pp. 175-203.

————, 2004, 'Pre-Angkorian and Angkorian Cambodia', in P. Bellwood and I.C. Glover (eds.), _Southeast Asia: from Prehistory to History_. London: RoutledgeCurzon, pp. 89-119.

Stark, Miriam T. and Sovath Bong, 2001, 'Recent Research on Emerging Complexity in Cambodia's Mekong', _Indo-Pacific Prehistory Association Bulletin_, 21, pp. 85-98.

Stark, Miriam T. and S. Jane Allen, 1998, 'The Transition to History in Southeast Asia: An Introduction', _International Journal of Historical Archaeology_, 2(3), pp. 163-74.

Tri Marhaeni, 2002, 'Pemukiman pra-Sriwijaya di Karangagung Tengah: Sebuah kajian awal', _Siddhayâtra_, 7(2), pp. 65-89.

Wolters, Oliver W., 1967, *Early Indonesian Commerce: A Study of the Origins of Sri Vijaya*. Ithaca: Cornell University Press.

————, 1999 [1982], *History, Culture, and Region in Southeast Asian Perspectives*. Ithaca/Singapore: Cornell University, Southeast Asia Program Publications/Institute of Southeast Asian Studies.

Wright, Henry T., 1998, 'Developing Complex Societies in Southeast Asia: Using Archaeological and Historical Evidence', *International Journal of Historical Archaeology*, 2(4), pp. 343-48.

Zakharov, Anton O., 2007, 'Constructing the Island Polities of Southeast Asia in the 5th–7th Centuries', *Journal of Historical, Philological and Cultural Studies*, 17, pp. 270-85.

————, 2009, 'Constructing the Polity of Sriwijaya in the 7th – 8th Centuries: The View According to the Inscriptions'. Indonesian Studies Working Papers #9. Sydney: The University of Sydney, 14 pages.

Zurndorfer, Harriet T., 1998, 'The Discipline of World History and the Economic and Social History of the Orient: A New Fashion in an Old Hat? Further Reflections on Forty Years of JESHO', *Journal of the Economic and Social History of the Orient*, 41(3), pp. 241-48.

PART I

New Archaeological Evidence from South Asia and Southeast Asia

1

Central Vietnam during the Period from 500 BCE to CE 500

Lam Thi My Dzung

INTRODUCTION

The time from 500 BCE to CE 500 (the protohistoric and early historic periods) is defined by scholars as the critical period in the cultural and historical process of Central Vietnam in particular and in Southeast Asia in general. According to scholars, this early historic period in mainland Southeast Asia straddled two critical junctures. The mid-first millennium BCE marks the transition to an 'Iron Age' and all the shifts that accompanied such a technological change. A second transition occurred in the later centuries BCE with the shift to the early historic period; changes during this time set the stage for the emergence of the region's first centralised polities (Stark and Bong Sovath 2001: 85).

Recent archaeological finds and discoveries lead us to recognise the dynamic cultural contacts of the area with the external world and strong acculturation between the exogenous and indigenous factors which led to formation of various kinds of early states. Due to these qualitative and critical changes, a big number of local cultural features disappeared, while the forms and behavioural patterns of the new cultural structure appeared to replace the old elements.

The main issues of this chapter are to provide:

- An overview on the archaeological cultures in Central Vietnam during the period from 500 BCE to CE 500.
- The transition processes from Sa Huynh to Champa reflected in the

archaeological sites and artefacts, and the discussion for the delimitation of the early historic period from 500 BCE to CE 500.

• Some opinions about the so-called Sinicisation, Indianisation and the impact of indigenous elements.

AN OVERVIEW OF THE ARCHAEOLOGICAL CULTURES IN CENTRAL VIETNAM, 500 BCE–CE 500

The Archaeological Sequences for Central Vietnam

According to Vietnamese archaeologists, archaeological sequences and chronologies for Central Vietnam could be reconstructed as follows:

1. *Pre-Sa Huynh* (or *Early Sa Huynh, Initial Sa Huynh*): It consists of some groups of sites (under the umbrella of Xom Con, Long Thanh, Binh Chau cultures). These cultures belong to the Early Metal Age from 3500 to 2600/2500 BP; all influenced each other and finally crystallised in one cultural tradition, which was represented by the Sa Huynh culture. It is believed that the jar burial tradition in Sa Huynh period originated in the Pre-Sa Huynh phase (Lam Thi My Dzung 2002: 53).

2. *The typical Sa Huynh culture* (*Archaic* or *Early Iron*): There are some contradictions about the spatial distribution and the forms of burial jars in the Sa Huynh culture (Nguyen Thi Hau 1997; Yamagata 2007: 4). According to the author of this paper, the typical Sa Huynh culture existed during the period from 500 BCE to CE 100 or 200. The sites were distributed in the area between Thua Thien – Hue and the Dong Nai Delta. The Sa Huynh culture consisted of two main local groups:

   i. The Northern group occupied the areas of Quang Tri, Thua Thien – Hue, Quang Nam, Quang Ngai, Binh Dinh provinces, and Da Nang city. This group was characterised by big cylindrical jars and conical, semi-conical lids; jar burial was predominant, and so were cremations and secondary burials.

   ii. The Southern group occupied the areas of Khanh Hoa, Ninh Thuan, and Binh Thuan provinces, down to the Dong Nai Delta. This group was characterised by various forms of burials; jar burials, ground burials; cremations, primary and secondary burials. The burial rites evidenced the strong and close relations with Tabon cave (Philippines) and Samui Island (Thailand).

3. *The Early Cham period from CE 100 to 500*: This is a period of establishment of Early States. It may be divided into two main phases:

     i. From 100 to 200: The Jinan Period
    ii. From 200 to 500: The establishment of Linyi and Linyi-like polities. From CE 500 onwards, we are in the Champa Kingdom period.

Due to many reasons, this chronological framework could not be fixed precisely. The upper and lower years of each period were not recognised clearly and it is worth noting the transitional nature of the end of the previous phase and beginning of the successive phase.

This study concerns the chronological phases from 500 BCE to CE 500 (i.e. Sa Huynh and Early Cham). The scholars use different terms such as Pre-Linyi to Linyi, Tra Kieu, Pre-Cham, Early Cham or Ancient Cham for indicating the period from CE 100 to 400, when the name Champa had not appeared yet in the ancient Chinese annals (Yamagata 1998, 2005).

There are some controversial views regarding the definition of the location and nature of Linyi and especially its relationship with successive Champa periods (Vickery 2005; Southworth 2001, 2004). The author would like to emphasise that up-to-date information allows the northern border of the Sa Huynh culture to be clearly positioned in Thua Thien – Hue province (in the Hue area, several large Sa Huynh cemeteries were found, such as Con Giang, Con Dai, etc.). In Quang Binh and Quang Tri provinces, only little information is available for the existence of Sa Huynh culture. Archaeological artefacts discovered accidentally in recent years in Quang Tri province show strong cultural acculturation between Dong Son and Sa Huynh cultures. For the period from CE 200 to 900 in Quang Tri province, this author's survey material (particularly pottery) evidences features similar to the pottery found in Quang Nam and other provinces in Central Vietnam. It fact, this could be interpreted as the unification of the culture in the large area ranging from Quang Tri to Khanh Hoa provinces. Focusing on the recent archaeological data, I prefer to use the term Early Cham for the period from CE 100 to 500 which means Cham culture and not only the Champa kingdom or Cham ethnics. It is important to note that this is mostly a working concept.

The Definition of Sa Huynh Culture Concept

The most notable characteristic of the Sa Huynh culture is its mortuary tradition with burial jars. In general, the Sa Huynh sites reveal a considerable use of iron and decorative items made from glass, semi-precious and precious stones such as agate, carnelian, rock crystal, amethyst, and nephrite. The sites (cemeteries and occupation sites) are located on sand dunes extending along the shore or along the rivers in the alluvial plains. A large number of Sa Huynh sites are distributed on the highland and mountainous area (Lam Thi

My Dzung 1998: 13). The sphere of the Sa Huynh culture extended from the Thua Thien – Hue province down to the Dong Nai Delta.

In this huge region, the author recognised three successive phases of Sa Huynh culture (Lam Thi My Dzung 2007a):

1. *The earliest phase, phase I.* The key sites are Go Ma Voi, Binh Chau II, Binh Yen pit 1, Thach Bich, Go Que cemeteries and Thon Tu occupation site. Jar burials existed with some extended ground burials. The grave goods include many bronze artefacts, some iron implements, a small number of beads, and no bronze containers or Han bronze mirrors. The artefacts and the burial type show strong relationships with the Dong Son culture from further north.

2. *The middle phase, phase II.* The key sites are Go Dua, Lai Nghi, Binh Yen pit 2, An Bang, Dai Lanh, Dong Cuom, Sa Huynh, Dien Khanh. This is the peak of the Sa Huynh culture. Common burial jars are cylindrical with everted rims, which are usually associated with semi-conical lids. Mortuary accessories consist of many iron artefacts, agate, carnelian, glass beads and earrings, and several gold ornaments. Among the ornaments and other kinds of grave goods, there are some imported items from the outside world such as bronze ritual vessels, bronze mirrors, etched beads. If compared with Phase I, the pottery is poorly decorated. The artefacts and some kind of burials show strong relationships with Han (Late Western and Early Eastern Han culture) from the north.

3. *The final phase, phase III.* The key sites are Lai Nghi, Hau Xa II, Xom Oc (the burials), Suoi Chinh, Rung Long Thuy, Hoa Diem (the burials), and the group of sites in Can Gio district and in Ho Chi Minh city. A variety of burial practices could be recognised. Jar burials are associated with extended graves. The grave goods reflect the dynamic trade and other forms of exchange with China, India and Southeast Asian islands.

The author also recognised two traditions for the evolution of burial patterns from Pre Sa Huynh to Sa Huynh and Epi Sa Huynh periods.

1. *Tradition I,* from Long Thanh to Sa Huynh. It is characterised by the existence of egg-shaped and cylindrical jars. In the final period, the grave goods consist of many iron implements and ornaments made from agate, carnelian and glass. This first tradition began at the end of the first millennium BCE and declined around the end of CE 100. It may be named Northern Sa Huynh.

2. *Tradition II,* from Bau Tram to Suoi Chinh, Hoa Diem, Giong Ca Vo. It is recognised by the presence of the spherical jars which contained the human

skeletons. This tradition began around 3500 BP and finished in CE 200 or 300. It may be named Southern Sa Huynh (Fig. 1.1).

The spatial division of Sa Huynh culture is flexible in some cases. In fact it could be recognised as two traditions in the same area. For example in Khanh Hoa province, Hoa Diem cemetery belongs to Tradition II and Dien Khanh cemetery to Tradition I.

FIGURE 1.1
The spatial distribution of two areas of Sa Huynh culture

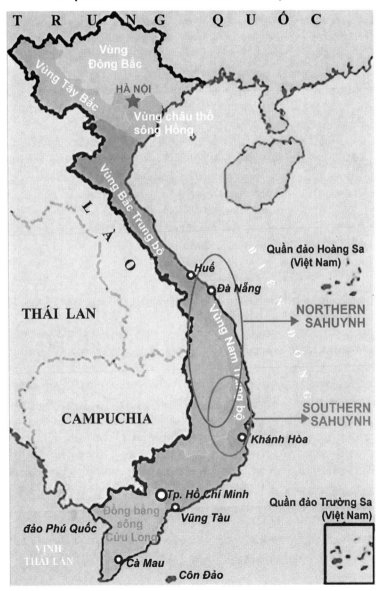

TRANSITIONAL PROCESSES FROM SA HUYNH TO CHAMPA, AS REFLECTED IN ARCHAEOLOGICAL SITES AND ARTEFACTS

Spatial Distribution of Sa Huynh and Cham Sites and the Connections between the Sites

Over 100 Sa Huynh sites and a dozen Early Cham sites have been discovered and studied in Central Vietnam. It is worth noting that the Cham sites are located closely to the area of Sa Huynh sites, and in many cases, the Cham cultural layer or at least the Cham artefacts were found above the Sa Huynh cemeteries. The end of the Sa Huynh cultural phase coincided with the beginning of Cham culture. The location of Cham sites overlaps with that of Sa Huynh sites. But we cannot explain this simply as the continuous cultural development from Sa Huynh to Cham. We do recognise the coincidence of dates, or that of location, but there are divergences in many aspects of material culture between Sa Huynh and Cham.

There are differences in the nature of the sites. The Sa Huynh sites as mentioned above are mostly cemeteries. Cham sites are varied in nature and include occupation sites, port sites and citadel sites. The differences in nature and function of Sa Huynh and Cham sites produces the differences of the features and artefacts brought to light during excavations.

The results of excavations of some Cham sites have also yielded substantial information regarding the ritual, economic and political activities of the people.

The Chronology of the Cham Excavated Sites

By using stratigraphic sequences and the evolution of artefact assemblages, at least two or three phases may be recognised for the first millennium CE Cham sites.

The early phase consists of the sites that reveal cultural layers of the CE 100 to the end of CE 200 or 300. The key sites are Go Cam (Duy Trung, Duy Xuyen, Quang Nam), the lowest and lower layers of Tra Kieu (Duy Xuyen, Quang Nam), the lower layer of Hau Xa I (Hoi An, Quang Nam), the upper layer of Vuon Dinh-Khue Bac (Da Nang), the lower layer of Co Luy-Phu Tho (Quang Ngai), the lower layer of Thanh Ho (Phu Yen). There are some debates about the dating of the lowest layer of Tra Kieu among scholars (Glover et al. 2005; Lam Thi My Dzung 2002, 2005; Yamagata 1998, 2005).

The middle phase consists of the sites that have cultural layers of CE 400 to 700. The key sites are the upper layers of Tra Kieu, of Co Luy-Phu Tho, and of Thanh Ho.

The later phase includes the site with dates between CE 900 and 1000, such as Bai Lang (Cu Lao Cham) and Nam Tho Son (Da Nang).

It is important to remember that a number of these sites contain various cultural layers dating from CE 100 to 700. The Cham sites are varied in nature and dates: the archaeological research documents an unbroken record of occupation during the first millennium CE, but it also recognises the process of organisational changes from CE 100 to 500.

ASSEMBLAGES OF ARTEFACTS

Radical changes occurred in the assemblages of artefacts between Sa Huynh and Cham cultures.

The Pottery

In comparison with Sa Huynh pottery (mostly from graves), the pottery found in Cham sites seem to be simpler in decoration, but varied in material and potting techniques. From CE 100, a new technique for pottery making was introduced in Central Vietnam (higher fired stamped ware). It is important to focus on the appearance of the fine clay pottery and new forms of pottery such as egg-shaped jars, pedestal cups, *kendis* (spouted vessels), and tiles with textile impression.

We can recognise during the first millennium three main groups of pottery based on differences in fabric, surface treatment, vessel-forming techniques, style and function (Lam Thi My Dzung 2005).

1. The 1st group includes the domestic wares, locally made and relatively low-fired. This group evidenced some common features with the Sa Huynh pottery.
2. The 2nd group consists of the locally made earthenwares, but under the influence of the new technique from the North (i.e Northern Vietnam or China). Some pottery forms seem to originate from the West.
3. The 3rd group presents the high-fired, stamped, glazed and unglazed Han pottery and probably some imported pottery from the West. These earthenwares were found in sites belonging to the early and middle phases as defined above.

The Ornaments

Indo-Pacific glass beads are found in abundance. Gold, silver jewellery and ornaments became more popular, but agate, carnelian, and nephrite beads became rare; the Ling-ling O and two animal headed earrings, trademarks of the Sa Huynh culture, totally disappeared.

The Other Artefacts

We do not have much information from the archaeological sites to evidence the evolution of metal and stone implements over this period; only by looking at private collections can we recognise great changes in the making and use of stone and metal tools.

In comparison with the previous Sa Huynh culture, the Early Cham and Cham artefact assemblages reflect the great changes in material, manufacturing techniques and form. According to us, there are two main groups of factors (inner and outer), which caused these shifts.

On the one hand, it is important to note the continuous cultural processes, especially in some domestic aspects from 500 BCE to CE 500, and on the other hand, we have to focus on the cultural changes over this time. The new forms of settlement patterns and artefacts derived from new social structures and newly acquired functions.

New social functions provide the opportunities and abilities for the development of quantitative and qualitative levels of organisation of production and distribution. These changes influenced the selection of imported items. The changes occurring in artefact assemblages and site structures led us to recognise tendencies and preferences in the ways people interacted with the outside world over this millennium long period.

For the first phase, the connection with Han China played an important role in the establishment of new social structures. Influence from China penetrated the Sa Huynh culture and became stronger in the beginning of the first millennium CE; it was caused by various factors, among which the political factor is most significant (Lam Thi My Dzung 2007b). In this same time, we cannot ignore the influence from India, but the connection with India seems to be weaker than that with China. The material culture of this phase also reflects some features which were inherited from the earlier Sa Huynh culture.

During the second phase, one is witness to the increase of complexity in the connections with the outside world, in comparison with the first phase. One must also emphasize the strength of the influence from India and the multiple connections with Insular Southeast Asia. All these factors brought about radical transformations in various facets of Cham societies.

ABOUT THE PROCESSES OF THE SO-CALLED 'SINICISATION' AND 'INDIANISATION' OF SOUTHEAST ASIA

Some Opinions about Sinicisation, Indianisation and their Social Impacts

There are three groups of scholarly opinions about the process of so-called Indianisation (and Sinicisation), which for more than a millennium, beginning from the early centuries of the Common Era, was accomplished time and again by Brahmin priests, Buddhist monks, scholars and artisans who were introduced into Southeast Asian indigenous societies by Indian merchants. They emphasise: (1) Southeast Asian initiatives; (2) colonisation theories; (3) the idea of a mutual sharing process in the evolution of Indianised statecraft in Southeast Asia.

Obviously, all early kingdoms were based on the Hindu conception of royalty; but never did they become Indian colonies. Up to now, Vietnamese archaeologists are of the opinion that much of the available data supports the third point of view. We suggest that trade with China and India played an important role, but that it was never the principal 'cause' of the emergence of early states. State power was an important addition, but not the result of the successful development of trade with the external world. I argue that the spread of goods and culture from India and China reflected the grafting of Indian and Chinese commerce onto a pre-existing infrastructure of Southeast Asian networks. Such an explanation implies that earlier phases of development in various areas of Southeast Asia were characterised by indigenous processes of trade expansion and increasing social stratification (Lam Thi My Dzung 2006).

The Earliest Archaeological Artefacts from India in Central Vietnam

We can mention a great number of carnelian and agate beads of Indian origin, which were found in the Iron Age sites in Thailand, Myanmar, and Vietnam: in particular, specific etched beads and beads with animal shape (lion, bird, tiger...). At Lai Nghi cemetery in Quang Nam province, two carnelian beads in the shape of bird and tiger and thousands of carnelian and agate beads were found as grave goods (Reinecke et al. 2003) (Fig. 1.2). Carnelian or tiger beads are a reference to Buddha as Sakyasimha (Lion of the Sakya Clan), and it is highly probable that the lion bead from Thailand, as well as similar ones (tiger, bird or deer) from Vietnam, Myanmar are early Buddhist icons, and as such probably the earliest witness to Buddhist ideas and values yet recognised in Southeast Asia (Glover 1994: 140; Lam Thi My Dzung 2006).

FIGURE 1.2
Agate and carnelian beads from India found in Sa Huynh sites
(a.c. Photos by Andreas Reinecke; b. Photo by Bui Van Liem)

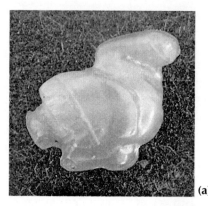
(a)

(b)

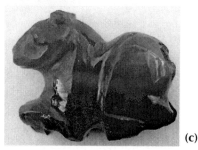
(c)

The pottery imported from South India appeared very early in Central Vietnam. It was evidenced in the early Cham sites such as Tra Kieu and Go Cam in Quang Nam province (Nguyen Kim Dzung 2005: 41) (Fig. 1.3).

So, through the unique process of acculturation, the ethnically different Southeast Asian peoples absorbed the Chinese and Indic cultural elements and adapted them to their own particular needs. The superimposition of Indian culture never derived from a policy of political subjugation nor to economic exploitation; rather the very process signified a peaceful outlook and a cooperative approach.

In summary, based on the archaeological and historical annals, one could apply the following cultural sequences for the period 500 BCE to CE 500:

1. *The Protohistoric period – Sa Huynh culture*: This culture ends around the beginning of the second century CE. But in some areas, especially in the southern part, the Sa Huynh culture only declined about CE 200 or 300, with some transformations in both burial rites and grave goods.

FIGURE 1.3
Trade pottery from South India found in ancient Cham site Go Cam
(Courtesy: Nguyen Kim Dzung)

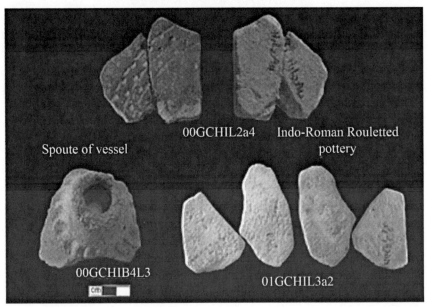

2. *The period from the end of first century CE to the end of the second or third centuries CE:* The Ancient Cham or Early Cham period is characterised by multi-cultural interactions with the outside world, among which the strongest connections were with the Chinese cultural sphere. These connections began in the final phase of Sa Huynh culture and increased during the Eastern Han period. According to the ancient annals, the sphere of Sa Huynh culture belonged to Jinan district (Quan Nhat Nam) of Eastern Han China. Cultural shifts are easily recognisable, particularly the total changes in burial rites and ceremonies. The jar burials and their associated grave goods disappeared and these shifts were reflected in the appearance of new cultural patterns. There are, therefore, some arguments to name this period as the pre-Linyi Period (Tien Lam Ap).

3. *The beginning of the third century CE – The Linyi state and similar states along Central Vietnam:* This is an intensive process of state formation. The appearance of the earliest Cham citadels, as evidenced by the vestiges found in the lower layers of Tra Kieu, the upper layer of Co Luy – Phu Tho and the Ho citadel. The cultural interaction with India and Southeast Asia Islands became most important.

4. *From the CE 600, the term Champa occurred:* There are some gaps in the evolution of these phases, particularly in the transitional stage from

Sa Huynh to Early Cham or Pre-Linyi (i.e., end of first century BCE to middle of second century CE); and in the transition from Linyi to Champa (i.e., the relationship between Linyi and similar polities, and Champa). In several cases, the interpretation of the historical annals finds no match in the archaeological evidence. From the archaeological point of view, it is important to note that the differences in archaeological records between the above-mentioned phases during period from CE 100 to 500 are smaller in comparison with the previous Sa Huynh culture.

We tend to accept the idea that the Linyi and Linyi-like polities of Central Vietnam from *c.* CE 100 to 400 were established under strong Han Chinese influence (in fact, the formation of these early states reflected the reaction of the local people fighting against the Chinese domination). The impact and influence of Indic civilisation increased around CE 400 and 500, and Champa appeared on the historical scene around CE 600. The archaeological materials do not bring evidence for such a radical change or the replacement of Linyi by Champa. On the contrary, one can observe continuities in the development of material culture between these periods. It is recognised both in the sites and in the artefact assemblages.

REFERENCES

Glover, Ian, 1994, 'Recent Archaeological Evidence for Early Maritime Contacts Between India and Southeast Asia', in H.P. Ray and J.-F. Salles (eds.), *Tradition and Archaeology: Early Maritime Contacts in the Indian Ocean*, New Delhi: Manohar, pp. 129-44.

Glover, Ian, Nguyen Kim Dzung and Ruth Prior, 2005, 'Mua khai quat 2000-2001 o pho Champa co o Tra Kieu va Go Cam, tinh Quang Nam – mien Trung Viet Nam' (The excavation season 2000-2001 at Ancient Champa citadel Tra Kieu and Go Cam, Quang Nam province, Central Vietnam), in *One Century of Vietnamese Archaeology*. Hanoi: Publishing House of Social Sciences (in Vietnamese), pp. 635-52.

Lam Thi My Dzung, 1998, 'The Sahuynh Culture in Hoi An: Southeast Asian Archaeology 1996', Proceedings of the 6th International Conference of the European Association of Southeast Asian Archaeologists, Leiden, 2-6 September 1996, Centre for Southeast Asian Studies, University of Hull, pp. 13-25.

———, 2002, 'Jar Burial Tradition in Southeast Asia', *Journal of Science*. English Issue for Social Sciences and Humanities. Vietnam National University, no. 1E. Hanoi: 44-55.

———, 2005, *Do gom thien nien ky I sau CN o Mien Trung Vietnam* (The pottery in the 1st millennium AD in Central Vietnam), *Khao co hoc*, no. 1, Hanoi (in Vietnamese): 50-70.

———, 2006, *Regional and Inter-regional Interactions in the Context of Sa Huynh Culture: With Regards to the Thu Bon Valley in Quang Nam Province, Vietnam*. IPPA Congress 4.2006, Manila, Philippine.

————, 2007a, *Gom di chi Giong Noi trong moi quan he voi phuc hop gom so su Nam Trung Bo*. (Giong Noi pottery in the proto-historical pottery complex of Southern part of Central Vietnam). *Khao co hoc*, no. 2, Hanoi: 79-86 (in Vietnamese).

————, 2007b, *Mot so y kien xung quanh van de giao luu va tiep bien trong van hoa Sa Huynh* (Some opinions about the relationships with the outside world of Sahuynh culture). The paper presented at the Conference on 'The Relationships and Acculturations in Sahuynh Culture', Institute of Archaeology, Hanoi, September (in Vietnamese).

Nguyen Kim Dzung, 2005, 'Di chi Go Cam va con duong tiep bien van hoa sau Sa Huynh khu vuc Tra Kieu' (Go Cam site and the ways of cultural acculturation epi - Sahuynh in Tra Kieu area'. *Khao co hoc*, no. 6. Hanoi (in Vietnamese): 17-50.

Nguyen Thi Hau, 1997, 'Di tich mo chum mien Dong Nam Bo - Nhung phat hien moi tai Can Gio TP.HCM' (Jar burials in Southeastern part of Southern Vietnam - The new discoveries in Can Gio District, Hochiminh City), Ph.D. thesis (in Vietnamese).

Reinecke, Andreas, Lam Thi My Dzung and Nguyen Chieu, 2003, 'Past lives'. *Heritage* March/April, Hanoi: 28-30.

Southworth, William A., 2001, 'The Origins of Campa in Central Vietnam: A Preliminary Review', Ph.D. thesis, Archaeology, SOAS, University of London.

————, 2004. 'The Coastal States of Champa', in Glover and Bellwood (ed.), *Southeast Asia from Prehistory to History*. London and New York: RoutledgeCurzon, 209-33.

Stark, Miriam T. and Bong Sovath, 2001, 'Recent Research on Emergent Complexity in Cambodia's Mekong', *Indo-Pacific Prehistory Association Bulletin* 21 (Melaka Papers, vol. 5).

Vickery, Michael, 2005, *Champa Revised*, ARI Working Paper, no 37, March, www.ari. nus.edu.sg/pub/wps.htm.

Yamagata, Mariko, 1998, 'Formation of Lin Yi: Internal and External Factors', *Journal of Southeast Asian Archaeology*, no. 18: 51-89, June.

————, 2005, 'Transition from Sahuynh to Linyi (Champa): Eith Special Reference to the Thu Bon River Valley'. *One Century of Vietnamese Archaeology*. Social Sciences Publishing House, Hanoi (in Vietnamese): 622-34.

————, 2007, 'Sahuynh Culture and the Human Migration Hypothesis', unpublished paper.

2

Ban Don Ta Phet and Khao Sam Kaeo: The Earliest Indian Contacts Re-assessed

Ian C. Glover
Bérénice Bellina

INTRODUCTION

This paper summarises the evidence from Ban Don Ta Phet (henceforth BDTP) in the light of recent studies on the site itself as well as of new discoveries in Thailand, and makes special reference to the analyses of metal, glass and hard stone artefacts from the excavations at Khao Sam Kaeo (henceforth KSK) in Chumphon Province, Peninsular Thailand (Fig. 2.1). The latter is the project of a joint French-Thai team with a strong focus on technological analyses of craft productions involved into Trans-Asiatic exchange.

Over thirty years ago a series of excavations commenced at BDTP, an Iron Age burial site in Kanchanaburi Province (west-central Thailand) which yielded, what at the time, was the earliest clear and dated evidence for contacts between Southeast Asia and India. A carnelian lion pendant provisionally identified by Glover (1990a) as a representation of Buddha as *Sakyasima* (Lion of the Sakya Clan) in the late centuries before the Christian Era, was interpreted as a precursor to the introduction of Buddhism into Southeast Asia. New data and analyses enable us to augment and revise previous interpretations of BDTP, to compare and contrast it to KSK, and to raise new issues on the timing and nature of early exchange between South and Southeast Asia and across the South China Sea.

FIGURE 2.1
Thailand locating BDTP and KSK (B. Bellina)

BAN DON TA PHET

This site was first excavated in 1975 with subsequent investigations up to 2000 by teams from the Archaeological Division of the Fine Arts Department of Thailand (henceforth FAD) and the Institute of Archaeology, University College London and many reports, booklets, journal and conference articles have been published over the years in Thai and English (Glover 1980, 1983, 1990; Glover et al. 1984 among others). New studies of the site and renewed analyses of the finds (Srinivasan and Glover 1995; Bellina 2007; Woods 2002; Lankton and Dussubieux 2006; Lankton pers. comm. May 2007) and comparisons with the excavations at KSK (Bellina and Silapanth 2006, 2008) both deepen, and to some extent change, our understanding of BDTP and allow us to raise new issues on the timing and nature of early exchange between South and Southeast Asia and across the South China Sea.

The archaeological site lies on the southern edge of the village, located at 8 km north of the district headquarters of Phanom Tuan, and 2 km west of route 324 between Kanchanaburi and U-Thong in (Fig. 2.2). The village is on a low mound rising above swampy ground that was under rice and sugar cultivation at the time of excavation. Antiquities were found there by school children in September 1975 in the course of erecting a perimeter fence for their school; excavations undertaken by the FAD identified a number of funerary deposits richly equipped with iron tools and weapons, bronze vessels and jewellery made from bronze, bone, ivory, glass and semi-precious stones (You-di 1976).

Further excavations were undertaken in 1980-81 and 1984-85, jointly by the Institute of Archaeology, London, and the FAD (Fig. 2.3) in which further funerary deposits were revealed with a generally similar range of furnishings (Glover et al. 1984; Glover 1990b). Yet another and limited excavation was made in 2000 by the Suphanburi branch of the FAD (Fig. 2.4) (Thepsuriyon 2001) but only a limited publication of this has so far been available.[1]

FIGURE 2.2
The archaeological site of BDTP is marked by a cross on the edge of the village (Drawing from I.C. Glover)

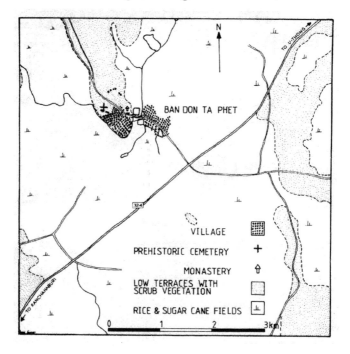

FIGURE 2.3
Excavations at BDTP in 1981 (Photo by I.C. Glover)

KHAO SAM KAEO

At KSK, local villagers have been unearthing bronze objects and semi-precious beads from the 1970s, discoveries that led the FAD to conduct archaeological surveys in 1981. Srisuchat (1986, I: 388-96; 1989; 1993: 131-43) listed the materials that the site yielded. The French-Thai programme led by Bellina (CNRS, Paris) and Silapanth (Silpakorn University) started surveying from 2003 and the first excavation campaign took place in 2005.

In contrast to the burial site of BDTP where no related settlement has been identified, excavations at KSK revealed a large settlement and an industrial

FIGURE 2.4
The 2000 FAD excavations at BDTP (Photo courtesy of FAD)

site but no cemetery yet.[2] Located on the east coast of the peninsula (at 99° 11'-12' East and 10° 31'-32' North), this Iron Age site is now 5 km distant from the sea. It consists of four hills whose height averages 30 m above the sea level. They are separated by ravines oriented North-South (20°) and East-West (110°). The tops of the hills are relatively flat and their size averages 150 × 150 m and 200 × 200 m, forming plateaux partially enclosed by ramparts, embankments and ditches partly using the natural ravines. To the west, the site is bordered by the Ta Thapao River that flows into the South China Sea. Excavation indicates that populations mainly settled on gentle slopes on the hills, apparently within ramparts, the extent and complexity of these find no equivalent so far for this period in Southeast Asia (Bellina and Silapanth 2008).

KSK AND BDTP REFLECT SOME OF THE SIGNIFICANT SOCIAL AND ECONOMIC CHANGES IN THE IRON AGE

Both are located on trade routes; BDTP is close to the rich tin belt of western Thailand and was formerly accessible by river, as well as close to the major land trade route from Burma through Three Pagoda Pass. KSK lies on the east coast of Kra Isthmus, the narrowest part of the Thai-Malay Peninsula (Fig. 2.1). Only short portages from the headwaters of the Ta Taphao River via a series of small streams may have provided a link from the site to the Kraburi estuary on the Bay of Bengal (Manguin 1983; Jacq-Hergoualc'h 2002: 44;

Wheatley 1961: xxvi) where sites such as newly-discovered Phukhao Thong provide abundant evidence of early exchange across the Bay of Bengal (see Chaisuwan's chapter in this volume).

Tin has long been considered as an important commodity along trans-asiatic routes and the uneven distribution of tin around the Eurasian World meant that any bronze-consuming region need to establish links, directly or indirectly, with tin producing areas. To date it is not possible to say when the Peninsula began to play a role in producing and exchanging tin and how much this exploitation influenced regional development in west-central Thailand (Pryce et al. 2008: 306-07). South Asia, we know, is deficient in tin, with only small deposits (Coote 1991). Even at such an early date, it is likely that tin was one of the major South Asia imports from Southeast Asia as it has been in historical periods. Within the upper part of the Thai-Malay Peninsula, the richest tin deposits are located near Ranong, on the west coast, less than 100 km southwest from Khao Sam Kaeo, and at the other end of a geological fault connecting the Andaman Sea and the Gulf of Thailand where several possible trans-peninsular exchange routes might have long been used.

Materials at these sites reflect their active involvement into exchange networks and their key positions on those. They also reveal major socio-economic changes at that time. Indeed, although intra-regional exchange networks are already in evidence in the Southeast Asian Bronze Age, they really expanded through the Iron Age (Higham 2002). By the end of this period, regional East Asian, Southeast Asian and South Asian exchange networks interconnected (Glover 1990a; Bellina and Glover 2004). For those Southeast Asian societies involved in these exchange networks, the increasing demands and contacts they generated appear to have been a catalyst for internal social restructuring.

As will be presented below, both BDTP and KSK reflect these changes. Burial goods evidence regional and inter-regional contacts of various Asian cultural horizons. These point towards South China and northern Vietnam with *lingling-o* and bi-cephalous ornaments made of nephrite, a raw material of Taiwanese origin (Hung et al. 2007)[3] and towards South Asia with glass and semi-precious stone ornaments whose raw materials and technologies stemmed from there (Bellina 2001, 2007; Bellina and Silapanth 2006). Some of those artefacts appear to be shared by different Southeast Asian groups in Thailand (BDTP and KSK), the Sa Huynh culture and related sites in central and southern Vietnam (such as Giong Phet and Giong Ca Vo), and, finally, the Tabon Caves, Palawan island, Philippines (Fig. 2.5). This distribution led Bellina (2001, 2003; 2007; Bellina and Silapanth 2006) to suggest that, since the late prehistoric period, a set of social groups in different and mutually distant Southeast Asian localities involved in exchange might have established a common symbolic system. The wide distribution of common prestige

FIGURE 2.5
KSK and BDTP are both located on important early trans-Asiatic trade routes.
Map displaying some of the Southeast Asian groups that shared many common artefact types from central Thailand (BDTP), Peninsular Thailand (KSK), from Sa Huynh Culture related sites in central and southern Vietnam (Giong Phet and Giong Ca Vo), and, finally from the Tabon Caves, Palawan island, Philippines. Some are illustrated here (Map B. Bellina 2007).

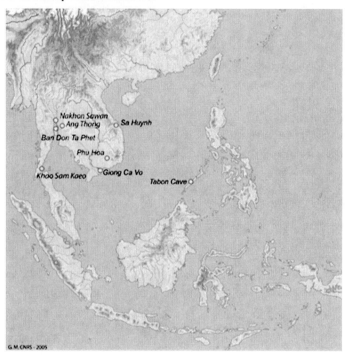

goods across disparate regions has been noted across various chiefdoms in Central America, in Hawaii (Earle 1990; Hantman and Plog 1982), and in the Philippines (Junker 1994; Bacus 2003). Both BDTP and KSK yielded several varieties of high technology prestige goods, widely distributed across Southeast Asian late prehistoric sites that could be considered to have led to the creation of the first common symbolic system across the region. Amongst these sites, KSK presents one special feature in so far as it has provided evidence for the production of some of those valuables previously believed to have been made at several different localities along the Trans-Asiatic networks.

In 2005, the French-Thai mission at KSK set up a programme largely dedicated to studying the transfer of complex technologies along these Trans-Asiatic routes. Focus was on the production and distribution of valuable artefacts in order to reconstruct early cultural exchanges from a period on which historical sources are mute (for further explanation of the theoretical frame and details on the programme, see Bellina and Silapanth 2008).

DATING BDTP AND KSK

Five radiocarbon dates calculated from organic temper obtained from pottery were dated to between cal. 390-360 BCE.[4] New calibrations of these samples confirms that the fourth BCE still provides the best fit for the dated samples although we are less confident of insisting on the narrow range of cal. 390-360 BCE earlier published[5] (Fig. 2.6).

FIGURE 2.6
Radiocarbon dates from BDTP (Courtesy of OAU)

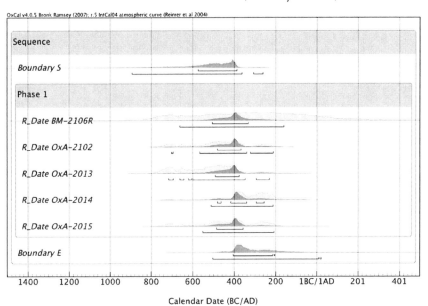

Calendar Date (BC/AD)

Although a few earlier dates (8000 and 6000 BCE) and finds such as Neolithic polished adzes, seals bearing a Brahmi script of the mid-fifth-seventh century CE, and a few sherds of Ayutthaya Period pottery (fourteenth-eighteenth century CE) which show that KSK had been occupied at different periods, 15 radiocarbon dates from KSK place the main activity at the site between the early fourth-second century BCE, making it almost exactly contemporary with BDTP (Bellina and Silapanth 2008) (Fig. 2.7).

STRUCTURE OF THE BDTP CEMETERY

A preliminary analysis by Alvey (1990) revealed some 20 funerary deposits from the 1980-81 alone, situated between 50 cm to 1 m below the present surface.[6] Because of the acid nature of the soil, few skeletons, or even bones,

FIGURE 2.7
Radiocarbon dates from Khao Sam Kaeo 4 seasons of excavation

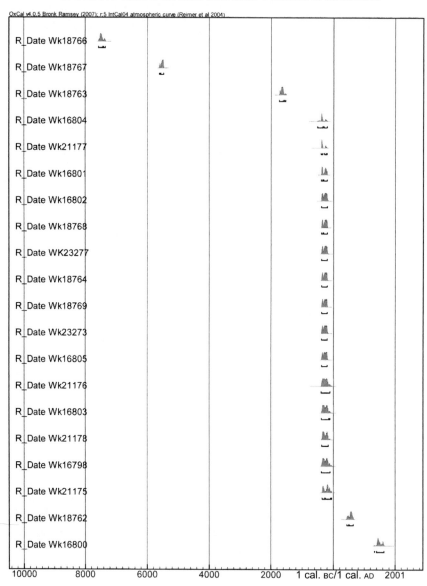

Calibrated date (cal. BCE/cal. CE)

were found except where they had been protected from the soil by bronze ornaments. Nevertheless, it seems that the total excavated area of the site[7] includes about 100 secondary burials with bones and funerary materials brought together and buried in regular rows some 50-70 cm apart, perhaps in one mass 'grave', and certainly over a very short time and within an area about 40 m across surrounded by a ditch and low bank.

Later, Woods (2002) used a bigger range of spatial and statistical analyses of the artefact distribution in the site in order to identify the burials, their orientation, depth and mode of burial and sequence of deposition and this made it possible the better to reconstruct the layout of the cemetery and to draw inferences regarding the social structure of the community buried there (Fig. 2.8). She argued that although the site is, in many ways, typical of other Iron Age sites in Thailand in having a range of unequal mortuary

FIGURE 2.8
Plan of the burial groups at BDTP trenches from the excavations in the 1980s
(from Woods 2002)

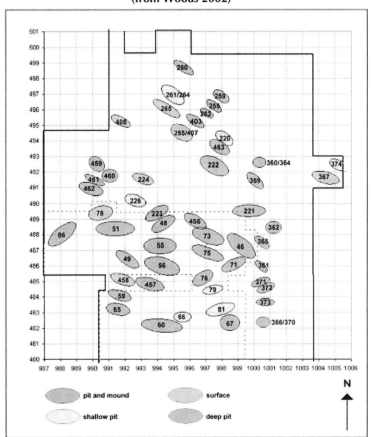

differentiation which might reflect power relationships, and possible evidence for hereditary relationships, there were some unique features, especially in the predominance of secondary burial.

Detailed spatial analysis again showed that in some instances, a single burial context represented two burials, and in other instances, several burial contexts separated during excavation represented a single burial. A total of fifty-three burials were identified from the 1980-81 and 1984-85 seasons[8] making it possible to identify various modes of burial – those laid on or very close to the then existing ground surface; those buried in shallow pits; ones in deeper pits, and yet others in pits which had been mounded. Apart from burials 371 and 372, and 463 and 229, no two burials overlay each other. This tends to confirm the suggestion made after the 1980-81 excavations season that above-ground markers were used.[9]

The richest burials, in the main, were those laid in pits with mounds and this may be significant; but more significant is the location of the deep pit burials. These are all located in two rows at either edge of the area analysed and are associated with a single pit and mound burial in each row.

That the burials had been laid out in rows confirms the evidence from the excavations and Alvey's earlier study, with the clearest examples in the northern part of the site. There is also a pattern in regards to orientation, with the rows in the northern part of the site being oriented NW-SE where orientation was discernable. Elsewhere, the orientation is less clear, but is either NW-SE, or roughly W-E directions, apart from five burials that are in a SW-NE direction. The orientations tend to be the same in the rows, but not in all.

Glover had earlier argued (Glover 1990b) that the whole cemetery represented a single event or at least had been laid out over a very short time, but the re-analysis by Woods raised the possibility that the site contains sequential burial events. Furthermore she suggested that some rows might represent descent groups – the presence of burials each with socketed spearheads in each of the three northern rows may support such an interpretation – but there is also some indication that burials adjacent to each other but in different rows might be linked. The clearest examples are burial contexts 457 and 458, which are associated with each other by clustering and multidimensional scaling, plus the fact that the position of different artefact types is extremely similar within both burials. This similarity also suggests these two burials were interred at the same time.

A group of five relatively wealthy burials (Fig. 2.9) are distinguished by the presence of agate and carnelian beads, etched or banded agate and carnelian beads, and crystal beads. The wealthiest burials are identified by the numbers and types of beads present, even though a few similar beads also occur with poorer burials.

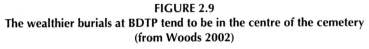

FIGURE 2.9
The wealthier burials at BDTP tend to be in the centre of the cemetery
(from Woods 2002)

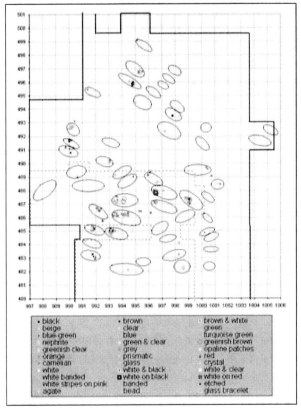

The distribution of artefact types also reveals a pattern between spindle whorls and socketed spearheads in that no burial contains both, even though spindle whorls are one of the commonest types of artefacts. One might be tempted to suggest that burials with spindle whorls represent female graves, however, during the Bronze Age in Northeastern Thailand, men, women and children were buried with spindle whorls (O'Reilly 2000). There are also patterns between the colour and types of glass beads in burials, most notably with '*mutisalah*' and prismatic beads. Their location in adjacent burials within rows, tends to support the idea of a relationship between these burials. If imported beads are heirlooms, the rows may represent hereditary relationships.

The spatial and statistical analysis of burials at BDTP by Woods has enabled a greater understanding of what is still a unique burial site in late Iron Age Thailand. Her analysis of the data from both the 1980-81 and 1984-85 excavations has confirmed some conclusions drawn from previous spatial studies and it has both clarified and contradicted other conclusions. That there is some social stratification within the burials is clear from the wealth analysis which may reflect a consolidation of power relationships represented in the distribution of artefacts in burials a pattern which is typical of hierarchical societies in the Iron Age (O'Reilly 2000: 291). Thus we can say that BDTP appears to be unique in Thailand as a cemetery dominated by secondary burial, although the layout of the burials in rows is consistent with other Iron Age sites in Thailand.

THE MATERIAL EVIDENCE FROM BDTP

Finds from BDTP include abundant locally-made low fired earthenware pottery vessels, iron tools and weapons, bronze containers and personal ornaments, glass and semi-precious stone beads, glass and ivory bracelets, and rare traces of textiles made from hemp, cotton and perhaps silk. Whereas the pottery and iron tools and weapons seem local in style and relate to everyday domestic and agricultural tasks, two categories of finds, bronze vessels and beads, are related more to display and ritual, and provide, together with that from KSK, some of the earliest evidence for exchange between India and Thailand in the late centuries of the pre-Christian period (Glover 1990b).

More than 3,000 beads of glass and semi-precious stone have been excavated; numbers in a single burial vary from two or three up to several hundred, and some burial deposits rich in beads had rather few bronze vessels or iron tools (Fig. 2.10). Beads were generally found in the lower part of the funerary deposits and mostly at the western end, glass and stone beads together although some groups indicated that they had been deposited as

FIGURE 2.10
Carnelian, agate and glass beads and iron tools below a crushed bronze bowl at BDTP, 1985 (Photo by I.C. Glover)

strung necklaces. Perhaps they were sewn onto clothing, of which traces remain on corroded bronze vessels.

SEMI-PRECIOUS STONE ORNAMENTS

Of the 3,000 or so beads found in the three seasons at BDTP, over 600 were made of hard, semi-precious stone such as agate, carnelian, rock crystal (varieties of siliceous stone) and rarely, nephrite. Morphologies of siliceous stone ornaments include spherical and small faceted carnelians, cylindrical and barrel-shaped banded agates (Fig. 2.11), small, unmodified rock crystals. Some semi-precious stone ornaments from the site bear close stylistic and technological similarities with the late prehistoric sites such as KSK, the Sa Huynh sites in central and southern Vietnam such as Giong Ca Vo, and with the Tabon caves in Palawan, Philippines. Those include flat hexagonal shaped carnelians which appear frequently in these sites, especially at KSK and also were found at Leang Buidane in the Talaud Islands of northeastern Indonesia (Bellwood 1976: 275, Fig. 2.10) as well as many Sa Huynh sites in central Vietnam, such as Go Mun (Reinecke et al. 2002: Fig. 2.14). The flat hexagonal beads in agate exploiting the natural colour zoning of the stone is more rare and can be compared to one found in the Tabon Caves (Fig. 2.12). Morphologies of nephrite or jade ornaments include small cylinders and few 'tiger claw' beads, and slotted and 'comma-shaped' nephrite pendants, found during the 1975-76 season only. 'Comma-shaped' ornaments have been found in Thailand and in Cambodia in glass and jade (Fig. 2.13). Complex geometric faceted beads with a double pyramid shape such as the octahedron and the icosaedre were also found as well as a double pyramid form with a hexagonal section made in agate, carnelian, green jasper and rock crystal (Fig. 2.14).

FIGURE 2.11
Etched and banded agate beads from BDTP (Photo by I.C. Glover)

FIGURE 2.12
Flat hexagonal carnelian and agate beads from Khao Sam Kaeo
(Photo by B. Bellina)

FIGURE 2.13
Colourless glass ear pendant from BDTP (Photo courtesy of FAD) and fragment of
a possible similar ornament found in KSK (Photo by B. Bellina)

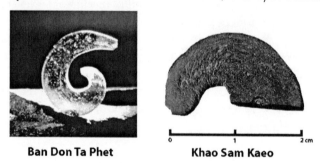

Ban Don Ta Phet   **Khao Sam Kaeo**

FIGURE 2.14
Complex geometric facetted beads of agate, carnelian, green jasper
and rock crystal (Photo and drawings by B. Bellina)

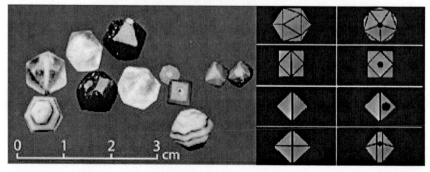

SMALL LION OR TIGER FIGURINES

Local villagers reported the discovery of few hard stone figurines at KSK such as the one almost complete and one broken excavated from burial context 46 at BDTP (Fig. 2.15). Similar figurines have also been found at Khuan Lukpad and Tha Chana in Peninsular Thailand, one in central coastal Vietnam in Lai Nghi near Hoi An dated of the second-first century BCE (Reinecke 2004) and more recently, some kept in private collections were reported such as one from near Chansen in Central Thailand. Yet others, also unprovenanced and undated, are reported from around Halin and in Ywa Htin and Hnaw Kan (Mandalay division) in Central Burma (Fig. 2.16) (Campbell Cole 2003; Glover and Bellina 2003). And they are also reported from Han period tombs in South China (Yokokura 1993).

FIGURE 2.15
Carnelian lion pendant in situ, BDTP context 73 (Photo by I.C. Glover)

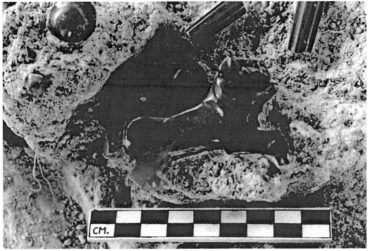

GLASS BEADS

A substantial number of the glass beads both at BDTP and KSK are prismatic transparent forms, resembling natural mineral crystals, suggesting that the bead makers were familiar with natural gemstones[10] and were perhaps imitating them for a provincial market (Fig. 2.17). Observation of their surface allowed us to recognise polishing marks indicating that they had been worked with lapidary techniques (Bellina and Silapanth 2006: 386). Only a few lapidary glass beads have been reported (or identified as such) in sites in India at Arikamedu, in Sri Lanka at Mantai (Francis 2002: 132), in Thailand at Ban Don Luang in the Lopburi area (Salisbury and Glover 1997) and at

FIGURE 2.16
Carnelian 'liger' pendants (lions and/or tigers) from various sites in Burma
(Photo courtesy of Bob Hudson)

FIGURE 2.17
Faceted glass beads from BDTP and KSK in imitation of natural gem stone forms
(Drawing from I.C. Glover & Photo B. Bellina).

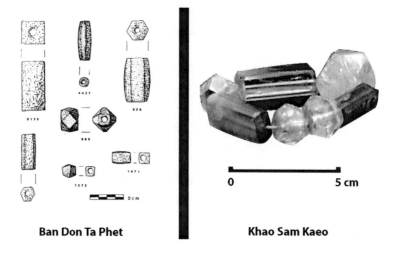

Ban Don Ta Phet   Khao Sam Kaeo

Khuan Lukpad in the Peninsula and finally in the Palawan in Uyaw Cave, Tabon (Fox 1970: 137; Francis 2002: 132).

COMPOSITION OF GLASS BEADS

The composition of the glass beads from BDTP has shown that many are made of a high potassium glass which is distinct from the potassium glass found in India at this time and almost unknown in the West at this time, leading to the possibility of an early tradition of glass manufacturing in Southeast Asia which is only now being recognised and investigated (Lankton and Dussubieux 2006). Other common bead types are small opaque red, green and blue glass beads, varieties of the well-known Indo-Pacific monochrome drawn beads which were made in great numbers in southeastern India from at least the third century BCE, traded along the East African coast, and have been widely found in southern and eastern Asia and as far as Korea and Japan (Gupta 2000; Lankton and Dussubieux 2006).

New analyses by Lankton and Dussubieux (2006) and Gratuze (2007) amplify and largely replace the earlier series of glass analyses by Basa, Glover and Henderson (1991), Glover and Henderson (1995), and Salisbury and Glover (1997). There are now over 200 analyses from glass beads from sites in Thailand, Cambodia and Vietnam dated to between the fourth century BCE and the second century CE, three quarters of these (including 97 specimens from Angkor Borei) come from the second century BCE-second century CE.[11]

The older sites (c. fourth century BCE) include BDTP, Ban Takhong, Ban Chieng, Giong Ca Vo and Giong Phet. According to the classification made by Dussubieux (2001), beads from these sites belong to two main compositional families. Of the total 207 analyses 113 are alumina-based glass and 57 potassium-based. Other groups include sodium-calcium – both plant and mineral derived glass; a few with mixed alkali; two lead based glasses. Only two of these glass types are typical of Arikamedu glass compositions and four cannot be classified being too corroded. The few glass analyses from Burma tend to support the conclusion that the most ancient glass ornaments so far known in Southeast Asia are predominantly potassium based and the later glass is mainly sodium-alumina glass.[12]

At BDTP, there seem to be two types of potash glass – one low in Al^2O^3 and rather high in CaO that Lankton calls mKC-lowA, and one much higher in Al^2O^3 and rather lower in CaO that he calls mKCA. The two types of potash glass, mKC-lowA and mKCA, are internally homogeneous with lapidary-worked beads made from mKC-lowA glass, and all but one drawn beads made from mKCA glass. However, it seems at present that neither of these are compositional types clearly related to potash glass at KSK. There is much variation in the preservation of the BDTP mKC-lowA glass beads, despite similarities in the compositions. As the larger beads are the least well preserved, improper annealing during manufacture could be the cause, indicating perhaps, an incipient bead-making technology.[13]

In conclusion it seems that neither of the two types of potash glass at BDTP are clearly related to potash glass at KSK, Giong Ca Vo in southern Vietnam or to Arikamedu in India despite the close similarities of the siliceous stone beads from the two Southeast Asian sites. It is rather surprising to find such a variety of types, and this may indicate non-centralised production of raw glass either in Thailand or Myanmar in the mid-first millennium BCE.

BRONZES FROM BDTP

Bronze was used for three categories of grave furnishings at BDTP: for containers, some with a raised-conical knob in the base (Fig. 2.18), bird figurines (Fig. 2.19), and for ornaments such as bracelets, anklets and small bells. Some of the more than 30 bronze vessels (Fig. 2.20) also present strong evidence for contacts with India. Most of the vessels were made of a high-tin bronze (23-28 per cent Sn), cast with thin walls, and were then hot-worked, quenched and annealed to varying degrees (Rajpithak and Seeley 1979). Some vessels had bands of fine incised decoration below the rims, a raised cone at the base, surrounded by incised lines and dots and a few included scenes of people, houses, horses, cattle and buffaloes (Fig. 2.21). It has been suggested that this intractable alloy was chosen because of its resemblance to yellow gold when freshly polished. Within Southeast Asia, bronze vessels with identical compositions and similar forms have been recovered from the tin-gravels of western Malaya; in Ongbah cave on the Kwae Yai River; from a site disturbed by tin mining at Khao Jamook, west of Chombung (Fig. 2.22) and at Khao Kwark, both in Ratchaburi province (Bennett and Glover 1992); at Ban Pong Manao in Lopburi Province; at Ban Mai Chai Mongkol near Chansen in Nakhon Sawan Province.[14] A knobbed high-tin bronze vessel (Fig. 2.23) was found at KSK by a villager next to the bank running along Hill 2 (Wall 2) in 2007. Its morphology and decoration, consisting in a series of concentric circles surrounding a central cone in the base of the vessel, are comparable to the examples known in BDTP. Knobbed ware, which has been argued to derive from Hellenistic ceramics decorated with an *omphalos*, appeared on the Indian subcontinent during the third-second centuries BCE. The appearance of knobbed wares in Southeast Asia supports the argument that relationships between the two regions were already firmly established during the last few centuries BCE (Bellina 1999, Bellina and Glover 2004).

In earlier publications Glover (1990a and b) suggested, perhaps too strongly, that the few high-tin bronzes reported to that time in India (Adichallanur and the Nilgiri Hills burials; Knox 1985) may have been imported from Thailand, India being rather short of tin ore sources. However, joint research

FIGURE 2.18
Knob-base bronze bowl from BDTP,
contexts 326 and 366
(Drawing by I.C. Glover)

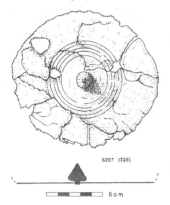

FIGURE 2.19
BDTP fighting cock figurine cage and from
BDTP context 46 (Photo by I.C. Glover)

FIGURE 2.20
Small, high-tin, bronze cup from
BDTP context 59
(Photo by I.C. Glover)

with Sharada Srinivasan (Srinivasan and Glover 1995; Srinivasan 1997) made it clear to us that rather similar compositional types and forms of high-tin bowls were both earlier and more widespread in India than we had realised. The question, therefore, is now open as to where this difficult alloy was first developed although far more have been found in Thailand than in India.

FIGURE 2.21
A and B: Decorated high-tin bronze bowl fragments from BDTP,
1975 FAD excavations (Drawing by I.C. Glover)

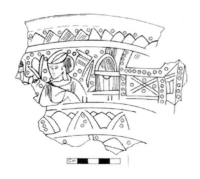

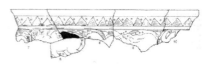

FIGURE 2.22
A and B: Decorated bronze vessel fragments from Khao Jamook
(Drawing by I.C. Glover)

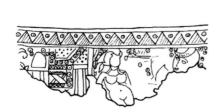

FIGURE 2.23
Knobbed high-tin bronze vessel found at Khao Sam Kaeo
(Photo by B. Bellina and drawing by V. Bernard)

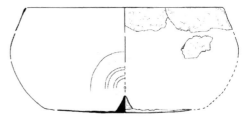

IRON TOOLS AND WEAPONS

Over 600 iron tools, weapons and fragments were recovered from the second two seasons of excavation at BDTP (Glover 1990b: 161) (Figs. 2.24, 2.25, 2.26). These include at least twenty-nine distinctive iron billhooks (while others have been reported at Old Kanchanaburi, at locations near Chansen and Lopburi). The function of these tools is uncertain, but Glover suggested

FIGURE 2.24
Iron socketed spearheads from BDTP (Photo by I.C. Glover)

Figure 2.25: Iron socketed billhooks from BDTP and KSK
(Photos by I.C. Glover and B. Bellina)

Ban Don Ta Phet   **Khao Sam Kaeo**

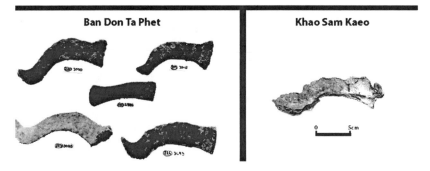

FIGURE 2.26
Iron socketed adzes or digging tools from BDTP (Photo by I.C. Glover)

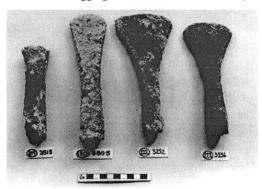

that they might have been an earlier type of harvesting sickle. KSK also yielded one similar socketed billhook now displayed in the National Museum of Chumphon (Fig. 2.25).

A preliminary study was made by Natapintu (1976) on finds from the 1975-76 season at BDTP and this was augmented by Bennett (1982) who studied the metallographic structure of thirteen iron tools and weapons. This showed that the tools, and most of the weapons, were made by simple techniques and no attention seemed to have been paid to the degree of decarburisation during forging. There was no evidence of the use of sophisticated quenching and tempering treatments. However, the implements appeared to be well adapted to their function. They were of sufficient hardness for their purpose. The working edges of some tools appear to have been hardened and sharpened during use. The one socketed spearhead examined had a piled structure and was of superior workmanship. This may be explained by the greater care that had been taken in its manufacture than in the less important, mainly agricultural, implements that were more commonly found. Alternatively, it is possible that, while everyday implements were locally produced, some, with more sophisticated requirements, were imported.

MATERIAL CULTURE FROM KSK

Excavations and survey at KSK yielded evidence for the manufacture of some siliceous and nephrite ornaments, in the form of raw material (agate and carnelian cores), sawn or knapped raw material, stone flakes, unfinished ornaments at different stages and grinding stones (Fig. 2.27) (Bellina and Silapanth 2006). All of these beads were drilled for suspension with carefully made cylindrical holes 1.0-1.5 mm in diameter. Studies of the drilling methods support the use of diamond-tipped drill bits – amongst the earliest evidence for this technique so far known in the world.

Technological analysis of stone ornament materials led Bellina to suggest that they were made with Indian technologies responding to the specific demands of Southeast Asian exchange networks. This interpretation is based on four arguments. First, such agate and carnelian ornaments were made with the most skilful Indian manufacturing techniques and correspond to the most sophisticated production, even rare in India (Bellina 2001, 2007). Based on ethno-archaeological studies, such kind of production requires several years of long apprenticeship (Roux 2000). Second, there is evidence for the production of these types of ornaments on the site. Third, there are in this region no known local sources of agate and carnelian, nor for the previous development of a local manufacture of semi-precious stone ornaments. Finally, because in terms of technology, quality and style, the beads of KSK are comparable to the types of ornaments found in other late prehistoric sites

FIGURE 2.27
Evidence of hard stone bead production at KSK (Bellina 2007)

in central Thailand such as BDTP and sites in the Lopburi area, in Sa Huynh
sites in Vietnam, and in the Tabon caves in the Philippines.

These arguments lead Bellina to propose the hypothesis that KSK was
a manufacturing centre for semi-precious ornaments, probably with Indian
craftsmen settled on the site at least at its initial stage (Bellina 2001, 2003,
2007). Of course one could argue that the hard stone bead production
could result from Southeast Asian craftsmen using Indian technologies; this
explanation implies that they had been taught by Indians for long enough to
be trained into highly skilled technologies. This seems to us unlikely, given the
guild and the apprenticeship systems controlling the luxury industry in South

Asia. Another explanation appearing more plausible to us is that of Indian craftsmen settled at KSK, at least at the initial period of the production, and who could have later transmitted their knowledge.

KSK excavations yielded a dozen lapidary glass beads as well as evidence for their manufacture, together with that of bracelets. Observations on the wasters led us to suggest the possible involvement of Indian stone knapping techniques in the manufacture of glass ornaments at KSK (Bellina and Silapanth 2006). Evidence consists of chunks, beads and bead fragments, bracelet fragments and fragments and flakes. The evidence for the hard stone ornament industry at KSK and potentially as well for some glass production points to the possible presence of Indian craftsmen and, taking a wider view, of different Indian social groups in the peninsula by the late prehistoric period.

CONCLUSION

The presence of several categories of material at BDTP and KSK such as metallic vessels and some specific hard stone and glass ornaments – some having symbolic functions in early Indian religious traditions – together with other strong evidence for interactions such as the identification of Indian complex technologies adapted to regional style, as well as the transmission of Indian decorative shapes strongly suggest to the authors that dynamic regional networks had established and sustained relationships with the Indian subcontinent as early as the fourth-second centuries BCE. The manufacture of specific Southeast Asian-style items, albeit with distinctive Indian technologies, could have taken place in Southeast Asia, as the evidence at KSK seems to indicate, possibly resulting from the presence of Indian craft persons, settled amongst local Southeast Asian social groups (Bellina 2003, 2007; Bellina and Silapanth 2006). This conforms to evidence from various South Asian historical epics and the *Jatakas* and precedes by several centuries the appearance of the temples, towns and written scripts of the Dvaravati Civilisation, indicating that 'Indianisation' in Thailand was a long drawn out process with its origins in the late prehistoric Iron Age.

NOTES

1. Glover saw some photographs and finds of this excavation in office of the FAD in 2001 when it was clear that a very similar range of material had been uncovered; however two infant jar burials were excavated, a type of disposal not recognised in previous work at the site. As far as I know, no new dates have been obtained from this excavation.
2. In 2007, excavation unearthed a cremation pot. Unfortunately, the area is extremely disturbed by looting, limiting the opening of further test pits in the vicinity. The cremated bones of two very young children were subjected to radiocarbon analysis;

those were also dated of the fourth-second centuries BCE and correspond to the first evidence for funerary practice found for this period in upper Peninsular Thailand.

3. Visual inspection of this ornament by Hung and others at the National Museum, Bangkok in April 2008 has confirmed that the green nephrite is from the Fengtian jade source in eastern Taiwan (Hung et al. 2007).

4. See Glover 1990b for a presentation and discussion of these dates.

5. Christopher Ramsey, Oxford Laboratory for Archaeological Research, Pers. Comm. 6 September 2007.

6. This had previously been leveled to make a school football ground, also disturbed and perhaps built up by the spoils from the 1975–76 FCE excavations. During excavation some burial deposits thought to be single were, after more study, recognised to be two and vice versa.

7. This includes all four excavation seasons.

8. Only 53 burials were identified in 1980-81 and 1984-85; the Figure of 100 burials is an estimate based on the total area excavated and a study of the incomplete plans made in 1976 and 2000.

9. The original excavation context numbers have been retained here as all drawings and finds are referred to by these. Some numbered excavation contexts were sterile earth or represent scattered finds.

10. A suggestion long since made by Malleret (1963) when reporting beads from Oc Eo.

11. Translated and summarised by ICG from Gratuze (2007).

12. Looking at the samples from Ywa Htin, Myo Hla and Ohh Min in the Samon Valley in Central Burma analysed by Gratuze and Dussubieux and sorted by date it is clear that the earlier samples are mainly potassium based and the later ones sodium-alumina based glass together with some other chemical types.

13. Additional information on glass technology and compositions received by email from Jim Lankton in May 2007.

14. I have to thank Podjanok Kanjanajuntorn, Roberto Ciarla (2004) and Surapol Natapintu (ND) for bringing us up to date on sites in this area with comparable finds.

REFERENCES

Alvey, B., 1990, 'Ban Don Ta Phet - Data Capture and Analysis', in I. and E. Glover (eds), *Southeast Asian Archaeology 1986*, Oxford: BAR International Series 561, pp. 185-94.

Bacus, E., 2003, 'Style of Alliance? Decorated Earthenwares in Late Prehistoric and Protohistoric Philippine Polities', in *Earthenwares in Southeast Asia* (ed. John Miksic). Singapore: Singapore University Press, pp. 39-51.

Basa, K., I.C. Glover and J. Henderson, 1991, 'The Relationship Between Early Southeast Asian and Indian Glass', in P. Bellwood (ed.), *Indo-Pacific Prehistory 1990*, vol. 1, pp. 366-85.

Bellina, B., 1999, 'La vaisselle dans les échanges entre le sous-continent indien et l'Asie du Sud-Est à l'époque protohistorique'. Notes sur quelques marqueurs archéologiques, *Bulletin de l'Ecole Française d'Extrême-Orient* 86: 161–84.

———, 2001, 'Témoignages archéologiques d'échanges entre l'Inde et l'Asie du Sud-Est, morphologie, morphométrie et techniques de fabrication des perles en agate et en cornaline' (VIe siècle avant notre ère – VIe siècle de notre ère), unpublished Ph.D. thesis, Université Paris III, Sorbonne Nouvelle, Paris.

————, 2003, 'Beads, Social Change and Interaction between India and Southeast Asia'. *Antiquity* 77 (296) : 285–97.

————, 2007, *Cultural Exchange between India and Southeast Asia: Production and Distribution of Hard Stone Ornaments (VI c. BC – AD VI c.)*. Editions de la Maison des Science de l'Homme (Editions Epistemes).

Bellina, B. and I.C. Glover, 2004, 'The Archaeology of Early Contacts with India and the Mediterranean World from the Fourth Century BC to the Fourth Century AD', in I.C Glover and P. Bellwood (eds), *Southeast Asia, From the Prehistory to History*, London: Routledge/Curzon Press, pp. 68-89.

Bellina, B. and P. Silapanth, 2006, 'Khao Sam Kaeo and the Upper Thai Peninsula: Understanding the Mechanism of Early Trans-Asiatic Trade and Cultural Exchange', in E.A. Bacus, I.C. Glover and V.C. Pigott (eds), *Uncovering Southeast Asia's Past*, Selected papers from the Tenth Biennial Conference of the European Association of Southeast Asian Archaeologists, London, 14–17 September 2004. Singapore: National University Press, pp. 379-92.

————, 2008, 'Weaving Cultural Identities on Trans-Asiatic Networks: Upper Thai-Malay Peninsula: An Early Socio-Political Landscape'. *Bulletin de l'Ecole Française d'Extrême-Orient*: 93 (2006) : 257–93.

Bellwood, P., 1976, 'Archaeological Research in Minahasa and the Talaud Islands, North-eastern Indonesia'. *Asian Perspectives* 19: 240-88.

Bennett, A., 1982, 'Metallurgical Analysis of Iron Artefacts from Ban Don Ta Phet, Thailand'. Unpublished report, Institute of Archaeology, London.

Bennett, A. and I.C. Glover, 1992, 'Decorated High-Tin Bronzes from Thailand's Prehistory', in I. Glover (ed.), *Southeast Asian Archaeology 1990*. Hull: Centre for Southeast Asian Studies, Hull University, pp. 187-208.

Campbell Cole, B., 2003, 'Ancient Hard Stone Beads and Seals of Myanmar', in *Ornaments from the Past: Bead Studies after Beck* (ed I.C. Glover, H. Hughes Brock and J. Henderson). London and Bangkok: Bead Study Trust, pp. 118-33.

Chaisuwan, Boonyarit (this volume), 'Early Contacts between India and the Andaman Coast in Thailand from the Second Century BCE to Eleventh Century CE'.

Ciarla, R., 2004, 'The Thai-Italian Lopburi Regional Archaeological Project: A Survey of Fifteen Years of Activities. *Atti di Convegno, La Cultura Thailandese e le Relazioni Italo-Thai*. Torino, 20–21 Maggio 2004, pp. 78–104.

Coote, V.S., 1991, *The Ultratrace Element Geochemistry of Tin Ores and Bronze Using ICP-MS, and the Mining and Metals Trade in Prehistoric Thailand*. UCL, Institute of Archaeology.

Dussubieux, L., 2001, 'L'apport de l'ablation laser couplée à l'ICP–MS à la caractéris-ation des verres: application à l'étude due verre archéologique de l'Océan Indien', unpublished Ph.D. thesis, Centre Ernest-Babelon, CNRS, Orleans, France.

Earle, T.K., 1990, 'Style and Iconography as Legitimation in Complex Chiefdoms', in *The Use of Style in Archaeology*, ed M. Conkey and C. Hastorf. Cambridge: Cambridge University Press, pp. 73-81.

Fox, R.B., 1970, *The Tabon Caves: Archaeological Explorations and Excavations on the Palawan Island, Philippines*. Manila: Monograph of the National Museum, No.1.

Francis, P. Jr., 2002, *Asia's Maritime Bead Trade: 300 B.C. to the Present*. Honolulu: University of Hawaii Press.

Glover, I.C., 1980, 'Ban Don Ta Phet and its Relevance to Problems in the Pre- and Protohistory of Thailand'. *Bulletin of the Indo-Pacific Prehistory Association* 2: 16-30.

————, 1990a, *Early Trade Between India and Southeast Asia - a Link in the Development of a World Trading System* (2nd revd. edn.) Hull: Centre for Southeast Asian Studies, Hull University.

————, 1990b, 'Ban Don Ta Phet: The 1984-85 Excavation', in I. and E. Glover (eds), *Southeast Asian Archaeology 1986*, Oxford: BAR International Series 561, pp. 139-83.

Glover, I.C., B.A.P. Alvey, P. Charoenwongsa and M. Kamnounket, 1984, 'The Cemetery of Ban Don Ta Phet, Thailand: Results from the 1980-81 Excavation Season', in *South Asian Archaeology 1981*, ed. B. Allchin, Cambridge: Cambridge University Press, pp. 319-30.

Glover, I.C. and J. Henderson, 1995, 'Early Glass in South and Southeast Asia and China', in R. Scott and J. Guy (eds), *China and Southeast Asia: Art, Commerce and Interaction*. London: Percival David Foundation of Chinese Art, pp. 141-69.

Glover, I.C. and B. Bellina, 2003, 'Etched Alkaline Beads in Southeast Asia', in *Ornaments from the Past: Bead Studies after Beck*, in I.C. Glover, H. Hughes-Brock and J, Henderson (eds), London and Bangkok: The Bead Study Trust, pp. 92-107.

Gratuze, B., 2007, 'Archaeometric study of éléments of Iron Age Glass Ornaments Discovered on Burmese Sites', in Pautreau et al. (eds), *Ywa Htin: Iron Age Burials in the Samon Valley, Upper Burma*. Chiang Mai: Mission Archéologique française au Myanmar, pp. 67-70.

Gupta, S., 2000, 'From Eastern Indian Ocean to the Yellow Sea Interaction Sphere: Indo-Pacific Beads in Japan', *Puratattva: Bulletin of the Indian Archaeological Society* 30: 93-8.

Hantman, J.L. and S. Plog, 1982, 'The Relationship of Stylistic Similarity to Patterns of Material Exchange', in *Contexts for Prehistoric Exchange*, ed. J. Ericson and T. Earle, New York: Academic Press, pp. 237-63.

Higham C.F.W., 2002, *Early Cultures of Mainland Southeast Asia*. Bangkok and London: River Books and Thames and Hudson.

Hung, H.C., Y. Iizuka, P. Bellwood, K.D. Nguyen, B. Bellina, P. Silapanth, E. Dizon, R. Santiago, I. Datan and J.H. Manton, 2007, 'Ancient Jades Map 3,000 Years of Prehistoric Exchanges in Southeast Asia', *Proceedings of the National Academy of Science* 104 (50): 19745-50.

Jacq-Hergoualc'h, M., 2002, *The Malay Peninsula: Cross-roads of the Maritime Silk-Road (100 BC–1300 AD)*, translated by V. Hobson. Leiden: Brill.

Junker, L.L., 1994, 'The Development of Centralised Craft Production Systems in A.D. 500-1600 Philippine Chiefdoms', *Journal of Southeast Asian Studies* 25 (1): 1-30.

Knox, B., 1985, 'Jewellery from the Nilgiri Hills: A Model of Diversity', in M. Taddei, and J. Schotsmans (eds), *South Asian Archaeology 1983*, pp. 523–34.

Lankton, J. and L. Dussubieux, 2006, 'Early Glass in Asian Maritime Trade: A Review and an Interpretation of Compositional Analysis', *Journal of Glass Studies* 48: 121-44.

Malleret, L., 1963, 'Classification et nomenclatures des "perles" archéologiques en function de la symétrie minerale'. *Bulletin de l'Ecole Française d'Extrême-Orient*, 51: 117-24.

Manguin, P.-Y., 1983, 'Comments on the Concept of Trans-Peninsular Routes', in *SPAFA, Final Report, Consultative Workshop on Archaeological and Environmental Studies on Srivijaya* (T-W3). Bangkok and South Thailand, 29 March-11 April 1983. Bangkok: SPAFA, Appendix 7d, pp. 297-98.

Natapintu, Surapol, 1976, 'Prehistoric Iron Implements from Ban Don Ta Phet'. B.A. Report, Faculty of Archaeology, Silpakorn University, Bangkok (unpublished).

Natapintu, S., (nd), 'Contribution of Archaeology to the Quality of Life Improvement at the Village of Ban Pong Manao, Lopburi Province, Central Thailand' (unpublished Ms.).

O'Reilly, D., 2000, 'A Diachronic Analysis of Social Organisation in the Mun River Valley, Thailand', Ph.D. dissertation, Department of Anthropology and Archaeology, University of Otago, Dunedin, New Zealand.

Pautreau, J.-P. et al. (eds.), 2007, *Ywa Htin: Iron Age Burials in the Samon Valley, Upper Burma*. Chiang Mai: Mission Archéologique française au Myanmar.

Pryce, T.O., B. Bellina-Pryce, and A.T.N. Bennett, 2008, 'The Development of Metal Technologies in the Upper Thai-Malay Peninsula: Initial interpretation of the Archaeometallurgical Evidence from Khao Sam Kaeo', *Bulletin de l'Ecole Française d'Extrême-Orient* 93 (2008): 295-315.

Rajpitak, W. and N. Seeley, 1979, 'The Bronze Bowls from Ban Don Ta Phet: An Enigma of Prehistoric Metallurgy', *World Archaeology* 11(1): 26-31.

Reinecke, A., Nguyen Chieu and Lam Thi My Dung, 2002, *Neue Entdeckungen zur Sa Huynh-Kultur*. Köln: Lindensoft, AVA-Forschungen 7.

Reinecke, A., 2004, 'Reiche Gräber – frühes Salz. 600 feldforschungen auf Dunen und Reisenfeldern (Vietnam)'. *AVA Forschungen*, Band 10: 209-41.

Roux, V., 2000, *Cornaline de l'Inde. Des pratiques techniques de Cambay aux techno-systèmes de l'Indus*. Paris: Editions des Maisons de Science et de l'Homme.

Salisbury, A. and I. Glover, 1997, 'New Analyses of Early Glass from Thailand and Vietnam', *Bead Study Trust Newsletter* 30: 7-14.

Srinivasan, S., 1997, 'Present and Past of South Indian Crafts for Making Mirrors, Lamps, Bells, Vessels, Cymbals and Gongs: Links with Prehistoric High-tin Bronzes from Mohenjodaro, Taxila, South Indian Megaliths and Later Finds', *South Asian Studies* 13: 209-25.

Srinivasan, S. and I.C. Glover, 1995, 'Wrought and Quenched, and Cast High-tin Bronzes in Kerala State, India', *Journal of Historical Metallurgy* 29 (2): 69-88.

Srisuchat, T. and A. Srisuchat (eds), 1986, *Encyclopaedia of Southern Culture*, vol. I, Bangkok: Amarin Printing Group (in Thai).

Srisuchat, T., 1989, 'Beads Reflecting Foreign Influence', *The Silpakorn Journal* 33(1): 4–19.

———, 1993, 'Ancient Community of Khao Sam Kaeo', *Journal of Southeast Asian Archaeology* 13: 131-43 (tr. Masayuki Yokokura).

Thepsuriyanon, W., 2001, *Ban Don Ta Phet Archaeological Site: The Result of the Excavation*, ed. Kemchat Thephachai, Fine Arts Department, The Office of Archaeology and National Museum II, Suphan Buri.

Wheatley, P., 1961, *The Golden Khersonese: Studies in Historical Geography of the Malay Peninsula before A.D. 1500*. Kuala Lumpur: University of Malaya Press.

Woods, M., 2002, 'A Spatial and Statistical Analysis of Ban Don Ta Phet', M.A. thesis, SOAS, University of London (Unpublished).

Yokokura, M., 1993, 'Objects in the form of a beast from Southeast Asia and Southeast China', *Journal of Southeast Asian Archaeology* 13: 144–50.

You-di, Chin, 1976, *Ban Don Ta Phet: Preliminary Excavation Report, 1975-76* (in Thai). Bangkok: National Museum.

3

Preliminary Study of Indian and Indian Style Wares from Khao Sam Kaeo (Chumphon, Peninsular Thailand), Fourth-Second Centuries BCE[1]

Phaedra Bouvet

INTRODUCTION

In the absence of textual evidence for the earliest periods of cultural exchange between South Asia and Southeast Asia, the technological analysis of ceramics from Khao Sam Kaeo (KSK) appears to provide convenient means with which to understand these interactions. Indeed, the technological approach, based on the 'chaîne opératoire' concept (Creswell 1996), permits the identification, starting from archaeological materials, of the technical practices used, and extends to the question of production centres, circulation networks and modalities of distribution (direct circulation, indirect, circulation of objects or ideas, circulation of craftsmen). This approach has already been employed in Southeast Asia to investigate distribution networks of hard stone beads and socio-technical exchange between South Asia and Southeast Asia (Bellina 2007). However, for this last region, it is the first time that it is applied to a ceramic assemblage. I propose, firstly, to describe ceramics that are distinctive of the local productions and which I suppose reflect exchange patterns. Secondly, to identify such exchanges, I will compare these ceramics to productions from the Indian subcontinent. Finally, the origin of KSK's ceramics will be discussed, along with the contacts they attest during the fourth-second centuries BCE.

METHODOLOGY

I employ a technological approach to the archaeological assemblages which refers to the concept of 'chaînes opératoires' as an analysis and observation tool. This methodology has been developed and used by V. Roux and M.A. Courty (Roux 2003: 1-30, Roux et al. 2005: 201-14). According to Creswell, the 'chaîne opératoire' is the result of 'a catalogue of steps which turn a raw material into a finished product' (Creswell 1996), or, for H. Balfet, it is 'the whole set of steps that a group of human beings creates and works out here and now, according to the skill this group has got, notably the technical ability this group masters, so as to get a result: the satisfaction of a need, socially recognized' (Balfet 1991: 12). Ideally, there are three stages in the study of the 'chaînes opératoires'. The first one consists in classifying the different shards in technical groups, according to the macrotraces that can be observed: they allow characterising the fashioning and/or finishing work phases. In order to distinguish a technical practice relevant to a tradition or an individual variability, I check the recurrence of these traces on the external and internal faces. Then, the different technical groups are made of shards related to the same fashioning 'chaîne opératoire'. The second step consists in classifying the different shards, within each technical group, according to their petrographic outline. The aim of this grouping is to find the origin of the clay materials. The third and last step consists in classifying the different shards according to morpho-stylistic and functional factors. Combined to a technological and petrographic study, this classification leads to appreciation of the types of containers made by different production units, characterised by various technical traditions and different types of clay.

Due to the poor state of preservation of the excavated shards in KSK, the fashioning macrotraces, which were very often concealed, could not be taken into account as a classifying factor. I have thus established a classification which is mainly based on the survey of the different pastes (fineness, colour: firing methods), surface aspects (lustrous or mat) and shapes. From the observation of these factors, four technical groups have emerged from the rest of the production.

CORPUS

Between 2005 and 2007, 81 test pits have been dug at KSK.[2] The four technical groups studied in this paper have been determined from the assemblages gathered from the 22 test pits that have been totally studied. For those, 26 different technical groups were set up. Moreover, regarding these four groups, the shards coming from the 59 other test pits and surface finds have also been taken into account (altogether 800 shards, see Table 3.1). The total number

Table 3.1: Proportion of KSK-Fine Wares 1, KSK-Fine Wares 2, KSK-Black Polished Wares and KSK-ECR 1 Groups, KSK

	Amount of sherds	%
KSK-Fine Wares 1	619	5.4
KSK-Fine Wares 2	2	0.02
KSK-Black Polished Wares	154	1.3
KSK-ECR 1	25	0.2
Amount of shards (4 groups)	800	
Total amount of studied shards	11,422	
Percentage of the 4 groups (Referring to the total amount of studied shards)		6.92

of shards studied amounts to 11, 422. These shards are extremely fragmented (about 3 cm²). The so-called four groups are therefore a minority. They show a preferential repartition on the four hills of the site (see Map 3.1). The comparative information concerning the Indian subcontinent derives from bibliographical sources.

RESULTS

KSK-Fine Wares 1 Group

In all, 619 shards belong to this group. 27 test pits provided shards (see Map 3.1).[3] They constitute 0.01 to 4.5 per cent of the total amount of shards per test pit, and are mainly coming from hills 3 and 4. This distribution is very significant, as it also exists in the surface finds, which delivered 114 shards: 80.5 per cent of these fragments also come from hill 4. Only 3.4 per cent come from hill 3. The percentage is nil for hills 1 and 2 (see Table 3.2). The radiocarbon calibrated dates of two archaeological layers with fragments of this group go back to fourth-second century BCE.

Technical Description

The *KSK-Fine Wares 1* group gathers shards, the paste of which is very fine and homogeneous. When inclusions are visible to the naked eye, tiny specks of mica can be noticed. The best preserved shards have got a lustrous surface (due to a vitrified slip),[4] with the same colouration as the paste, depending of firing in an oxidising and/or a reducing atmosphere (red and/or black).[5] The less preserved shards are mat, pale red and/or grey:[6] the colours of the paste and the typology being not different from the lustrous shards, I think that they were, at the very beginning, lustrous red and/or black as well. In this group, the wares are of high quality. I do not have proof that rotary kinetic energy was used for the fashioning (see Map 3.1).

MAP 3.1
Topographic map, Khao Sam Kaeo
(French-Thaï mission of Khao Sam Kaeo, 2007)

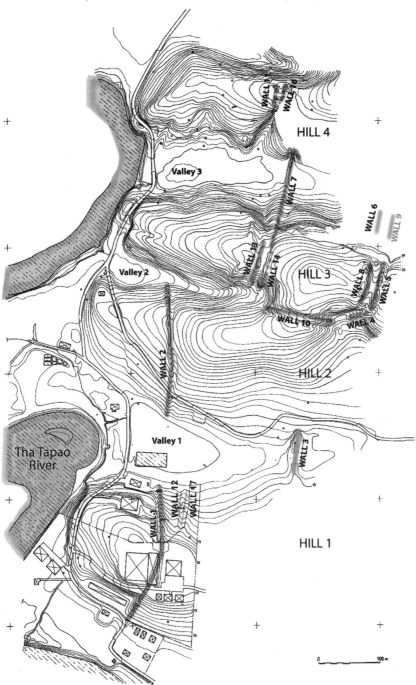

TABLE 3.2: DISTRIBUTION OF KSK-FINE WARES 1 AND 2 GROUPS, KSK

	Amount of shards	%	Weight of the amount of shards (grams)	%
Hill 1	5	0.8	7	0.3
Hill 2	2	0.3	23	0.9
Hill 3	200	32.3	504	19.9
Hill 4	395	63.6	1,892	74.6
Unknown	19	3	110	4.3
Totals	621	100	2,536	100

Schema 3.1: KSK-Fine Wares 1 Group

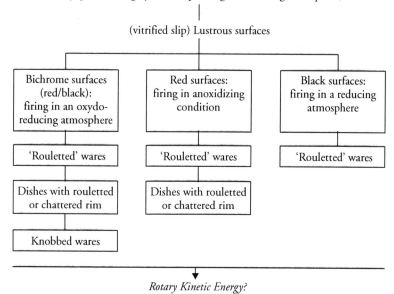

Very fine and homogeneous paste,
tiny specks of mica can be noticed.
Grey, pale red or grey core (depending on the firing atmosphere).

(vitrified slip) Lustrous surfaces

Bichrome surfaces (red/black): firing in an oxydo-reducing atmosphere

Red surfaces: firing in anoxidizing condition

Black surfaces: firing in a reducing atmosphere

'Rouletted' wares

'Rouletted' wares

'Rouletted' wares

Dishes with rouletted or chattered rim

Dishes with rouletted or chattered rim

Knobbed wares

Rotary Kinetic Energy?

Morpho-stylistic Classes

Among ten or so morpho-stylistic types belonging to the *KSK- Fine Wares 1* group (see Figs. 3.1, 3.2, 3.3 and 3.4), I will discuss three of them: 'rouletted' wares, dishes with rouletted or chattered rim and knobbed wares. I have prioritised their study, because similar specimens can unquestionably be found among the assemblages in the Indian subcontinent.

A. The 'Rouletted' Ware

'Rouletted Ware' describes a type of ceramic dish characterised by circular rouletted or chattered (Begley 1988) bands of indentations in the centre of the interior base (see Fig 3.1). It has not been possible to firmly associate any rim shards with base fragments, due to the fragmentary nature of the corpus. 60.1 per cent of the shards from the group designated *KSK-Fine Wares 1* (402 shards) have been identified as 'rouletted' wares; and of those 75.2 per cent were discovered on hill 4 (test pits and surface finds). Rim shards display variation in the formation of the lip; most commonly (92.3 per cent of 'rouletted' ware rim shards) the rim is inverted and the lip faceted on the inside (see. Fig. 3.1). More rarely (7.7 per cent of 'rouletted' ware rim shards) the rim is inverted and the lip rounded. The rims also show different colour patterning (see Table 3.4). The most common variation (79.2 per cent of 'rouletted' ware rim shards) of bichrome rims show, on their external face, a colour extending from mid lip to mid-body. Wholly grey or lustrous black rims (19.2 per cent of 'rouletted' ware rim shards) are unusual, and fully red dishes are very rare. Decorated base fragments (58 shards) also show variation in their colour, but bichrome bases are not the norm (see Table 3.4a). The different morphological types of 'rouletted' wares have, on the interior mid-body of the dishes, series of wrinkles perpendicular to the diameter of the vessel and forming a band of ~2 cm. Moreover, irregular wrinkling can be noticed on the external side of the bases: impressions of mats sometimes prevent their description. Those macro-traces indicate a fashioning method that does not use rotary kinetic energy and which may indicate a finishing technique.

FIGURE 3.1
'Rouletted' wares, *KSK-Fine Wares 1* group, KSK. From the top to the bottom: Dishes with an inverted rim and a lip faceted on the inside (Surface find; Surface find; Testpit 68, SU 8, hill 4). Dish with an inverted rim and a rounded lip (Testpit 67, SU 2, hill 4). Drawings: P. Bouvet.

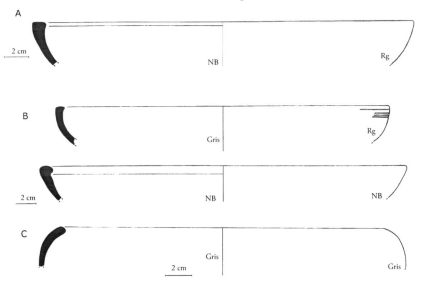

TABLE 3.3: DISTRIBUTION OF KSK-BLACK POLISHED WARE GROUP

	Amount of shards	%	Weight of the amount of shards (grams)	%
Hill 1	2	1.3	13	0.75
Hill 2	7	4.5	40	2.3
Hill 3	110	71.5	1329	76.5
Hill 4	29	18.8	246	14.15
Unknown	6	3.9	110	6.3
Totals	154	100	1738	100

TABLE 3.4: MORPHO-STYLISTIC DESCRIPTION OF RIMS OF 'ROULETTED'
WARES FROM KSK

Inverted rims, lip faceted on the inside:

Internal side of the rim	External side of the rim	Amount of shards	%
Pale red/lustrous red	Pale red/lustrous red	2	1.7
Pale red/lustrous red	Grey/lustrous black	1	0.8
Grey/lustrous black	Grey/lustrous black	20	16.7
Grey/lustrous black	Pale red/lustrous red	97	80.8
	Totals	120	100

Inverted rims, rounded lip:

Internal side of the lip	External side of the lip	Amount of shards	%
Pale red/lustrous red	Pale red/lustrous red	0	0
Pale red/lustrous red	Grey/lustrous black	1	10
Grey/lustrous black	Grey/lustrous black	5	50
Grey/lustrous black	Pale red/lustrous red	4	40
	Totals	10	100

B. Dishes with a Rouletted or Chattered Rim

A shard of an externally projecting flaring rim decorated with parallel and oblique ridges was discovered on the site (see Fig. 3.3), together with another piece of rim (see Fig. 3.2, third example starting from top), probably a part of this type of dish itself. These two shards show a distinct combination of colours (see Table 3.5). No macro-trace can be seen on these shards.

C. Knobbed Wares

Two pieces of vessels with a central knob were excavated on the site. The first item is a fragment of a flat base. It is a surface find (see Fig 3.6). Four rows of incised concentric circles decorate its inner circumference. The second item, derived from a disturbed archaeological context, is a small cup with a foot-

FIGURE 3.2
Morphological types included in the *KSK-Fine Wares 1* group, KSK. From the top
to the bottom: Testpit 66 SU 1, hill 4; Testpit 64 SU 3, hill 4; Testpit 55 SU 2,
hill 3; Testpit 64 SU 3, hill 4; Surface find; Testpit 62 SU 1, hill 4;
Testpit 57 SU 1, hill 4. Drawings: P. Bouvet

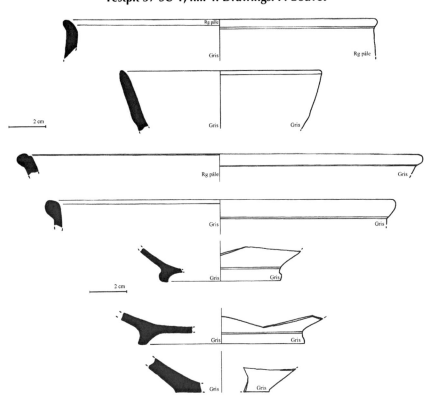

FIGURE 3.3
Jars included in *KSK-Fine Wares 1* group, KSK. From the top to the bottom: Testpit
67, SU 2, hill 4; Surface find; Testpit 77, SU 1, hill 3. Drawings: P. Bouvet. These
jars can typologically be compared to Arikamedu type 6 (Begley 2004: 257,
276-77, 278-79, Figs. 3.303 and 3.304) and type 8 (Begley 2004: 257,
278-79, Fig. 3.308)

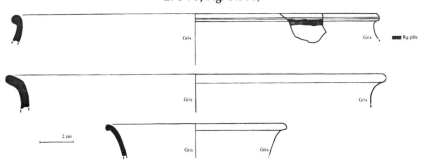

TABLE 3.4a: STYLISTIC DESCRIPTION OF BASES OF 'ROULETTED' WARES FROM KSK

Internal face	External face	Amount of shards	%
Grey/lustrous black	Grey/lustrous black	54	93.1
Grey/lustrous black	Pale red/lustrous red	3	5.2
Pale red/lustrous red	Pale red/lustrous red	1	1.7
	Totals	58	100.0

TABLE 3.4b: DESCRIPTION OF MAIN STYLISTIC TYPES OF 'ROULETTED' WARES FROM ARIKAMEDU (AFTER BEGLEY 1988: 430)

	Interior surface and half of the lip	Rest of the lip and of the contiguous upper exterior surface	Base
'Variety 1'	Black	Brown/pale brown/grey	Black
'Variety 2'	Grey	Red	Grey

TABLE 3.4c: MORPHO-METRIC DESCRIPTION OF 'ROULETTED' WARES FROM ARIKAMEDU (AFTER BEGLEY 1988: 430)

High	Diameter	Thickness of the walls	Thickness of the lips	Thickness of the walls below the rims	Thickness of the bases
~5.5 cm	24/32 cm	0.7/1.4 cm	1/1.2 cm	0.7/0.9 cm	0.3/0.4 mm

TABLE 3.4d: DESCRIPTION OF EXCEPTIONAL STYLISTIC TYPES OF 'ROULETTED' WARES FROM ARIKAMEDU: BODY SHARDS AND BASE SHARDS (AFTER BEGLEY 1988: 431)

Body shards	Interior surface and half of the lip	Rest of the lip and of the contiguous upper exterior surface	Base	Amount of shards
	Black	Black	x	4
	Red	Red	x	2
	Grey	Grey	x	1
	Black	Black	Brown	3
	Grey	Grey	Red	1

Base shards	Internal face	External face	Amount
	Red	Red	1
	Black	Red	1

FIGURE 3.4
**Dish with rouletted or chattered rim, *KSK-Fine Wares 1* group, KSK: Testpit 66,
SU 8, hill 4. Drawing: P. Bouvet**

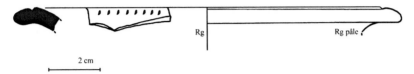

2 cm

TABLE 3.5: Stylistic Description of Rims of Dishes with Rouletted or
Chattered Rim from KSK

Internal face	External face	Amount
Pale red/lustrous red	Grey/lustrous black	1
Pale red/lustrous red	Pale red/lustrous red	1
	Total	2

TABLE 3.5a: Stylistic Description of Dishes with Rouletted or Chattered
Rim from Arikamedu (after Begley 1996: 380)

	Internal face	External face	Class
Fig. 8.21	Dark grey	Light reddish brown to very dark grey discoloration	Fine Wares 1
Fig. 8.22	Yellowish-red	Light reddish brown	Possibly Fine wares 1
Fig. 8.23	Dark grey	Dark grey	Possibly Fine wares 1

ring, the knob of which is not surrounded by circles (see Fig 3.6). These
potteries show a similar combination of colours (see Table 3.6). No macro-
trace can be noticed on these shards. However, the extreme evenness of the
incised circles on the first fragment suggests the use of a rotary movement.

THE KSK-FINE WARES 2 GROUP

Only two shards are representative of this group. They come from surface
finds.[7]

Technical description

As for the paste, they present the same characteristics as the shards in the
KSK-Fine Wares 1 group. However, its colour is always grey, which appears to
indicate a firing in a reducing atmosphere. The outer side of the shards is not
lustrous. On the inner side, embossings could indicate a shaping due either to
the technique of moulding on concave shapes, or the use of paddle and anvil
technique (see Schema 3.2). For the first technique, the macro-traces could

FIGURE 3.5
Fragments of rims of dishes with rouletted or chattered rim, Phu Khao Thong:
Surface finds (French-Thai archaeological mission of KSK, April 2006)
(Photo.: P. Bouvet)

FIGURE 3.6
Knobbed wares, *KSK-Fine Wares 1* group, KSK. From the top to the bottom:
Surface find, hill 4; Testpit 66, SU 6, hill 4 (Drawings: P. Bouvet)

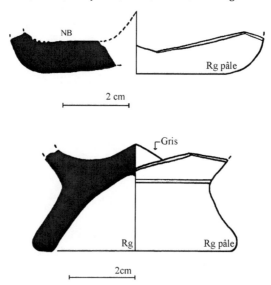

TABLE 3.6: STYLISTIC DESCRIPTION OF KNOBBED WARES FROM KSK

	Internal face	External face	Below the ring-foot	Amount of sherds
Flat base Cup with ring-foot	Grey/lustrous black	Pale red/lustrous red	x	1
	Grey/lustrous black	Pale red/lustrous red	Pale red/lustrous red	1
			Total	2

TABLE 3.6a: STYLISTIC DESCRIPTION OF KNOBBED WARES FROM ARIKAMEDU

	Bibliographical references	Internal face	External face	Class
Cups with ring-foot	Begley 1991: 185, Fig.10.28	Black	Lustrous red	Possibly Fine Wares 1
	Begley 1996: 232	?	?	Fine Wares 2
Bowls with short ring-foot	Begley 1991: 184, Fig.10.27	Lustrous black?	Lustrous black	Fine Wares 1
	Begley 1996: 170, 266 and 302: Fig. 4.106, Fig. 4.312, and Fig. 5.10	Lustrous black/ Lustrous black/ Dark grey to black	Pink to light grey/ Pale brown/ Dark red	Fine Wares 1
Dish	Casal 1949, Pl. 15,c and 8,d	Mat, grey	Mat, grey	x

then be 'prints due to the method of applying on the matrix' (Pierret 2000: 43); for the second technique, macro-traces could be the prints of a counter-beetle or of a tool used as a counterforce (Pierret 2000: 43).

Morpho-stylistic class

Only one piece is listed in this group: Shards with linear prints.

Their external surface shows drawings made of geometrical, parallel and criss-crossed impressions (see Fig. 3.8). The shape of these vases is unknown.

The KSK-Black Polished Wares Group

This group averages 0.5 to 6.5 per cent of the totality of shards found in the test pits.[8] It was mostly discovered on hill 3 (see Map 3.1 and Table 3.3). Fourteen test pits gave samples.[9] The radiocarbon analysis of two archaeological layers with fragments of this group provide calibrated dates of the fourth-second centuries BCE.

Schema 3.2: KSK-Fine Wares 2 group

Very fine and homogeneous paste,
tiny specks of mica can be noticed. Grey core.

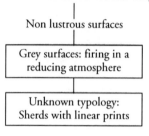

Non lustrous surfaces

Grey surfaces: firing in a
reducing atmosphere

Unknown typology:
Sherds with linear prints

Rotary Kinetic Energy?

FIGURE 3.7
Knobbed wares, Phu Khao Thong: Surface finds
(Boonyarit Ghaisuwan, October 2006) (Drawings: P. Bouvet)

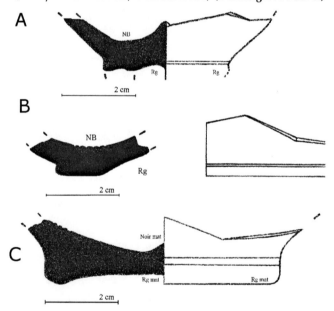

Technical Description

The paste is characterized by an important density of organic temper (rice husks). It is very aerated, not very thick, light and friable. Its dark grey colour[10] leads me to think of a firing in a reducing atmosphere. Most of the shards have a black, carefully polished external and inner surface. Besides, there are bichrome shards in a subgroup. Their external side is red and

FIGURE 3.8
Shard with linear prints, *KSK-Fine Wares* 2 group, KSK: Surface find, hill 3
(Photo.: P. Bouvet)

FIGURE 3.8a
Shard with linear prints, Phu Khao Thong: Surface find (French-Thai
archaeological mission of KSK, April 2006) (Photo.: P. Bouvet)

lustrous (due to a vitrified slip;[11] see Schema 3.3), whereas their inner side
is black and polished. The red surface lies on a white one,[12] leading me to
think of an oxidised surface (see Fig. 3.12, second example starting from top;
Fig. 3.14, third example, starting from top). This type of surface is sometimes decorated with incised drawings, with lines and circles (see Fig. 3.9).

Schema 3.3: KSK-Black Polished Wares Group

Paste with an important density of organic temper (rice husks),
very aerated, not very thick, light and friable.
Dark grey core (firing in a reducing atmosphere)

Lustrous surfaces (polishing/ vitrified slip)

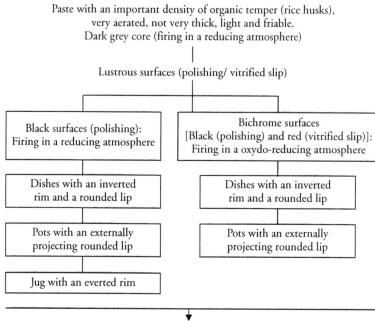

Black surfaces (polishing): Firing in a reducing atmosphere	Bichrome surfaces [Black (polishing) and red (vitrified slip)]: Firing in a oxydo-reducing atmosphere
Dishes with an inverted rim and a rounded lip	Dishes with an inverted rim and a rounded lip
Pots with an externally projecting rounded lip	Pots with an externally projecting rounded lip
Jug with an everted rim	

Rotary Kinetic Energy?

FIGURE 3.9
Decorated shard, KSK-Black Polished Wares group, KSK. Left: External face (residual red painting); Right: internal face (polished surface). Testpit 34, SU 1, hill 3 (Photo.: P. Bouvet)

Rotary kinetic energy was not in use for the fashioning. The location of voids inside the edges of shards corresponding to plates linked together, indicate that the coiling method was used for the fashioning.

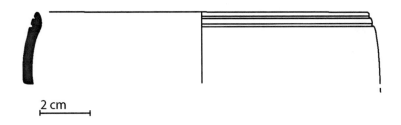

2 cm

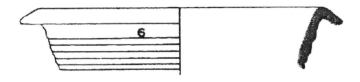

Stylistic Description: Morphological Items

The *KSK-Black Polished Wares* group includes a wide range of shapes. The most representative, in our study, are dishes with an inverted and rounded rim, a jug with an everted rim and pots with an externally projecting rounded rim (see Figs. 3.12, 3.13 and 3.14). Items with similar typological aspect and style can be found in the Indian subcontinent.

A. Dishes with an Inverted Rim and a Rounded Lip

There are many of these in this group. Two parallel incised lines encircle under their external lip. The shape of the dishes varies (see Fig. 3.12). One item is bichrome (Fig. 3.12, second example starting from top).

B. Jug with an Everted Rim

Only one item of this morpho-stylistic type has been found, from a disturbed archaeological context.[13] Its neck has an external wavy surface (see Fig. 3.13).

FIGURE 3.12

Dishes with an inverted rim and a rounded lip – typological variations can be noticed – KSK-Black Polished Wares, KSK. From the top to the bottom: Testpit 69, SU 3, hill 3; Testpit 57, SU 15, hill 4; Testpit 77, SU 2, hill 3; Testpit 69, SU 1, hill 3; Testpit 77, SU 2, hill 3 ; Testpit 69, SU 3, hill 3 (Drawings: P. Bouvet)

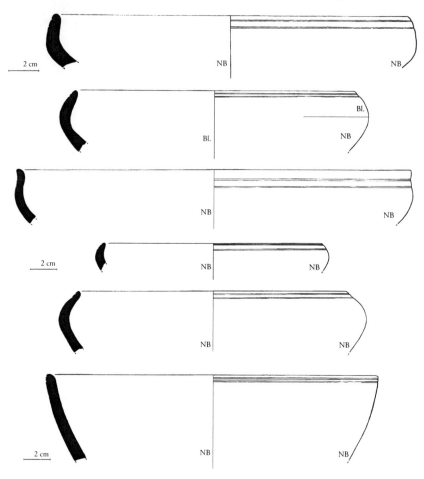

FIGURE 3.13

Jug with an everted rim, KSK-Black Polished Wares group, KSK: Testpit 34, SU 1, hill, 3. Maximum diameter: 24 cm (Drawing: P. Bouvet)

C. Pots with an Externally Projecting Rounded Lip

As for the dishes with an inverted rim and a rounded lip, this morphological type is common in the group (see Fig. 3.14). One item is bichrome (Fig. 3.14, third example starting from top).

FIGURE 3.14
Pots with an externally projecting rounded lip, *KSK-Black Polished Wares* group, KSK. From the top to the bottom: Testpit 69, SU 3, hill 3; Testpit 69, SU 4, hill 3; Testpit 69, SU 4, hill 3 (Drawings: P. Bouvet)

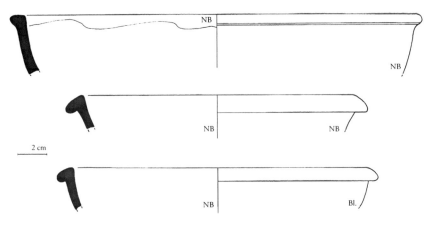

FIGURE 3.15
Morphological types included in *KSK-Black Polished Wares* group, KSK. From the top to the bottom: Testpit 77, SU 1, hill 3; Unknown; Testpit 77, SU 2, hill 3; Testpit 69, SU 3, hill 3 (Drawings: P. Bouvet)

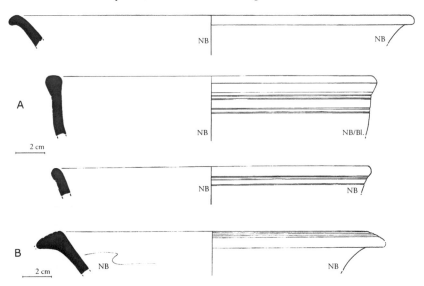

THE KSK-ECR 1 GROUP

The evidences of this group are very much in the minority (see Table 3.1), and were dug out on hills 1 and 2 only.[14] In two archaeological layers, with radiocarbon calibrated dates going back to fourth-third centuries BCE, shards belonging to this group were discovered.

Technical Description

The paste of this group is off-white, friable, and has got a rather important mineral tempering part (see Fig. 3.17). The surfaces are always mat (see Schema 3.4). Oblique compression fold can be seen inside the neck of the jars. This means rotary kinetic energy was in use for the fashioning.[15]

Schema 3.4: KSK-ECR 1 Group

Paste with a rather important mineral tempering part, friable.
Off-white core

|

Non lustrous surfaces

|

Necks with a ridge lip

Rotary Kinetic Energy?

Morpho-stylistic Description

Only one morpho-stylistic class takes place in this group: Necks with a ridge lip.

The shards are part of four vases, the shape of which is unknown: the rim is externally projecting and down-turned, the lip shows an outline with two rounded and successive protrusions (see Fig. 3.16).

FIGURE 3.16
**Neck with a ridge lip, *KSK-ECR* 1 group, KSK: Testpit 1, SU 17, hill 2
Maximum diameter: 13 cm (Drawing: V. Bernard)**

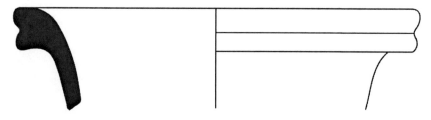

FIGURE 3.17
Paste of the group KSK-ECR 1, detail. KSK (Photo.: P. Bouvet)

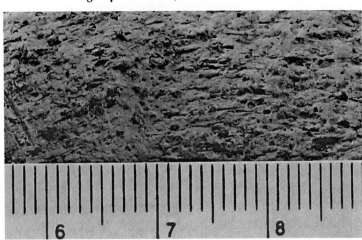

COMPARATIVE DATA FROM THE INDIAN SUBCONTINENT

Fine Wares from Arikamedu (Tamil Nadu)

Regarding the coastal site of Arikamedu, V. Begley's classifications are a reference work on account of their far-reaching consequences (Begley 1996, 2004). The site provided different types of fine wares characterized by a very fine paste, homogeneous, with mica inclusions visible to the naked eye (see Schema 3.5). They are called *Fine Wares*. Morpho-stylistic criteria are the basis of their classification (Begley 1996, 2004). The singular combination of colours (firing in oxidizing and/or reducing atmosphere) and the different aspects of the surfaces (lustrous[16] or non lustrous surfaces) of *Fine Wares* represent basic criteria to lay down subdivisions. I will only deal with the classes (*Fine Wares* 1 to 4) which include techno-morphological types fitting with vessels from the techno-morphological groups from KSK described in this paper. Actually, their index of shapes is much wider (Begley 1996, 2004).

Fine Wares 1 from Arikamedu

The containers in this class are characterized by bichrome and lustrous surfaces. Less often, they are completely black. The colour of oxidized surfaces changes (see Schema 3.5). 'Rouletted' wares (type 1), dishes with rouletted or chattered rim (type 18), and knobbed wares (type 11) are listed in this group (Begley 1996, 2004). The two main stylistic types of 'rouletted' wares (Begley 1988: 430) are bichrome (see Table 3.4b). Wholly black or grey rims

Schema 3.5: Fine Wares 1 to 4 from Arikamedu (after Begley 1996, 2004). The colours of paste are linked to the firing atmosphere (oxidizing or/and reducing): pale red/pink/red/brown-red/reddish-yellow/pale brown or/and black/grey

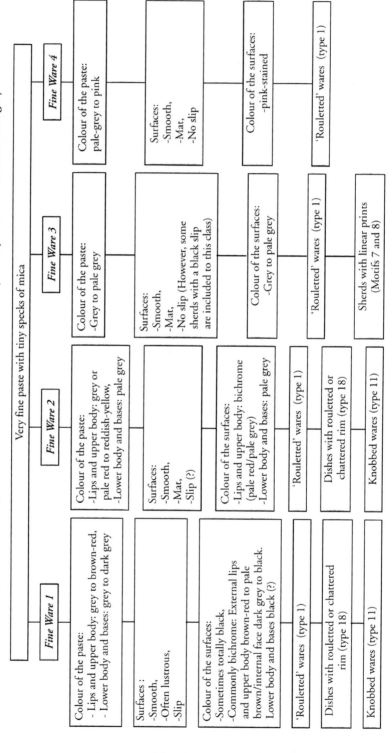

were in the minority. Totally red dishes were very much in the minority, as well as those with a bichrome base (see Table 3.4d). The inverted rims with a lip faceted on the inside would be the most common (Begley 1988: 430). Dishes with rouletted or chattered rim have a decorated rim with ridges positioned slantwise or perpendicular to the rim. The base, equipped with a ring-foot, is, on its inner face, decorated with stamped leaves around a central medallion made of a tracery of concentric lines or an incised helix. The orderly combination of colours of the surfaces changes (see Table 3.5a). The fashioning methods used in India for these dishes are unknown. Three morphological types of knobbed wares exist in Arikamedu. Most of them are classified in *Fine Wares 1* (see Table 3.6a). These are cups with a ring-foot (Begley 1991: 185, Fig. 10.28; 1996: 232), bowls with a short ring-foot (Begley 1991: 184, Fig. 10.27; 1996: 170, 266 and 302, Figs. 4.106, 4.312 and 5.10), and a dish (Casal 1949, Pl.15.C, Fig. 8, d).

The characteristics of paste and surfaces of the *KSK Fine Wares 1* group match with those of the wares in the *Fine Wares 1* class. However, unlike this last one, the colours of the paste and surfaces are always homogeneous. Typological similarities exist between both groups. The 'rouletted' ware from KSK show a morphology which can be compared to that of dishes from Arikamedu (size, shape, diameter, thickness of the walls, see Table 3.4c and Fig. 3.1). The most common stylistic types are the bichrome ones. Moreover, the orderly combination of colours is similar, and they have a lip faceted on the inside (see Table 3.4). The morphological types with a rounded lip are in the minority, and the information given by exceptional morpho-stylistic types agree with the data from Arikamedu (see Tables 3.4 and 3.4a). The rim shards of dishes with rouletted or chattered rim coming from the Thai site have a morphology similar to that of dishes from Arikamedu. Their colours, identical on both sites, differ in their combination (see Table 3.5). Only one rim shard, completely oxidised, has its true stylistic replica in Arikamedu (see Table 3.5a: Fig. 8.22). The knobbed cup with foot-ring discovered in Khao Sam Kaeo shows a shape and an orderly combination of colours similar to the one of the cup published by V. Begley, in 1991 (see Fig. 3.6, second example and Begley 1991: 185, Fig. 10.28). The knobbed ware with a flat base has no typological replica in Arikamedu (see Fig. 3.6, first example). Nevertheless, its technical description appears to indicate that this type of vessel may belong to the group of *Fine Wares 1* (ware, colours, state of surfaces).

Fine Wares 2 from Arikamedu

In this group, there are ceramics, the surfaces of which are always mat and bichrome. The colour of the oxidised paste shows differences. Shards coming from the *KSK Fine Wares 1* group, bichrome as well, are made of a similar paste – the colours of which, on the other hand, do not show variation –, and have similar surface characteristics. However, I took into account the fact that the lack of lustre was the result of erosion of surfaces, which could have been lustrous at the very beginning, by reference to some shards which still have, in a very residual state, a lustrous surface, corresponding to a protrusion averaging 1 mm. Moreover, it is noticeable that the *Fine Wares 2* class includes morphological types similar to the ones of *Fine Wares 1* and *KSK Fine Wares 1*, such as 'rouletted' wares, dishes with a rouletted or chattered rim, and knobbed wares. Concerning the main morpho-stylistic types of 'rouletted' wares she describes, V. Begley does not specifically state whether the surfaces are lustrous or not (I believe they are similar in the *Fine Wares 1* and *2* classes). I therefore propose that the *Fine Wares 1* and *2* from Arikamedu correspond to a same technical group of the Thai site: *KSK-Fine Ware 1*.

Fine Wares 3 from Arikamedu

This class contains ceramics with mat surfaces and grey paste. It includes 'rouletted' wares and shards with linear prints.[17] In her classification of ornaments of the assemblage, V. Begley put these last ones, the corpus of which is small, in *Motifs* 7 and 8 (Begley 1996: 204). The author translates the designs of the first set as 'impressions of baskets, cord or other woven objects' (Begley 1996: 204). According to her, pots of the second set could have been shaped in a mould such as a basket. The *KSK Fine Wares 1* group also includes grey 'rouletted' wares which are, according to me, originally black and lustrous ware. The *KSK-Fine Wares 2* group includes the shards with linear prints. They are part of a different technical group, because the macro-traces I observed – with embossings on the inner surface – make them different from the containers of the *KSK-Fine Wares 1* group. Besides, their surfaces, better preserved than the ones of this last group, seem to have been originally mat. In fact, *KSK-Fine Wares 2* group can be put together with the *Fine Wares 3* from Arikamedu.

Fine Wares 4 from Arikamedu

In this class are grouped shards, the non-lustrous surfaces of which are pink-stained. It includes 'rouletted' ware. The characteristics concerning the ware match those of the *KSK-Fine Wares 1* group, which includes shards with comparable surface conditions. In KSK, I attributed the pink stains to the gradual fading of the oxidised surface, laying unaltered on a grey surface, which is the non-oxidised core of the shard. According to me, these marks testify that these wares were, at the very beginning, lustrous and bichrome. That is why I have listed this category of shards in the *KSK-Fine Wares 1* and that another group has not been created, like in Arikamedu.

Northern Black Polished Ware of the Indian Subcontinent (NBP)

Technical Description

Archaeological publications describe the *NBP* as a ware with fine paste, grey most of the time and sometimes red in its core. Its characteristic surfaces are black and lustrous. However, some other items (grey, steel blue, brown, orange, gold and so on) are linked to its corpus (Ghosh 1957: 24; Thapar 1969: 73). Sometimes, *NBP* is bichrome. In this case, the inner and external parts have distinct colours (Thapar 1969: 73). The lustrous aspect of the surface led to hypothesis and technical conclusions that are as numerous as they are contradictory.[18] Nevertheless, the researchers do agree on the firing methods – a firing in a reducing atmosphere – to explain the black colour (Bhardwaj 1979; Gillies et al. 1983: 40; Mitchell 1979). The eventuality of a post-firing smoke-blackening action was considered (Ghosh 1956). The variety in the aspects of surfaces of *NBP* involves a technical multiplicity which is most probably at the origin of the mix-up and the multiple explanations given. As a matter of fact, all the technical groups of *NBP* are named by the same generic term. The alluvial clay coming from the Ganges could have been used for the fashioning. As far as I know, no mineralogical analysis backs up this hypothesis, often taken into account by the researchers (Sahay 1969). The different techniques of fashioning of *NBP* are unknown, and its wide typology was, up to now, the basis of its classification, which has never been summarised. Nevertheless, the classifying work carried out on finds from Mahasthangarh by S. Elaigne-Pardon does provide a reference grid (Elaigne-Pardon 1995-96).[19]

I have not been able to link technically the *KSK-Black Polished Wares* group with the *NBP* productions, except from a morpho-stylistic point of view. Actually, dishes with an inverted rim and a rounded lip from KSK (see Fig. 3.12), have their morphological replica listed in the shapes index of the *NBP*, as for example, samples from Ujjain (Madhya Pradesh), from Chandraketugarh (Bengal) or from Mahasthangarh (Bangladesh) (Ghosh 1957: 26; Ghosh 1957a: 29 and Fig. 10). This morphological type was previously listed as the so-called 'megalithic black and red ware',[20] and was therefore described as bichrome (Thapar 1967: 70). Therefore, from a shape and colour point of view, the Thai dishes can be included into an Indian tradition: I have noticed that a dish coming from KSK was bichrome (Fig. 3.12, second example starting from top), and that sometimes *NBP* could also be bichrome (see Fig. 3.17). Again, considering morpho-stylistic criteria, I compared the shards of a jug with an everted rim from KSK with a vase of *NBP* from Mahasthangarh (see Fig. 3.11). From the latter site also come vases similar to the pots with an externally projecting rounded lip from KSK, they are considered as cooking pots and listed in this *NBP* group (Elaigne-Pardon 1995-96: 287).[21]

Necks with a Ridge Lip from the Indian Subcontinent

These necks from the *KSK-ECR 1* group have morphological replicas in the Indian subcontinent. Actually, they fit in well with fragments of the *kendi* morphological type (Adhyatman 1987, Polunin 1994: 100). Of Indian origin, these earthenware jars, with an egg-shaped body and a flat or round base are noticeable on account of the porosity of their paste (which allows the formation of a thin layer of water onto the external surface, so as to keep the inside cool). In Buddhism, *kendis* were used as ceremonial vessels (Adhyatman 1987: 5). In India, these jars are listed among the ceramic assemblages of the second millennium BCE. Their typology is plural and changes according to the chronological phase. The type of *kendi* with a neck with a ridge lip appears in jars from Brahmagiri (Karnataka), which are dated to around the third century BCE (see Fig. 25). Some other examples come from Arikamedu. They belong to the *Fine Wares 3* class (Begley 2004: 226-27); their dating and their shapes are unknown.

DISCUSSION

Starting from the analogies in technical outlines and shapes, we can now undertake the study of the exchange patterns between the Indian subcontinent and KSK. The first stage is an approach in chronological terms, the synchronism of dating leading us to conclude that the different groups studied were contemporary, and so were the exchange networks. The second stage studies the intrinsic nature of the exchanges themselves: items (potteries), style (shapes and decoration) and the craftsmen as well.

Synchronism of Comparative Data Regarding the Indian Subcontinent and the Groups KSK-Fine Wares 1-2, KSK-Polished Wares and KSK-ECR 1

Fine Wares from Arikamedu and KSK-Fine Wares 1 and 2

In 1945, when Wheeler first discovered 'Rouletted' Ware in Arikamedu, he dated it back to the first-second centuries CE (Wheeler et al. 1946). Thanks to new excavations led between 1989 and 1992, V. Begley moved this date back in time, and suggested a chronological range from the second century BCE up to the third century CE (Begley 1996: 381, 2004: 54). Few dishes with a rouletted or chattered rim were discovered during the excavations conducted in Arikamedu. They are dated from the first century BCE to the first-second centuries CE (Begley 1996: 381, 2004: 259; Wheeler et al. 1946). Finally, the *terminus post quem* of a fragment belonging to a knobbed ware (a bowl with a short ring-foot) is dated – together with amphora and sigillates – from the first century BCE up to CE 25 (see Table 3.6a and Begley 1996: 101, Fig. 4, 106). An inscribed shard of the same morphological type is dated from BCE 50 up to CE 50 (Begley 1996: 302, Fig. 5.10).

In KSK, the radiocarbon dating of the shards discovered in two stratigraphic units of the *KSK-Fine Ware 1* group of 'rouletted' wares goes back to fourth-second century BCE. Therefore, the observation of the synchronism of dating of *Fine Wares* from Arikamedu and KSK, in the vicinity of the second century BCE, allows us to consider that the technical analogy provides evidence for exchange between the two areas.

Northern Black Polished Ware from the Indian Subcontinent and KSK-Black Polished Wares Group

NBP was first discovered in an archaeological layer in Taxila (Pakistan) and was then considered as a Greek ceramic. It is usually acknowledged as appearing around the seventh-fifth centuries BCE in the Bihar area (in the Ganges valley). It would have spread as early as the fifth century BCE into the surrounding areas. Its production would have run out of steam in the second-third centuries CE (Narain 1969; Sahay 1969). Present research thus posits a two-stage production with no precise dating (Elaigne-Pardon 1995-96: 25; Gaur 1969: 314; Kumar 1987: 217):

- The first stage corresponds to the development of the NBP's typology. It links a proto-urban stage together with a production of NBP regarded as 'basic' ('canonique' in the French text: Elaigne-Pardon 1995-96: 26).
- The second stage is often regarded as a stage of distinct decline of NBP. Less produced than previously, it then presents a miscellaneous typology. Its quality is always described as being less fine. It was then produced in urban environments and communities (terracotta bricks houses, wells, fortifications).[22] The more recent NBP are sometimes said to have deteriorated in quality. (ex. Kumar 1987: 217).

The shards from the *KSK-Black Polished Wares* group, found in dated contexts, prove that this group did exist as early as the fourth-second centuries BCE, at a time when *NBP* production is attested: this is a good indicator of contact with the *NBP* producing populations.

Necks with a Ridge Lip from the Indian Subcontinent and KSK-ECR 1 Group

In the Indian subcontinent, the items from Brahmagiri bring evidence for the existence of this morphological type, dated as early as the third century BCE. The samples from Arikamedu were found in disturbed archaeological contexts. However, their link with *Fine Ware 3* class leads me to think that they did exist together with 'rouletted' ware. The shards from *KSK-ECR 1* group are dated to as early as fourth-third centuries BCE. This dating brings evidence for the synchronism of a morphological types in KSK and in India, at least during the third century BCE, leading us again to the conclusion that there were established relationships with the Indian subcontinent during this period.

Origin of KSK-Fine Wares 1 and 2, KSK-Black Polished Wares and KSK-ECR 1 Groups

KSK-Fine Wares 1 and 2

Regarding the *KSK-Fine Wares* groups, the noticeable homogeneity of colours of containers (paste and surfaces) and the recurrence of macro-traces, which can be seen on some morphological types ('rouletted' wares, shards with linear prints), appear to indicate that there was only one centre of production. For these groups, it is certain that there is a techno-morpho-stylistic similarity with the *Fine Wares* from Arikamedu, which means that the 'chaîne opératoire' of the *Fine Wares* from KSK is similar in all ways to the one describing the *Fine Wares* from Arikamedu, which must have been made in India. In the 1990s, there appeared a strong will to ascertain the location of the production centres of 'rouletted' wares in India; this opened a new way for mineralogical analyses. They led us to suppose that there was a local use of clay and the working of only one clay source – still undetermined – for their production (Gogte 1997;[23] Krishnan et al. 1995;[24] Pollard et al. 2005). It is therefore reasonable to assume that the *KSK-Fine Wares* from KSK were made in India, and to suppose they were imported from one and the same centre.

The spread of *Fine Wares* is a widely known fact, both in India and in Southeast Asia. 'Rouletted' ware, generally dated comparatively to similar 'rouletted' wares from Arikamedu, have been identified in Bengal and in Bangladesh, in the North, and as far as Sri Lanka in the South. Nowadays, it is established that this morphological type did exist in some fifty sites.[25] Recent studies led in Anuradhapura (Sri Lanka) have showed that it was still there in the archaeological layers dated from fourth century BCE till the beginning of fourth century CE (Coningham 1999). Dishes with a 'rouletted' or chattered rim are known to have been found in Alagankulam (Tamil Nadu, Begley 2004: 155, Fig. 3.49 and 3.50) and in Nattamedu (Karaikadu) (Begley 1991: 182). Some other shards, discovered in Chandraketugarh, seem to belong to this morphological type (Ghosh 1957: 29, Pl. 55B). Finally, a shard with linear prints and a fine paste is said to have been discovered in Karaikadu, on the Coromandel Coast, north of Arikamedu (Begley 1996: 205).

Potteries belonging to the same morpho-stylistic description as the *Fine Wares* groups from KSK were discovered in various Southeast Asian sites. Their Indian origin is obvious. So as to establish the source of these 'rouletted' wares, some mineralogical analyses were again carried out. They reveal that the composition of their paste corresponded to that of Indian and Sri Lankan shards of the same morpho-stylistic type, whereas it differed from the paste of local shards and sediments (Ardika et al. 1991; Glover et al. 1996). 'Rouletted' wares were reported from Central Thailand (Chansen, CE 460-600; Bronson 1976), in Bali (Sembiran, first-third centuries CE; Ardika et al. 1991), in Vietnam (Tra Kieu, fourth-first century BCE; Glover et al. 1996) and in North West Java (Kobak Kendal and Citubak)[26] (Walter et al. 1977). The latter two sites also provided fragments of knobbed wares. Recent field work on the site of Phu Khao Thong (Peninsular Thailand)[27] led me to notice, based on techno-morpho-stylistic criteria, the presence of productions similar to *Fine Wares 1* and *2* from KSK: 'Rouletted' wares, dishes with 'rouletted' or chattered rim (cf. Fig. 3.5), knobbed wares (cf. Fig. 3.7), and shards with linear prints. Another recent study carried out in Batujaya (West Java) also delivered 'rouletted' wares.[28] All this data gathered from Indian and Southeast Asian archaeological sites alike allow us to conclude that vessels from *KSK-Fine Wares 1* and *2* groups were part of a widespread exchange network linking India to Southeast Asia, which may have started in the fourth-third century BCE.

KSK-Black Polished Wares Group

The analysis of technical and stylistic outlines lead me to venture the hypothesis of a local production of the *KSK-Black Polished Wares* group. First of all, its paste is completely similar (fineness and homogeneity of the paste, firing atmosphere) to one group of common wares coming from the site, named *KSK-Common Wares 2*.[29] These wares are also fashioned without using kinetic rotative energy (coiling method) and sometimes are bichrome (pink[30] and mat external surface), which provides evidence for the use of oxidizing-reducing firing techniques. However, the aspect of the oxidised surfaces is not attributable to the same technical processing in the *KSK-Black Polished Wares* and the *KSK-Common Wares 2* groups: in the first group, the red surfaces of bichrome wares are a vitrified slip resultant;[31] in the second group, what we have is a slip. Apart from the *KSK-Fine Wares*, this technique (vitrification of a slip) is not established in any other contemporary local technical group on the site, which leads me to think of an exogenous know-how, the origin of which could be India. During the technical processing, it was combined with local know-how (paste preparation, fashioning, polishing of inner faces, oxidising-reducing firing atmosphere), so as to make wares inspired by Indian models (*NBP*); this, however, is not always the case, as the *KSK-Black Polished Wares* shapes are not only inspired by productions from the subcontinent: some morphological types do not have true stylistic replica among the Indian *NBP* productions (see Fig. 3.15). It appears therefore that local potters did appropriate an imported style, but that the wares did not circulate. The borrowing of techno-stylistic outlines shows that there were established relationships with populations producing *NBP*. Until now, the assemblage form Mahasthangarh, located in Bangladesh, has delivered most of the comparative data for the *KSK-Black Polished Wares* group. It is interesting to recall, as did B. Bellina, that it was possible 'to move upstream along the Tha Tapao river (...)' which borders KSK in the South, 'to reach the Tenasserim range, from where it was possible to move downstream along the different rivers which led to the Kraburi estuary, located in the Bay of Bengal' (Bellina 2005: 10). Thus, Mahasthangarh is directly connected to it via the Brahmaputra and the Korotoya rivers (Alam et al. 1991). Links with the different sites leading to the Bay of Bengal should therefore be considered as early as the fourth-second centuries BCE.

KSK-ECR 1 Group

This group is the only one among local contemporary productions to display the use of kinetic rotary energy for its fashioning. We have already noticed that the index shapes of this group amounted to no more than one shape with an Indian origin. However, its paste is similar (fineness, homogeneity, firing atmosphere) to the one out of a group of common wares from the site named *KSK-Common Wares 1* (see Fig. 3.17).[32] According to me, this similarity of paste could indicate the work of Indian craftsmen working on this site: they could have used the locally available raw materials and fashioned *kendis* using their technical know-how.

For these periods, in keeping with our study, the circulation of Indian craftsmen in Southeast Asia has already been considered (Bellina 2003, 2007). In fact, as a result of her studies on beads made of agate and cornelian, B. Bellina has established that, as early as the last centuries before the Common Era, some 'prestige' possessions, such as hard stone beads, locally made with the use of Indian technical traditions, could have been means of official recognition of Southeast Asian communities having an interest in exchanges. It is perfectly conceivable that *kendis* from KSK, together with the beads, could have been devices of power for the local elite involved in exchanges with the subcontinent.

CONCLUSION

This study has led me: (1) to show that the site of KSK took part in a trans-Asian trade in ceramics made in the Indian subcontinent, as early as the fourth-second centuries BCE; (2) to establish the borrowing of stylistic Bengalese outlines and of an Indian technique (vitrification of a slip) to some of KSK's local productions, during the same period; (3) to suggest the circulation of Indian craftsmen, potters in this case, in the Thai peninsula, during the same period.

It is now important to proceed with further field researches, so as to establish in more precise terms the network of distribution of *Fine Wares*, and then the areas in contact during different periods. Technological analysis, in both Indian subcontinent and Southeast Asian sites, should allow us to ascertain whether one or several Indian centres of production, contemporary or not, dealt with the production of *Fine Wares*. Besides, it appears as necessary to deepen our studies about *NBP*, so as to discover if the borrowing of techno-morpho-stylistic outlines by the potters of KSK could have been the result of a continuous relationship with some other producing communities of *NBP*, different from the one of Mahasthangarh. Finally, mineralogical analysis with a view to compare the pastes of the *KSK-ECR 1* and *KSK-Common Wares 1* would allow us to confirm that *kendis* were locally produced.

NOTES

For Figures 3.1 to 3.4, 3.6, 3.7, 3.12 to 3.15, the abbreviations of surface's colours are to be understood as follow:

NB: lustrous black,
Rg: lustrous red (P37 referring to the index of colours of Cailleux),
Gris: mat, grey (N73 referring to the index of colours of Cailleux),
Rg pâle: mat, pale red (M11 referring to the index of colours of Cailleux),
Bl.: lustrous red layer on a white surface,
NB/Bl.: lustrous black layer on a white surface.

For the Tables 3.4, 3.4a, 3.5 and 3.6, as for the schemas 3.1 to 3.4, the colours grey, dark grey, pale red and red correspond to the references N73, N31, M11, P37 of the index of colours of Cailleux.

1. I thank Praon Silapanth and Bérénice Bellina, co-directors of the French-Thai mission of Khao Sam Kaeo (Peninsular Thailand) to have allowed me to study the

ceramic assemblage of the site, starting in 2006. I thank Mrs Bérénice Bellina and Valentine Roux, for their valuable advices all along the writing of this paper. I also sincerely thank the late Christine Jarrige who kindly translated this paper from the French.

2. 27 test pits on hill 1, 17 on hill 2, 16 on hill 3 and 21 on hill 4.

3. 3 test pits on hill 1, 3 test pits on hill 2, 8 test pits on hill 3 and 13 on hill 4.

4. It is about a mineral coating made of finely levigated clay. The fineness of the clay and the presence of specific elements allow to get a beginning of vitrification in low temperature (900 °) (Blondel 2001: 50).

5. Red: P37, referring to the index of colours of Cailleux.

6. Grey: N73; pale red: M11, referring to the index of colours of Cailleux.

7. Hills 3 and 4.

8. Percentages got once considered the number of shards per test pits.

9. 1 test pit on hill 1, 1 on hill 2, 7 on hill 3, 5 on hill 4.

10. N31, referring to the index of colours of Cailleux.

11. It is about a mineral coating made of finely levigated clay. The fineness of clay and the presence of specific elements allow to get a beginning of vitrification in low temperature (900 °; Blondel 2001: 50).

12. L92, referring to the index of colours of Cailleux.

13. Test pit 34 (SU 1, hill 3).

14. 25 shards (test pits 9 and 14, hill 1; test pits 1 and 29, hill 2).

15. A survey led by A. Pierret has shown that these folds (*'a micro oblique fold (80 %) with regard to a horizontal line'*) are due to compression (Pierret 2000: 98). In his bibliographical index of macrotraces, this oblique fold can also be seen on the inner surface of wheel-shaped wares. In both cases, there are better preserved when the aperture is narrower (Pierret 2000: 41).

16. The brightness of surfaces was supposed to be the result of the application of a slip – the components of which would be different from the body clay – on a smoothed surface (Begley 1998: 431).

17. On the site, other shards with linear impressions were listed. They are linked to a group named *Fine Wares* 5, the paste of which is less fine than the fine wares 1 to 4 (Begley 1996: 123). I therefore do not take them into account for the comparative data. They are also noticeable in coarser pastes.

18. Addition of lead-oxide or ferrous silicates to a slip or burnishing work (Elaigne-Pardon 1995-96: 23-24); 'The lustre on the surface of the Ware appears to be composed of some easily fusible material, possibly of organic origin, which undergoes incipient fusion at low heat' (Ghosh 1956: 56); '(…) the black colouration of the "NBPW" slip examined is predominantly due to the presence of an iron-rich biotite or related mica (…) The surface gloss is attributed to the alignment of such mica platelets parallel to the slip surface' (Gillies et al. 1983: 41); Application of a 'carefully-sifted liquid clay, peptised by the addition of alkaline material' (Thapar et al. 1967: 73).

19. This was a two-stage classification work. The first step consisted in classifying the shards in 'categories', according to their inclusions (kinds, size, abundance: microscopic and macroscopic scale observations), firing methods and surface treatments (care done to surfaces before the application of a slip, quality of the 'gloss'). The second step consisted in determining the typological variability inside the different 'categories' (Elaigne-Pardon 1995-96).

20. This production is supposed to have appeared some time around 1500 BCE, in Occidental Bengal. It could have been made until the third century BCE. These dates

are the ones generally taken into account by the Scientific Community (Wheeler 1948: 208, Begley 1988: 433, Thapar 1969: 68).

21. 'Small cooking pot with flared neck', inv. MAH 99168.1, Fig. 3.15.

22. For further information about the different stages of production of *NBP* and their links with the development of towns in Indian world, see Elaigne-Pardon 1995-96: 25-26.

23. X-ray diffraction analyses.

24. Thin section analysis.

25. See Begley 1991, Map 10.2, Bellina 1999, Bouvet 2006.

26. Relative dating: beginning of Christian era.

27. Three survey campaigns conducted on the site of Phu Khao Thong delivered about 300 such shards: about 50 shards of 'rouletted' wares; 10 shards of dishes with 'rouletted' or chattered rim; about 5 shards of knobbed wares; about 10 shards with linear prints; fragmentation of the shards: ~6 cm². The two first campaigns were led by the French-Thai team of KSK, in April 2006 and 2007. The third one was led by M. Boonyarit Ghaisuwan, from the Fine Arts Department in Phuket (Thailand), in October 2006. We did not study the material discovered during the excavations he supervised on the site, in 2005 and 2006. The chronological sequence of Phu Khao Thong is still unknown. Nevertheless, the site gave a lot of evidence for exchanges with the Indian subcontinent, such as glass fineries, or shards, with inscriptions in Tamil-Brahmi, the study of which indicates developments starting in the fourth and the third century BCE and until the first half of the first millennium CE.

28. Data collected during a study conducted in April 2006 in Jakarta and Batujaya; shards gathered during excavations at Batujaya from 2002 to 2006 by Pierre-Yves Manguin (Ecole française d'Extrême-Orient) and Agustijanto Indrajaya (Pusat Penelitian dan Pengembangan Arkeologi Nasional, Indonesia). About 350 shards of presumed Indian wares were sampled by the excavators from the site of Batujaya (West Java), some 60 out of which turned out to be shards of 'rouletted' wares; fragmentation of the shards: ~7 cm². The site was occupied from the first century to the seventh century CE (P.-Y. Manguin, personal communication).

29. See group III (Bouvet 2006b and 2007).

30. M25 on the index of colours of Cailleux.

31. It is about a mineral coating made of finely levigated clay. The fineness of clay and the presence of specific elements allow a beginning of vitrification at a low temperature (900 °; Blondel 2001: 50).

32. See group I (Bouvet 2006b and 2007).

REFERENCES

Abbreviations

AI: Ancient India, Bulletin of the Archaeological Survey of India
AP: Asian Perspectives
APA: Ancient Pakistan
IAR: Indian Archaeology, A Review
JAMT: Journal of Archaeological Method and Theory
JMBRAS: Journal of the Malayan Branch of the Royal Asiatic Society
JSS: Journal of the Siam Society

Adhyatman, S., 1987, *Kendi: Wadah air minum tradisional. Traditional Drinking Water Container*, Jakarta: Himpunan Keramik Indonesia.

Alam, S. and J.-F. Salles, 2001, *France-Bangladesh Joint Venture Excavations at Mahasthangarh*, Dhaka: Dept. of Archaeology, Ministry of Cultural Affairs, Govt. of the People's Republic of Bangladesh.

Ardika, I.W. and P. Bellwood, 1991, 'Sembiran: The Beginnings of Indian Contact with Bali', *Antiquity* 65, pp. 221-32.

Balfet, H. (ed.), 1991, *Observer l'action technique*, Paris: CNRS.

Begley, V. (ed.), 1988, 'Rouletted Ware at Arikamedu: A New Approach', in *AJA 92*, pp. 427-40.

——, 1991, 'Ceramic Evidence for pre-*Periplus* Trade on the Indian Coasts', in V. Begley, R.-D. De Puma, (eds.), *Rome and India, the Ancient Sea Trade*, Madison: The University of Wisconsin Press, pp. 157-96.

——, 1996-2004, *The Ancient Port of Arikamedu: New Excavations and Researches 1989-92*, Paris: Ecole française d'Extrême-Orient (Mémoires Archéologiques 22), 2 vols.

——, 2004a, 'Critique of Gogte's Interpretations of Arikamedu Pottery', in V. Begley, (ed.), *The Ancient Port of Arikamedu: New Excavations and Researches 1989-92*, Paris: Ecole française d'Extrême-Orient (Mémoires Archéologiques 22.2).

Bellina, B., 2003, 'Beads, Social Change and Interaction between India and South-East Asia', in *Antiquity* 77 (296), pp. 285-97.

——, 1999, 'La vaisselle dans les échanges entre le sous-continent indien et l'Asie du sud-est à l'époque protohistorique. Note sur quelques marqueurs archéologiques', in *BEFEO* 86, pp. 161-84.

——, 2005, 'Mission archéologique franco-thaïe de Khao Sam Kaeo (province de Chumphon, Thaïlande péninsulaire)'. *Rapport préliminaire de la campagne 2005* (unpublished report).

——, 2007, *Echanges culturels entre l'Inde et l'Asie du Sud-Est. Production et distribution de parures en roches-dures du VI*ᵉ *siècle avant notre ère au VI*ᵉ *siècle de notre ère*, Paris: MSH, collection Référentiels, no. 3.

Bhardwaj, H.-C., 1979, *Aspect of Ancient India Technology: A Research based on Scientific Methods*, Delhi: Motilal Banarsidass.

Blondel, N., 2001, *Céramique. Vocabulaire technique*, éd. Centre des monuments nationaux, Paris: Editions du patrimoine Monum.

Bouvet, P., 2006, 'La céramique des échanges entre le sous-continent indien et l'Asie du sud-Est (5ᵉ s. av. E.-C.-5ᵉ s. E.-C.)', DEA dissertation supervised by Serge Cleuziou (Université Panthéon-Sorbonne, Paris, France) and tutored by Bérénice Bellina (CNRS, UMR 7528 'Mondes iranien et indien', Ivry-sur-Seine, France), 2 vols. (unpublished dissertation).

——, 2006b, *La variabilité technique de Khao Sam Kaeo* (unpublished report).

——, 2007, *Etude préliminaire de la céramique archéologique de Khao Sam Kaeo : Deuxième saison* (unpublished report).

Bronson, B., 1976, 'Excavations at Chansen: The Cultural Chronology of Protohistoric Central Thailand', Ph.D. thesis, University of Pennsylvania, UMI Dissertation Service.

Coningham, R.A.E., 1999, *Anuradhapura: The British-Sri Lankan Excavations at Anuradhapura Salgaha Watta 2*, 2 vols., BAR International Series 824, éd. Oxford, Archaeopress.

Creswell, R., 1996, *Prométhée ou Pandore ? Propos de technologie culturelle*, Paris: Kimé.

Elaigne-Pardon, S., 1995-96, *Etude des céramiques fines de Mahasthangarh (Bengale) aux époques Maurya et Shunga dans des perspectives techniques et culturelles*, DEA supervised by J.-F. Salles (University of Lyon II, France).

Ghosh, A. (ed.), 1956, 'Ceramics', in *IAR* 55-56, pp. 56-57.

——, 1957, 'Excavation at Ujjain', in *IAR* 56-57, pp. 20-28.

——, 1957a, 'Excavation at Chandraketugarh, district 24-Parganas', in *IAR* 56-57, pp. 29-30.

Gillies, K.J.S. and D.S. Urch, 1983, 'Spectroscopic Studies of Iron and Carbon in Black Surfaced Wares', *Archaeometry* 25 (1).

Glover, I.C. and M. Yamagata, 1996, 'The Cham, Sa Huynh and Han in Early Vietnam: Excavations at Buu Chau Hill, Tra Kieu, 1993', in P. Bellwood (ed.), *Indo-Pacific Prehistory 1994 (1). Proceedings of the 15ᵗʰ Congress of the Indo-pacific Prehistory Association, Chiang Mai, Thailand, 5-12 January 1994*, Canberra: Indo-Pacific Prehistory Association, Australian National University, pp. 166-76.

Gogte, V.D., 1997, 'The Chandraketugarh-Tamluk Region of Bengal : Source of the Early Historic Rouletted Ware from India and Southeast Asia', *Man and Environment* 22 (1), pp. 69-85.

Krishnan, K. and R.A.E. Coningham, 1995, 'Microstructural Analysis of Samples of Rouletted Ware and Associated Potteries from Anuradhapura, Sri Lanka', in F.R. Allchin and B. Allchin, *South Asian Archaeology 1995*, New Delhi: Oxford and IBH, vol. II, pp. 925-37.

Kumar, B., 1987, *Archaeology of Patliputra and Nalanda*, Delhi: Ramanand Vidya Bhawan.

Mitchell, L., 1979, 'Surface Analysis of N.B.P.W.', B.A dissertation, Institute of Archaeology of the University of London.

Narain, L.A., 1969, 'Associated Antiquities of the *NBP* Ware with Special Reference to Bihar', in B.P. Sinha (ed.), *Potteries in Ancient India*, Patna: The Department of Ancient Indian History and Archaeology, Patna University, pp. 193-202.

Pierret, A., 2000, *Analyse technologique des céramiques archéologiques: Développements méthodologiques pour l'identification des techniques de façonnage. Un exemple d'application : Le matériel du village des arènes à Levroux (Indre)*, Villeneuve d'Ascq, Presses Universitaires du Septentrion.

Pollard, A.M., L.A. Ford, R.A.E. Coningham and B. Stern, 2005, 'A Geochemical Investigation of the Origin of Rouletted and Other Related South Asian Fine Wares', *Antiquity* 79, pp. 909-20.

Polunin, I., 1994, 'Kendi: Pouring Vessels in the University of Malaya Collection', *JMBRAS* 67 (1), pp. 100-01.

Roux, V., and M.A. Courty, 2005, 'Identifying Social Entities at a Macro-Regional Level: Chalcolithic Ceramics of Southern Levant as a Case Study', in A. Livingstone Smith, D. Bosquet and R. Martineau (eds.), *Pottery Manufacturing Processes: Reconstitution and Interpretation*, Actes du XIVᵉ congrès UISPP, Colloque 2.1, Université de Liège, Belgique, 2-8 Septembre 2001, Oxford, BAR International Series 1349, éd. Archaeopress, pp. 201-14.

Roux, V., 2003, 'A Dynamic Systems Framework for Studying Technological Change: Application to the Emergence of the Potter's Wheel in Southern Levant', *JAMT* 10 (1), pp. 1-30.

Sahay, S., 1969, 'Origin and Spread of the *NBP* Ware', in B.P. Sinha (ed.), *Potteries in Ancient India*, Patna: The Department of Ancient Indian History and Archaeology, Patna University, pp. 145-54.

Thapar, B.K. et al., 1967, 'Prakash 1955: A Chalcolithic Site in the Tapti Valley', *AI* 20-21, pp. 1-167.

Walter, M.J. and S. Santoso, 1977, 'Romano-Indian Rouletted Pottery in Indonesia', *AP* 22(2), pp. 228-35.

Wheeler, R.E.M., 1948, 'Brahmagiri and Chandravelli 1947: Megalithic and Other Related Cultures in the Chitaldrug District, Mysore', *AI* 4, 1948, pp. 181-310.

Wheeler, R.E.M., A. Ghosh and D. Krishna, 1946, 'Arikamedu: An Indo-Roman Trading Station on the East Coast of India', *AI* 2, pp. 17-125.

4

Early Contacts between India and the Andaman Coast in Thailand from the Second Century BCE to Eleventh Century CE

Boonyarit Chaisuwan

The Andaman Coast of the southern region of Thailand displays numerous evidences that reveal the long history of trade and cultural contacts between Thailand and other countries. By the early part of the Common Era these trade routes reached out to bring together the previously rather disparate Southeast Asian exchange systems, linking them into a vast network stretching from Western Europe, via the Mediterranean Basin, the Persian Gulf and the Red Sea, to India, Southeast Asia and China. This period saw the first appearance of what has been called the World System (Glover 1996: 59). The contacts caused the communities located along the Andaman Coast to rapidly become a significant trading-station in Southeast Asia (Fig. 4.1).

EARLY SEAPORTS ON THE ANDAMAN COAST

The southern region of Thailand is geographically part of the Thai-Malay Peninsula, forming a natural wall stretching into the sea. The area became a meeting point for the ships sailing between the east and the west. This led to the establishment of the early trading-stations on the Andaman Coast. During the uncomfortable journey along the coastline, resting points were essential for tired sailors and crews. Consequently, commercial connections fostered cultural exchange and engendered settlements of foreign sailors and traders, especially Indian people, during early times. The foreigners gradually

FIGURE 4.1
Map of the Indian Ocean (after K. Hall)

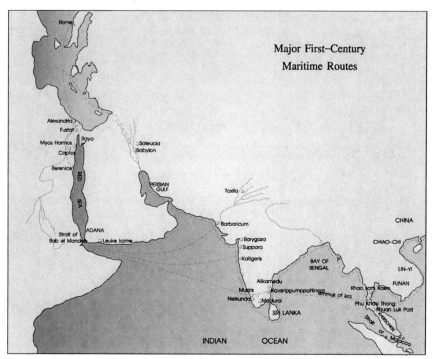

Revised from *Maritime Trade and State Development in Southeast Asia* by Kenneth R. Hall

merged with the local people. Later on Indian merchants established trading-stations at many ports in Southeast Asia. In ancient Indian literature, the area was called Suwannaphumi (*Swarnabhumi*). The trading stations founded by Indians did not distribute only Indian goods, but also Roman products and items that imitated the original Roman goods. The Roman items came to Southeast Asia because at that time the Romans had already founded many trading stations in India (Phasook Indrawooth 2005: 37). The archaeological site Khuan Luk Pat at Khlong Thom, Krabi Province, is located on the coast of the Andaman Sea. There is archaeological evidence that illustrates the contacts with overseas regions since the beginning of the Common Era. The number of beads found at this site is ample enough to say that this place was once significant bead-making site in Thailand. Archaeologists also found there many overseas artefacts. Some were amulets and ornaments, which may have been carried to the Andaman Coast by merchants or travellers. They may have used them to exchange with local products, such as spices, herbs, fragrant plants, ivory, animal horns and tin. One important type of artefact is the glass 'face beads': they are adorned with a sun-like figure, while its colours and stripes are similar to Roman beads (Fig. 4.2). Roman carnelian intaglios with scenes from mythology, popular among the Greeks and Romans, were also found (Fig. 4.3). They were an important product exported to many countries that had trading connections with the Roman empire. That is the reason why the Roman carnelian intaglios were found at the ancient trading stations in India and the seaports where there is evidence of Roman settlement in the first-second centuries CE. Moreover, archaeologists also found Indian seals from the first to fourth centuries CE, which were extensively used among

FIGURE 4.2
Face bead, found at Khuan Luk Pat

FIGURE 4.3
Carnelian intaglio, Perseus holding the head of Medusa, found at Khuan Luk Pat

the Greeks, Romans and Persians. The seals were probably used as tools for communicating with Southeast Asian people (Phasook Indrawooth 2005: 54, 57). One piece of evidence that proved the existence of a Tamil settlement in this area is an ancient inscription: this early Tamil inscription is an inscribed touchstone belonging to a goldsmith of the third century CE. The text reads 'Perumpadan Kal' which means 'the stone of Perumpadan' (transliterated by Prof. Subrayalu of Tamil University, Tanjavur, India, 1993; Amara Srisuchat 1996: 269) (Fig. 4.4).

The archaeological group of Phu Khao Thong is a remarkable archaeological site located on the Andaman Coast (Figs. 4.5 and 4.6). The group contains four featured minor sites. They are Phu Khao Thong, Ban Kluai Nok, Khao Kluai and Rai Nai. They represented large trading communities in Suksamran district, Ranong Province. They are not very well known among scholars, although the dating reveals that their ages overlap with Khlong Tom. Phu Khao Thong seemed to be the centre of the communities because

FIGURE 4.4
Tamil inscription found at Khuan Luk Pat

FIGURE 4.5
The Phu Khao Thong archaeological site

FIGURE 4.6
Map of Phu Khao Thong

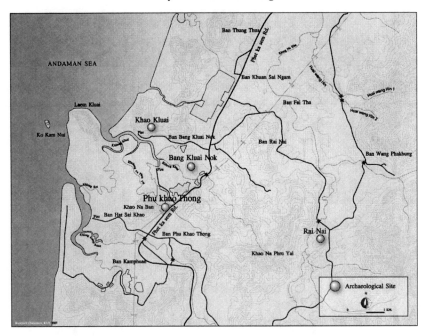

most ancient artefacts were found there (the place was named after the gold ornaments found at the site). The huge amount of glass and stone beads prove that it was a local bead making site, comparable to Khuan Luk Pat. The beads manufactured from the site specifically belong to the so-called Indo-Pacific beads family (Francis 1996: 139). People in the past made the beads by pinching off short segments of glass tubing. After that the beads were reheated to un-sharpen the edges of the glass. This method was used to make monochrome beads, yellow, blue, black, green, etc. The significant finds that convinced archaeologists that Phu Khao Thong was a bead making site are clumps of glass, specific types of stones for making beads, unfinished glass and stone beads and large quantities of melted beads (Figs. 4.7 and 4.8). However, there is no evidence of glass beads and vessels made by more sophisticated techniques such as mosaic glass. Some glass beads and wares were scientifically analysed by James W. Lankton (UCL Institute of Archaeology). The result revealed that the composition of both the green and yellow mosaic glassware at Phu Khao Thong was Roman mosaic glass. The scientific analysis thus proved the connection of trading systems that spread throughout the Ancient World.

A piece of a half crouching-lion pendant elaborately made of rock crystal was also found at Phu Khao Thong (Fig. 4.9). There are a couple of

FIGURE 4.7
Clumps of glass and stone from Phu Khao Thong

FIGURE 4.8
Melted beads from Phu Khao Thong

archaeological sites in Thailand where carnelian lions appeared, such as Ban Don Ta Phet (Kanchanaburi Province) and Tha Chana (Surat Thani Province). However, the stone lions were extensively found in Taxila, the Buddhist centre in North-West India (first-eighth centuries CE). It was also found in many western ancient towns, such as Sanbhar and Nasik, during the Satavahana dynasty. The lion pendant was a symbol of power and grandeur. During the Kushana dynasty (first-third centuries CE), it was the symbol of

FIGURE 4.9
Rock crystal lion pendant from Phu Khao Thong

Buddha as Sakya Singha (Phasook Indrawooth 2005: 48). Other auspicious emblems were conch shells, *srivatsas*, *svastikas*, and gold (Figs. 4.10-4.12).

A most important artefact was a carnelian *triratna* bead, similar to the one found at Khao Sam Kaeo, Chumphon Province (Figs. 4.13-4.16). In India, before Buddha images were created as human figures, *triratnas* were found on the necks of ancient stone figures. At Arikamedu, it was used to create stripes on pottery (Wheeler 1946: XXXI/A; Ray 1996, 50). Those religious emblems were the sign of the arrival of Buddhism in Suvarnabhumi 2,000 years ago.

There are other artefacts from Phu Khao Thong sites that are obviously from overseas, such as the ring top gorgeously carved as a man sitting on a horseback (Fig. 4.17), and the Roman intaglios which were also found at many early seaports such as Khuan Luk Pat (Mayuree Veeraprasert 1992: 159), Anuradhapura in Sri Lanka (Schroeder 1990: 68-71) and Oc Eo in Vietnam (Phasook Indrawooth 2005: 54). The most significant artefacts were granulated gold beads that were also found in Iran (Dubin 1987: 21).

Evidence that strongly emphasizes the importance of the Phu Khao Thong archaeological sites as a trading station is the range of pottery imported from India. Their production technique, clay composition and shapes are totally different from the local pottery. Some of them were inscribed and comparable to those found at Arikamedu (Wheeler 1946: 110-14). The first discovery at Phu Khao Thong was made by the Thai-French team of archaeologists led by Bérénice Bellina. The pottery inscription is in Tamil and written in Tamil-Brahmi script of about the second century CE. Only three letters have survived on the pottery fragment (Fig. 4.18). They read '*Tu Ra O...*', possibly a part of the Tamil word 'turavon' meaning 'monk'. The presence of the characteristic letter 'Ra' confirms that the language is Tamil

FIGURE 4.10
Gold ornaments from Phu Khao Thong

FIGURE 4.11
Conch shell seal from Phu Khao Thong

FIGURE 4.12
Srivatsa seal from Phu Khao Thong

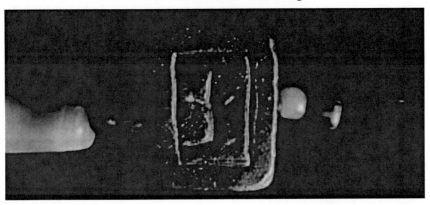

FIGURE 4.13
Yaksi with triratna from Bharhut, India

FIGURE 4.14
Gold triratna bead from
Phu Khao Thong

FIGURE 4.15
Fragment of red ware from Sonkh (Kushan) with impressed triratna symbol
(Ray 1996)

FIGURE 4.16
Carnelian triratna bead from Phu Khao Thong

FIGURE 4.17
The ring carved with a man sitting on horseback from Phu Khao Thong

and the script is Tamil-Brahmi. It is possible that the inscription recorded the name of a Buddhist monk who travelled to Thailand from Tamil Nadu. This is the earliest Tamil inscription found so far in Southeast Asia. Another one, assuming it is writing, can be read, somewhat speculatively, as '*pu aa*' in Brahmi characters of *c.* fourth century CE. Both pieces were translated by Iravantham Mahadevan, the expert in ancient Indian language from the Indian Council of Historical Research (Fig. 4.19).

Rouletted ware is another feature of the site (Fig. 4.20). It was the first time that we found this type of ware on the Andaman Coast. It is recorded in large quantities at 50 sites both in India and in Sri Lanka, and dated to about the third to the first centuries BCE (2,000-2,200 BP; Begley 1988: 427). In Southeast Asia, rouletted wares were also found at the Buni Complex

FIGURE 4.18
Inscribed shards in Brahmi script from Phu Khao Thong

FIGURE 4.19
Inscribed shards in Tamil-Brahmi from Phu Khao Thong

on the northern coast of Java, at Sembiran on the northern coast of Bali (Indonesia) and at Tra Kieu (the central region of Vietnam). The rouletted ware was probably made in Tamil Nadu, South India (Bellina 2004: 78). X-ray diffraction (XRD) and Neutron activation (NAA) were the scientific methods applied to analyse the samples of the rouletted wares chosen from Anuradhapura, Arikamedu, Karaikadu, Sembiran and Pacung. The results proved that the composition from all samples is very close. This seems to confirm that the rouletted wares from different sites were originally from one same source of production before being exported to different countries (Ardika 1991: 224).

Moreover, there are other types of potteries found at Phu Khao Thong. Some of them are similar to those found in Arikamedu (Wheeler 1946: 17-25) (Fig. 4.21). All evidences mentioned above illustrate the close trade and cultural relationship between India and the Andaman Coast of Thailand. It also contradicts the old theories of Wheeler and Raschke (Wheeler 1954: 206-07, Raschke 1978: 653) who once believed that the well organised mercantile commerce of the Indian Ocean only extended across the Bay of Bengal at the beginning of Common Era (Glover 1996, 62).

FIGURE 4.20
Rouletted ware from Phu Khao Thong

FIGURE 4.21
Dish with floral pattern on the base from Phu Khao Thong

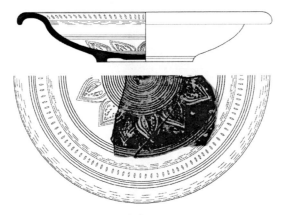

THUNG TUK: LINK OF GLOBAL SEA TRADE

The Andaman Coast played an outstanding role in the sea trade, along the so-called 'Silk Route of the Sea', between the west and the east, and successfully flourished at that time. The Thung Tuk or Muang Thong archaeological site is located at Ko Kho Khao, Ta Kua Pa District, in Phang Nga Province (Fig. 4.22). When the maritime routes changed from sailing along the coast to sailing across the oceans, the ships from South India sailed across the Indian Ocean by making use of the southwest monsoon. Thunk Tuk is at a perfect geographical location, on the eastern side of the island of Ko Kho Khao, where merchantmen could moor and upload the goods all year round, even during the monsoon season. For convenient travel across the peninsula and along the river to the Laem Pho archaeological site, which was the seaport located on the Gulf of Thailand (Chaiya district, Surat Thani Province), it is possible to assume that when early contacts with the Andaman Coast began (as evidenced at Khuan Luk Pat and Phu Khao Thong), sailors may have taken some time to explore and learn about geographic features and landscapes of the region. They first learned about the direction of the northeast and southwest monsoons that blew regularly throughout the year. They then discovered the rivers that become the trans-peninsular routes between the Andaman Coast and the towns located along the Gulf of Thailand. They did not need to sail past the Straits of Malacca that was infested by pirates. As a result, the trans-peninsular trade-route called 'Ta Kua Pa – Ban Don Bay' developed.

Thung Tuk was a place where sailors stopped for a break and to transfer their goods from sea-going ships to small boats before continuing the journey along the Ta Kua Pa River. At the same time, the goods were transferred from the small boats to the ships, too. When the process was over, the ships sailed into the sea. However, travel by sea was dependent on wind power.

FIGURE 4.22
Ganesha from Thung Tuk

This was the reason why Thung Tuk needed to have resting places for sailors who waited for the annual monsoons. This town was also a market where people exchanged their goods with local products, such as spices, rare items gathered from forests and probably also including tin. There were also Chinese products, such as different styles of vessels and silk, and Middle-East beads and glass wares. All luxurious goods entered the region by the ancient trade system. Although ancient artefacts from Thung Tuk displayed different cultures, the communities clearly grew up under the shade of both Hinduism and Buddhism adopted from India, as proved by the religious images found there.

NEW EVIDENCE FROM THUNG TUK ARCHAEOLOGICAL SITE

In 1981-82, Thung Tuk was severely damaged by people who hunted for precious treasures and ancient beads. Plenty of pottery shards, bricks, rocks and stone column bases were scattered all over the surface. The result of the archaeological excavation carried out in 2003 revealed considerable new evidence. Eight monuments were discovered. Although their conditions were not good, it was the first time that we knew how the ancient architectural style of the Andaman Coast culture looked like. It also emphasised Thung Tuk's important role as a seaport.

The monuments face to the east. There are many chambers in the central space inside the monument for enshrining religious images. Their architectural characteristics are very similar to the monument at Bujang Valley in Malaysia, including holes on stone column bases that supported wooden columns and earthenware tiles. Some artefacts are similar to those found at Thung Tuk, such as beads, glass, Persian wares, etc. (Nik Hassan Shuhaimi 2005: 143). This evidence shows close connections between the two archaeological sites, particularly between monuments 4 and 8 of Thung Tuk (Figs. 4.23-4.29).

Remarkable artefacts include numerous Chinese wares from the late Tang dynasty (eighth-ninth centuries CE). They were also found at the Laem Pho archaeological site on the Gulf of Thailand. There are ten types of Chinese wares from these two sites. Some of them have never been found in Southeast Asia before. Chinese wares found there are Ding wares from the north, Changsha wares from the central region, Yue wares from the east, Meixian wares from the south. There are some from Feng Kai, Yang Kang and Guangdong, kiln sites that are not well known. Three colours glazed wares from the Tang dynasty were also found. There is no evidence in the whole of South Thailand for Chinese wares that are older than the eighth century CE. Similar Chinese wares were recorded in other sites of Southeast Asia, Sri Lanka and the Middle East (Ho Chuimei 1989: 27-28).

Persian ware (or Basra Turquoise wares) is made of a soft paste, coated blue or cyan inside and outside the vessels; even finger nails can cause abrasion (Fig. 4.30). Feng Xianming concluded that it was made in the Middle-East and dated to around the eighth-ninth centuries CE. It was also found at Fuzhou, Hangzhou, Yangzhou and Beijing in China (Pornchai Sujit 1986: 19).

Beads are also among the important archaeological artefacts of the site (Fig. 4.31). It can be said that the most beautiful beads found in Thailand are from Thung Tuk, especially mosaic beads, products of a sophisticated technology which allowed many colours to be applied to a single bead (Fig. 4.32). This kind of bead was found only at important seaports, like Laem Pho, the seaport on the Gulf of Thailand. It was believed that the glass beads were brought to the region by the trading system from the Middle-East or the Mediterranean Sea, as they are different from those monochrome beads found at inland sites. Outstanding styles are carnelian beads, striped beads with several colours, such as black, white, red and blue, cylindrical

FIGURE 4.23
Map showing the location of Thung Tuk, Khao Phra Neur and
Khao Phra Narai archaeological sites

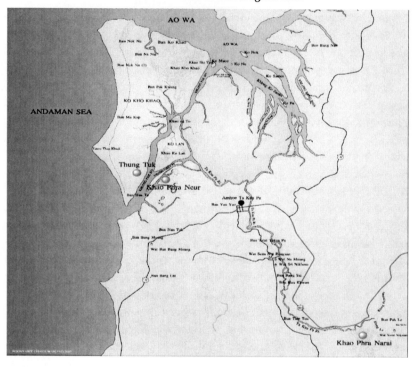

FIGURE 4.24
Monument no. 4, Thung Tuk

FIGURE 4.25
Plan of monument no. 4, Thung Tuk

Bricks
Stones

FIGURE 4.26
Monument no. 8, Thung Tuk

FIGURE 4.27
Plan of monument no. 8, Thung Tuk

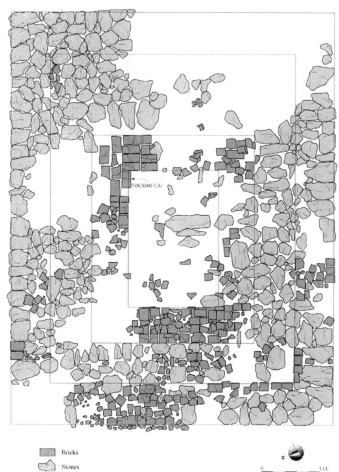

Bricks

Stones

0   1 M.

FIGURE 4.28
Monuments at Bujang Valley, Malaysia

FIGURE 4.29
Shards of Changsha ware of the late Tang dynasty, from Thung Tuk

FIGURE 4.30
Shard of Persian ware from Thung Tuk

beads in different sizes and colours, such as blue, green, yellow, azure, black and transparent white, segment beads and gold glass beads (Amara Srisuchat 1986: 3212-14)

At Thung Tuk, a very large number of glass pieces was found. They were probably imported from the Middle-East or the Roman Empire. Some of them are small glass bottles, which may have been imported from Syria, the principal source for glass bottles for perfume and medicine. Large quantities of Syrian glass bottles were found at many ancient markets and seaports (Pornchai Sujit 1985, 38) (Figs. 4.33-4.34). Syrian glass bottles were also found at Fustat and Raya, in Egypt. Archaeologists also found luster-

FIGURE 4.31
Stone and glass beads, from Thung Tuk (Private Collection)

FIGURE 4.32
Mosaic glass beads (Private Collection)

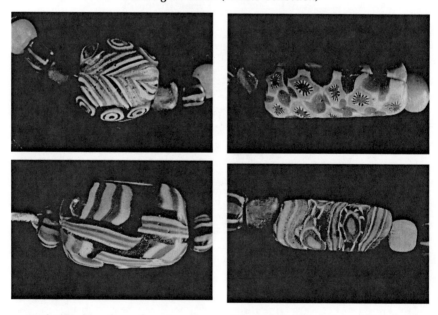

stained glass like those found at Fustat, Raya, Raqqa and other Islamic sites (Fig. 4.35). They were polychrome and dated around the ninth-tenth centuries CE (Scanlon and Pinder-Wilson 2001, 110-14; Shindo 1992: 584-85). Glass wares with incised decorative and continuous triangle designs were also found at Fustat and Raya (Shindo 2001: 184) (Figs. 4.36-4.37).

Regarding the archaeological excavation in 2003, two pits were dug.

FIGURE 4.33
Fragments of glass ware from Thung Tuk

FIGURE 4.34
Fragments of small glass bottles from Thung Tuk

Anthropic deposits were found only in the second stratigraphical layer. Its thickness was 30 cm. Charcoal from the first excavation square was dated by the Carbon 14 method (at the Office of Atoms for Peace) to 1,000-1,300 BP, i.e. the ninth-eleventh centuries CE, which was concordant with the result of the comparative study of ancient artefacts. The earlier Chinese wares date from the late Tang and the early Song dynasties (late eighth to eleventh centuries), while the Persian wares were dated around the eighth-ninth centuries. Thus, to combine both evidences together, the site should be dated to around the eighth-eleventh centuries.

FIGURE 4.35
Lustre-stained glass from Thung Tuk [two pictures together]

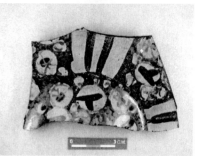

FIGURE 4.36
Glass ware with incised decoration from Thung Tuk

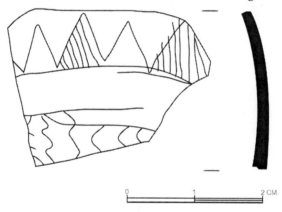

FIGURE 4.37
Glass ware with incised decoration from Leam Pho

THE TRANS-PENINSULAR ROUTE FROM
TA KUA PA TO BAN DON BAY

Many scholars have suggested that the trans-peninsular route was used as a shortcut to avoid the Straits of Malacca (Chaiwut Piyakul 2003, 50-62; Nongkram Suksom 2002, 25; Preecha Noonsuk 1997, 349-50; Wheatley 1969: XXVI-XXVII). Yet the route from Ta Kua Pa to Ban Don Bay or Thung Tuk to Laem Pho is also the most acceptable route because of the following reasons:

1. They were contemporary seaports located on the opposite coasts of the peninsula: Thung Tuk was the seaport on the Andaman Coast while Laem Pho was on the Gulf of Thailand. As a result of similar evidences found at both sites, it could be said that they obviously were contemporary (Amara Srisuchat 1989: 3237; Bronson 1996: 181-97).

2. Many contemporary sites were found along the way from the Andaman Coast to the Gulf of Thailand, along the trans-peninsular route. Significant landmarks are monuments on the hills that are close to the estuary, headwaters and confluents. These must have been resting spots along the route, as 1,000 years ago it was impossible to travel through the trans-peninsular route without taking a rest.

To draw the overall image of the trans-peninsular route it is necessary to mention some archaeological sites and monuments located along the way (Fig. 4.38).

Khao Phra Neur (Bang Nai Si sub-district, Ta Kua Pa district, Pang Nga province) is a small mountain located on the estuary of the Ta Kua Pa River, opposite to Thung Tuk. On the top of the mountain lies a religious monument where a beautiful sculpture of the god Vishnu was found. It is dated to the Pallava period (sixth-seventh centuries CE) by Pierre Dupont, to the seventh century by H.G. Quaritch Wales, while Stanley O'Connor believed that it was post-Gupta and therefore dated from the late seventh to the middle of the ninth century (Tharapong Srisuchat 1986: 1224-26).

Khao Phra Narai or **Khao Wieng** (Le sub-district, Kapong district, Pang Nga province) is also a small mountain located where the Le Canal and the Rommani Canal join and become the headspring of the Ta Kua Pa River. On the top of the mountain is an ancient monument with a group of three Figures: Vishnu, Rishi Markandeya and Phu Dhevi. The group of images was inspired by the Pallava Dynasty style of India, in the early tenth century (Piriya Krairiksh 2001: 152-53), and a Pallava inscription was written in Tamil and dated to around the seventh century (Kongkaew Weeraprajak 1999: 7460-61).

FIGURE 4.38
Map of the trans-peninsular route, from Ta Kua Pa to Ban Don Bay

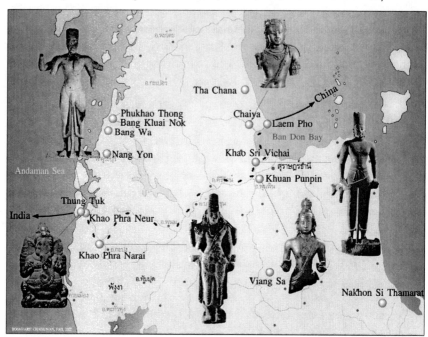

Khuan Punpin or **Khuan Saranrom** (Thakam sub-district, Phun Phin district, Surat Thani), is a small hill near the meeting point of many rivers, among which the Phum Duang and the Ta Pi rivers. The archaeological evidences found here are a square brick monument, 7 m wide, a sculpture of Avalokiteshvara, a pre-fired votive tablet, the head and the body of a Buddha image, and an Arabian silver coin produced in the year 767 (Nongkram Suksom 2002: 94-95).

Khao Srivichai or **Khao Phra Narai** (Srivichai sub-district, Punpin district, Surat Thani province), is an isolated hill located 400 m away from the Phum Duang River. There are 8 monuments found on the hilltop ridge. Important artefacts are the large sculpture of the god Vishnu dated to about the eighth century. There are also Chinese wares from the late Tang dynasty, Persian wares, glass vessels, local earthen wares, beads, etc. (Nongkram Suksom 2002: 96-100).

Laem Pho (Phum Riang sub-district, Chaiya district, Surat Thani province), delivered outstanding artefacts such as various types of Chinese ceramics from the late Tang and Five dynasties (ninth-tenth centuries), Persian wares (tenth century), huge amounts of local earthen wares, beads, glass vessels, and also wooden boat rudders and many freshwater wells (Khemchart Thepchai 1986: 4163).

The passage across the trans-peninsular route from Ta Kua Pa peninsula to Ban Don Bay started after sailors and merchants finished transferring goods from sea-going ships to smaller boats. They first sailed past the estuary of the Ta Kua Pa River, where Khao Phra Neur was located. The river was about 30 km long and they then reached Khao Phra Narai, which was the headspring of the Ta Kua Pa River. After that, they had to sail along the Rommani Canal until they arrived in Ban Tha Han. From Ban Tha Han, they had to walk along the bank of the Hin Lab Canal, which was a shallow creek, across Khao Sok (this route was only abandoned when highway 401 that links Ta Kua Pa and Surat Thani Province was constructed in 1975). It took 4 hours to walk or use elephants to carry luggage across Khao Sok to Ban Sok. People could then transfer their luggage into a boat at Tha Sok and sail along the Klong Sok, which flowed into the Phum Duang River. At Khuan Punpin, the Phum Duang and Ta Pi rivers joined together and then sailed pass Khao Srivichai and reached the sea at Ban Don Bay. The ship would journey along the coast line to Laem Pho. People normally stopped here for a break. Laem Pho was a large exchange market. Many merchants and sailors stopped here to transfer their goods to the ships and continued the trip to other seaports of Southeast Asia or China.

Laem Pho was a remarkable seaport on the Gulf of Thailand. It was only 9 km away from Chaiya Town and it could be said that it was specifically Chaiya's seaport. Although it was 20 km from the estuary of the Phum Duang River and 35 km by sailing, there are several factors that made Laem Pho the eastern seaport. The most probable reason was that it was more practical for Chaiya to administrate and earn *pike* (tax) from middlemen who used the trans-peninsular route. Chaiya was probably acting as middleman to exchange goods between the eastern side and the western side of the Thai-Malay Peninsula, including transporting the goods across the peninsula, because of its better knowledge of local routes. Accordingly, merchants from the east and the west of the Thai-Malay Peninsula had no need to be in direct contact.

THUNG TUK AND TAKOLA

Thung Tuk includes the ancient communities along the Ta Kua Pa River. It is an archaeological site that some scholars believed that it meant 'Takola' as it corresponded to 'Ta Kua Pa', which was named after the river and district in Pang Nga province, the main reasons invoked being that both the sculpture of Vishnu and ancient monuments that clearly reflected Indian culture were found there. The reference to 'Takola' and other similar names in textual sources convinced some scholars that they were the same town.

'Takola' was mentioned in the *Milindapanha* in 43 BCE (Manit Walli-

phodom 1982, 68; Tanith Yupho 2002, 44-45; Wheatley 1961, 269), in
Claudius Ptolemy's *Geography* in CE 150, and in the *Mahaniddesa* in the
second-third century CE (Tanith Yupoh 2002: 44; Wheatley 1961: 268-
69). Sylvain Lévi referred to other scholars' assumptions on Takola: for
example, Kanakasabhai believed that Ptolemy's Takola was Talaittakolam,
which appeared on the inscription of Tanjore. This told about the battle and
victory of King Rajendrachola over many Southeast Asian seaports between
1012 and 1042 (Tharapong Srisuchat 1986: 1223-26). George Coedès also
claimed, based on the same inscription of Tanjore, that in 1025 the Chola
army sailed across the Indian Ocean to attack Srivijaya and her dependencies
including Takola and Tambralinga (i.e. Nakhon Sri Thammarat; Coedès
1964).

According to the information above, Thung Tuk cannot be the Takola that
was referred to in the *Milindapanha*, in Claudius Ptolemy's *Geography* and in
the *Mahaniddesa*, all texts dated the turn of the first millennium, a period for
which the site provides no contemporary archaeological evidence. However,
names similar to Takola appeared continuously in many documents until the
eleventh century CE, such as the Chinese source citing a place called Geluo
or Geguluo in the seventh-tenth centuries and the inscription of Tanjore of
the eleventh century. If these names really referred to the same town, Takola
probably was active between the first century BCE and the eleventh century
CE.

If we consider the literary evidence together with the archaeological
artefacts, the 'Takola' in Ptolemy's text, dated to about the second century
CE should be found either at Khuan Luk Pat or at Phu Khao Thong, as both
sites have delivered artefacts that could be dated back to the second century.
However, Khuan Luk Pat and Phu Khao Thong could not uphold their status
as important seaports between the eighth-eleventh centuries, since only few
contemporary artefacts, such as Persian and glass wares, were found there.
It is also noticeable that there is no evidence of Chinese ware from the late
Tang dynasty. Moreover, no signs of religious influence, such as respected
Figures and sacred monuments appeared at the site. In contrast, Thung Tuk
flourished in those times. Buddhism and Hinduism were practised, as attested
by many sacred monuments.

Roman carnelian intaglios and Indian rouletted ware, however, were never
brought to light at this site. Archaeological excavations at Thung Tuk found
no evidence older than the eighth century CE. We may be able to assume that
Khuan Luk Pat, Phu Khao Thong and Thung Tuk were occupied in turn.
Thus 'Takola' may have been a general term to designate the seaports on the
Andaman Coast of what is now Thailand. When the trans-peninsular route
from Ta Kua Pa to Ban Don Bay was discovered, the centres would have been
moved to Thung Tuk and Khuan Luk Pat. Consequently, Phu Khao Thong

would have played a decreasing role. This assumption may explain why 'Takola' coincided with the name recorded in Arabian and Chinese sources and in the inscription of Tanjore between the eighth and eleventh centuries. The site of Thung Tuk may, therefore, have then been 'Takola' too. It is also possible that it was Talaittakolam that was invaded by King Rajendrachola, and this battle possibly caused the people to finally abandon the town.

CONCLUSION

The Indian Ocean was not an obstacle for trade between the towns along the Andaman Ocean and India. Phu Khao Thong was dated to around 1,200-2,200 BP (third century BCE to eighth century CE) during archaeological excavations in 2005-06. It was an important bead making site comparable to Khuan Luk Pat. Many artefacts displayed overseas contacts, especially with India. Among the notable artefacts found at the site, we have the rock crystal lion pendant (which was also found at Taxila), inscribed shards in both Tamil-Brahmi and Brahmi scripts dated to the second-fourth centuries CE, rouletted wares dated to the second century BCE-first century CE, and other potteries similar to those found at Arikamedu. All illustrate the close cultural and trade contacts between the two regions during the early Common Era.

Phu Khao Thong and Khuan Luk Pat played a decreasing role during the ninth-tenth centuries CE. Artefacts of the period were rarely found, except a few Persian ceramics and glass wares from the Middle-East. No evidence of Indic religious monuments and statues, and no Chinese ware from the late Tang dynasty were found in Phu Khao Thong and Khuan Luk Pat at this time. In contrast, they were found in large quantities at Thung Tuk. It could be said that the importance of Phu Khao Thong and Khuan Luk Pat was reduced and replaced by Thung Tuk when people started travelling by the trans-peninsula route from Ta Kua Pa to Ban Don Bay in the ninth-eleventh centuries CE (during the Srivijaya period). Thung Tuk then became a very important step in 'the Silk Route of the Sea' that linked the trade systems of the west and the east of the Thai-Malay Peninsula, where communities grew up under the shade of Buddhism and Hinduism, adopted from India.

Some scholars believed that only Thung Tuk and the ancient communities along the Ta Kua Pa River could be identified as 'Takola'. However, results of archaeological excavations revealed that there was no evidence older than the eighth century CE at Thung Tuk, so that Takola could not be the town that was mentioned in the textual sources of the first to eighth centuries CE. On the other hand, considerable archaeological evidence for the period was brought to light at both Phu Khao Thong and Khuan Luk Pat. We may thus assume that in the past the name Takola was in generic reference for the port-towns along the Andaman Coast.

REFERENCES

Amara Srisuchat, 'Ancient Beads', in *Cultural Encyclopedia of Southern Thailand*, vol. 8, 1976, pp. 3212-44 (in Thai).

Ardika, I.W. and P. Bellwood, 'Sembiran: The Beginning of India Contact with Bali', *Antiquity* 65: 247, 1991, pp. 221-32.

Begley, V., 'Rouletted Ware at Arikamedu: A New Approach', *American Journal of Archaeology*, vol. 92, no. 3 (July), 1988, pp. 427-40.

Bellina, B., 'The Archaeology of Early Contact with India and Mediterranean World, from the Fourth Century BC to the Fourth Century AD. Southeast Asia', in *Prehistory to History*, ed. Ian Glover and Peter Bellwood, 2004, pp. 68-89.

Bronson, B., 'Chinese and Middle Eastern Trade in Southern Thailand During the 9th Century AD', in *Ancient Trades and Culture Contacts in Southeast Asia*, Bangkok: The Office of the National Culture Comission, 1996, pp. 181-200.

Chaiwut Piyakul and Klin Kongmuenphet, 'Across the Malay Peninsula: From Khlong Thom, Krabi Province- Ban Don Bay, Surat Thani Province', *Taksin Kadee Magazine*, vol. 6, no. 3, 2003, pp. 50-62 (in Thai).

Coedès, G., *The Empire of the Southern Sea*, written for the Siam Society, tr. Prince Pitthayalab Pruttiyakorn, Thailand, 1954.

Dubin, L. Sherr, *The History of Beads from 30,000 B.C. to the Present*, New York: Harry N. Abrams, 1987.

Francis, P., 'Bead, the Bead Trade and Development in Southeast Asia', in *Ancient Trades and Culture Contacts in Southeast Asia*. Bangkok: The Office of the National Culture Commission, 1996, pp. 139-52.

Glover, I.C., 'The Southern Silk Road: Archaeological Evidence for Early Trade Between India and Southeast Asia', in *Ancient Trades and Culture Contacts in Southeast Asia*, Bangkok: The Office of the National Culture Comission, 1996, pp. 57-94.

Ho Chuimei et al., 'Early Chinese Ceramics in Southern of Thailand', *Silpakorn*, vol. 33, no. 4, 1989, pp. 15-29 (in Thai).

Khemchat Thepthai, 'Laem Pho Archaeological Site', in *Cultural Encyclopedia of Southern Thailand*, vol. 10, 1986, pp. 4159-63 (in Thai).

Kongkaew Weeraprajak, 'Inscription from Khao Phra Narai: Ta Kua Pa', in *Cultural Encyclopedia of Southern Thailand*, vol. 15, 1999, pp. 7460-61 (in Thai).

Manit Walliphodom, 'The Empires on the South of Thailand before the Rise of Srivijaya', in *Seminar on the History and Archaeology of Srivijaya*, Bangkok: Kanesha Publishing, 1982 (in Thai).

Mayuree Verapasert, 'Khlong Thom: An Ancient Bead-Manufacturing Location and An Ancient Entrepot', in *Early Metallurgy Trade and Urban Centres in Thailand and Southeast Asia*. Bangkok, 1992, pp. 149-60 (in Thai).

Nik Hassan Shuhaimi Nik, Abd. Rahman, 'Hindu and Buddhist Art in Northern Peninsular Malaysia', in *Proceeding of the Seminar on Thailand-Malaysia: Malay Peninsular Archaeology Programme*, Bangkok, 2005, pp. 140-87.

Nongkran Suksom, *Historical Archaeology of Surat Thani*, Bangkok: Artit Communication, 2002 (in Thai).

Phasook Indrawooth, *Suwannaphumi from Archaeological Evidences*, Bangkok: Sak Sopha Printing, 2005 (in Thai).

Piriya Krairiksh, *Thai Civilization: Introduction to Art History*, vol. 1, *Arts before the 19th Century*, Bangkok: Ammarin Printing, 2001 (in Thai).

Pornchai Sujit, 'Ancient Glass in Asia', *Muang Boran*, vol. 11, no. 1 (January-March), 1985 (in Thai).

————, 'Persian Ware in Thailand', *Muang Boran*, vol. 12, no. 4 (October-December), 1986 (in Thai).

Preecha Noonsuk, 'Ko Kho Khao Archaeological Site', in *Cultural Encyclopedia of Southern Thailand*, vol. 1, 1976, pp. 229-36 (in Thai).

Raschke, M.G., 'New Studies in Roman Commerce with the East', in *Aufstieg und Niedergang der Romischen Welt*. Berlin and New York: de Gruyter, vol. 2, no. 9, 1978.

Ray, Himanshu Prabha, 'Trans-oceanic contacts between South and Southeast Asia', in Amara Srisuchat (ed.), *Ancient Trades and Cultural Contacts in Southeast Asia*, Bangkok, The Office of the National Culture Commission, 1996.

Scanlon, G.T. and R.H. Pinder-Wilson, *Fustat Glass of the Early Islamic Peroid-Finds Excavated Reported by The American Research Center in Egypt 1964-1980*, London: Altajir World of Islam Trust, 2001.

Schroeder, U. von, *Buddhist Sculptures of Sri Lanka*, Hong Kong: Visual Dharma Publications, 1990.

Shindo, Y., 'Glass', in *Egyptain Islamic city, al Fustat: Excavation Report 1978-1985*, Tokyo: Waseda University Press, 1992. pp. 304-35, 572-617 (in Japanese).

————, 'Islamic Glass Finds from Raya, Southern Sinai', in *AIHV Annales du 15 Congres*, New York: 2001, pp. 180-84.

Thanit Yupho, 'Takola: Gigantic Ancient Seaport', *Silpakorn*, vol. 11, no. 4, 1967 (in Thai).

Wheatley, P., *The Golden Khersonese*. Kuala Lumpur: University of Malaya Press, 1961.

Wheeler, R.E.M., A. Ghosh and Krishna Deva, 'Arikamedu: An Indo-Roman Trading Station on the East Coast of India', Ancient India, *Bulletin of the Archaeological Survey of India*, vol. 2, 1946, pp. 17-125.

5

The Batujaya Site: New Evidence of Early Indian Influence in West Java

Pierre-Yves Manguin
Agustijanto Indradjaja

INTRODUCTION

West Java has always been known as an area with very sparse archaeological remains from the Hindu-Buddhist period, if compared to Central and East Java, although written sources – both inscriptions and manuscripts – state that in West Java there were once two kingdoms, known as Tarumanagara and Sunda. The Tarumanagara polity, known from the famous group of seven Sanskrit inscriptions dated paleographically to the fifth century CE appears to have still been in existence in the 660s, when two embassies were sent to China by a country named *To Lo Mo* (*Duolomo*) in Chinese sources. The fifth-century stone inscriptions repeatedly refer to the City of Taruma (Tarumanagara), to King Purnavarman, and to gods Vishnu and Indra.[1]

After the seventh century, little is known about events in West Java, until a polity named Sunda is mentioned in the inscription of Rakyan Juru Pangambat (CE 932); it is written in Old Malay and refers to a king of Sunda 'regaining his power'. There is therefore a distinct possibility, evoked long ago by Cœdès and reasserted by Indonesian historians, that we have, in between the demise of Tarumanagara and the rise of Sunda, a period of domination by Srivijaya (if the CE 686 inscription of Kota Kapur mentioning a Malay expedition to *bhumi Jawa* is to be understood as referring to West Java, which is so far not proved). This kingdom of Sunda survived until the sixteenth century, when it succumbed to the newly dominant Islamic political powers.[2]

The discovery in West Java in the 1980s of the large temple complex of Batujaya brought a considerable amount of new data to document the history of the first millennium CE in West Java, though it does not necessarily bring answers to the above historical questions (Fig. 5.1). The site is now in the middle of a large scale restoration programme and many research projects were carried out on and around the temples. The site is situated some 2 km away from the present-day course of the Tarum River (Citarum), but appears to have been traversed by a now extinct branch of this same river flowing north into the sea, now 4 km away. [3]

A cooperation programme between the National Research and Development Centre of Archaeology and the Ecole française d'Extrême-Orient (EFEO, French School of Asian Studies) was designed in 2002 to carry out systematic excavations on the site, so as to better document its chronology and to explore the long neglected proto-historical and early historical periods, during which contacts with India developed and resulted in the Indianisation of Southeast Asia. [4] Excavations were stopped after the 2006 campaign; the artefacts collected between 2002 and 2006 are now under study.

This programme (and the work carried out before it started) progressively revealed the existence of a remarkably large complex of some thirty sites at Batujaya, of which thirteen are now unmistakably identified as brick temples.

FIGURE 5.1
The Batujaya site in West Java

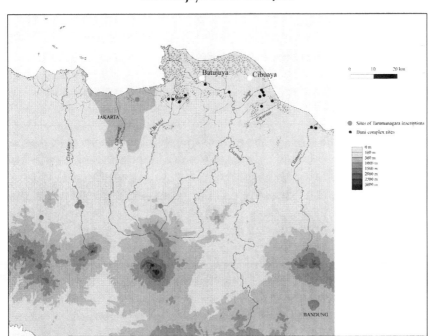

Recent excavations, however, also revealed that the Batujaya area, before the construction of the first Buddhist temples, had been part of the culture complex revealed in the 1960s at the eponymous site of Buni (some 15 km to its west), known for its singular pottery with incised, geometrical decoration, and because its assemblages also yielded the first Indian rouletted fine wares in Southeast Asia.[5] The 2005 and 2006 excavation campaigns brought to light stratigraphic levels which suitably document the passage from an indigenous culture with access to some Indian goods, to a Buddhist culture. In our excavations at Batujaya, the occupation of the region by Buni culture settlers starts around the turn of the first millennium, in the form of a dense burial ground. Then, after the fourth or fifth century and before the end of the eighth century, a phase of dense occupation revealing clear indications of the adoption of Buddhism, during which period the first temples were built in the surroundings of this sector. It should be remembered at this point that the first textual references to Buddhism in Java by Fa Xian and Gunavarma indicate that the religion was practically unknown in 413 but was spreading quickly a few years later, before 424. It is unfortunately impossible to determine whether these travellers landed in West Java or elsewhere on the island, or for that matter if they landed on the same place.[6]

Only some of the results of the 2005-06 excavations can be described in this short presentation; we have chosen to present those that best document the transition from a local to a fully Indianised culture (i.e. showing attributes associated with Indianisation: the adoption of India inspired writing, religion, art styles, architecture).

BUDDHIST TEMPLES AND ASSOCIATED STRUCTURES

The larger temples of Batujaya and associated structures are to be found on three tells (locally called *unur*) situated in the central part of the site, on both sides of the now extinct northern branch of the Tarum River. All are made of bricks (stone is only used for the stairs of the main Blandongan shrine and as bases for wooden columns). The main features of the principal temples and their chronology have been described in a previous paper by the same two authors (Manguin and Agustijanto 2006). There are no extant statues that can be linked to these temples. It is clear, however, that the main temples uncovered so far are Buddhist: they were built in the shape of stupas; votive tablets and all inscriptions found so far can be linked to Buddhism.

Many temples and associated brick buildings reveal two distinct phases of construction: the first phase dates between the fifth and eighth centuries; it has not been possible so far to objectively narrow down this time interval. Circumstantial evidence, however, points to a *c.* sixth-seventh centuries main period of activity and most probably of temple building. Two main arguments can be produced to strengthen this last point, but will need further research: a cache of baked clay votive tablets excavated in 1995 and 2001 by Indonesian archaeologists was found in a layer now associated with the first phase of the Blandongan temple: they belong to a broad group of votive tablets found in a variety of sites in Continental Southeast Asia, from Burma, Thailand and Champa which are conventionally dated to the sixth-seventh centuries; by analogy we will for the time being retain this sixth-seventh centuries date to narrow down the first temple phase at Batujaya.[7] The tablets represent a Buddha seated on a throne, with hands in *abhaya mudra*, with two standing side figures in *tribhanga* and three seated Buddhas on the top part of the tablet. The edges of the tablet carry multi-layered *sikharas*. Some also carry on their bottom part a few lines of an unreadable text. These tablets may depict either the miracle of Sravasti or the first sermon episodes of the life of the Buddha (Agustijanto 2005; Manguin and Agustijanto 2006).

This early building phase was followed at Blandongan by a phase of destruction and abandonment, during a period of time that remains un-determined, before large scale renovation and reconstruction took place in the early ninth century. The whole site appears to have then been abandoned for good, around the end of the tenth century or in the early eleventh century (following evidence from the few Chinese ceramics retrieved in the top levels of the excavated sites: they all belong to the Guangdong, Changsha and Yue-type wares).

One interesting preliminary remark about the ground plan of the Blandongan (Segaran V) temple is that it is comparable not so much to Central Javanese temples, but to Dvaravati temples such as Wat Phra Men at Nakhon Phatom (Dupont 1959, I, Pl. I). Furthermore, other temples at Batujaya (though not Blandongan) were decorated with high reliefs carved out of stucco, which again brings us to comparisons with Dvaravati temples and reliefs rather than to Central Java or elsewhere in Indonesia, where this kind of stucco decoration is so far unknown (Manguin and Agustijanto 2006). This also brings further arguments in favour of a sixth to seventh centuries dating of such reliefs, which checks well with the fact that, in Batujaya, stucco decoration is associated with the first phase of temple building.

Excavations carried out in 2005-06 focused on the Segaran II mound (Unur Lempeng). It covers an area of 4,800 m², about 100 m southwest of Unur Blandongan on which the principal temple of Batujaya was built. Parts of the Segaran II site were recently levelled and transformed into rice fields. The northern part of the mound culminated at 3.58 m above sea level before excavations, along two embankments extending towards Unur Blandongan, whereas the average altitude of the southern area is 2.30 m.

The excavation of these higher sectors (Segaran IIB, IIC and IID) revealed that two long parallel brick walls, with a southwest-northeast orientation extended across and beyond Unur Lempeng in the direction of Unur Blandongan (the southern wall is not built along a continuous line) (Fig. 5.2). These walls are 1.10 m wide. Respectively 67.5 m (N) and 88.6 m (S) of their length have been excavated, but they no doubt extend further to the southeast (towards the ancient river bank?) and to the northeast towards the Blandongan temple. Both walls are adjacent to or incorporate brick structures in the form of chambers, floors and other so far unexplained structures, some of them incomplete (rice growing activities along these structures have heavily damaged them). The three chambers in Segaran IID are adjacent to the northern wall, which is incorporated into their structure; they belong to a building the remaining length of which is 24.4 m and the width 5 m; they have a brick floor covered with a mortar of stucco and pebbles (which most probably indicates their use during the post-800 occupation phase of Batujaya, always associated with such a feature at the nearby Blandongan

FIGURE 5.2
Site plan of Segaran II (Unur Lempeng)

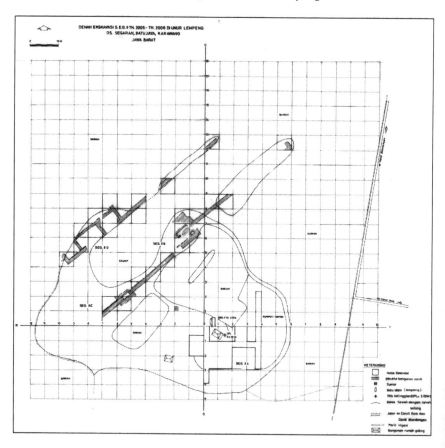

temple). They must have been used for habitation purposes, in connection with the neighbouring temple of Blandongan.

One hypothetical interpretation of this odd parallel structure is that of a pathway, flanked by or incorporating additional buildings, leading from the ancient river bank towards the central temple of Blandongan. We have seen that these structures were employed until the last phase of Batujaya (post-CE 800); the building adjacent to the southern wall in Segaran IIB, like that of Segaran IID, was in use during the two successive phases of temple building at Batujaya, with obvious renovations in the second phase (with levelling of the brick floors with pebble and stucco mortar, as in the second phase at Blandongan). There is therefore a distinct possibility that the walls and the buildings were first built in the early phase. However, further excavations are needed to provide firm explanations of the functions and dates of such unusual and complex buildings. Excavations were carried out in very difficult conditions due to the immediate proximity of wet rice fields and a very high water table (Figs. 5.3, 5.4).

At Segaran IID, a human skeleton in stretched position was revealed during excavations; it lay parallel to the wall at the level of its foundations. It is incomplete and was probably damaged during the construction of the wall foundations. This level produced a Cal (BCE 90-CE 80) radiocarbon date.[8] Further dispersed remains of human skeletons were found in the bottom levels of Segaran IIB. These provide clear indications that the cemetery excavated in sector Segaran IIA must have extended over a larger part of Unur Lempeng (see below).

THE EXCAVATIONS AT SEGARAN IIA

The remaining, low lying (alt. 2.30 m) part of the Unur Lempeng (the Segaran IIA sector) attracted our attention during previous campaigns as it obviously contained no massive structure and therefore stood a good chance

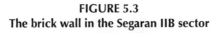

FIGURE 5.3
The brick wall in the Segaran IIB sector

FIGURE 5.4
The brick wall and attached halls in the Segaran IID sector

of providing unobstructed access to earlier Buni culture layers. Local people told us about some looting of the site in the 1960s, when Buni sites were the centre of much attention from tomb raiders because of the gold and beads found in them (some of the looters' pits were revealed during excavation). Moreover, if the usual permanence of sacred sites in Southeast Asia is taken into consideration, this particular sector also showed more than one sign of association with ancient religious rituals. First, two large stone slabs still lay on the surface and a third standing stone was still revered as a *kramat* (only the tip of the seemingly large stone is visible from the surface). A brief test excavation in 2004 revealed that the largest slab had been flattened by chiselling on one of its surfaces. Stones are only available from the mountains lying tens of kilometres south of Batujaya, and must have been brought to inhabitants of this area with a clear purpose in mind. The Segaran IIA sector thus clearly presented features associated with megalithic practices. It is also, in this low lying, coastal region, the only mound with an ancient well of very clear, non-brackish water, a feature often associated with significant sites. Finally, our test excavations brought to light, in a disturbed sub-surface environment, two shards of fine Indian rouletted ware.

The post-CE 800 'Market Place'

As soon as excavations commenced, the Segaran IIA sector appeared to be fully covered, some 20 cm below the surface, by a 20 cm thick layer of brick rubble and reused bricks (Fig. 5.5). This was verified by extending two north-south and east-west trenches across the site. To fully understand the function of this floor, further clearing would be needed. After fully clearing the central part of the sector and the two long trenches, though, it appeared that this brick floor was divided into small compartments, leaving some space for paths in between and a few uncovered 'yards'. The brick rubble used to build this floor was clearly taken from the ruins of the earlier abandonment/destruction phase of the monuments.

Detailed analysis of the rich and dense assemblage of artefacts found above this floor is not yet complete and falls outside of the scope of this paper. In brief, it can be said that the brick structure could have been used as a solid floor for an array of small wooden sheds used by merchants and artisans (glass bead makers, particularly), activities no doubt linked with the daily life of a large Buddhist temple complex. For practical purposes, we named this feature the 'market-place' of Unur Lempeng. The presence above this floor (never under) of a few early ninth- and tenth-century Chinese ceramics is proof that its usage was contemporaneous to the second (re)construction phase of the temple complex of Batujaya, i.e. between *c.* 800 and the end of the tenth or the early eleventh century.

The pre-CE 800 'Early Buddhist' Phase

Excavations of the preceding (pre-800) phases of Batujaya (early Buddhist/ first temple construction phase and Buni phase) were carried out in 2005

FIGURE 5.5
The post-CE 800 'market place' at Segaran IIA (2005 campaign)

and 2006 on three neighbouring spots in the central part of this sector, over approximately 35 m², including 2 'yards' left uncovered when the said brick floor was built, and some 15 m² uncovered during excavation after dismantling of this brick floor. We can only give a summary account of the rich and complex finds brought to light during excavations of these pre-800 levels. The ceramic evidence gathered from these excavations (more than ten thousand shards) is now under study and cannot therefore be fully integrated into our analysis, which remains preliminary.[9]

The top levels (approx. 30 cm thick) of the pre-800 stratigraphic sequence are made of a dark brown soil, with an abnormally high density of (mostly) ceramic artefacts. It appears that these levels must have been utterly depleted during the phase of abandonment that preceded the construction of the brick floor around 800. Some post holes dating from this phase were isolated during excavation, but the surface excavated is not large enough to discern a pattern. Apart from ceramics, these levels produced only two objects that can be objectively associated with an Indic religion: one small, fragmentary limestone mould with one motif representing a conch; and, more specifically, a small, single line inscription in difficult, probably sixth century writing, on an elongated piece of gold foil; it appears, contrary to other similar inscriptions found at Batujaya, not to carry the *Ye dharmā* ... or *Ajñānāc cīyate karmma*... Buddhist mantras, but an invocation to a name of a divinity (so far undeciphered) (Fig. 5.6).[10]

The ceramic assemblage of these Indic levels appears, on the base of incomplete counts, to differ markedly from the earlier, Buni levels. Buni ceramics, which make the vast majority of earlier levels, are found in residual numbers only. Before in depth analysis is carried out on the ceramic and overall assemblages of these levels, it remains impossible to determine if these changes are due to the arrival and settlement of a new group of Indianised people who would therefore be the Buddhist temple builders, or if they attest to the adoption by the same people of Indic religions, together with a new material culture set.

Radiocarbon dates taken in these levels from charcoal samples produced dates ranging between the fourth and the sixth centuries CE: Cal CE (330-

FIGURE 5.6
The gold foil inscription at Segaran IIA

540), Cal CE (390-550), Cal CE (340-540).[11] Information gathered from both dates and artefacts therefore appear to indicate that Indic religious rituals were familiar to people who settled or worked on the Segaran IIA sector in this early phase. It is most probable that they were associated, possibly only in the sixth century, with the first phase of Buddhist temple building occurring in other sectors of Unur Lempeng and elsewhere in Batujaya.

The Buni Culture Levels

Further down, some transition stratigraphic levels in a lighter brown soil produced charcoal samples that have been radiocarbon dated from the first century BCE to the third century CE: Cal BCE 40-Cal CE 140, Cal CE (20-220).[12] Ceramics now appear to all belong to the Buni culture complex assemblage. No other identifiable artefacts have been found in these levels.

The lowest stratigraphic levels of Segaran IIA take us a few more centuries back in time, with calibrated radiocarbon dates ranging from the second century BCE to the third century CE: Cal BCE 160-Cal CE 70; Cal BCE 40-Cal CE 140; Cal BCE 60-Cal CE 90; Cal CE (50-230).[13] The soil, as one goes down, turns into a greenish/yellowish, hard clay mixed with sand; it has a brownish colour only in the denser and more recent levels of the burial grounds.

We brought to light, from these stratigraphic levels, twenty six burials, in various states of preservation, representing individuals of both sexes and of varied ages (Fig. 5.7). Only partial anthropological studies of some of their skeletons have been carried out so far (Harri Widianto 2006) and analysis of DNA sampling is still pending. Radiocarbon dates of bones or teeth are only now being produced.

All burials delivered a variable number of grave goods. All of them comprised potteries and metal tools, the two older ones having only one coarse Buni ceramic pot with a lid and one iron tool. As time passed, burial assemblages grew in complexity. One infant wore a gold eye mask (Fig. 5.8), others wore gold jewellery (earrings and a bracelet), another one a carved bone hair pin. The richest burial of an adult male had burial goods positioned at the arms, the waist (above and under the skeleton), the knees and the feet; it comprised one 18 gr. gold wrist-bracelet (Fig. 5.9), 4 iron tools (totalling 3 kg of iron, with concretions) (Fig. 5.10), three large Buni pots with two lids, two grey burnished bowls and two coarse dishes with rouletted decoration (the latter two categories are either of Indian origin or local copies of Indian wares).

The Buni Culture Complex Assemblage

Taken together, the artefacts brought to light in the lower levels of Segaran IIA and neighbouring sectors largely confirm the early descriptions that resulted

FIGURE 5.7
Burial (UF98), Segaran IIA

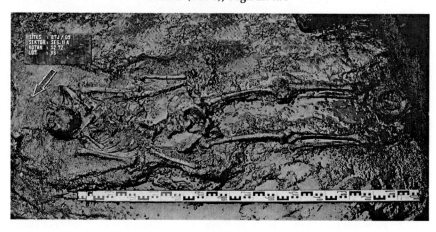

FIGURE 5.8
Gold eyeshade and earring, Segaran IIA

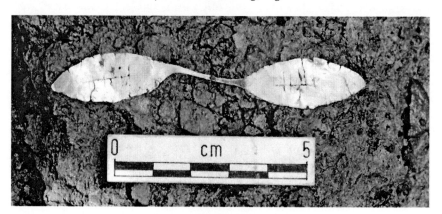

FIGURE 5.9
Gold bracelet burial (UF106)

FIGURE 5.10
Iron tool (burial UF106), Segaran IIA

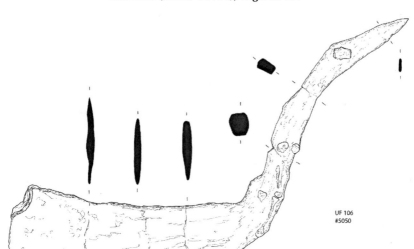

UF 106
#5050

in the identification of a proto-historic Buni culture complex.[14] The overall Buni assemblage is very similar to assemblages gathered elsewhere along the northern coasts of Java, in Bali or in other islands of Indonesia in more or less contemporary sites (i.e. in the early centuries CE), often classified as paleo-metallic. Gold foil eye-shades were found at Gilimanuk (Bali), at Plawangan (East Java) or in South Sulawesi.[15] Iron tools and glass and semi-precious stone beads are also a common denominator of most such sites. At Batujaya as in Buni and other proto-historic sites, artefacts surviving from a Neolithic culture are also found in small quantities: a few stone adzes, stone arrow-heads, and tools made of bone.

The Buni complex, however, distinguishes itself from the other proto-historic (or paleo-metallic) sites by its pottery assemblage. The outstanding, unique repertoire of paddle and anvil geometric decoration and the overall quality of pot making in the Buni area is remarkable at first sight (Figs. 5.11, 5.12). It is this pottery which allowed archaeologists of the 1960s and 1970s to identify this culture complex, based only on artefacts produced during a looting spree. Buni pottery has been reported in West Java in coastal sites ranging from Anyer in the west to Cirebon in the east, but goods collected during the 1960s and 1970s were all found between Jakarta and the Cilamaya River (see Fig. 5.1, Map).[16] Buni pottery comes in multiple shapes, the most

FIGURE 5.11
Early Buni pots and lid (burials UF80 & UF98, Segaran IIA)

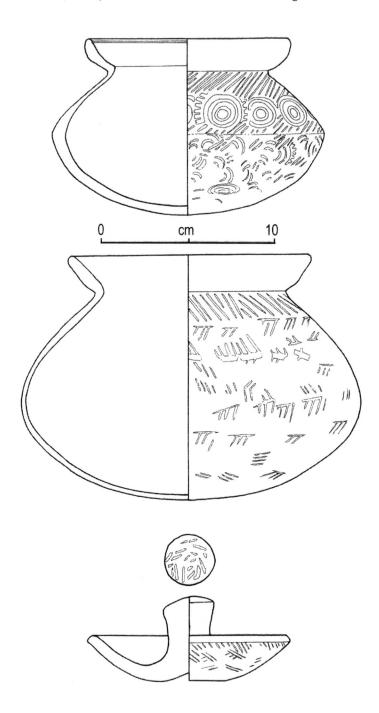

FIGURE 5.12
Late Buni spoutless flask (burial UF304, Segaran IIA)

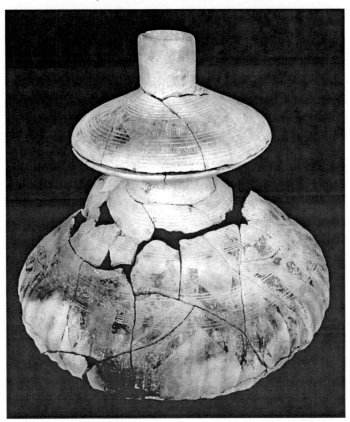

common, by far, being the pot-like containers, together with their typical concave lids with a vertical knob.

The Evidence for Long Distance Exchange

One feature that drew attention in the 1960s to the Buni sites is the presence, in their assemblage, of Indian wares. Three well preserved 'rouletted ware' dishes were then collected by the National Museum in Jakarta, where they remain as permanent exhibits. They were quickly identified and compared to similar finds revealed in Mortimer Wheeler's famous excavation at Arikamedu, and remained for long the only early Indian wares known to have been found in Southeast Asia.[17] Similar Indian wares have now been reported from a variety of sites in coastal Southeast Asia and their spread in archaeological sites in India proper is now much better known (though their place of production remains elusive).[18] Sembiran, on the north coast of Bali, was the first systematically excavated site to have produced such wares, but it was soon followed by excavations at Tra Kiêu (in Central Vietnam), and more recently at Khao Sam Kaeo (Chumphon, Peninsular Thailand), which produced the largest collection of similar potteries.[19] This is not the place to describe in detail such wares, which first appear in India and soon also in Southeast Asia in the last four centuries BCE. The best known such ceramic ware is the above mentioned 'rouletted ware' family, usually dishes made of a hard, dark grey, fine paste and carrying circular 'rouletted' motifs in its internal, central part (Fig. 5.13). They appear in Segaran IIA in the lower levels, therefore in the last century BCE or the first century CE. We have never found them in grave goods, though, which may be significant; with only two dozen burials to work on, however, negative evidence of this sort is far from reliable. A few odd shards of Indian stamped wares would appear to be contemporaneous to these fine paste rouletted dishes (Fig. 5.14).[20]

However, by the time non-Buni wares start appearing in burial goods and in contemporary levels outside of burials, which is around the second century CE, fine rouletted ware seems to have no longer been produced in India. What we then get in Batujaya is a variety of Indian wares of a coarser type, either crude copies of the earlier fine ware dishes with a rouletted décor (Fig. 5.15), or bowls and small dishes with a burnished surface, usually grey, but also buff or orange in some cases. Similar coarse wares are reported from other sites in Southeast Asia (at Khao Sam Kaeo, Tra Kiêu or Oc Eo), but not much attention has so far been given to these lower quality potteries. Visual

FIGURE 5.13
Shards of Indian fine paste 'rouletted' ware, Segaran IIA

FIGURE 5.14
Indian stamped ware, Segaran IIA

FIGURE 5.15
Indian (?) coarse 'rouletted' ware, Segaran IIA

similarities in pastes of such coarse wares and of local Buni wares raises the possibility that they are local copies of the finer and earlier Indian wares, thus Indianised rather than Indian wares. On the other hand, the fact that they are also found at Tra Kiêu or Oc Eo, as well as in Arikamedu proper, may well indicate that such coarser wares were also produced in India before finding their way to Southeast Asia.[21]

Pottery and other artefacts brought to light at Batujaya (in Segaran IIA as well as in other sites) also provide evidence for contacts with remote sites and cultures. A few ceramic shards are clearly reminiscent of contemporary finds at Oc Eo and elsewhere in the Mekong Delta. A gold, octahedral filigree bead is possibly of Persian origin, but similar examples have been found at Oc Eo (Fig. 5.16).

FIGURE 5.16
Gold filigree bead, Segaran V.

cm

DISCUSSION

The evidence brought to light at Batujaya spans more than ten centuries, with data from two main phases: a Buni phase (*c.* first century BCE to *c.* fourth century CE) and an Indianised phase (*c.* fifth to late tenth century CE). It is the first systematically excavated archaeological sequence in Java that can be used to document the transition from local (Austronesian?) to Indianised cultures.

The Buni phase shows evolutions in ceramic and grave good assemblages, with improved technical standards as time passes (particularly regarding pottery), but the overall horizon remains within the same Buni culture complex: a local population, sharing burial rituals and overall material culture traits with many other contemporary populations of Island and even Continental

Southeast Asia. Judging from the variations in the total amount and quality of burial assemblages (based on twenty-six burials only), it also appears that they belonged to a ranked society. The iron tools they used indicate they were dry field (*ladang*) farmers, in an environment where forest still needed to be cleared. We have no direct evidence for rice cultivation in the Buni phase. On the basis of the fauna finds, it appears that sea and mangrove products (turtles, sea-shells and fishes), were also consumed in large quantities, which is not surprising as the site is only some 4 km away from the sea. Bovidae, Cervidae, suinae and canidae bones are also present in Buni levels, as well as those of reptiles.

In common with contemporary societies in Central Vietnam, in the Mekong Delta, in Central and Peninsular Thailand, in South Sumatra (Karang Agung and Air Sugihan), and in Bali, the Buni people had direct or indirect access to goods from India and from Continental Southeast Asia.[22] Indian (or Indianised) pottery must have been highly valued, for it took a prominent place in burial goods of those deceased people of higher rank. The small quantity of Indian wares found in Batujaya, as in many other Southeast Asia sites, can only attest to direct or indirect contact or exchange with India. They could, of course, be a by-product of overseas trade of a different nature: spices (one single clove was found in the lower levels) or textiles (minute pieces of loosely knit, whitish textile were found in two burials, and will soon be analysed); this, however, remains very speculative, at least in Batujaya.

The appearance of signs of Indianisation in the Batujaya settlement, after four or five centuries of contact with Indian material culture, coincides with the disappearance of Buni ceramics and of proto-historic/paleo-metallic burial rituals at Segaran IIA. As discussed earlier on, it is also impossible to determine at this stage of research if the adoption of Indic religious features was associated with the arrival of a new population or if it was the result of the conversion of the populations formerly belonging to the 'Buni culture'. For lack of evidence precise enough to date the first building of brick structures, it is impossible to determine how long it took for this newly Indianised population to invest in the construction of a major Buddhist complex of temples. It appears, though, that, in the sixth-seventh centuries, the temple complex was highly active and architectural and art forms were shared with Continental Southeast Asia, rather than with the rest of Java (or rather, because of lack of comparable early evidence in Central and East Java, they may be said to have little in common with what is known from eighth- to ninth-century Java).

Stratigraphic observations at the Blandongan temple site and several other sectors reveal that the first phase of the construction of the temple complex (some time between fifth and eighth century CE) was contemporary with the polity of Tarumanagara (*c.* fifth to seventh century), which is so far only known by the fifth-century inscriptions written by king Purnavarman, all of them found at Tugu (not far from the coast, near Tanjung Priok), and in the mountains south of Jakarta, hence some 50 to 70 km to the west and south-west of Batujaya. We know from this set of inscriptions that the said king was of Vaishnava obedience. The Cibuaya site, some 20 km east of Batujaya – where three *c.* sixth-century 'mitred' Vishnu statues were found and where a few small brick shrines were also excavated – is therefore a better candidate for an association with Tarumanagara.[23] It is, however, a modest site, in no way comparable in size to the Batujaya complex. So far, however, despite the absence of any Buddhist statue at Batujaya, all the available evidence indicates that we are in the presence of a strictly Buddhist complex. Did both religions find their place in the Tarumanagara polity? The first temple building may have been as late as the end of the seventh century, and one could, therefore, argue for the possibility of an association with the early expansion of Buddhist Srivijaya in the 680s, as discussed earlier on. The older Indianised levels at Batujaya, however, appear to have been active in pre-Srivijaya times. Apart from their being contemporary and neighbours, the links between pre-800 Indianised Batujaya and the Tarumanagara polity can therefore be said to be, at best, unsubstantiated. If CE 932 is considered as the beginning of the Sunda kingdom, on the basis of the Rakyan Juru Pangambat inscription, then again the link with Tarumanagara is similarly tenuous, as the reconstruction of the temples and their consequent use cannot date to much later than CE 800 and we have therefore a gap of more than a century to account for.

NOTES

1. On Tarumanagara epigraphy, see Vogel 1925, Sarkar 1959, de Casparis 1986.
2. Marwati Djoenoed Poespononegoro et al., 2008: 77-78; Hasan Djafar 2000: 73-74; Bosch 1941. There are multiple reports (many unpublished) on early finds at Batujaya, among which Hasan Djafar, McKinnon and Soeroso 1998; Hasan Djafar 2000, 2007; Ferdinandus 2002; and Agustijanto, Bambang and Eka 2006 are the prominent ones. The history of Tarumanagara before the discovery of Batujaya is best summarised in the relevant passages of Coedès' reference work (Coedès 1964, 1968). The Indonesian institutions involved in the effort to reveal this site include the National Research and Development Centre of Archaeology (Pusat Penelitian dan Pengembangan Arkeologi Nasional or Puslitbang Arkenas), the Office of Protection and Conservation of Archaeological Remains (Balai Perlindungan dan Pelestarian Purbakala or BP3), and the Archaeology Department of the Faculty of Cultural Sciences in the University of Indonesia (Departemen Arkeologi FIB UI).
3. The site of Batujaya is administratively situated in the province of West Java, in the regency of Karawang; it encroaches upon two districts (Batujaya and Pakisjaya), in the villages of Segaran and Telagajaya.
4. A first publication of the results of this programme appeared in 2006, which described our research until 2004 (Manguin & Agustijanto 2006). See also Agustijanto, Bambang Budi Utomo and Eka Asih Putrina Taim 2006.

5. On the Buni complex, as then known, see Sutayasa 1972, 1975; Soejono 1962; Walker and Santoso 1977a, 1977b. On more recent finds of rouletted ware in Indonesia, see Ardika 2003 and Ardika and Bellwood 1991, 1993; Manguin and Agustijanto 2006.
6. Damais 1989: 814.
7. For other similar votive tablets, see Moore 2007; Manguin and Agustijanto 2006; Agustijanto 2005; Nandana Chtiwongse 2005; Ferdinandus 2002; Pattaratorn Chirapravati 1997, 2000; Brown 1999; O'Connor, 1974; Luce 1985.
8. 1998±34 BP (Wkt 21319).
9. Guillaume Epinal is studying Segaran IIA ceramics for his Ph.D. dissertation at the EHESS, Paris.
10. Preliminary decipherments of this small inscription were carried out by Arlo Griffiths (EFEO) and Titi Surti Nastiti (Pusat Penilitian dan Pengembangan Arkeologi Nasional). Other inscriptions are discussed in Hasan Djafar 2007, Machi Suhadi 2005.
11. 1637±37 BP (Wkt 21320), 1596±33 BP (Wkt 21322), 1622±37 BP (Wkt 21323).
12. 1932±38 BP (Wkt 21324), 1907±34 BP (Wkt 21328).
13. 2019±34 BP (Wkt 21317), 1933±34 BP (Wkt 21326); 1989±34 BP (Wkt 21327); 1885±34 BP (Wkt 21321).
14. Soejono 1962; Wahyono 1967, 1993-94; Ali Akbar 2006, 2008.
15. Soejono 1977: 208; Santoso Soegondho 1995; Tim Penyusun 1970: 22; see also Wahyono 1999: 27.
16. On which see, among others: Sutayasa 1969, 1972, 1975; Wahyono 1967, 1993-94; Hasan Djafar 1983, 1988, 2007; Ali Akbar 2006, 2008.
17. The Indian wares were first identified by Walker and Santoso 1977a, 1977b.
18. See Wheeler 1949, Begley 1996-2004, Nigam 2001, among many others.
19. Ardika 2003, Ardika and Bellwood 1991, 1993, Ardika et al. 1993; Bouvet 2006; Glover and Yamagata 1994, 1995, 1998; Glover, Yamagata and Southworth 1996; Manguin 2004; Bellina-Pryce and Praon Silapanth 2006.
20. Bellina 1999.
21. Phaedra Bouvet is now putting a finishing touch to a Paris I University dissertation on Indian and 'Indianised' wares found in Indian and Southeast Asian sites, which will no doubt bring much needed new data (including laboratory analyses of pastes) for the resolution of this problem.
22. Manguin 2004.
23. On the dates of the Cibuaya Vishnus, see Dalsheimer and Manguin 1998. The Bojongmenje temple at Rancaekek in the regency of Bandung, and the Cangkuang temple in the regency of Garut, based on architectural styles, are assumed by Indonesian archaeologists to be Hindu and to date from the seventh century. Their links with Tarumanagara, however, are no better documented than those between Batujaya and Tarumanagara.

REFERENCES

Ali, Akbar, 2006, 'Prehistoric Artefacts in Jakarta and nearby', in Truman Simanjuntak et al. (eds.), *Archaeology: Indonesian Perspective. R.P. Soejono's Festschrift*, Jakarta: Indonesian Institute of Sciences, International Center for Prehistoric and Austronesian Studies, pp. 212-22.

————, 2008, *Zaman Prasejarah di Jakarta dan sekitarnya*, Jakarta: Universitas Indonesia.

Ardika, I. Wayan, 2003, 'Archaeological Excavations at Pacung, Northeastern Bali, Indonesia', in A. Karlström and A. Källén (eds.), *Fishbones and Glittering Emblems: Southeast Asia Archaeology 2002*, Stockholm: Museum of Far Eastern Antiquities, pp. 207-11.

Ardika, I. Wayan and Peter Bellwood, 1991, 'Sembiran: The Beginnings of Indian Contact with Bali', *Antiquity*, 65, pp. 221-32.

Ardika, I. Wayan, Peter Bellwood and I. Made Sutaba, 1993, 'Sembiran and the First Indian Contacts with Bali: An Update', *Antiquity*, 71, pp. 193-95.

Ardika, I. Wayan et al., 1993, 'A Single Source for South Asian Export-Quality Rouletted Ware?', *Man and Environment*, 18(1), pp. 101-09.

Begley, Vimala, 1988, 'Rouletted Ware at Arikamedu: A New Approach', *American Journal of Archaeology*, 92, pp. 427-40.

Begley, Vimala et al., 1996-2004, *The Ancient Port of Arikamedu: New Excavations and Researches, 1989-1992*, Pondicherry, Paris: Ecole française d'Extrême-Orient (Mémoires archéologiques), 2 vols.

Bellina, Bérénice, 1999, 'La vaisselle dans les échanges entre le sous-continent indien et l'Asie du Sud-Est à l'époque protohistorique. Note sur quelques marqueurs archéologiques', *Bulletin de l'Ecole française d'Extrême-Orient*, 86, pp. 161-84.

Bellina-Pryce, Bérénice and Praon Silapanth, 2006, 'Weaving Cultural Identities on trans-Asiatic Networks: Upper Thai-Malay Peninsula: An Early Socio-political Landscape', *Bulletin de l'Ecole française d'Extrême-Orient*, 93, pp. 257-93.

Bosch, F.D.K., 1941, 'Een Maleische inscriptie in het Buitenzorgsche', *Bijdragen van het Koninklijk Instituut voor Taal-, Land- en Volkenkunde*, 100, pp. 49-53.

Bouvet, Phaedra, 2006, 'Étude préliminaire de céramiques indiennes et 'indianisantes' du site de Khao Sam Kaeo, IVe-IIe siècles av. J.-C', *Bulletin de l'Ecole française d'Extrême-Orient*, 93, pp. 353-90.

Brown, Robert (ed.), 1999, *Art from Thailand*, Mumbai: Marg Publications.

Casparis, Johannes G. de, 1986, 'Some Notes on the Oldest Inscriptions of Indonesia', in C.M.S. Hellwig and S.J. Robson (eds.), *A Man of Indonesian Letters: Essays in Honour of Professor A. Teeuw*. Dordrecht: Koninklijk Instituut, VKI 121, pp. 242-56.

Coedès, George, 1964, *Les Etats hindouisés d'Indochine et d'Indonésie*, Paris: de Boccard, 2nd rev. edn.

————, 1968, *The Indianized States of Southeast Asia* (ed. W.F. Wella, tr. S.B. Cowing), Kuala Lumpur/Honolulu: University of Malaya Press/University of Hawaii Press.

Dalsheimer, Nadine and Pierre-Yves Manguin, 1998, 'Visnu mitrés et réseaux marchands en Asie du Sud-Est : nouvelle données archéologiques sur le Ier millénaire apr. J.-C.', *Bulletin de l'Ecole française d'Extrême-Orient*, 85, pp. 87-123.

Damais, Louis-Charles, 1959, 'Le Bouddhisme en Indonésie', *France-Asie*, 153-57 (Special number: *Présence du Bouddhisme*), pp. 813-28.

Dupont, Pierre, 1959, *L'archéologie mône de Dvaravati*, Paris: EFEO, 2 vols.

Eka Asih Putrina Taim, 2006, 'The Batujaya Pottery: Early Hindu Buddhist Pottery in West Java', in Truman Simanjuntak et al. (eds.), *Archaeology: Indonesian Perspective. R.P. Soejono's Festschrift*, Jakarta: Indonesian Institute of Sciences, International Center for Prehistoric and Austronesian Studies, pp. 334-44.

Ferdinandus, Peter, 2002, *Recent Archaeological Excavations in Blandongan Site, Batujaya, Karawang, West Java*, Jakarta: Badan Pengembangan Kebudayaan dan Pariwisata.

Glover, Ian C. and Yamagata Mariko, 1994, 'Excavations at Buu Chau Hill, Tra Kieu, Viet-nam 1993', *Journal of Southeast Asian Archaeology*, 14, pp. 48-57.

————, 1995, 'The Origins of Cham Civilization: Indigenous, Chinese and Indian Influences in Central Vietnam as Revealed by Excavations at Tra Kieu, Vietnam 1990 & 1993', in C.T. Yeung and B. Li (eds.), *Southeast Asian Archaeology*, Hongkong: Hongkong University Museum, pp. 145-69.

————, 1998, 'Excavations at Tra Kiêu, Viêtnam 1993: Sa Huynh, Cham and Chinese influences', in Pierre-Yves Manguin (ed.), *Southeast Asian Archaeology 1994*, Hull: University of Hull, Centre for Southeast Asian Studies, vol. I, pp. 75-93.

Glover, Ian C., Yamagata Mariko and William Southworth, 1996, 'The Cham, Sa Huynh and Han in Early Vietnam: Excavations at Buu Cau Hill, Tra Kieu, 1993', *Bulletin of the Indo-Pacific Prehistory Association* (*The Chiang Mai Papers*, vol. I), 14, pp. 166-76.

Gupta, Sunil, 1995-96, 'Beyond Arikamedu: Macro Stratigraphy of the Iron Age-Early Historic Transition and Roman Contact in South India', *Puratattva: Bulletin of the Indian Archaeological Society*, 26(1-2), pp. 50-61.

Harri Widianto, 2006, 'Cranio-Morphological Aspects of the Recent Discovery of Human Remains from Batujaya, West Java', in Truman Simanjuntak et al. (eds.), *Archaeology: Indonesian Perspective. R.P. Soejono's Festschrift*. Jakarta: Indonesian Institute of Sciences, International Center for Prehistoric and Austronesian Studies, pp. 124-35.

Hasan Djafar, 1983, 'Gerabah prasejarah dari situs-situs arkeologi di daerah aliran Sungei Ciliwung, DKI Jakarta', in *Pertemuan Ilmiah Arkeologi III*, Jakarta: Pusat Penelitian Arkeologi Nasional, vol. 1, pp. 42-67.

————, 1988, *Daftar inventaris peninggalan arkeologi masa Tarumanagara*, Jakarta: Universitas Tarumanagara (Proyek penelitian tarpadu Sejarah Kerajaan Tarumanagara).

————, 2000, *Percandian di Situs Batujaya, Karawang: Kajian Arsitektur, Kronologi dan sistemnya*, Depok: Lembaga Penelitian Universitas Indonesia.

————, 2007, 'Kompleks Percandian Batujaya: Rekonstruksi Sejarah Kebudayaan Daerah Pantai Utara Jawa Barat', Ph.D. dissertation, Jakarta, Universitas Indonesia, Fakultas Sastra (in press at the EFEO, Jakarta).

Hasan Djafar, Edward McKinnon and E. Soeroso, 1998, 'Tarumanegara? A Note on Discoveries at Batujaya and Cibuaya, West Java', in *Southeast Asian Archaeology 1994: Proceedings of the 5th International Conference of the EurASEAA, Paris 1994* (ed. P.-Y. Manguin), Hull: University of Hull, Centre for Southeast Asian Studies, pp. 147-60.

Indradjaya Agustijanto, 2005, 'Votive tablet Tipe Ketiga dari Situs Batujaya, Karawang, Jawa Barat', in *Pertemuan Ilmiah Arkeologi ke-X*. Yogyakarta (unpublished).

Indradjaya Agustijanto, Bambang Budi Utomo and Eka Asih Putrina Taim, 2006, 'Laporan Penelitian Arkeologi Situs Batujaya Kab. Karawang, Propinsi Jawa Barat', Jakarta: Puslitbang Arkenas (unpublished)

Luce, Gordon H., 1985, *Phases of Pre-Pagan Burma: Languages and History*, Oxford: Oxford University Press, 2 vols.

Machi Suhadi, 2005, 'Prasasti-prasasti temuan baru pada tiga dasawarsa terakhir', paper presented at the *Diskusi Epigrafi*, Jakarta, Asisten Deputi Urusan Arkeologi Nasional, 15 June 2005, unpublished.

Manguin, Pierre-Yves, 2004, 'The Archaeology of the Early Maritime Polities of Southeast

Asia', in *Southeast Asia: From Prehistory to History* edited by P. Bellwood and I.C. Glover. London: RoutledgeCurzon, pp. 282-313.

Manguin, Pierre-Yves and Agustijanto Indradjaja, 2006, 'The Archaeology of Batujaya (West Java, Indonesia): An Interim Report', in *Uncovering Southeast Asia's Past: Selected Papers from the 10th International Conference of the European Association of Southeast Asian Archaeologists*, edited by Elizabeth Bacus, Ian C. Glover and Vincent Piggott. Singapore: National University of Singapore Press, pp. 245-57.

Marwati Djoenoed Poesponegoro, et al. (eds.), 2008, *Sejarah Nasional Indonesia, Jilid II: Zaman Kuno*, Jakarta: Balai Pustaka (rev. edn.).

Moore, Elizabeth and San Win, 2007, 'The Gold Coast: Suvannabhumi? Lower Myanmar Walled Sites of the Firts Millennium A.D.', *Asian Perspectives*, 46(1), pp. 202-30.

Nandana Chutiwongs, 2005, 'Le bouddhisme du Champa', in Pierre Baptiste and Thierry Zéphir (eds.), *Trésors d'art du Vietnam. La sculpture du Campa, Ve-XVe siècles*. Paris: Musée national des arts asiatiques Guimet, pp. 65-87.

Nigam, J.S., 2001, 'The Rouletted Pottery and its Distribution', in A.V. Narasimha Murty et al. (eds.), *Recent Researches in Archaeology and Museology (Shri C.T.M. Kotraih Felicitation Volume)*, Delhi: Bharatiya Kala Prakashan, vol. I, pp. 129-41.

O'Connor, Stanley, 1974, 'Buddhist Votive Tablets and Caves in Peninsular Thailand', in *Art and Archaeology in Thailand: Commemoration of the 100th Anniversary of the National Museum*. Bangkok: Fine Arts Department, pp. 67-84.

Pattaratorn Chirapravati, 1997, *Votive Tablets in Thailand: Origins, Styles, and Uses*, Kuala Lumpur: Oxford University Press.

———, 2000, 'Development of Buddhist Traditions in Peninsular Thailand: A Study Based on Votive Tablets (Seventh to Eleventh Centuries)', in *Studies in Southeast Asian Art: Essays in Honour of Stanley J. O'Connor* (ed. N.A. Taylor), Ithaca, New York: Southeast Asia Program, Cornell University, pp. 172-93.

Santoso Soeghondo, 1995, *Tradisi Gerabah di Indonesia dari masa Prasejarah hingga masa kini*, Jakarta: Himpunan Keramik Indonesia, 1995.

Sarkar, H.B., 1959, 'Four Rock Inscriptions of Batavia', *Journal of the Asiatic Society*, 1(2), pp. 135-41.

Soejono, R.P., 1962, 'Indonesia', *Asian Perspectives*, 6(1-2), pp. 34-43.

———, 1977, 'Sistem-sistem penguburan pada akhir masa prasejarah di Bali', Ph.D. dissertation, Universitas Indonesia, Jakarta.

Sutayasa, I. Made, 1969, 'Ragam hias gerabah prasedjarah dari komplek Buni', *Manusia Indonesia*, 3(1-6), pp. 127-35.

———, 1972, 'Notes on the Buni Pottery Complex, Northwest Java', *Mankind*, 8(3): pp. 121, 182-84.

———, 1975, 'Sebuah tinjauan tentang kompleks kebudayaan Buni di pantai Utara Jawa Barat', *Manusia Indonesia*, 6(5-6), pp. 83-103.

Tim Penyusun, 1970, 'Projek Penggalian di Sulawesi Selatan', Jakarta: Jajasan Purbakala (unpublished).

Vogel, Jean Philippe, 1925, 'The Earliest Sanskrit Inscriptions of Java', in *Publicaties van de Oudheidkundige Dienst in Nederlandsch-Indie*, 1, 1925, pp. 15-35.

Wahyono Martowikrido, 1967, 'Penemuan dari Buni', *Manusia Indonesia*, 1(5), p. 31.

———, 1993-94, 'Pottery of the Buni Complex as Shown by the Collection of the Museum Nasional', *Kalpataru*, 10 (Saraswati, Esai-Esai Arkeologi, 2), pp. 95-112.

———, 1999, 'The Gold of the Archipelago', in *Indonesia Gold*, South Brisbane: Queenland Art Gallery, pp. 26-33.

Walker, M.J. and Santoso Soegondho, 1977a, 'Romano-Indian Rouletted Pottery in Indonesia', *Asian Perspectives*, 20(2), pp. 228-35.

————, 1977b, 'Romano-Indian Rouletted Pottery in Indonesia', *Mankind*, 11, pp. 39-45.

Wheeler, Robert Eric Mortimer, A. Ghosh, and Krishna Deva, 1946, 'Arikamedu: An Indo-Roman Trading Station on the East Coast of India', *Ancient India*, 2, pp. 17-124.

6

Continuity and Change in South Indian Involvement in Northern Sumatra: The Inferences of Archaeological Evidence from Kota Cina and Lamreh

E. Edwards McKinnon

INTRODUCTION

The earliest evidence for medieval Tamil involvement in northern Sumatra currently comes from Lobu Tua near Barus on the west coast of the island. An inscription with a date equivalent to CE 1088 (Sastri 1932) announces the presence of the *ticai ayirattu annurruvar* – 'The Five Hundred of a Thousand Directions' who at Vorōcu, agreed amongst themselves certain dues (Subbarayalu 1998, 2002). Vorōcu, i.e. Barus, also called Fansur, was well known to Arab and Persian traders of the ninth century as a source of valuable forest products, benzoin and camphor, that came from the mountainous forested hinterland of this coast. It seems, however, that the profits to be made from the camphor trade attracted many different groups of traders who made their way to Barus, and these included Tamils as well as Javanese and others (Guillot 1998).

Not only has a Tamil inscription been found at Lobu Tua, but about one hundred years ago a Buddha image was recovered from this site (Anon 1899, 12). The image was destined to be sent to the museum in Batavia but it somehow disappeared en route. Unfortunately no description or illustration of the image has survived, but if one may speculate, based on the archaeological context in which it was found and what has been recovered at Kota Cina, then it was, in all likelihood, a provincial Chola style figure set up by the Tamil trading community. That a Buddha figure was recovered from this site is important in understanding the overall context of Tamil involvement at Barus, for like that at Kota Cina, it was in all probability erected by merchants who were adherents of a form of syncretic mercantile Buddhist/Saiva cult known as *Cholappauttam*, originally imported from Kerala to Tamilakam (southern India) and Ilam (Sri Lanka). This syncretic form of Buddhist/Saiva religion was practiced in mercantile port communities in southern India and northern Sri Lanka (Schalk 2005, 776, 841). Membership composition of the guilds was of a composite character, mostly being adherents of cults within the fold of Hinduism, but at the same time, eclectic, extending patronage to Saivaite, Vaisnavite and Buddhist institutions. It was the result of intensive mercantile and martial interaction between Tamilakam and Ilam and specific in that it was transmitted in Tamil but disappeared by the fourteenth or early fifteenth centuries in Sri Lanka when conditions changed for the benefit of Pali-Sinhala traditions (Schalk 2005, 841).

Merchants belonging to one or other of the great *vira valanjar* or Tamil trading guilds, the Ainnurruvar or Nanadesi, were wealthy and powerful figures in South Asian medieval society (Abraham 1988, Stein 1965, 56) between the eighth to seventeenth centuries with maritime trading networks extending from the Red Sea, south India, Sri Lanka, Burma, the Thai peninsula through Indonesia to south China. They traded in all manner of day to day goods,[1] including grains, salt, pepper, ginger and other spices, areca nuts, horses, and precious items such as camphor used for medicinal purposes, as well as other resins such as benzoin of great value for the preparation of incense. Cloth and iron were also important items as well as precious and semi-precious stones, such as rubies, sapphires and moonstones from Sri Lanka and gold from Sumatra and probably elsewhere in the archipelago. Moreover, inscriptional evidence from southern India and Sri Lanka over a period of several hundred years, suggests that these same guilds were generous patrons of Buddhism, Hinduism and in some instances, Jainism (Schalk 2005), and who provided support for Sanskrit learning (Stein 1965, 59).

Merchant communities operated in a variety of urban and rural settings, the market towns being known as – *pattinam*, though there were also seasonal locations – such as that at Lobu Tua, known as *velapuram*, and regular periodic or weekly markets known as *katikaitavalam*.

More recent archaeological work in Sumatra suggests that Lobu Tua was occupied from the mid/late ninth century through to the end of the eleventh or possibly early twelfth centuries CE, though whether a permanent settlement was established or the site was occupied only intermittently as suggested by the above terminology has yet to be fully ascertained – the inference of the Buddha image, and what may have been a permanent religious institution is, however, that it may have been continuously occupied by at least a nucleus of Tamil settlers for a period of some two to three hundred years. Importantly, unlike the Arabs who appear to have kept to coastal connections, Tamil merchants supported by armed mercenaries made their way deep into the hinterland,[2] perhaps to the sources of the forest resins that were traded on the coast and to the Karo plateau where folk memories suggest the appearance of south Indian merchants accompanied by numerous well-armed guards. Among the ceramics recovered at Lobu Tua, Kota Cina and Ujung Batee Kapal, accumulations of earthenware with south Indian stylistic affiliations emphasise such a presence, as I will explain below.

Guillot (2002) notes that there are two legends that relate to the demise of trading at Lobu Tua by about the end of the eleventh century, one which is attributed to supernatural intervention that took place on Islamisation of the region and the second, more detailed, that was due to an attack by an enemy referred to as *Garagasi*, a term which in Malay means 'monster' or 'giant'! Whether such an attack, if indeed such an event took place, was launched by a group of booty-seeking Batak warriors from the hinterland, for the Batak, self-admitted cannibals were often regarded by outsiders as somewhat monstrous beings, or there was some other group of people involved such as those from the northern part of the island or from elsewhere is not known. The sacking of a trading settlement such as that at Lobu Tua may not, perhaps, have been such an unusual event in a coastal world that was probably subject to raiding and piracy. Indeed, it was the inherent instability of life that caused the merchants of the guilds to protect themselves with bodies of armed mercenaries.

As Tamil guild activity at Lobu Tua came to an end, so then a new site appears on the north eastern coast of Sumatra. By about the late eleventh century, if indeed not some time earlier, these same merchants or others of a similar origin established themselves at a riverine harbour site, a short distance inland of the Belawan estuary, at a point near where the Deli and Sunggal rivers met. This place is now known as Kota Cina. At some point after their arrival in the Barus area the merchants seem to have learnt about the possibility of contact with the east coast by means of trans-insular portages and that the same sources of forest resins were accessible from the east as well as the west coasts (McKinnon 2006). This strategically located riverine harbour settlement at Kota Cina gave access to the rich mountainous hinterland that had been formerly accessed through the river valleys and mountain trails of the Pakpak lands from Lobu Tua but, at the same time, was located on the main maritime sailing route from India to China through the Selat Melaka.

Although marketing aromatic resins such as benzoin and camphor in the Middle East was undoubtedly a highly profitable business, and ships could sail directly from the west coast of Sumatra or the north western tip of Aceh across the Indian ocean to Sri Lanka, south India and the Middle East, by about the beginning of the ninth century even greater profits could be made in China where there was an insatiable demand for such exotic products. To access the China route, ships from Barus had either to turn southeast along the coast of Sumatra to the pirate-infested Selat Sunda and then northwards through the Java Sea, past the islands of Bangka and Belitung towards Singapore and thence to the South China Sea[3] or alternatively turn back in a north-westerly direction to Aceh Head (Ujung Pancu) and then sail north eastwards into the Selat Melaka. Sailing was of course seasonal and entirely dependent upon the direction of the monsoon winds.

In north-western Aceh there were seemingly two ancient harbours, one located in the bay close to Ujung Pancu at Kuala Pancu immediately east of Aceh Head, possibly also known as Pancu or Fansur (the Boluo of Faxian ?, conceivably an early collecting centre for goods to be transported across the ocean), and a second known to the Arabs as Rami or Ramni, and to the eleventh century Tamils as Ilamuridesam, in all probability located in and around the Krueng Raya or 'great bay' of Aceh Besar. Many of these early toponyms are, however, rather vague and the name Ramni might well at different times have referred to the whole coastline of north-western Aceh. Elsewhere in the archipelago, archaeological evidence suggests that the reality of life was actually rather unstable and there was periodic transition of activity among several different port-polity centres. Furthermore, Hall (2006) in discussing eastern Indonesia, has come to a similar conclusion that historical Chinese references to toponyms (such as Barus or Fansur, for example) must be considered as 'regional or coastline inclusive' rather than to a single and continuous port location. In other words, harbour settlements tended to relocate over time. Something similar appears to have happened in Aceh and northern Sumatra.

By the mid-twelfth century, Chinese records affirm that the coast of Aceh was an important resting point for Chinese shipping waiting for the monsoon winds to go westwards (Hirth & Rockhill 1911) and may also have acted as a landfall for shipping arriving from Sri Lanka and Cape Comorin. In all likelihood, however, shipping had already made use of this particular landfall for some time. I shall return to this point later in this essay.

KOTA CINA

A legend current among the local inhabitants of the modern village of Kota Cina, near Labuan Deli in north east Sumatra, ascribes the origin of the name to the settlement having once been occupied by the Chinese who had chased away a group of Indians who were there earlier, and it thus became known as 'China town' or a place fortified and occupied by the Chinese. Recoveries from this site with 'Chinese' connotations are large quantities of good quality northern and southern Song and Yuan period Chinese export ceramics from the kilns of Fujian, Guangdong, Zhejiang and elsewhere and numerous Tang and Song dynasty coins. Whether or not the story as related is true, or whether there is some other explanation is difficult to say. This north-east coast of Sumatra appears in thirteenth century Chinese records as 'Batta', the Batak coast, and was indeed frequented by Chinese shipping. Along with other numerous contemporary polities, a small Islamic polity known as Aru (equated with Deli) sent tribute to the Yuan emperors during the early part of the fourteenth century (Wade 2005).[4] Ma Huan, writing in the early fifteenth-century records that the Belawan estuary was known to the Chinese at that time as the 'freshwater estuary' and that Aru was a small country with few products. In the sixteenth century Aru had the unwelcome attention of the expanding sultanate of Aceh, and was subjugated in 1539, but soon reasserted itself until it finally succumbed to the forces of Sultan Iskandar Muda of Aceh in 1612. The Acehnese reportedly took away some 20,000 people as slaves from this and other places on the east coast of Sumatra at this time, leaving these coastal areas virtually devoid of population. The numbers killed in these invasions are not recorded.

Work at Kota Cina has revealed the occupation of a riverine harbour site that began in the eleventh century and flourished until the late thirteenth or early fourteenth centuries when it was either abandoned or destroyed. Finds of imagery and brick foundations suggest that there are the remains of three brick-built religious structures, one of which was a Siva shrine; a second a Visnu temple, and the third a Buddhist complex, suppositions borne out by the recovery of a Siva linga of a type found at Polonarruva (see Fig. 6.3) during the Tamil occupation; a headless Visnu image together with a female deity, both in provincial Chola style (see Figs. 6.4 and 6.5); and two provincial Chola style Buddha images (see Figs. 6.1 and 6.2), all of which reflect a range of beliefs and deities that parallel many found in contemporary mercantile religious sites in southern India and Sri Lanka. There are, moreover, fragments of smashed stone imagery at Kota Cina that chemical tests suggest come from rock found in southern India, but not in Sumatra (McKinnon: 1984, 70).

Although an early nineteenth-century British report suggests that there was a large stone with an inscription on it to be found at Kota Cina (Anderson 1971, 294), the stone has never been recovered. Whether it ever existed at all has been questioned (Miksic 1979). Several large roughly shaped stones have been recovered from the site but none of them bears any trace of an inscription. These stones may have been used as anchor stones or ballast, though one at Keramat Pahlawan was clearly incorporated into the fabric of a brick-built structure. The archaeological evidence points strongly, however, to a Tamil presence with the existence of syncretic Hindu/Buddhistic religious beliefs, of exactly the type found in contemporary mercantile settlements in Sri Lanka. At Kota Cina, a small bronze temple lamp (*vilaku*) with a bird-headed suspension (see Fig. 6.6), stylistically similar to one in the site museum at Polonarruva, was recovered within the confines of the area of what appears to be a Buddhist sanctuary. Dedications of similar 'perpetual' lamps in which the flame was to be kept burning for ever were a common occurrence by members of the Guilds and several such donations are recorded in their inscriptions found in Tamil Nadu and Sri Lanka. Yet another significant find at Kota Cina was the tip of an iron javelin, one of the favourite weapons of the mercenaries (often derived from communities of potters) who were in constant support of the Tamil mercantile community. Moreover, a *tali*, or marriage token, made from gold foil in the form of an Abbasid or Fatimid dinar of about the middle of the twelfth century was also recovered here.

Much of the red slipped earthenware pottery recovered at Kota Cina has close stylistic affinities to relatively coarse medieval red wares produced in southern India and Sri Lanka (see Fig. 6.13), both in the carinated form of many of the open-mouthed cooking pots (see Fig. 6.14) and some of the globular water pots. Some are almost indistinguishable from earthenware found at medieval coastal sites south of Pondicherry where contemporary Chinese stonewares are also to be found. The paste of this south Indian earthenware contains mica but lacks the volcanic glass found in earthenware produced locally in Sumatra and the Malay peninsula.

With both Indic and Chinese (see Fig. 6.7) associations, is there perhaps, an alternative source of the name Kota Cina, a term that one might translate loosely as 'China town'? The religious structural remains, the imagery, a few copper coins and much of the glass and earthenware recovered at Kota Cina have south Indian or Sri Lankan connotations. Tamil merchant guilds were established in the northern and eastern parts of Sri Lanka, at Anuradhapura, Polonarruva and Trincomalee, during the medieval period. Could it be that with the strong south Indian connotations found here, suggesting the presence of Tamil merchants and mercenaries, the name was originally *Cinna Kotta?*, meaning 'little town' from the Tamil word *cinna*, meaning small or little? Had the term 'cinna' become confused with 'Cina', or was the site ultimately also occupied by a group of Chinese settlers as suggested by the legend, or perhaps was it at some time a cosmopolitan community with both ethnic groups living side by side?

As I mentioned earlier, the Tamils were not content to remain in the harbours of the west and east coasts but ventured far into the rugged interior, probably following jungle trails by which forest produce was brought down to the coast by inhabitants of the upland areas. The presence of place names with Tamil affinities, such as Lingga, Cingkam, etc., on the Karo plateau, and the presence of several Tamil words in the Karo vocabulary in all probability came about due to a long-standing association between the indigenous people of the interior and Tamil merchant communities over a period of some two or three hundred years or more. For instance, the Karo word for a traditional weekly market is *tiga*, as opposed to the Malay word *pasar*, in all probability derived from the Tamil term *katikaitavalam*, a weekly or periodic market. The *tiga* was held on a regular basis at specific locations throughout the plateau. It is these sites, apparently located on 'neutral' ground, but usually in proximity to established settlements, that have entered into the local geographic terminology, giving rise to names such as Tiga-binanga, Tiga-juhar, Tiga-nderket, Tiga-panah, etc. It appears that some, if not most of these weekly market sites may be of considerable antiquity. Locations may have changed over time as economic and social conditions changed, but the basic principle of a periodic market where a free exchange of goods took place remained the same. There are so many coincidences of words, names and perhaps even customs that some longstanding contact seems inevitable. Another example is the name *cingkeru* for Job's tears (*Coix lacryma jobi Linn.*), a type of grain often planted in upland areas. There are also words for days, months and directions, etc., of Sanskritic derivation that may have entered the Karo language from Tamil ceremonial usage.[5]

The Karo are known among themselves as the Merga Si Lima, the five clans, comprising the Karo-karo, Ginting, Perangin-angin, Sembiring and Tarigan. Coincidentally, a similar arrangement of five clans existed in medieval southern India where the *Panca Marga* were to be found (Stein 1965, 54). Among the Sembiring, there are two groups, the Kembaren (incidentally a term meaning 'potter' in Tamil) who, along with the other Karo clans, are allowed to eat dog meat, and the Sinyombak, who unlike the other groups are forbidden to do so (*pantangen*) – The Sinyombak are a group of Sembiring septs or sub-clans who 'let drift the remains of their ancestors' in an elaborate periodic ceremony on the upper reaches of the Lau Biang, the Dog River, at Siberaya, one of the largest villages on the plateau. Among the Sembiring Sinyombak one finds sub-clan or sept names with Dravidian associations such as Colia, i.e. Chola; Meliala, Malāya, Muham, Pandia, etc., and several others. This is yet another coincidence – during medieval times, it was apparently common for Tamil military units to be named after the titles or epithets of Cōla royalty (Pathmanathan 1976, 122), so possibly the naming of these Karo groups follows a contemporary tradition. The Karo origin stories admit to descent from a mysterious Indian ancestor.

Two, now long-defunct ceremonies, one mentioned above and formerly celebrated by the Karo Sembiring clan, the *Pekualuh* – a death ceremony involving the construction of specially-made ships and the *Artelebuh* celebrated by the Perangin-angin, appear to have Indic affinities or origins. Formerly in addition to independent villages on the plateau, there were groups of Karo villages that were organised into *urung*, a term that appears to have derived from the medieval Tamil term *urom*, a council for a group of sudra class villages.

No inhumations were discovered at Kota Cina, which suggests that cremation may have been the common practice among the inhabitants. A human skull was reportedly discovered during ditch-digging operations at some point in the village but it was never possible to establish any context for this find. A single Yuan period jar burial, a form of secondary burial, is known from a rice *sawah* near Percut, some distance east of Kota Cina, but due to the acid nature of much of the soil in these often swampy coastal areas, finds of other burials are unlikely.

Although all the so-called 'Batak' groups appear to have had some contact with Indian mercantile activity, it is the Karo who portray the most signs external of influence, in their traditions and folk tales, their vocabulary and in their metal-working skills which, they say, they obtained from their mystical Indian ancestor (Neumann 1903, 1926). The archaeological evidence from Kota Cina, including metal working, strongly suggests that a community of Tamil traders established a long-term symbiotic relationship with the people of the hinterland which left its mark in the social organisation, the vocabulary and customs of the Karo clans.

UJUNG BATEE KAPAL

Located on a headland (the name means literally 'Ship rock point') that forms the eastern edge of the Krueng Raya, the 'Great bay of Aceh' this site was discovered only in 1996 and has yet to be topographically surveyed. Systematic, controlled excavations are yet to be undertaken. The following comments are therefore based entirely upon observations made through extensive walking over the site and recoveries of surface finds of ceramics and other artefacts. The most striking feature of this coastal settlement site is the numerous early Islamic grave markers associated with good quality Chinese export wares of the Yuan and Ming periods and south Indian style earthenware. The grave markers or *nisan* are to be found at numerous locations over the headland that is perhaps to some 60 hectares or more in extent. Importantly, however, much of the earthenware material that is exposed here and there at different points on the headland is of a type that in the context of Kota Cina, I have denoted as 'South Indian redware', being typologically similar to 'Indianising' earthenwares that appear at Lobu Tua, Kota Cina, at various sites in Kedah on the Malay peninsula, in a fourteenth-century context in Singapore, and at numerous medieval sites in Sri Lanka and on the south-east (Coromandel) coast of India. This distinctive type of earthenware may well have been copied locally in Southeast Asia, where the locally-made paste contains traces of mica and volcanic glass, the latter seemingly absent in southern India. Published medieval material from the Chola port of Kaveripattinam and sites such as Polonarruva in Sri Lanka, as well an examination of unpublished material from elsewhere in Tamil Nadu, suggests that several of the ceramic forms found in India are the same as, or very similar to, those recovered at sites in Southeast Asia.

This north-western part of the coast of Aceh appears under the name of Rami or Ramni in Arab writing of the ninth century and it is mentioned under one name or another in various sources on numerous occasions thereafter. The early eleventh century Rajendrachola Thanjavur inscription (equivalent to CE 1030) mentions Ilamuridesam as one of the locations subjected to the unwelcome attentions of the Tamil raids into Southeast Asia (Sastri 1949). The name appears also in Malay texts as Lamuri or Lamiri and it is mentioned by Marco Polo as Lambri. The Chinese knew it as Lan-li, Lan-wu-li, Nan-wu-li and Nan-po-li (Cowan 1933, Tibbets 1979, McKinnon 1988).

Many of the grave markers to be seen at Ujung Batee Kapal are of an early genre that would appear to predate most of the so-called *batu Aceh* or Aceh (grave) stones and a typographical analysis of the funerary monuments is a subject that is still virtually unresearched. A few grave markers have been described by Montana (1997), who states (incorrectly) that they are known in Aceh as *plakpling*, a term that is virtually unknown to most modern day Acehnese and should perhaps more correctly be *plang pleng*, meaning 'of varied decoration'.[6] One grave marker, situated behind a sixteenth century fortification known as Kota Lubhok,[7] bears an inscription that commemorates the demise of the Sultan Suleiman bin Abdullah bin al-Basir who died in 608 H, equivalent to CE 1211,[8] almost ninety years prior to the Islamic date 696 H, that is equivalent to CE 1297, on a stone erected on the tomb of the first Islamic sultan of Samudera-Pasai on the east coast of Aceh.[9] Many of the grave markers that lie scattered over this headland bear what appear to be both stylistic and decorative design linkages to southern and eastern India. The concept of form, which is a generally, though not always a small, tapered, obelisk-like pillar (see Fig. 6.8) may well relate to the south Indian hero stone tradition, though of course without any depiction of a human image, or are similar to towers of temple gateways. Others bear design motifs that suggest an affinity with Buddhistic designs, displaying elements of lotus and jasmine motifs, intertwined stems or an endless knot (see Fig. 6.11). A common element among these designs may be a stylised *tri ratna* or three jewel motif.[10] Some bear inscriptions in Arabic script (see Figs. 6.9, 6.10 and 6.12), though I understand not all the inscriptions actually constitute funerary memorials but comprise lettering that does not add up to proper sentences,[11] suggesting that the carvers of these memorials were less than conversant with Arabic script.

A number are squat but otherwise plain and undecorated forms though displaying design concepts that can almost assuredly be of an Indic origin and there are yet others that may display Persian influence. Yet others are small, plain, slab-like forms with rounded or slightly stepped or shouldered tops cut from volcanic tuff which suggests that they have been brought from elsewhere.

Unfortunately it appears that little systematic analysis work has been done on the forms of early Islamic grave markers in southern India or Sri Lanka to enable direct physical typological comparisons to be made with these stones. It should be remembered, however, that Nagapattinam, a medieval port site with Sumatran connections, was taken by Malik Kafur in the early fourteenth century and that Islam was in the process of being established in southern India and northern Sri Lanka long before this. Although their presence is apparently not that well documented, by CE 875, Arab settlers were already established in southern India, as a Tamil copper plate from that time issued by the ruler of Madura which granted asylum to an Arab community goes to prove. A south Indian tradition asserts early contacts with Arabia – the king Shakaravarti was converted to Islam when the miracle of the splitting of the moon occurred. Other more tangible evidence suggests that Islam was certainly well-established in parts of Tamil Nadu by the early thirteenth century, and that by this time there were Muslim elements working with, or within the Tamil guilds of that period (Schalk 2005). Muslim traders were established in Malabar or Kerala on the south-west coast of India at an even earlier period. By the late thirteenth or early fourteenth centuries, Islamic ports such as Kayal east of Cape Comorin (for Kayal is Marco Polo's Cail), in addition to carrying the horse trade from Arabia to the Pandyan kingdom, were doing a flourishing trade with China.

There are, moreover, numerous communities of Muslim Tamils living in northern Sri Lanka who have been there for centuries. The thirteenth and fourteenth centuries were a period of great disruption in southern India and the commercial activities of the mercantile guilds may well have been in disarray. Some of those who at that time converted to Islam maintained their pre-Islamic Hindu caste titles in their new names though whether the term *nai'na*, for example, reflected a specific caste association or was simply used mean 'Lord', 'Master' or 'Father' is not known (Lambourn 2004: 219, 220).

Equally important, Islam was already well established at the north-eastern terminus of the medieval maritime route through the Selat Melaka. Initially established at Guangzhou,[12] by the thirteenth century Muslim merchants had established themselves in Quanzhou, the greatest port in the world at that time.[13] It was also frequented by south Indian merchants who built Hindu temples there. Chinese sources affirm that by the ninth century Muslim merchants were also established in Champa (Wade 2007, 2).

The grave markers at Ujung Batee Kapal are made of several different types of stone, ranging from a relatively soft (fossiliferous) and easily eroded chalky limestone available at Ujung Batee Kapal itself, to a harder form of the same rock, possibly also local, – as well as some specimens carved from granitic rock, andesite and/or basalt and, as noted earlier, volcanic tuff. Some were undoubtedly carved locally. Others may well have been imported from elsewhere. Among the several *batu Aceh* to be found at this site, which on stylistic grounds may be dated to the early part of the fifteenth century,[14] some are carved from a medium hard greyish-yellowish sandstone from an, as yet, unidentified origin.

Quite apart from the grave markers, it is, however, the earthenware that strongly suggests a south Indian and/or northern Sri Lankan connection for the Ujung Batee Kapal site. Several large shards of carinated vessels, decidedly similar to those found at Kota Cina, and allied to forms from Kaveripattinam and Polonarruva have come to light here (see Fig. 6.15). As earthenware makes up the most common element of domestic rubbish recovered from most Indonesian medieval coastal archaeological sites, this suggests that either the inhabitants of the settlement were of Indian or Sri Lankan origin or, that they perhaps imported large quantities of such earthenware. Both alternatives should be considered. The possibility thus arises that the founders of the Ujung Batee Kapal settlement were members of the *Anjuvannam*, an Islamic merchant guild organisation that flourished in the thirteenth and fourteenth centuries and who were, in effect, heirs to the earlier Hindu Buddhist traders who had dominated the South Asian China trade for some four centuries.[15]

On their return voyages from China, Indian ships no doubt carried large quantities of Chinese ceramic wares (see Figs. 6.16, 6.17 and 6.18), primarily as merchandise but possibly also as a form of ballast. The coastal trading communities into which these ships entered used considerable amounts of these same goods themselves, which accounts for the relatively large amounts of shard material to be found in these sites, whilst passing on saleable utilitarian items such as jars and bowls to others in their hinterlands. Thus such ceramics are of common occurrence in coastal settlements generally but often relatively rare in the interior.

It appears also that there is no reason why consignments of good quality earthenware might not have been carried across the Indian ocean to sites in Southeast Asia, either as cargo or possibly as containers for items such as salt. Some pots were, of course, required for the use of the crew to prepare their own food or to carry water. It is interesting to note that fine paste ware (a light, somewhat brittle type of earthenware usually either pale whitish grey or light reddish creamy brown in colour) *kendis* were traded from either east Java or possibly from a source in southern Indo-China (Champa) to points throughout the Indonesian archipelago. A number of wrecks have been found in Southeast Asian waters with these same items making up part of the cargo alongside higher fired ceramics.

As noted earlier, Islamic communities were established in the Champa region from at least the ninth century but many fled in 1377 when the country was overrun by the Vietnamese. It was possibly a Cham Muslim merchant who founded the Sultanate of Aceh in the early fifteenth century. It is worth noting also that a Hindu temple is thought to have continued to exist in Banda Aceh until the sixteenth or early seventeenth centuries and that a thirteenth-century Tamil language guild inscription was discovered in Banda Aceh in 1990.[16]

CONCLUSION

Covering a period of more than five hundred years of close association with South Asia, a range of sites including initially Lobu Tua, from the ninth to the late eleventh or early twelfth; followed by Kota Cina from the eleventh to the late thirteenth or early fourteenth; and finally Ujung Batee Kapal from the thirteenth to the fifteenth centuries, have all yielded evidence of cultural influences from overseas sources. All three above-mentioned coastal settlements have produced similar kinds of red slipped carinated earthenware which has its origins in south India and Sri Lanka; both Lobu Tua and Kota Cina provide evidence of Hindu Buddhistic religious activity in the earlier part of the period and towards the end of the time spectrum, originating at a time when many political disruptions occurred in southern India and Islamic influences became stronger, Ujung Batee Kapal is an interesting example of an early Islamic settlement with southern Indian connotations, seemingly one of the first of its kind in Sumatra.

The inference of all this is that Islam arrived in Sumatra from Tamil Nadu or Sri Lanka, not from Gujarat as is often thought. Different groups of Muslim merchants were apparently competing for trade along the northern and western coasts of Sumatra, and the fact that Lambri (or Lamri), as personified by the site at Ujung Batee Kapal, was already Islamic by the early thirteenth century and occupied by 'Tamil' merchants, could account for the seeming misinformation provided to Marco Polo at Samudera Pasai, for he describes Lambri as still heathen. It should be remembered that by the early fifteenth century Samudera was strongly influenced by Gujaratis who seem to have dominated the scene and who were selling ornate reworked Hindu marble sculptures as tombstones to the Muslim rulers there!

It is my belief that the ethnic groups involved in inter-regional trade reflected by recoveries at both Kota Cina and Ujung Batee Kapal, were essentially one and the same. By the early thirteenth century, however, some merchants had, due to force of circumstance, converted to Islam but continued sailing and trading along the same maritime routes as their Hindu Buddhist predecessors and probably, to a large extent using some of the same harbours where these still continued to exist, as they had done in earlier centuries. Changing conditions meant, however, that over time some settlements were abandoned and new ones established, or as in the case of Samudera Pasai, the indigenous local ruler converted to Islam, thus changing the religious environment of the port. There is, in effect, an 'ethnic continuity' – though with a changing religious situation. As Tamil Buddhism weakened and gradually disappeared from southern India and northern Sri Lanka, the Brahmanical proscription of sea travel strengthened, so that the Hindu element in seagoing mercantile activity although possibly always present to some extent (as in Melaka) also lessened and gradually faded until there was a resurgence of activity by the Chettis of Chettinad during the colonial period.

Coincidentally, in conclusion, it is interesting to note that according to the *Sejarah Melayu* or Malay Annals, Islam was introduced to Lamri (Aceh), Aru (the Kota Cina area), Peureulak (Perlak) and Samudera Pase by a fakir named Muhammad who was formerly the Sultan of Ma'abri (Ma'bar = a kingdom on the south-east coast of India) but who abdicated his throne in order to bring Islam to 'Semudra' (Brown: 1970, 32).

ACKNOWLEDGEMENTS

All photographs by the author. I am greatly indebted to Prof. M. Shohooky for advice and translation of the Islamic inscriptions and texts (MS01a and LE01).

NOTES

1. Items of trade were often mentioned in inscriptions, for example, Stein (1965, 51), quotes the Ayyavole Shikapur inscription dated to CE 1050.
2. A bilingual Tamil/Malay inscription was formerly known from the highlands of Minangkabau, but seems to have now disappeared. Other Tamil inscriptions are known from the interior of Sumatra and elsewhere in Southeast Asia (Christie 2002).
3. Whether this route was in regular use during medieval times is yet to be ascertained. Sailing along the west coast of Sumatra at that time may well have been a particularly hazardous journey, as there are few natural harbours. The straits of Sunda were infested with pirates.
4. An extensive early Islamic site with numerous *batu Aceh* type funerary monuments dating to the *c.* 15 or earlier has been identified at Kota Rentang, no more than 8 km west of Kota Cina and linked to it through tidal swamp lands. Ceramic recoveries suggest contemporary linkages with the Kota Cina site.

5. Parkin (1978) who discussed the Sanskritic terms appearing in various Batak languages and who otherwise made useful analyses of the various vocabularies, does not appear to have appreciated the fact that Sanskrit was used in Tamil religious ceremony or that Tamil could have been a source for these words in the various Batak languages.

6. I am grateful to Dr Nurdin A.R., Director of the Museum Negeri Aceh for this explanation.

7. Montana suggests that the graves are within the confines of the fortress. This is not the case, however, as they are situated at the foot of the Ujung Batee Kapal escarpment, beyond the trace of the rear wall of the fort, of which only the foundations remain. There are four or five rather disturbed ancient burials in a cluster at this point. Fragments of carved nisan from this location have recently been deposited in the provincial museum in Banda Aceh. By 2006, however, due to further disturbance, this memorial stone had seemingly disappeared, making it impossible to verify the early thirteenth century date attributed to it.

8. Wade notes that there is much dispute over the dating and other aspects of this gravestone (Wade 2007, 4). The overall archaeological context has not, however, been understood until recently.

9. For a full discussion on the stylistic affinities of these Gujarati grave markers, see: Elizabeth Lambourn, 'From Cambay to Samudera-Pasai and Gresik: The Export of Gujarati Grave Memorials to Sumatra and Java in the Fifteenth Century C.E.' *Indonesia and the Malay World*, 31, no. 90 (2003), 221-89. As far as can be ascertained at the moment, none of the Ujung Batee Kapal stones would appear to relate to this Gujarati tradition.

10. This symbol is either a triangle (*trikona*) or three-pronged element which is connected with the *trisula* and the *vajra*, representing in Buddhism the Buddha, the dharma and the sangha. The Islamic adaptation of this element, if this is what it is, displays a central lozenge shape with a pair of curved 'horns'.

11. Mike Feener, personal communication.

12. An Arab trader, Sulaiman, who visited Guangzhou (Canton) in 851 noted the existence of a Muslim community there and Muslims were among those slaughtered in the Huang Jao rebellion of CE 878 (Lo 1967, 177; Wade 2007, 2).

13. Al-Idrisi, E. Cerulli et al. (eds), *Opus Geographicam*, 2 vols., Rome, 1970 I, p. 62, cited in Wade, 2007, p. 2.

14. I am gratefully to Dr Elizabeth Lambourn for this information and for discussing this phenomenon.

15. Karashima and Subbarayalu (2002) note that the term is usually interpreted as an organisation of 'foreign' merchants who were Jews, Christians or Muslims but I understand that the term would also apply to south Asian Muslims. The Anjuvannam were also active in Sri Lanka.

16. The inscription, now in the Museum Negeri Aceh is badly worn and most difficult to decipher. Interestingly, some of the early nisan at Ujung Batee Kapal are almost miniature replicas of this stone being similar in shape, a small slab with a rectangular cross section and having a rounded top.

REFERENCES

Abraham, Meera, 1988, *Two Medieval Merchant Guilds of South India*, New Delhi: Munshiram Manoharlal.

Anonymous, 1899, 'Bodhisatwa, gevonden te Loboe Toewa', *Notulen van het Bataviaasch Genootschap*, 38, 12.

Ayappan, A., 1960, *Story of Buddhism with Special Reference to South India*, Madras: Madras Museum.

Brown, C.C., 1970, *Sejarah Melayu 'Malay Annals'*, Kuala Lumpur: Oxford University Press.

Christie, Jan Wisseman, 1998, 'The Medieval Tamil-language Inscriptions in Southeast Asia and China', *Journal of Southeast Asian Studies* 29 (2), 239-68.

Cowan, H.K.J., 1933, 'Lamuri-Lambri-Lawri-Ram(n)i-Lan-li-Lan-wu-li-Nan-po-li', *Bijdragen tot de Taal-, Land en Volkenkunde van Nederlandsch-Indie*, 90, 421-24.

Edwards McKinnon, E., 1980, 'A Note on a Gold "Tali" from Kota Cina', *JMBRAS*, 53, no. 2, 117.

———, 1981, 'Kota Cina: Its Context and Meaning in the Trade of Southeast Asia during the 12th to 14th Centuries', Ithaca, N.Y. Cornell University, Ph.D. dissertation.

———, 1988, 'Beyond Serandib: A Note on Lambri at the Northern Tip of Sumatra', *Indonesia* 46, 103-21.

———, 1994, 'Tamil Imagery in Northeast Sumatra', *Oriental Art*, XL, 3, 15-24.

———, 1996, 'Tamil Involvement in Northern Sumatra: The Gold and Resin Trade', JMBRAS 69, 1, 95-99.

———, 2006, 'Medieval Landfall Sites in Aceh, North Sumatra', in *Uncovering Southeast Asia's Past: Selected Papers from the 10th International Conference of the European Association of Southeast Asian Archaeologists*, ed. Elisabeth A. Bacus, Ian C. Glover and Vincent C. Piggot, Singapore: Singapore University Press, 325-34.

Guillot, Claude, 1998, *Histoire de Barus, Le Site de Lobu Tua I Études et Documents*, Paris: Cahiers d'Archipel.

———, 2004, *Histoire de Barus, II*, Paris: Cahiers d'Archipel.

Hall, Kenneth R., 2006, 'Sojourning Communities, Ports-of-Trade, and Agrarian-based Societies in Southeast Asia's Eastern Regions, 1000-1300', paper presented at IEHC in Helsinki.

Hirth, F. and W.W. Rockhill, 1911, *Chau Ju-Kua: His Work on the Chinese and Arab Trade in the Twelfth and Thirteenth Centuries, Entitled Chu-fan-chi*, St. Petersburg: Imperial Academy of Sciences.

Hourani, George F., 1995, *Arab Seafaring* [Expanded edition by John Carswell], Princeton, New Jersey: Princeton University Press.

Karashima, Noboru, 2002, *Ancient and Medieval Commercial Activities in the Indian Ocean: Testimony of Inscriptions and Ceramic-sherds*, Tokyo: Taisho University.

Karashima, Noboru and Y. Subbarayalu, 2002, 'Ainūrruvar: A Supra-local Organization of South Indian and Sri Lankan Merchants', in Noboru Karashima (ed.), *Ancient and Medieval Commercial Activities*, 72-87.

Lambourn, Elizabeth, 2003, 'From Cambay to Samudera-Pasai and Gresik: The Export of Gujarati Grave Memorials to Sumatra and Java in the Fifteenth Century C.E.', *Indonesia and the Malay World*, 31, no. 90, 221-89.

——— 2004, 'The Formation of the Batu Aceh Tradition in Fifteenth-Century Samudera-Pasai', in *Indonesia and the Malay World*, 32, no. 93, 211-48.

Leong Sau Heng, 1990, 'Collecting Centres, Feeder Points and Entrepôts in the Malay Peninsula, c. 1000 B.C.-A.D. 1400', in *The Southeast Asian Port and Polity: Rise and Demise*, ed. J. Kathirithamby-Wells and John Villiers, Singapore: Singapore University Press, pp. 17-38.

Lo Hsiang-Lin, 1967, 'Islam in Canton in the Sung Period', in F.S. Drake (ed), *Historical,*

Archaeological and Linguistic Studies in South-East Asia, Hong Kong: Hong Kong University Press, 177-79.

Miksic, J.N., 1979, 'Archaeology, Trade and Society in Northeast Sumatra', Ithaca, N.Y. Cornell University Ph.D. dissertation.

Montana, Suwedi, 1997, 'Nouvelles données sur les royumes de Lamuri et Barat', *Archipel*, 53, 85-95.

Parkin, Harry, 1978, *Batak Fruit of Hindu Thought*, Madras: Christian Literature Society.

Pathmanathan, S., 1976, 'The Vēlaikkārar in Medieval South India and Sri Lanka', *Sri Lankan Journal of the Humanities*, 2, 2. 120-37.

Sastri, K.A.N., 1932, 'A Tamil Merchant-Guild in Sumatra', *Tijdscrift v. h. Bataviaasch Genootschap* 72, 314-27.

——, 1949, *The History of Srivijaya*, Madras: University of Madras.

Schalk, Peter (Editor in Chief), 2002, *Buddhism among Tamils in Pre-colonial Tamilakam and Ilam*, Uppsala: Uppsala University: 2 vols. Pt. 1, *Prologue: The Pre-Pallava and the Pallava Period*. Pt. 2: *The Period of the Imperial Cōlar: Tamilakam and Ilam*.

Srinivasan, P.R., 1960, 'Buddhist Images of South India', in A. Aiyappan (ed.), *The Story of Buddhism with Special Reference to South India*, Madras: Department of Information and Publicity, Government of Madras, 62-101.

Subbarayalu, Y., 1998, 'The Tamil Merchant-Guild Inscription at Barus: A Rediscovery', in Guillot (ed.), *Histoire de Barus I*, 25-33.

——, 2002, 'The Tamil Merchant-Guild Inscription at Barus, Indonesia: A Rediscovery', in Noboru Karashima (ed.), *Ancient and Medieval Commercial Activities*, 19-34.

Tibbets, G.R., 1979, *A Study of the Arabic Texts Containing Material on South-East Asia*. Leiden and London: E.J. Brill for the Royal Asiatic Society.

Wade, Geoff, 2006, Translator, *Southeast Asia in the Ming shi-lu: An Open Access Resource*, Singapore: Asia Research Institute and the Singapore E-Press, National University of Singapore. http://epres.nus.edu.sg/msl/entry/, 2009.

——, 2007, 'Quan-zhou and Southeast Asian Islam in the Second Half of the 14th Century: A Moment of Change', paper presented at Moments in the Making of Southeast Asian Islam, Singapore: Asia Research Institute, National University of Singapore, 5-6 February 2007.

MAP 6.1
India and China with Sumatra

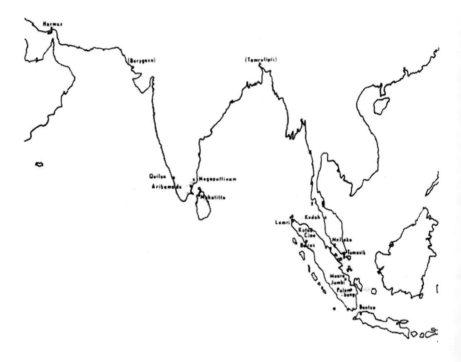

FIGURE 6.1
Kota Cina, Buddha 1 Chola style (Cholapauttam)

FIGURE 6.2
Kota Cina, Buddha 2 Chola style (Cholapauttam)

FIGURE 6.3
Kota Cina, Siva linga, Chola Polonarruva style

FIGURE 6.4
Kota Cina, Visnu, Chola style with 'sri vatsa' symbol on right breast

FIGURE 6.5
Kota Cina, Sakti, Chola style: lower portion with drapery

FIGURE 6.6
Kota Cina, Bronze bird-headed 'perpetual' votive lamp, Polonarruva style

FIGURE 6.7
Kota Cina, Chinese gold with impressed characters, 'shi fen'

FIGURE 6.8
Lamreh, Islamic nisan, plang pleng style (LZ 04) with lotus and jasmine motifs

FIGURE 6.9
Lamreh, Islamic nisan, plang pleng style (BT 02 a) panel, unread

FIGURE 6.10
Lamreh, Islamic nisan, plang pleng style (LE 04 a), unread

FIGURE 6.11
Lamreh, Islamic nisan, plang pleng style (MS 01), Malik Zin al-din, the holy
warrior, stylistically early fifteenth century but accompanying inscription defaced

FIGURE 6.12
Lamreh, Islamic *nisan*, slab type with inscription (LE 01),
Syeik Al-din 838 H. = CE 1435

FIGURE 6.13
South Indian coarse red ware (Kota Cina)

FIGURE 6.14
Outline of course red ware (Kota Cina)

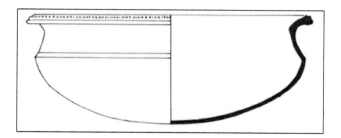

FIGURE 6.15
South Indian coarse red ware (Lamreh)

FIGURE 6.16
Zhejiang Longquan ware (Kota Cina and Lamreh)

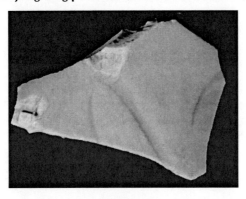

FIGURE 6.17
Jiangxi Jingdezhen qingbai shufu ware (Kota Cina and Lamreh)

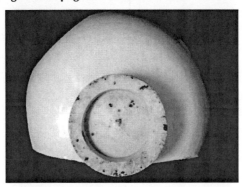

FIGURE 6.18
Jiangxi Jingdezhen blue on white ware (Lamreh)

7

South Asia and the Tapanuli Area (North-West Sumatra): Ninth-Fourteenth Centuries CE

Daniel Perret
Heddy Surachman

In North Sumatra, archaeological excavations on settlements dating from the historical era started at the beginning of the 1970s with researches conducted in Kota Cina, a site located on the east coast, between Medan and Belawan. This settlement, dated between the end of the eleventh century CE and the first half of the fourteenth century CE, notably yielded imagery almost certainly of south Indian origin (McKinnon 1984, 1994, 1996, 2003).

Some ten years later, a team of archaeologists at the National Research Centre for Archaeology of Indonesia conducted the first test pits in Barus on the opposite coast. The outcome of this initiative led to the launch in 1995 of a joint French-Indonesian archaeological research programme focused on the coastal site of Lobu Tua. It was completed in 2000 after five stages of excavations on this settlement dated between mid-ninth and the end of the eleventh century (Guillot (ed.) 1998; Guillot et al. 2003).

A new joint research programme was set up the following year involving the École française d'Extrême-Orient and the National Research Centre for Archaeology of Indonesia,[1] in order to study the main ancient settlements of Tapanuli, an area covering roughly the western half of the North Sumatra province. The first phase, between 2001 and 2005, was focused on other settlements in the Barus area, especially the site of Bukit Hasang founded during the twelfth century (Perret & Surachman (eds.) *forthcoming*). With the knowledge accumulated during these eleven years on the west coast, the team then started a second phase in 2006, moving to the study of inland sites. Padang Lawas, an area well known for its numerous Hindu-Buddhist temple remains, was the logical choice for this phase. From that year, excavations have been conducted twice in the site of Si Pamutung.

When combined with previous discoveries, the finds collected during recent surveys and excavations bring new perspectives on the nature and intensity of the relations between Tapanuli and South Asia, especially south India and Sri Lanka, between mid-ninth century and the beginning of the fourteenth century. This aspect will be examined here through five indicators, which, more or less clearly, throws light on the direct involvement of South Asian populations in the ancient history of this area, and more generally in the ancient history of North Sumatra. These indicators are inscriptions, place names, *marga* (descent group) names, techniques and artefacts.

THE EXCAVATED SITES

More than a century has elapsed since the discovery in 1873 of the famous Lobu Tua Tamil inscription, before the launch of comprehensive archaeological excavations focused on the ancient settlement of Lobu Tua. So far, this is the earliest well attested settlement of the Barus area. In fact, since the sixth century CE at least, the name of Barus was associated in various sources with the product which made its reputation for more than a millennium, from China to the Mediterranean region, that is the camphor found in its hinterland. Located a few hundred metres away from the ocean, its central part, which covered an area estimated between 7.5 and 14 hectares (ha), was protected by a system made up of earthen walls and ditches (Guillot et al. 2003). This central part accommodated a dense population, whereas its surroundings seem to have had only a sparse population, perhaps on a 200 ha area. More than 1,000 m² were excavated on this site.[2]

Lobu Tua was suddenly deserted by the turn of the twelfth century. A local Malay chronicle written at the end of the nineteenth century recounts that Lobu Tua was attacked by giants, without giving more details. This chronicle is an outstanding source because, certainly without knowing the existence of the ancient settlement of Lobu Tua and even less that of the Tamil inscription, it relates that Barus was founded by Chettis and Hindus (Drakard (ed.) 2003: 142), thus preserving in the collective memory an event 1,000 years old, only now confirmed by archaeology.

The account in the same chronicle of later settlements founded in the Barus area lead us to Bukit Hasang, a few kilometres away from Lobu Tua. From the physical point of view, this site is very similar to Lobu Tua, with a fortified central area estimated at some 15 ha and a surrounding sparse settlement estimated at a maximum of 50 ha. Nearly 700 m² were excavated on this site,[3] which yielded more than 43,000 shards of imported ceramics and more than 120,000 shards of pottery. Although the analysis of these artefacts is not completed yet, we suggest that the site was founded at the beginning of the twelfth century, and reached its peak between mid-thirteenth century and the beginning of the fifteenth century. It should be added that two successive settlements existed on the seashore at the time of Bukit Hasang; however, because of the coastal erosion, only about 1 ha is left today of each site (Perret & Surachman (eds.) *forthcoming*).

Padang Lawas, on the other hand, is a textbook case in the historiography of the Malay World. Since its discovery in the mid-nineteenth century and during the next century and a half, researches were exclusively focused on monuments, statuary, inscriptions and bronze artefacts. As the presence of temples attracted all the attention, the interest for the ancient settlements of this area was aroused even later than in Kota Cina and Barus. It is in fact less than a decade old.

So far, 19 sites showing a complex of buildings or a single building have been spotted in the Padang Lawas area, and 17 of them are still visible today. All these sites, except one, are located above the confluence of the Barumun and the Batang Pane rivers. The architecture usually mixes bricks and ornaments made of tuff, but some buildings seem to have been made exclusively of stone.

The Medan Office for Archaeology conducted the first test pits dealing with the ancient settlements of Padang Lawas in 1999 (Susilowati et al. 1999; Susilowati, Wiradnyana & Koestoro 2000; Susilowati, Oetomo & Sutrisna 2003). In fact, this new approach was motivated by the rediscovery during its restoration of a system made of earthen walls and moats around the Si Pamutung temple (Susilowati 2001). Si Pamutung is at a strategic location, on a height overhanging the confluence of the Barumun and Batang Pane rivers. The inner space of this system is estimated at some 35 ha, and it is divided in six sections by these earthen walls and moats. Made of six buildings of bricks and tuff, the main temple complex of Si Pamutung stands in the centre of one of these sections.

During the two stages of excavations conducted so far, the team[4] has spotted several brick-mounds, has excavated part of the foundations of another brick building, and has identified remains of dwellings, including dwellings built on posts. The site is relatively rich in finds. So far, 75,000 shards of local pottery, 10,000 shards of imported ceramics, more than 900 shards of glass, 60 shards of imported glazed pottery, metal artefacts and a few beads have been collected. The first precise chronological data regarding this settlement are drawn from the recent analysis of the imported ceramics found during the first stage of excavations (Dupoizat 2007). It shows a foundation during the tenth century; the settlement reached its peak during the eleventh century, until the beginning of the twelfth century, before experiencing a decline and becoming deserted at the beginning of the fourteenth century.

THE INSCRIPTIONS

The strongest indicator to suggest the presence in Tapanuli of populations originating from South Asia is represented by two Tamil inscriptions. The first one is the famous inscription dated CE 1088, found in Lobu Tua. Most of the text, made of 26 lines written in Tamil script and language, was deciphered and published only a few years ago (Subbarayalu 1998). It is now confirmed that its content deals with the payment of taxes by the ships calling at Barus to the local representative of the merchant guild Ayyavole. Therefore, it is clear that a community of traders from south India was living in Barus at that time. Among the very interesting aspects of this inscription, the first occurrence of the word *marakkala-nayan* is noteworthy. During the sixteenth century it was used to refer to the high seas Muslim traders living on the coasts of Tamil Nadu and Kerala. It cannot be ascertained that this word already referred to Muslim seafarers by the end of the eleventh century, but it is known that there were several settlements of Arab traders, with their trade guilds called *anjuvannam* or *hanjamana*, all along the West and East coasts of India right from the ninth century onwards (Subbarayalu 1998: 32). Thus the people living in Lobu Tua and related to the Ayyavole guild were possibly of various origins.

The second inscription is a stone pillar decorated with a head of Ganeśa at the top. It was spotted around 1920 a few kilometers down the source of the Barumun River, quite far inland. It is a bilingual inscription with its upper part in old-Malay language using old-Javanese script, and its lower part in Tamil language and script. Both texts seem to have the same meaning: a Javanese (?) commander-in-chief makes offerings for the merit of a king named 'Pāduka śrī Mahārāja' in the old-Malay inscription, and 'Peritu śrī Mahārāja' in the Tamil inscription. The date found in both inscriptions provides a time range from CE 1213 to 1265.[5] Among several interesting aspects, this inscription first reveals that Tamil people frequented the hinterland of Tapanuli at least since the second half of the thirteenth century. This observation contradicts a common assumption maintaining that since ancient times, foreigners were prevented to enter the hinterland of North Sumatra. This ban, if it ever prevailed, was perhaps brought in by foreigners directly involved in the exploitation of the hinterland itself, in this case Tamil and Javanese people. Furthermore, this inscription is another testimony of the existence and continuity of a large cooperation network between Javanese and Tamil people, a network already suggested for a previous period in Barus (Guillot et al. 2003: 49, 68).

PLACE NAMES

A study of the present topographical maps of Tapanuli reveals the use of place names such as Mahligai, Pane, Sunggam, Singkam, all showing a Tamil origin. The toponym Batu Mundam, at the mouth of the Batang Toru River delta, may be added to this list because one of its components is of Tamil origin. Bahal, a toponym occurring several times in Padang Lawas, is still used in Nepal to indicate a Buddhist monastery. Furthermore, several places named Pijor (or Pijar[6]) Koling very probably indicate a south Indian settlement. An example is 'Picar Koling', at the mouth of the Batang Gadis River, reported to have yielded 'antiquities' (*Notulen van de Algemeene en Directievergaderingen van het Bataviaasch Genootschap van Kunsten en Wetenschappen*, 25, 1887: 56).

Some of the Padang Lawas remains stand along the Pane River, a tributary of the Barumun River. F.D.K. Bosch, a Dutch scholar, was probably the first to link them with the name 'Pane' at the mouth of the Barumun River, some 200 km downstream, and to the 'Panai', whose conquest is claimed by the Cholas during the yet-to-be confirmed 1025 expedition.[7] According to Bosch, the occurrence of the toponym Panai[8] could only be explained by the presence of a Tamil colony settled there for some time, probably traders using to cross the island (Bosch 1930: 147-48). As the Thanjavur inscription mentions that Panai is 'watered by *the* river' (Cœdès 1918: 5), the present state of knowledge would lead us to suggest that the Panai mentioned in the inscription should be the one at the mouth of the Barumun River. A survey conducted in 2006 in order to spot ancient settlements between Si Pamutung and the present mouth of the Barumun River turned out negative results. But this question needs to be addressed after a study on the fluctuations of the lower course of the river. Therefore, the link between the Thanjavur inscription and the Barumun River Basin is so far limited to the similarity of the toponyms, without any stronger basis.

Another aspect, which needs a thorough study, is the history of several *marga*, the patrilineal descent groups found in Tapanuli. Kern was the first, as early as 1903, to draw attention to the Dravidian names borne by several subdivisions of the Sembiring *marga*, located north of Lake Toba. To follow up this question, we think that an investigation of the history of the Tapanuli *margas* showing Tamil influence in their names, such as Daulay, Pane or Pulungan, could be very useful.

TECHNIQUES

Except 1½ m³ of bricks, no remains of a permanent building was ever found in Lobu Tua. Yet, this material is interesting because some of these bricks show traces of lime mortar. This technique was common in India at that time, but still unknown in Java (Guillot et al. 2003: 41-42). Almost no bricks were found during the excavations at the nearby site of Bukit Hasang. On the other hand, lime mortar was not used in the building of the brick temples in Padang Lawas.

Barus was the first settlement in Sumatra and the second in the whole Malay World, after Java, to have struck coins. The technique to make these gold coins was very similar to the one known in south India at that time. It used casts made of terracotta showing several hemispherical holes very similar to the casts found in the excavations of Gangaikondacholapuram, near Thanjavur, the royal town of the Cholas during the eleventh century. The gold hemispheres were struck in order to show the sandalwood flower on one side and a character on the other side (Guillot et al. 2003: 45, 67, 289). This type of coin has not been found in later coastal sites of the Barus area and has yet to appear in the Padang Lawas area.

It is well known that the Indians had a great experience of gold-mining in India itself. It looks like this experience was used in the gold mines of Sumatra. The local literature offers a few indications regarding the direct exploitation of gold by South Asian people. The *Hikayat Raja Pasai*, a fifteenth-century Malay text related to the northern tip of Sumatra, gives a clear indication of their involvement. Relating the arrival in Pasai of a ship carrying Indian traders, the text recounts that one of them was able to detect gold. Claiming to have spotted seven gold deposits unknown to the local people, he was given customary dresses by the king and sent with a royal guard to look for these places. The story ends with the foreigner managing to find a lot of gold (Jones, ed. 1999: 21). A similar idea occurs north of the Toba Lake, in a Karo tale, which recounts that in former times gold was owned by the god of the intermediate world, Tuan Banua Keling, and a recurrent theme in the Karo tales is the presence of an 'Indian' with supernatural powers (Edwards McKinnon 1984: 29).

This assumption regarding the direct exploitation by Indians of gold located in the hinterland of Sumatra is strengthened by an inscribed gold ring found in Lobu Tua. The Sanskrit inscription on this ring is dated from the tenth century and leads us to think that its owner was working in a mine. It has been read 'In the darkness, I have chosen to work' by Friederich, whose conclusion is that the ring was owned by an 'Indian miner, who came to become rich by working in the gold mines of Sumatra' (Guillot et al. 2003: 45, 52, 288-89; Friederich 1858). There are some indications showing that this Indian expertise probably led miners based in Lobu Tua to extract gold in the Bengkulu area, in cooperation with Javanese workers (Guillot et al. 2003: 290).

A fourth technique could be of Indian origin. It is the use of square section iron nails in house and temple building and perhaps in boat building, whereas at that time, the local technique in Sumatra was based on vegetal binding material. More than 200 of them were found in Lobu Tua, with an example exceeding 20 cm in length. Such long nails were also used in the contemporary site of Gangaikondacholapuram (Guillot et al. 2003: 45, 52, 276). Square section nails are also common finds in Bukit Hasang, and nails showing a quadrangular section in their lower half were found in Si Pamutung during the restoration of the main temples.

THE ARTEFACTS

Some of the finds collected during recent excavations in the Tapanuli area probably originate from South Asia. Several shaped fragments of artefacts made of pink and black granite have been found in Lobu Tua. The common use of this material in India at the time is well known, whereas this type of stone does not seem to have been worked locally (Guillot et al. 2003: 295, 297, 298). Lobu Tua is not the only place of Sumatra to have imported granite. At least one image made of granite and supposedly imported from South Asia has been identified in Kota Cina, to the north of Medan (Edwards McKinnon 1984: 67). Another example is the stone found in 1990 in the vicinity of Banda Aceh, at the northern tip of Sumatra, which bears a Tamil inscription dating from the very end of the thirteenth century.[9] Three fragments of black granite were also found in Bukit Hasang. Another type of stone very probably imported from India is garnetiferous gneiss. The Lobu Tua site has yielded some shaped fragments of this stone, which looks very similar to the stone used at that time in Orissa for statuary.[10] As far as we know, so far no artefacts made of granite or gneiss has ever been found in the Padang Lawas area. Most of images there are made of tuff, a material still quarried and used locally.

Most of the Lobu Tua earthenwares show strong similarities regarding shapes and decorations with pottery found in south India and Sri Lanka. We would like to point out here the difficulty to make comparisons as very few studies on medieval pottery have been conducted so far in India or in Sri Lanka. The paste often shows brick-red inclusions and small glittering mica flecks, reminding us of earthenwares of the Kaveri Valley. Yet, if compared to pottery observed in South Asia, the fabrics of the earthenwares found in Lobu Tua are more heterogeneous and the firing is of inferior quality. Some twenty-two different types identified according to the general features of the paste, slip and shape have been suggested as imports from South Asia (Guillot et al. 2003: 69-101). The most common South Asian type found in Lobu Tua is probably the round cooking pot with a wide mouth showing a pattern made of stamped parallel grooves on the external side of the lower part. Sri Lanka is the highly probable origin of this type. Another common ware in Lobu Tua is the carinated cooking-pot or *kadhai*, an earthenware well-known all over South Asia. The excavations in Lobu Tua also yielded plates or dishes without any decoration which are also found in south India and in Sri Lanka; round *kendis* with a very short spout, also found in the Tamil area; *kendis* with short coarse pyramidal spouts commonly found in Sri Lanka. Other types include jars, pots, lids, bowls and an oil lamp with a shape common in south India.

Compared to Lobu Tua, Bukit Hasang probably yielded more types of earthenwares believed to originate from South Asia,[11] but the proportion of these wares to the total amount of collected shards is far lower, as it should not exceed 25 per cent.

The situation is again different in Padang Lawas. In fact, so far, these types of earthenwares rarely occurred during the first two stages of excavations in Si Pamutung.

Other artefacts supposedly imported from South Asia and worth mentioning here are double teeth iron or bronze combs found in Lobu Tua, which are on display in several museums of south India (Guillot et al. 2003: 280-81).

What should be emphasised here is that these earthenwares and combs made for a daily use are not known to have been traded in the Malay world, and thus were probably brought by South Asian people for their own needs.

As the studies of these three sites of the Tapanuli area are now at different stages, it is not yet possible to provide definitive answers regarding the position and the importance of South Asia in the history of the region between mid-ninth century and the fourteenth century. We will only suggest several hypotheses based on data available so far.

THE SOUTH ASIAN POPULATION IN BARUS

A body of indicators suggests that a significant population coming from South Asia settled in the coastal site of Lobu Tua between mid-ninth century and the end of the eleventh century. Lobu Tua could even have been dominated by South Asian populations. At least part of this population asserted the permanent authority of a traders' guild by setting up a stone inscription related to the payment of taxes. This event happened a few years before the destruction of the site.

The site of Bukit Hasang, founded at the beginning of the following century a few kilometres away from Lobu Tua, shows continuity in the use of pottery believed to have been brought from South Asia. Unfortunately, due to disturbances of the site and the lack of precise dating for medieval earthenwares in South Asia itself, it is not yet possible to determine precisely the trends in the use of these earthenwares between the twelfth century and the beginning of the sixteenth century. Therefore, the fact that on the one hand several types observed in Lobu Tua are also found in Bukit Hasang, and on the other hand the mention by Tomé Pires of Gujarati traders, and probably merchants from south India and Bengal coming to Barus by the beginning of the sixteenth century suggest that South Asian people settled in Barus during the entire period.[12] Then, one can only guess the factors which could explain a much lower proportion of earthenwares probably brought from South Asia, compared to Lobu Tua: a much more cosmopolitan site, the presence of indigenous people, the acculturation of South Asian people settled permanently or semi-permanently in Barus leading to the rejection in daily use of South Asian pottery, or migrations to other trading places. Perhaps the development or the success of another centre for Tamil trading activities on the northern tip of the island, precisely in the present suburbs of Banda Aceh, could have attracted part of this population. In fact, from the few words that have been deciphered so far in the Tamil inscription of Neusu (at the very end of thirteenth century), it seems that the text refers to a decision made by a group of people.[13] Activities related to gold trade are mentioned,[14] and the occurrence of the word *mandapam* could refer to the foundation of a temple or to a donation to a temple, at the time a common practice among trade guilds (Christie 1998: 258-59). A major trading place with a quite different evolution, that is Pasai, probably attracted South Asian people settled in Barus starting in the fourteenth century.

THE END OF SOUTH INDIAN TRADERS' GUILDS IN NORTH SUMATRA

Researches conducted so far on the history of the hinterland of Tapanuli between the tenth and the fourteenth centuries show that the Tamil population was ready to show its presence through the use of foreign place names and through permanent inscriptions written in Tamil language, at least in the thirteenth century. On the other hand, South Asian people appear far more restrained regarding the daily material culture.

Both coastal inscriptions of Lobu Tua and Neusu bear a single language and highlight the community and its authority on a particular area in the context of trade. On the other hand, three other inscriptions found in Sumatra show different features. They are bilingual, not directly related to trade and were set up in the hinterland. The one on the Barumun River has been discussed earlier. The bilingual inscription of Batu Bapahat near Suruaso,[15] carved on a rock near an old channel, is dated from the end of the thirteenth century. The text is made of ten lines in Sanskrit using 'Adityawarman' or 'old-Sumatran' script, and 13 lines in Tamil language using the Grantha script. Unfortunately, this inscription, never fully transcribed or translated, has completely disappeared today. It probably referred to the building of some structure for irrigation, therefore showing that a Tamil speaking population was involved in the exploitation of the agricultural environment of the hinterland of Sumatra at the time. The third bilingual inscription bearing Tamil language is the Batubasurat inscription near Buo, again in the Minangkabau area. It is dated to the thirteenth-fourteenth centuries (Edwards McKinnon 1996: 97). Unfortunately, so far, this text appears not to have been deciphered.

Even if these Tamil inscriptions of the Sumatra hinterland do not refer to the trade guilds, we would like to point out that they occur simultaneously with the peak of prosperity of the Ayyavole guild in the Pandya kingdom of Madurai at the end of the thirteenth century. Like the Colas, the Pandyas too supported Ayyavole and the coast of the Pandya kingdom became the hub of the trade with Southeast Asia. In fact, the inscriptions related to the Manigramam and Ayyavole guilds give the general impression of a huge increase regarding the importation of Southeast Asian products (spices, aromatic products, wax, elephants, precious stones, etc.) and the exportation (cotton fabric, iron, dyes, etc.) to this region at the end of the thirteenth century (Abraham 1988).[16] This increase in the volume of trade would have been possible through the intensification of the direct exploitation of the hinterland of Sumatra, and especially of Tapanuli, by people more or less connected to the guilds. Tamil inscriptions of the hinterland could thus be a testimony of this dynamism.

We suggest the occurrence of a major turning point in the middle of the fourteenth century, marked by the collapse of the old south Indian trade guild activities and the rise of the Pasai Sultanate, at the northern tip of Sumatra, to the detriment of other trading places like Barus, Kota Cina and the Bujang Valley in the Malay Peninsula.

So far, no Tamil inscription dated later than the thirteenth century and related to these guilds has ever been found in Southeast Asia. In India itself, Ayyavole seems to have changed completely its nature during the fourteenth century, while the Manigramam guild disappeared, an evolution which took place at the same time as the collapse of the Pandya Kingdom. Ayyavole disappeared in the Tamil area, but the name was reused by a new group of traders based in the Telugu area and probably without any relation with the former guild (Abraham 1988: 2-3, 67-68). The end of the Pandya Kingdom also saw an increasing fragmentation of the old economic networks in the region (Christie 1982: 78). The place is then left free, in the new kingdom of Vijayanagar, for powerful businesses managed by great trading castes of the Tamil area – Chettis, Komattis and Balijas – and also for Muslim trading communities, whether foreign, mixed or local (Arasaratnam 1994: 41).

Therefore, it was maybe at this time that large-scale family economic networks and temporary associations took over the overseas trade with the Malay World. It is in these groups, probably dominated by Muslims settled along the coast from Gujarat to Bengal and belonging to a cosmopolitan society including Persians, Arabs, Turks, Yemenites, Omanis, Iraqis, Armenians, Abyssinians and local people converted to Islam, that we have to look for the driving forces, if not the founders of the Pasai sultanate.

It is probably no coincidence that this mid-fourteenth-century turning point occurred at the same time as the expansion of the pepper cultivation in the northern tip of Sumatra. We suggest therefore that the trading places apparently not involved in pepper cultivation at the time, such as Kota Cina and Barus, were progressively deserted by foreign traders for major pepper centres such as Pasai and Pedir. Regarding these pepper centres themselves, we would like to underline the similarities between the system of port city-state they have developed and the system, probably unique in South Asia, developed by several kingdoms of Malabar, where pepper was a major commodity.

On the other hand, the middle of the fourteenth century saw the end of Padang Lawas. It is too early, at the present stage of our research on this area, to suggest a direct relation between this fact, the collapse of the old south Indian trade guilds, and the rise of Pasai. Very recent indications would suggest that the focalisation on religious aspects has completely overlooked the economic potential of Padang Lawas itself. Local economic difficulties could be among the reasons of the decline of the area.

CONCLUSION

Excavations already completed or in progress in three sites of the Tapanuli area bring new data regarding the role played by South Asian populations in the north of Sumatra between the ninth and the fourteenth centuries. In Barus, the Tamil inscription of Lobu Tua dating from the end of the eleventh century stands now in a clearer context through the identification of South Asian techniques and artefacts, as well as mentions in local traditions. This environment sets this coastal site as a major settlement probably dominated by South Asian people from its foundation by the mid-ninth century until its destruction at the end of the eleventh century.

Data regarding the nearby site of Bukit Hasang (twelfth-beg. of the sixteenth centuries) seems less clear to interpretation as the site has been settled for a longer period of time and artefacts believed to have been brought from South Asia are generally not precisely dated. We can only suggest that South Asian communities were present there during the entire period, but probably not dominant. Bukit Hasang may have been ethnically much more balanced than Lobu Tua, with a significant indigenous population, a situation encouraging the acculturation of foreigners settled permanently or semi-permanently. Others may have been attracted by the dynamism of flourishing trading centres at the northern tip of the island from the second half of the thirteenth century.

So far, the Padang Lawas area, where a programme of excavations has just started at Si Pamutung (tenth-beg. fourteenth centuries), reveals very few indications of a daily material culture originating in South Asia, whereas South Asian traces left on the landscape or territory of Padang Lawas are highlighted by several place names and an inscription dating from the thirteenth century. The addition of two other almost contemporary inscriptions in the hinterland of the Minangkabau area leads us to think that these texts could reveal an increase in the direct exploitation of the hinterland of North Sumatra by South Asian people when the trade guild Ayyavole reached its peak of prosperity.

We suggest the existence of a major turning point in North Sumatra by mid-fourteenth century characterised by the collapse of the old south Indian trade guild activities and the rise of the sultanate of Pasai at the northern tip of the island. This rise was probably stimulated by large-scale economic family networks and temporary associations involved in the overseas trade. These predominantly Muslim groups, based along the coasts of India, were probably involved in the rise of Pasai. As a major pepper centre, Pasai managed to supersede other trading places such as Barus in Tapanuli, which did not take part in the early developments of this cultivation in Sumatra.

POSTSCRIPT, MAY 2010

Since the presentation of this paper, the results of the second phase of excavations conducted in the Barus area (2001-05) have been published.

NOTES

1. Both archaeological research programmes in cooperation have been and are supported by the consultative committee for archaeological research abroad under the French Ministry of Foreign Affairs.
2. Claude Guillot, Heddy Surachman, Daniel Perret, Untung Sunaryo, Mohamad Ali Fadillah, Sugeng Riyanto and Sonny Ch. Wibisono have been involved in the excavations. Imported ceramics have been studied by Marie-France Dupoizat.
3. Daniel Perret, Heddy Surachman, Untung Sunaryo, Sophie Péronnet, Ery Sudewo, Nenggih Susilowati, Deny Sutrisna and Repelita Wahyu Oetomo have been involved in the excavations. Imported ceramics have been studied by Marie-France Dupoizat.
4. Daniel Perret, Heddy Surachman, Sukawati Susetyo, Véronique Degroot, Ery Sudewo, Deny Sutrisna, Repelita Wahyu Oetomo and Mujiono have been involved

in the excavations. Imported ceramics are studied by Marie-France Dupoizat. On the results of the first stage (2006), see Perret et al. 2007.

5. Collection of the National Museum in Jakarta, no. D.181 (Callenfels, 1920: 70; Bosch, 1930: 147; Krom, 1931: 304; Damais, 1952: 100-01; 1955: 208-09; Sedyawati, 1994: 556; Karashima, 2002: 14).

6. *Pijar* is a local word related to smelting. *Pijar-pijar* is borax, a white, water-soluble powder or crystals, hydrated sodium borate used to lower the melting point of gold.

7. Before Bosch, the Panai of the Thanjavur inscription was put side by side exclusively with the Pane of the mouth of the Barumun River (see for example Cœdès, 1918: 9; Krom, 1926: 245). Moreover, in some local traditions, Padang Lawas is not related to Pane but to Aru (Parlindungan, 1964: 590-92, 618; Lubis, 1993: 3, 31).

8. 'Cleared land' or 'colony' in Tamil language, according to this author. For Y. Subbarayalu, its meaning in Old Tamil is 'rice field' or a species of palm tree (pers. comm.).

9. *Kecamatan* Baiturrahman. It was first dated on palaeographic grounds to the twelfth-thirteenth centuries and read by L. Jhyagarajan (Ariyalur) in 1995, based on a rubbing and pictures. We thank Pierre-Yves Manguin to have made this unpublished analysis available to us. The more precise dating given here is provided by Y. Subbarayalu, based on the observation of a casting available in Singapore (pers. comm.).

10. For examples of ancient images coming from Orissa using this type of stone, see Okada, 2000: 97-101.

11. The great variety of fabrics, as revealed by X-ray diffraction analysis, supports the idea of various origins.

12. Pires, 1990, I: 161; Guillot, Surachman, Perret et al. 2003: 49.

13. According to the unpublished analysis done by L. Jhyagarajan in 1995.

14. Y. Subbarayalu, pers. comm.

15. *Kabupaten* of Tanah Datar, which is part of the Minangkabau area.

16. Gold, ivory and tin should be added to this list of importations by South Asia.

REFEFENCES

Abraham, Meera, *Two Medieval Merchant Guilds of South India*, New Delhi: Manohar, 1988.

Arasaratnam, Sinappah, *Maritime India in the Seventeenth Century*, New Delhi: Oxford University Press, 1994.

Bosch, F.D.K., 'Verslag van een reis door Sumatra', *Oudheidkundig Verslag uitgegeven door het Bataviaasch Genootschap van Kunsten en Wetenschappen* (1930): 133-57.

Callenfels, P.V. van Stein, 'Rapport over een dienstreis door een deel van Sumatra', *Oudheidkundig Verslag uitgegeven door het Bataviaasch Genootschap van Kunsten en Wetenschappen* 2 (1920): 62-75.

Christie, J. Wisseman, 'The Medieval Tamil-Language Inscriptions in Southeast Asia and China', *Journal of Southeast Asian Studies* 29, no. 2 (1998): 239-68.

Cœdès, George, 'Le Royaume de Çrivijaya', *Bulletin de l'École française d'Extrême-Orient* 18, no. 6 (1918): 1-36.

Damais, Louis-Charles, 'Études d'épigraphie indonésienne. – III. Liste des principales inscriptions datées de l'Indonésie', *Bulletin de l'École française d'Extrême-Orient* 46, no. 1 (1952): 1-105.

——, 'Études d'épigraphie indonésienne. – IV. Discussion de la date des inscriptions', *Bulletin de l'École française d'Extrême-Orient* 47, no. 1 (1955): 7-290.

Drakard, Jane (ed.), *Sejarah Raja-Raja Barus*, Jakarta: École française d'Extrême-Orient, Angkasa, 1988, 2nd edn. Jakarta: École française d'Extrême-Orient, Gramedia Pustaka Utama, 2003.

Dupoizat, Marie-France, 'Essai de chronologie de la céramique chinoise trouvée à Si Pamutung, Padang Lawas: Xe-début XIVe siècle', *Archipel* 74, 2007: 83-106.

Friederich, R.H.Th., 'Over eenige inskriptien op ringen en gesneden steenen (meest afkomstig van Sumatra)', *Tijdschrift voor indische Taal-, Land- en Volkenkunde* 7 (1858): 141-46.

Guillot, Claude (ed.), *Histoire de Barus. Le Site de Lobu Tua: I. Études et Documents*, Paris: Cahiers d'Archipel 30, 1998.

Guillot, Claude et al., *Histoire de Barus, Sumatra, Le site de Lobu Tua. II: Étude archéologique et Documents*. Paris: Cahier d'Archipel 30, 2003.

Jones, Russell (ed.), *Hikayat Raja Pasai*, Kuala Lumpur: Yayasan Karyawan dan Penerbit Fajar Bakti, 1999.

Karashima, N., 'Tamil Inscriptions in Southeast Asia and China', in *Ancient and Medieval Commercial Activities in the Indian Ocean: Testimony of Inscriptions and Ceramics-shards*, ed. N. Karashima, Tokyo: Taisho University, 2002, 10-18.

Krom, N.J., *Hindoe-Javaansche Geschiedenis*, 1926, 2nd edn., 's-Gravenhage: Martinus Nijhoff, 1931.

Lubis, Mhd. Arbain, *Sejarah Marga-Marga Asli di Tanah Mandailing*, Medan: 1993.

McKinnon, E. Edwards, 'Tamil Imagery in Northeast Sumatra', *Oriental Art* XL, no. 3 (1994): 15-24.

———, 'Mediaeval Tamil Involvement in Northern Sumatra, C11-C14 (The Gold and Resin Trade)', *Journal of the Malaysian Branch, Royal Asiatic Society* 69, no. 1 (1996): 85-99.

———, 'Historic Period Earthenware from the Island of Sumatra', in *Earthenware in Southeast Asia*, ed. J.N. Miksic, Singapore: Singapore University Press, 2003, 162-72.

McKinnon, E. Edwards, 'Kota Cina: Its Context and Meaning in the Trade of Southeast Asia in the Twelfth to Fourteenth Centuries', Ph.D. thesis, Cornell University, New York, 1984.

Okada, Amina. *Sculptures indiennes du musée Guimet*, Paris: Réunion des Musées Nationaux, 2000.

Parlindungan, Mangaradja Onggang, *Tuanku Rao*, Jakarta: Tandjung Pengharapan, 1964.

Perret, D. and H. Surachman (eds.), *Histoire de Barus-Sumatra. III: Regards sur une place marchande de l'océan Indien (XIIe-milieu du XVIIe s.)*, Paris, EFEO/Archipel (cahier d' Archipel 38), 2009.

Perret, Daniel, Heddy Surachman, Lucas P. Koestoro, Sukawati Susetyo, 'Le programme archéologique franco-indonésien sur les sites d'habitats anciens de Tapanuli (Sumatra Nord): réflexions préliminaires sur Padang Lawas', *Archipel* 74, 2007: 45-82.

Sedyawati, Edi, *Pengarcaan Gaṇeśa Masa Kadiri dan Siṅhasāri*, Jakarta: LIPI-RUL, École française d'Extrême-Orient, 1994.

Subbarayalu, Y., 'The Tamil Merchant-Guild Inscription at Barus: A Rediscovery', in *Histoire de Barus. Le site de Lobu Tua. I: Etudes et documents*, ed. C. Guillot, Paris: Cahier d'Archipel 30, 1998, 25-33.

Susilowati, Nenggih, 'Benteng Tanah, Bidangan, dan Penataan Ruang di Kompleks Kepurbakalaan Si Pamutung, Padang Lawas', *Berkala Arkeologi "Sangkhakala"* (Medan) 9 (2001): 68-81.

Susilowati, Nenggih, K. Wiradnyana and L.P. Koestoro, 'Laporan Penelitian Arkeologi dan Pemetaan Situs Candi Sipamutung dan Sekitarnya, Kecamatan Barumun Tengah', Medan: Balai Arkeologi, 1999.

Susilowati, N., K. Wiradnyana; L.P. Koestoro, 'Laporan Penelitian Arkeologi di Tempuran Sungai Barumun dan Batang Pane', Medan: Balai Arkeologi, 2000.

Susilowati, N., R.W. Oetomo and D. Sutrisna, 'Laporan Penelitian Arkeologi di Kompleks Kepurbakalaan Sipamutung, Kecamatan Barumun Tengah', Medan: Balai Arkeologi, 2003.

8

Emergence of Early Historic Trade in Peninsular India

K. Rajan

INTRODUCTION

One geographical area dealing with transoceanic trade covers the present states of Kerala and Tamil Nadu. It formed a distinctive linguistic identity and cultural homogeneity, particularly during the early historic period. The Tamil language and Tamil-Brahmi script is found engraved on memorial stones, caves, coins, seals, rings and on ceramics in the above geographical zone with great uniformity. These inscribed objects clearly suggest a common language with its own script, established as a native language well before the third century BCE, one of the prerequisites for trade. This linguistic uniformity would not have been achieved without minimum, continuous cultural interaction. The striking similarity observed in various Iron Age monuments clearly points to the emergence of cultural homogeneity. The available archaeological sites further suggest that human occupation was widespread and transcended different ecological zones (Fig. 8.1). The continuous human occupation led to resource mobilization leading in turn to resource transactions through trade. The long survival of trade centres and port towns located in an economically viable resource zone are fine indicators of its natural growth and expansion (Fig. 8.2). The exploitation of natural resources like iron ore, pearl fishery, gemstone industry, spices, forest products, etc., transformed the cultural matrix of the place through the introduction of new technology in the area of production and in transportation. The state protection and formation of trade guilds had an indirect impact on development of trade. These multiple factors played a crucial role in maintaining these commercial activities over a

FIGURE 8.1
Map showing Archaeological Sites in Tamil Nadu

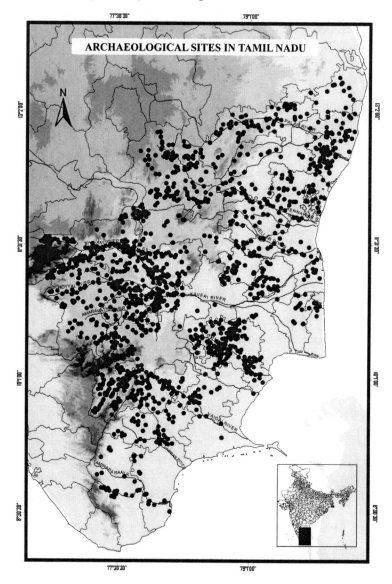

period. The present study attempts to focus on the trade that existed between fifth century BCE and third century CE. These dynamic trading activities have been discussed in the backdrop of recent archaeological evidence that surfaced in India, Sri Lanka, Southeast Asia and the West.

The long survival of Iron Age monuments spanning over one thousand years shows the establishment of settlements in different ecological zones. It

FIGURE 8.2
Map showing Trade Centres and Port Towns

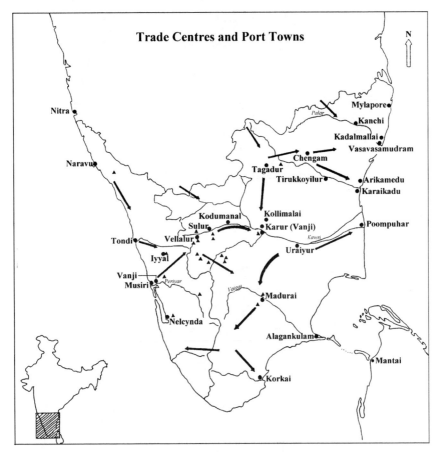

shows no cultural break between the Iron Age and early historic phase though there is a marked difference in ways of life. The manifold activities of the Iron Age people have been observed in the late phase of Iron Age. Iron Age cults, such as the system of venerating departed souls, were continued in early historic villages, capital cities, trade centres and port towns, in advanced stages both in content and in quality. For instance, at Kodumanal, transepted cists yielded potsherds with Tamil-Brahmi script reading *visaki* (Rajan 1996: 72-86) (Fig. 8.3); the Sulur grave yielded punch marked coins (Beck 1930:166-82); one should also recall the bronze seal with two-line inscriptions collected from a burial at Anaikottai in Jaffna Peninsula (Fig. 8.4) (Raghupathy 1987: 200-02). Recently, three memorial stones with Tamil-Brahmi inscriptions were found installed as part of an urn burial discovered at Pulimankombai and Thathapatti (Rajan 2007: 51-61). All these denote the continuation of the custom of erecting Iron Age monuments in early historical period. One

FIGURE 8.3
Kodumanal: Russet coated ware inscribed with visaki

FIGURE 8.4
Anaikottai seal from Sri Lanka

may therefore visualise that in the last stage of the Iron Age phase, people became settled; a clan based society slowly emerged; exploitation of minerals and ores culminated; industrial activities intensified; specialised craftsman-ship developed; new scripts developed or the earlier one (graffiti) got modified; trade routes were formed in the potential agricultural and mineral rich zones; various religions took shape and literature proliferated. This cultural transformation is reflected in archaeological, epigraphical, numismatics and literary records. Capital cities like Uraiyur, Madurai, Karur, Tagadur and Koyilur, trade centres like Kodumanal and Vellalur and ports like Musiri, Korkai, Alakankulam, Kaveripattinam and Arikamedu witnessed the same cultural transformations. Keeping these factors in mind, an emerging trade scenario can be observed.

It is widely accepted that trade is considered as one of the indicators for the existence or the formation of state. Trade played an important role in the formation of inter-regional networks and for territorial expansion during the early historic period. For instance, Cheras made a territorial advance into the Kongu country (Coimbatore region) from the Periyar river valley of present Kerala State to keep control of economic products like semi-precious stones, iron ore and spices that brought considerable amounts into their treasury (Rajan 1991: 111-12). It seems that the building of Karur-Vanji as their second capital on the Amaravathi riverbank was primarily in the interest of trade. The production of cash crops and the introduction of new technologies in the manufacture sectors like textile, gem and iron industries further increased economic viability and sustained trading activities. The merchants dealing exclusively in salt, sugar, ploughshare, cloth, gold, oil and gem mentioned in Tamil-Brahmi inscriptions as potential donors suggest organised trade (Mahadevan 2003: 141-42). Besides, terms like *nikama* (Fig. 8.5) and *cattu* are related to trade guilds. The term *Vellarai-nikamattor* (trade guild of Vellarai) noticed at Mangulam suggests that the trade guild came into existence well before the third century BCE. The second term *cattu* (meaning 'caravan') probably indicates that different traders moved in groups for longer distances. These are all indicative of well-established trade networks and trade routes connecting important trade centres, capital cities and port towns. The occurrence of punch-marked coins, Prakrit terms, products of other regions like carnelian, lapis lazuli, agate, copper, bronze, lead, silver, etc., are moreover suggestive of intra-regional trade interactions.

FIGURE 8.5
Kodumanal: Inscribed potshard with nikama

The collection of numerous luxury objects, particularly beads (in some occasions more than 2,000 beads from a single Iron Age or Early Historic grave), point to accumulation of wealth. Such items are suggestive of extensive inland trade network. The host of coin hoards unearthed along trade routes, particularly Roman coins and punch-marked coins, are another pointer of external trade networks. The occurrence of large amounts of punch marked coins carrying the fish symbol (*insignia* of the Pandya rulers) suggests that they were minted for local consumption. Whether the authority to mint these coins lay with the king or with traders or trade guilds is not clear in the present context. However, the coins issued in the name of Pandya king Peruvaluthi (Fig. 8.6) and Chera kings Kolliporai, Makkotai and Kuttuvan Kotai suggest they had such authority (Fig. 8.7). Whether these coins were used as a currency in the trade transaction is not clear. The concentration of punch marked coins, Roman coins and other local issues in trade centres and on trade routes is a fine indicative of the existence of both internal and

FIGURE 8.6
Square Pandya copper coin reading Peruvaluti

FIGURE 8.7
Kodumanal: Punch-marked coin

external trade. These trade networks exclusively depend on a supply and demand system on one hand, and on a favourable trade atmosphere on another. The production, procurement and transportation of trade goods through well-established trade routes to potential consumption areas are a prerequisite for trade. The production of trade items like gemstones, spices, forest products, pearls, steel and other related objects requires technical skills. For instance, gemstones need a comprehensive mineral zone and highly specialised artisans; spice production needs a controlled environment; pearl fishing needs specialised divers and favourable sea conditions where pearl oysters can grow; steel production requires a specialised technical know-how. As all these items were potential trade goods during early historic times, a brief attempt is made here to understand the level of industrial production of some of them.

PRODUCTION OF TRADE GOODS

Pearls

A recent ethno-archaeological study made on traditional diving practices in the Gulf of Mannar helps us to understand the economic viability of pearl fishing as it existed in the pre-Christian era. Even today, the people of the Gulf of Mannar dive without any breathing aids to the depth of six fathoms and usually stay on the sea floor for about 54 seconds (Athiyaman 1997). Though the method of diving is not adequately recorded, many of the Sangam literary works like *Kalitokai* (131: 22) and *Akananuru* (350: 10-11) talk of the fishing community Paratavar (Barata in Sri Lanka) who resided at the Pandya capital Korkai and was involved in pearl fishing (*Cirupanarruppadai* 56-58). The *Mahavamsa* refers to eight kinds of pearls presented to King Ashoka by King Devanampiya Tissa (250-210 BCE). Duttagamani (161-137 BCE) decorated his hall with pearls that establishes the existence of pearl fishing in the Gulf of Mannar (Geiger 1950: 78; 207). The *Periplus of the Erythrean Sea* relates that condemned criminals were used at the Pandya port of Korkai in the Gulf of Mannar (McCrindle 1984: 140). Strabo, Pliny and Ptolemy also refer to pearl fishing. The ports of Korkai (Tamil Nadu) and Mantai (Sri Lanka) are the two important ports in the Gulf of Mannar. The pearl oysters of the *Pinctada fucata* type grow on pearl beds or banks (*paar* in Tamil), but it is a seasonal activity. The frequent migration of pearl oysters to opposite beds in the Gulf of Mannar, in Tamil Nadu or Sri Lanka, forced the pearl divers to move frequently between the two coasts.

Gem Stones

Another industry which has brought great amounts of external wealth to the Tamil region is gem stones production. The recent study carried out on traditional bead-making industry at Kangayam proved the continuity of this industry (Rajan 2004: 385-414). The gem stone industry of the Kongu region (Chera country) played a crucial role in exchanges with the Mediterranean. Beads of sapphire, beryl, agate, carnelian, amethyst, lapis lazuli, jasper, garnet, soap stone, quartz, onyx, cat eye, etc., found in different manufacturing stages in the excavation at Kodumanal, stand as a testimony to their production (Rajan 1991: 111-12) (Fig. 8.8). The Sangam literary work *Patirruppattu* (67: 1; 74: 5) referred to this site as *Kodumanam*, famous for gems. During early historic times, beryl carried a higher value than gold; finished beads were sent down to Musiri through the Palaghat gap on the Kerala coast for final shipment to the Roman world. Such beads also made their way to Southeast Asia.

FIGURE 8.8
Beads of Early Historic times

Metallurgy

Another important industry that brought wealth to the treasury is that of iron and steel production. Recent chemical analysis and metallurgical studies carried out on iron objects collected from an iron producing site at Guttur, Mallapadi, Kodumanal by Raghunatha Rao and Sasisekaran (1997: 347-59) showed the evidence of cast iron. The study further reveals that they not only smelted wrought iron and carburized it into steel but also fabricated iron bar by forge welding low carbon steel strips with wrought iron strips to bring strength to the artefacts (Sasisekaran 2004: 61). The study of the steel-producing site at Mel-Siruvalur in Tiruvannamalai district (Srinivasan 1994: 44-59) clearly proves that high quality iron and steel were produced in Tamil Nadu. The discovery of separate furnaces like conical furnaces for iron and crucible furnaces for steel at Kodumanal (Fig. 8.9) accords well with this process (Rajan 1991: 111-12). This high quality steel was in greater demand in the West for a long period.

FIGURE 8.9
Kodumanal: Crucible furnace

Forest Products

Forest products like spices, cardamom, sandalwood, etc., also played a crucial role both in internal and external trade. The recent excavations at Thandikudi in Palani hills clearly proved that people reached and settled at such high altitudes starting in Iron Age times. The archaeological vestiges identified at Thandikudi suggest that this site lay in an ecological niche perfectly adapted to large scale pepper and cardamom cultivation. The occurrence of large numbers of carnelian (Fig. 8.10), quartz (Fig. 8.11) and agate (Fig. 8.12) beads at this altitude suggests the existence of an extensive trade network. Most of the elite items recovered from the graves were of products of the plains. These extravagant items might have been exchanged for local products such as pepper and cardamom or other forest products such as ivory. The concentration of large numbers of archaeological sites noticed in Vaigai basin, particularly in the Kambam valley, suggests that the whole western ghat may have been well-connected with the trade centres and routes of the plains (Rajan 2005: 49-65). These products may have found their way to remote countries through well established networks.

FIGURE 8.10
Carnelian Beads

FIGURE 8.11
Kodumanal: Quartz beads

FIGURE 8.12
Kodumanal: Agate beads

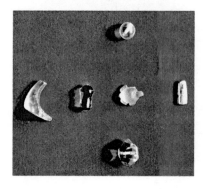
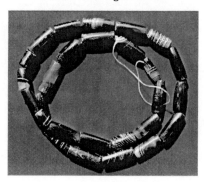

Besides the above objects, glass beads were exported to Southeast Asian countries. In addition to Arikamedu, two glass bead production centres at Manikollai (*mani* > bead and *kollai* > field) and Porunthal have been identified (Fig. 8.13). Like glass beads, the occurrence of terracotta spindle whorls and woven cotton pieces at Kodumanal (Rajan 1996: 72-86) and of dyeing vats at Uraiyur (Raman 1964-65: 25-26) and at Arikamedu (Begley 1993: 93-108) further strengthen the existence of textile industries in early historic times.

The objects for export recovered from archaeological sites located in different ecological zones demonstrate the existence of well-established trade networks. The exchange of export items from inland trade centres to port towns by the *nigamattor* and the *cattu* (trade guilds) or the *vanikan* (traders) is well attested in archaeological, epigraphical and numismatic records. These port towns played a vital role in accelerating the maritime trade contacts

FIGURE 8.13
Porunthal: Glass beads

with both the West and the East. Maritime trade would not have taken place without the knowledge of sea voyaging, boat building and port installation. Navigational terms like *ampi* (*Ainkurunuru* 98: 1-2), *punai* (*Akananuru* 186: 8) and *timil* (*Narrinai* 111: 5-9) points to the existence of different types of boats or ships. Lionel Casson, who examined the ship motif collected at Alagankulam, identified it as one of the largest types of Graeco-Roman three masted ships used in trans-oceanic voyages (Sridhar 2005: 67-73). One must also recall here the Vienna Museum papyrus, a trade contract written in Greek executed between Musiri and Alexandria traders, which specifies the volume of goods carried to Alexandria in a single ship (Rajan 2000: 93-104). This was strengthened with identifications of extensive port infrastructures like wharfs, lighthouses and warehouses at Kaveripattinam (Soundrarajan 1994: 21-42; Kasinathan 1999: 54-60) and at Pattnam (Musiri) (Shajan, Selvakumar and Tomber 2005: 66-73).

EXTERNAL TRADE

The above findings suggest that the exchange of goods through sustained trade contacts with mutual benefit between two cultural groups is seen as a dynamic process. Well-established trade networks and production centres are a prerequisite for sustained trade contacts over a long period. A close view of the archaeological evidence encountered in recent years will help document the existence of such networks.

Trade with Southeast Asia

Indian cultural contacts with foreign countries, next to Sri Lanka, are best observed in Southeast Asian countries. Elements of Indian culture in Southeast Asia appear around the fifth century BCE. As pointed out by B. Bellina, the study of the proto-historic period or Iron Age has been neglected and has not so far been considered to be a significant period of cultural exchange (Bellina 2007: 11). However, recent works have brought to light tangible evidence of early maritime contacts between peninsular India and Southeast Asia. The mercantile communities dealing with salt, textiles, metals, gems, gold, pearls and spices were integrated into a trading system. The frequent references to trade guilds in Peninsular India indirectly points to this same scenario. Glover felt that the great expansion of Southeast Asian exchange was closely connected with the demand in exotic and luxury items by the urban people of the Mediterranean basin, which induced the mercantile community to venture into the sea towards Southeast Asia (Glover 1996a: 129-58). Among the spices, cloves from the Moluccas received much of the attention of traders. The unopened aromatic flower buds of the tree *Eugenia aromatica* would have been exported through south Indian ports to the Western world. The Sangam literary work *Pattinappalai* (lines 191-94) refers to the item of Kalakam (*kalakattu akkam* meaning 'objects from the region of Kalakam') and red coral from the Eastern sea (*gunakkadal tukir*). The exact location of such places has not been identified, but scholars believe that they could be in the area covering southern Thailand and northern Malaysia, where important archaeological sites with Indian goods were recovered.

The site of Khlong Thom (Khuan Luk Pat or Bead mound) is known for its glass and semi-precious stone beads (Glover 1996: 64). A number of agate and etched carnelian beads, carnelian lion pendents, glass collar beads, Roman intaglios and other intaglios with elephants, lions and the god Perseus are among the items found at this site (Veraprasert 1987: 323-33; Bronson 1990: 213-30). One of the interesting findings is that of a tortoise or a turtle made of quartz from Srikshetra in Myanmar (Di Crocco 1996: 164, Pl. 5). Identical pieces were recovered at Kodumanal. The objects of carnelian and agate recovered in Southeast Asia, particularly in graves, are considered to be of Indian origin. One of the largest deposits and the oldest to be quarried comes from the Deccan plateau of India. Recent evidence, particularly that from Kodumanal, suggests that carnelian beads were manufactured in other industrial centres by importing raw material from the Deccan. Bellina's recent studies on beads, particularly those collected from the earlier Southeast Asian sites like Khuan Luk Pat, Kuala Selinsing, Khao Sam Kaeo in the Thai-Malay Peninsula, the Buni area of West Java and in the Oc Eo area of the Mekong Delta of southern Vietnam, point to the existence of high quality carnelian beads of Indian origin. Further, she identifies Khao Sam Kaeo as one of the local Indian production centres (Fig. 8.14). On technological grounds, she suggests that the finishing techniques of Indian beads usually involved the use of rotary grinding stones, whereas the bead manufacturing in Southeast Asia more generally involved the use of drum. The technical analysis of beads along with other archaeological evidence for exchange makes it possible to infer the existence of firmly established trade relationships (Bellina 2007: 22-35).

Another item of exchange was bronze with a high tin content. The abundant sources of tin both in Thailand and Malaya and its scarcity in India would have induced trade with Southeast Asia (Bennett and Glover 1992: 206). A few high tin bronze objects were found in India, at Adichallanur, at Kodumanal and in the Nilgiri hills. These bronze objects would have been exported to India in exchange for gem stones (Fig. 8.15) and for glass. The high-tin bronze bowls found at Adichallanur and Kodumanal would have been imported from Southeast Asia as these high-tin cast bronze vessels were not part of Indian metallurgy (Glover 1996: 77). However, Sharada Srinivasan's joint research with I. Glover made it clear that such high tin

FIGURE 8.14
Map showing the Southeast Asian sites

FIGURE 8.15
Kodumanal: Copper bowl

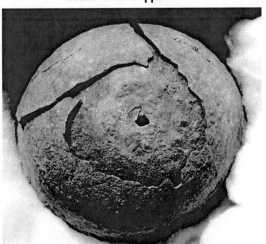

bronzes were also available in India, but the area of production has yet to be identified (Srinivasan 1997: 209-25). Indian made glass and stone beads datable to the fourth century BCE found in Thailand in burials at the bronze producing site of Ban Don Ta Phet and at the tin-rich deposit areas near Khao Sam Kaeo suggests that Tamil Nadu bronze materials would have been imported from Thailand (Srisuchat 1996: 237-74). The lead and tin ingots found at Khuan Luk Pat found their way to Sri Lanka. The excavations carried out at Abhayagiri Vihara in Anuradhapura show the presence of tin ingots (Abeyratne 1990), which incidentally suggests that the lead and tin ingots would have reached Tamil Nadu coast either through Sri Lanka or directly from Thailand (Srisuchat 1996: 237-74).

Noboru Karashima brought to light an inscribed small flat rectangular touchstone of third-fourth centuries CE at the temple Museum of Wat Khlong Thom. The eight letters in Tamil-Brahmi reads *perumpatankal* meaning '(this is) the (touch) stone of Perumpatan'. *Perum* means big and *patan (pattan)* means goldsmith. Therefore, Perumpatan is a title or the name of the goldsmith who possessed this touchstone (Karashima 1995: 1-25). A square copper coin with a tiger (*insignia* of the Sangam Age Cholas) on the obverse and an elephant on the reverse can safely presume that this coin belongs to the Sangam period (Shanmugam 1993: 81-84; Krishnamurthy 1997). Pallava coins with bull on the obverse and double masted ship motif on the reverse were also unearthed at this place. The next Tamil inscription originally discovered in Kho Kor Khao island and presently preserved in the Nakhorn Si Thammarat Museum is the famous Takuapa (ancient Takkola of Ptolemy) inscription of Pallava Avaninaranam (Nandivarman III CE 846-69). The above evidence shows the continuous activities of peninsular Indian traders with Thailand.

Glass is considered as one of the export items. Chemical and spectrographic analysis suggests that potassium-silica based glass beads were manufactured at Arikamedu and at Mantai in Sri Lanka. Now, in addition to Arikamedu, the author has identified two glass bead-manufacturing sites at Manikollai and Porunthal. The monochrome beads produced out of hollow tubes are more common in south India. The lead-barium had its origin in China and soda-lime in the west. Based on these chemical compositions, one could easily locate its origin. For instance, the single coloured small potassium bearing glass beads of Arikamedu, Manikollai, Porunthal and Mantai might have reached Southeast Asia through transoceanic trade. The tombs of the Han dynasties yielded quite a number of glass beads which were very popular between 200 BCE and CE 200. Along with lead-barium glass beads of China, potassium-silica glass beads were also found at Guangdong and Guangxi. Among the objects, glass bowls, cups and plates are quite interesting. Even the historical records of the Han dynasty say that Emperor Wu (140-87 BCE) sent people to

Southern Sea to buy glass. It seems that these glass beads would have reached China via sites like Mantai, Khlong Thom and Oc-Eo (Francis 1991: 28-43). The Indian traders would even have carried Roman glass objects after trans-shipment at Musiri, Arikamedu or Kaveripattinam. P. Francis felt that the potassium-silica based glass beads were first manufactured at Arikamedu (third century BCE to third century CE); then the craftsmen moved from Arikamedu to Mantai in Sri Lanka and then to Khuan Luk Pat in Thailand and to Oc-Eo in Vietnam. From Khuan Luk Pat, they went to Kuala Selinsing in Malaysia. Further, he felt that due to the complexity of the process and difficulties in transferring the technology, this industry would have been in the hands of Tamils (Francis 1996: 139-60). It is widely believed that Arikamedu was the production centre of glass beads, particularly for those exported to Southeast Asia. As stated earlier, two glass bead manufacturing centres, one at Manikollai and another at Porutal, have recently been identified. Large numbers of beads at various stages of manufacture along with glass crucibles were collected. Interestingly, quite a number of hollow tubes were recovered from the site. Glass cullet, carnelian, agate, steel would have been exported from the south Indian coast. Among them glass occupied an important position. Glass and semi-precious stone beads were also collected from the site at Gilimanuk in West Bali of Indonesia (Ratna Indiraningsih 1985: 133-41). The regular concentric grooves found in the drill holes of the semi-precious stone beads found at Khlong Thom and Ban Don Ta Phet are clearly indicative of an Indian origin.

On the ceramic side, rouletted wares were identified at Tra Kieu (Vietnam), Darussalam (Brunei), in Buni culture graves (at Kobak Kendal) and in Sembiran (Indonesia), at Mantai, Kandarodai, Tissamaharama and Ambalantota (Sri Lanka) (Glover 1989: 4-5; 1996: 59-94; Gogte 1997: 69-85; Walker 1980: 225-35). Ardika unearthed 79 shards of rouletted ware in which 78 came from Sembiran and a solitary example from Pacung. The X-ray diffraction and neutron analysis carried on the rouletted ware from Sembiran, Anuradhapura and Arikamedu indicate that they all have one geological source in terms of their clay and temper compositions (Ardika et al. 1993: 101-09).

Trade with the West

The material evidences suggest that trans-oceanic voyages between the ancient Tamilakam and Mediterranean goes back to pre-Augustus period. The availability of Republican coins from Lakshadweep (Suresh 1992: 71), Kallakinar (Raman 1992: 19-24) and Tiruppur (Suresh 1992: 68) found in the vicinity of semi-precious stone bearing area strongly suggests that trade with the Roman world would have been initiated in the pre-Augustus period.

The major items of export shipped from the west coast ports were pearls, semi-precious stones, particularly aquamarine beryl, gems, steel, forest goods like teak, akil, sandalwood, spices, ivory and pepper. The archaeobotanical evidence of black pepper from Berenike (Cappers 1998: 289-330) and Myos Hormos (van der Veen 2000: 59) demonstrates the importance of products from the Malabar coast. The fine ware of Indian origin found at the above ports brings further evidence for contacts between the two regions (Tomber 2002: 27-31). All these items, except the pearls, are primarily the products of the Kongu region and its adjoining western ghat. Naturally, there is no surprise in seeing the largest number of Roman coin hoards in Kongu country.

Much has been said about export goods based on the classical Graeco-Roman accounts and it need not be repeated here except for recent findings. Those of Mediterranean origin include coins, terracotta figurines, jewellery, intaglios and Arretine wares. The maximum number of Roman coins found so far in India comes from the site Vellalur located on the left bank of the river Noyyal on the ancient trade route connecting Karur and Musiri. In association with coin hoards, a few Roman objects like a gold ring representing a lady dressing her hair, another ring having a dragon and the head of a Graeco-Roman soldier with an elaborate headgear, and two carnelian objects representing a horse and a fish are noteworthy (Suresh 1992: 57). Also at Karur, gold objects such as a chariot rider, a horse rider, a bowl with an unidentified animal, and an unusual figure of a man wearing a headgear, converted from the neck downwards into a scorpion tail, have recently surfaced. The terracotta figurine of Mediterranean origin unearthed along with a Roman coin and a shard of rouletted ware needs a special mention here, as it was found at Kodumanal, one of the biggest industrial sites actively involved in gemstone production and steel industry. Though Indian merchants had continuous trade relations with the West, it seems that the traders themselves rarely migrated to the West, particularly during early historic times. In contrast, there are quite number of references of Graeco-Roman settlements in Indian soil mentioned in literary and epigraphical records. The material evidence suggests that Arikamedu and Kaveripattinam had such Roman settlements. Likewise, Tamil traders would have also made a visit to Red Sea ports. The recent findings of Tamil-Brahmi inscribed potshards yielding Tamil merchants' names like *kanan* and *catan* from Red Sea ports at Myos Hormos (Qusier al Qadim) and *panai ori* and *korpuman* from Berenike (Mahadevan 1998: 17-19; Whitecomb 1979; 1982) further supports this view. The Musiri-Alexandria trade contract found in the Vienna papyrus has to be seen against this background. The mid-second century CE papyrus clearly emphasises the volume of goods exchanged between the Chera ports of Musiri and the Roman port of Alexandria (Harraur and Sijpesteiju 1985: 124-55; Sidebotham 1989: 195-223). Unfortunately, the names of the merchants are lost; otherwise it would have been easier to reconstruct the trading community of the mid-second century CE. However, the recovery of Tamil personal names such as *panai ori, korpuman, kanan* and *catan* suggests the ethnic group involved in this maritime trade. In the light of the Vienna papyrus, one may visualise the large amount of Roman antiquities in the form of coins, jewellery, ceramics, intaglios and terracotta figurines that brought to export oriented economic zones (Rajan 2000: 93-104).

The above discussion clearly indicates that multiple factors played an important role in the transoceanic trade during early historic times. Littoral states of peninsular India lay between the Mediterranean in the west and China in the east and played a dominant role in the origin, growth and spread of trade. The emerging scenario points to the fact that it is difficult to understand the trade and cultural matrix of any country without understanding the global nature of the trade.

REFERENCES

Abeyratne, M. and O.C. Wickramasinghe, 1990, 'Emission Spectroscopy in Determining the Origin and the Composition of Ancient Glazed Tiles Found during Excavation at Abhayagiri Vihara, Anuradhapura', paper presented in the International Seminar, Sri Lanka, 7-13 July.

Ardika, I.W., P.S. Bellwood, R.A. Eggleton and D.J. Ellis., 1993, 'A Single Source for South Asian Export-Quality Rouletted Ware?', *Man and Environment* XVIII(1): 101-09.

Arunachalam, S., 1952, *The History of the Pearl Fishery of the Tamil Nadu Coast*, Annamalai Historical Series No.10, Annamalainagar: Annamalai University.

Athiyaman, N., 1997, 'Traditional Pearl and Chank Diving in Mannar Gulf', Report submitted to the Nehru Trust, New Delhi.

Beck, Horace C., 1930, 'Notes on Sundry Asiatic Beads', *Man* 30 (34): 166-82.

Begley, V., 1993, 'New Investigations at Port Arikamedu', *Journal of Roman Archaeology* 6: 93-108.

Bellina, Berenice, 2007, *Cultural Exchange between India and South East Asia: Production and Distribution of Hard Stone Ornaments (VI c. BC - VI c. AD)*, Paris: Editions de la Maison des sciences de l'homme, Editions Epistemes.

Bennett, A.N. and I.C. Glover, 1992, 'Decorated High-Tin Bowls from Thailand's Prehistory', in *Southeast Asian Archaeology 1990*, ed. I. Glover, Hull: Hull University, Centre for Southeast Asian Studies, pp. 187-208.

Bronson, B., 1990, 'Glass and Beads at Khuan Lukpad, Southern Thailand', *Southeast Asian Archaeology 1986*, Oxford: BAR International Series, pp. 213-30.

Cappers, R.T.J., 1998, 'Archaeobotanical Remains', in *Berenike '96. Report of the Excavations at Berenike (Egyptian Red Sea Coast) and the Survey of the Eastern Desert*, ed. S.E. Sidebotham and W.Z. Wendrich, Leiden: Centre of Non-Western Studies, pp. 289-330.

Casson, L., 1992, 'Ancient Naval Technology and the Route to India', in *Rome and India: The Ancient Sea Trade*, ed. Vimla Begley and R. De Puma, New Delhi: Oxford University Press, pp. 8-11.

Di Crocco, Virginia, M., 1996, 'References and Artefacts Connecting the Myanmar Area with Western and Central Asia and China Proper via the Ancient Southwestern Silk

Route from ca. 3rd century BC to the 13th century CE', in *Ancient Trades and Cultural Contacts in Southeast Asia*, ed. Amara Srisuchat, Bangkok: Office of the National Culture Commission, pp. 161-80.

Francis, Jr. P., 1991, 'Bead making at Arikamedu and Beyond', *World Archaeology* 23(1): 28-43.

——, 1996, 'Beads, the Bead Trade and State Development in Southeast Asia', in *Ancient Trades and Cultural Contacts in Southeast Asia*, ed. Amara Srisuchat, Bangkok: Office of the National Culture Commission, pp. 139-60.

Geiger, W. and M.H. Bode, 1950, *The Mahavamsa or the Great Chronicle of Ceylon*, Colombo: Ceylon Government Information Department.

Glover, I.C., 1989, *Early Trade Between India and Southeast Asia*, Hull: The University of Hull.

——, 1996, 'The Southern Silk Road:Archaeological Evidence for Early Trade between India and Southeast Asia', in *Ancient Trades and Cultural Contacts in Southeast Asia*, ed. Amara Srisuchat, Bangkok: Office of the National Culture Commission, pp. 57-94.

——, 1996a, 'Recent Archaeological Evidences for Early Maritime Contacts between India and Southeast Asia', in *Tradition and Archaeology: Early Maritime Contacts in the Indian Ocean*, ed. H.P. Ray and J.F. Salles, New Delhi: Manohar, pp. 129-58.

Gogte, D. Vishwas, 1997, 'The Chandraketugarh-Tamluk Region of Bengal: Source of the Early Historic Rouletted Ware from India and Southeast Asia', *Man and Environment* XXII(1): 69-85.

Harrauer, H. and P. Sijpesteiju, 1985, 'Ein Neues Dokument Zu Roms Indienhandel P. Vindob G.40822', *Anzhien* 122: 124-55.

Jiayao, An, 1996, 'Glass Trade in Southeast Asia', in *Ancient Trades and Cultural Contacts in Southeast Asia*, ed. Amara Srisuchat, Bangkok: Office of the National Culture Commission, pp. 127-38.

Karashima, Noboru, 1995, 'Indian Commercial Activities in Ancient and Medieval South East Asia', paper presented in the Plenary Session of the VIIIth International Conference – Seminar of Tamil Studies, Tamil University, Thanjavur, pp. 1-25.

Kasinathan, Natana, 1999, *Poompuharum Katal akazhaivum* [Poompuhar and Underwater Excavations], Chennai: Then Indiya Saiva Siddhanta Nurpatippuk Kazhakam.

Krishnamurthy, R. 1997. *Sangam Age Tamil Coins*, Madras: Garnet Publications.

Mahadevan, I.,1998, 'Ekiptu nattil Tamilil elitiya taali' (An amphora with Tamil characters found in Egypt), *Avanam, Journal of Tamil Nadu Archaeological Society* 9: 17-19.

——, 2003, *Early Tamil Epigraphy: From the Earliest Times to the Sixth Century A.D.*, Chennai: CRE-A and Cambridge MA: Department of Sanskrit and Indian Studies, Harvard University.

Majeef, Abdul A., 1987, 'A Note on Korkai Excavations', *Tamil Civilization* 2(1-2): 73-77.

McCrindle, J.W., 1984, *The Commerce and Navigation of the Erythraean Sea: Being a Translation of the Periplus Maris Erythraei / by an anonymous writer. And of Arrian's Account of the Voyage of Nearkhos from the Mouth of the Indus to the Head of the Persian Gulf* (with introductions, commentary, notes and index by J.W. McCrindle), Calcutta: Thacker, Spink; London: Trübner, 1879 (rpt. 1984).

Raghunatha Rao, B. and B. Sasisekaran, 1997, 'Guttur: An Iron Age Industrial Centre in Dharmapuri District', *Indian Journal of History of Science* 32(4): 347-59.

Raghupathy, P., 1987, *Early Settlements in Jaffna*, Madras: Thillimalar Raghupathy.

Rajan, K. 1991, 'Iron and Gemstone Industries as Revealed from Kodumanal Excavations', *Puratattva* 20: 111-12.

——, 1996, 'Kodumanal Excavations: A Report', in *Gauravam: B.K. Gururajarao Felicitation Volume*, ed. K.V. Ramesh et al., New Delhi: Harman Publishing Company, pp. 72-86.

——, 2000, 'Musiri-Alexandria Trade Contract: An Archaeological Approach', *Pondicherry University Journal of Social Sciences and Humanities* 1 (1&2): 93-104.

——, 2004, 'Traditional Gemstone Cutting Technology of Kongu Region in Tamil Nadu', *Indian Journal of History of Science* 34(4): 385-414.

——, 2005, 'Excavations at Thandikudi, Tamil Nadu', *Man and Environment* 32(2): 49-65.

——, 2007, 'The Earliest Hero Stones of India', *International Journal of Dravidian Linguistics* 36 (1): 51-61.

Raman, K.V., 1964-65, 'Excavation at Uraiyur, District Tiruchirappalli', *Indian Archaeology – A Review*, New Delhi: Archaeological Survey of India, pp. 25-26.

——, 1992, 'Roman Coins from Tamil Nadu', *Studies in South Indian Coins* 2: 19-34.

Ratna, Indraningsih, 1985, 'Research on Prehistoric Beads in Indonesia', *Bulletin of the Indo-Pacific Prehistory Association* 6: 133-41.

Sasisekaran, B., 2004, *Iron Industry and Metallurgy: A Study of Ancient Technology*, Chennai: New Era Publications.

Shajan, K.P., V. Selvakumar and R. Tomber, 2005, 'Was Pattnam Ancient Muziris?', *Man and Environment* 30(2): 66-73.

Shanmugam, P., 1993, 'Tamilnaadum Thailandum: Tonmai Todarpukal (Ancient Relation between Tamil Nadu and Thailand)', *Avanam, Tamil Nadu Archaeological Society* 3: 81-84.

Sidebotham, E. Steven, 1989, 'Ports of the Red Sea and the Arabia-India Trade', *L'Arabia Preislamique Et Son Environnement Historique Et Cultural*, ed. T. Fahd, Strasbourg: Universite des Sciences Himaines de Strasbourg Travaux du Centre de Recherche, pp. 195-223.

Soundrarajan, K.V., 1994, *Kaveripattinam Excavations 1963-1973 (A Port City on the Tamil Nadu Coast)*, New Delhi: Archaeological Survey of India.

Sridhar, T.S. (ed.), 2005, *Alagankulam: An Ancient Roman Port City of Tamil Nadu*, Chennai: Department of Archaeology.

Srinivasan, Sharada, 1994, 'Wootz Crucible Steel: A Newly Discovered Production Site in South India', *Papers from the Institute of Archaeology* 5: 44-59.

——, 1997, 'Present and past of South Indian Crafts for Making Mirrors, Lamps, Bells, Vessels, Cymbals and Gongs: Links with Prehistoric High-tin Bronzes from Mohenjadaro, Taxila, South Indian Megaliths and Later finds', *South Asian Studies* 13: 209-25.

Srisuchat, Amara, 1996, 'Merchants, Merchandise, Markets: Archaeological Evidence in Thailand Concerning Maritime Trade Interaction between Thailand and Other Countries before 16th century AD', in *Ancient Trades and Cultural Contacts in Southeast Asia*, ed. Amara Srisuchat, Bangkok: Office of the National Culture Commission, pp. 237-74.

Suresh, S., 1992, *Roman Antiquities in Tamil Nadu*, Madras: The C.P. Ramaswami Aiyar Institute of Indological Research.

Tomber, Robert, 2002, 'Indian Fine Wares from the Red Sea Coast of Egypt', *Man and Environment*, 27(1): 27-31.

Van der Veen, M., 2000, 'The Plant Remains: Roman Imports from India', in *Myos Hormos - Quesir al-Qadim: A Roman and Islamic Port Site on the Red Sea Coast of Egypt. Interim Report, 2000*, ed. D.P.S. Peacock, L. Blue, N. Bradford and S. Moser, Southampton: University of Southampton, p. 59.

Veraprasert, Mayuree, 1987, 'Khlong Thom: An Ancient Bead and Manufacturing Location and an Ancient Entrepot', Seminar in Prehistory of Southeast Asia, SPAFA Final Report, Bangkok, SEAMEO Project in Archaeology and Fine Arts: 323-31.

Walker, M. and S. Santoso, 1980, 'Romano-Indian Rouletted Pottery in Indonesia', *Asian Perspectives* 20(2): 225-35.

Whitecomb, D.S. and J.H. Johnson, 1979, *Quseir al-Qadim 1978: Preliminary Report*, Cairo: Nafeh Press.

9

Contacts between India and Southeast Asia in Ceramic and Boat Building Traditions

V. Selvakumar

INTRODUCTION

Any analysis seeking a holistic understanding of the nature of contacts between India and Southeast Asia needs to encompass the interactive dynamics in the larger Indian Ocean region. The Indian Ocean region is geographically divisible into the Western Indian Ocean region consisting of the littoral of Africa, Arabia, Persia and Pakistan and the west coast of India; and the eastern Indian Ocean region covering the east coast of India, Bangladesh and Southeast Asia (Fig. 9.1). The Indian subcontinent, due to its central location, acted as an important meeting locus for the south-western and the south-eastern Indian Ocean regions. The Indian subcontinent was also an important region of cultural production that had lasting impact on the Indian Ocean region. People, ideas, goods, and animal and plant species travelled across the Ocean, perhaps from prehistoric times and such interactions have impacted the socio-cultural formations, directly or indirectly (McPherson 1993; Gupta 2002; Ray 2003; Blench et al. 2005; Dick-Read 2006). Why did people look/travel beyond the Ocean? A number of factors, such as the demand for prestige goods – rather than subsistence goods – and the boost in trade induced by the efflorescence of 'civilisations' or early states or population pressure in one region or another, interest in material wealth, curiosity, and the adventurous nature of humans to explore far-off lands, probably, gave impetus to the interactions across the Ocean.

FIGURE 9.1
Map of Indian Ocean region with select sites mentioned in the text

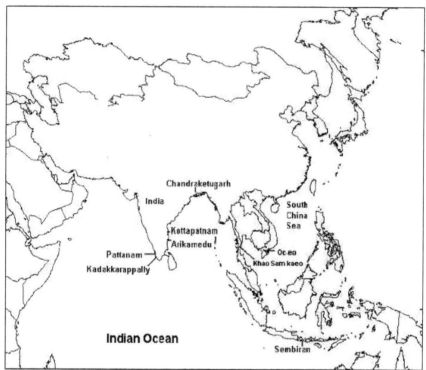

In the area of interactions between India and Southeast Asia, the contributions of India have a higher visibility and often it is not clear in what
way Southeast Asia influenced India. This paper presents a discussion on the
probable Southeast Asian origin of two technological elements – namely,
the 'carved paddle beating' technique in ceramic tradition and 'lashed-lug
technique' of securing planks in boat building tradition – that are represented
in archaeological and/or ethnographical contexts in India. For the interactions
between India and Southeast Asia, textual sources and archaeological evidence
such as architecture, pottery and a variety of artefacts are available. The paper
primarily focuses on the two technological elements mentioned above, and
hence it is not the intention here to present an exhaustive survey of the entire
evidence for the contacts between India and Southeast Asia in ceramic and
boat building traditions.

CERAMIC EVIDENCE FOR INDIA-SOUTHEAST ASIA CONTACTS

India-Southeast Asian Contacts in Ceramic Traditions

With the exploration and excavation of new archaeological sites across India
and Southeast Asia, fresh material evidence for the contacts between India and

Southeast Asia is unearthed in the form of ceramics. Ceramic vessels dispersed as items of trade (tableware), media (storage jars) that carried commodities, personal collection of travellers and ritual vessels. Fine rouletted ware and a few other forms in identical fabrics and knobbed vessels are the known Indian ceramics reported from Southeast Asia; the former is datable to *c.* the second century BCE to *c.* the second century CE, while the latter occurs in a slightly later context as well (Bellina and Glover 2004). The only ceramic group from India that suggests Southeast Asian impact is the carved paddle impressed pottery, which mainly occurs on the coastal sites of south India.

Indian Fine Ware (Rouletted Ware and Related Fabrics)

The fine ware group of ceramics comprising of the rouletted ware dish, stamped bowl (Wheeler et al. 1946, Arikamedu Type 10) and other related fabrics (Wheeler et al. 1946, Arikamedu Types 18 and 141) is the earliest known Indian pottery to occur in Southeast Asia (Bellwood 1997: 292). Rouletted ware is reported at several sites in the Indian Ocean rim such as Wari Bateshwar and Mahastangarh (Jahan 2002) in Bangladesh; Anuradhapura, Tissamaharama (Schenk 2000; Gogte 2001) and Kantarodai in Sri Lanka (Deraniyagala 1992); Khao Sam Kaeo in Thailand (Bellina and Silapanth 2006); Sembiran in Bali (Ardika and Bellwood 1991, Ardika et al. 1993); at Kobak Kendal, Cibutak and Cibango known as Buni complex in north-western Java (Walker and Santoso 1977) and Batujaya east of Buni also in Java (Bellwood 1997: 292); and Oc-Eo (Malleret 1959-63; Miksic 2003) and Tra Kieu (Smith 1999) in Vietnam. This fine ware group has also been reported as far as Berenike (Tomber 2000) and Quseir al Qadim (Tomber 1999) on the Red Sea Coast (Begley and Tomber 2001). Besides, pottery graffiti of Tamil Brahmi/Brahmi/Kharoshti have been identified from the Red Sea coast down to Southeast Asia (Mahadevan 2003; *The Hindu*, 16 July 2006, Chennai edition; Bellwood 1997). Earlier the rouletted ware was thought to be non-Indian in origin, but Vimala Begley argued that it must have been manufactured in India (Begley 1988). Gogte (1997, 2002), based on X-Ray Diffraction (XRD) analysis of pottery and ceramic clay, proposed that this group of ceramics was manufactured in the Ganga-Brahmaputra delta. The author's observation of the ceramics from Arikamedu and Chandraketugarh also suggests such a possibility (Selvakumar 2008). While some researchers accept the findings of Gogte, there are contrary viewpoints (Bellina and Glover 2004; see Begley 2004 for a critique). On the basis of XRD-analysis and evidence such as identical bricks and other artefacts, Gogte is of the view that the traders from Bengal had set up ports on the Tamil Coast in the Early Historic period (*c.* 500 BCE-CE 300). Although substantial research is needed on the origin of the rouletted ware and the dynamic factors that led to its spread, the results of this analysis have certainly forced us to rethink about the trade networks in the Bay of Bengal region (Morrison 1997: 95).

'Knobbed ware' refers to a vessel form (bowl) in ceramics as well as high-tin bronze with a small knob-like projection on the interior base. Such vessels are considered Indian in origin, and probably had ritual functions. It is found at Wari-Bateshwar in Bangladesh and at a few sites on the east coast of India including Sisupalgarh (Tripathi 2002) and also in Southeast Asia (Glover 1990, 1996), and a granite specimen from Taxila is in the British Museum. The ceramic form bottle-necked sprinkler (*kundika*) found in Indian sites seems to have been adopted in Burma, Thailand, Java and Vietnam (Bellina and Glover (2004: 80). Bellina and Glover (2004: 78) report the presence of a shard resembling the russet coated and painted ware in the Buni Complex. Besides, stamped and moulded pottery comparable to Indian ceramics is reported in Southeast Asia (Bellina and Glover 2004: 80-81).

Medieval Ceramics

While the medieval Chinese ceramics occur more frequently on the Indian coast, very limited finds of Southeast Asian ceramics have been reported so far in India (Karashima 2004). Kottapatnam in Andhra Pradesh produced Thai celadon and Thai iron-painted wares of the fifteenth century manufactured at Sisachanalai kilns (Sasaki 2004: 17). A lone Thai shard of the Late Medieval period was found at Cheramanparambu near Kodungallur on the Malabar Coast (Aoyagi and Ogawa 2004: 49). Sasaki (2004) reports that the Thai, Myanmar and Vietnamese shards were found in West Asia, and hence it is worth a while to closely look for these ceramics on the Indian coast. Impressed and stamped ceramics also occur along with the imported glazed ceramics in large numbers in the Medieval context at Kottapatnam (Karashima 2004; Rao 2004).

THE PADDLE IMPRESSED POTTERY IN INDIA AND SOUTHEAST ASIA

Carved Paddle Beating Technique

Paddle, also referred as 'mallet', is a small, flat wooden plank with a handle that is used by potters to shape the leather-hard pottery before firing. In the Indian ethnographic context, beating with a paddle is done to close the hole left at the bottom of the vessel when it is removed from the wheel and also to shape the hand-formed vessels. Paddle is carefully beaten on the exterior of the leather-hard pottery against a polished stone anvil resting on the interior surface. While the method of shaping pottery with a plain paddle is known as 'paddle and anvil' method, the use of paddles carved with grooves or other designs can be labelled as 'carved paddle beating' method.

The ceramics grouped under 'paddle impressed' variety includes pottery with impressions obtained by beating grooved or carved paddles and paddles wrapped with cord or woven fabric. Such impressed shards are not often recognised by the excavators, who casually label them as 'mat impressed', 'basket impressed', 'incised', 'stamped' or decorated pottery (e.g. Wheeler et al. 1946; Sharma 1960). It is not clear if woven basket was actually used for obtaining impression on the pottery in India and often, repeated beating of grooved paddles gives pseudo basket-impression. The term 'stamped' is also invariably used to describe the paddle beaten/impressed pottery. The term 'stamped' may be used only in the case of impression of images and complex decorations, which were carefully stamped (e.g. stamped bowl of the Early Historic period, Wheeler et al. 1946: Type 10; Bellina and Glover 2004). In the case of stamped pottery, the decorations do not overlap, while in the paddle-impressed variety they do. But there are exceptions to this.

Function

The exact intention of using the carved paddle is not clear and the contemporary Indian potters are not unanimous on its use. While a few potters claimed that it was mainly ornamental, there were others who felt that carved paddle gave better grip than the plain paddle, while shaping the vessel. The function of the carved paddles might not have been universal and it could have depended upon the cognition of the potters who use them.

Distribution of Paddle Impressed and Related Pottery

India

The technique of 'carved paddle beating' has not been common in historical as well as contemporary India, though it is present in certain archaeological and ethnographic contexts. The earliest occurrence of a comparable variety is the cord-marked pottery in the central Indian or Vindhyan Neolithic sites (Sharma et al. 1980). The central Indian Neolithic site of Koldhiwa had early dates in the seventh millennium BCE (Sharma et al. 1980; Singh 2002). Since most of the C-14 dates from this region fall within the range of 2400 BCE to 1700 BCE, the early dates are questioned (Singh 2002: 144). Recent research has dated this Neolithic culture, which produced cord-marked pottery to the seventh millennium BCE, based on the C-14 dates from Lahuradewa in Uttar Pradesh (Tewari et al. 2006: 35-36). Parallels are often drawn between the eastern Indian and the Southeast Asian-East Asian Neolithic cultures

(Driem 2001: 290; Misra 2001). Only more C-14 dates obtained from different laboratories could help to fix the precise chronology of this culture. The decorations on ceramics from Chopani Mundo (*Indian Archaeology a Review* 1977-78: Pl. XXVA) do show some similarities with the East Asian Neolithic pottery. Although, there is a possibility of indigenous origin of this culture, its exact relationship with the East Asian Neolithic culture has not been investigated systematically. However, from the publications it appears that there was no paddle-impressed pottery in this Neolithic complex.

What is described as 'cord-marked' pottery is reported from the Neolithic context in north-eastern India at sites such as Deojali Hading (Sharma 1967), Charutaru (Rao 1977) and Ambari (*IAR* 1968-69: 3; Goswami and Roy 1977) and the source of this ceramic tradition is often attributed to Southeast Asian contacts (Behera 1994; Misra 2001; Bellwood 2005: 94). The Neolithic cultures of north-eastern India are later in date and survived into the Historical period (Singh 2002: 139). On the contrary, Bellwood argues that the Neolithic element came to this region 'soon after' 3000 BCE from Southeast Asia (Bellwood 2005: 94). From the published references the author does not find much similarity between the cord-marked pottery of the central Indian Neolithic cultures and the eastern Indian Neolithic cultures in Ceramic traditions. The eastern Indian Neolithic ceramics have paddle-impressed variety, which is not reported in the central Indian Neolithic sites. More systematic studies are necessary for understanding chronology of the eastern Neolithic cultures and its interactions with the East Asian-Southeast Asian Neolithic cultures.

At a few sites of the Cholistan Desert in Pakistan unmistakable specimens of paddle impressed pottery are found along with the Painted Grey Ware (Mughul 1982: Pl. 7.12), though Mughul labels them as 'stamped and relief designs'. But these finds are from a surface context and hence I am not in a position to comment on them. The probability of the use of carved paddle techniques in the Painted Grey ware contexts in north India needs to be researched further.

In the southern Neolithic sites of India, neither cord-marked nor carved paddle impressed pottery is known to occur, though accidental mat impression does occur on the exterior base of vessels. But the carved paddle impressed pottery is present in the Early Historic context at Arikamedu in Pondicherry (Fig. 9.2; Begley 1996: 202-4; Begley et al. 1996, 2004); Kudikkadu (Raman 1991); Alagankulam (Nagaswamy 1991); and Karur (Nagaswamy 1995) in Tamil Nadu; at Pattanam in Kerala with the Mediterranean imports (Fig. 9.3; Shajan et al. 2004; Selvakumar et al. 2005; Cherian et al. 2007). It is also found at a few other sites on the east coast including Chandraketugarh in West Bengal (personal observation; Chakraborty 2000), Sisupalgarh in Orissa and in north India (e.g. Kausambi; Sharma 1960: Pl. 53) and western

FIGURE 9.2
Paddle impressed pottery from Arikamedu

FIGURE 9.3
Paddle impressed pottery from Pattanam

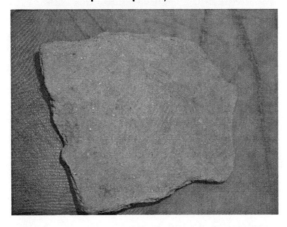

India in Early Historic levels, though in a limited number. Along with carved paddle-impressed, a few shards of cord-impressed variety also occur at some of these sites. In the Medieval context, it appears at Periyapattinam (Karashima 1987, 1988; Subbarayalu 1996), Manappattu near Pondicherry (Begley 1996: Fig. 4.231) and at Ariyankunru in the Rameshwaram Island in Tamil Nadu (Begley 1996; Selvakumar 2004); Kottapatnam in Andhra Pradesh (Rao 2004); Cheramanparambu and Taikkal (Achan 1946; *IAR* 68-69:10, Pl. XIII; Selvakumar 2006) in Kerala, and also in Maharashtra (Sushma Deo, personal communication). No diagnostic vessel forms have been found in the impressed pottery group. It mostly has storage jars, vases and cooking vessels, but rarely tableware. Generally, there is a concentration of these ceramics in the coastal region and they are not frequently encountered in the interior settlements. The site of Pattanam in Kerala first brought to light the presence of pottery with carved paddle impression in the Late Iron Age context or in the beginning of the Early Historic period. Similarly these ceramics are not known to occur in the 'megalithic' burial pottery from the Upper Gundar basin in Madurai district (Selvakumar 1996), but at Kodumanal (Rajan 1994), some of the russet coated and painted ware ceramics bear carved paddle impressions. The author also personally observed this in 2007. However, among the megalithic burial sites in the neighbourhood of Arikamedu, the use of carved paddle was not noticed. In general, this pottery has not been a common feature as revealed from the author's survey of the Iron Age and Historical sites in Tamil Nadu. In the patterns of decoration, variation is seen between those from the Early Historic and the Medieval sites. More intricate patterns and what appeared to be 'stamped' decoration, rather than overlapping carved paddle impression, are noticed on the Medieval sherds from the east coast, especially at Manappattu and Kottapatnam. Compared to the Early Historic period, the cord-impressed decorations seem to be less frequent in medieval contexts. At Arikamedu in the total collection of c. 430,877 ceramic shards from the 1989-92 excavations (Begley et al. 1996, 2004), there were only 874 impressed shards forming about only 0.2 per cent of the collection and this indicates that the impressed pottery was not a major ceramic group in the Early Historic period in south India. At the site of Pattanam in Kerala too it was not very frequent.

In ethnographic context, the use of carved paddle exists among some of the contemporary potters of India in the states of Karnataka, Andhra Pradesh, Kerala, Goa and West Bengal (Saraswati and Behura 1966: 22). The survey of potters undertaken in the 1990s as part of the Arikamedu Excavation Project revealed the use of carved paddle among the potters of Kerala (Begley 1996). The author's archaeological survey across Kerala and ethnographic survey of potters at Eroor near Ernakulam, Padukkadu near Trissur (Fig. 9.4), Kolappuram near Malappuram (Figs. 9.5, 9.6) and nearby Ponnani in Kerala from 2003 to 2007 exposed the frequent use of carved paddles in the historical and ethnographic contexts in Kerala. This survey further revealed that in Kerala the carved paddle beating technique was used by the Malayalam-speaking potters as well as the Telugu-speaking migrant potters from Andhra Pradesh, known as Andhra Nayanmars or Andhur Nayars. The Kerala potters reported that they used the carved paddle to get the surfaces of the pottery decorated. Enquiries among a few potters in Madurai and Thanjavur districts in Tamil Nadu revealed that this technique was not in use in these regions. Carved paddle impressed pottery also survives among the potters of north-eastern India (Selvakumar 2004).

Western Indian Ocean Region

The carved-paddle impressed pottery occurs at a few sites in the western Indian Ocean region. In Sri Lanka, it is reported at several sites (Deraniyagala 1956;

FIGURE 9.4
A potter beating leather-hard pottery with a carved paddle
at Padukkadu, Kerala (after Begley 1996)

FIGURE 9.5
A potter beating leather-hard pottery with a carved paddle
at Kolappuram, Kerala

Deraniyagala 1972a, 1972b; Ragupathy 1987). Solheim and Deraniyagala (1972) considered the impressed pottery in Sri Lanka to be of Southeast Asian origin, but Vimala Begley differed with them in this regard and called for detailed investigations (Begley 1975).

In Egypt, this pottery is found at Quseir al Qadim (Whitcomb and Johnson 1982; Tomber 1999, 2000) and also at Berenike along with the rouletted ware and other Indian ceramics (Tomber and Begley 2001). While some of the paddle-impressed shards in the Red Sea sites are similar to those from India, there are certain varieties that are quite different from impressed pottery from India. It is reported that carved paddle technique was in use in

V. Selvakumar

FIGURE 9.6
Potter's tools (carved paddles) at Kolappuram, Kerala

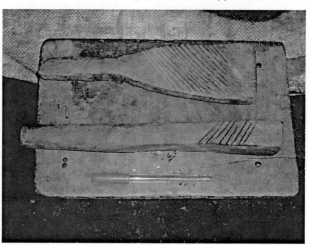

Western Africa (Meyers 1999) and also in other areas of the Indian Ocean region (e.g. Yemen, Posey 1994).

Southeast Asia

The ceramics with stamped/carved paddle impression occur in early contexts in Southeast Asia (Rooney 1987; Solheim 2003). The earliest pottery from Southeast Asia (part of the Hoabinhan culture, dated to 8400 BP, from Spirit Cave in north-western Thailand) had the impressions of net-wrapped paddles (Gormon 1971; Solheim 2003: 1). Despite this discovery, some scholars attribute the introduction of Neolithic cultures and the cord marked pottery in Southeast Asia to the migration of groups from the Yangzi Valley (Higham 1996). The incised and stamped ceramics were in use between 2500 BCE and 1500 BCE in southern China, Thailand and Vietnam (Bellwood 2005: 133). In Philippines, impressed potteries are dated from 1500 BCE to 1000 BCE (Fox 1970; Ronquillo 2003; Yankowski 2005: 41) and they continued to exist till the third or fourth centuries CE (Solheim 1957). Around the early centuries of the Common Era, impressed pottery is reported along with the rouletted ware in the Buni complex in Java (Walker and Santoso 1977) and at Sembiran in Bali (Solheim et al. 1956; Peacock 1959; Solheim 1990; Ardika and Bellwood 1991; Ardika et al. 1993). In Southeast Asia, the stamped designs do occur in later contexts as well (Lertrit 2004). Ethnographic parallels for this tradition exist at several areas in Southeast Asia including Sagaing near Mandalay in Burma (Adhyatman 1985), Lao potters in Northern and East Laos (Solheim 1964) and in East Sumbawa (Sukarto 1973).

Discussion

From the available evidence, it is certain that the use of carved paddle beating technique was absent among the Neolithic people of south India, and it appeared here only from the Late Iron Age context along with 'megaliths' and more prominently in the Early Historic context onwards in the coastal settlements. Earlier it was thought that the carved paddle technique was unknown to the 'megalithic' or Iron Age population, based on the ceramics from Arikamedu and its neighbourhood (Selvakumar 2004, 2008); but recently carved paddle impressed pottery has been identified by the author in the ceramics from Late Iron Age context datable to the later centuries of the first millennium BCE at Pattanam 2007 excavations (Cherian et al. 2007). Subsequently this impressed decoration was recognized on the megalithic pottery in Madurai district (Selvakumar 1996) and also at Kodumanal collections from the Tamil University, Thanjavur (Rajan 1994).

The fabric of the impressed variety from Arikamedu and Pattanam suggests that most of the impressed potteries of the Early Historic period were locally produced. Some of the fine ware ceramics from Arikamedu with fabric similar to the ceramics from the Ganga-Brahmaputra delta had the impressed decoration, which suggests that this technique was used in that region too. Not all the impressed pottery in India was imported, while the local potters did imitate this technique, some of the ceramics were perhaps also imported. Rao argues that Neutron Activation Analysis and XRD-analysis suggest that the impressed pottery from Kottapatnam in Andhra Pradesh was not locally produced (Rao 2004). Further petrographic analysis of ceramics from Indian sites that produce carved paddle impressed pottery would reveal if some of the impressed ceramics were actually imported from Southeast Asia.

Currently there are two lines of arguments; Solheim considers the carved paddle impressed pottery had its origin in south China and refers to this pottery tradition as 'Bau-Malay', while Bellwood (1997, 2005) suggests a possible Indian source for this techno-tradition. From the absence of this tradition in the pre-Iron Age context in South India, and its widespread occurrence in Southeast Asia in early context, it can be argued that the source of carved paddle impressed technique found in India could be Southeast Asia. This technique could have reached South India from Southeast Asia either through the land via eastern India in the Neolithic period or through the coast route of Bengal or by overseas. It is plausible that this technique reached India through/during more than one spatial and temporal context, and also independently developed in certain regions. However, more research is necessary by mapping the spatio-temporal distribution of this ceramics in archaeological and ethnographical context and scientific analysis of ceramic fabrics.

BOAT BUILDING TRADITIONS:
THE LASHED-LUG TECHNIQUE

India-Southeast Asian Contacts in Boat Building Traditions

The exact nature of interactions between India and Southeast Asia in boat building traditions is not known. Interestingly the Dravidian terms such as *pataku* and *kappal*, which refer to watercrafts, resemble the Austronesian (also Malay) terms (e.g. *padaw/perahu*). However, there is an inherent problem in the origin of terms, as researchers tend to argue the source of these terms either way (Manguin 1996; Mahdi 1999: 172). The early watercrafts of Southeast Asia developed sewn planks with 'lashed lug' technique (Horridge 1982; Andaya 1992: 372-74; McCarthy 2005), and at a later stage, wooden dowels were fixed in the holes drilled on the opposite faces of the plank edges (Horridge 1982). The Maldivian dhonis having hulls with multiple planks, dowels joining the edges, the lugs and thwart beams are considered to be an adoption from the Southeast Asian 'lashed lug' boat building tradition (Manguin 1996; Green 2001: 76). The Taikkal-Kadakkarappally boat on the Malabar Coast of India is the first archaeological example for the use of 'lashed lug' technique in India.

Taikkal-Kadakkarappally Boat on the Malabar Coast

The Kadakkarappally boat is the first significant example of a large watercraft excavated in India in a waterlogged deposit. The village is located near Taikkal (Thaikkal or Thyckal – N Lat. 9° 41.470; E Long. 76° 18.095), *c.* 35 km south of Kochi/Ernakulam, in Chertala taluk of Alappuzha district of Kerala close to the Arabian Sea. The Taikkal boat was accidentally unearthed by workers, who were digging a rice field, in the early 1990s. The Kerala State Department of Archaeology and the Centre for Heritage Studies, Tripunithura jointly excavated the boat in 2002, and in 2003, the researchers from the University of Southampton, UK, and the Institute of Nautical Archaeology, USA, documented and studied the boat (Nair et al. 2004; Pedersen 2004; Selvakumar et al. 2004; Tomalin et al. 2004). The intact portion of the nearly flat-bottomed plank-built boat measured *c.* 18.67 m in length and *c.* 4.05 m in width (Fig. 9.7). The stern portion of the boat was completely disturbed by the local people who were prospecting for treasure, while the bow and amidships were preserved to a limited extent. The boat had a transom stern and a curvilinear, pointed bow. From the mast-steps available, it appeared that the boat had at least two masts; one in the bow and the other amidships. The boat displayed a mixture of technologies, some of which are not found in the traditional sailing crafts of Kerala. It was mostly made of Anjily wood (*Artocarpus hirsutus* Lamk.) (Gulerija et al. 2003) and for the bulkhead *Cassia*

FIGURE 9.7
A general view of the excavated boat at Kadakkarappally

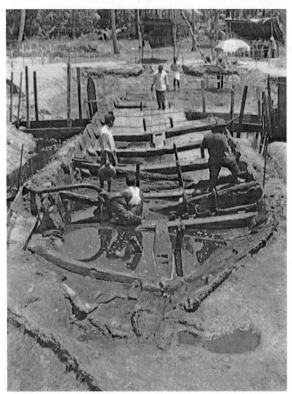

fistula has been used (Selvakumar 2006). Two wood samples from the boat were dated using the radiocarbon dating method, at Birbal Shahni Institute of Palaeobotany, Lucknow, India (Cal CE 920-1160, average 990±70 years), and Beta Analytic, USA (Cal CE 1020-1270). Based on the radiocarbon analysis, a date of twelfth to fifteenth centuries CE was proposed. The interior of the boat has been completely exposed, while the base remains unexcavated due to a number of reasons such as the delay in acquiring the necessary land, preparation of conservation and exhibition plans and raising the necessary funds. The Kerala State Government has agreed to set up a site museum at Kadakkarappally, but nothing has happened till 2010.

While it is certain that the boat was locally made and meant for transport on the inland waterways, certain technological elements used in the construction appear to be non-local. One of the remarkable aspects of the boat is the combination of technologies – fastening with iron nails, treenails and ropes through lashing of the lugs/cleats – used in the construction. The Taikkal-Kadakkarappally boat could be described as a hybrid version like the 'hybrid South China Sea' tradition.

The traditional Sri Lankan watercraft Madel Paruwa is also similar in design in the use of chine strakes (Devendra 1995; Kentley 2003). But the Madel Paruwa uses 'C' shaped chine strakes, unlike the 'L' shaped chine strakes of the Kadakkarappally boat. However, in their design, both they show similarities with log boats and Kentley (2003) argues that boats with such designs appear in the areas with log boat traditions.

The boat is divided into 11 compartments with the help of 10 solid frames, which support the bulkheads and in-between, these frames, a row of lugs/cleats has been provided across. Above the row of lugs, a crossbeam was attached to the chine strake with mortise-tenon lock. The lugs on the floor are flush with the surface, while those on the walls have prominent midribs. Many of the lugs had rope made of coconut fibre intact. However, no other frames or ribs or thwarts were found *in situ* or in the vicinity of the boat. Hence, it is not certain if the boat had any lashed ribs and thwarts other than the cross beams fixed with mortise-tenon lock, placed above the row of cleats and the solid frames, which support the bulkheads. Pedersen (2004) is of the view that no additional thwarts/ribs were used in the Taikkal boat and the rope was directly lashed through the lugs.

The lugs/cleats are an interesting feature of the boat that has not been encountered so far from ethnographic or archaeological contexts in Kerala or other parts of India (Fig. 9.8) (Greeshmalatha and Rajamanickam 1993). This feature is found mainly in the traditional boats of Southeast Asia, which are built, using the 'lashed-lug' technique (Horridge 1982, 1986; Barnes 2002; Brown and Sjostrand 2002), and also in the boats of north-western Europe. For example, in the 3,550 year-old Bronze Age boat from Dover in England, two central planks are put together using cleats and wedges (McGrail 2002).

FIGURE 9.8
A view of the lugs on the Kadakkarappally boat

'Lashed lug' Boat Building Traditions of Southeast Asia

The technique of 'lashed lug' or cleat survives in Southeast Asia in ethno-graphic context (Horridge 1982, 1986; Fig. 9.9) and it is also reported from the archaeological contexts datable to the early first millennium CE onwards (e.g, Pontian boat, Manguin 1996; Green et al. 1992). Recently, the Cirebon shipwreck off-Indonesia has revealed a lashed-lug boat datable to the tenth century CE (Liebner 2007) and the lashed-lug construction is also represented in rock art in East Timor (Lape 2007). The lashed lug construction is considered to be a characteristic Austronesian boat building technique (Horridge 1995). The Austronesian speakers who used the Lapita pottery seem to have made long journeys through Melanesia using the boats with lugs and internal thwarts around 2500 BCE (Horridge 1982). These lashed lug boats of Southeast Asia display similarities with the Scandinavian watercrafts (Horridge 1982, 1995: 147). Certain components of the 'lashed lug' method are considered to have been developed by the Indo-European speakers in the Bronze Age (Horridge 1982: 57; Barnes 1996) and it was also used in Viking and pre-Viking boats (Hornell 1946). In the medieval boat building tradition named 'hybrid South China Sea tradition' the characteristics of both the Chinese and Southeast Asian traditions are noticed (Manguin 1984, 1996; Wade 2003: 5) in the coastal India.

FIGURE 9.9
Patterns of lashing in Southeast Asian boats (after Horridge 1982)

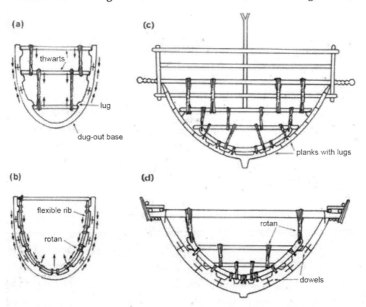

Discussion

The use of 'lashed lug' technique was not reported in historical/archaeological context in India till the discovery of the Taikkal-Kadakkarappally boat, and it is also not found in the ethnographic context. From the comparatively early occurrence of this technique in Southeast Asia, it can be argued that the 'lashed lug' technique used in the Kadakkarappally boat might have derived from Southeast Asian lashed lug boats. The adoption of this technique here is no surprise, since the Malabar Coast had regular contacts with Southeast Asia and China in the Medieval period (Raghava Varier 1990). The Chinese ships used to visit Kerala coast regularly and similarly the Southeast Asian ships must have visited the Malabar Coast, which perhaps influenced the boat building traditions of the Malabar Coast. Or it is possible that this region as well as Southeast Asia had the identical techno-tradition in the early period (see, Manguin 1996). Only further archaeological evidence from South Asia could shed more light on the nature of contacts in boat building traditions within the eastern Indian Ocean region. The recent discovery of a dug out canoe in the Early Historic context at Pattanam in Kerala (Cherian et al. 2007) suggests the possibilities of finding more such boats in waterlogged archaeological contexts.

GENERAL DISCUSSION

Techniques are solutions to certain problems or means to achieve certain intended functions. Each culture evolves different or identical methods for solving an identical problem or for achieving identical functions (e.g. the method of joining the planks in water crafts). Often people imitate, modify techniques of other cultures to suit their purpose. However, diffusion alone cannot always explain the appearance of new technique in a particular region and independent origin could not be ruled out. There could be more than one source or independent sources of origin for the same technique. Considering the historical and geographic (spatio-temporal) contexts of the above-mentioned ceramic and boat building techniques, it is argued that they might have derived from Southeast Asia. These views are proposed as hypotheses, rather than definite conclusions. Further research is necessary for a better understanding of these techno-traditions and their origin and distribution.

How did these ceramics and boat building techniques disperse across such a long distance? Perhaps ceramics such as the rouletted ware and other fine wares were collected by traders/travellers visiting Southeast Asia for their personal use or they were items of trade. The impact of the rouletted ware on the local ceramic traditions of Southeast Asia is not certain. However, imitated varieties of rouletted decorations are seen on coarse wares of local origin across south India (Begley 1996). The carved paddle technique could have reached India through trade. In the boat building traditions, the local shipwrights must have involved in the repairing of the foreign ships, which must have given them ample opportunity to familiarise with the non-local shipping technology. A number of factors would have induced the copying of alien ship design or experimentation of new designs.

While diffusion can definitely be a useful model for investigating cultural formations, preoccupation with this model alone would not improve our understanding. It is well known that the processual or new archaeology of the 1960s argued for the study of cultural processes and functioning of cultures rather than mere diffusion. Diffusion oriented researches focusing on 'Austronesian linguistic tree' and the construction of 'monolithic cultural categories' have been criticised by researchers (Szabo and O'Connor 2004). With the enrichment of archaeological research by the processual and post-processual theories there has been a paradigm shift in the researches which focus on social formations and a number of theoretically relevant issues (e.g. Stark 2006). However, migration and diffusions are vital agents of change.

Indianisation, i.e. the influence of Indian cultural traditions on the cultural formations in Southeast Asia, has been a matter of great debate and discussion among scholars for several decades now (Mabbett 1997; Smith 1999; Bellina and Glover 2004; Stark et al. 2006). Within the Indian context, the influence of the Ganga Valley on the Early Historic south India is an issue somewhat comparable to the process of 'Indianisation' in Southeast Asia. The study of the influence of a particular region's cultural traditions on other region is always fraught with difficulties for a number of reasons: (1) often the nature of evidence is scanty; (2) the textual and material evidence does not display the complex, hidden historical processes; (3) the researchers' cognition of reality is unconsciously conditioned by their contemporary socio-cultural milieu. Sometimes, bias unconsciously creeps into the interpretation of reality. When on a visit to a town within India, I remember a friend of mine observed – based on the few people and symbols that he encountered there – that numerous people of his ethnic identity were in the town. Whereas I could not perceive the same, since I was an outsider to the reality that he perceived. The few shreds of evidence found here and there may mislead us to build an over-emphasised picture of the reality. The study of socio-cultural formations of the past societies is a very complex issue and often insiders and outsiders view the reality differently. In the analysis of such contacts, contemporary national and regional boundaries/identities influence and distort the perception of the reality. Only sustained research with a broader database, holistic perspective, deconstruction of regional boundaries and identities, critical outlook and methodical approach could help us to move closer to the so-called 'objective reality', i.e. the 'subjective objectivity'.

REFERENCES

Achan, A.P., 1946, *Annual Report of the Archaeological Department of Cochin State for the Year 1121 M.E. (1945-46)*, Cochin: Government Press.

Adhyatman, S., 1985, *Burmese Ceramics*, Jakarta: The Ceramic Society of Indonesia.

Andaya, L.Y., 1992, 'Interactions with the Outside World and Adaptation in Southeast Asian Society – 1500-1800', in *The Cambridge History of Southeast Asia*, vol. 1, *From Early Times to c. 1800*, ed. Nicholas Tarling, Cambridge: Cambridge University Press, pp. 345-401.

Aoyagi, Y and H. Ogawa, 2004, 'Chinese Trade Ceramics of the Thirteenth and Fourteenth Centuries Discovered on the Malabar Coast', in *In Search of Ceramic-Sherds in South India and Sri Lanka*, ed. N. Karashima, Tokyo: Taisho University Press, pp. 47-55.

Ardika, I.W. and P. Bellwood, 1991, 'Sembiran: The Beginnings of Indian Contact with Bali', *Antiquity* 65: 221-32.

Ardika, I.W., P.S. Bellwood, R.A. Eggleton and D.J. Ellis, 1993, 'A Single Source for South Asian Export-quality Rouletted Ware?', *Man and Environment* 18(1): 101-9.

Barnes, R.H., 1996, *Sea Hunters of Indonesia: Fishers and Weavers of Lamalera*, Oxford Studies in Social Cultural Anthropology, Oxford: Clarendon Press.

——, 2002, 'Yami Boats and Boat-building in a Wider Perspective', in *Ships and the Development of Maritime Technology in the Indian Ocean*, ed. D. Parkin and R. Barnes, London: Routledge Curzon, pp. 291-314.

Begley, V., 1975, Review of *Archaeological Survey to Investigate South-East Asian Prehistoric Presence in Ceylon* by Wilhelm G. Solheim II and S. Deraniyagala, *American Anthropologist* NS 77(3): 685.

——, 1988, 'Rouletted Ware at Arikamedu: A New Approach', *American Journal of Archaeology* 6: 93-108.

——, 1996, 'Pottery from the Northern Sector, 1989-1992', in Begley et al., *The Ancient Port of Arikamedu: New Excavations and Researches 1989-1992*, Pondicherry: Ecole française d'Extrême-Orient, pp. 115-286.

——, 2004, 'Critique of V.D. Gogte's Interpretations of X-Ray Diffraction Analyses of Arikamedu Pottery', in V. Begley et al., *The Ancient Port of Arikamedu: New Excavations and Researches 1989-1992*, vol. 2, Paris: Ecole française d'Extrême-Orient, pp. 631-42.

Begley, V. and R. Tomber, 2001, 'Chapter 3. Indian Pottery', in *Berenike '98. Report of the 1998 Excavations at Berenike and the Survey of the Egyptian Eastern Desert, Including Excavations in Wadi Kalalat*, ed. S. Sidebotham and W. Wendrich, Leiden, pp. 161-81.

Begley, V. et al., 1996, *The Ancient Port of Arikamedu: New Excavations and Researches 1989-92*, vol. 1, Pondicherry: Ecole française d'Extrême-Orient.

——, 2004, *The Ancient Port of Arikamedu: New Excavations and Researches 1989-92*, vol. 2, Paris: Ecole française d'Extrême-Orient.

Behera, K.S., 1994, 'Maritime Contacts of Orissa: Literary and Archaeological Evidence', *Utkal Historical Research Journal* 5: 59-60.

Bellina, B. and I.C. Glover, 2004, 'The Archaeology of Early Contact with India and the Mediterranean World, from the fourth century B.C. to the fourth century A.D.', in *Southeast Asia: From Prehistory to History*, ed. I. Glover and P. Bellwood, New York: Routledge/Curzon, pp. 68-88.

Bellina, B. and P. Silapanth, 2006, 'Preliminary Report on the First Season of Excavation at Khao Sam Kaeo (Chumphon Province, Peninsular Thailand), *European Association of Southeast Asian Archaeologists, 11th International Conference*, Bougon, France, 25 au 30 September 2006.

Bellwood, P., 1997, *Prehistory of the Indo-Malaysian Archipelago*, Honolulu: University of Hawaii Press.

Bellwood, P.S., 2005, *First Farmers: The Origins of Agricultural Societies*, Oxford/Malden (MA): Blackwell Publishing.

Blench, R., L. Sagart and A. Sanchez-Mazas, 2005, *The Peopling of East Asia: Putting Together Archaeology, Linguistics and Genetics*, London: Routledge.

Brown, R.M. and Sten Sjostrand, 2002, *Maritime Archaeology and Shipwreck Ceramics in Malaysia*, Kuala Lumpur: The Department of Museums and Antiquities.

Chakraborty, S., 2000, 'Chandraketugarh: A Cultural and Archaeological Study (500 BC to 500 AD)', unpublished Ph.D. dissertation, Pune: University of Pune.

Cherian, P.J., K.P. Shajan and V. Selvakumar, 2007, 'In Pursuit of Missing Links – Pattanam and the Maritime History of Malabar Coast: A Report of 2007 Excavations, paper presented at the *EASSA conference* in Revanna, Italy, 4-8 July 2007.

Deraniyagala, P.E.P., 1956, 'Land Oscillation in the Northwest of Ceylon', *Journal of Ceylon Branch of Royal Asiatic Society* NS 4(2): 127-42.

Deraniyagala, S., 1972a, 'Archaeological Explorations in Ceylon', part 2, Kollankanata, Vilpattu, *Ancient Ceylon* 2: 1-17.

——, 1972b, 'The Citadel of Anuradhapura: Gedige 1984, a Preliminary Report', *Ancient Ceylon* 6: 39-47.

Deraniyagala, S.U., 1992, *The Prehistory of Sri Lanka: An Ecological Perspective*. Colombo: Department of Archaeological Survey.

Devendra, S., 1995, 'Pre-Modern Sri Lankan Watercrafts: The Twin Hulled Log-boats', in *Sesquicentennial Commemorative Volume of the Royal Asiatic Society of Sri Lanka 1845-1995*, ed. G.P.S.H. De Silva and C.G. Uragoda, Colombo: Royal Asiatic Society of Sri Lanka, pp. 211-38.

Dick-Read, R., 2006, 'Indonesia and Africa: Questioning the Origins of Some of Africa's Most Famous Icons', *The Journal for Transdisciplinary Research in Southern Africa* 2(1): 23-45.

Driem, George van 2001, *Languages of the Himalayas*, vol. 1, Leiden: Brill.

Fox, Robert B., 1970, *The Tabon Caves: Archaeological Explorations and Excavations on Palawan Island, Philippines*, Manila: National Museum of the Philippines.

Glover, I., 1990, 'Early Trade Between India and Southeast Asia: A Link in the Development of World Trading System', *Occasional Paper No. 16*: 1-45, London: University of Hull.

——, 1996, 'Recent Archaeological Evidence for Early Maritime Contact between India and Southeast Asia', in *Tradition and Archaeology: Early Maritime Contacts in the Indian Ocean, Proceedings of the International Seminar Techno-Archaeological Perspectives of Seafaring in the Indian Ocean*, ed. H.P. Ray and J.F. Salles, New Delhi: Manohar, pp. 181-97.

Gogte, V.D., 1997, 'The Chandraketugarh-Tamluk Region of Bengal: Source of the Early Historic Rouletted Ware from India and Southeast Asia', *Man and Environment* 22(1): 69-85.

——, 2001, 'XRD Analyses of the Rouletted Ware and Other Fine Grey Ware from Tissamaharama', in H.-J. Weisshaar, H. Roth and W. Wijeyapala (eds.), *Ancient Ruhuna*, vol. 1, Mainz am Rhein: von Zabern, 197-202.

——, 2002, 'Ancient Maritime Trade in the Indian Ocean: Evaluation by Scientific Studies of Pottery', *Man and Environment* 27(1): 57-67.

Gorman, C., 1971, 'The Hoabinhian and After: Subsistence Patterns in Southeast Asia during the Late Pleistocene and Early Recent Periods', *World Archaeology* 2: 300-20.

Goswami, M.C. and S.K. Roy, 1977, 'A Report on the Selected Potsherds from Ambari, Assam, India', *Bulletin of the Department of Anthropology, Guwahaty University* 1:122-27.

Green, J., 2001, 'The Archaeological Contribute to the Knowledge of the Extra-European Shipbuilding at the time of the Medieval and Modern Iberian-Atlantic Tradition', in *Trabalhos de Arqueologia 18 - Proceedings. International Symposium on Archaeology of Medieval and Modern Ships of Iberian-Atlantic Tradition. Hull Remains, Manuscripts and Ethnographic Sources: A Comparative Approach*, ed. Francisco Alves, Centro Nacional de Arqueologia Náutica e Subaquática / Academia de Marinha. Lisbon – Septembre 7th to 9th 1998, pp. 63-102.

Green, J., Tom Vosmer, Paul Clark, Rey Santiago and Mauro Alvares, 1992, 'Interim Report on the Joint Australian–Philippines Butuan Boat Project', October 1992. Report—Department of Maritime Archaeology, Western Australian Maritime Museum, No. 64.

Greeshmalatha, A.P. and G. Victor Rajamanickam, 1993, 'An Analysis of Different Types of Traditional Coastal Vessels Along the Kerala Coast', *Marine Archaeology* 4: 36-50.

Gulerija, J.S., B. Sekar and M.V. Nair, 2004, 'A Report on the Identification of a Wood Sample of a Ship Excavated from Thaikkal, Alappuzha District, Kerala', *Science and Culture* 70(3-4): 169-70.

Gupta, S., 2002, 'The Archaeo-Historica Idea of Indian Ocean', *Man and Environment* 27(1): 1-24.

Higham, C.F.W., 1996, 'A Review of Archaeology in Mainland Southeast Asia', *Journal of Archaeological Research* 4(1): 3-49.

Hornell, J., 1946, 'The Sailing Craft of Western India', *Mariner's Mirror* 32: 195-217.

Horridge, A., 1982, *The Lashed-Lug Boats of the Eastern Archipelagoes*, London: National Maritime Museum Monograph 54.

——, 1986, *The Sailing Craft of Indonesia*, Oxford: Oxford University Press.

——, 1995, 'Austronesian Conquest of the Sea—Upwind', *The Austronesians: Historical and Comparative Perspectives*, ed. Peter Bellwood, James Fox and Darrell Tryon, Canberra: Australian National University, pp. 143-60.

Jahan, S.H., 2002, 'Early Maritime Trade Network of Bengal', *Man and Environment* 27(1): 127-38.

Karashima, N., 1987, 'Trade Relations between Tamil Nadu and China During the 13th and 14th Centuries', paper read on the International Seminar on Tamil Studies, Plenary Session 1987, Kuala Lumpur, Malaysia.

——, 1988, 'Periyapattinam: South Indian Coastal Village: Discovery of Chinese Potherds and its Identification with Ta Pa-tan and Fattan', *Tohogaku (Eastern Studies)* 75: 81-98.

——, 2004, *In Search of Ceramic-Sherds in South India and Sri Lanka*, Tokyo: Taisho University Press.

Kentley, E., 2003, 'The *Madel Paruwa* of Sri Lanka: A Sewn Boat with Chine Strakes', in *Boats of South Asia*, ed. S. McGrail, London: Routledge Curzon, pp. 167-83.

Lape, Peter V., 2007, 'Rock Art: A Potential Source of Information about Past Maritime Technology in the South-East Asia-Pacific Region', *The International Journal of Nautical Archaeology* 36(2): 238-53, doi: 10.1111/j.1095-9270.2006.00135.x

Lertrit, S., 2004, 'Late Prehistoric and Early Historic Ceramic Chronology for Central Thailand', *Silpakorn University International Journal* 4 (1-2): 5-37.

Liebner, H., 2007, 'Cirebon Shipwreck', *The Oriental Ceramic Society of the Philippines Newsletter*, January 2007.

Mabbett, I., 1997, 'The "Indianization" of Mainland Southeast Asia: A Reappraisal', in *Living a Life in Accord with Dhamma: Papers in Honor of Professor Jean Bois-selier on his Eightieth Birthday*, ed. N. Eilenberg, M.C. Subhadradis Diskul and R.L. Brown, Bangkok: Silpakorn University, pp. 342-55.

Mahadevan, I., 2003, *Early Tamil Epigraphy: From the Earliest Times to the Sixth Century AD*, Harvard Oriental Series, 62, Chennai: CRE-A.

Mahdi, W., 1999, 'The Dispersal of Austronesian Boat Forms in the Indian Ocean in Archaeology and Language', in *Archaeology and Language*, ed. R. Blench and M. Spriggs. New York: Routledge.

Malleret, L., 1959-63, '*L'archéologie du Delta du Mékong*', Paris: Ecole française d'Extrême-Orient, 7 vols.

Manguin, P.-Y., 1984, 'Relationship and Cross-Influence between South-East Asian and Chinese Shipbuilding Traditions', in *Final Report. SPAFA Workshop on Shipping and Trade Networks in Southeast Asia*, Bangkok, pp. 197-212.

——, 1996, 'Southeast Asian Shipping in the Indian Ocean During the First Millennium A.D.', in *Tradition and Archaeology: Early Maritime Contacts in the Indian Ocean*, Proceedings of the International Seminar Techno-Archaeological Perspectives of Seafaring in the Indian Ocean, ed. H.P. Ray and J.F. Salles, New Delhi: Manohar, pp. 181-97.

McCarthy, M., 2005, *Ships' Fastenings: From Sewn Boat to Steamship*, College Station: Texas A&M University Press.

McGrail, Sean, 2002, *Boats of the World: From the Stone Age to Medieval Times*, Oxford: Oxford University Press.

McPherson, Kenneth, 1993, *The Indian Ocean: A History of People and the Sea*, New Delhi: Oxford University Press.

Meyers, A.D., 1999, 'West African Tradition in the Decoration of Colonial Jamaican Folk Pottery', *International Journal of Historical Archaeology* 3 (4) 1999: 201-23.

Miksic, John, 2003, 'Introduction: The Beginning of Trade in Ancient Southeast Asia: The Role of Oc-Eo and the Lower Mekong River', in *Art and Archaeology of Fun Nan. Pre-Khmer Kingdom of the Lower Mekong Valley*, ed. James C.M. Khoo, Bangkok: Orchid Press/The Southeast Asian Ceramic Society, pp. 1-34.

Misra, V.N., 2001, 'Prehistoric Human Colonization of India', *Journal of Biological Science* 26(4): 491-531.

Morrison, K.D., 1997, 'Commerce and Culture in South Asia: Perspectives from Archaeology and History', *Annual Review of Anthropology* 26: 87-108.

Mughul, R., 1982, 'Recent Archaeological Research in Cholistan Desert', in *Harappan Civilization: A Contemporary Perspective*, G. Possehl, pp. 85-95, New Delhi: Oxford IBH.

Nagaswamy, R., 1991, 'Alagankulam: An Indo-Roman Trading Port', in *Indian Archaeological Heritage, K. V. Soundara Rajan Felicitation Volume*, ed. C. Margabandhu et al., New Delhi: Agam Kala Prakashan, pp. 247-54.

——, 1995, *Roman Karur: A Peep into Tamil's Past*, Madras: Brahad Prakashan.

Nair, M.V., V. Selvakumar and P.K. Gopi, 2004, 'Excavation of a Unique Sailboat at Kadakkarappally, Kerala', *Current Science* 86.5: 709-12.

Peacock, P.V.A., 1959, 'A Short Description of Malayan Prehistoric Pottery', *Asian Perspectives* 3: 121-56.

Pedersen, R., 2004, 'Shipwreck in the Coconut Grove: The Kadakkarappally Boat', *Institute of Nautical Archaeology Quarterly* 31.2: 3-9.

Posey, S., 1994, *Yemeni Pottery: The Littlewood Collection*, London: British Museum Press.

Raghava Varier, M.R., 1990, 'Trade Relations between Kerala and China 1200-1500 AD', *Proceedings of the Indian History Congress* 51: 690-98.

Ragupathy, P., 1987, *Early Settlements in Jaffna: An Archaeological Survey*, Madras: CRE-A.

Rajan, K., 1994, *Archaeology of Tamil Nadu (Kongu Country)*, Noida: Book India Publication Company.

Raman, K.V., 1991, Further Evidence of Roman Trade from Coastal Sites in Tamil Nadu', in *Rome and India: The Ancient Sea Trade*, ed. V. Begley and R.D. DePuma New Delhi: Oxford University Press, pp. 125-33.

Rao, K.P., 2004, 'I-2: Kottapatnam – A South Indian Port Trading with Eastern Lands', in *In Search of Ceramic-Sherds in South India and Sri Lanka*, ed. N. Karashima, Tokyo: Taisho University Press, pp. 11-15.

Rao, S.N., 1977, 'Excavations at Sarutaru: a Neolithic Site in Assam', *Man Environment* 1: 39–43.

Ray, H.P., 2003, *The Archaeology of Seafaring in Ancient South Asia*, London: Cambridge University Press.

Ronquillo, W.P., 2003, 'Philippine Earthenware Pottery from the Early Prehistoric Period', in *Earthenware in Southeast Asia: Proceedings of the Singapore Symposium on Premodern Southeast Asian Earthenwares*, ed. John N. Miksic, Singapore: Singapore University Press, pp. 32-38.

Rooney, D.F., 1987, *Folk Pottery in South-East Asia*, Singapore: Oxford University Press.

Saraswati, B. and N.K. Behura, 1966, *Pottery Techniques in Peasant India*, Calcutta: Anthropological Survey of India.

Sasaki, H., 2004, 'I-3: Chinese and Thai Ceramics in Kottapatnam', in *In Search of Ceramic-Sherds in South India and Sri Lanka*, ed. N. Karashima, Tokyo: Taisho University Press, pp. 16-21.

Schenk, H., 2000, 'Rouletted Ware and Other Imports of Tissamaharama: Observations on the Pottery Sequence from Southern Sri Lanka', in M. Taddei and G. De Marco (eds.), *South Asian Archaeology 1997*. Proceedings of the Fourteenth International Conference of the European Association of South Asian Archaeologists, held in the Istituto Italiano per l'Africa e l'Oriente, Palazzo Brancaccio, Rome, 7-14 July 1997. 653-77.

Selvakumar, V., 1996, 'Investigations into the Prehistoric and Protohistoric Cultures of the Upper Gundar Basin, Madurai District, Tamil Nadu', Ph.D. dissertation, University of Poona.

——, 2004, 'Impressed pottery from 1989-92 Excavations, Appendix B', in V. Begley et al., *The Ancient Port of Arikamedu*, vol. 2, Paris: Ecole française de'Extrême Orient, pp. 613-21.

——, 2006, 'Nature and Characteristics of the Sailboat Excavated at Taikkal-Kadakkarappally, Alappuzha District, Kerala', in *Glimpses of Marine Archaeology in India*, ed. A.S. Gaur and K.H. Vora, Goa: Society for Marine Archaeology, pp. 4-14.

——, 2008, 'Ceramic Traditions of the Iron Age-Early Historic Tamil Country', in *Early Historic Archaeology of South Asia*, ed. Sengupta and Chakrabarty, Kolkata: CASTEI, 421-49.

Selvakumar, V., M.V. Nair, P. K. Gopi, and P. Sridharan, 2004, 'Spatio-Temporal Contexts of the Sailboat Excavated at Kadakkarappally', *Journal of the Centre for Heritage Studies* 1: 75-82.

Selvakumar, V., P.K. Gopi and K.P. Shajan, 2005, 'Trial Excavations at Pattanam: A Preliminary Report', *The Journal of the Centre for Heritage Studies* 2: 57-66.

Shajan, K.P.R., Tomber, V. Selvakumar and P.J. Cherian, 2004, 'Locating the Ancient Port of Muziris: Fresh Findings from Pattanam', *Journal of Roman Archaeology* 17: 312-20.

Sharma, G.R., 1960, *The Excavations at Kausambi 1957-59*, Allahabad: University of Allahabad.

Sharma, G.R. et al., 1980, *From Hunting and Food Gathering to Domestication of Plants and Animals, Beginnings of Agriculture*, Allahabad: University of Allahabad.

Sharma, T.C., 1967, 'A Note on the Neolithic Pottery of Assam', *Man* NS 2(1): 126-28.

Singh, P., 2002, 'The Neolithic Cultures of Northern and Eastern India', in *Indian Archaeology in Retrospect: Prehistory*, ed. S. Settar and R. Korisettar, New Delhi: ICHR and Manohar, pp. 127-50.

Smith, M.L., 1999, '"Indianization" from the Indian Point of View: Trade and Cultural Contacts with Southeast Asia in the Early First Millennium C.E.', *Journal of the Economic and Social History of the Orient* 42(1): 1-26.

Solheim II, Wilhelm G., 1957, 'The Kulanay Pottery Complex in the Philippines', *Artibus Asiae* 20(4): 279-88.

——, 1964, 'Pottery Manufacture in Sting Mor and Ban Nong: Sua Kin Ma, Thailand', *Journal of the Siam Society* 52(2): 151-61.

——, 1990, 'Earthen Ware Pottery: The Ta'i and Malay', *Asian Perspectives* 2: 167-76.

——, 2003, 'Southeast Asian Earthenware Pottery and Its Spread', in *Earthenware in Southeast Asia: Proceedings of the Singapore Symposium on Premodern Southeast Asian Earthen Wares*, ed. John N. Miksic, Singapore: Singapore University Press, pp. 1-21.

Solheim II, W.G. and S. Deraniyagala, 1972, *Archaeological Survey to Investigate Southeast Asian Prehistoric Presence in Ceylon: Ancient Ceylon Occasional Paper No. 1*.

Solheim, W.G., B Harrison, and L Wall., 1956, 'Niah Three Coloured Ware and Related Prehistoric Pottery from Borneo', *Asian Perspectives* 2: 167-76.

Stark, Miriam T., 2006, 'Early Mainland Southeast Asian Landscapes in the First Millennium A.D.', *Annual Review of Anthropology* 35: 407-32.

Stark, M.T., D. Sanderson and R.G. Bingham, 2006, 'Monumentality in the Mekong Delta: Luminescence Dating and Implications', *Bulletin of the Indo-Pacific Prehistory Association* 26: 110-20.

Subbarayalu, Y., 1996, 'Chinese Ceramics from Tamil Nadu and Kerala Coast', in *Tradition and Archaeology: Early Maritime Contacts in the Indian Ocean*, Proceedings of the International Seminar Techno-Archaeological Perspectives of Seafaring in the Indian Ocean, ed. H.P. Ray and J.F. Salles, New Delhi: Manohar, pp. 109-14.

Sukarto, K.A.M.M., 1973, 'Note on Pottery Manufacture near Raba, East Sumbava', *Asian Perspectives* 16: 71-77.

Szabo, K. and S. O'Connor, 2004, 'Migration and Complexity in Holocene Island Southeast Asia', *World Archaeology* 36(4): 621-28.

Tewari, Rakesh, R.K. Srivastava, K.K. Singh, K.S. Saraswat, I.B. Singh, M.S. Chauhan, A.K. Pokharia, A. Saxena, V. Prasad, M. Sharma, 2006, 'Second Preliminary Report of the Excavations at Lahuradewa District Sant Kabir Nagar, U.P. 2002-2003-2004 & 2005-06', *Pragdhara* 16: 35-68.

Tomalin, V., V. Selvakumar, M.V. Nair and P.K. Gopi, 2004, 'The Thaikkal-Kadakkarapally Boat: An Archaeological Example of Medieval Shipbuilding in the Western Indian Ocean', *International Journal of Nautical Archaeology* 33(2): 253-63.

Tomber, R., 1999, 'The Quseir al-Qadim Project: Report 1999 - Pottery', URL: http://www.arch.soton.ac.uk/Research/QuseirDev/getpage.asp?PageID=88&Style=Default

——, 2000, 'Indo-Roman Trade: The Ceramic Evidence from Egypt', *Antiquity* 74: 624-31.

Tripathi, S., 2002, 'Early Maritime Activities of Orissa, East Coast of India: Linkages in Trade and Cultural Developments', *Man and Environment* 27(1): 117-26.

Wade, G., 2003, *The Pre-Modern East Asian Maritime Realm: An Overview of European-Language Studies*. Asia Research Institute Working Paper Series No. 16, Singapore: Asia Research Institute of the National University of Singapore.

Walker, M.J. and S. Santoso, 1977, 'Romano-Indian Rouletted Pottery in Indonesia', *Asian Perspectives* 20(2): 228-35.

Wheeler, R.E.M., A. Ghosh and Krishna Deva, 1946, 'Arikamedu: An Indo-Roman Trading Station on the East Coast of India', *Ancient India* 2: 17-124.

Whitcomb, D. and Janet H. Johnson, 1982, *Quseir al-Qadim 1980: Preliminary Report*. Malibu, ARCE Reports, vol. 7.

Yankowski, A., 2005, 'Trade, Technologies and Traditions: The Analysis of Artifacts Recovered from a Metal Age Burial Site In District Ubujan, Tagbilaran City, Bohol', unpublished M.A. thesis, Department of Anthropology, San Francisco State University, San Francisco.

10

Marine Archaeological Investigations along the Tamil Nadu Coast and their Implications for Understanding Cultural Expansion to Southeast Asian Countries

Sundaresh
A.S. Gaur

The ancient ports on Tamil Nadu coast have played a dominant role in the transoceanic trade and commerce with the Mediterranean and the Southeast Asian countries since very early times. Important ports such as Kaveripoompattinam, Mahabalipuram, Nagapattinam, Korkai, Alagankulam are noted not only for brisk maritime trade but also for the establishment of the Hindu kingdoms and spread of the Indian culture in the foreign lands from beginning of the Christian Era up to the eleventh century CE. Many such port towns that existed on the coastal region vanished or were submerged by the sea, maybe due to coastal erosion, sea level changes, neo-tectonic activities, etc. Ancient literary sources across the country refer to the submergence of prosperous cities. These traditions, like the submergence of the Golden City of Dwarka mentioned in the *Mahabharata*, the Sangam literature refers to the submergence of Poompuhar and popular beliefs about the submergence of the temples of Mahabalipuram, the '*Kumari Kandam*' traditions of Tamil Nadu, etc., are well known as they are passed on from father to son as local traditions. It may well be impossible to search for their roots or find proof that such beliefs are based on facts. Nevertheless, many archaeological explorations have been taken up in an attempt to verify the historicity of these traditions.

Sangam literature, one of the richest ancient literary bodies, preserved in Tamil Nadu, gives ample historical accounts of maritime trade and commerce prior to the Christian era. Sangam literature mentions about the flourishing port town of Poompuhar, the capital of the early Cholas. The maritime trade with the Southeast Asian countries through the port of Kaveripattinam was confirmed with the item of Kalakam (*Kalakattu akkam* means 'the goods from the place of Kalakam') (Rajan, this volume). According to Nagaswamy (2007) Hindu images of Shiva, Vishnu along with Tamil inscription mentioning Nangur, Manigramattar, Avani Naranam and Sena mukattars were found at the ancient port town of Takuapa, Thailand; they prove close contact with the Kaveripattinam trade network and with the Pallava kings. The *Manimekhalai* mentions that Poompuhar was swallowed by the sea due to the wrath of goddess Manimekhalai. Though the reference is only to a supernatural incident, it may be taken as an echo of some actual sea erosion due to high tidal wave surge that engulfed the city.

Mahabalipuram, also known as Mamallapuram, is well known for its architectural marvels carved during the Pallava period. This place was still famous among the mariners for its 'Seven Pagodas' during the early seventeenth century CE. Mahabalipuram, 'the city of the great wrestler' was controlled by Pallava kings from Kanchipuram, the capital of the Pallava dynasty from the third to ninth centuries CE (Rabe 2001). Mahabalipuram literally means 'city of the Great Bali' in memory of the tradition when Vamana (Vishnu's dwarf incarnation) humbled the demon king Bali and caused his splendid beachfront palaces to collapse beneath the sea (Rabe 2001). According to the local tradition, six out of seven temples got submerged in the sea and the surviving one is the shore temple.

Marine archaeological explorations have been carried out by the National Institute of Oceanography, Goa at Poompuhar and Mahabalipuram (Fig. 10.1) to find out the submerged structural evidences of the famous port towns, which carried out maritime trade with other countries in general and Southeast Asian countries in particular.

These two famous sites are being surveyed to find out the remains of the ancient ports and their locations. Marine archaeological investigations are not only providing the information on submerged structures and cultural expansion, but also provide scientific results regarding coastal erosion, shoreline changes, etc. The details of the findings are described below.

POOMPUHAR

Poompuhar or Kaveripoompattinam is located on the east coast of India, at the point where the river Kaveri joins the Bay of Bengal. Sangam period texts such as *Silappatikaram*, *Pattinapalai* and later ones including *Manimekhalai*

FIGURE 10.1
Map showing the survey area on the Tamil Nadu coast

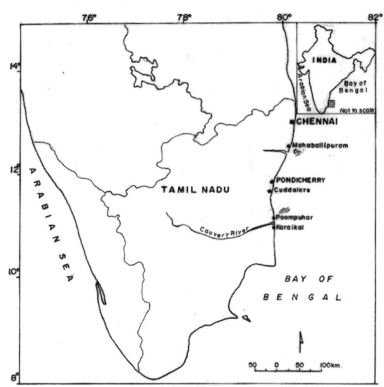

and *Ahananaru* vividly describe Poompuhar as the port capital of the Early Cholas.

Land excavations at Poompuhar brought to light two brick structures that have been described as wharves (Rao, 1987; Athiyaman, 1999), possibly located on an ancient channel of the river Kaveri.

Coastal Archaeological Explorations at Poompuhar

During the course of explorations, a brick structure of eleven courses running parallel to the coast was exposed (it is 1.2 m in width, 1.2 m in height and 4 m in length) (Fig. 10.2). A terracotta ring well with three courses was exposed in the inter-tidal zone at Poompuhar (it is 25 cm high, 4 cm thick at the rim, and has a diameter of 75 cm) (Fig. 10.3).

Four aligned brick structures of 25 m in length, 3.4 m in width were noticed at an under water depth of 1 m, about 60 m from the high water line, opposite to present Cauvery temple. The size of the bricks of the structures is 22 × 13 × 6 cm.

FIGURE 10.2
Brick structure exposed near the Kannagi statue in the
intertidal zone at Poompuhar

FIGURE 10.3
Terracotta ringwells exposed in the intertidal zone at Poompuhar

Vanagiri

Vanagiri is located on the coast about 1 km south of Poompuhar. The eleventh century CE Yellaiyamman temple has collapsed and the remains are scattered in the inter-tidal zone. Three terracotta ring wells (75 cm in diameter, 15 cm high and 6 cm thick at the rim) were exposed about 300 m south of the Yellaiyamman temple at Vanagiri. A neatly paved structure made of bricks, probably the floor of a house, was exposed in the inter-tidal excavation (Fig. 10.4).

FIGURE 10.4
Brick paved structure exposed in the inter-tidal zone at Vanagiri

Chinnavanagiri

Chinnavanagiri is located on the coast about 3 km south of Poompuhar. In a trench at a beach site near Chinnavanagiri, a terracotta ring well with rings of 25 cm in height, 5 cm rim thickness and 115 cm in diameter, was found surrounded with burnt bricks, and associated with megalithic black and red ware and other materials like beads of semi-precious stones (agate, crystal, carnelian) and varieties of glass and terracotta. The other important finds from this site are a potsherd with an inscribed Brahmi letter 'Ma' (Fig. 10.5), an early Chola square coin (completely eroded), and a few later Chola coins.

FIGURE 10.5
Inscription on a potsherd found at Chinnavanagiri

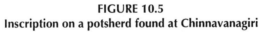

Findings of brick structures, terracotta ring wells, storage jars and brick paved platforms prove the existence of a settlement in the inter-tidal zone. A ring well was excavated near Chinnavanagiri where a habitation site was also noticed. The pottery from the site suggests that the ring well can be dated to the second century BCE, as one of the potsherds is inscribed in Brahmi with the letter 'Ma'. The other ring wells found at Vanagiri and Poompuhar are of the same period. Similar kinds of ring wells found at Arikamedu and Vasavasamudram are dated to the second century BCE to the third century CE (Rao et al. 1995-96). The size of the bricks used is 36 × 18 × 6 cm and closely corresponds to the bricks used in the Buddha Vihar at Kaveripoompattinam.

Tranquebar

Tranquebar is situated about 15 km south of Poompuhar and has a continuous habitation commencing from the late Chola period until today. The entire Tranquebar was well protected by a fort wall including the Masilamani temple and the Dansborg Museum, with a sufficient distance from the shoreline as shown in the map prepared by the Danish rulers in the mid-seventeenth century. The Masilamani temple of the thirteenth century CE is under threat as the sea has destroyed more than 50 per cent of the temple (Fig. 10.6) and is likely to engulf the entire temple in the near future. Two brick wells were completely exposed in the inter-tidal zone. There is also evidence in Tranquebar about the destruction of modern houses due to the encroachment of the sea (Sundaresh et al. 1997). The coins of Chola, Dutch, and Danish periods were collected in the inter-tidal zone of Tranquebar.

A mid-seventeenth-century map of Tranquebar is displayed in the Dansborg Museum. It shows a complete plan of the town along with the

FIGURE 10.6
Partly collapsed Masilamani temple at Tranquebar

then shoreline. A careful study of the map suggests that Tranquebar town was well protected by a sea side fort wall, and that the Shiva temple was situated sufficiently landward from this wall. It is estimated from the seventeenth-century map, that the shoreline was then at least 50 m away from the fort wall. The Masilamani temple located around 250-300 m from the shoreline (Fig. 10.7). This observation unequivocally suggests that the shoreline has transgressed about 300 m in the last 300 years, therefore infringing at an average rate of one metre per year.

FIGURE 10.7
A seventeenth-century map prepared by the Danish rulers where the shoreline and the protection walls are indicated at Tranquebar

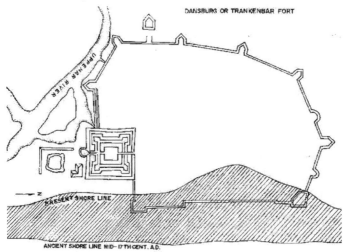

Offshore Explorations

Underwater explorations were conducted between Tranquebar and Nayak-ankuppam for a distance of about 25 km with small grids of 250 m at Poompuhar. The survey revealed several isolated objects such as rock boulders at a depth of 7-8 m and 11-13 m opposite to the Masilamani temple (Vora 1987; Rao 1992; Rao 1991a). Further south of Tranquebar, sonograms and echograms recorded the extension of submerged river valleys of Nandalar and Uppanar (Rao 1991). Off Poompuhar, near the southern bank of the river Cauvery, off Pudukuppam and off Nayakankuppam, between water depths of 5.5 to 10.5 m, the presence of three major sites of interest was observed.

A few dressed stone blocks measuring 90 × 40 × 15 cm, a semi-circular stone with a L-shape cut on its surface and many other irregular blocks of sandstone were noticed in 5 to 8 m water depth off the river Cauvery's mouth. The other findings during airlifting operations are brickbats and the early historic pottery of black and red ware, red ware, buff ware and grey ware (*NIO Technical Report* 1995).

The airlifting operations in the north of Poompuhar revealed a few dressed stone blocks in three general dimensions (30 × 20 × 5 cm, 65 × 40 × 10 cm and 60 × 35 × 10 cm), and brought to light potsherds of grey ware and huge storage jars at 1 m below the sea bed. The echograms of the sub-bottom profiler revealed a submerged palaeo-channel of the river Kaveri to the north of Poompuhar at 10 to 15 m water depth, with a width of 300 to 500 m, buried 20 m below the sea bottom (*NIO Technical Report* 1997).

Three structures identified with the help of geophysical surveys between 22 and 24 m water depth off Poompuhar were later confirmed by diving (Vora 1987; Rao 1992; Rao 1991). They are lying in a north-south direction. The first structure was located at a water depth of 23 m about 5 km offshore and is oval in shape. The total periphery of the object is 140 m. North-south length of the object is 40 m and east-west length is 20 m. The height of the object on the outer edge is 3 m while on the inner side it has a maximum height of 1 m. The height of the eastern arm is greater than that of the western arm. The width of the arm varies from 3 to 6 m. The middle portion of the object is covered with sediments and rock patches. About 40 m north of the above object, two smaller objects of the same material were noticed. These two objects are lying in east-west direction within a distance of 10 m. The circumference of each object is not more than 15 m and their height is about 2 m. They have a maximum height in the centre and their edges are sloping down. There are a number of wide cracks on the structures. A few blocks are of 2 m in length, 1.5 m in breadth and 1 m in height. A few smaller blocks measure 100 × 60 × 20 cm (*NIO Technical Report* 1995, 1997).

Significance of Submerged Structures

Underwater exploration in shallow water revealed a few well-dressed stone blocks. One of them is semicircular in shape along with a number of eroded blocks. This evidence suggests that stones were also used for construction of buildings, but whether they were used for habitation or some other kind of building is still not confirmed. Sangam literature mentions that buildings were constructed of bricks. Airlift operation suggests that habitation site was buried at least 1 m below sediment. The ceramic evidence suggests that the habitation belongs to the early Christian era. In the Bay of Bengal the high-energy zone can be considered up to a depth of 8-9 m. As this area is much more disturbed by high waves, currents and tides, it is very difficult to presume that some structures particularly of bricks that were mostly used in Sangam Period would have survived in the high-energy zone. Only the stone structures are likely to provide a clue to understand the plan.

The explorations at Poompuhar and Tranquebar demonstrate that the sea has gradually encroached upon the land to a great extent in recent years. It is worth mentioning here that the Kannagi statue, said to have been installed in 1973 about 200 m from the high water line and was shifted for about 150 m landward from its original place after it was destroyed by the sea during 1994; this is a clear indication of the fast advancement of the sea. Similarly, other monuments were destroyed in the vicinity by wave activity.

The erosion on sandy coastlines is due to less sediment supply from the rivers, especially where dams have been built for reservoirs, and also due to the shifting of river mouths (Bird 1984). Subsequently, the sea began to erode the coastline, leading to submergence of several ancient coastal structures at Poompuhar (Sundaresh et al. 1997). The Bay of Bengal is subjected to a large number of high intensity cyclones, causing immense amounts of destruction on the coastline. More than 42 major cyclones or depressions have been reported from this area. The narrowness of the eastern continental shelf is also another factor responsible for the coastal erosion. This shelf is less than 50 km wide. Wave propagation over a narrow shelf results in low frictional loss of energy and thus expends much energy on the coastline, causing great coastal erosion. The removal of sand from the beaches results in destabilization and destruction of coastal structures.

The archaeological evidence recovered in the inter-tidal zone as well as offshore belongs to the Sangam period (third century BCE to third century CE). Evidence in the inter-tidal zone, hydrographic charts, and the seventeenth-century map at Tranquebar all confirm the shoreline recession. This suggests that about 300 m recession of shoreline occurred in last 300 years at an average rate of 1 m per year. If the same rate was continued for the last 2000 years, then ancient Poompuhar must definitely have extended much further towards the sea from the present coastline. Relative sea level rise has also undoubtedly been taking place on coasts where the land is subsiding.

MAHABALIPURAM

Mahabalipuram is situated on the seashore about 55 km south of Chennai and is famous for its architectural marvels such as the Shore Temple, the Chariot Rathas carved out of single rock, Arjuna's Penance bas-relief, and several cave temples built by the Pallava king Narasimha Varman during the eighth century. It is recognised as a World Heritage Monument by UNESCO. A discussion has arisen due to the belief that six temples out of seven may have been submerged. It is to verify this fact that underwater explorations were taken up.

Mahabalipuram is said to have been a seaport right from the beginning of the Christian era. An eighth-century Tamil text written by Tirumangai

Alwar described this place as Kadal Mallai (Ramaswami 1989). A few Roman coins of Theodosius (fourth century CE) suggest that Mahabalipuram then had trade contacts with the Roman world (Dayalan 1992). The epigraphical sources mention that the Pallava Kings had an active contact with Sri Lanka, China and Southeast Asia. Pallava King Sihmavarman led two expeditions by embarking on two ships from Mamallapuram. The Pallava embassy and Vajradanthi, the famous Buddhist monk who introduced Mahayana Buddhism to Sri Lanka sailed to China from the port of Mamallapuram (Ramaswami 1989). Archaeological excavations near Punjeri village, about 1.5 km west of Mahabalipuram, revealed remains of the early historic and medieval periods. The excavator has suggested that this place could have served as an ancient port (Dayalan 1992).

Mahabalipuram was well known to earlier mariners as 'Seven Pagodas' since the seventeenth century. It is generally believed that out of seven temples originally constructed, all but one were submerged by the sea over a period of time, and that only the one known as 'Shore Temple' remains visible. European travellers in the eighteenth and nineteenth century have recorded this folk tradition (Ramaswami, 1989). Carr (1869) refers to the account given by William Chambers (1869) after his second visit to Mahabalipuram in 1776:

according to the natives of the place, the more aged people among them, remembered to have seen the tops of several pagodas far out in the sea, since being covered with copper, probably gilt, they were particularly visible at sunrise as their shining surface used to reflect the sun's rays, but that now the effect was no longer produced, as the copper had since become incrusted with mould and Verde grease.

To confirm the popular tradition, underwater investigations were carried out at Mahabalipuram. The survey comprised geophysical methods and underwater visual inspection by diving.

Underwater Findings

The seabed off Mahabalipuram in depths ranging from 6 to 15 m is highly undulating, with variation in height from 1 to 6 m. Granitic rocks with patches of coarse-grained sand carpet the floor.

Several rectangular and square shaped structures appeared on most of the sonagraphs, particularly in the northern part, showing groups and clusters of blocks arranged in a systematic pattern, mostly discontinuous short linear structures parallel to each other. Strong reflections of the images suggest that they are massive hard bodies that are well shaped. Some natural irregular rock outcrops are also associated with these linear structures. It appears from the entire sonagraphs in the study area that some significant parallel discontinuous rocky structures exist on the seafloor at some places in addition to the dominant occurrence of natural rock outcrops.

The interesting findings were explored by diving on the basis of the sonagraphs and important archaeological evidence was discovered including structures and sections of walls more than 10 m in length.

Site I: Among many submerged structures, a big structure was found about 700 m east of the Shore Temple under 6 m of water which comprises several small structures. The upper portion of the structure is above sea surface during low tide and is visible from shore or from a boat. The structure covers an area of approximately 75 × 35 m. The structure is broader on the northern side where a heap of stone blocks are also observed, while on the southern side scattered small stone structures of various sizes were observed. The structure has several N-S oriented wall sections (Fig. 10.8).

Dressed granite blocks were used for the construction of this structure. A wall, about 25 m in length and 65 cm in width with two to four courses is noticed. The dimensions of the blocks varies between 95 × 65 × 90 cm and 45 × 50 × 50 cm. Huge rectangular blocks measuring approximately 2 × 1 × 1.5 m were also noticed on the upper portion of the structure along with a few blocks having joinery projections. The structures are covered with marine growth; a few blocks were cleaned and chisel marks were observed. Another wall, measuring about 5.40 m in length was noticed on the northern side along with two parallel walls on the southern side of the main structure, with a stair like structure leading up. There was a small platform along with a wall towards the north-eastern side of the main structure. Further on the

FIGURE 10.8
Underwater submerged structure at Mahabalipuram

northern side remains of a wall extended up to 15 m in length. Some of the stone blocks of the western side were cleaned. One of the blocks shows that it has the joinery projections for interconnecting the blocks. The length of some of these six walls varies from 7 to 32.5 m; other walls are shorter in length. Large sized square and rectangular blocks are noticed in the middle of the structure, which had a height of 4 m above seabed. A floor measuring 2 × 2.5 m was also noticed towards the north-western side of the structure. The entire structure has a thick marine growth of sponges, shells, barnacles and mussels.

Site II: Another site is located about 200 m towards the NNE of the former structure. The water depth varies between 5-8 m. The site has remains of a wall, dressed stone blocks and natural boulders. Some of the stone blocks appear to have figurines carved on them; however, identification was not possible due to thick marine growth. There was a wall 2 m wide and 5 m in length running in an E-W direction and many fallen dressed stone blocks were found scattered around it. One of the most important finding of this location is a wall running more than 10 m, with a width of 2.5 m.

Apart from the above structures there were many more found in the vicinity which includes different types of structures, fallen walls (Fig. 10.9), dressed square and rectangular stone blocks, a square platform reached by stairs (Fig. 10.10), stone figurines, etc.

FIGURE 10.9
Underwater fallen wall of the structures at Mahabalipuram

Significance of Underwater Structures

The underwater investigations off Mahabalipuram revealed the presence of submerged fallen and scattered long walls, structures at various locations, large number of dressed stone blocks of rectangular and square type of building

FIGURE 10.10
Steps found in underwater leading to a platform at Mahabalipuram

materials at several places and perhaps a quarry. Many of them are man-made in nature. Sometimes the extension of these structures can be noticed at least a few hundred metres parallel to the shore at various depths between 5 to 10 m. A few continuous remains of walls have been noticed at all the places. Structures running sometime more than 25 m in length suggest that they are part of some building complex. At several places high platforms and steps leading to platforms are also noticed. It is, however, difficult to determine the layout for all sites as the structures have been badly damaged and are covered with a thick biological growth.

The plan of the structures indicates that this construction could be part of a big complex, as the huge stone blocks and several fallen walls were noticed *in situ* (Fig. 10.11). It appears that construction has been carried out on a raised platform with several walls and a floor made of granite blocks. An opening between two walls with steps has been noticed which probably may be an entrance to the complex from the southern side. The natural rock boulders noticed on the SW side are similar in shape and size to those found on land on the hill at Mahabalipuram. Similarly, the construction style observed in the structures underwater is identical to that observed on adjacent land. It was not possible, however, to verify the binding material of underwater structure due to huge marine growth and the damaged condition of structures. There were many wall sections observed at different locations including the 'quarry area' on a huge rock. The dressed stone blocks required for the construction were probably extracted from the quarry found near by. In fact, most of the religious or ceremonial constructions, including the present shore temple at Mahabalipuram, have been built with granite. The stone was extensively used for the construction of temples during Pallava rule.

FIGURE 10.11
Plan of a submerged structure of Mahabalipuram

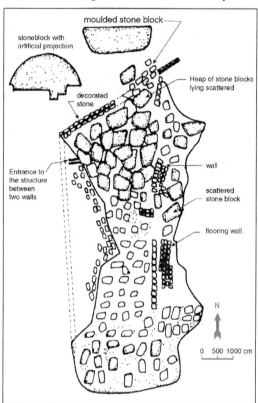

Dating of Underwater Structures

Ancient Tamil literature does not mention Mahabalipuram but the poem
Perumpanarrupadai, dedicated to Tondaiman Ilamtiraiyan, a king of
Kanchipuram, describes a port called Nirppeyarvu that could either be
identified with Kanchipuram or with Mamallapuram. The place has been
dated to the end of second century CE (Ramaswami 1980). Similarly, early
foreign travellers also do not mention this site, but the author of *Periplus of
the Erythrean Sea* (Schoff 1974) mentioned a port called Sopatma, which may
be identified with Sadras, situated about 20 km south of Mahabalipuram,
and which was a small port during the early centuries of the Common Era.
Ramaswami (1980) mentions that the Pallava King Mamalla set his workers
working on the rocks for the first time here in the seventh century CE; thereafter,
this place became known as Mamallapuram. The name Mahabalipuram,
therefore, is of late origin.

The archaeology of Mahabalipuram commences from the early centuries of the Christian Era as a few Roman and Chinese coins were found (Ramaswami 1980). Two Pallava coins bearing legends read as *Srihari* and *Srinidhi* have been reported in and around Mahabalipuram (Dayalan 1992). One of the inscriptions of Narasimha I mentions that he (Narasimha I) is the first person to introduce the construction of cave temples in granite. The zenith of human habitation around Mahabalipuram was during the Pallava dynasty, therefore, these temples may not be less than 1,500 years old.

Ramaswami (1980) refers to several accounts of the Europeans about the submergence of the city and the tradition that 'a large city and 5 magnificent pagodas have been swallowed up at this place by the sea'. Rabe (2001), Chambers (1869), Hancock (2002), Mohan and Rajamanickam (2002) believe that out of seven temples carved out of granite during eighth century CE only one has survived and the rest have submerged. However, based on the facts that the rock art sculpture was encouraged by the Pallavas at this place and most of them were made during that period, these structures may be 1,200-1,500 years old.

Mahabalipuram as an Ancient Port

On the western side of Mahabalipuram, about 1.5 km within the hill region known as Mallar, at Punjeri, just on the western bank of the Bunkingham canal, Early Historic and Medieval period habitations were discovered (Dayalan 1992). Probably, this Mallar area could have been the ancient harbour situated in the backwaters, an place for safe mooring. The boats might have entered either from Sadras, where there is a channel between the river and the sea, or by the existing canal 3 km south of Mahabalipuram.

Considering this evidence, it may be concluded that Mahabalipuram was a port before the Pallavas. It became the principal port during Pallava rule, from which voyages to Sri Lanka and Southeast Asia were started. The port functioned until the early British period, when there are mentions of British ships anchored at Mahabalipuram (Ramaswami 1980). With this evidence at hand it may be said that Mahabalipuram was an active port for 2,000 years.

Possible Causes of Submergence

Geological studies carried out in the water depths between 20 and 30 m in the central eastern continental shelf of India have indicated the evidences of submerged beaches and beach ridges formed during lower sea level times (Mohan Rao et al. 2001 & 1989; Mohan Rao and Rao 1994). Srinivasa Rao et al. (1990) obtained a radiocarbon date of 8,200 years BP for the carbonate sample recovered at 17 m water depth in the Nizamapatnam bay in the east coast of India. Banerjee and Sengupta (1992) have broadly identified two low stands, one at around 30 m and other at around 100 m depth based on anomalous sediment, geomorphic, palaeontological and geological criteria. However, the shelf of Tamil Nadu coast is believed to have undergone severe tectonic activities, because of which the sea level history varies from place to place.

It has been observed that many places that were along the shore some centuries ago are now a few miles inland. Coringa, near the mouth of the Godavari, Kaveripattinam in the Cauvery delta and Korkai on the coast of Tinnevelly, were all flourishing seaports about 1,000-2,000 years ago, but are now defunct due to siltation or erosion. Their present position some distance inland may be attributed to the gradual growth of deltas of the rivers at whose mouths they lie. Similarly on the Tinnevelly coast, in the Valinokkam bay, a submerged forest has been noticed, with numerous tree trunks of about 0.6 m diameter at the base, getting exposed at low tide over a bed of black clay containing oyster and other marine shells, a clear indication of earlier prevalence of marine environment (Krishnan 1968).

These references clearly indicate the violent fluctuations in the sea levels and shoreline in the last few thousand years and a clear trend of changing shorelines at places in Tamil Nadu.

Sea level and shoreline changes and the tectonic history of the region are very critical in determining the dates of the structures. The sea level has fluctuated between 2-6 m about 2-3 times during the mid-Holocene period on both the coasts of India (Merh 1987). The history of sea level fluctuation has been documented on the East Coast of India for the last 5,000 years (Banerjee 2000). Krishnan (1968), Mahapatra and Hariprasad (1999) also point out that the major and important factor affecting the Mahabalipuram coast is erosion: severe erosion at Kalpakkam, south of Mahabalipuram, due to long shore sediment drift, has also been reported (Mahapatra and Hariprasad 1999). A recent study suggests the rate of coastal erosion in and around Mahabalipuram is 55 cm/year (Ramiyan et al. 1997). If the same rate has prevailed since the last 1,500 years, then the shoreline at that time might have been around 800 m eastward and all the structures noticed underwater would have been on the land. If the rate of coastal erosion derived for Poompuhar, located 125 km to south, were applied for Mahabalipuram, then the structures in -5 to -8 m must have been on land 1,500 years ago (Sundaresh et al. 1997).

Interestingly, due to the recent construction of semi-circular breakwater, the shoreline over a stretch of 3 km north of the Shore Temple is experiencing accelerated erosion (Subramanyam & Selvam 2001). There is evidence of tectonic activity around Mahabalipuram during the early Quaternary period (Murthy et al. 1995). However, there is no evidence of tectonic activity on the coast during the past 1,200 years, as the Shore Temple has not been affected (Mohapatra and Prasad 1999).

From the above discussions, it can be concluded that coastal erosion has played a major role in the submergence of these structures and sea level changes might have played a contributory role.

The underwater structures, especially the long walls having 2 to 3 courses, the scattered dressed stone blocks of various sizes, and the stones with projections considered to be man-made may well be the remains of huge complexes or the temples of the so-called 'Seven pagodas'. As the Pallavas encouraged temple architecture at Mahabalipuram during the eighth century, these structures may be assigned to the same period. Mahabalipuram has served as a port during the Pallava period. Part of earlier Mahabalipuram town may have been submerged in the sea. Further investigations, however, are required to fully understand the nature of these submerged structures and their dates.

CONCLUSION

Poompuhar and Mahabalipuram flourished as port towns and led maritime activities with Rome, China, Sri Lanka and South East Asia. The potsherds of Rouletted ware, the Chola coins, Brahmi inscribed artefacts were also found in Southeast Asian countries and were probably carried through Poompuhar, from which similar coins were reported. Glass beads were also exported to Southeast Asia during the early historical period from Poompuhar through the Kaveripattinam ports, as the Manigramam was located in the vicinity. The maritime archaeology evidence is further confirmed by the findings at Kalakattu. The gopurams of temples of Kampong Prea of eighth century CE and Prasat Bayang of Cambodia are said to closely resemble the Mamallapuram temples. The early sculptures of Cambodia of the ninth century also resemble Pallava sculptures at Mamallapuram (Nagaswamy 2007). Based on all this evidence, it is clear that cultural expansion through maritime trade started during the early historical period, if not earlier.

The marine archaeological exploration off Poompuhar and Mahabalipuram brought to light several underwater remains and the traditions mentioning the submergence of these towns have been partially confirmed.

ACKNOWLEDGEMENTS

The authors are grateful to the Director, NIO for his support and encouragement. Thanks are also due to Dr K.H. Vora for suggestions and critically reviewing the manuscript, to Dr Sila Tripati, Shri S.N. Bandodker, Shri S.B. Chitari for their help in fieldwork and to Dr Mohan Rao and Shri Prem Kumar for their bathymetric study. And finally to Shri R. Uchil for line drawings. This is the NIO contribution number 4576.

REFERENCES

Athiyaman, N., 1999, 'Two Wharves at Poompuhar: A Technical Study', paper presented at Second International Conference on Marine Archaeology, held at Thane, 8-10 January 1999.

Banerjee, P.K., 2000, 'Holocene and Late Pleistoene Relative Sea Level Fluctuations Along the East Coast of India', *Marine Geology*, 167, 243-60.

Banerjee, A. and R. Sengupta, 1992, *Evidences of Law Stands on the Continental Shelf of East Coast of India*, in Recent Geoscintific Studies in the Bay of Bengal and Andaman Sea, special Publication of Geological Survey of India, Pub. No. 29, 163-70.

Bird, E.C.F., 1984, *Coasts: An Introduction to Coastal Geomorphology*, 3rd edn., Oxford: Basil Blackwell.

Carr, M.W., 1869, *The Seven Pagodas*, Madras: Foster Press. Reprinted New Delhi: Asian Educational Services, 1999.

Chambers, W., 1869, 'Some Account of the Sculptures and Ruins at Mavelipuram, a Place a Few Miles North of Sadras, and Known to Seamen by Name of the Seven Pagodas', in *The Seven Pagodas*, ed. M.W. Carr, New Delhi: Asian Educational Services, pp. 1–29.

Dayalan, D., 1992, *Punjeri: A Pallava Sea Port Near Mamallapuram*, ed. Natana Kashinathan, Seminar on Marine Archaeology, State Department of Archaeology, Madras, 52-56.

Hancock, Graham, 2002, *Underworld: The Flooded Kings of the Ice Age*, London: Penguin Books.

Krishnan, M.S., 1968, *Geology of India and Burma,* 5th edn., Madras: Higginbotham.

Mahapatra, S.P. and M. Hariprasad, 1999, 'Shoreline Changes and Their Impact on the Archaeological Structures at Mahabalipuram', *Gondwana Goel Magazone*, Spl. vol. 4, 225-33.

Mahapatra, S.P. and M. Hariprasad, 2002, 'Historical Sea Level Changes in Relation to Archaeological Structures on the East Coast of India', Proccedings of *Four Decades of Marine Geosciences in India: A Retrospect*, Special Publication No. 74, Kolkata: Geological Survey of India, 132-36.

Merh, S.S., 1987, 'Quaternary Sea Level Changes: The Present Status vis-a-vis Record Along Coast of India', *Indian Journal of Earth Science*, vol. 14 (3-4), 235-51.

Mohan, P.M. and Victor Rajamanickam, 2002, 'Importance of Studies on the Recent Sea Level Changes in the Southern Part of East Coast of India', in *Proceedings of Four Decades of Marine Geosciences in India – A Restrospect*, Special Publication No. 74, Kolkata: GSI, pp. 77-79.

Mohan Rao, K. and T.C.S. Rao, 1994, 'Holocene Sea Level of Visakhapattanam Shelf, East Coast of India', *Journal of Geological Society of India*, vol. 44, 685-89.

Mohan Rao, K., G.V. Rajamanickam and T.C.S. Rao, 1989, 'Holocene Marine Transgression as Interpreted from Bathymetry and Sand Grain Size Parameters off Gopalpur', *Proc. Ind. Acad.Sci*, 98, 59-67.

Mohan Rao, K., K.S.R. Murthy, N.P.C. Reddy, A.S. Subrahmanyam, S. Lakshminarayana, M.M.M. Rao, KVLNS Sarma, M.K. Premkumar, A. Sree and M. Bapuji, 2001, 'Submerged Beach Ridge Lineation and Associated Sedentary Fauna in the Inner Shelf of Gopalpur Coast', Orissa, Bay of Bengal, *Current Science*, 81(7), pp. 827-33.

Murthy, K.S.R., K. Venkataswarulu, and T.C.S. Rao, 1995, 'Basement Structures Beneath the Inner Shelf off Mahabalipuram to Palar River, East Coast of India', *Indian Journal of Marine Science*, 24 (2), 223-24.

Nagaswamy, R., 2007, 'Migration if Folk and Classical Tradition from South India to Southeast Asia', paper presented at the conference on Early Indian Influences in Southeast Asia: Reflections on Cross-Cultural Movements, 21-23 November 2007 at Singapore.

NIO Tech. Report, 1993, 'Marine Archaeological Explorations in Poompuhar Waters', National Institute of Oceanography, Goa.

——, 1995, 'Marine Archaeological Explorations in Poompuhar Waters', National Institute of Oceanography, Goa, No. NIO/SP/13/95

——, 1997, 'Marine Archaeological Explorations in Poompuhar Waters', National Institute of Oceanography, Goa, No. NIO/SP/13/97

——, 2003, 'Underwater Explorations of Poompuhar and Mahabalipuram, Tamil Nadu', Goa, No. NIO/SP-2/2003.

Rabe, M., 2001, *The Great Penance at Mamallapuram*, Chennai: Institute of Asian Studies.

Ramaiyan, M., E. Krishna Prasad and P.K. Suresh, 1997, 'Shoreline oscillation of Tamil Nadu Coast', in *Proceedings of Second Indian National Conference of Harbour and Ocean Engineering (INCHOE - 97)*.

Ramaswami, N.S., 1980, *Mamallapuram: An Annotated Bibliography*, Madras: New Era Publications.

——, 1989, *2000 Years of Mamallapuram*, New Delhi: Navrang.

Rao, S.R., 1987, *Progress and Prospects of Marine Archaeology in India*, Goa: National Institute of Oceanography.

——, 1991a, 'Marine Archaeological Explorations of Tranquebar-Poompuhar Region on Tamil Nadu Coast', *Journal of Marine Archaeology*, 2, 5-20.

——, 1991b, 'Underwater exploration of submerged towns near Tranquebar Tamil Nadu', *Recent Advances in Marine Archaeology*, 60-64.

Rao, T.C.S., 1991c, 'Marine Archaeological Surveys of Kaveripattinam for Archaeological investigation', *Journal of Marine Archaeology*, 2, 21-31.

——, 1992, 'Marine Geophysical Surveys of Kaveripattinam for Archaeological Investigations', *Seminar on Marine Archaeology*, ed. Natana Kashinathan, Madras: State Department of Archaeology, 17-22.

Rao, S.R., T.C.S. Rao, A.S. Gaur, S. Tripati, Sundaresh and P. Gudigar, 1995-96, 'Underwater Explorations of Poompuhar', *Journal of Marine Archaeology*, NIO Goa, 5-6, 7-22.

Schoff, W.H., 1974, *The Periplus of the Erythrean Sea: Travel and Trade in the Indian Ocean*, Delhi: Oriental Books.

Srinivasa Rao, P., G. Krishna Rao, N.V.N. Durgaprasada Rao, and A.S.R. Swamy, 1990, 'Sedimentation and Sea Level Variations in Nizamapatnam Bay, East Coast of India', *Indian Journal of Marine Sciences*, 19, 261-64.

Subramanyam, K.S. and T.A. Selvan, 2001, *Geology of Tamil Nadu and Pondicherry*, Bangalore: Geological Society of India.

Sundaresh, A.S. Gaur, R.R. Nair, 1997, 'Our Threatened Archaeological Heritage: A Case Study from Tamilnadu Coast', *Current Science 73* (7): 593-98.

Vora, K.H., 1993, *Marine Archaeological Explorations off Poompuhar*, A Technical Report of National Institute of Oceanography, Goa.

——, 1987, 'A Note on the Geophysical Explorations for Marine Archaeology of Tamil Nadu Coast, India', *International Journal of Nautical Archaeology*, 16(1), 159-64.

PART II
Localisation in Southeast Asia

11

Tamil Merchants and the Hindu-Buddhist Diaspora in Early Southeast Asia

John Guy

It is generally accepted that the dissemination of Hindu-Buddhist beliefs and ritual practises in first millennium Southeast Asia were largely the result of initiatives of local rulers to recruit Brahman priests and Buddhist monks able to secure their political and personal welfare. Yet it remains equally self-evident that the medium of transmission of both an awareness of Indian culture, and of its agents and propagators, were the merchant vessels which linked the Indian Ocean diaspora. It follows that a study of early traces of Indian merchant activity in the region should provide clues to the early entry of Indic religious systems into the emerging states and kingdoms of Southeast Asia.

The legacy of these early contacts and engagements are indicated by the scattering of Indic script stone stele inscriptions, both royal and mercantile, and by the regional distribution of the earliest Indic religious imagery, imported and locally produced. The vast majority of the inscriptions identify the patron, usually a local ruler who had assumed the trappings of Hindu culture, often including obeisance to Shiva or Vishnu and a Sanskritised honorific title and name-form. Religious imagery is, after the inscriptions, our single most important source of knowledge of the religious allegiances assumed by these rulers and has, through the study of style and iconography, the potential to clarify the regional origins of the propagators from the subcontinent (Figs. 11.1 and 11.2).

One of the earliest examples of a local ruler with clear Hindu religious affiliations is known from the Purnavarman inscription. This rock-cut inscription was located in a river-bed at Ciaruteun, near Bogor, West Java,

FIGURE 11.1
Ivory comb, a probable Indian import from Andhra Pradesh,
c. third-fourth centuries, excavated at Chansen, Lopburi, Thailand

FIGURE 11.2
Gaja-Laksmi, terracotta, probable Indian import, excavated at
Chansen, Lopburi, Thailand (Photo: J. Guy 1998)

and dedicated by a local ruler titled Purnavarman, who declared himself as the famous king of Tarumanagara [kingdom] and a devotee of Vishnu, and represented himself by a pair of footprints (*pada*), the same device used to evoke a divine presence (Fig. 11.3).[1] This Sanskrit inscription is written in a cursive Tamil Grantha script in a style associated with the period, c. 450. The ruler, presumed to be local, has adopted an Indic name-form, and consistent with most ruler-names appearing in Sanskrit inscriptions of this early period,

FIGURE 11.3
Rock-cut inscription of King Purnavarman, *c.* 450, *in-situ* Ciaruteun River,
near Bogor, West Java (Photo: Indonesian Archaeological Service)

has the south Indian word-ending 'varman', a convention associated with the
Pallava-clan of Tamil Nadu.

This rock-cut inscription prominently displays, in the midst of the
expressive cursive letters, a *Vishnupada*, the 'sacred footprint' device used in
early South Asian religions to evoke a deity's presence. This is the earliest
representation of *pada* in Southeast Asia. This inscription and footprint,
which is integral to the inscription's meaning, are remarkable for they are the
earliest instance of a Southeast Asian ruler invoking not only the authority of
an Indic deity, but seemingly personally identifying himself with that god –
we are told that the footprints are those of the ruler King Purnavarman, whilst
simultaneously being identified as those of Vishnu. Through this inscription
Purnavarman asserted his allegiance to, and a close personal identification
with, Vishnu, so both evoking and sharing in his divine authority. This is
the language of the Puranas, invoked by a new convert to the concept of
Indian kingship. Vishnu's *avatar* as the revered ruler Rama, a role model of
just kingship, is often represented by footprints, specifically to denote Rama's
temporary absence from the throne of Ayutthaya. Such *pada* can therefore
have royal as well as divine associations, and this was understandably a
popular insignia for royal devotees to employ, intended to invoke the dual
meanings. Further, Purnavarman's inscription describes the king as 'capable of
destroying his enemies but beneficent to loyal princes'. The threatening tone
is in keeping with other early Sanskrit inscriptions from western Indonesia,
the so-called 'curse inscriptions', which invoke dark magic against those who
display disloyalty to a ruler. The power of these magic spells and invocations
has strong tantric overtones. Similar language is employed at the naga-stele
inscription from Telaga Batu, Palembang, dated to the late seventh century,
where subjects are commanded to 'drink the curse' which would be activated
by acts of disloyalty (Fig. 11.4).[2]

The earliest Indic inscriptions in Southeast Asia are almost certainly the
seven steles from Kutei, eastern Borneo, attributed on palaeographic grounds
to the late fourth century (Fig. 11.5).[3] They were installed by a local ruler

FIGURE 11.4
Telaga Batu stele, seventh century, Palembang, South Sumatra,
Nasional Museum, Jakarta

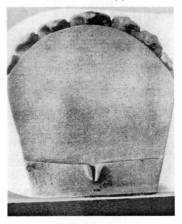

FIGURE 11.5
Yupa **post installed by King Mulavarman, late fourth century,**
Kutei, eastern Kalimantan. Nasional Museum, Jakarta

who titled himself Mulavarman. Highly significantly, they record animal sacrifice and gift-giving rituals performed by Brahmans at a designated site, on behalf of the king. It is remarkable that here we have – from the outset of an Indic written record in Southeast Asia – clear evidence of Brahmanic ritual activities and, by implication, the presence of Indian Brahman priests in a 'court context'. The simultaneous appearance of Sanskrit and Brahmans was a necessary coincidence. The inscriptions explicitly refer to these steles as *yupa*, sacrificial posts employed in Vedic animal sacrifice, and to the existence of designated sacred space where these rituals were performed; the latter may be presumed to be of a temporary nature, as Vedic ritual dictate, perhaps a temporary placement of fired bricks. According to Brahmanic prescriptions, *yupa* posts should be wooden, and were only rarely rendered in stone as a commemorative record of the enactment of a highly significant ritual sacrifice. In the archaeological records of early northern India up to this period only around four such stone posts are known, two from Kushana Mathura.[4] One of these carries an inscription recording the event it commemorates together with a depiction, carved into the trunk of the post, of the rope used to secure the sacrificial animal. It is curious that the Kutei examples are not post-like, but rather rough-hewn monoliths bearing relatively refined inscriptions in a box-head style Grantha script. How they related to sacrifice in Kutei is unknown.

These epigraphs are the earliest record of a local ruler assuming the trappings of Hindu kingship in insular Southeast Asia. The development of Kutei from a fiefdom to a small 'Indic' kingdom was in all probability linked to contacts with Indian merchants seeking the natural wealth of the region. That the kingdom grew in importance, sustained by the export of Borneo's natural riches, is witnessed by the discovery of a series of Hindu stone sculptures, first reported in 1907 and the more recent discovery of a series of high quality bronze Buddhist images, the latter in a Central Javanese style and therefore attributable to the late first millennium.[5] The latter images could be imports from the metropolitan centre of Java, but another possibility should also be considered, that Kutei, with its abundance of copper and gold, served not only as a source of raw materials for Java's religious institutions, but may have been a production centre.

This hypothesis is supported by two new forms of evidence; first, the reporting by Edwards McKinnon of quantities of discarded bronze images and metal scrap artefacts found in the Kutei region some years ago.[6] This included a Buddhist Bodhisattva image of a type known from Javanese finds.[7] Secondly, recent evidence from two shipwrecked cargoes excavated in the Java Sea, known as the Intan and Cirebon cargoes, supports the notion of multiple production nodes in the 'Sailendra world', centres close to the sources of raw materials.[8] These vessels appear, on the balance of evidence, to have been sailing from Sumatra to Java with international cargoes that included consignments of metal ingots, 'scrap' copper alloy, *and* cast bronze religious images and ritual objects. Kutei could have assumed a similar role in the supply of religious imagery to Java. This raises the possibility that a wealthy metropolitan centre like Java was being supplied from its periphery with not only the raw materials for the manufacture of religious paraphernalia, but also with actual finished images and ritual objects made in the client's designated style.

Locating Tamils in Southeast Asia

Tamils appear to have been dominant amongst the earliest Indian traders to operate in insular Southeast Asia, supported by successive kingdoms in southern India. This is supported both by the nature of the earliest Indic inscriptions found which, as noted, consistently exhibit south Indian affiliations, and by the distribution of these inscriptions. They chronicle the centres of commercial activity and by implication the trade routes – indeed they are one of the few sources for an understanding of these early trade routes and their commercial nodes. The distribution of these inscriptions thus may be accepted as faithfully mirroring the centres of most intensive mercantile contact.

This model would suggest that the earliest sustained contact between India and Southeast Asia took place at riverine coastal sites, as witnessed by the fourth to seventh centuries inscriptions of Java, Borneo, Sumatra, the Malay peninsula and coastal Vietnam. The religious activity is predominantly Hindu but also, especially in the Srivijayan territories of southern Sumatra, Buddhist.[9] The early inscriptions in Southeast Asia have been consistently located at coastal sites served by riverine systems which allowed access to the commercial riches of the hinterlands whilst linking them to the international exchange system. These locales must have been important to both intra-regional trading and to the long-distance trade which served to link India and China through Southeast Asia.

Inscriptions from a variety of sources make clear that Tamil participation in long distance trade to Southeast Asia and beyond was sustained over most part of the historical period, beginning in the early centuries CE. The goldsmith's touchstone from Wat Klong Thom, Krabi province, peninsular Thailand, is the earliest Tamil inscription; it is written in Tamil Brahmi script of the third or fourth centuries CE (Fig. 11.6). The archaeological work currently being done on the Thai peninsula, at Khao Sam Kheo in Champhun province on east coast and the finds at Takuapa on the west coast, indicate levels of processing and production which went beyond the activities of traders alone.[10] The excavations at Khao Sam Kheo indicate the extent to which early trading settlements undertook the processing of raw materials sourced in the region, such as gold, and the fabrication of imported materials such as glass into artefacts for re-sale.

A number of Sanskrit inscriptions appear in mainland Southeast Asia from the same period, the earliest being the Vo Canh stele, found near the coastal city of Nha Trang, central Vietnam in Cham territory. The Vo Canh

FIGURE 11.6
Goldsmith's touchstone from Wat Klong Thom, Krabi province, peninsular
Thailand, with the earliest Tamil inscription in Southeast Asia, third or fourth
century. Phra Kru Athon Sangarakit Museum, Khuan Luk Pat, Klong Thom district
(Photo courtesy: Tsugisato Omura)

stele, close in date to the Kutei *yupa* steles but written in a cruder Sanskrit,
signals the importance of the early trading states that were emerging along the
India-China sea route. Three additional inscriptions from My Son, a major
religious centre from the early northern Cham kingdoms, are all associated
with the oldest recorded Cham ruler, Bhadravarman I, who employed the
honorific title 'Dharmamaharaja'. They are attributed to *c.* CE 400, and have
been interpreted as referring to sacrifices to Shiva as Bhadesvara.

A little later in date – probably mid-fifth century – is the highly important
Devanika inscription at Champasak, located on the Mekong River in southern
Laos, the earliest Sanskrit inscription belonging to the Chenla Kingdom
and so representing the beginning of the Khmer epigraphic record. Recent
investigations of this stele have revealed that it is inscribed on a tripartite
pillar of square, octagonal and round section; that is, a *linga*-form stele, the
earliest occurrence of an inscribed *linga* in early Southeast Asian epigraphy.[11]

Lands of Gold

Indian merchants were drawn to Southeast Asia by its legendary natural
wealth, of spices, resins and other forest products, and by its precious metals,
especially gold. They were also attracted to the region because it served as the
gateway to trade with China. As the maritime routes were mastered, so trade
between southern India and China expanded. Chinese silk was imported
at Pompuhar in the early centuries CE, according to the *Shiappadikaram*,[12]
probably by Tamil merchants operating via entrepôts in the Malay peninsula.
Southeast Asia featured early in Indian literature as an important source of
gold, especially in Buddhist Jataka stories. Therein the region is identified by

the title *Suvarnadvipa* (Island of Gold) and *Suvarnabhumi* (Land of Gold).
Western Indonesia in particular yielded a steady supply of gravel and river-
borne alluvial gold; Sumatra, Kalimantan and the peninsula all played a role
in this trade. Evidence of gold working activity in Sumatra and the Malay
peninsula in particular confirm that Tamils were active in this process: the
goldsmith's touchstone newly deciphered inscription found at one of the
earliest identified entrepôts of peninsular Thailand, Wat Khlong Thom,
indicates it was the property of a Tamilian identifying himself as 'Perum
patan' [the great goldsmith].[13]

The ongoing link between Tamil merchants, gold trade and a religious
presence is further underscored by the important discoveries at Takuapa,
on the west coast of the Malay peninsula, of an early ninth-century Tamil
inscription and three large-scale stone Hindu sculptures in the Pallava style
(Fig. 11.7). The sculptures are remarkable for their iconographic and stylistic
completeness and for their scale, the principal male figure standing at over
2 m. These monumental icons could only have been completed under
Brahmanical direction, though we only speculate as to the ethnicity of the
artisans responsible. Given the scale of these sculptures, we may reasonably
assume that a temple or shrine existed to house them, though no traces have
been recorded of a structure which seems adequate to this purpose. The
Takuapa inscription provides some important clues on this question: it is
dedicated to the foundation of a new tank, named as *Sri Avani naranam*,
which Nilakanta Sastri, who published his revised translation in 1949, links
to the reign of the Pallava king Nandivarman III (r. 826-50).[14] The presence
of a tank clearly implies the pre-existence of a temple or shrine, as a tank is
integral to the ritual life of a Hindu temple, essential for the performance of
purification activities. If the temple was also new, it would undoubtedly have
been mentioned in the inscription, so we may assume a temple or shrine of
some sort predated the tank inscription.

FIGURE 11.7
The Pra Narai Hindu sculptures, mid-ninth century, *in situ*, Takuapa, Thai
Peninsula. Photograph mid-twentieth century (after Quaritch Wales, 1976)

The inscription further states that this project was the work of the members of three Indian merchant guilds, two of whose names have been deciphered: the *manigri ramattar* and the *sena mugattar*. The *mani giraman* was one of the most prominent itinerant merchant organisations whose activities are well recorded in Tamil Nadu and Kerala, and inscriptions indicate that they were most active from the ninth to fourteenth centuries.[15] The name *sena mugattar* does not appear in Indian sources but is known in Javanese inscriptions where it refers to employees of a guild, possibly the militia/armed guards (Tamil: *viran kodiyar*) who were employed to protect the guild member's godowns and caravans. Bronze weapons excavated in Sumatra have been identified as south Indian in type, and may be associated with such merchant militia.[16]

A clue as to the activities of the Tamil residents of Takuapa is found in the form of traces of processed gold in the soil, evidence that this location had served as a gold working centre. Taken together with the goldsmith's 'anvil' found at Krabi, we get an emerging picture of the nature of the Indian mercantile presence, extending beyond sourcing of materials to engaging in their processing and refinement. The Takuapa inscription and its implied Hindu activity together with the style of the associated statuary relate this phase of the site to the ninth century. When the gold working sites were active is less clear.

A Tamil settlement in Southeast Asia at a place named 'Takola' is confirmed as early as the third century CE by a Buddhist canonical text, the *Mahanidessa*. This refers to trade with 'Takola', a place of riches in Suvarnadvipa, which may correspond with Takuapa. Irrespective of whether this identification is correct – other sites have a claim to this title – the text confirms the continuity of Tamil commercial activity in the Thai peninsula over most of the first millennium. It is interesting that the earliest reference is in a Buddhist source, but that much of the archaeological evidence, especially from the second half of the millennium, is of Hindu activity. This pattern is mirrored elsewhere, as seen in the Indian settlements in the riverine sites of the Bujang valley, Kedah, on the west coast of the Malayan peninsula.

Another Tamil inscription, belonging to the height of the Chola period – the eleventh century – was recorded from Lobu Tua, Barus, on the west coast of Sumatra. This is a region rich in camphor, benzoin and alluvial gold. It was dedicated in February-March 1088, and records the activities of the famous Indian merchant guild the *ainurruvar*, whose members resident at Barus committed to a charitable fund for the benefit of members and their families ('our sons'). The inscription makes clear that it is enforceable by the withdrawal of trading rights should anyone fail to pay the *anchutuntayam* [proportion of revenue] fee in gold. This right to trade is described as having the privilege to 'step on the spread cloth'.[17] A further three Tamil inscriptions have been reported from Sumatra, one from Aceh, one from Barus and one from an inland site in Minangkabau province, the latter indicating that Tamil traders both penetrated and settled in the hinterland as well as at coastal centres.

South Indian communities, including communities of Brahmans, settled in peninsular Thailand also left an inscriptional record. A Sanskrit inscription in Grantha script is recorded from Wat Mahaeyong, Nakhon Si Thammarat, and now displayed in the National Museum, Bangkok. George Coedès attributed it to the seventh century and provided a translation which indicates a Buddhist affiliation, invoking all to uphold the Dharma, dissolve desire and passion, and to be impartial to happiness and grief.[18] A rock-cut inscription at Chong Koi, Nakhon Si Thammarat province, identifies the existence of a community of Saivite Brahmans and extols them to both practise the rituals correctly and to live harmoniously with their host community.[19]

Whilst Brahmanical ritual and its accoutrements came to be associated with kingship and statecraft in early Southeast Asia, the Buddhist presence appears to be more linked to commerce. Monumental stupa buildings were underway in mainland and peninsular Southeast Asia in the early centuries CE; the great stupas at Sri Ksetra and Nakhom Pathom bear witness to this, as do the foundations of other stupas dating to the early centuries CE at Beikthano and other Pyu sites.[20] These great foundations, no doubt understood in their day to house Buddha relics, were commemorated on miniature clay devotional icons and meditation plaques (Fig. 11.8).

Among the earliest Buddhist inscriptions in Southeast Asia are two steles found in the Lembah Bujang valley area of Kedah (Fig. 11.9). Both steles follow the same form: an engraving of a stupa with Buddhist creed in Sanskrit around the border. Epigraphically the south Indian Grantha script is datable to around CE 450-500. The inscription found at Seberang Perai is unique amongst finds of this kind in that it names the donor. He is identified as 'the great sea-captain Buddhagupta', 'a resident of Raktamrittika', possibly a

FIGURE 11.8
Votive tablet depicting a stupa, Pyu, c. eighth century,
probably Sri Ksetra, Prome, Burma

FIGURE 11.9
Buddhist commemorative stele, c. sixth century, Bujang valley, Kedah, Malaysia

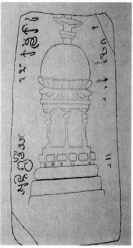

Sanskrit form of the Malay place name 'Tanah Merah', meaning 'Red Earth', presumably another entrepôt located in the Malay peninsula.[21] The remaining text is of Buddhist creed and has an appeal that 'He and his fellow travellers by all means … be successful in their voyage'. The stele was found by Col. James Low in the 1840s near the Muda River, in Kedah close to what he described as the ruins of a Buddhist temple. Along this same river valley the remains of a number of Hindu shrines and temples have been excavated and restored, identifying the valley as a major first millennium entrepôt, patronised by Indian merchants, amongst others.[22] Traces of Hindu-Buddhist religious imagery have been recovered, along with late Tang and Five Dynasties Chinese ceramics, and glassware from the Islamic Middle East.

The excavated trade goods in the Bujang valley mirror, in part, the Belitung shipwreck cargo recently discovered in the Java Sea.[23] It is an early ninth century vessel and has been identified as a *dhow* built in the Arab-shipbuilding tradition, built of African hardwoods. Judging from its cargo, it was active in the China-Persian Gulf trade.[24] It is significant that this is the first Arab *dhow* to be identified in Southeast Asian waters.[25] By the time of its sailing, entrepôts in south-east Sumatra had emerged to compete with Kedah, most notably Srivijaya, centred in the Musi River estuary in the vicinity of Palembang.

The Tamil Presence in China

As early as CE 510, a foreign trading mission to the Chinese court identified as Indian, is described in the Tang annals. By the mid-eighth century the

Indian presence in Guangzhou had expanded to the extent that they supported three temples, complete with resident Brahman priests.[26] In CE 750 the Buddhist monk Kanshin recorded that on the river at Guangzhou 'There are merchantmen [ocean-going ships] belonging to the *Bolomen* [Indians], the *Posi* [Persians] and the *Kunlun* [Malays] ... of which it is difficult to determine the number.' It continues to explain that there are 'three monasteries of the *Bolomen* [Indians] where Brahmans reside'.[27] These Hindu religious establishments must have existed alongside places of worship for other expatriate communities, notably Buddhist shrines and monasteries, and mosques for the Arab-Persian traders (and for an emerging indigenous Chinese Muslim community).

The pervasive presence of Indian priests and monks in court and temple life in Southeast Asia and, by extension in the expatriate communities in south China, is clear from the archaeological evidence of Hindu temples and sculptures in Quanzhou.[28] According to Zhao Rugua's *Zhufanzhi* (Description of Barbarian Peoples), in the Yongxi period (984-88) of the Northern Song a Buddhist monk from India (Tianzhu) purchased land in the southern suburbs of Quanzhou for the purpose of building a Buddhist shrine. This structure still existed at the time that Zhao Rugua was writing in the early thirteenth century.[29] Funds were presumably provided by both the Indian merchant community and Chinese Buddhists, but the Song administration also provided tracts of land for the use of foreign communities, to create the 'foreign quarters' (*fanfang*). These communities acquired a degree of legal autonomy, with the post of *Shahbandar* (Persian: harbourmaster) to act as the legal intermediary between the foreign communities and the Chinese authorities.

The beginning of the eleventh century saw the expansion of the Cholamandala through a combination of military conquest and commercial acumen. The commercial importance of long distance trade to the Cholas was acknowledged in the reign of Rajendrachola (1012-44), with the sending in 1015 of the first diplomatic mission of the Chola period to China. These missions continued on an irregular basis until the close of the thirteenth century. The Chinese presence in Tamil Nadu was acknowledged by the royal endowment of a Buddhist temple at Nagapattinam. A place of Chinese worship appears to have existed there since the reign of the Pallava king Narasimhavarman II, but the structure known as the 'Chinese Pagoda' was probably constructed under Chola patronage in the early thirteenth century (Fig. 11.10). According to the fourteenth-century writer on Chinese overseas trade Wang Dayuan, it was built in 1267 to encourage the visits of Chinese merchants.

The Chola missions were effectively in competition with those from Srivijaya, in all likelihood the principal reason for the punishing raids sent

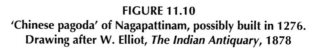

FIGURE 11.10
'Chinese pagoda' of Nagapattinam, possibly built in 1276.
Drawing after W. Elliot, *The Indian Antiquary*, 1878

by the Cholas in 1026 and 1068. The 'kingdom of Sanfoqi' (Srivijaya) is recorded in the famous Canton inscription of 1079 as funding the renovation and maintenance of several Buddhist temples in that port-city.[30] Srivijaya may be assumed to have still been under a degree of Chola suzerainty at this time, and if this was the case, then this inscription may be interpreted as an attempt by merchant delegations under Chola control to enhance the standing of their expatriate community in Guangzhou. The presence of south Indian merchants belonging to the Chola-mandala was in turn actively encouraged by the Song administration

Archaeological evidence exists of Chola-period south Indian trading community settlements at intermediate locations in the Thai-Malay peninsula. The scale of the ongoing role of Tamil merchants in this period is confirmed by several important discoveries. A dated Tamil inscription preserved in the Buddhist temple of Wat Boroma That, Nakhon Si Thammarat, and first translated and published by Noboru Karashima records the donation (*brahmadeya*) by a named individual, Danma Senapati, probably a merchant, of funds to endow a Hindu temple and/or community of *brahmanas* in three shares.[31] Importantly, a site north of Nakhon Si Thammarat has yielded architectural elements from a substantial Hindu temple in the late Chola style (Fig. 11.11). Architectural fragments, including a capital with inverted pendant lotus bud designs, are now displayed in the National Museum at Nakhon Si Thammarat. First reported by Quaritch Wales in the 1930s, this site has not, to my knowledge, been fully investigated. Possible associations between the Wat Boroma That inscription and these architectural fragments warrants close examination and in all probability share a common ancestry. The inscription is cyclically dated, most probably to 1258 or 1265.

FIGURE 11.11
Pillar capital, late Chola style, from Nakhon Si Thammarat, National Museum,
Nakhon Si Thammarat (Photo: after Quaritch Wales, 1976)

The second site to yield evidence of Chola-period temples in Southeast Asia is the Lembah Bujang, the riverine valley site in Kedah described earlier, which has a continuous archaeological record of international entrepôt trade from at least the sixth century. The recovery of a Chola-period balustrade incorporating a lion design makes clear that south Indian merchant community activity continued in the valley well into the Chola period (Fig. 11.12).

Quanzhou

The most spectacular indicator of Tamil merchant activity outside India in the Chola period is the remains of Hindu temple, or temples, at the southern Chinese port-city of Quanzhou, Fujian, which I have discussed at length elsewhere.[32] Like the contemporary sites in Southeast Asia, the Hindu temple(s) at Quanzhou had all but disappeared from the city landscape by

FIGURE 11.12
Balustrade section, late Chola period, from Lembah Bujang, Kedah.
Site Museum, Lembah Bujang (Photo: J. Guy, 2001)

the Ming period. This became clear from 1940 when the city wall – a Ming construction – was demolished during the Sino-Japanese war, and a large quantity of 'Hindu relics' and other foreign religious stone artefacts, were recovered from the core of the wall, where these cut granite stones had been used as filler.[33]

The Tamil identity of a Hindu temple is confirmed by an inscription also discovered in association with these architectural remains (Fig. 11.13). It consists of five lines of Tamil and a final line in Chinese. It is dated to April (month of Chittirai) in the Saka era 1203, equivalent to CE 1281. The dedication is to Shiva (Hara), and the donor identifies himself as Sambandh Perumal, but also uses an honorific name 'Tava-chchakka-tavar-ttigal', perhaps a devotee of the Saiva saint [Sambandar], which suggests he may be a native of Kumbakonam, in the Tanjavur district of Tamil Nadu. Other fragments of Hindu architecture have been found integrated into the fabric of domestic dwellings in the southern district of Quanzhou, particularly in the vicinity of the Tonghuai city-gate where we may therefore assume the temple was located. The site itself has disappeared beneath urban expansion.

The most complete series of architectural elements to be preserved *in situ* was two pillars and a series of basement reliefs integrated in a Ming-period renovation of the Kaiyuan temple (Fig. 11.14). This is a remarkable instance of cultural syncretism, in which alien architectural elements – late Chola style pillars decorated with cartouche panels depicting scenes from Hindu mythology and basement stones with lotus petal mouldings and decorated with lions – are integrated into the fabric of a Chinese Ming-style Buddhist temple. Turning briefly to the subject matter of the Hindu reliefs, they concern themselves with themes associated both with Shiva and Vishnu. Those scenes depicted on the pillars are exclusively devoted to Vishnu, both as supreme Lord enthroned with his consorts Sri Devi and Bhu Devi, and in some of his more popular avatars (manifestations/appearances), notably as Narasimha, as the infant and youthful Krishna, and Krishna subduing the *naga* Kaliya.

FIGURE 11.13
Tamil inscription, from an untraced Hindu temple, Quanzhou, dated 1281.
Xiamen University Museum of Anthropology, Xiamen

FIGURE 11.14
Kaiyuan temple, Ming-period renovation, incorporating Hindu pillars from a lost
thirteenth-century temple, Quanzhou (Photo: J. Guy, 1984)

Only one medallion depicts Shiva, as the wandering mendicant. In addition, one freestanding sculptural image of Vishnu survives, an unfinished image over 1 m in height.

The relatively lifeless rendering of these most dynamic and gracious subjects makes clear the nature of manufacture at the Hindu temple. It is obvious that the sculptures are not the work of Indian artisans, but of stonemasons trained in the Chinese tradition. Such is the complexity of Indian temple building that it must be assumed that an Indian architect versed in the *sastric* traditions was responsible for directing their construction. Such a skilled *sthapati* must have been recruited by the Tamil merchant community, in all likelihood from within their own community in south India.

The iconographic content of the Hindu reliefs of Quanzhou are of especial interest because they depict localized versions of Hindu myths, and legends associated with known saints of south India (Fig. 11.15). In my 2001 paper I examined the extent to which localising the origins of the scenes depicted could throw light on the regional affiliations of the Tamil merchant active in Quanzhou, and hence enable us to suggest the guild organisations to which they may well have been aligned.[34] The localising of these subjects to sites in proximity of the Kaveri River in Tamil Nadu provided some tentative indications as to the origins of the merchants and their priests who

FIGURE 11.15
Elephant worshipping a *linga* with flowers; relief from an untraced Hindu temple,
Quanzhou, thirteenth century. Maritime Museum, Quanzhou

commissioned and directed the construction of the temples in southern China.

The Quanzhou Hindu temple remains are not an isolated phenomenon, but rather a final and spectacular manifestation of a long process of dissemination of a Tamil presence along the maritime trade route that stretched from the ports of the Coromandel and Malabar coasts, to Southeast Asia and ultimately to those of southern China.

NOTES

1. Vogel, 1925.
2. See J. de Casparis, 1956 and Kulke, 1993 for a discussion of the inscriptions meaning, and J. Guy, 2004a for the acculturation of Indian naga-imagery in early Southeast Asia.
3. First published by Vogel, 1918, and further finds by Chabbra, 1949.
4. Two are on display in the Government Museum, Mathura, Uttar Pradesh.
5. Nieuwenhuis, 1907, vol. II: 115, Pl. X, cited in Bosch, 1926. The bronzes appeared on the art market in the 1990s.
6. McKinnon, 2000, and verbal communication.
7. Guy, 2005: Fig. 8.
8. Guy, 2004b.
9. McKinnon, 1985-86, provides a valuable overview of the distribution of inscription and images for southern Sumatra.
10. See Glover and Bellina, and Boonyarit Chaisuwan, in this volume.
11. Coedès, 1954. This author was instrumental in having the *linga* 'excavated' from the garden of the late Prince of Champasak's residence in 2005, revealing its tripartite form; it is now displayed in the Champasak site museum. Inscribed *lingas* are very rare in India, but occur more frequently in Southeast Asia, especially in Java.
12. Wolters, 1967: 82-83.
13. Shanmugan, 1996: 101.
14. Sastri, 1949.
15. Abrahams, 1988.
16. Personal communication, E. Edwards McKinnon.
17. Subbarayalu, 2002.
18. Coedès, 1961: 32-33.

19. Ibid.: 38-40.
20. Aung Thaw, 1968.
21. 'Red Earth' is also the meaning of the name by which the Chinese knew a small entrepôt at this time on the east coast of the Malay Peninsula, *Chi tu*. It is referred to in the seventh-century *Sui shu*, see Guy, 2004a.
22. Rahman and Yatim, 1990.
23. Guy, 2003.
24. Guy, 2006
25. Flecker, 2000.
26. Sastri, 1937.
27. This and the other Chinese sources that follow are discussed in Guy, 2001.
28. Guy, 1994.
29. Hirth and Rockhill, 1911.
30. Lo, 1967. See also H. Kulke, K. Kesavapany and V. Sakhuja (eds.), *Nagapattinam to Suvarnadwipa: Reflections on the Chola Expeditions to Southeast Asia*, Singapore, ISEAS, 2009.
31. Dated either 1183 or 1283; see Karashima, 2002: 13.
32. Guy, 1994, 2001, 2010.
33. Published by Wu, 1956.
34. Guy, 2001: 296-302.

REFERENCES

Abraham, M., *Two Medieval Merchant Guilds of South India*, New Delhi: Manohar, 1988.

Aung Thaw, *Report on the Excavations at Beikthano*, Rangoon: Government of Burma, 1968.

Bosch, F.D.K., 'Oudheden in Koetai', *Oudheidkundigen Dienst in Nederlandsch-Indie, Oudheidkundig Verslag 1925*, 1926: 132-46, Pls. 29-36.

Casparis, J.G. de, *Prasati Indonesia II: Selected Inscriptions from the 7th to the 9th Century*, Bandung, 1956.

Chabbra, B. Ch, 'Three More Yupa Inscriptions of King Mulavarman from Kutei (East Borneo)', *Bijdragen van het Koningklijeke Instituut*, no. 83, 1949: 370-74.

Coedès, G., 'Nouvelles données sur les origines du royaume Khmer. La stèle de Vat Luong Kau près de Vat P'hu', *Bulletin de l'Ecole française d'Extrême-Orient*, 48, 1954 : 209-20.

——, *Prachum silā chārūk Sayām. phāk thī 2, čhārūk krung Thawārawadī mūang Lavō lāe mūang prathētsarāt khūn kāe krung Srīwichai / Recueil des Inscriptions du Siam. Deuxième partie: Inscriptions de Dvāravatī, de Çrīvijaya et de Lăvo*, Bangkok: Department of Fine Arts, 2504 (1961).

Flecker, M., 'A 9th-century Arab or Indian Shipwreck in Indonesian Waters', *The International Journal of Nautical Archaeology*, vol. 29, no. 2, 2000, pp. 199-217.

Guy, J., 'The Lost Temples of Nagapattinam and Quanzhou: A Study in Sino-Indian Relations', *Silk Road Art and Archaeology*, 1994, vol. 3: 291-310.

——, 'Tamil Merchant Guilds and the Quanzhou Trade', in A. Schottenhamer (ed.), *The Emporium of the World: Maritime Quanzhou 1000-1400*, Leiden: Brill, 2001: 283-308.

——, 'Early Asian Ceramic Trade and the Belitung ("Tang") Cargo', *Transactions of the Oriental Ceramic Society*, vol. 66, 2003: 13-27.

——, 'South Indian Buddhism and its Southeast Asian Legacy', in A. Pande and P.P. Dhar (eds.), *Cultural Interface of India with Asia*, New Delhi: National Museum Institute Monographs Series, no. 1, 2004a: 155-75.

——, 'The *Intan* Shipwreck: A 10th century Cargo in South-east Asian Waters', in S. Pearson (ed.), *Song Ceramics: Art History, Archaeology and Technology*, University of London, Percival David Foundation of Chinese Art Colloquies on Art & Archaeology in Asia, No. 22, 2004b: 171-92.

——, 'Early Ninth-century Chinese Export Ceramics and the Persian Gulf Connection: The Belitung Shipwreck Evidence', in *Chine - Méditérranée, routes et échanges de la céramique jusqu'au XVIe siècle*, *TAOCI*, 2006, vol. 4: 9-20.

——, 'Southern Buddhism: Traces and Transmissions', in C. Jarrige and V. Lefevre (eds,), *Proceedings of the 16th European Association of South Asian Archaeology Conference, College de France, Paris, 2001*, Paris: L'Hartmann, 2005: 495-503.

——, 'Quanzhou: Cosmopolitan City of Faiths', in J. Watt (ed.), *The World of Khubilai Khan: Chinese Art in the Yuan Dynasty*, New York: The Metropolitan Museum of Art/Yale University Press, 2010: 158-78.

Hirth, F. and W.W. Rockhill, *Chau Ju-kua; his Work on the Chinese and Arab Trade in the Twelfth and Thirteenth Centuries*, St Petersburg: Imperial Academy of Sciences, 1911.

Karashima, N. (ed.), *Ancient and Medieval Commercial Activities in the Indian Ocean: Testimony of Inscriptions and Ceramic-sherds*, Tokyo: Taisho University, 2002.

Kulke, Hermann, 1993, '"Kadatuan Srivijaya"—Empire or Kraton of Srivijaya? A Reassessment of the Epigraphical Evidence', *Bulletin de l'Ecole française d'Extrême-Orient*, 80, 1993: 159-81.

Lo Hsiang-lin, 'Islam in Canton in the Sung Period: Some Fragmentary Records', in F.S. Drake (ed.), *Symposium on Historical Archaeological And Linguistic Studies in Southeast Asia*, Hong Kong: Hong Kong University Press, 1967: 176-79.

McKinnon, E. Edwards, 'Early Polities in Southern Sumatra: Some Preliminary Observations based on Archaeological Evidence', *Indonesia*, 40, 1985-86: 1-36.

——, 'Buddhism and the Pre-Islamic Archaeology of Kutei in the Mahakam Valley of East Kalimantan', in N.A. Taylor (ed.), *Studies in Southeast Asian Art: Essays in Honor of Stanley J. O'Connor*, Ithaca: Cornell University, 2000: 217-40.

Quaritch Wales, H.G., *The Malay Peninsula in Hindu Times*, London: Bernard Quaritch, 1976.

Sastri, K.A. Nilakanta, *Foreign Notices of South India: From Megasthenes to Ma Huan*, Madras: University of Madras, 1937.

——, 'Takua Pa and its Tamil Inscription', *Journal of the Malayan Branch of the Royal Asiatic Society*, XXII (i), 1949: 25-30.

Shanmugan, P., 'An Early Tamil Brahmi Inscription from Thailand', *Journal of the Epigraphical Society of India*, vol. 22, 1996: 101.

Shuhaimi, N.H. and O.M. Yatim, *Antiquities of Bujang Valley*, Kuala Lumpur: Museum Association of Malaysia, 1990.

Subbarayalu, Y., 'The Tamil Merchant-Guild Inscription at Barus, Indonesia: A Rediscovery', in N. Karashima (ed.), *Ancient and Medieval Commercial Activities in the Indian Ocean: Testimony of Inscriptions and Ceramic-sherds*, Tokyo: Taisho University, 2002: 19-26.

Vogel, J.Ph., 'Yupa Inscriptions of King Mulawarman from Kotei (East Borneo)', *Bijdragen van het Koninklijk Instituut voor Taal-, Land- en Volkenkunde*, 74, 1918: 167-233.

——, 'The Earliest Sanskrit Inscriptions of Java', *Oudheidkundigen Dienst in Nederlandsch-Indie, Oudheidkundig Verslag 1925*: 15-35.

Wolters, O.W., *Early Indonesian Commerce*, Ithaca: Cornell University Press, 1967.

Wu Wen Liang, *Quanzhou Zongliao Shilo* (Religious stone inscriptions in Quanzhou), Beijing: Academy Publishing House, 1956.

12

The Spread of Sanskrit in Southeast Asia*

Johannes Bronkhorst

Sanskrit makes its first appearance in inscriptions in South Asia during the early centuries of the Common Era. It then gradually takes over and becomes the inscriptional language par excellence in the whole of the South Asian subcontinent and much of Southeast Asia. For almost a thousand years Sanskrit 'rules' in this enormous domain. Sheldon Pollock (1996, 2006) speaks for this reason of the 'Sanskrit cosmopolis', which he dates approximately between CE 300 and 1300.

How do we explain the strange vicissitudes of the Sanskrit language? Was it a *lingua franca* for trade, international business and cultural promotion? Is the spread of Sanskrit into Southeast Asia to be explained by the same reasons that also explain its spread within the Indian subcontinent?

Pollock, by using the expression 'Sanskrit cosmopolis', draws attention to the political dimension of the spread of Sanskrit. One defining feature of the Sanskrit cosmopolis, he states (1996: 197), 'is that Sanskrit became the premiere instrument of political expression in the polities that comprised it, those of most of South and much of Southeast Asia'. He rightly points out that Sanskrit was not a lingua franca:[1]

Sanskrit's spread was effected by traditional intellectuals and religious professionals, often following in the train of scattered groups of traders and adventurers, and carrying with them disparate and decidedly uncanonized texts of a wide variety of competing religious orders, Śaiva, Buddhist, Vaiṣṇava, and others. [...] There is little to suggest [...] that Sanskrit was an everyday medium of communication in South let alone Southeast Asia, or that [it] ever functioned as a language-of-trade, a bridge-, link-, or koiné language or lingua franca (except among those traditional intellectuals) [...]

Pollock continues: 'We have little direct evidence that Sanskrit actually functioned as a language of practical imperium – the medium of chancellery communication or revenue accounting, for example – certainly not in Southeast Asia, almost certainly not in peninsular India or the Deccan [...]'

The hypothesis he then goes on to propose (pp. 198-99) is

that Sanskrit articulated politics not as material power – the power embodied in languages-of-state for purposes of boundary regulation or taxation, for example, for which so-called vernacular idioms typically remained the vehicle – but politics as aesthetic power. To some degree the Sanskrit 'cosmopolis' I [i.e. J.B. Pollock] shall describe consists precisely in this common aesthetics of political culture, a kind of poetry of politics.[2]

Further explanation follows on p. 199: 'Constituted by no imperial power or church but in large part by a communicative system and its political aesthetic, the Sanskrit ecumene is characterised by a transregionally shared set of assumptions about the basics of power, or at least about the ways in which power is reproduced at the level of representation in language, and Sanskrit's unique suitability for this task.' Having discussed the epigraphical and related evidence from a number of regions, Pollock then depicts the situation around CE 1000 in the following passage (pp. 229-30):

A traveler around the year 1000 [...] would have seen, from the plain of Kedu in central Java to the basin of Tonlé Sap in Cambodia, from Gaṅgaikoḍacoapuram in Tamil Nadu to Patan in Gujarat and beyond, imperial formations that had many features in common. The material and social ones I have ignored here: their largely hierarchized societies, administered by a corps of functionaries, scribes, tax collectors, living in grand agrarian cities geometrically planned in orientation to the cardinal points and set within imaginary geographies that with their local mountains, rivers, and springs recapitulated the geography of India, urban structures 'freighted with cosmic symbolism, helping one to visualize the order of things' [...] It is their common political-cultural, especially literary-cultural, features I have emphasized: the existence of cultural and political élites assiduously mastering the intricate codes and protocols of Sanskrit poetry, and the publication of their works throughout these cities, in varying degrees of density and grandeur – stately public poems in Sanskrit engraved on the ubiquitous copper-plates recording gifts and donations, or on stone pillars looming up from gigantic architectural wonders.

There was thus, I think, a certain concrete reality to the 'Sanskrit cosmopolis', one that does not exist only in the retrospective gaze of the historian. For a millennium, and across half the world, élites participated in a peculiar supralocal ecumene. This was a form of shared life very different from that produced by common subjecthood or fealty to a central power, even by shared religious liturgy or credo. It was instead a symbolic network created in the first instance by the presence of a similar kind of discourse in a similar language deploying a similar idiom and style to make similar kinds of claims about the nature and aesthetics of polity – about kingly virtue and learning; the dharma of rule; the universality of dominion. A network, accordingly, wherein the élite shared 'a broadly based communality of outlook', and could perceive 'ubiquitous signs of its beliefs'.

Readers may be surprised to see that this passage makes no reference to

Brahmans. Isn't there an old and well-established link between Sanskrit and Brahmans? Can one speak about the spread of Sanskrit without speaking about Brahmans that presumably travelled with the language? Pollock speaks very little of Brahmans in these publications.[3] Where he does so, his aim appears to be to weaken or even deny the link between the two. He does so, for example, where he criticises the notion of 'legitimation'.[4] He cites (p. 236) in this connection the following passage from an article by Hermann Kulke (1990: 20 ff.):

> At a certain stage of this development Brahmins 'came hither' [to mainland Southeast Asia] in order to legitimize the new status and wealth of these chiefs. Obviously there existed a tremendous need of additional legitimation which obviously no other traditional institution was able to provide fully ... Brahmins appear to have been invited particularly as a sort of 'extra' legitimators of a new and more advanced type of authority which was not sanctioned by the traditional societies of South-East Asia. ... Obviously in both [South India and Southeast Asia] there had existed the same or at least similar socio-political needs for a new type of legitimation.[5]

Pollock is very critical about the notion of 'legitimation', and he argues that 'there is no reason to accept legitimation theory'.[6] However, he seems to think that the rejection of 'legitimation theory' also does away with the question of the connection between Brahmans and Sanskrit in south India and Southeast Asia, for he does not return to it. And yet, there is ample evidence to show that there were Brahmans in virtually all the regions that were affected by the spread of Sanskrit. Even if one were to accept that legitimation theory does not explain their presence in all those regions, this hardly justifies leaving their presence altogether out of consideration. Innumerable Sanskrit inscriptions, both in India and in Southeast Asia, testify to the presence of Brahmans, who were no doubt involved in many, if not most, Sanskrit inscriptions. It is a fair question to ask whether the users of Sanskrit in all these regions were not preponderantly Brahmans. Even if one were to admit that 'legitimation' was not the reason why these Brahmans were there, this is no reason to deny that they were there, and that their presence was intimately connected with the use of Sanskrit in those regions.

By disconnecting Sanskrit from Brahmanism and from Brahmans, Pollock can formulate the questions relating to the spread of Sanskrit in terms of the language itself rather than in terms of its users. This allows him to propose his hypothesis of 'politics as aesthetic power'. A consequence of this disconnection is that 'we cannot simply read off automatically from the choice to express political will in Sanskrit any particular social consequences (e.g., hierarchization, hegemony; the production of false belief)' (p. 245). No, the qualities of the language itself have to account – if not fully, then at least to a large extent – for its extraordinary expansion: 'This had to be a language of transethnic attraction; a language capable of making translocal claims [...];

one powerful not so much because of its numinous qualities [...], but because of its aesthetic qualities, its ability somehow to make reality more real. [...] These aesthetic qualities, moreover, are authenticated by the language's possessing a tradition of literary texts that embody and realize them' (pp. 239-40). Indeed, 'the unique expressive capabilities of Sanskrit poetry allow the poet to make statements about political power that could be made in no other way' (Pollock 2006: 139).[7]

All this leaves one with the apprehension that the traditional connection between Sanskrit and Brahmans has been too hastily disposed off. Pollock is no doubt right in rejecting 'the received account that imagines a "resurgence of Brahmanism" leading to a "re-assertion of Sanskrit" as the language of literature and administration after the Maurya period'. Indeed, one of the consequences of the main argument of my book *Greater Magadha* (2007) is that Brahmanism did not resurge after the Maurya period but commenced at that time its spread over the subcontinent and beyond for the first time. We are, as a matter of fact, confronted with two remarkable instantiations of spread: the spread of Brahmanism and the spread of Sanskrit. And the question that cannot be avoided is, were these two really unconnected? Is it not more likely that they had something to do with each other?

In order to answer these questions we must be clear what we are talking about. Pollock's observations about the spread of Sanskrit are enlightening and, by and large, sufficient for our present purpose. But what is meant by 'spread of Brahmanism'? The expression Brahmanism can be used to designate the religion and culture of the Veda, but it is only in a very limited sense that these can be said to have spread during the period following the Mauryas. No, the spread of Brahmanism was primarily the spread of Brahmans as Brahmans. That is to say, a region is Brahmanised when its population, or its rulers, accept the Brahmans that have settled there as by right the most eminent members of society. This population, or these rulers, are not so much converted to a different religion: no converts are made to Vedic religion or to any other specific religion promulgated by the Brahmans. No, these populations or rulers are made to accept a different vision of society, in which Brahmans are highest because they have access to the supernatural. An important instrument in the hands of the Brahmans is their knowledge of the Veda, a collection of texts which the vast majority of the population is not even allowed to hear recited, much less study. It is their often secret knowledge that gives them the power to work for the good of a kingdom, its ruler and its population. It also allows them to do the contrary, and this is an important reason to humour them.

For reasons that are not at all clear at present, Brahmans succeeded in the course of time to convince many rulers that it was a good thing to provide them with what they needed to carry out their rites and do whatever else would benefit the kingdom. The growing presence of Brahmans all over South Asia is well documented, but they also showed up in Southeast Asia, even in countries that became Buddhist: 'even in states where Hinayana Buddhism prevailed, Brahmans played an important ceremonial part, especially at Court, and still do so in Burma, Siam and Cambodia, though themselves strikingly different from their counterparts in India'.[8]

The oldest known inscriptions in Indonesia – we read in *The Economic and Administrative History of Early Indonesia* (Van Naerssen & De Iongh 1977: 18) – are those of East Borneo. Here there are seven stone sacrificial posts, called *yūpas* by archaeologists, that date from around CE 400. What is written on them is described in the following terms:[9]

In clear, well written Sanskrit verses Mūlavarman 'the lord of kings', his father – Aśvavarman, 'the founder of a noble race' – and his grandfather, 'the great Kulotunga, the lord of men' – are mentioned on the occasion of a sacrifice. 'For that sacrifice', we read on one of the stone poles, 'this sacrificial post has been prepared by the chief amongst the twice-born [dvija, JB]'. ('Twice-born' is applied to the members of the brahmanical or priestly caste.) Apparently these 'priests [vipra, JB] who had come hither' (as is written on the second pole) were rewarded by king Mūlavarman for their religious services. Thus the third inscription sounds: 'Let the foremost amongst the priests and whatsoever other pious men hear of the meritorious deed of Mūlavarman, the king of illustrious and resplendent fame – (let him hear) of his great gift, his gift of cattle, of a wonder-tree [...], his gift of land. For this multitude of pious deeds this sacrificial post has been set up by the priests.'

A Sanskrit rock inscription in West Java dating from about CE 450 deals with an occasion on which the Brahmans were presented with 1,000 cows.[10]
About Cambodia we read:[11]

In Cambodia the Brahmans for many centuries maintained a powerful hierarchy. They were the only one of the four castes that was really organized, this caste having taken form in the fifth century and been constantly augmented by immigrants from India.[12] In the days when Yaśovarman was king (acceded A.D. 889), Saivism was predominant, and we learn from the following inscription that the Brahmans still enjoyed a position similar to that which was theirs in India:
'This king, well-versed (in kingly duties), performed the Koṭi-homa and the Yajñas (Vedic sacrifices), for which he gave the priests magnificent presents of jewels, gold, etc.'[13]

The cult of the Royal God, though founded by Jayavarman II (CE 802), did not reach the height of its development until some two centuries afterwards, and was especially associated with Vaisṇavism and the temple of Angkor Vat. This cult led to the Brahmans enjoying an even more exalted position. The Cambodian hierarchy was established by Jayavarman II, and the priesthood became hereditary in the family of Śivakaivalya, who enjoyed immense power; indeed, this sacerdotal dynasty almost threw the royal dynasty into the shade.[14] Brahmans were depicted on the reliefs of Angkor Vat and Coedès has identified Droṇa and Viśvāmitra amongst them.[15] In one of the reliefs that illustrate a royal procession, it is interesting to note that the Brahmans are the only onlookers who do not prostrate themselves before the king, as was also the case in India.[16] [...] Another point of interest that we learn from the reliefs of Angkor Vat and Angkor Thom is that not only the Brahmans, but also the aristocracy wore the chignon, the lower classes having short hair.[17]

One very remarkable sign of the power of the Brahmans during the Angkor period is that, contrary to the modern custom, by which princesses of the royal blood rarely marry, formerly alliances were common with the Brahmans;[18] and up to the present day there is a tradition amongst the Bakus, who are the descendants of the ancient Brahmans, that in the event of the royal family failing, a successor would be chosen from amongst them.[19]

As early as the reign of Jayavarman V (CE 968) we find evidence of the admixture of Mahāyāna Buddhism with the cult of the Royal God.

'The purohita should be versed in Buddhist learning and rites. He should bathe on the days of the festivals the image of the Buddha and should recite Buddhist prayers'.[20]

And the rites and duties of the purohitas remained a mixture of Hinduism and Mahāyānism until the introduction of Pāli Buddhism in the thirteenth century,[21] after which this powerful sacerdotal caste degenerated with their religion to the position occupied by the modern Bakus.[22] But the Brahmans of Cambodia perhaps never sank so low as did those of Campā, where 'In the Po Nagar Inscription (No. 30) we read that the king's feet were worshipped, even by Brāhmaṇas and priests'.[23]

King Yaśovarman of Cambodia created numerous *āśramas*, among them some that were specifically meant for Vaiṣṇavas, Śaivas and Buddhists. Interestingly, in all three, including the Buddhist *āśrama*, Brahmans had to be honoured more than anyone else: 'In the Saugatāśrama, too, the learned Brāhmaṇa should be honoured a little more than the āchārya versed in Buddhist doctrine [...]'.[24]

The situation in Thailand was not independent from the one prevailing in Cambodia:[25]

Though the Thai were Buddhists, their kings surrounded themselves with the appurtenances of Khmer royalty, and recruited their Court Brahmans from Cambodia. For centuries, indeed, Brahmanism enjoyed quite an important position; for although Buddhism was the religion of the people, and was protected by the kings, Hinduism was still considered as essential to the monarchy, and so received a great share of royal favour. The famous inscription (about A.D. 1361) of King Dharmarāja I mentions the king's knowledge of the Vedas and of astronomy;[26] while the inscription on the Śiva statue found at Kānbèn Bejra records the desire of King Dharmaśokarāja to exalt both Hinduism and Buddhism. And this is as late as A.D. 1510.[27]

It would be a mistake to think of the Brahmans in Southeast Asia as an endogamous group of people, as they were in India. Indeed, G. Coedès (1964: 54) cites a Chinese text from the fifth century which states that 'dans le royaume de Touen-siun [Dun-sun] il y a plus de mille brahmanes de l'Inde. Les gens de Touen-siun pratiquent leur doctrine et leur donnent leurs filles en mariage; aussi beaucoup de ces brahmanes ne s'en vont-ils pas.[28] (In the kingdom of Dun-sun there are more than a thousand Brahmans of India. The people of Dun-sun practice their doctrine and give them their daughters in marriage. Consequently, not many of these Brahmans go away.)

De Casparis & Mabbett (1992: 287) sum up present knowledge about the role of Brahmans in Southeast Asia:

Brahmins had great influence in the Southeast Asian courts in various capacities. As they had access to the sacred texts, the lawbooks and other literature in Sanskrit, they were employed as priests, teachers, ministers and counsellors: the principal advisers of the kings. Government, particularly in early centuries, depended upon such men, who were the chief available sources of literacy and administrative talent and experience. As in the early Indian kingdoms, an important office was that of the purohita, a chief priest with ritual and governmental functions. The epigraphic record of the mainland kingdoms demonstrates the powerful influence of purohitas, notably in Burma and Cambodia, where they often served under several successive rulers and provided continuity to the government in troubled times. In ninth-century Angkor, for example, Indravarman I had the services of Śivasoma, who was a relative of the earlier king Jayavarman II and was said to have studied in India under the celebrated Vedānta teacher Śaṅkara.

About the origins of these Brahmans – where they Indians or not? – De Casparis and Mabbett have the following to say:[29]

If such brahmins were Indians (the Indian brahmins are indeed occasionally mentioned in Southeast Asian inscriptions), one wonders how or why they should have left India. This is the more surprising since Indian lawbooks contain prohibitions for brahmins against overseas travel, which was regarded as ritually polluting. These prohibitions may have had little practical effect, and would not have deterred ambitious men lured by the hope of honour and fortune in a distant land. It has been suggested that some learned brahmins were invited by Southeast Asian rulers at a time when commercial relations between Indian and Southeast Asian ports had spread the fame of such brahmins to the courts. It is indeed likely that this happened sometimes, but probably not on a large scale. It is, for example, striking that the Indian gotra names, never omitted in Indian inscriptions, are not normally mentioned in Southeast Asia. On the other hand, in the few cases where they are mentioned it is likely that they refer to Indian Brahmins. It therefore follows that the great majority of Southeast Asian brahmins would have been Southeast Asians, many of whom had acquired their knowledge of the Sanskrit texts and of brahmanic ritual in Indian ashrams.

The services of the Southeast Asian Brahmans extended beyond the limits of any single religion:[30]

Not only in the 'Hindu' courts, such as Angkor, but also in the Buddhist courts, such as those of Pagan in Burma and Sukothai in Thailand, the brahmins conducted the great ceremonies, such as the royal consecration, and functioned as ministers and counsellors, but had to share their influence with that of the Buddhist monks. By its very nature Buddhism was concerned with the acquisition of spiritual merit and moral perfection rather than with the rites and ceremonies of a royal court, which were left to the brahmins. The grand ceremonies in Pagan [...] required the services of numerous brahmins, although Theravāda was then well established. In Cambodia, as late as the thirteenth century [...], Jayavarman VIII built a temple for the scholar-priest Jayamaṅgalārtha, and likewise for the brahmin Vidyeśavid, who became court sacrificial priest. The Chinese visitor Chou Ta-kuan refers to the presence of brahmins wearing the traditional sacred thread.

De Casparis and Mabbett (1992: 288) draw the following conclusion:

What is shown by the role of such brahmins is that it is appropriate to speak of Brahmanism as distinct from the specific cults of Śiva or Viṣṇu, or any of their innumerable kin: the priests stood for a social order and for the rituals that gave to the political or local community a sense of its unity and its place in the world.

The part of this conclusion which must be emphasised is that Brahmanism is distinct from the specific cults of Śiva or Viṣṇu, or any of their innumerable kin, and that the Brahmans stood for a social order.[31] This seems obvious and undeniable. It is yet often overlooked by scholars who wish to assign Brahmanism to the category 'religion'. In reality, Brahmanism is primarily a social order. Only this way can we make sense of the evidence from Southeast Asia as well as of the evidence from South Asia.

It appears, then, that some of the proposals made already in 1934 (in Dutch) by J.C. van Leur still hold good.[32] About South Asia he said (van Leur 1955: 97):[33]

The chief disseminator of the process of 'Indianization' was the Brahman priesthood; the aim of the 'Brahman mission' was not the preaching of any revealed doctrine of salvation, but the ritualistic and bureaucratic subjugation and organization of the newly entered regions. Wherever the process of 'Indianization' took place, 'religious' organization was accompanied by social organization – division in castes, legitimation of the ruling groups, assurance of the supremacy of the Brahmins. The colossal magical, ritualistic power of the Brahman priesthood was the most characteristic feature of early Indian history. The rationalistic, bureaucratic schooling of the priesthood as the intellectual group, which went to make up its great worth, its indispensability even, for any comprehensive governmental organization, was [...] interwoven with the sacerdotal function. The Brahman priesthood developed high qualities in that field as well, but its decisive influence came from the magical, ritualistic power of domestication it in the absoluteness of its power was able to develop.

The spread of Brahmanical institutions to Southeast Asia was hardly more than a continuation of this process (pp. 103-04):

The Indian priesthood was called eastward – certainly because of its wide renown – for the magical, sacral legitimation of dynastic interests and the domestication of subjects, and probably for the organisation of the ruler's territory into a state.

Pollock may object to the word legitimation in these two passages. Nothing much is lost by removing it.[34] The factual situation remains the same. Brahmans were called to Southeast Asia (or were found in Southeast Asia; there is no reason to insist on the Indian origin of these Brahmans), and these Brahmans brought with them their sacred language, Sanskrit.[35]

We see that it will be hard to separate Sanskrit from Brahmans, both in South and Southeast Asia. The one complicating factor is Buddhism. What was the relationship between Buddhism and Sanskrit, and why had Buddhists already in South Asia adopted Sanskrit for their texts? These questions require a detailed discussion, which cannot be provided within the limits imposed upon this article.

NOTES

* This is part of a more encompassing study 'The Spread of Sanskrit', dealing with the phenomenon in both South and Southeast Asia, which will appear in the Felicitation Volume for Dieter Schlingloff.

1. Pollock, 1996: 198.
2. Similarly Pollock, 2006: 14.
3. This in spite of the fact that he observes in another article that 'to choose a language for literature [...] is at the same time to choose a community' (Pollock, 1998: 9).
4. Nemec (2007: 210), reviewing Pollock's *The Language of the Gods in the World of Men* (2006), expresses some reservations about the rejection of legitimation.
5. See, however, Kulke, 1986: 274: 'legitimation was not the only attraction of Hinduism for tribal leaders. As pointed out by Wolters, Hinduism must have been particularly attractive for "men of prowess" because of its highly developed system of magical power derived from meditation (tapas)'.
6. Elsewhere Pollock calls it a 'functionalist explanation [which] is not only anachronistic, but really is a mere assumption, and an intellectually mechanical, culturally homogenizing, and theoretically naive assumption at that' (1998: 13; cp. 2006: 18). And again: 'It is typical [...] to reduce one of these terms (culture) to the other (power) – a reduction often embodied in the use of the concept of legitimation of power. There is no reason to assume that legitimation is applicable throughout all human history, yet it remains the dominant analytic in explaining the work of culture in studies of early South and Southeast Asia.' See further Pollock, 2006: 511 ff.
7. See further Pollock, 2006: 254 f.
8. Hall, 1968: 12. About Champa, Mabbett (1986: 294) observes: 'Except for a short while around the end of the ninth and the beginning of the tenth centuries, Buddhism in Champa never really rivalled Hinduism. Epigraphic statistics give some idea of the relative importance of the two faiths, at least in royal and courtly circles: of 130 inscriptions published, 21 are not sectarian, 92 refer to worship of Śiva, 3 are directed to Viṣṇu, 5 to Brahmā, 7 to Buddhism, and 2 to Śiva and Viṣṇu jointly.' (These numbers correspond to those given in Mus, 1934: 369.) For the fate of Sanskrit after the introduction of Theravāda Buddhism in Burma, see Bechert & Braun, 1981: xxxviii f.: this language continued to be used for some time for the secular sciences, i.e., grammar, lexicography, metrics, poetics, medicine, pharmacology, astrology, gemmology, logic. Interestingly, in Burma a work dealing with the right conduct of a king (*Rājanīti*) was composed in Pāli by court Brahmans (Bechert & Braun, 1981: lxi). However, 'it seems that all Rājanīti verses are direct translations from Sanskrit' (Bechert & Braun, 1981: lxxvii).
9. Van Naerssen & De Iongh, 1977: 18. Cf. Vogel, 1918.
10. Ibid.: 23.
11. Quaritch Wales, 1931: 58-60.
12. Aymonier, 1900-04: III: 548. Even though the system of four varṇas does not seem to have taken root in Southeast Asia, this may not be due to lack of trying.

In Cambodia, according to Chatterji (1928: 239), Sūryavarman I is stated to have 'established the division of castes', and Harshavarman III boasts of having made the people observe strictly the duties of the four castes. Chatterji adds, however (p. 240): 'We do not get much substantial evidence of the other [i.e., different from Brahmins] castes however.' See further Mabbett, 1977 (p. 439: 'varṇas [in Angkor] were largely ceremonial orders'). A text which seems to have been issued in the fourteenth century CE by King Kṛtanagara of East-Java prescribes: 'The Śivaite's son shall be a Śivaite, the Buddhist's son a Buddhist, the rāja's son a rāja, the manuh's (common layman's) son a manuh, the Śūdra's son a Śūdra, and so on all classes shall follow their own avocations and ceremonies.' (Ensink, 1978: 188)

13. Chatterji, 1928: 114.
14. Chatterji, 1928: 80 f.
15. Coedès, 1911: Pls. XII and XIII.
16. Delaporte, 1878.
17. Groslier, 1921: 58.
18. Aymonier, 1900-04: III: 531. Cp. Coedès, 1964: 219: 'Jayavarman V [Cambodia, 10th century] maria sa soeur Indralakshmī au brahmane hindou Divākarabhaṭṭa, né dans l'Inde sur les bords de la Yamunā, auteur de diverses fondations çivaïtes'; p. 223: 'Les familles brahmaniques s'alliaient souvent avec la famille royale: les mariages entre brahmanes et kshatriyas semblent avoir été fréquents, ces deux castes constituant, au-dessus de la masse, une classe à part, représentant l'élément intellectuel et la culture hindoue, sans qu'il faille en conclure que, du point de vue racial, cette aristocratie ait été très différente du reste de la population'.
19. Aymonier, 1920: 178.
20. Chatterji, 1928: 163. Pāsādika (2006: 468), referring to an unpublished lecture by Peter Skilling, provides the following information about the second Sambor-Prei Kük inscription in Chenla: 'A Sanskrit inscription ... from the reign of Āśānavarman I, records the erection of a *liṅga* in Śaka 549 = CE 627, by the high official Vidyāviśeṣa, a Pāśupata Brahman, who was versed in grammar (śabda), the Brahmanical systems of Vaiśeṣika, Nyāya, and Sāṅkhya, and the doctrine of the Sugata.'
21. Aymonier, 1900-04: III: 591. An inscription from Arakan, which Johnston (1944: 365) dates to the beginning of the ninth century, speaks of a king named Ānandacandra, who was a Mahāyāna Buddhist and an *upāsaka*. This did not prevent him from having four monasteries (*maṭha*) built for fifty Brahmans, 'provided with lands and servants, furnished with musical instruments and musicians' (pp. 381-82).
22. Aymonier, 1900-04: III: 614.
23. Majumdar, 1927: Chapter 14.
24. Goyal, 2006: 221.
25. Quaritch Wales, 1931: 60.
26. Coedès, 1924: 98.
27. Coedès, 1924: 159.
28. Coedès explains in a note (1964: 54, n. 6): 'Le Touen-siun était une dépendance du Fou-nan, probablement sur la Péninsule Malaise'.
29. De Casparis & Mabbett, 1992: 287.
30. Ibid.: 288. Cp. Golzio, 2003: 79 f.
31. Pāsādika (2006: 465), referring to Bhattacharya (1997), mentions the 'synthesis of Śaivism and gruesome local cult or possibly "the" indigenous religion of Cambodia'. 'Originally this cult culminated in human sacrifices to the mountain-spirit performed

by the king himself. [...] The early Cambodian kings could have had no objection to the assimilation of a primitive and gruesome cult by Brahmanism thanks to which [...] the mountain-spirit [...] became Bhadreśvara, i.e. Śiva [...]'

32. Cp. Kulke, 1986a: 256 f.
33. On the 'Indianization' of Southeast Asia, see further Mabbett, 1977a.
34. Or one might replace it with protection: 'protection of the ruling groups' and 'sacral protection of dynastic interests' may give less reason for objections.
35. They also brought with them the information about the consecration of temples that we find in Indian texts such as the Kāśyapaśilpa, information which was also used in the building of Buddhist structures; see Ślączka, 2007, esp. Chapters 7.3 and 7.4.

REFERENCES

Bayly, Susan, 1999, *Caste, Society and Politics in India from the Eighteenth Century to the Modern Age* (The New Cambridge History of India IV.3.), Cambridge: Cambridge University Press.

Bechert, Heinz & Heinz Braun, 1981, *Pāli Nīti Texts of Burma: Dhammanīti, Lokanīti, Mahārahanīti, Rājanīti,* (Pali Text Society, Text Series no. 171) London: Henley: and Boston: Routledge & Kegan Paul.

Bhattacharya, Kamaleswar, 1997, 'Religious Syncretism in Ancient Cambodia', *Dharmadūta. Mélanges offerts au Vénérable Thich Huyên-Vi à l'occasion de son soixante-dixième anniversaire,* ed. Bh. T. Dhammaratana, Bh. Pāsādika, Paris, pp. 1-12. (not seen)

Bronkhorst, Johannes, 2007, *Greater Magadha: Studies in the Culture of Early India,* (Handbook of Oriental Studies, Section 2 South Asia, 19.) Leiden - Boston: Brill.

Chatterji, Bijan Raj, 1928, *Indian Cultural Influence in Cambodia,* Calcutta: University of Calcutta.

Coedès, George, 1911, *Les bas reliefs d'Angkor Vat,* BCAI II, pp. 170-220.

——, 1924, *Les inscriptions de Sukhodaya,* Bangkok: Bangkok Times Press.

——, 1932, 'Études cambodgiennes, XXV. Deux inscriptions sanskrites du Fou-nan', *Bulletin de l'École Française d'Extrême-Orient* 31 (1931), 1-12.

——, 1964, *Les états hindouisés d'Indochine et d'Indonésie,* Nouvelle édition revue et mise à jour, Paris: E. de Boccard.

Das, Rahul Peter, 2005, "Kaste". *Gemeinsame kulturelle Codes in koexistierenden Religionsgemeinschaften: Leucorea-Kolloquium 2003,* ed. Ute Pietruschka. Halle (Saale). (Hallesche Beiträge zur Orientwissenschaft 38 (2004).), pp. 75-116.

De Casparis, J.G. & I.W. Mabbett, 1992, 'Religion and Popular Beliefs of Southeast Asia before c. 1500', *The Cambridge History of Southeast Asia,* Volume One: *From Early Times to c. 1800,* ed. Nicholas Tarling, Cambridge: Cambridge University Press, pp. 276-339.

Ensink, Jacob, 1978, 'Śiva-Buddhism in Java and Bali', *Buddhism in Ceylon and Studies on Religious Syncretism in Buddhist Countries* (Symposien zur Buddhismusforschung, I.), ed. Heinz Bechert, Göttingen: Vandenhoeck & Ruprecht (Abhandlungen der Akademie der Wissenschaften in Göttingen, philologisch-historische Klasse, Nr. 108.), pp. 178-98.

Golzio, Karl-Heinz, 2003, *Geschichte Kambodschas,* München: C.H. Beck.

Gopinath Rao, T.A., 1926, 'Kanyākumāri Inscription of Vīra-Rājendra-Deva', *Epigraphia Indica* 18 (1925-26), 21-55.

Goyal, S.R., 2006, 'History and Cultures of Kambuja and Champā as known from Their Inscriptions', *India's Interaction with Southeast Asia*, ed. G.C. Pande, New Delhi: Munshiram Manoharlal (History of Science, Philosophy and Culture in Indian Civilization, I.3), pp. 201-60.

Hall, D.G.E., 1968, *A History of South-East Asia*, London: MacMillan; New York: St Martin's Press.

Johnston, E.H., 1944, 'Some Sanskrit Inscriptions of Arakan', *Bulletin of the School of Oriental and African Studies*, 11(2), 357-85.

Kulke, Hermann, 1986, 'The Early and the Imperial Kingdom in Southeast Asian History', *Southeast Asia in the 9th to 14th Centuries*, ed. David G. Marr and A.C. Milner, Singapore: Institute of Southeast Asian Studies / Canberra: Research School of Pacific Studies, Australian National University, pp. 1-22. Reprint: Kulke, 1993: 262-93. (References to the reprint.)

——, 1986a, 'Max Weber's contribution to the study of "Hinduization" in India and "Indianization" in Southeast Asia', *Recent Research on Max Weber's Studies on Hinduism*, ed. D. Kantowsky, Munich: Weltforum-Verlag, pp. 97-116, Reprint: Kulke, 1993: 240-61. (References to the reprint.)

——, 1990, 'Indian Colonies, Indianization or Cultural Convergence? Reflections on the Changing Image of India's Role in South-East Asia', *Semaian* 3, 1990, pp. 8-32.

——, 1993, *Kings and Cults: State Formation and Legitimation in India and Southeast Asia*, Reprint 2001, Delhi: Manohar.

Mabbett, I.W., 1977, 'Varṇas in Angkor and the Indian Caste System', *Journal of Asian Studies*, 36(3), 429-42.

——, 1977a, 'The "Indianization" of Southeast Asia: Reflections on the Historical Sources', *Journal of Southeast Asian Studies* 8(2), 143-61.

Mabbett, Ian, 1986, 'Buddhism in Champa' *Southeast Asia in the 9th to 14th Centuries*, ed. David G. Marr and A. C. Milner, Singapore: Institute of Southeast Asian Studies/ Canberra: Research School of Pacific Studies, Australian National University, pp. 289-313.

Mus, P., 1934, 'Cultes indiens et indigènes au Champa', *Bulletin de l'École Française d'Extrême-Orient* 33 (1933), 367-410.

Nemec, John, 2007, 'Review of Pollock', 2006, *Journal of the American Academy of Religion*, 75, 207-11.

Ostler, Nicholas, 2005, *Empires of the Word: A Language History of the World*, New York: HarperCollins.

Pāsādika, Bhikkhu, 2006, 'The Development of Buddhist Religion and Literature in Cambodia and Vietnam', in *India's Interaction with Southeast Asia*, ed. G.C. Pande, New Delhi: Munshiram Manoharlal. (History of Science, Philosophy and Culture in Indian Civilization, I.3.), pp. 463-88.

Pollock, Sheldon, 1996, 'The Sanskrit Cosmopolis, 300-1300: Transculturation, Vernacularization, and the Question of Ideology', *Ideology and Status of Sanskrit: Contributions to the history of the Sanskrit language* (Brill's Indological Library, 13), ed. Jan E.M. Houben, Leiden: E.J. Brill, pp. 197-247.

Pollock, Sheldon, 1998, 'The cosmopolitan vernacular', *Journal of Asian Studies* 57(1), 6-37.

——, 2006, *The Language of the Gods in the World of Men: Sanskrit, Culture, and Power in Premodern India*, Berkeley – Los Angeles – London: University of California Press.

Quaritch Wales, H.G., 1931, *Siamese State Ceremonies: Their History and Function*, London: Bernard Quaritch.

Ślączka, Anna A., 2007, *Temple Consecration Rituals in Ancient India: Text and Archaeology*, (Brill's Indological Library, 26), Leiden – Boston: E.J. Brill.

Van Leur, Jacob Cornelis, 1955, *Indonesian Trade and Society: Essays in Asian Social and Economic History*, The Hague. Reprint: Foris Publication Holland, Dordrecht/ U.S.A., Cinnaminson, 1983.

Van Naerssen, F.H. & R.C. De Iongh, 1977, *The Economic and Administrative History of Early Indonesia*, (Handbuch der Orientalistik 3.7), Leiden/Köln: E.J. Brill.

Vogel, J.Ph., 1918, 'The Yūpa Inscriptions of King Mūlavarman, from Koetei (East Borneo)', *Bijdragen tot de Taal-, Land- en Volkenkunde* 79, 167-232.

13

The Early Inscriptions of Indonesia and the Problem of the Sanskrit Cosmopolis

Daud Ali

The original aim of this paper, following from my own work in early medieval Indian history, was to explore the role that South Asian political ideas and practices played in the transformation of early Southeast Asian societies. Partly inspired by Hermann Kulke's work on state-formation, partly by Sheldon Pollock's recent theory of the 'Sanskrit cosmopolis', both of which, in different ways, have argued for strong continuities in the cultural and social development of South and Southeast Asia in early medieval times, I sought to correlate the literary, ideological and administrative aspects of early Indonesian inscriptions against their wider social contexts. The research, however, threw up some major analytical problems which have proved very instructive, the most pertinent of which was the difficulty of linking language practice and ideologies on the one hand and state 'structures' and social formations on the other. My findings, which seem clearly as relevant for South as for Southeast Asian history, suggest that the relations between 'cultural practices' and state structures are highly complex and shifting. While this may seem like a point of almost staggering banality, I hope to show more precisely how such an analytical awareness may add a new perspective on highly-touted theories of linguistic and cultural 'cosmopolitanism' inspired by Pollock's work. Before turning to the evidence, this essay will place the discussion within an analytical environment through a brief survey of major approaches to understanding the role of South Asian culture in Southeast Asian history.

SANSKRIT AND STATE FORMATION IN SOUTHEAST ASIA:
FROM EMPIRE TO COSMOPOLIS

The historiography of South and Southeast Asian interactions, and indeed the conceptualization of the conference itself, 'Early Indian influences in Southeast Asia', has a well-established pedigree. Since at least the end of the nineteenth century, but more clearly since the rise of nationalist historiography in India, the topic has been of great interest to both scholars of South and Southeast Asian history. While there is no space here for a complete review of this work, it will be useful to present a brief account of the major approaches in order to situate my own concerns. Earlier generations of nationalist scholarship in India forwarded the idea of Hindu colonies in the Far East, of a vast cultural 'empire' known as 'Greater India'. Scholars of this generation, like R.C. Majumdar and H.B. Sarkar initiated grand research projects and marshalled the materials which French and Dutch scholars had assembled in ways that tended to portray Indian influence in Southeast Asia as a politico-cultural imperialism, a sort of eastward *mission civilisatrice*.[1] Notwithstanding some careful empirical and long lasting work forwarded by such scholars, history conspired to overtake this view. With the gradual collapse of colonial empires and the rise of nationalist assertion in Southeast Asia, the concepts of 'Greater India' and 'Hindu colonies' were deemed outmoded vestiges of a colonial mindset.[2] European historians instead forwarded the theory of 'Indianisation' as an alternative, debates around which raged for nearly three decades. Perhaps its most well known proponent was the eminent historian and epigraphist George Coedès, who rejected the notion that Southeast Asia was colonized by Hindu kings (by this time dubbed the 'kṣatriya' thesis) in favour of the role of brahman advisors, ritual specialists and merchants, who 'transplanted' Indic civilisation in the region (the so-called 'brahman' and 'vaiśya' theories).[3] The upshot of these debates was to establish conclusively that any process of 'Indianisation', to whatever extent it occurred, was not effected through political dominion but through various complex interactions between South Asian intellectuals, merchants or ritual specialists on the one hand, and local Southeast Asian elites on the other. It became widely accepted that cultural contact probably followed commercial interaction between south India and Southeast Asia, which was in turn connected to wider trade networks in the Indian Ocean. What has been a matter of debate, on the other hand, and has been far more difficult to decide, is the relative agency that various parties exercised in the process of cultural transmission.

In ensuing discussions, it was argued that the theory of Indianization was too 'Indo-centric' in its basic assumption of the transplantation of a superior and dynamic civilization upon relatively inert local cultures. Scholars making this argument, like J.G. de Casparis and O.W. Wolters, sought not so much to exclude Indic influences as to show how local peoples had been able to absorb, translate and recontextualise such external elements for their own ends.[4] What 'Indianisation' actually facilitated was not so much adopting practices and making their own culture 'Indian', but the consolidation of already existing indigenous concepts and practices under new terminology. Wolters, for example, argued that the Hindu concept of bhakti was grafted onto the local cult of the 'man of prowess', creating a new status of overlordship, and thereby effectively bringing 'persisting indigenous beliefs into sharper focus'.[5] This scholarship, with its far more complex theories of cultural interaction, has rightly left an indelible mark on the field of Southeast Asian studies to date. Consequently, Indo-centric models and theories of 'Indian influences', have quite correctly been less emphasised paradigms for research in Southeast Asian history.

Wolters' perspectives have drawn various criticisms from Southeast Asianists over the years. But more recently, the Sanskritist Sheldon Pollock has launched an apparently more withering and polemical critique against what he labels the 'civilisationalist indigenism' of Wolters and others. Pollock argues, like Craig Reynolds and Victor Lieberman, that 'indigenist' historiography is deeply flawed in its projection of some ahistorical and unitary essence back into history.[6] But more pointedly, he suggests that Wolters' theory of the persistence of indigenous ideas through the process of Indianisation is both empirically unjustified and theoretically misguided. Pollock asserts that as far as 'the key conceptions that underwrote many Southeast Asian polities' like universal sovereignty and *bhakti*, 'there is a lot of Indian evidence but none from non-Indian Southeast Asia'.[7] In fact, Pollock continues, 'it is from the Sanskrit evidence that Wolters derives much of his interpretation of Southeast Asian kingship and political systems more generally'.[8] Perhaps most profoundly, Pollock accuses Wolters of presuming that a particular historical 'thought-world' could exist somehow separated from the language in which it is embodied.[9] For Pollock, Sanskrit could never signify local ideas, because ideas themselves must be constituted through language and in being expressed in Sanskrit, become ipso facto, Sanskrit ideas. I will have occasion to return to this point.

Pollock provides his own account of this transformation, or 'transculturation' as he calls it, in Southeast Asia. He does so against the backdrop of his wider theory of Sanskrit literary culture, which begins from the observation that, from about CE 300, classical Sanskrit poetry (*kāvya*) quite suddenly became the preferred public proclamatory and prestige language at courts across South Asia itself. Departing from ahistorical literary studies and traditions of Indology that have tended to root all Indian cultural developments in hoary antiquity, Pollock argues that the rise of Sanskrit *kāvya* was a cultural phenomenon so remarkable and consequential that it requires a theorisation all its own. Pollock documents the spread of Sanskrit *kāvya* through its rise in inscriptions as public courtly documents almost simultaneously at the courts of South and Southeast Asia in the first half of the first millennium CE. Pollock calls this cultural formation the 'Sanskrit cosmopolis' – a world in which perduring political claims were articulated in a grammatically regularised language, which made claims to be eternal, universal, and non-placeable. A key feature of cosmopolitan language use in these inscriptions, according to Pollock, was a neat division of linguistic labour between Sanskrit and local languages. Inscriptions show a strong tendency to relegate non-literary, everyday and 'documentary' discourse to local languages, while reserving the diplomatic and rhetorical parts of inscriptions where claims about universal kingship were made for Sanskrit. The effect of this was to emphasise the superordinate and universal quality of Sanskrit and to link political power and aesthetic expression. The importance of this trans-regional cosmopolitanism, for Pollock, does not simply derive from its distinct configuration of language, locality and power largely at odds with our own. In history, the Sanskrit cosmopolis left a strong imprint on the rise of regional 'vernacular' literatures in the first half of the second millennium CE. Far from welling up from popular sources, these literatures were self-consciously fashioned by elites who patterned them on a cosmopolitan, Sanskrit, prototype. Sanskrit, in other words, taught the vernaculars how to be literary.

Many interpretive implications of Pollock's thesis have yet to be fully discussed. At first glance, the Sanskrit cosmopolis would seem to rehabilitate older notions of a 'Greater India' or India's 'cultural empire' which Southeast Asian historians for the last twenty-five years have worked so hard (and so effectively) to overturn. But such a conclusion would be hasty, as Pollock is emphatic to note that Sanskrit influences in the region did not arrive through military presence, political subordination, material exploitation, or even through substantial Indian settlements. For Pollock, this makes the spread of Sanskrit *kāvya*, through the agency of merchants, adventurers and itinerant religious entrepreneurs, all the more remarkable. The attraction of Sanskrit *kāvya*, according to Pollock, was the same in both South and Southeast Asia: it served as a language of power par excellence, with its eternal moral claims and notions of universal overlordship, and most importantly, its aestheticization of power itself. Sanskrit *kāvya*, originally patronised by Śakas and Kūṣāṇas (then-recent migrants to the South Asian subcontinent), was in any event hardly the property of the national state of 'India', and extended far beyond its modern borders. Most profoundly, Sanskrit never identified itself as the language of a particular region – in other words, the ideology of Sanskrit, like other premodern cosmopolitan languages, asserted its provenance as universal and not local. For Pollock, the adoption of Sanskrit by the courts of South and Southeast Asia did not represent a 'Hinduisation' or 'Indianisation' of these regions, but instead a participation in the cosmopolitan culture of Sanskrit itself – a world where claims to self-identification, representation and sovereignty were articulated in a common poetic language.

The theory of a spreading Sanskrit cosmopolitanism becomes particularly interesting when set against the background of recent (or perhaps not so recent) theories of state formation in South and Southeast Asia. That Pollock himself did not undertake this task is significant – in fact, the extensive literature on states and state formation in early South and Southeast Asia is conspicuously absent from his otherwise exhaustive account of the Sanskrit cosmopolis. Pollock's indifference to this scholarship is hardly accidental, being connected to his sustained criticism of the regnant social scientific approaches to 'ideology'. While his disagreement with historians for their banalisation of Sanskrit sources through the paradigm of 'legitimation' may be justified, his own attempt to connect Sanskrit and power would have been enhanced considerably by attention to this literature. Pollock suggests that Sanskrit serves to aestheticise power – a wholly acceptable first premise. But, in side-stepping the ideological content of Sanskrit literature beyond its self-referential nature, Pollock in the end focuses on literary-language choice alone, 'conversion to the Sanskrit literary complex' as the primary descriptor of power. Literariness itself serves as the sign of power. The trajectory of Pollock's argument leads him to postulate such tantalising but perhaps tenuous ideas as 'cosmopolitan' and 'vernacular' polities. Beyond highlighting the indisputably important point of literary language use, it is not clear what such terms could possibly describe.

Interestingly, studies of state-formation in Southeast Asia have provided their own, equally compelling, critique of the Indianisation theory. The influential reassessments of the nature and structure of early Southeast Asian states by Wolters, Tambiah, and Kulke (among others) over the last thirty years, along with the emphasis on local, long-term historical development, partly driven by archaeology, have involved serious reconsiderations of the idea of 'Indianisation'.[10] As long as pre-Indianised Southeast Asia was viewed as a primitive region populated by small tribes and bands and the early states as full-fledged empires and kingdoms, then, according to Kulke, 'it was an obvious, if not the only rational conclusion to regard India as sole origin and transmitter of civilisation to Southeast Asia and initiator of its history'.[11] With these certainties undermined, new frameworks were required.

Particularly important has been the work of the historian of India Hermann Kulke, who, drawing on his own extensive research on Orissa, suggested the point that the experience of local societies receiving impetus toward state-formation by 'Indianising' elites was not unique to Southeast Asia but also applied to the eastern and southern regions of the South Asian subcontinent. The markers of what is called 'Indianisation' in the historiography of Southeast

Asia – Sanskrit inscriptions, Hindu temples, social stratification and the spread of intensive wet-rice agriculture – appeared simultaneously in various regions of South and Southeast Asia at roughly the same time.[12] The ideology of kingship which emanated from the courts of the Gupta empire found fertile ground in Southeast Asia for the same reasons that it did in eastern and southern India, suggesting a social 'nearness' or convergence on both sides of the Bay of Bengal. The intellectuals and scribes who formed the conduits of Sanskrit *kāvya* and the Pallava script to Indonesia in *c.* CE 400 were not the civilising 'emissaries' or agents of powerful south Indian kingdoms, but arrived with experience at nascently formed princely courts which had shared similar backgrounds and faced similar problems in establishing authority. This led Kulke to postulate a social 'convergence' between the regions which made them part of the same historical development. Drawing on a seminal but neglected line of enquiry outlined by de Casparis in the early 1980s, in which he proposed in lieu of the theory of Indianisation 'a complicated network of relations, both between various parts of each of the two great regions and between the two regions themselves', Kulke suggested that once the regions were viewed in this manner, it was clear that Indian culture did not reach Southeast Asia through any moment of 'transplantation', but through a continuous and complex set of networks of relations within and between the regions, by mutual processes which linked both sides of the Bay of Bengal.

It is notable, and in fact the premise for my discussion so far, that Kulke's theory of social circulation, networks and convergence clearly in some ways provides a sociological complement to Pollock's Sanskrit cosmopolis. But how well, if at all, do the two theories really fit? In the remainder of this paper I will review the evidence of early Indonesian inscriptions to evaluate different forms of localizing political discourse in Sanskrit and their implications for a Cosmopolis in Southeast Asia.

THE INSCRIPTIONS OF THE EARLY STATES OF JAVA AND SUMATRA

Before beginning, it is perhaps worth noting just how important Southeast Asia is for any theory of early Indic or Sanskritic 'cosmopolitanism'. This is the case for at least two reasons. The first is obvious – it would be difficult to imagine any claim that Sanskrit was cosmopolitan if it had not indeed spread across geographically and culturally diverse regions. Had the Sanskrit Cosmopolis been confined to South Asia alone, then it is hard to imagine that the theory would have its current leverage, though theoretically, as I have hinted, this would hardly render it incoherent or useless, if we were to simply prise ourselves away from nationalist frameworks. But it does, I think, explain, why one might want to look outside the modern state of India to make the case. And between the two major options for exploration in this regard, Central and Southeast Asia, it is the latter that provides the most copious and useful evidence for the theory. Indeed, and the second reason, more connected to our concern here, is that Southeast Asia forms a perfect test case for the theory itself, both in terms of the adaptability of cosmopolitan culture, but more specifically, as a region which seems to conform perfectly to Pollock's model of the neat division of Sanskrit and local languages in epigraphy. Indeed, to the extent that the idea of the Sanskrit Cosmopolis relies on this purported division of labour in epigraphic discourse – between cosmopolitan and regional languages, between the literary/symbolic aspects of inscriptions carried in Sanskrit and the quotidian/documentary parts of inscriptions set out in local languages – it is perhaps an embarrassing fact that most of Indian epigraphy does not in fact conform to this framework. North Indian epigraphy from Gupta times is entirely in Sanskrit, and in south India, it is only some of the dynasties of the early medieval Deccan, along with the Pallavas, that divide their inscriptions between Sanskrit and local languages in this way. Inscriptions of such powerful dynasties as the Pāṇḍyas and Cōḷas, again, do not conform in any clear way to Pollock's model.[13]

But despite the impression one gets from Pollock's account of Sanskrit in Southeast Asia, the evidence again is highly variable and complex. Angkor inscriptions seem to fit the linguistic division more clearly, with Sanskrit and Khmer apparently conforming neatly to rhetorical and documentary roles. When we come to Indonesia, however, the situation is much less clear. Bilingual records, with a few notable exceptions, are unusual. Monolingual Sanskrit inscriptions tend, like the early fifth-century records of Borneo and the fifth- and later eighth-century inscriptions from Western and Central Java, to be entirely in verse, sometimes including the documentary details of gifts in a manner similar to that of north Indian inscriptional practice.[14] Inscriptions in Sumatra at the end of the seventh century are either Sanskrit verse fragments or larger prose inscriptions in Old Malay with Sanskritised vocabulary. An important exception to this is the remarkable bi-lingual curse inscriptions we will have occasion to consider below, but significantly, they do not conform to Pollock's model. They do not separate their labour between 'cosmopolitan Sanskrit' and a local tongue, but between Old Malay and a still unidentified Austronesian language. In Java, soon after the appearance of the first Old Javanese prose inscription at the beginning of the ninth century in Central Java (after which Javanese becomes the official court language of the kings in the region), we find a rare bi-lingual inscription and then, some thirty years later, the first versified inscription in Old Javanese.[15] While Pollock may be correct to describe this as a seizure 'of the place of Sanskrit in the domain of royal inscription', one which inaugurated what he calls the 'cosmopolitan vernacular',[16] this state of affairs did not arise from a long-standing division of labour between Sanskrit and local languages in public discourse, as we find in Cambodia, a fact which may point to significant differences in the way we should conceive of the history of Sanskrit and its relations with 'vernaculars' in these regions.[17] Another problem of considerable bearing on the life of Sanskrit in Southeast Asia is the presence of Sanskrit loan words in Old Khmer, Old Malay and Old Javanese, a phenomenon readily apparent in the earliest epigraphic occurrence of these languages, and one distinct from Pollock's theory of a linguistic division of labour between them and Sanskrit. The diachronic documentation and analysis of such 'loan words' in Southeast Asian languages, still in its initial stages,[18] may help us understand the 'life' of Sanskrit as a literary prestige language in Southeast Asian contexts, not to mention processes of putative 'literisation' and 'vernacularisation' in later times. The point of such evidentiary nitpicking and empirical complication is not, I should hasten to add, to detract from Pollock's thesis on the rise of Sanskrit as a language of power, or its eventual displacement by vernaculars. These are, it seems to me, both indisputable and invaluable observations. It does, however, seriously question, I think, how we conceive of this power in relation to local contexts and political practice. This will become particularly clear when we look at some specific epigraphic examples from the earlier period in Indonesia.

I would like to compare the earliest inscriptions of Java and Borneo on the one hand with those of Sumatra and the Malay peninsula on the other. Among the earliest inscriptions in Island Southeast Asia are those found in south western Borneo and Western Java: the so-called *yūpa* inscriptions of Mūlavarman in Kutei, Borneo, and the 'footprint' inscriptions of Pūrṇavarman, near modern day Jakarta. These records share several features linguistically and palaeographically and are generally ascribed to the mid- to late-fifth century CE.[19] Both sets of inscriptions are entirely in Sanskrit verse and in the Pallava-Grantha script. In them we find kings with Sanskritised names ending in the suffix -*varman*, indicating a putative kṣatriya status. The inscriptions use a number of generic terms in Sanskrit meaning 'king' (*rāja*, *avanipati*, *narapati*, *narendra*) to refer to these men. They also associate the rule of each of these kings with a 'state' (*nagara*). They record gifts to Brahmans and refer to Indic deities and religious ideas. Both Mūlavarman and Pūrṇavarman are praised for having defeated rival kings (called *pārthiva* or *nṛpa*) in battle. The Tugu rock inscription uses the term *rājādhirāja*, 'king over kings' to describe Pūrṇavarman.[20] Finally, the inscriptions seem to suggest, as the term *rājādhirāja* itself implies, the existence of some sort of regularised hierarchy among subordinate rulers. The rendering of tribute (*karada*) and the distinction of being 'loyal' (*bhakta*) as opposed to refractory are explicitly mentioned. The idealisation of the monarch's feet and the mention of royal paraphernalia like banners suggest the presence of at least rudimentary political protocols and court rituals common elsewhere in the Sanskrit cosmopolis. But given the paucity of the epigraphic evidence, we cannot be certain about this. It may be concluded, then, that some elements of Indic political culture existed in these kingdoms – in a configuration similar to that found in parts of the Indian subcontinent at roughly the same time (from the middle and later Gupta period) – a point noted by Hermann Kulke some 20 years ago.[21]

For many years the appearance of Sanskrit inscriptions in fifth-century Borneo and Java was assumed to be the commencement of 'Indian contact' with insular Southeast Asia. But archaeologists in the last 20 years have been able to show that these early inscriptions emerged only after regular exchange with the Indian subcontinent 'had become the rule'.[22] What led to the rather sudden appearance of these inscriptions in the fifth century and a new spurt of cultural transformation must be sought, as O.W. Wolters first suggested, in the re-organisation of inter-regional trade networks between Chinese and Western Asian ports between the fifth and seventh centuries in which insular ports came to replace those associated with Funan and Champa as conduits for the flow of goods from Western Asia to China.[23] More than this, goods sourced in insular Southeast Asia, particularly aromatics and resins, came to replace certain West Asian goods in Chinese markets, giving traditional chiefdoms in coastal towns the impetus to develop elementary state structures.

Most scholars have pointed out, however, that it would probably be hasty to consider these small kingdoms 'empires' or even 'states' in the sense usually implied by the terms. While the inscriptions suggest that there was an attempt to subordinate rival rulers (chiefs) and even extract tribute from them, there is no evidence of the collection of taxes nor regularised relations between these town-courts and hinterland areas, though some sort of relations had to be developed with inland groups to source indigenous commodities for Chinese markets. Chinese sources mention a number of 'kingdoms' in the region who sent emissaries and even paid 'tribute', though this evidence needs to be read carefully, as many of these places cannot be clearly correlated with known coastal polities like those of Pūrṇavarman and Mūlavarman, and, perhaps just as importantly, Chinese accounts of their trading partners were often strongly coloured by the expectations of their authors.[24] The archaeological evidence of the kingdoms of Mūlavarman and Pūrṇavarman is sparse, almost non-existent in the case of Borneo and somewhat better in the case of Java, where continuous settlement has been documented from the early centuries CE at the nearby 'Buni' complex and some temple remains have been found at Batujaya near an ancient bed of the Tarum River.[25]

What is significant for our purposes, however, is that when 'incipient' state structures do emerge in sixth-century coastal regions as a result of trade dynamics with China, the palpable evidence is Indic-Sanskrit inscriptions and Vaiṣṇava and Buddhist sculpture. The adoption of Indic political terminology, royal rituals and religious practices was surely, given the existing contact with South Asia, a deliberate policy, no doubt partly motivated by the need to gain dominance over local rivals, as Hall has noted. Miksic has pointed out that the absence of any local language in these early inscriptions suggests a transformation of policies almost entirely confined to the highest reaches of these societies.[26] If this was indeed the scenario, we may rightly question the degree to which concepts and practices represented in the inscriptions had effective social referents in early Borneo and Java. It is difficult, in other words, to decide whether the usage of terms like *vaṁśa*, *kula*, *nagara* and *pura* reflect new social phenomena or 'map' onto existing institutions.[27] The newly acquired vocabulary, rituals and paraphernalia which accompanied this status may have had little 'significance for the workings of these political systems', being 'grafted', as it were, onto social realities very different from those in the societies that produced them.[28] Whatever the rhetoric of the inscriptions, in reality Pūrṇavarman and Mūlavarman may have remained 'primus inter pares among the local leaders',[29] with the difference that they now claimed putative kṣatriya status in the prestige language of Sanskrit.

The earliest inscriptions of Sumatra appear somewhat later than their Javanese and Borneo counterparts, in the seventh century, and are associated with the now famous and comparatively richly researched 'maritime empire' known as Śrīvijaya.[30] Most of these inscriptions have been found in the region of Palembang in southeastern Sumatra, the presumed centre of the state, with some important finds in outlying regions (including the island of Bangka off the east coast of Sumatra). These inscriptions, along with three further epigraphs (on the Malay peninsula and the adjoining Riau Archipelago), one of which is dated to the eighth century, constitute the bulk of the corpus of evidence for the state of Śrīvijaya.[31] It has been noted that this epigraphic legacy is remarkably thin by any standards for a state whose existence is said to span nearly half a millennium, and that without the 'external' evidence of Chinese, Arab and Indian sources, it would be difficult indeed to conclude on the basis of epigraphy, that Śrīvijaya was vastly different than the proto-states of Pūrṇavarman and Mūlavarman some two centuries before.[32]

Yet the differences in the inscriptions, as we shall see, are substantial and significant. The majority of the seventh-century inscriptions of Śrīvijaya are not in Sanskrit, but Old Malay, though they contain extensive Sanskrit vocabulary. The most important of these records is undoubtedly the Sabokingking (Telaga Batu) inscription dated reliably on palaeographic grounds to the environs of CE 686.[33] Abbreviated versions of this inscription have been found at Kota Kapur on the island of Bangka, Karang Berahi, in Jambi province, and at Palas Pasemah and Bungkuk in Lampung province, near the Sunda Straits –

suggesting some form of communications network between Palembang and these outlying regions.[34] The inscription takes the form not of praise verses to the king but instead a long prose imprecation directed against potential malefactors and subordinates disloyal to the king. The inscription is uttered in the voice of an unidentified (Śrīvijaya) king, warning a list of officials and subordinates against disobedience and treachery through an elaborate curse 'which was to be drunk by you' (*niminumāmu*). The inscription begins with several sentences in an Austronesian language which has not been definitively identified but which seems to include the words of the curse itself.[35] De Casparis surmised that the peculiar stele on which the inscription was carved, a sort of upright tablet or headstone crowned by a row of snake hoods with a bottom lip and spout, may have itself been used to produce the 'imprecation' water referred to in the text.[36] Water poured across the stone draining into the spout was infused with the power of the words contained in the inscription. Officials and subordinates were presumably offered this water, the drinking of which bound them to its stipulations on pain of activating the curse. While water or poison-drinking rituals are not unknown in early Indian sources, they are typically associated with ordeals or oaths resolving uncertainty and providing purification in legal matters, and do not appear in courtly and inscriptional sources for the purpose of establishing bonds of loyalty in this manner.[37]

Historians have naturally used these inscriptions to reconstruct the structure of the Śrīvijaya state, which by all accounts seems to have been more complex in its organisation than any previous archipelagic polity. Putting aside older interpretations of a great 'empire', more recent formulations have seen the Śrīvijaya state as a small but dynamic maritime kingdom with 'central' and 'district' administration.[38] Hermann Kulke, in an important re-assessment of the epigraphical evidence relying heavily on the Sabokingking (Telaga Batu) inscription, has suggested that Śrīvijaya was characterised by a central core, composed of a palace (*kadātuan*) and its immediate urban-rural environment (*vanua*) surrounded by a series of concentric rings of decreasing authority and political control – a hinterland area (*samaryyada*) where the centre shared authority with local princely chiefs (*dātus*) and geographically more distant outlying regions (*maṇḍalas*) beyond the Musi River system where local polities had been subdued (but not annexed) by the military power of the centre and whose chiefs expressed loyalty to the king.[39] Ultimately, according to Kulke, Śrīvijaya's reluctance (or inability) to consolidate itself into a more centralised structure may have allowed it to survive for nearly five centuries and to outlive many more centralised empires in the region and beyond.[40]

The Sabokingking inscription is addressed to a large list of classes of individuals frequently encountered in South Asian epigraphy from post-Gupta times, including *yuvarāja* (crown prince), *rājaputras* (princes of royal blood), *bhūpati*s (chiefs or kings), *nāyaka*s, *daṇḍanāyaka*s and *senāpati*s (types of military leaders), *kumārāmātya*s (high ministers), *vaṇiyāga* (merchants), *cāṭa*s and *bhaṭa*s (soldiers and police), *adhikaraṇa*s (officers), *kāyastha*s (scribes), and *sthāpaka*s (architects). While many of the Sanskrit names for officials are well known from contemporary Indian epigraphy, and may have been of uncertain reality in various contexts even within South Asia, the list is unlikely to have been an entirely rootless imposition on local political structures, because of the fact that the Sanskrit terms, unlike the earlier inscriptions from Java and Borneo we have noted above, are interspersed with local Indonesian or Old Malay terms such as *dātu* (chief), *marsī hāji* (royal intimates or vassals),[41] *hulun hāji* (royal servants or slaves), *hulun tuhān* (senior servants or slaves),[42] *puhāvaṃ* (shipmasters), and in one case a Sanskrit and Old Malay compound term, *hājipratyaya*.[43]

The hierarchy, institutions, and concepts represented in the Sabokingking inscription and its cognates constitute a hybrid political vocabulary, with a complex distribution of Sanskrit and Old Malay lexical items across the inscription. So while many of the men reporting to the king are given Sanskrit titles, where we find a differentiation of roles and functions typical of South Asian court polities, certain social groups (ship masters, for example) and particularly servants and relations who enjoyed great intimacy and physical proximity to the king's person – his intimates, servants or slaves, but also the women of his household (*vini hāji*) – retain Old Malay designations – an important lexical pattern. Fundamental political building blocks like the royal residence (*kadātuan*) and chief (*dātu*) and village settlement area (*vanua*) were expressed through (presumably long-standing) Old Malay terms, while other political (presumably new) divisions indicated by Sanskrit words like *maṇḍala*, *samaryyada* and *bhūmi*. Categories of servants or slaves (*hulun*) co-existed not only with the diverse functional hierarchies of offices but with family and lineage units invested with Sanskritic vocabulary (*kula*, *gotra*, *vaṃśa*). *Dātu*s could be held by varieties of lords with 'princely' designations drawn from the Sanskrit lexicon (*yuvarāja*, *pratiyuvarāja*, *rājakumāra*) whose local connotations are far from clear. Affiliative and dispositional vocabulary remains equally mixed, with words for concepts like disloyalty (*tīda bhakti*) and 'traitor' (*drohaka*) being taken from Sanskrit usage. The inscription warns against the use of artificial means of controlling people (*vaśīkaraṇa*) and spells (*mantra*) using terms well-known from Sanskrit sources, but the more important words for the curse and imprecation constituted by the body of the inscription itself, are indigenous terms (*maṃmaṃ*, *sumpaṃ*). Other concepts, like command and the delegation of power (*nigalarku*, *nisaṃvarddhiku*) use both Old Malay and Sanskrit and still other Sanskritic terms seem to denote meanings not at all widespread in South Asian epigraphy.[44]

In short, the evidence of the Sabokingking inscription indicates a deep entanglement of Sanskritized 'cosmopolitan' elements with local usage. Even taking into account the existence of seventh-century Sanskrit verse epigraphs (surviving in fragments) found in southern Sumatra and the famous Ligor (Nakhon si Dhammarat) Sanskrit inscription associated with Śrīvijaya in the eighth century, the evidence suggests, firstly, that the political culture and expressive registers of Śrīvijaya were decidedly not derived solely from a Sanskrit lexicon of cosmopolitan vocabulary. The picture is far more complex and calls for the sort of study carried out by Lustig, Evans and Richards (though with an admittedly larger database). While Sanskrit words denoted some of the most quotidian elements of everyday administrative and material culture (belying any claim for a neat linguistic division of labour), some of the most exalted and highly 'symbolic' terminology was expressed in indigenous vocabulary.

If the early inscriptions of Java and Borneo are compared with those of Śrīvijayan Sumatra, it will be noticed that the earlier records present a more exalted and 'pristine', if somewhat spare, political rhetoric, one that might be largely indistinguishable, to follow Pollock's claim, from its South Asian counterparts. Yet the political reality behind such early records was undoubtedly quite different than that of our later Sumatra inscriptions. Indeed, the early inscriptions seem to represent a political rhetoric at one level apparently 'misaligned' with the social contexts in which they functioned. This, of course, did not diminish the utility of Sanskritic discourse for these early chiefly lineages. Sanskrit and its world clearly functioned as a source of prestige, but one that was perhaps ideologically 'over-calibrated' for the society in which it functioned and thus effectively 'blunt' in its social implications, when compared to the more 'embedded', Sanskritised, vocabulary found in the Old Malay inscriptions of Śrīvijaya. Indeed, Sanskritic discourse perhaps precisely because of its rootless and transposable universality, could function as a rhetorical storehouse for social formations of considerably less complexity than those that generated it. The corpus of Śrīvijaya inscriptions indicates a world in which Sanskrit terminology had taken a much firmer hold on political reality, not as a rootless prestige object but a vocabulary 'translated' and imbricated into a local discursive context, bearing considerably more semantic 'weight' in social reality. Old Malay cannot be said to have functioned, at least at this point, as a 'cosmopolitan' or 'literised' vernacular in Pollock's sense, where local languages come into literary existence through the adoption and localisation of Sanskrit models, as in the case of Old Javanese. The Old Malay inscriptions are not in fact in verse and do not try to occupy the place of poetry. Nor is there any clear evidence to demonstrate a vernacularised 'literisation' of Old Malay from a prehistory of Indic or Khmer-style cosmopolitanism in Sumatra.

Yet there is a certain sense in which the appearance of Sanskrit in the region does seem to bring with it a sea-change in political practice – a change best indicated by the Sabokingking inscription itself. While this important record and its cognates have effectively been seen (in the manner of Indian copper-plate grants) as revealing a kind of 'state structure' composed of ranks and functions, scholars have tended to pass over an important feature of this inscription. In contrast to the thousands of royal land grants and laudatory inscriptions from South and Southeast Asia, preceded by *prasastis*, which functioned as legal deeds of economic entitlement, the Sabokingking inscription seems to have an explicitly performative or constitutive element for the political realm. As a sort of 'oath', it served the explicit function of 'binding' servants and subordinates to the king. By imbibing water that had passed across the inscribed face of the stele – the text of the inscription – individuals pledged loyalty and made themselves subject to the power of its words. The Sabokingking inscription, then, served as something of a 'charter' or 'constitution' for politico-economic relations in early Śrīvijaya.[45] What is perhaps most significant about this document from the vantage point of the concerns of this essay is that it seems to be forging an entirely new political dispensation, one in which older but hitherto undocumented social identities and relationships marked by terms like *dātu, hāji, hulun*, take on a new social being, indicated at the very least by the fact of their first appearance in the historical record. It is indeed significant that the first epigraphical evidence of such presumably pre-existent elements of political culture occurs precisely at the historical conjuncture of the new – and here Pollock is right to emphasise the watershed of Sanskrit in the region and to raise questions about any strong claims to ancient, sedimented realities. Existing political terminologies clearly gained a new 'being' through their imbrication and alignment with the Sanskrit-based language of political identity which had been circulating in the region. The relations being forged in this inscription between the traditional roles of *dātu* and *hāji* cannot be understood, in other words, without appreciating the importance of apparently hitherto 'unthematised' concepts of affiliation, like *bhakti* and *droha*. But by the same token, Sanskrit in seventh-century Sumatra does not simply impose itself as a seamless and self-referential sign system. Indeed, the significant point may be that in the end, Sanskrit's career in Palembang seems to have stimulated the local, rather than effaced it.

The analysis above has suggested two related points. First, that the apportioning of symbolic and quotidian functions to Sanskrit and local languages, respectively, is too simple a paradigm for epigraphic reality, either in South Asia or beyond, but particularly in the case of Southeast Asian epigraphy. Sanskrit in Southeast Asia was hardly reserved for exclusively 'eternal' rhetorical claims; it also articulated quotidian, material ones, particularly as a language of formal affiliation among elites, where it rubbed shoulders with and stimulated the development of other, existing vocabularies of power. Southeast Asian languages, by the same token, very often took part in the ongoing construction of symbolic registers and terminologies of lordship from the very outset, as is very clear from the Śrīvijaya epigraphs. Second, and perhaps more importantly, Sanskrit, as a set of discursive claims and symbolic practices, did not express a single set of 'meanings', or have an inevitable set of implications for a given thought world and its relation to social structures. The comparison between the inscriptions of early Java and Borneo and those from Sumatra suggest that various elements of Sanskrit cosmopolitanism could function very differently in divergent political environments. The relevant point is perhaps that expressive registers, literary formations, and ideologies, in their journeys across social landscapes, articulate with different social realities in a variety of ways. Indeed, ideology should be conceived, to use the insight of V.N. Vološinov, not as monological utterance, but as an unstable and multivalent sign system.[46] Despite its cosmopolitan transposability, Sanskrit in Southeast Asia gained its ideological 'traction' and local meaning through a diversity of imbrications with existing ideologies and language practices. The examples presented demonstrate clearly that there were different ways in which localisation could work in the process of Sanskritic 'transculturation'. In the end, Wolters' approach may be more helpful than Pollock would have us believe, and I hope here to have vindicated him.

NOTES

1. R.C. Majumdar, *Hindu Colonies in the Far East*, Calcutta: Firma K.L. Mukhopadhyay, 1944; and the much more finely researched works of H.B. Sarkar, including *Indian Influences on the Literature of Java and Bali*, Calcutta: Greater India Society, 1934.
2. There had been critiques of these ideas as early as the 1930s, most notably by the Dutch scholar van Leur, but his was published posthumously after an untimely death and gained due recognition only in the 1960s, Hermann Kulke, 'Indian Colonies, Indianization, or Cultural Convergence? Reflections on the Changing Image of India's Role in South-East Asia', *Semaian* 3, 1990, p. 11.
3. George Coedès, *The Indianized States of Southeast Asia* (Honolulu: East-West Center Press, 1968). The distinction between *kṣatriya*, *vaisya* and *brahmin* 'theories' was first made by See F.D.K. Bosch, *Selected Studies in Indonesian Archaeology*, The Hague: Hijhoff, 1961.
4. J.G. de Casparis, *India and Maritime South East Asia: a Lasting Relationship*, Kuala Lumpur: University of Malaya, 1983 and O.W. Wolters, *History, Culture and Region in Southeast Asian Perspectives*, Singapore: Institute of Southeast Asian Studies, 1982.
5. Wolters, *History, Culture and Region*, p. 9.
6. See Craig J. Reynolds, 'A New Look at Old Southeast Asia', *Journal of Asian Studies* 54, 2, 1995: 424 ff. and Victor Lieberman, *Strange Parallels: Southeast Asia in Global Context, 800-1830*, Cambridge: Cambridge University Press, 2003, p. 19.

7. Sheldon Pollock, *The Language of the Gods in the World of Men: Sanskrit, Culture and Power in Premodern India*, Berkeley: University of California Press, 2006, p. 531.

8. Pollock, *Language of the Gods*, p. 531.

9. Here Pollock seems to misread Wolters who does not so much suggest that Sanskrit terminology signified something completely different in local contexts, as that Sanskrit sensibilities were grafted onto local meanings, thereby accentuating and giving greater endurance to them, albeit through new vocabulary. The implication of Pollock's criticism, that Sanskrit words could not be invested with local meanings seems to presume a sort of monovocality for language at odds with his historical approach.

10. As Paul Wheatley commented, 'it was in the pre- and protohistoric paramountcies that much of the dynamism of the so-called Hinduization process should be sought'. Paul Wheatley, 'Presidential Address: India beyond the Ganges: Desultory Reflections on the Origins of Civilization in Southeast Asia', *Journal of Asian Studies* 42, no. 1, 1982, p. 18.

11. Kulke, 'Indian Colonies', p. 21.

12. 'The socio-political development of Eastern India during the first half of the first millennium AD…resembles in many respects the development in parts of Southeast Asia': Kulke, 'Indian Colonies', p. 24.

13. The copper plate inscriptions of the Pāṇḍyas from the eighth century begin with Sanskrit *praśasti*s but are often followed by sometimes quite elaborate Tamil verse portions providing eulogistic geneaologies of the Pāṇḍya kings. See the Velvikudi, Srivaramangalam, Chinnamanur, and Dalavaypuram copper plate grants, in K.G. Krishnan, ed., *Inscriptions of the Early Pāṇḍyas*, Delhi: Indian Council of Historical Research, 2002. The Cōḷas continue this practice, though their inscriptions are typically entirely in Tamil from an early stage, and from the reign of Rājarāja I (985-1014) a specifically designated, and officially sanctioned and standardised Tamil eulogistic poem praising the reigning king called *meykkīrtti* was prefixed to many royal orders. In the few Cōḷa copper plate inscriptions with a Sanskrit *praśasti*, these Tamil *meykkīrtti*s typically introduce the operative portions of the grant in Tamil. Herman Tieken has contended with reference to Pāṇḍya inscriptions, that the Tamil eulogies, present universal claims of their Sanskrit counterparts, provide detailed 'local histories', a point which, while it would seem to corroborate Pollock's claims, is highly debatable (see Herman Tieken, *Kāvya in South India: Old Tamil Caṃkam Poetry*, Groningen: Egbert Forsten, 2001, pp. 135-36. Nevertheless, the fact remains that both Tamil and Sanskrit here are in literary mode, and should both be distinguished from the operative portions of inscriptions. In other words, the neat dichotomy between Sanskrit as a symbolic and Tamil as administrative discourse, is not sustainable. Epigraphically, Tamil very early on had strong pretensions toward poetic claims and symbolic association – even in the presence of literary Sanskrit.

14. See verses 6-7 of the Kanjuruhan stone inscription of King Gajayāna, Sarkar, *Corpus of Inscriptions of Java*, vol. 1, pp. 25-33.

15. On the first Old Javanese prose inscription, see P.J. Zoetmulder, *Kalangwan: A Survey of Old Javanese Literature*, The Hague: Martinus Nijhoff, 1974, p. 3. For the first Sanskrit/Old Javanese bilingual inscription, dated to CE 824 from Karangtengah, see H.B. Sarkar, *Corpus of the Inscriptions of Java*, vol. 1, Calcutta: Firma K.L. Mukhopadhyay, 1971, pp. 64-75. For the first Old Javanese metrical inscription, see

J.G. de Casparis, *Prasasti Indonesia II: Selected Inscriptions from the 7th to 9th Century AD*, Bandung, 1956, pp. 280-330.

16. Pollock, *Language of the Gods*, pp. 387-89.

17. See the remarks of Zoetmulder, *Kalangwan*, pp. 15-17.

18. For Khmer inscriptions, see the innovative and suggestive study by Eileen Lustig, Damian Evans, and Ngaire Richards, 'Words Across Space and Time: An Analysis of Lexical Items in Khmer Inscriptions, Sixth-Fourteenth Centuries', *Journal of Southeast Asian Studies* 38, 1, 2007, esp. pp. 15-16.

19. For texts of the Kutei inscriptions, see B.C. Chhabra, *Expansion of Indo-Aryan Culture During Pallava Rule*, Delhi: Munshiram Manoharlal, 1965, appendix I; for the Western Java inscriptions, see Sarkar, *Corpus of the Inscriptions of Java*, vol. 1, pp. 1-12. The palaeographical dating of these inscriptions is problematic, because 'there was not much change in Pallava-Grantha characers betewen 400-750 AD,' Sarkar, p. 2. This may mean that they were in fact closer in date to the inscriptions of Sumatra than is otherwise assumed.

20. Sarkar, *Corpus of the Inscriptions of Java*, p. 6.

21. See Hermann Kulke, 'The Early and Imperial Kingdom in Southeast Asian History', in Kulke, ed., *Kings and Cults: State Formation and Legitimation in India and Southeast Asia*, New Delhi: Manohar, 2001 (1st pub. 1986), pp. 262-93; see also Hermann Kulke, 'Indian Colonies, Indianization, or Cultural Convergence? Reflections on the Changing Image of India's Role in South-East Asia', *Semaian* 3, 1990: 8-32.

22. Pierre-Yves Manguin, 'The Archaeology of Early Maritime Polities of Southeast Asia', in Ian Glover and Peter Bellwood, eds., *Southeast Asia: From Prehistory to History*, London: Routledge Curzon, 2004, p. 283.

23. See O.W. Wolters, *Early Indonesian Commerce: A Study of the Origins of Śrīvijaya*, Ithaca: Cornell University Press, 1967.

24. See the remarks of Keith Taylor on Chinese accounts of Champa, in Nicolas Tarling, ed., *The Cambridge History of Southeast Asia*, vol. 1, part 1, Cambridge: Cambridge University Press, 1999, pp. 153-54.

25. For summaries of archaeological evidence from Kutei in eastern Kalimantan and the Tarum river basin in western Java, see Manguin, 'The Archaeology of Early Maritime Polities of Southeast Asia', pp. 301-04.

26. John Miksic, 'The Classical Cultures of Indonesia', in Ian Glover and Peter Bellwood, eds., *Southeast Asia: From Prehsitory to History*, London: Routledge Curzon, 2004, p. 237.

27. See the remarks of Hermann Kulke, 'Epigraphical References to the "City" and "State" in Early Indonesia', in Kulke, *Kings and Cults: State Formation and Legitimation in India and Southeast Asia*, New Delhi: Manohar, 2001, pp. 308-09.

28. Cf. the remarks on Funan by Kenneth Hall, *Maritime Trade and State Development in Early Southeast Asia*, Honolulu: University of Hawaii Press, 1985, p. 67.

29. Kulke, 'Early and Imperial Kingdom', p. 274

30. Key early studies of this empire are K.A. Nilakanta Sastri, *History of Sri Vijaya*, Madras: University of Madras, 1949; O.W. Wolters, *Early Indonesian Commerce*; ibid., *The Fall of Śrīvijaya in Malay History*, Ithaca: Cornell University Press, 1970. Important studies in the last two decades include Hermann Kulke, '"Kadātuan Śrīvijaya" Empire or Kraton of Śrīvijaya? A Re-assessment of the Epigraphical Evidence', *BEFEO* 80, 3, 1993: 159-80; Edwards E. McKinnon, 'Early Polities in Southern Sumatra: Some

Preliminary Observations Based on Archaeological Evidence', *Indonesia*, 40, 1985: 1-36; *Studies on Srivijaya*, Jakarta: Pusat Penelitian Arkeologi Nasional, 1981; Nik Hassan Shuhaimi, 'The Kingdom of Srivijaya as a Socio-political and Cultural entity', in J. Kathirithamby-Wells and J. Villiers, eds. *The Southeast Asian Port and Polity: Rise and Demise*, Singapore: Singapore University Press, 1990, pp. 61-82. Pierre-Yves Manguin, 'Palembang and Sriwijaya: an Early Malay Harbour-City Rediscovered', *Journal of the Malayan Branch, Royal Asiatic Society*, 66, 1 (1993): 23-46; and Pierre-Yves Manguin, 'Sriwijaya, entre texte historique et terrain archéologique: un siècle à la recherche d'un État évanescent', *BEFEO*, 88, 1 (2001): 331-39. See also Pierre-Yves Manguin, *A Bibliography for Sriwijayan Studies*, Jakarta: EFEO, 1989.

31. For texts of the inscriptions in Palembang, see Nilakanta Sastri, *Sri Vijaya*, Appendix I, pp. 113-15 and de Casparis, *Prasasti Indonesia II*, pp. 1-15. For the Sabokingking inscription, see de Casparis *Prasasti Indonesia II*, pp. 15-46, for the inscription on the island of Bangka, see Nilakanta Sastri, *Sri Vijaya*, pp. 115-16. The much studied 'Ligor inscription' on the Malay Peninsula is available in Nilakanta Sastri, *Sri Vijaya*, pp. 119-21, 125.

32. See the remarks of Bennet Bronson, 'The Archaeology of Sumatra and the Problem of Srivijaya', in R.B. Smith and W. Watson, eds., *Early South East Asia: Essays in Archaeology, History and Historical Geography*, Oxford: Oxford University Press, 1979, pp. 395-405. Bronson's skepticism was based partly on what proved to be incorrect assumptions about the 'lateness' of archaeological remains at Palembang. See Pierre-Yves Manguin, 'Palembang and Sriwijaya: An Early Malay Harbour-City Rediscovered', *Journal of the Malaysian Branch of the Royal Asiatic Society* 66, 1, 1993: 23-46.

33. de Casparis, *Prasasti Indonesia II*, pp. 15-46.

34. For the Kota Kapur and Karang Berahi inscriptions, see Nilakanta Sastri, *Sri Vijaya*, pp. 115-16. For the Palas Pasemah inscription, see Boechari, 'An Old Malay Inscription at Palas Pasemah (South Lampong)', in *Pra Seminar Penelitian Sriwijaya*, Jakarta: Puslit Arkenas, 1978, pp. 19-42. For the badly weathered inscription at Bungkak, see Boechari, 'New Investigations on the Kedukan Bukit Inscription', in *Pusat Penelitian Arkeologi Nasional, Untuk Bapak Guru. Persembahan para murid untuk memperingati Usia Genup 80 Tahun Prof. Dr. A.J. Bernet Kempers*, Jakarta: Puslit Arkenas, 1986, pp. 33-56.

35. See Louis-Charles Damais, 'Language B of the Sriwijaya Inscriptions', *BEFEO* 54 (1968): 523-66.

36. See the remarks of de Casparis, *Prasasti Indonesia II*, pp. 28-29.

37. Oaths in early Indian society seem largely restricted to juridical or quasi-juridical contexts where they were used to exonerate an individual from some legal or social accusation. See P. V. Kane, *History of Dharmaśāstra*, vol. 3, Pune: Bhandarkar Oriental Research Institute, 1993 [repr], pp. 356-59; S.N. Pendse, *Oaths and Ordeals in Dharmaśāstra*, Baroda: University of Baroda, 1985, p. 200; and most recently Robert Yelle, 'Poetic Justice: Rhetoric in Hindu Ordeals and Legal Formulas', *Religion* 32, 2002, pp. 259-72, esp. p. 267.

38. See Hall, *Maritime Trade and State Development*, pp. 90-96, esp. the diagram on p. 96.

39. See Kulke, 'Kadātuan Śrīvijaya', see diagrame on p. 172.

40. Kulke, 'Kadātuan Śrīvijaya', p. 176.

41. de Casparis translates *marsī hāji* as 'royal washerman', on the basis of a presumed Old/modern Malay correspondence of *mar-* : *bər-* (*bərsih*, clean) but Adelaar has more convincingly argued for the sense of a reciprocal prefix, 'you who would treat each other as royal', i.e. intimates or relatives. See K. Alexander Adelaar, 'The Relevance of Salako for Proto-Malayic and for Old Malay Epigraphy', *Bijdragen tot de Taal-, Land- en Volkenkunde* 148, 3/4, 1992, pp. 394-96. Arlo Griffiths (personal communication) has suggested that the reflexive prefix may more likely mean 'those who consider each other King', i.e. fellow vassals.

42. de Casparis reads *huluntuhāṃku* as 'my empire', but Adelaar ('Relevance of Salako', p. 397) corrects to 'my senior servants'.

43. For a discussion of these terms, see de Casparis, *Prasasti Indonesia II*, pp. 19-20. The final compound, *hājipratyaya*, translated as 'royal sheriffs' by de Casparis, but perhaps more likely some sort of royal lessee, is unusual, its form following that of a *tatpuruṣa* compound in Sanskrit reversing the order of the Old Malay *hulun hāji*.

44. See the remarks on *samaryyada* and *bhūmi* in Kulke, 'Kadātuan Śrīvijaya', pp. 171, 175-76.

45. I am indebted to discussions with my colleague Whitney Cox for a number of the ideas expressed here.

46. See V.N. Vološinov, *Marxism and the Philosophy of Language*, trans. Ladislav Matejka and I.R. Titunik, Cambridge Massachusettes: Harvard University Press, 1973, pp. 14-16, 65-82.

REFERENCES

Adelaar, Alexander, 1992, 'The Relevance of Salako for Proto-Malayic and for Old Malay Epigraphy', *Bijdragen tot de Taal-, Land- en Volkenkunde* 148, nos. 3/4: 381-408.

Boechari, 1986, 'New Investigations on the Kodukan Bukit Inscription', in *Pusat Penelitian Arkeologi Nasional. Untuk Bapak Guru. Presembuhan para murid untuk memperingati Usia Genup 80 Tahun Prof. A. J. Bernet Kempers*, pp. 33-56. Jarkata: Arkenas.

———, 1978, 'An Old Malay Inscription at Palas Pasemah (South Lampong)', in *Pra Seminar Penelitian Sriwijaya*, pp. 19-42. Jakarta: Puslit Arkenas.

Bosch, F.D.K., 1961, *Selected Studies in Indonesian Archaeology*. The Hague: Nijhoff.

Bronson, Bennet, 1979, 'The Archaeology of Sumatra and the Problem of Srivijaya', in *Early South East Asia: Essays in Archaeology, History and Historical Geography*, ed. R.B. Smith and W. Watson, pp. 395-405. Oxford: Oxford University Press.

de Casparis, J.G., 1983, *India and Maritime South East Asia: A Lasting Relationship*. Kuala Lumpur: University of Malaya.

———, 1956, *Prasasti Indonesia II: Selected Inscriptions from the 7th to 9th Century AD*. Masa Baru, Bandung.

Chhabra, B.C., 1965, *Expansion of Indo-Aryan Culture During Pallava Rule*. Delhi: Munshiram Manoharlal.

Coedès, George, 1968, *The Indianized States of Southeast Asia*. Honolulu: East-West Center Press.

Damais, Louis Charles, 1968, 'Language B of the Sriwijaya Inscriptions', *BEFEO* 54: 523-66.

Hall, Kenneth, 1985, *Maritime Trade and State Development in Early Southeast Asia*. Honolulu: University of Hawaii Press.

Kane, P.V., 1993, *History of Dharmaśāstra*, 5 vols. Pune: Bhandarkar Oriental Research Institute [repr].

Krishnan, K.G., 2002, *Inscriptions of the Early Pāṇḍyas*. Delhi: Indian Council of Historical Research.

Kulke, Hermann, 2001, 'Epigraphical References to the "City" and "State" in Early Indonesia', in *Kings and Cults: State Formation and Legitimation in India and Southeast Asia*, ed. H. Kulke, pp. 294-326. Delhi: Manohar.

——, 2001, 'The Early and Imperial Kingdom in Southeast Asian History', in *Kings and Cults: State Formation and Legitimation in India and Southeast Asia*, ed. Hermann Kulke, pp. 262-93. Delhi: Manohar.

——, 1993, '"Kadātuan Śrīvijaya" Empire or Kraton of Śrīvijaya? A Re-assessment of the Epigraphical Evidence', *BEFEO* 80, no. 3: 159-80.

——, 1990, 'Indian Colonies, Indianization, or Cultural Convergence? Reflections on the Changing Image of India's Role in South-East Asia', *Semaian* 3: 8-32.

Lieberman, Victor, 2003, *Strange Parallels: Southeast Asia in Global Context, 800-1830*. Cambridge: Cambridge University Press.

Lustig, Eileen, Damian Evans, and Ngaire Richards, 2007, 'Words Across Space and Time: An Analysis of Lexical Items in Khmer Inscriptions, Sixth-Fourteenth Centuries', *Journal of Southeast Asian Studies* 38, no. 1: 1-26.

Majumdar, R.C., 1944, *Hindu Colonies in the Far East*. Calcutta: Firma K.L. Mukhopadhyay.

Manguin, Pierre-Yves, 2004, 'The Archaeology of Early Maritime Polities of Southeast Asia', in *Southeast Asia: From Prehistory to History*, ed. Peter Bellwood and Ian Glover, London: Routledge Curzon, pp. 282-313.

——, 2001, 'Sriwijaya, entre texte historique et terrain archéologique: un siècle à la recherche d'un État évanescent', *BEFEO* 88, no. 1: 331-39.

——, 1993, 'Palembang and Sriwijaya: An Early Malay Harbour-City Rediscovered', *Journal of the Malaysian Branch of the Royal Asiatic Society* 66, no. 1: 23-46.

——, 1989, *A Bibliography for Sriwijayan Studies*. Jakarta: EFEO.

McKinnon, Edwards E., 1985, 'Early Polities in Southern Sumatra: Some Preliminary Observations based on Archaeological Evidence', *Indonesia*, 40: 1-36.

Miksic, John, 2004, 'The Classical Cultures of Indonesia', in *Southeast Asia: From Prehistory to History*, ed. Peter Bellwood and Ian Glover. London: Routledge Curzon, pp. 234-56

Nilakanta Sastri, K.A., 1949, *History of Sri Vijaya*. Madras: University of Madras.

Pendse, S.N., 1985, *Oaths and Ordeals in Dharmaśāstra*. Varoda: University of Baroda.

Pollock, Sheldon, 2006, *The Language of the Gods in the World of Men: Sanskrit, Culture and Power in Premodern India*. Berkeley: University of California Press.

Reynolds, Craig J.,1995, 'A New Look at Old Southeast Asia', *Journal of Asian Studies* 54, 2: 419-446.

Sarkar, H.B., 1971, *Corpus of the Inscriptions of Java*, vol. 1. Calcutta: Firma K.L. Mukhopadhyay.

——, 1934, *Indian Influences on the Literature of Java and Bali*, Calcutta: Greater India Society.

Shuhaimi, Nik Hassan, 1990, 'The Kingdom of Srivijaya as a Socio-political and Cultural Entity', in *The Southeast Asian Port and Polity: Rise and Demise*, ed. J. Kathirithamby-Wells and J. Villiers, pp. 61-82. Singapore: Singapore University Press.

Tarling, Nicholas, ed., 1999, *The Cambridge History of Southeast Asia*, vol. 1, part 1. Cambridge: Cambridge University Press.

Tieken, Herman, 2001, *Kāvya in South India: Old Tamil Caṇkam Poetry*. Groningen: Egbert Forsten.

Wheatley, Paul, 1982, 'Presidential Address: India beyond the Ganges—Desultory Reflections on the Origins of Civilization in Southeast Asia', *Journal of Asian Studies* 42, no. 1: 13-28.

Wolters, O.W., 1982, *History, Culture and Region in Southeast Asian Perspectives*. Singapore: Institute of Southeast Asian Studies.

——, 1970, *The Fall of Śrīvijaya in Malay History*. Ithaca: Cornell University Press, 1970.

——, 1967, *Early Indonesian Commerce: A Study of the Origins of Śrīvijaya*. Ithaca: Cornell University Press.

Yelle, Robert, 2002, 'Poetic Justice: Rhetoric in Hindu Ordeals and Legal Formulas', *Religion* 32: 259-72.

Zoetmulder, P.J., 1974, *Kalangwan: A Survey of Old Javanese Literature*. The Hague: Martinus Nijhoff.

14

Indian Architecture in the 'Sanskrit Cosmopolis': The Temples of the Dieng Plateau

Julie Romain

The temples of the Dieng plateau (Dataran Tinggi Dieng) in Central Java represent some of the earliest Indian related architecture in Indonesia, but the precise date of their construction is unknown (Fig. 14.1). Scholars have dated them anywhere from the middle of the seventh to the end of

FIGURE 14.1
Candi Arjuna Complex, Indonesia, Central Java,
Dieng Plateau, eighth century (Photo by author)

the eighth centuries. This range places the Dieng temples on the timeline of Javanese temple architecture as the immediate predecessors to the larger temple building programmes such as those at Borobodur and Prambanan that begin in the late eighth/early ninth century, parallel to the rise of the Central Javanese kingdom of Mataram.

Where the dating of the Dieng temples becomes problematic is in the discussion of Indian influence on Javanese temple architecture. The Dieng temples contain stylistic referents to Indian stone temple forms and architectural motifs that only appear in India for the first time in the seventh century. The conventionally held view of scholars is that the Dieng temples were heavily influenced by the south Indian *drāvida* style temples and specifically those of the Pallavas who dominated the Coromandel coast from the fourth to ninth centuries CE. The Dieng temples have been compared to Pallava temples that were produced roughly around the mid-seventh to the early eighth century.

While the Dieng temples are clearly related to south Indian style temples, there are no exact counterparts that allow for a one to one comparison of Pallava and Dieng temples. Rather, the structures at Dieng incorporate an amalgamation of architectural motifs found across south India at this time with local stylistic elements which make them uniquely Javanese. Thus in the seventh century there is evidence in Java of an awareness of Indian temple models simultaneous to the evolution of free-standing stone temples on the Indian subcontinent. It is, therefore, difficult to determine the starting point for the diffusion of south Indian architecture traditions in Java. The degree of 'cultural convergence' of Indian and Javanese visual art traditions challenges the traditional model of influence used to explain Indian cultural diffusion in Southeast Asia (Kulke 1990).

Sheldon Pollock's recent work on the formation of a 'Sanskrit Cosmopolis' is a useful framework for thinking about the diffusion of Indian art tradition in Southeast Asia.[1] According to Pollock, the formation of a shared world-view across South and Southeast Asia took shape in the first millennium CE through the widespread adoption of Sanskrit as the primary language of political expression. By the fifth century CE, royal inscriptions exclusively used Sanskrit in the writing of *praśasti* (panegyric) and *kāvya* (literary composition, but particularly poetic verse), while local language was employed only for the purposes of documentation. This practice continued through the end of the first millennium; thereafter political eulogistic statements were expressed in vernacular languages. In Java, this process of 'vernacularization' began around the ninth century when Sanskrit was replaced by Old Javanese, a language that was itself formulated by integration of many aspects of Sanskrit language into traditional Javanese.

The universal adoption of Sanskrit as the primary language of political expression may have been a factor in the rapid adoption of Indian style art and architecture in Southeast Asia. In fact, Pollock conceives of South and Southeast Asia as all part of the same cultural matrix in which the formation of the Sanskrit Cosmopolis takes place simultaneously across an incredibly diverse landscape which extends as far west as Pakistan and as far east as Cambodia, including all of island Southeast Asia. However, unlike the exclusive use of Sanskrit as the language of royal political expression, there was not an exclusive Indian art style that was adopted across Southeast Asia in the production of Indian related art. Indian art was not confined by the same restrictions applied to royal inscriptions at the time. In extant Indian related art and architecture of Southeast Asia, it appears that certain regional Indian art traditions had a stronger impact on Southeast Asian art than others. There were times when north Indian art was more influential and other times when south Indian art was more influential. At times there may have been more than one Indian regional style referenced in Southeast Asian art at the same time. Southeast Asian artists chose from whichever Indian school best suited local predilections.

The purpose of this paper is to problematize the notion of Indian influence by looking at the dating of the earliest Indian related temples in Java in relation to contemporary temple production in India itself. My paper is based on a preliminary comparison of seventh- and eighth-century temple sites in Central Java, Tamil Nadu, Karṇāṭaka and Orissa. I have focused on Indian temple sites associated with the Cālukyas of Bādāmi (ruled *c.* CE 550-750) and the Pallavas of Kāñcīpuram (ruled *c.* third/fourth century-ninth century CE) because they were the predominant producers of temple architecture in south India during this time. In spite of ongoing territorial disputes between the Cālukyas and Pallavas, a significant amount of 'sharing' or 'borrowing' is evident among the artistic productions of both courts, while each maintained distinct regional 'Karnataka' and 'Tamil' identities (Tartakov 1980; Tartakov and Dehejia 1984). The height of Cālukya and Pallava court art immediately follows the rise of Pollock's 'Sanskrit Cosmopolis', so one of the questions to be addressed here is to what extent artistic production was impacted by the diffusion of Sanskrit literary culture in India and Southeast Asia.

DATING THE TEMPLES OF THE DIENG PLATEAU

Located in a caldera on the southern foot of Mt. Prahu and the western slopes of Mount Ungaran, Dieng, or 'Di-Hyang' in Old Javanese, means 'abode of the Gods.' The Dieng Plateau was a religious centre marked by temple building from the mid-seventh to the early thirteenth century. However, all that remains today are eight stone temples, including the five temples of the Candi Arjuna complex and three other temples located in their vicinity –

Candi Bima, Candi Davaravati and Candi Ghatotkaca. All the temples were constructed as individual shrines dedicated to Shiva; each is assumed to have once had a *liṅga* sculpture inside. One temple, Candi Srikandi, has relief sculptures of Shiva (east), Brahma (north) and Vishnu (south) still remaining on the outer walls of the shrine (Fig. 14.2). Another temple, Candi Semar, located directly in front of Candi Arjuna, may have been a subsidiary shrine for Nandi (Fig. 14.3). The temples were constructed in small clusters, and were configured like rows of small, individual shrines, delineated as a sacred precinct by a small brick-laid perimeter that encloses the structures.

The temples on the Dieng plateau were a pilgrimage centre where ascetics took residence in the foothills surrounding the Telega Warna (coloured lake), and made small meditation caves. Scholars believe the Dieng Plateau was probably a site of traditional ancestor worship, in which mountains were the dwelling of the gods. Dieng is mentioned as a sacred mountain in a CE 919

FIGURE 14.2
Vishnu, Candi Srikandi, Indonesia, Central Java, Dieng Plateau, eighth century
(Photo by author)

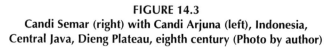

FIGURE 14.3
Candi Semar (right) with Candi Arjuna (left), Indonesia,
Central Java, Dieng Plateau, eighth century (Photo by author)

inscription where it is referred to as 'a priestly city,' accessible by stairways leading from the plains of Pekalongan to the north, and Bagelen to the south. A stairway made of igneous rocks was discovered in both areas between the years 1860 and 1870 (van Goor and Banner 1922: 23).

The Dieng plateau was re-inhabited around 1830 after which many of the temple remains were excavated. Evidence of roughly 400 temples was discovered with inscriptions dating from the ninth to the thirteenth century. Today the Dieng plateau is an agriculture centre with terraced farmlands along the valleys and foothills. Farmers reclaimed most of the land in the nineteenth century, and carted away the majority of the temple remains for building purposes. The eight remaining temples were named after characters in the Javanese version of the *Mahābhārata* in the modern era.[2]

Initial dating of the Dieng temples was based on a theory first put forth by the Dutch scholar E.B. Vogler (1949) that there were two phases of construction at Dieng: Candi Arjuna, Semar, Srikandi, and nearby Ghatotkaca were built in the early phase; Candi Puntadeva, Sembadra, and Davaravati were built in the later phase.

One temple, Candi Bima, poses problems of dating and classification because stylistically it is not consistent with other temples at Dieng. It more closely resembles north Indian *nāgara* style temples, and has often been compared to the seventh-century Paraśurameśvara temple at Bhubaneśvara

(Fig. 14.4). Most scholars place it in the later phase of construction at Dieng or the mid to late eighth century. If this is accurate, than the impact of north Indian models at Dieng cannot be ruled out, and this underlines another ongoing issue underlying the discourse of Indian influence which is to determine which regional Indian art tradition had the greatest impact on Southeast Asia.

Dating the Dieng temples is problematic also because although many inscriptions have been discovered on the plateau, none can be ascribed with certainty to any of the temples. Scholars have thus relied primarily on archaeological evidence and stylistic analysis to date the temples. The earliest dated inscription found near the Dieng temples is from the year CE 809 and the latest is dated CE 1210, indicating the possible continuation of temple activity well after the centre of political power in Java shifted to the east in the tenth century from Mataram (Dumarçay 1996).

The table provided below charts the dating of the Dieng temples by previous scholars, which I have identified with two different approaches (Table 14.1). The first type of analysis – represented here by the work of R. Soekmono (1979) and Joanna Williams (1981) – relies primarily on Indonesian archaeological and inscriptional evidence. The second type of analysis – represented by the work of Daigoro Chihara (1996) and Jacques Dumarçay (1993) – utilizes the same Indonesian evidence but relies heavily on comparisons to south Indian Pallava temples. I will begin by discussing

FIGURE 14.4
Paraśurāmeśvara temple, India, Orissa, Bhubaneśwara,
seventh century (image copyright American Institute of Indian Studies,
Varanasi, accession no. 1387, negative no. 48.45)

the approaches used by Soekmono and Williams and then deal with Chihara and Dumarçay in the following section.

Soekmono states that the earliest temples were built in the 'Old Dieng Style' between 650 and 730. Candi Canggal, located near Borobudur at Gunung Wukir (Mount Wukir), is the earliest temple associated with an inscription dated 732; however, only the base of this structure survives (Soekmono 1979: 471-72). Thus the Dieng temples are the earliest stone monuments available for study, and Soekmono believes these were completed prior to Candi Canggal. Temples of the Old Dieng Style include Candi Arjuna, Semar, Srikandi, and Ghatotkaca. A second phase of temple production or the 'New Dieng Style,' took place between 730 and 800, in which Candi Puntadeva, Sembadra, and Bima were built. The nearby Gedong Songo temples are also dated to this period as well as Candi Badut, which is the only temple made during this period in East Java.

Williams builds a chronology of Central Javanese monuments by analysing two architectural motifs – the profiles of mouldings and the presence of dentils found on the temple plinth, and the roof finials.[3] She notes that these motifs start out simple and become more elaborate over time. According to Williams, the style of the moulding profiles and finials of the Dieng temples are consistent with the earliest monuments of Central Java, which she argues were built between 732 and 778 (Williams 1981: 38-40). This date range is supported by inscriptional evidence – the 732 Candi Canggal inscription is the starting point, and a 778 inscription from Candi Kalasan in Prambanan marks the ending point.[4] The exception to this is Candi Bima, which Williams believes was built after 800.

TABLE 14.1

	Soekmono	Williams	Chihara	Dumarçay
Dieng Phase 1	*c.* 650-730	begins *c.* 732	±680 - ±730	650-750
Arjuna				
Semar				
Srikandi				
Ghatotkaca				
	*732 Candi Canggal inscription			
	*778 Candi Kalasan I inscription			
Dieng Phase 2	±730 -±800	ends ±778	±730 -±800	750-850
Puntadeva				
Sembodro				
Davaravati				
Bhima				

MAMALLAPURAM AND THE PALLAVA QUESTION

Chihara and Dumarçay follow a similar methodology to Soekmono and Williams to analyse the Dieng temples, but they rely heavily on comparisons with south Indian models to support their dating, and draw from specific Pallava structures based on the assumption that the earliest Sanskrit inscriptions in Java, attributed to the mid-fifth century, were written in Pallava script, and thus provide evidence of a long-standing relationship between the Pallavas and the Javanese.

Like Williams, Chihara analyses the profiles of the Dieng temple podia and plinths surmounting the podia, as well as ground plans and construction materials.[5] The early temples are identified by flat podia, while later temples are divided into 'northern' and 'southern' style designed podia (Chihara 1996: 102-05). Maintaining the two-phase construction scheme set forth by Vogler and then Soekmono, Chihara dates the earliest temples at Dieng to *c.* 680, and the second phase of construction between 730 and 780.

Chihara's dating of the Dieng temples hinges on a theory that the mid-seventh century Pañca Rathas, built by the Pallavas at Māmallapuram (known by its popular name Mahabalipuram), are the prototype for Dieng. Chihara says the basic ground plan of Javanese temples is the same *caitya-grha* plan found in India and mainland Southeast Asia (that is, any temple that provides interior shelter for housing a deity or *liṅga*), and that the specific prototypes for the Dieng temples are the Dharmarāja Ratha and the Arjuna Ratha monolithic structures (Chihara 1996: 97-99) (Figs. 14.5 and 14.6). His theory is supported by inscriptional evidence of undated Pallava script found near the Arjuna complex at Dieng (Chihara 1996: 106-07).

Chihara's study illustrates, however, a common misconception shared by previous studies of Dieng. Scholars have argued that the Dieng temples are primarily modelled after south Indian Pallava temples. This theory has been perpetuated by the conventional view that the earliest Indian inscriptions found in Southeast Asia were written in the same Pallava script associated with the Tamil Nadu kingdom, which has since been challenged by recent scholars.[6] While there may be strong resemblances between the Pallava script and the early Southeast Asian inscriptions, there are certain attributes of the latter which are completely absent in the Indian Pallava inscriptions. For example, Pollock notes in his study of the Sanskrit Cosmopolis that the earliest inscriptions found in Southeast Asia also share affinities with Early Cālukyan inscriptions, which used the north Indian Shaka dating system as well as verse, two attributes that are non-existent in the Pallava inscriptions of Tamil Nadu (Pollock 2006: 123, nn. 19 and 21). Finally, the earliest dated Dieng inscription of 809 is written not in Pallava script but in Old Javanese, in an early form of Kawi script.

FIGURE 14.5
Dharmarāja Ratha, India, Tamil Nadu, Māmallapuram, seventh century
(Photo by author)

FIGURE 14.6
Arjuna Ratha, India, Tamil Nadu, Māmallapuram, seventh century
(Photo by author)

Unfortunately, stylistic analysis of the Pañca Rathas and the Dieng temples does not yield overwhelming evidence to suggest that the former were the model for the latter. First, the Pañca Rathas are not free-standing temple structures but stone-carved monoliths, designed to emulate free-standing structures. Therefore, they cannot be considered an appropriate architectural prototype for the free-standing Dieng temples. Second, stylistically there are few similarities between the Dieng temples and the Pañca Rathas, except perhaps that the temples are raised on a high plinth with S-shaped staircases, but this is not an exclusive feature of Pallava temples. In fact, these are a common structural component of many Cālukya temples in Karṇāṭaka that are contemporary with Mamallapuram. Third, the tiered *śikharas* of the Pañca Rathas are comprised of miniature domed shrines instead of the multi-tiered shrines such as those reconstructed at Candi Arjuna (Fig. 14.3). Finally, covered porticos with pillars such as those found in the Pañca Rathas are non-existent in Central Javanese architecture.[7] There are also no lion pillars such as those found on the Pañca Rathas found at Dieng or any extant monuments of the Central Javanese period, except in relief sculptures at the Buddhist Candi Borobodur.

Finally, if – as Chihara suggests – the Dieng temples were started in the late seventh century, they could very well have been built at the same time the Pañca Rathas were built at Māmallapuram. While there has been much scholarly debate over the dating of Māmallapuram, most scholars now accept the following chronology: that the site was started by Māmalla I (Narasimhavarman I, ruled 630-68), who in addition to building several rock-cave temples, commissioned the narrative relief of Arjuna's penance and the Pañca Rathas some time after his victory over the Cālukya ruler Pulakeśin II (ruled 610-42) in 642, and the Shore temple was built by Māmalla's grandson, Rājasimha (Narasimhavarman II, ruled 700-28) in the early eighth century (Rabe 1997: 189, n. 3). However, the Pañca Rathas were never consecrated (their *śikhara* finials still lay on the ground beside each structure) and if, as others have argued, the Pañca Rathas were actually commissioned by Rājasimha and not Māmalla I, then they could not have been built any earlier than 690 (Nagaswamy 1962; Tartakov 1980: 98). The fact that the Pañca Rathas have the sedant lion capitals associated with Māmalla I indicates they were at least started during his reign; but work probably continued on them into Rājasimha's reign. Thus the proximity between the building of the Dieng temples and the Pañca Rathas makes the latter an unlikely candidate for influence on the former.

Dumarçay's analysis also maintains the two-phase construction scheme at Dieng, with the first phase beginning in the mid-seventh century and the second phase ending at the turn of the ninth century.[8] He also states that subsidiary shrines were added to the Arjuna complex later, and construction probably continued at this site through the year 850, with ongoing renovations.

Dumarçay's dating of the Dieng temple hinges on the assumption of a lost tradition of wooden temple construction in India and Java. Dumarçay maintains that proof of wood temple architecture in Java is evident from the aforementioned architectural reliefs that adorn the gallery walls of Candi Borobudur (Dumarçay 1977) (Fig. 14.7). He argues the transition from wood to stone architecture took place in Java in the late seventh century, and mirrors the transition from wood to stone temple architecture of the Pallava dynasty. Like Chihara, Dumarçay's theory is supported with the inscriptional evidence of Pallava script being used in Indonesia from the mid-fifth century (Dumarçay 1993: 57).

FIGURE 14.7
Drawing of Borobudur relief (from Dumarçay 1977, Pl. VII MA 139:
'Architecture figurée sur le relief E/I/10a, relevé FG')

Dumarçay notes a strong affinity between the Borobudur reliefs and
Pallava architecture, such as the Talagiriśvara temple at Panamalai in Tamil
Nadu (Fig. 14.8). He maintains the shape of the temple and its columns with
rampant lions at the base imitate wood architecture which was then translated
in stone. Clearly there are affinities between the Borobudur architecture reliefs
and the stone temple at Panamalai, and in this sense it is a much stronger
comparison than Chihara's comparison of the Dieng temples to the Pañca
Rathas. However, the Panamalai temple was built in the eighth century, which
is confirmed by the capitals with the rampant lions that adorn the temple that
are typically associated with Rājasimha's reign. Without material evidence
one cannot say with certainty that the temple in the Borobudur relief is based

FIGURE 14.8
Talagiriśvara temple, India, Tamil Nadu, Panamalai, eighth century (image
copyright American Academy of Benares, Varanasi, accession no. 7949,
negative no. 91.2)

on a wooden prototype from the seventh century. Given wood prototypes, one might expect to see subsequent examples in stone containing the same portico configured with rampant-lion pillars, but as stated above these do not exist in Central Javanese architecture.

Based on my own stylistic analysis of the Dieng temples and comparison of these to the nearby site of Gedong Songo (nine temples), where construction began slightly later than at Dieng in *c.* CE 750, I have concluded that the Dieng temples were probably made in the early eighth century. If I am correct, the earliest Dieng temples date to almost the same time as the earliest central Javanese temple (considering the date for Candi Canggal of 732).

While there is no supporting evidence to support the hypothesis of an exclusive Pallava Indian influence at Dieng, there is a strong likelihood that the temples are related to south Indian forms. With the exception of Candi Bima, all the Dieng temples have the distinctive *drāvida* style *śikhara*, or pyramid-like tower which is constructed in tiers of miniature shrines with finials as well as the aforementioned raised plinth and S-shaped staircases.

In effect, those aspects of the Dieng temples that are 'Indian' constitute an amalgamation of architectural motifs associated with various regional south Indian temple styles. Hence any study of Indian influence on Dieng temples must consider the broader landscape of temple building activity across south India in the seventh and eighth centuries, to which I now turn.

THE CHRONOLOGY OF EARLY STONE TEMPLES IN SOUTH INDIA

The earliest experimentation with free-standing stone architecture in India appears *c.* mid to late sixth century, with early *nāgara* style temples in the north and the *drāvida* style temples in the south developing from the seventh century onward.[9] Still unresolved is the discussion of which south Indian dynasty had a greater impact on the development of south Indian architecture – the Pallavas of Kañci or the Cālukyas of Bādāmi. The next phase of my research will examine this relationship in more detail. My preliminary research focused on the major seventh and eighth centuries sites associated with the Cālukyas (Bādāmi, Aihoḷe, Mahākūṭa and Paṭṭadakal) and the Pallavas (Kañci and Mamallapuram). Still to be researched are additional sites of the Cālukyas and Pallavas located outside their political centres, such as the various seventh and eighth century sites in Andhra and Tamil Nadu, as well as sites of the Early Pandyas, the third major regional south Indian court competing for territory at this time.

The earliest examples of free-standing stone architecture in south India are not found among Pallava sites but rather at the Cālukya site of Aihoḷe in northern Karṇāṭaka. The earliest dated free-standing south Indian temple is the Meguti temple, which has an inscription dated 634. The Upper Shivalaya temple, another Cālukya temple at Bādāmi, was made slightly later, in the mid-seventh century, and the Mahakuteśvara temple at Mahākūṭa is attributed to the late seventh century (Tartakor 1980).

By contrast, the earliest Pallava free-standing architecture is the Shore Temple in Mahabalipuram, which is dated to the reign of Rājasimha between 700 and 725. The Talagiriśvara temple at Panamalai referred to by Dumarçay is also attributed to this period. The last example of early eighth-century Pallava architecture is the Kailāsanātha temple at Kāñcīpuram. The latest temples of the Cālukyas of Bādāmi are the Virūpakṣa and Mallikarjuna temples of Paṭṭa-ḍakal, which were built during the reign of Vikramāditya II (ruled 733-42).

More important than the earlier dating of the first Cālukya temples relative to Pallava temples, what this brief chronology illustrates is that by the time the earliest Dieng temples were being built around 732, large temple complexes were being produced across south India. Given the unlikelihood of exclusive Pallava influence on the Dieng temples which was discussed above, one can suggest the possibility of various streams of regional south Indian temple styles coming to Indonesia including the Cālukyas.

This is borne out further by studies of architectural motifs by M.A. Dhaky (1974). Dhaky's study of *akśalinga* finials describes a motif that appears primarily in the seventh and eighth centuries in Orissa, Hill States, Andhra Pradesh and Karṇāṭaka (Dhaky 1974: 307). South Indian sites such as Mahabubnagar in Alampur incorporate the *akśalinga* motif also contain eclectic *nāgara-karṇāṭa* style shrines (Dhaky 1974: Pls. 3 and 4) (Fig. 14.9). Most of these sites are associated with the Cālukyas of Bādāmi. This not only suggests that there was among the Cālukya court artists a knowledge of north Indian style temples, but also implies a conscious decision to mix northern and southern style temple motifs. This may be helpful when considering the eclectic style of the Dieng temples. It could help explain the presence of the northern style *śikhara* at Candi Bima, which again raises the issue of north Indian versus south Indian prototypes for Dieng. It is possible that the Dieng temples are related to an eclectic style associated with the Cālukyas. It then becomes nearly impossible to trace Indian influence to an exact source.

RE-ASSESSING INDIAN INFLUENCE AT DIENG

After conducting fieldwork at key Cālukya and Pallava sites I concluded that in the time period under consideration (seventh and eighth centuries), the major temples produced in south India do not bear a strong resemble to those of the Dieng plateau. Rather it is the small, individualised shrines scattered among the larger south Indian temple complexes that most closely resemble those at Dieng. What is the significance of the small size and scope of the

FIGURE 14.9
Svarga Brahma temple, a *'nāgara-karṇāṭa'* style with an *akśaliṅga* finial, India,
Andhra Pradesh, Alampur, Mahabubnagar, seventh century (image copyright
American Academy of Benares, Varanasi, Accession no. 18611,
Negative no. A17.29)

Dieng temples within the larger context of temple building of the Central
Javanese period? To answer this it is necessary to separate out which aspects of
the temples are more universal or 'cosmopolitan' from those that are local or
a regional 'vernacular'. Perhaps this will help art historians understand how
visual art functions within Pollock's 'Sanskrit Cosmopolis.'

The value of Pollock's theory for art historians is that it shows a parallel
process of cultural transformation taking shape simultaneously as a result
of increased interaction between India and Southeast Asia, and that the
process is not imposed by one culture over another but rather adopted from
one culture and adapted by another. Pollock's timeline for the Cosmopolis
also maps well onto the timeline of Indian related art in Indonesia – by
the seventh-century Sanskrit was universally employed in the expression of

political power (through *kāvya* and *praśasti*) across South and Southeast Asia. Likewise the earliest free-standing stone architecture appears simultaneously in India and Java. Thus there is a plausible connection between the spread of Indian literary and artistic culture in Southeast Asia.[10]

However, whereas Sanskrit language is a constant within the Cosmopolis, it appears from the above analysis that the process of diffusion of Indian visual art is more fluid, and is vernacular from the start. As Pollock points out in the inscriptional record, Sanskrit is the main language used for political expression (from ritual to expressive), while local Prakrit was used for description for documentary purposes. Not until the end of the first millennium is there a major shift toward use of vernacular languages for political expression, and Sanskrit is what gives birth to written vernacular languages in many parts of Southeast Asia (Pollock 2006). By contrast, the first Indian related visual art in Southeast Asia is already a 'vernacular' or local adaptation related to several regional Indian art styles from the north and south. At the same time the Indian temple was a universally recognised symbol in South and Southeast Asia.[11]

While this may help us understand the significance of the Dieng temples within the larger context of the 'Sanskrit Cosmopolis,' it does not explain their importance at the local level for the Javanese. What is needed is a more thorough examination of Dieng as a site in relation to the political centre of Central Java at Prambanan.[12] After all, there once were as many as 400 temples at Dieng when it was first excavated and inscriptions indicate it was an important sacred centre for an extended period of time. While the structures are no longer available for study, a significant number of sculptures contemporary with the temples that are now housed in the Dieng site museum have not yet received extensive scholarly attention. A combined study of Dieng and Gedong Songo could also reveal something about the nature of local patronage and religious pilgrimage during the Central Javanese period.

My discussion and conclusions on the Dieng temples is preliminary, and my research is still ongoing. My goal here instead has been to question the perpetuated use of influence for understanding the process of diffusion of Indian art in Southeast Asia. I have stated above that India related temples in Java appear almost simultaneously with the rise of free-standing stone architecture in South Asia itself. Furthermore, the earliest temples at Dieng are uniquely Javanese in style, and were designed by selection from a range of architectural motifs found across the Indian subcontinent rather than a specific model. Thus Indian art diffusion must be considered as a polymorphous process which took place within the larger context of the transmission of Indian culture across the 'Sanskrit Cosmopolis.'

NOTES

1. Pollock's theory of the Sanskrit Cosmopolis is first discussed in *Ideology and Status of Sanskrit: Contributions to the History of the Sanskrit Language* (Pollock 1996). It has been expanded in his recently published *Language of the Gods in the World of Men: Sanskrit, Culture, and Power in Premodern India* (2006).
2. Van Goor and Banner (1922: 24), recount a local legend recorded in 1825 that the Dieng plateau was the ancestral home of Pandu Dewa Notto, and his son Rajuno.
3. The dating of Javanese temples through architectural motifs was first undertaken by Vogler through analysing the *kala-makara* doorway motifs of Javanese temples, which Williams uses to support her argument (Williams 1981: 42).
4. This inscription is associated with the first phase of Candi Kalasan. The temple was later converted into a Buddhist temple and was significantly enlarged.
5. For example, Chihara states that stone temples constructed with *padas* (tuff – volcanic ash) used on the interior and andesite (volcanic rock) is a technique that only appears at the end of the Central Javanese period (Chihara 1996: 101).
6. In particular by J.G. de Casparis (1979).
7. This was brought to my attention by Dr. Robert Brown.
8. Dumarçay's dating of the earliest Dieng temples has progressively moved toward a later date: 650-730 in his *Histoire Architecturale du Borobudur* (1977: 25), in accord with Soekmono); late seventh/730 in his *Temples of Java* (1986: 9); and 'before 750' in his *Histoire de l'architecture de Java* (1993: 59).
9. According to Gary Tartakov, the South Temple at the Ravana Phadi cave temple complex in Aihoḷe, Karṇāṭka, represents what may be the earliest experimentation with free-standing *dravida* style architecture in stone, which he dates to the mid-sixth century. Tartakov concedes this kind of 'experimentation' could be traced in Pallava territory as well but he makes a strong case for earliest evidence at Ravana Phadi (Tartakov 1980: 87 and n. 124).
10. Robert Brown reflects on this in his study of the *dharmacakrastambha* of the Dvaravati period in Thailand, suggesting that 'Indian cultural styles supplied a shared vocabulary that allowed the elite (from the disparate South East Asian cultures) for the first time to communicate, interact, and compete in a fully intra-regional context' (Brown 1996: 187-88).
11. Again Brown's analysis of the *dharmacakrastambha* is noteworthy for describing the same phenomenon in Dvaravati Thailand (Brown 1996: 197).
12. Jan Wisseman Christie's study of early Javanese political formations and lack of urban centres is helpful here (Christie 1991: 23-40).

REFERENCES

Brown, Robert L., *The Dvaravati Wheels of the Law and the Indianization of South East Asia*, Leiden: E.J. Brill, 1996.

Casparis, J.G. de, 'Paleography as an Auxiliary Discipline in Research on Early South East Asia', in *Early South East Asia: Essays in Archaeology, History and Historical Geography*, ed. R.B. Smith, New York, Kuala Lumpur: Oxford University Press, 1979, pp. 380-94.

Chihara, Daigoro, *Hindu-Buddhist Architecture in Southeast Asia*, tr. Rolf. W. Giebel. Leiden: E.J. Brill, 1996.

Christie, Jan Wisseman, 'States Without Cities: Demographic Trends in Early Java', *Indonesia* 52 (October 1991): 23-40.

Dhaky, M.A., 'The Akasalinga Finial', *Artibus Asiae* 36, no. 4 (1974): 307-15.

Dumarçay, Jacques, 'Temples of the Dieng Plateau', in *Indonesian Heritage*, vol. 1: *Ancient History*, ed. John Miksic, Singapore: Archipelago Press, 1996, pp. 66-67.

——, *Histoire de l'Architecture de Java.* Paris: École française d'Extrême-Orient (Publications de l'École française d'Extrême-Orient, Mémoires archéologiques XIX), 1993.

——, *The Temples of Java*, tr. and ed. Michael Smithies. Singapore, New York, Oxford University Press, 1986.

——, *Histoire architecturale du Borobudur,* Paris: École française d'Extrême-Orient (Publications de l'École française d'Extrême-Orient, Mémoires archéologiques XII), 1977.

van Goor, M.E. Lulius and H.S. Banner, *A Short Guide to the Ruined Temples in the Prambanan Plain, the Dieng Plateau, and Gedong Sanga,* Weltevreden: Landdrukkerij, 1922.

Kulke, Hermann, 'Indian Colonies, Indianization or Cultural Convergence? Reflections on the Changing Image of India's Role in South-East Asia', *Semaian* 3 (1990): 8-32.

Nagaswamy, R., 'New Light on Mamallapuram', in *Silver Jubilee volume: Transactions for the Period 1960-1962: The Archaeological Survey of India.* India: Archaeological Survey of India, 1962, 1-50.

Pollock, Sheldon, 'The Sanskrit Cosmopolis, 300-1300: Transculturation, Vernacularization, and the Question of Ideology', in *Ideology and Status of Sanskrit: Contributions to the History of Sanskrit Language*, ed. Jan E.M. Houben, Leiden, New York, Koln: E.J. Brill, 1996, pp. 197-247.

——, *Language of the Gods in the World of Men: Sanskrit, Culture, and Power in Premodern India*, Berkeley: University of California, 2006.

Rabe, Michael, 'The Mamallapuram Prasasti: A Panegyric in Figures', *Artibus Asiae* 57: 3/4 (1997): 189-241.

Soekmono, R., 'The Archaeology of Central Java before 800 A.D.', in *Early South East Asia: Essays in Archaeology, History and Historical Geography*, ed. R.B. Smith and W. Watson, New York, Kuala Lumpur: Oxford University Press, 1979, pp. 457-72.

Tartakov, Gary, 'The Beginning of Dravidian Temple Architecture in Stone', *Artibus Asiae* 42, no. 1 (1980): 39-99.

Tartakov, Gary and Vidya Dehejia, 'Sharing, Intrusion, and Influence: The Mahisasuramardini Imagery of the Calukyas and the Pallavas', *Artibus Asiae* 45, no. 4 (1984): 287-345.

Vogler, E.B., *De monsterkop uit het omlijstingsornament van tempeldoorgangen en-nissen in de Hindoe-Javaanse bouwkunst.* Leiden: E.J. Brill, 1949.

Williams, Joanna, 'The Date of Barabudur in Relation to Other Central Javanese Monuments', in *Barabudur: History and Significance of a Buddhist Monument (Berkeley Buddhist studies series 2)*, ed. Luis O. Gomez and Hiram W. Woodward, Jr. The Regents of the University of California, 1981, pp. 25-46.

15

The Importance of Gupta-period Sculpture in Southeast Asian Art History

Robert L. Brown

The importance of Gupta-period sculpture to the art of South Asia, Southeast Asia, and East Asia has been stressed by many scholars for over a century.[1] The Gupta Period is roughly the fourth-sixth centuries during which the Gupta dynasty controlled much of north India. The Gupta-period artistic style was fairly consistent and emphasised an idealised naturalism that has been praised for its artistic excellence. It is also seen to have relationships with some of the earliest art that developed in Southeast Asia. My paper outlines how these relationships can be defined. It places the Gupta-related art into the context of other Indian art, of Sri Lankan art, of Chinese art, and then each of these with Southeast Asian art. It aims to question several of the standard scholarly assumptions made in regard to the relationship of Gupta-period and Southeast Asian art.

WHAT IS GUPTA-PERIOD ART?

The Gupta dynasty began rule in 320, reached its political zenith around 400, and was losing its strength a century later, by around 500. There is very little art that can be attributed to the fourth century, during the initial decades of Gupta political growth. Indeed there is little art in north India that can be placed in this century, following the end of the Kushan dynastic control and the rise of the Guptas. The Guptas themselves appear not to have been patrons of sculpture or temples, as we have no sculpture and only a few temple remains that were patronized by them.[2] Their interest in visual arts seems limited to coins, with their gold coins reaching a high level of artistic excellence.[3] Members of the Vakataka dynasty, linked through marriage with the Guptas, were, on the other hand, major patrons of both Hindu and Buddhist sculpture and temples.[4] The Buddhist cave temples at Ajanta were done under the Vakatakas in the second half of the fifth century.[5] By the middle of the sixth century we can say the Gupta-period style of art is ending, and during the seventh-century, sculpture in north India will become transformed into a much more formalised, flattened, and conceptual style. Indeed, the seventh century shows a rather radical break in terms of political and cultural styles as well, with a new type of court culture developing in north India.[6]

I will focus on the Gupta-period Buddha image for purposes of this paper in order to make the comparisons with other areas of India, and with Sri Lanka, China, and Southeast Asia. The Buddha image works best for these comparisons because of its large numbers, consistent iconography, and appearance in areas (such as Sri Lanka and China) where Hindu sculpture is scarce or non-existent. The initial question to ask is if the Gupta-period Buddha image represents a new style or type of image, one that we can clearly identify as of this period? The answer here is yes, that there was a new type of Buddha image created at Sarnath in the second half of the fifth century (Fig. 15.1). The Sarnath image type has several novel characteristics, which together I have identified as creating a feminised Buddha image.[7] These characteristics include a lowered gaze, the loss of the male genitals, a rearrangement of body

FIGURE 15.1
Buddha, Sarnath c. 470–90

proportions, and a robe without indication of folds. These changes can be fairly precisely attributed to the second half of the fifth century at Sarnath, and are seen in comparison with the Mathura type of Buddha image from which the Sarnath image develops. I propose that it is this type of Buddha image that will be of most importance in much of the Asian Buddhist world.

One interesting point to keep in mind when thinking of how the Sarnath type of image might have spread to other areas is in terms of the medium used to produce the images. The movement of icons is, of course, the assumed way they would have entered new territory. We have numerous references in texts about monks taking images from place to place. Xuanzang brought back with him from India to China six images of the Buddha, although their number pales into insignificance when compared to what was of real importance for Xuanzang, Buddhist texts, that were so numerous that he needed twenty-two horses to carry them.[8] Xuanzang's images were of gold, silver, and wood, and the assumption is that the travelling images would be of wood or metal, not of the very heavy stone. There are hundreds of Sarnath style Buddha images of stone at the site itself, and many more in museum and private collections throughout the world. If we consider stone Buddha images from Mathura and other sites in India, we have thousands of images. There are no wood images extant. Of most interest is that there is only a very tiny number of metal images as well. A total of thirty-two Indian metal images dating to the fifth-sixth centuries are known from collections throughout the world, with twenty-seven of these Buddha images, four Jain images, and one Brahmanical image.[9] There are no known metal images of bodhisattvas.

India had no well-defined bronze making tradition until the sixth and seventh centuries. There are very few early bronze images in India from the Mauryan through the Kushan periods. As we shall see, there were no early Amaravati bronzes either. Although the thirty or so images noted above do not represent the total number of Gupta bronze images made, only those that are extant and known, it is still a startlingly small number of objects. There has been no Indian Gupta-period imported bronze found in Southeast Asia or China. That the Indian corpus is almost entirely made up of Buddha images should also be noted, all of which are standing except for one example.

WHAT IS HAPPENING IN SOUTH INDIA AND SRI LANKA DURING THE GUPTA PERIOD?

The Buddhist artistic tradition of south India is often misunderstood in scholarship that deals with Indian artistic relations with China and Southeast Asia. One misunderstanding comes from the mis-dating of a group of bronze Buddha images that has traditionally been called Amaravati style images. The Dong-duong Buddha (Fig. 15.2) that was found in Champa is one of this

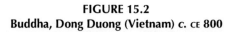

FIGURE 15.2
Buddha, Dong Duong (Vietnam) c. ce 800

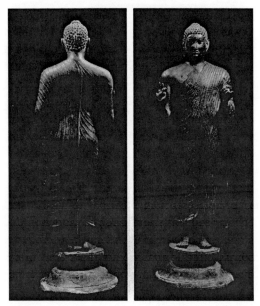

type, which was dated to the third century by Ananda Coomaraswamy who notes that it is probably an imported image and is in style 'very near that of Amaravati and Anuradhapura'.[10] Today most scholars would date the image to the eighth or ninth century. The dating is based on stylistic analysis, but the conservative style and wide geographical distribution (particularly of bronze images) has made precise dating difficult, and the controversy continues up to this day.

The reason for the initial early dating of the Dong-duong style of Buddha was simply because it 'looked like' the stone Buddha images from the Andhran sites of Amaravati and Nagarjunakonda, which are dated to the third-fourth centuries (Fig. 15.4). The most obvious stylistic feature was the way in which the robe was worn, which went under the right arm and had a distinct swag of cloth at the bottom hem in front. Amaravati is the earlier site. Douglas Barrett argues that the anthropomorphic Buddha image first occurs at Amaravati during the last two decades of the second century CE,[11] appearing in relief carvings. The stone three-dimensional Buddha images are later, he suggests around CE 225-50.[12] This is about when the Ikshvaku dynasty is taking political control of the region from the Satavahana dynasty that had ruled at Amaravati. The Ikshvakus ruled in the third century, building both Hindu and Buddhist monuments at Nagarjunakonda, and making Buddha images in the Amaravati style. Construction appears to have ceased by the end of the third century, although there is no reason to suppose the sites did

FIGURE 15.3
Buddha, Northern Qi, 550–77

not continue to be used. Indeed, we have ample evidence that Amaravati was used up until the fourteenth century.

But identifying any art, including Buddha images, at either site that dates after the third century is difficult, at least before the eighth century. There is no evidence that bronze images were being made at this early third-fourth century period. Remember that the fourth century in the north was a period when there was a relative dearth of art, and this appears to be true for Andhra as well.

It was Douglas Barrett writing in 1954 who first argued that the Dong-duong type of Buddha image, of which there were a number of images scattered across Southeast Asia, was not a product of the early Amaravati artistic school but was dated much later to what he called the 'later school of Amaravati'.[13] He thought that images of this type were imports from either south India or Sri Lanka, and served as the source for the Southeast Asian type of Buddha image. Barrett specifically calls the Dong-duong Buddha an Indian image that dates to *c.* 800. The point then is that there were no Buddha images of a south Indian style that were exported to Southeast Asia before the eighth century, and these later metal images had nothing directly to do with the stone Buddha images from Amaravati and Nagarjunakonda of the second and third centuries.

It may be helpful to look again at the Dong-duong image in comparison with a stone Buddha image from Nagarjunakonda to outline the stylistic differences that scholars use to differentiate them so radically in date (Fig. 15.4). The major stylistic difference is in the relation of the body to the robe. The earlier Buddha's body barely shows through the heavy robe, whereas the later image has a thin robe that hugs the contours of the right side of the body. Another detail is how the left hand is held. It is held with the palm inward and the robe draped over the wrist on the early image, while it is palm outward and holding the end of the robe on the later image. There are several other important stylistic differences that scholars have identified,[14] but for our purposes we want to ask where, considering this dating, does the Gupta-period Buddha image come into play?

A date before the fifth century for the Dong-duong type of Buddha is ruled out as it is at this date that the asexual body with the thin, tight fitting robe was invented in India. The appearance then is theoretically possible for such image types to occur in India, Southeast Asia, or China at any time from, say, the mid-sixth century on. The development of the Gupta-style image type in the post-Gupta period in India has been one way to explain how the Gupta-style reached outside of India, to Southeast Asia and China. Sculptures in China of the Tang Period of the ninth century, for example, are explained as not reflecting Gupta art directly, but via post-Gupta Indian artistic styles. For Southeast Asia the model for this approach is Pierre Dupont's detailed study of Mon-Dvaravati art.[15]

As already mentioned, the Dong-duong Buddha is accepted by all scholars as being an import, but there has been no consensus on whether it comes from south India or from Sri Lanka. The latest discussion of the image, by Thierry Zephir in the Musee Guimet's Cham catalogue lists various scholars' opinions of geographical origin, and ultimately leans slightly more towards a Sri Lankan source, and a date of the ninth century.[16] Interestingly, Zephir proposes that the image was re-cut around the eyes after importation to Champa in an eye-opening ceremony, an action that gave the sculpture a 'Cham' look with the eyebrows brought together in a single line.[17]

What, then, might art from Sri Lanka play during the Gupta-period? Much remains to be researched with the art of Sri Lanka. Scholarly progress has been slow as there are very few scholars working on Sri Lankan art today, and archaeological excavations (with some important exceptions such as Sigiria) have been rare. The difficulty in determining what is Sri Lankan and what is south Indian, such as with the Dong-duong Buddha, also stems in part from the almost total absence of artistic remains in south India itself. A rich Buddhist tradition existed in south India after the early Amaravati and Nagarjunakonda periods as described in numerous textual sources, but there is almost no Buddhist art extant today from this later time.[18] There has never been an adequate explanation proposed for this, but the result is that we do not have enough south Indian Buddhist art to compare to that in Sri Lanka to determine a difference.

The Buddha image development in Sri Lanka that I propose is that only imported stone images from Andhra were used during the early Amaravati period in Sri Lanka, third and fourth centuries. The earliest locally made Buddha images (made in stone) date perhaps to the fourth century. Ulrich Von Schroeder has proposed five badly damaged seated images as the earliest extant, dating CE 250-350.[19] He then dates an additional ten seated images, all of very indifferent quality, as fifth-sixth century, with all other Buddha images found on the island dating to sixth-seventh century or later.[20] In other words, Von Schroeder has proposed a very small number (a total of 14) stone images as the earliest Buddha images made on the island, with dates before the sixth-seventh centuries. The sixth-seventh century period is also the date, according to Von Schroeder, of the earliest Sinhalese bronze images of the Buddha.[21]

If this scenario is correct, the making of Buddha images in Sri Lanka appears more-or-less to parallel in date the making of images in Southeast Asia, although Sri Lanka had a rich tradition of imported Indian sculpture that Southeast Asia did not have. It also would mean that the presence of Sri Lankan images in Southeast Asia before the seventh century is highly unlikely.

WHAT IS HAPPENING IN CHINA
DURING THE GUPTA PERIOD?

China during the fifth and sixth centuries presents to me, as a South and Southeast Asian specialist, an entirely different world. Unlike the rare historical information available when researching ancient South and Southeast Asian art, the Chinese record is rich in written historical documents. The self-consciousness of people's motivations is recorded. Art styles carry stated political meanings. There is an awareness of what art is Chinese and what is foreign with preferences of taste and intentions of power. Artists are named, their styles described, their influence discussed in texts of the period. And art objects are repeatedly and precisely dated.[22]

This detailed historical and artistic record demonstrates that for China Gupta-period art had a direct impact on Chinese Buddha images. This impact can be very precisely dated to the sixth century, even to certain decades that reveal more intense influence. This demonstrates that, for China, we do not have to propose a post-Gupta Indian artistic relationship to explain Chinese Gupta-related images. It also means that Gupta styles were reaching China almost at the same time they were created in India.

The sudden change in style of Buddha image during the Northern Qi

(550-77) has been emphasized by several scholars, particularly following the discovery in 1996 of over 400 images that had been buried in Qingzhou in Shandong Province.[23] Most of the 400 sculptures can be dated to the sixth century, and many of them are dated by inscription (Fig. 15.3). They overall show a rejection of the earlier Chinese style of Buddha image for a different style that is defined in very clear Gupta stylistic terms. Su Bai refers to the 'abrupt change in style in the mid-sixth century', as defined by changes in the 'garments depicted and in the treatment of the body'.[24] He writes that:

In the first half of the sixth century Buddha wears a monk's robe with a sash, and a mantle of a thick material. In the second half of the century this typically Chinese attire, inspired by the robes of Confucian officials, is replaced by a close-fitting monk's garment of thin, light material, clearly influenced by Indian dress.[25]

Su Bai goes on to note the new emphasis on 'the three-dimensional fullness of the body and sometimes . . . a slight indication of movement'.[26]

Both the reasons for and sources of the Northern Qi style are contested among scholars. Su Bai is clear in his identification of the source: 'I believe that these Northern Qi figures with their thin robes were influenced directly by contemporary, Gupta-period images of the Buddha in India'.[27] But this is not the only scholarly opinion. Katherine R. Tsiang Mino in a recent University of Chicago dissertation rejects foreign artistic influences. She writes that 'the

FIGURE 15.4

| Buddha, Nagarjunakonda, | Buddha, Dong Duong |
| 3rd century CE | c. CE 800 |

appearance of the Indianising tendencies in officially sponsored Northern Qi sculpture is not likely to be the result of a sudden infusion of foreign influence but of a reconsideration of Buddhism in light of various modes of representation of Buddha images that were already known'[28] (Mino, p. 133). The topic of Northern Qi Buddha image style deserves extended discussion, but our focus on the fourth-fifth centuries in India art argues strongly against Mino, as the Northern Qi style could not have developed from already existent Chinese styles as the Gupta style did not exist before the end of the fifth century. Mino would have to argue that the Gupta style was a creation of Chinese art to be correct.

Indeed, an almost certain direct relationship with Sarnath Buddha images occurs in the Northern Qi examples in which the robe is completely without folds. The removal of indications of robe folds occurs at Sarnath in the last decades of the fifth century, and on Buddha images in China it appears only on sculptures from the Qingzhou region.[29] This does not necessarily mean there were no intermediary images outside of India, but they would have to be almost of the same date (within a 50-year period, first half of the sixth century), and none has been found. The absence of drapery folds on the Chinese Buddha sculptures that date to the mid-sixth century can only be from Indian models.

WHAT IS HAPPENING IN SOUTHEAST ASIA DURING THE GUPTA PERIOD?

Alexander Soper wrote in 1960 a brilliant essay on the neglected importance to understanding Six Dynasties Buddhism of the art and culture of Southern China.[30] He proposed that South China served as a conduit for developments in North China for Buddhist art and culture derived from Southeast Asia. The notion that South China at this early period was as much a part of the cultural sphere of Southeast Asia as of what we today categorise as China is, of course, an old and intriguing proposal. The role that Funan and other Southeast Asian states named by the Chinese played in their dated and recorded interchanges with China, some beginning as early as the third century, have been repeatedly reviewed and considered.[31] In other words, Southeast Asia in the first half of the first millennium CE clearly had frequent contact with China, and has long been considered as a possible source of Buddhist thought and culture, including art, for South China.

If we focus on Buddha images, however, it is very difficult to argue that Southeast Asian sculptures could have been of importance during the Funan period, or any time earlier than about the sixth or seventh century. For one thing, all Southeast Asian Buddha images show Gupta-period stylistic characteristics, so must date after the fifth century.

What I want to ask here is if there is evidence that Southeast Asia Buddha images display the kind of direct relationship with Gupta style Buddha images that we find in Northern Qi? The date that this might happen is the sixth century. It appears that there is evidence that Southeast Asia sculptures demonstrate a close relationship with Gupta-period Indian sculpture at about the same time as did the Chinese sculpture, which I will suggest through a series of comparisons of certain examples.

We first need to return to the issue of Gupta-period bronze images. The geographical origins of only a few of the small number of Gupta-period bronzes are known. Indeed, the bronzes are small and easily carried, so even their archaeological context does not tell us where they were made. Indian art styles are defined by geographical locations, so the lack of locations makes classifying the bronzes impossible. Nor have any bronze making workshops been identified. Two hoards of bronze Buddha images with a total of ten images are known from sites in the Deccan, seven from Phophnar in Madhya Pradesh and three from Ramtek in Maharashtra. A.P. Jamkhedkar feels the seven Phophnar bronzes are close in style and probably indicate a local workshop.[32] Still, they vary considerably in terms of iconography, such as the way in which the robe is worn, and particularly in their facial characteristics. The three Ramtek bronzes are very different from one another, and are unlikely to have been made in the same workshop unless a variety of styles were produced at the same time. The simultaneous production of different sculptural styles in one geographical location does not appear to happen with stone sculpture, but we do not have enough evidence to say if the bronze working tradition was similar. The Phophnar and Ramtek bronzes are associated with the Vakataka sphere of artistic patronage, and are usually dated to the fifth century, although they may be sixth century, and of course need not all date to the same period.

Using the fifth-sixth century bronze Buddha images to look at images produced in China and Southeast Asia can at least suggest relationships. One initial point is that I am comparing small bronze Indian images to stone images, many of which are very large, even life-size, which may seem problematical. There are, in fact, a number of other concerns that underlay such a comparison that I will make here. But with the lack of evidence we have, there is no real alternative.

We can divide the images into two groups, depending on whether they wear the robe over both shoulders or under the right arm. I have chosen one Indian bronze of each type and will compare it to possible Chinese, Khmer, and Mon images that suggest a close relationship.

This Gupta-period Buddha wears the robe in the covering mode (Fig. 15.5). It clings to the body in the wet drapery convention so that the body clearly shows through the cloth. The clinging cloth does not reveal any male

FIGURE 15.5

| India | China | Cambodia | Thailand |

sex. The figure shifts the weight onto one leg with the other leg relaxed so that the knee protrudes slightly. Also noteworthy is the very low *ushnisha*. The low *ushnisha* particularly compares with that of the Northern Qi Buddha. The robe of the Chinese image is worn in the covering mode. It reveals the body, although not as forcefully as the robe of the Indian image. And the Chinese example also still displays drapery folds, although they are reduced to simple wide-spaced groves. There are, however, other Northern Qi Buddha images with tightly clinging robes and no folds, an example of which I showed in Fig. 15.3. One point in regard to the Chinese examples is that China had a two-centuries old tradition of making Buddha images before the Northern Qi examples. Any foreign artistic model will be filtered through this already rich tradition.

The Khmer example from Vat Ramlok is very close to the Indian model, but takes the clinging robe even further to an almost abstract series of concave and convex forms. The body has become simplified, although the stance is very naturalistic with the weight on the left leg, allowing the thigh on the right leg to be relaxed and the knee projecting. The *ushnisha* remains low. The Buddha image from Si Thep in Central Thailand, which may or may not be related to the Mon, is very close to the Gupta-period Buddha type. Indeed, it is so close that Stanislaw Czuma, the Curator of the Cleveland Museum in whose collection it belongs, argues that it was made by Indian immigrant artists.[33] While I completely disagree with this suggestion, it does underline how closely a curator, known for his connoisseurship, can identify the two styles.

This exercise of comparisons can also be done with a Gupta-period bronze Buddha who wears the robe in the open mode and examples from China and Southeast Asia (Fig. 15.6). The Ramtek Buddha wears the robe under the right arm. The robe clings to the sexless body in the same convention as that shown on the covering mode. The robe has no drapery folds. The open mode shown here should not be confused with that of the robes of the Amaravati and the Dong-duong Buddha images we have seen. Both represent the robe worn under the right arm, but the northern example lacks the swag of cloth at the bottom hem and the vertical way in which the robe falls when thrown over the back. In the southern tradition, the end of the robe thrown over the back hangs in a straight vertical line, but it is pulled to the front and held in the hand in the northern tradition.[34] Note also the low *ushnisha* of the Indian bronze.

The Northern Qi Buddha relates closely to the Indian example. The robe without folds is worn in the same way, and the rather odd arrangement of the hair reflects the low *ushnisha*. The Chinese robe was once painted. There are a number of other examples with the paint still in good condition.[35] The Khmer Buddha image demonstrates similar traits that relate to the Indian prototype, although the very awkward lowered right arm is unusual. And it

FIGURE 15.6

is again Si Thep in Thailand that supplies another comparative example, and as with the Cleveland image, is one of the masterpieces of Southeast Asian sculpture.

In conclusion, the comparisons of Chinese and Southeast Asian sculpture with possible Gupta-period Indian images can be expanded and repeated, although not greatly. What it appears to show is that there was direct contact in the sixth century with Gupta Indian art. There is perhaps then no need to argue for post-Gupta Indian art to have been strongly influential on the seventh and eighth centuries in China and Southeast Asia. Also, the influence from Indian art reached China and Southeast Asia at the same time, primarily in the sixth century. This means that Southeast Asia is an unlikely source for artistic styles, at least for Buddha images, for China. Finally, there are few South Indian or Sri Lankan artistic relationships with Southeast Asia at this point (fifth and sixth centuries). Any relationship would begin more probably in the seventh century. The relationship of sixth-century Buddha images in China and Southeast Asia appear related to north Indian art of the Gupta Period.

NOTES

1. One of the most accessible arguments for the importance of Gupta-period sculpture in South and Southeast Asian art history is Pratapaditya Pal's exhibition catalogue *The Ideal Image: The Gupta Sculptural Tradition and its Influence*, New York: The Asia Society, 1978.
2. See Vidula Jayaswal, *Royal Temples of Gupta Period: Excavations at Bhitari*, New Delhi: Aryan Books International, 2001.
3. Barbara Stoller Miller, 'A Dynasty of Patrons: The Representation of Gupta Royalty in Coins and Literature', in *The Powers of Art: Patronage in Indian Culture*, ed. Barbara Stoller Miller, New Delhi: Oxford University Press, 1992, pp. 54-64.
4. See Hans Bakker, ed., *The Vakataka Heritage: Indian Culture at the Crossroads*, Groningen: Egbert Forsten, 2005 and Hans Bakker, *The Vakatakas: An Essay in Hindu Iconology*, Groningen: Egbert Forsten, 1997.
5. See Walter Spink, *Ajanta: History and Development*, 5 vols., Leiden: E.J. Brill, 2005-07.
6. See Daud Ali, *Courtly Culture and Political Life in Early Medieval India*, Cambridge: Cambridge University Press, 2004 and Sheldon Pollock, *The Language of the Gods in the World of Men: Sanskrit, Culture, and Power in Premodern India*, Berkeley: University of California Press, 2006.
7. Robert L. Brown, 'The Feminization of the Sarnath Gupta-Period Buddha Images', *Bulletin of the Asia Institute*, vol. 16 (2002), pp. 165-79.
8. Samuel Beal, *Buddhist Records of the Western World*, rpt., Delhi: Motilal Banarsidass, 1994, p. xx.
9. M. C. Joshi, 'The Gupta Art: An Introduction', in *The Golden Age of Classical India: The Gupta Empire*, Paris: Reunion des musees nationaux, France, 2007, pp. 53-55.
10. Ananda K. Coomaraswamy, *History of Indian and Indonesian Art*, New York: Dover Publications, 1965, p. 197.

11. Douglas Barrett, *Sculptures from Amaravati in the British Museum*, London: The Trustees of the British Museum, 1954, p. 58.

12. Ibid., p. 61.

13. Douglas Barrett, 'The Later School of Amaravati and its Influences', *Arts and Letters* 28 (1954): pp. 41-54.

14. See Sara Schastok, 'Bronzes in the Amaravati Style: Their Role in the Writing of Southeast Asian History', in *Ancient Indonesian Sculpture*, ed. Marijke J. Klokke and Pauline Lunsingh Scheurleer (Leiden: KITLV Press, 1994): pp. 33-56 and Pauline Lunsingh Scheurleer and Marijke J. Klokke, *Divine Bronze: Ancient Indonesian Bronzes from A.D. 600 to 1600*, Leiden: E.J. Brill, 1988, pp. 1-15.

15. Pierre Dupont, *L'Archeologie Mone de Dvaravati*, 2 vols., Paris: Ecole Francaise d'Extreme-Orient, 1959.

16. Pierre Baptiste and Thierry Zéphir, *Trésors d'art du Vietnam: La Sculpture du Champa Ve-XVe siècles*, Paris: Musée des arts asiatiques Guimet, 2005, pp. 207-09.

17. Ibid., p. 209.

18. Vidya Dehejia, 'The Persistence of Buddhism in Tamilnadu', in *A Pot-Pourri of Indian Art*, ed. Pratapaditya Pal, Bombay: Marg Publications, 1988, pp. 53-74.

19. Ulrich Von Schroeder, *Buddhist Sculptures of Sri Lanka*, Hong Kong: Visual Dharma Publications, 1990, pp. 118-19.

20. Ibid., pp. 120-22.

21. Ibid., pp. 171-84.

22. See for example Alexander C. Soper, *Literary Evidence for Early Buddhist Art in China*, Ascona: Artibus Asiae, 1959 and James C.Y. Watt et al., *China: Dawn of a Golden Age, 200-750 AD*, New York: Metropolitan Museum of Art, 2004.

23. See *Return of the Buddha: The Qingzhou Discoveries*, London: Royal Academy of Arts, 2002 and *Buddhist Sculptures from Shandong Province, China*, n.p.: Miho Museum, 2007.

24. Su Bai, 'Sculpture of the Northern Qi Dynasty and its Stylistic Models', in *Return of the Buddha: The Qingzhou Discoveries*, ed. Lukas Mickel, p. 54.

25. Ibid.

26. Ibid.

27. Ibid., p. 55.

28. Katherine R. Tsiang Mino, 'Bodies of Buddhas and the Princes of Xiangtangshan Caves: Image, Text, and Stupa in Buddhist Art of the Northern Qi Dynasty (550-577)', University of Chicago Ph.D. dissertation 1996, p. 133.

29. Su Bai, 'Sculpture of the Northern Qi Dynasty and its Stylistic Models', p. 57.

30. Alexander Soper, 'South Chinese Influence on the Buddhist Art of the Six Dynasties Period', *Bulletin of the Museum of Far Eastern Antiquities, Stockholm*, vol. 32 (1960), pp. 47-112.

31. For a recent look at some of the early cultural relationships between Southeast Asian and China see *Art & Archaeology of Fu Nan: Pre-Khmer Kingdom of the Lower Mekong Valley*, ed. James C.M. Khoo, Bangkok: Orchid Press, 2003.

32. A.P. Jamkhedkar, 'The Buddha in Bronze: Phophnar and Ramtek', in *The Great Tradition: Indian Bronze Masterpieces*, New Delhi: Festival of India, 1988, pp. 47-53.

33. Stanislaw J. Czuma, 'The Cleveland Museum's Krsna Govardhana and the Early Phnom Da Style of Cambodian Sculpture', *Ars Orieintalis: Professor Walter M. Spink Felicitation Volume*, ed. Stephen Markel, Ann Arbor: Department of the History of Art, University of Michigan, 2000, pp. 127-35.

34. See Alexander B. Griswold, 'Prolegomena to the Study of the Buddha's Dress in Chinese Sculpture with Particular Reference to the Rietberg Museum's Collection', *Artibus Asiae*, 26/2 (1963), pp. 85-131; 27/4 (1965), pp. 335-40.
35. See, for example, *Return of the Buddha: The Qingzhou Discoveries*, Figs. 16 and 17.

16

Individuals under the Glaze: Local Transformations of Indianisation in the Decorative Lintels of Angkor[1]

Martin Polkinghorne

When medieval Khmer artists chiselled into the sandstone lintel, components of the lintel design were entirely of their own making. The sovereign, project superintendent, and team supervisor all possessed the requisite power to tell artisans what to carve, but idiosyncratic differences in every work indicate that the majority of the specific decision-making was left to the artist. Control over every small detail of artistic creation would have been difficult to realise and administer. The patrons of the sculptural and architectural commissions apparently trusted the ability of the artists to produce work with the requisite symbolic and aesthetic power. Most of the time, artists selected and rendered iconography from a repertoire of forms known to them from training and tradition. But the medieval Khmer artistic tradition also facilitated innovation and difference between objects. The most important decorative lintels, situated on the most visible *prasat* and façades were often a chance for artists to demonstrate their creativity and skill by distinguishing their work. Even lintels that were carved at modest village shrines possess eccentricities in iconography and form. The recognition of the multitude differences in decorative lintels opens the way for a more exuberant and humane perspective of artistic change in the Angkorian world. When variation in the different components of artistic and material culture are assessed, change can be perceived as dynamic and constant, where medieval Khmer artists actively make novel associations of iconography and form.

The monuments of Cambodia abound with Indian derived motifs and deities. The medieval inscriptions likewise reveal a profound familiarity with the corpus of Indian Sanskrit literature. The substantial influence of Indian cultures on Southeast Asia, known as 'Indianisation' has framed much research on the Angkorian world. In order to understand medieval Khmer culture, repeated reference has been made to Indian meanings and texts which may have had little association with specific Southeast Asian contexts. This has created a problematic and uneasy dichotomy where the indigenous elements of medieval Khmer culture were determined by subtracting the correspondences with India. There is a body of contemporary scholarship, however, that seeks to emphasise Southeast Asian initiative through recognition of detail in the historical process. Rather than the rigid application of a definable set of cultural traits, Indianisation operated in various and different objects and contexts and was constantly renegotiated (see Brown 1992, 1994, 1996; Kulke 1990; Mabbett 1977a, 1977b, 1997; Maxwell 2007; Sanderson 2003-04; Smith 1999; Vickery 1998). Studies that adopt a realist epistemology have been a necessary post-colonial reaction to the legacy of earlier views, which at their most extreme posited Southeast Asian civilisation as the direct result of Indian colonisation (e.g. Majumdar 1927a, 1927b, 1953, 1963; also cf. Reynolds 1995). If Indianisation is now appraised as local innovation, then it is feasible to perceive small scale changes in material culture that are the actions of individuals as components in the complex process of cultural transformation.

'MEANING' AND MATERIAL CULTURE

Appraisal of Indianisation through the elaboration of Angkorian material culture is a challenging task, especially as the political and artistic 'fluorescence' of Angkor began approximately one thousand years after initial contact between India and Southeast Asia. Because the epigraphic and material record indicates a continuous and dynamic dialogue between India and Southeast Asia it is possible to consider the changing character of this relationship (Casparis 1983; also see Brown 1992). Despite the dismissal of colonisation, the operation of the Indian influence on the material culture of Southeast Asia has continued to be considered as unchanging and repetitive. That which could not easily be explained is deferred *deus ex machina* to what is supposed about medieval India. Analogies have been proposed for numerous aspects of the Angkorian world from the structure of political, religious, administrative, and economic systems to the creation and meaning of its art and architecture. The certainty and justification of the correspondence was the declaration of these matters to text. The medieval Khmer epigraphic corpus attested an intimate knowledge of Indian Sanskrit literature, including elements of the prescriptive *śāstric* tradition. These texts outlined procedures to realise political administration and fabrication of the material world in accordance with 'correct' religious and moral law.

The analysis of text has contributed greatly to the interpretation of an Angkorian historical narrative and the sequence of monuments. But from a contemporary philosophical acknowledgement that 'meaning' is individual and contextual, it follows that what was written in India did not have the same meanings in Cambodia, nor the same meanings to everyone in Cambodia, even amongst the literate elite. This is the case even if the texts were exactly the same, or if those who transmitted, wrote and thought them considered that they were equivalent. For instance, when administrative texts such as the *Dharmaśāstra, Arthaśāstra,* or '*The Laws of Manu*' (Barth 1885: 67; Cœdès 1932: 98; Bhattacharya 1997: 43) are cited in the Khmer inscriptions there is little evidence to suggest to what degree they were known, or how the medieval Khmer may have actualised them. The critical issues for scholars who have begun to deconstruct the detail of the Khmer inscriptions are the internal inconsistencies of text, ritual and materiality (e.g. see Sanderson 2003-04; Maxwell 2007; Vickery 1998). The corollary of the importance of words in perceiving past cultures is the presumption that text can also be directly related to artistic culture.[2] Because 'meaning', comprehension of instructions, and physical action are all intrinsically individual, the application of verbal prescriptions to create art is not universal or fixed. There is a 'non-correspondence' between verbal declarations and material outcomes, where the variation can be read as artistic idiosyncrasy. In medieval Cambodia an artistic milieu of many players produced a vibrant and dynamic artistic record with myriad combinations of iconographies and forms.

ART HISTORY, 'INDIANISATION' AND DECORATIVE LINTELS

Indian influence is especially apparent in the art and architecture of Southeast Asia. Therefore the discipline of art history is indispensable in understanding the character of the relationship between the regions. Brown (1996: 69) argued that the forms and meanings of Indian art have been modified in almost every case according to Southeast Asian contexts. Southeast Asian art was not a pastiche of Indian regional designs, but developed from a handful of Southeast Asian styles that modified the Indian forms immediately (Brown 1992: 49, 1996: xxvi). In this view the selection and adaptation of Indian forms were part of the continuous process of Southeast Asian artistic transformation. Elite patrons and project supervisors could specify the 'Indian' and syncretic character of the works according to religious and political requirements, but many large-scale changes in form and iconography also developed from the combination of individually produced creative decisions

and actions. Instead of the imposition of declared 'ideals', the choice and
modification of Indian motifs and forms was part of the multifaceted process
of local artistic innovation and change. Southeast Asians can be seen as the
generators of artistic change and their transformation of Indian motifs. In the
context of early trade in prestige and luxury goods from the end of the first
millennium BCE, it is maintained here, following Helms (1988, 1998) and
Mus (1975 [1933], 1977) among others, that the subsequent Indian forms
and symbols were embraced in early Southeast Asia because their 'foreignness'
conferred legitimate authority, and because they resonated with the existing
supernatural Southeast Asian requirements to ensure agricultural prosperity.

Consistent with philological and epigraphic studies, elaborating the
process of Indianisation by resolving a chronology has been a fundamental
undertaking of medieval Khmer art history. By the mid-twentieth century,
scholars had effectively accomplished the task of ordering the decorative
material (Coral-Rémusat 1935a, 1935b, 1940, 1951; Stern 1927, 1932,
1934, 1938a, 1938b, 1965). In doing so, it was necessary to impose 'styles'
or classificatory horizons that distinguished one group of artworks from
another. Scholars did not believe that these categories were real, or knowingly
adopted by Khmer artists. However, they were a good way of organising the
material. The decorative lintel, in particular, has been used as an invaluable
diagnostic tool to unravel the complex artistic sequence (Bénisti 1968, 1974;
Boisselier 1966, 1968; Coral-Rémusat 1934, 1940, 1951; Dupont 1952; and
Stern 1934a) (Fig. 16.1). These studies have perceived the artistic culture of
the Angkorian world as a pattern of stages and the stylistic categories have
become 'things' in their own right, standards, which define the transformation
of Khmer art. Objects are customarily discussed in terms of their relation

FIGURE 16.1
Decorative Lintel from Lolei, Prasat 2, east façade

to stylistic norms, which act to inhibit scholars from organising artistic culture in other ways. But the change from one style to another is not as clear-cut as the descriptions indicate and this approach seems at odds with contemporary historical and archaeological research which tends to look at the historical and material record in terms of contextual detail rather than deferring to general trends (e.g. Brown 1992, 1994, 1996; Pottier 1999, 2000; Pottier and Lujàn-Lunsford 2005; Sanderson 2003-04; Vickery 1998, 2003-04). Transitions were often indistinct, variable and inconsistent. Actual artistic transformation is much richer than a generalised account or a broad categorisation can encompass.

To demonstrate the operation of individual action in the process of artistic transformation and the complex expression of Indian derived influences, decorative lintels are an especially appropriate example. Lintels have been used to chart long-term change, but they also incorporate small-scale variations, which for the most part have remained undocumented. Because artistic themes often begin as subtle motif recombinations or experimentations with form, the small-scale variations actually play an important role in the transformation of art. Moreover, the differences in every lintel are not reducible to a fixed ideal or rigidly applied textual model and are therefore evidence of the actions of individual artisans and workshops. Consideration of artist-driven variation is consistent with the notion of Southeast Asian enterprise and autonomy in the process of Indianisation. Rather than application of 'top-down' directives or inflexible models, artists, workshops and patrons historically selected and adapted Indian iconography and forms as part of the unique Khmer artistic development.

'STYLISTICS' AND STATISTICAL ANALYSIS

To consider the creativeness of the Angkorian artists this study draws together data from approximately five hundred decorative lintels and lintel fragments from nearly one hundred sites dispersed across the medieval Khmer landscape between the seventh and the early eleventh centuries CE. At a structural level, medieval Khmer decorative lintels are groupings of iconographic characteristics. The motifs range from divine personages of the Brahmanic and Buddhist pantheon to stylised vegetal scrolls derived from the natural world. Nearly every lintel is unique in its combination of motifs and morphology. The easiest way to distinguish the elaborateness of decorative lintel is to observe the presence (or absence), tally, and position of each discrete motif.[3] Documentation of these motifs in a relational database allows the assembly of an enormous corpus of decorative material, beyond the ability of unaided visual memory. Whilst the style, representation, and meaning of motifs changed over time, each isolated motif is recorded in the database so that it cannot be mistaken for any other motif. Subsequently, each motif may be compared with every other motif, lintel with lintel, and site with site.

To assess the transformation of changing composition of decorative lintels both simple and complex statistical methods are available. Straightforward measures can chart the appearance of disappearance of single motifs, or the changing number of motifs between lintels and across time. But in order to compare the total combination of motifs on each lintel to every other lintel, a more complex statistical measure can be used. Each complete lintel contains anywhere between 5 and 28 discrete measured motifs (an average of approximately 13). To measure each lintel as a combination of its motifs, the multivariate statistical method of Principal Components Analysis (PCA) is an appropriate tool. PCA is a technique of statistical analysis that simplifies complex groups of data. It reduces multidimensional data sets to lower dimensions for analysis. Typically, PCA deals with large numbers of interrelated variables while retaining as much as possible of the variation in the original data (Jolliffe 1986: 1). PCA is commonly used in investigations of 'scientific' data, but in examination of human behaviour it is equally applicable to 'artistic' cultural outputs.[4] In fact, the statistical analysis of literature for the purposes of stylistic and authorship attribution has a thirty-five year history (see Potter 1991: 401-29; Holmes, 1994: 87-106). In a recent analysis, Craig (2007: 273-88) concludes that PCA is an indispensable methodology to examine the authenticity of Shakespearian plays. Reedy's (1997) application of discriminant statistical analysis to stylistic and 'technical' aspects of medieval Himalayan region copper alloy sculptures greatly improved the regional attributions of these works to specific casting centres. In the example of medieval Khmer decorative lintels, PCA measures how lintels relate to each other based on their motif composition. Each lintel as a combination of its motifs is assigned a *xy* weighting based on the original values. The 'line of best fit', or the direction of maximum variation through the entire data set statistically determines the axes of the PCA plot. In the PCA of the lintel data set (Fig. 16.2) the *x*-axis, or first principal component, is a statistical expression of the maximum amount of variation in the data (in this case 4.4 per cent of the total variance in the data set).

The *y*-axis is the second principal component, explaining the second largest degree of variance (3.6 per cent) within the data. The value that each lintel receives is based upon its difference or similarity to the motif combinations of every other lintel in the dataset. Therefore, by this measure lintels that are most similar in motif assemblage have similar PCA values and are clustered together. The more dissimilar the lintels, the further apart they will appear on the plot. Although PCA does not provide measures of the equally important, but more subjective artistic characteristics of form, skill

FIGURE 16.2
**A Principal Components Analysis plot of all complete lintels in the data set.
The PCA measures the difference or similarity of each lintel reduced to an
expression of its combination of motifs**

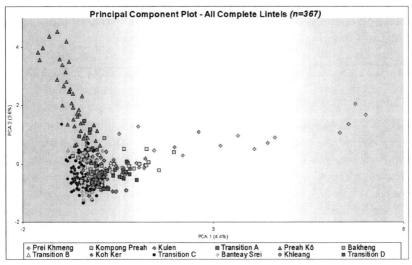

and meaning, it is a suitable way to verify the adequacy of the conventional
stylistic divisions, which were largely determined on the basis of changing
combinations of motifs. Moreover, its novel use upon medieval Khmer
art provides alternative avenues to appraise the transformation of material
culture. The plot represented in Fig. 16.2 illustrates PCA of 367 complete
lintels spanning the seventh to the early eleventh centuries. Only entire lintels
are considered in the analysis. Fragments, incomplete, and eroded lintels with
indiscernible elements are removed from the data-set as they would change
the relationality of each lintel to another. The analysis considers every motif
on every lintel, and gives each lintel a statistical 'weight' according to its
similarity or difference to every other lintel in the data set. Overall, the PCA
patterns are consistent with Coral-Rémusat's (1940, 1951) categorisations and
this analysis supports the stylistic methodologies of earlier scholarship. Figure
16.2 illustrates that the conventional stylistic categories in general cluster
together. Yet the styles are not clearly defined or separated. Each lintel may
be grouped into the same style based upon a particular piece of iconography,
or series of key motifs, but its location within that group is based upon the
variation and difference of additional motifs. Very few lintels possess exactly
the same motif combinations. Lintel decorative assemblages tend to blend
into each other and are not bounded by definable stage horizons. The stylistic
categories are suitable to describe general changes in medieval Khmer art and

compare lintels that are separated by substantial time periods. The 'blurred edges' demonstrate, however, that while the stylistic groups are related, the boundaries themselves are imposed artefacts of analysis to describe the transformation of Khmer art. Lintels are rarely all one style and not another. Each lintel is part of a broader dynamic continuum of artistic culture that was constantly changing at differing rates at different times.

Because the PCA groups similar lintels together, and similar lintels are generally dated to the same period, the plot can be interpreted as a time series. The axes do not, however, specifically measure the passage of time but only the statistical relationship of each lintel to every other lintel. The dispersion of the values indicates the degree of similarity and difference between the lintels. Figure 16.2 begins in the seventh century with a dispersed cluster of Prei Khmeng style lintels that appears to move along the *x*-axis towards the confluence of the graph. During the Preah Kô style the lintels make an upward vertical movement on the *y-axis*, before returning to the centre left of the graph until the termination of the dataset in the early eleventh century. The relatively wide range of values from Prei Khmeng to Preah Kô 'styles' suggests that there was a large degree of difference between the motif combinations on lintels during these periods. Tight clustering from late ninth and into the tenth centuries retains additional significance regarding the design standardisation suggestive of developments in the organisation and administration of workgroups responsible for their production (Polkinghorne 2007, 2007b, 2008).

The PCA plot is illustrative of the dynamic and unique process of artistic transformation and the difficult task of precisely dating decorative material on its motif composition alone. Lintels that share the same or similar motif combinations can cross stylistic boundaries and date ranges. For example, Fig. 16.3 (a detail of Fig. 16.2) illustrates lintels from epigraphically dated sites are not chronologically ordered according to the combination of their motifs (Fig. 16.3). Decorative lintels of tenth-century sites at Koh Ker[5] (CE 921-44), East Mebon (CE 953), Pre Rup (CE 961), and Preah Enkosei (CE 967) share interrelated motif assemblages, but their artistic culture does not follow a direct trajectory. Instead, change in the lintels involves experimentation and recombination of motifs. Illustration of inconsistent transformation can be given by the specific motif of 'brass ring with a chakachan shape flower' that divides the foliage branch of decorative lintels (Fig. 16.4). This motif appears at Koh Ker (Chen, Damrei, Dei Chnan, Prasat Thom and Krachap), and at the East Mebon, but is not used at the next monument in the chronological sequence at Pre Rup. It is adopted again at Preah Enkosei[6] fourteen years later, representing the changeable pattern of motif selection and artistic change.

FIGURE 16.3
The PCA plot illustrates that change from one period to the next is not linear. There are blurred boundaries between time periods and sites that draw from the same pool of motifs

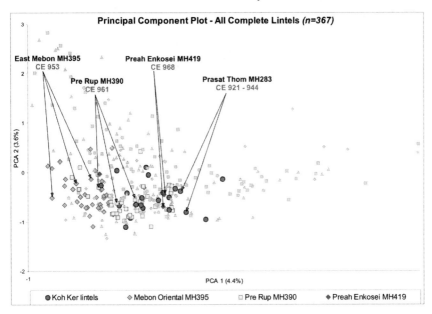

FIGURE 16.4
The 'brass ring with chakachan flower shape' motif that appears on the central foliage branch

Krachap MH265
Western Gopura, west façade

East Mebon MH395
Prasat B15, west façade

Preah Enkosei MH419
South Prasat, east façade

ARTISTS AND ARTISTIC CHANGE

Art historian Meyer Schapiro (1994: 55) asserted that when quantitative measurements are made, they tend to confirm the conclusions reached through direct qualitative description. Along the lines of this view, the largely quantitative methodology advocated here corroborates the conventional stylistic sequence and classification of decorative lintels. Support for the general trajectory of Khmer art formulated by 'stylistics' is particularly noteworthy in regard to the appearance of new and unusual artistic objects that appear to question earlier categorisations (e.g. Bunker and Latchford 2004). The analysis of detailed artistic change can concurrently consider long term transformations and accommodate idiosyncratic variation and anomaly. Nevertheless, the principal purpose of quantitative analysis is not to verify the qualitative assessments which posited the stylistic categorisations in the first place. Rather, quantitative analysis facilitates measuring the different magnitudes of artistic change between periods and styles. The notion that the artistic record was characterised by diverse degrees of change was acknowledged by historians of medieval Khmer art (Coral-Rémusat 1935a, 1935b, 1940, 1951; Stern 1927, 1932, 1934, 1938a, 1938b, 1965), but no relative measure was introduced to account for it. Quantitative analysis widens the capacity of art historical analyses to examine the detail of the artistic record so that variety is perceptible. It addresses transformative changes in the artistic culture difficult to express with traditional approaches. These include dynamic measures of variation, rates of change, transition, archaism, and stylisation, which can be charted across time and space. In addition, quantitative analysis can deal with a new suite of questions which investigate the association between change in artistic culture and its historical context.

Embracing intrinsic variation in artistic transformation recognises the medieval Khmer artists as the progenitors of their tradition. When the detail of motif assemblages can be perceived with quantitative methodologies like PCA, the artistic trajectory is not bound to the arbitrarily defined stylistic boundaries. The categories are a practical way of organising and comparing the large corpus of decorative material, but do not adequately express the process of artistic change. Appreciation of transformation can be found in the detail. Despite the pervasiveness of iconographic and religious traditions that had their origins in India, few scholars have ever conceived the Indian influence as absolute. But the conventional art historical tendency to describe art in categories separated by imagined boundaries acted against scholars from considering the process by which Southeast Asians were social agents in the transformation of their own art. Hence, the large-scale patterns in the artistic material are typically described as a consistent reference to imported and universally understood forms or texts. Rather than the consistent application of 'artistic rules', quantitative analysis perceives the variety of transformation as the operation of selective process which develops historically and from the actions of artists and workshops. The use of Indic iconographic and decorative elements is viewed as contextual selection and adaptation rather than passive acceptance of the 'foreign'. The quantification of variation is not an end in its own right, but a starting point to recognise the tangible process of material change and to posit new questions of medieval Khmer art.

Whether informed by training and tradition, or directed by superiors, it was artists acting upon material that interpreted and adapted the Indian influence. Identifying indigenous elements in Angkorian art is not a task of subtracting the Indic iconography and appraising that which remains, but rather celebrating the creativeness of the medieval Khmer artistic process and creators.

NOTES

1. This research was made possible with financial support from an Australian Postgraduate Award and the Carlyle Greenwell Bequest. The author acknowledges the continued and generous assistance of The Greater Angkor Project, APSARA Authority, the École française d'Extrême-Orient (Siem Reap), and the Archaeological Computing Laboratory of the University of Sydney. Thanks to Bob Brown, Roland Fletcher, Pam Gutman and Dan Penny for commenting on drafts of this paper.
2. See also Schopen (1997 [1991]: 1-22) who similarly observes the scholarly tendency to privilege that which is written in text by appraising the difference between the ideal and material reality of private property ownership by Buddhist monks and nuns.
3. There are 'shape analysis' methodologies that deal with morphology, where statistical analyses describe geometrical properties from similar shapes and different groups (Costa and Cesar Jr. 2001, Dryden and Mardia 1998). These techniques have been employed for examining the difference and similarity of skeletal shapes (e.g. Golland, Grimson, and Kikinis 1999; Lu et al. 2007), but require complex statistical computations and tight control over the 'shape' data itself.
4. For examples of scientific applications of PCA in mainland Southeast Asia see Penny (2001: 97-128), who uses the parallel technique of Detrended Correspondence Analysis (DCA) on palynological records in northeast Thailand. Latinis (2004: 108-31) uses PCA to chart trace materials in a glass bead assemblage from the EFEO Prei Khmeng excavations. Dussubieux and Gratuze (2003: 135-48) apply PCA to the study of glass trade between India and Southeast Asia.
5. A sample of lintels: Neang Khmau, Chen, Daung Kuk, Dei Chnan, Krachap, Prasat Thom, Prasat Kraham, Rolum, and Damrei.
6. And also at Banteay Srei.

REFERENCES

Barth, A., 1885, *Inscriptions sanscrites du Cambodge*, Paris: Imprimerie nationale.
Bénisti, M., 1968, 'Recherches sur le premier art khmer I. Les linteaux dits de Thala Borivat', *Arts asiatiques* XVIII: 85-101.
———, 1974, 'Recherches sur le premier art khmer VI. Linteaux inédits et linteaux méconnus', *Arts asiatiques* XXX: 131-72.
Bhattacharya, K., 1997, 'The Religions of Ancient Cambodia', in *Sculpture of Angkor and Ancient Cambodia: Millennium of Glory*, ed. H.I. Jessup and Thierry Zephir, New York: Thames & Hudson, pp. 34-52.
Boisselier, J., 1966, *Asie du Sud-est: I. Le Cambodge*, Paris: Picard, Manual d'archéologie d'Extrême-Orient, Paris.
———, 1968, 'Les linteaux khmers du VIIIe siècle nouvelles données sur le style de kompong prah', *Artibus Asiae* XXX(2/3): 101-44.
Brown, R.L., 1992, 'Indian Art Transformed: The Earliest Sculptural Styles of Southeast Asia', in *Indian Art and Archaeology: Panels of the VIIth World Sanskrit Conference*, ed. E.M. Raven, and Karel R. van Kooij, Leiden: E.J. Brill, pp. 40-53.

——, 1994, '"Rules" for change in the transfer of Indian art to Southeast Asia', in *Ancient Indonesian Sculpture*, ed. M.J. Klokke and P.L. Scheurleer, Leiden: KITLV Press, pp. 10-32.

——, 1996, *The Dvāravati Wheels of the Law and the Indianization of South East Asia*, Leiden: E.J. Brill.

Bunker, E.C. and D. Latchford, 2004, *Adoration and Glory: the Golden Age of Khmer Art*, Chicago: Art Media Resources.

Casparis, J.G. de 1983, *India and Maritime Trade in Southeast Asia: A Lasting Relationship*, Third Sri Lanka Endowment Fund Lecture, Kuala Lumpur: University of Malaya.

Cœdès, G., 1932, 'Études Cambodgiennes: 30. À la recherche du Yaçodharaçrama', *Bulletin de l'École Française d'Extrême-Orient (BEFEO)*, 32(1): 84-112.

Coral-Rémusat, G., de, 1934, 'De l'origine commune des linteaux de l'Inde Pallava et des linteaux khmèrs préangkoriens', *Revue des arts asiatiques* 8(3): 242-51.

——, 1935a, 'L'évolution de la décoration khmère et le fronton dans l'art d'Angkor', *Bulletin de la société des amis de l'EFEO*: 49 sqq.

——, 1935b, 'Quelques notes sur l'évolution du pilastre dans l'art d'Angkor', *Revue des arts asiatiques* 9(3): 158-64.

——, 1940, *L'art khmer. Les grandes étapes de son évolution*, Paris: Études d'art et d'ethnologie asiatiques.

——, 1951, *L'art khmer. Les grandes étapes de son évolution* (2nd edn.), Van Oest, Les Éditions d'Art et d'histoire, Paris.

Costa, L. da Fontoura and Roberto Marcondes Cesar Jr., 2001, *Shape Analysis and Classification: Theory and Practice*, Boca Raton: CRC Press.

Craig, H. 2007, 'Stylistic Analysis and Authorship Studies', in *A Companion to Digital Humanities*, ed. S. Schreibman, Ray Siemens and John Unsworth, Oxford: Blackwell, pp. 273-88.

Dryden, I.L. and K.V. Mardia, 1998, *Statistical Shape Analysis*, New York: John Wiley & Sons.

Dupont, P., 1952, 'Les linteaux khmers du VIIIe siècle', *Artibus Asiae* 15(1-2): 31-83.

Dussubieux, L. and B. Gratuze, 2003, 'Non-Destructive Characterization of Glass Beads: An Application to the Study of Glass Trade Between India and Southeast Asia', in *Fishbones and Glittering Emblems: Southeast Asian Archaeology 2002*, ed. A. Karlström and Anna Källén, Stockholm: Museum of Far Eastern Antiquities, pp. 135-48.

Golland, P., W.E.L. Grimson and R. Kikinis, 1999, 'Statistical Shape Analysis Using Fixed Topology Skeletons: Corpus Callosum Study', *Proceedings of 16th International Conference of Information Processing in Medical Imaging 1999*: 382-387.

Helms, M.W., 1988, *Ulysses' Sail: An Ethnographic Odyssey of Power, Knowledge, and Geographical Distance*, Princeton: Princeton University Press.

——, 1998, *Access to Origins: Afines, Ancestors, and Aristocrats*, Austin: University of Texas Press.

Holmes, D.I., 1994, 'Authorship Attribution', *Computers and the Humanities* 28(2): 87-106.

Jolliffe, I.T., 1986, *Principal Component Analysis*, New York: Springer-Verlag.

Kulke, H., 1990, 'Indian Colonies, Indianization or Cultural Convergence? Reflections on the Changing Image of India's Role in South-East Asia', in *Ondersoek In Zuidoost-Asië*, ed. H.S. Norholt, Leiden: Vakgroep Talen en Culturen van Zuidoost-Asië en Oceanië, Rijksuniversiteit te Leiden, pp. 8-32.

Latinis, D. K., 2004, 'Prei Khmeng Glass Beads Preliminary EDXRF Report', *From Mission*

archéologique franco-khmère sur l'aménagement du territoire angkorien (MAFKATA).
Campagne 2004, Rapport: École française d'Extrême-Orient (EFEO).

Lu., C., M. Stephen Pizer, Sarang Joshi and Ja-Yeon Jeong, 2007, 'Statistical Multi-Object Shape Models', *International Journal of Computer Vision* 75(3): 387-404.

Mabbett, I.W., 1977a, 'The "Indianization" of Southeast Asia: Reflections on the Prehistoric Sources', *Journal of Southeast Asian Studies* 8(1): 1-33.

——, 1977b, 'The "Indianization" of Southeast Asia: Reflections on the Historical Sources', *Journal of Southeast Asian Studies* 8(2): 143-61.

——, 1997, 'The "Indianization" of Mainland Southeast Asia: A Reappraisal', in *Living a Life in Accord with Dhamma: Papers in Honor of Professor Jean Boisselier on his Eightieth Birthday*, ed. N. Eilenberg, M.C. Subhadradis Diskul and R. Brown, Bangkok: Silpakorn University, pp. 342-55.

Majumdar, R.C. 1927a, *Ancient Indian Colonies in the Far East*, vol. 1, *Champa*, Lahore: Greater India Society Publication.

——, 1927b, *The Inscriptions of Champa*, Lahore: Greater India Society Publication.

——, 1953, *Inscriptions of Kambuja*, Calcutta: The Asiatic Society.

——, 1963, *Hindu Colonies in the Far East*, 2nd edn., Calcutta: Firma K.L. Mukhopadhyay.

Maxwell, T.S., 2007, 'Religion at the Time of Jayavarman VII', in *Bayon: New Perspectives*, ed. J. Clark, Bangkok: River Books, pp. 74–121.

Mus, P., 1975 [1933], *India Seen from the East: Indian and Indigenous Cults in Champa*, tr. I.W. Mabbett, ed. Ian W. Mabbett and D. Monash Chandler, papers on Southeast Asia, no. 3, Melbourne.

——, 1977, *L'angle de l'Asie*, Paris: Hermann.

Penny, D. 2001, 'A 40,000 Year Palynological Record from North-East Thailand; Implications for Biogeography and Palaeo-environmental Reconstruction. *Palaeogeography, Palaeoclimatology, Palaeoecology* 171: 97-128.

Polkinghorne, M., 2007a, 'Makers and Models: Decorative Lintels of Khmer Temples, 7th to 11th centuries', unpublished Ph.D. thesis, Department of Art History and Theory, Department of Archaeology, University of Sydney.

——, 2007b, 'Artists and Ateliers: Khmer Decorative Lintels of the Ninth and Tenth Centuries', in *Udaya – The Journal of Khmer Studies* 8: 219-41.

——, 2008, 'Khmer Decorative Lintels and the Allocation of Artistic Labour', in *Arts Asiatiques* 63: 21-35.

Potter, R.G., 1991, 'Statistical Analysis of Literature: A Retrospective on Computers and the Humanities, 1966-1990', *Computers and the Humanities* 25(6): 401-29.

Pottier, C. 1999, 'Carte archéologique de la région d'Angkor Zone Sud', 2 vols, unpublished Ph.D. thesis, Université Paris III - Sorbonne Nouvelle.

——, 2000, 'À la recherche de Goloupura', *BEFEO* 87(1): 79-107.

Pottier, C., and R. Lujàn-Lunsford, 2005, 'De brique et de grès. Précisions sur les tours de Prah Kô', *BEFEO* 92: 457-95.

Reedy, C.L. 1997, *Himalayan Bronzes: Technology, Style, and Choices*, Newark: University of Delaware Press.

Reynolds, C.J., 1995, 'A New Look at Old Southeast Asia', *The Journal of Asian Studies* 54(2): 419-46.

Sanderson, A., 2003-04, 'The Saiva Religion Among the Khmers', *BEFEO* 90-91: 349-462.

Schapiro, M., 1994, 'Style: In Theory and Philosophy of Art: Style, Artist, and Society', *Selected Papers*, vol. IV, New York: George Braziller, Inc., pp. 51-102.

Schopen, G., 1997 [1991], 'Archaeology and Protestant Presuppositions in the Study of Indian Buddhism', in *Bones, Stones, and Buddhist Monks: Collected Papers on the Archaeology, Epigraphy, and Texts of Monastic Buddhism in India*, Honolulu: University of Hawaii Press, pp. 1-22.

Smith, M.L., 1999, '"Indianization" from the Indian Point of View: Trade and Cultural Contracts with Southeast Asia in the Early First Millennium CE', *Journal of the Economic History of the Orient* 42(1): 1-26.

Stern, P., 1927, *Le Bayon d'Angkor et l'évolution de l'art khmer*, Paris: Paul Geuthner.

——, 1932, 'La transition de l'art préangkoréen à l'art angkoréen et Jayavarman II', in *Études d'Orientalisme*, vol. 1, Paris: Musée Guimet, Mélanges Linossier, Ernest Leroux, pp. 507-24.

——, 1934, 'Évolution du linteau khmer', *Revue des arts asiatiques* 8(4): 251-56.

——, 1938a, 'Le style des Kulen', *BEFEO* 38(1): 111-49.

——, 1938b, 'Hariharalaya et Indrapura', *BEFEO* 38(1): 175-97.

——, 1965, *Les monuments Khmers du style du Bayon et Jayavarman VII*, Paris: Presses Universitaires de France.

Vickery, M., 1998, *Society, Economics, and Politics in Pre-Angkor Cambodia*, The Toyo Bunko, Tokyo: Centre for East Asian Cultural Studies for UNESCO.

——, 2003-04, 'Funan Reviewed: Deconstructing the Ancients', *BEFEO* 90-91: 101-43.

17

Early Musical Exchange between India and Southeast Asia

Arsenio Nicolas

From the first centuries CE, the more important relations between Southeast Asia and India can be found in the shastras (religion, scripts, literature, politics, law) and architecture (Cœdès 1968: 254-56), while that with China, Korea and Japan, in music structures, musical instruments and ensembles (Picken 1981-90; Maceda 1995d). In Southeast Asia, after an extended period of adapting Hindu and Buddhist rites and ceremonies, courts and temples developed a parallel repertoire of music for court ceremonies, separate from the repertoire used for religious rites in the temples. In Java and Bali, the extensive use of musical forms, musical instruments and vocal music attested to in Old Javanese and Old Balinese inscriptions, literatures, and in temple reliefs (Kunst 1968), as can also be found in Burma, Thailand, Laos, Kampuchea, and Vietnam, are early records of music in the area. Religious transformation in the two islands of Java and Bali allowed for the reworking and recasting of old rites into new forms suitable for Hindu or Buddhist ceremonies both in the temples and in the courts. The manifold reworking of rites and ceremonies, and how the musical arts were integrated into these systems has yet to be described and analysed – what indigenous structures were perceived to be malleable for new Hindu and Buddhist liturgical forms, and how these were all incorporated into the ritual repertoire of both the courts and the temples and other sacred sanctuaries, and what musical, theatrical or dance forms were integrated into these systems.

If the courts and the temples exuded an aura of exclusivity and sacrality, the surrounding villages which constituted an even larger system nurtured their own musical traditions, rites and festivities that were of two orientations

– the persistence of indigenous repertoire, and the slow intrusion of Hindu, Buddhist, Islamic and Christian modes of ritual and ceremonial procedures. In these contexts, the musics of Southeast Asia developed into at least three distinct areas: first, the village which until today remains the repository of ancient religious and musical practices; second, the courts; and third, the temples, which together established a new form of centralised organisation and power, and consequently assumed the position as centres of musical activity, where musicians and dancers, players and puppeteers were employed in the service of the ruler, the aristocracy and the religious hierarchy. A new music culture based on ritual developed concurrent with monument building and the institution of the *devaraja* cult. However, while primary Indic rites were central to temple activities, indigenous rituals, music and dances were utilised to construct new ritual procedures. A new temple system and a new music culture then emerged after the introduction of Hinduism and Buddhism, and which can be characterised as follows (Nicolas 1993).

First, the construction of court and temple complexes formed closed relationships with the villages. Second, the introduction of sacred chanted texts in Sanskrit and Pali and later, the use of indigenous languages or Sanskritised local languages and scripts built two parallel musical repertoires, one preserving indigenous musical genres and the other, derived from Indic texts. Third, a shift from a bamboo music culture to a bronze music culture with the use of gongs and bells developed in the courts and temples, while the villages maintained a bamboo and wood tradition in music-making (Maceda 1977). Gongs assumed a sacred and prestigious position as a technology of bronze casting developed and diversified into larger musical ensembles that are extant today. In the villages, bamboo musical ensembles and other heterogeneous types evolved a separate repertoire (Nicolas 1987).

The introduction and spread of Hinduism and Buddhism into Asia branched off into two main streams – one took a northern route towards the direction of the land of the Sino-Tibetan peoples, towards Tibet, China, Korea and Japan, and the other, a southern route towards the direction of the land of the Mon-Khmer, Thai, and the Austronesian peoples. During these transcontinental journeys, the first accounts of musical change in the region were recorded in inscriptions and literary texts. The introduction of Indic, Arabic, Chinese and European musical ideas, their reception in the various regions in Asia and their amalgamation into the local musical systems represent four major phases in the history of music in Asia. Occurring in a serial fashion, each phase introduced into the indigenous base new languages and ritual literatures, the corpus of which became the basis for the performance of state rituals and ceremonies, of rites to fight the forces of nature, of disease, or to conjure the efficacy of power and ancestral blessings. Musical instruments likewise were transported from one frontier to another, evolving into various forms and styles, both musical and iconographic. One important task, therefore, remains the identification and description of what may be called the indigenous base, which is to be found in the hundreds of societies with diverse languages, ritual practices, beliefs, artistic and musical systems.

MUSIC IN LITERARY AND EPIGRAPHICAL SOURCES

Paleographical and literary evidence describe a formalisation of the courts and the temples as the first centres of new musical activity. Musical terms that are recorded in these documents may be classified into the following: names of musical instruments, names of vocal types, names or terms referring to musicians, dancers, musical genres, forms, names of tunes or melodies, rites and ritual where music, dances and theatrical presentations are held, terms referring to the nature or aesthetic of sound or music, terms describing sounds produced by natural phenomena, or describing the onomatopoeic phenomena of language representation of sound (Nicolas 1994). In Java and Bali, musical terms start to appear in inscriptions by the ninth century during the Central Javanese Period, which can all be classified as Old Javanese, Old Balinese and Sanskrit or Sanskrit derived (Kunst 1968; Zoetmulder 1982; Nicolas 2007). By the beginning of the tenth century, that is, during the East Javanese Period, Sanskrit terms are no longer mentioned. The disappearance of Sanskrit musical terms for musical instruments in tenth century Java thus signaled a new music culture in the region (Nicolas 2007: 92 ff.).

TWO SANSKRIT MUSICAL TERMS

In this study, I focus on two Sanskrit derived musical terms that are found in the Philippines and Indonesia, with cognates in Burmese, Thai, Khmer, Cham and Malay. The first musical term, *kacchapi*, is the Sanskrit form of boat lutes found in the Philippines and Indonesia, known in various languages as *kudyapi, kecapi, husapi, sampeq* among others. The second term, *kamsa*, meaning bell-metal, has a more limited distribution, which today is known as *gangsa*, referring to flat gongs in northern Luzon, metallophones in Java and Bali, musical ensemble in high Javanese (*kromo*) or more commonly known as *gamelan* (*ngoko*) and as bronze in high Javanese. Flat gongs are well represented in temple reliefs in India, as well as in Java, and were found in shipwrecks dating to the tenth, eleventh and thirteenth centuries. References to lutes are mainly found in literary works and are not mentioned in Old Javanese and Old Balinese inscriptions. Boat lutes are made up of wooden material and as such, archaeological artefacts are virtually non-existent. Lutes of diverse types are etched in temple reliefs in India, China, Cambodia, Thailand, Champa and Java.

LUTES

The Sanskrit term *kacchapi* is used for a variety of lutes in the Philippines and Indonesia, with the number of strings varying from two to four. Two-stringed lutes in Indonesia and the Philippines are widely distributed. In an early study of Sanskrit words in the Philippines, Kern listed *kudyapi* or *kotsapi* as a Sanskrit derived word both for Tagalog (1880: 267) and Bisaya (1881: 283). In 1663, Colin wrote about a stringed instrument called *coryapi* in Luzon (Blair & Robertson, 1903-09, vol. 40, p. 68). An ancient Tagalog term on Luzon, *kudyapi*, is still used in songs and poetry today, but the instrument no longer exists. The term had already meant guitar by late nineteenth century, and has remained so until today. However, in the case of Bisaya, *kodyapi* or *kotsapi* meant lute.

Farther south, the wide distribution of boat-lutes starts on the island of Mindoro, then on Palawan and Mindanao, Borneo, Sulawesi, Java, Sumatra and a few eastern Indonesian islands. There are no two-string lutes on Basilan Island and the Sulu archipelago. There are as well variations in the number of strings and the shape of the body of the lute. On Borneo, three-stringed lutes are found among the Modang and Kenyah and are called *sampeq*, or *sapeq*. On Java, we find bas-reliefs of two-, three- and four-string lutes on the Borobudur temple, as well as on Candi Sari. On Java, the terms *kacapi* or *kecapi* refer to zithers. Most of the lutes are plucked either with the fingers or with a plectrum. Lutes are either played alone, or as a duet (as in Palawan and Borneo), or with one other instrument like a polychordal bamboo zither in Palawan and Mindanao. The term, however, is not known in Bali and Lombok, which is significant, considering the fact that the Balinese in these two islands practice a religion based on ancient Balinese and Hindu religious systems and had an extended contact with India since the first century CE (Ardika 1997).

Java

Kunst provides a very detailed discussion of lutes based on his studies of bas-reliefs in Candi Borobudur, Prambanan and Candi Sari (1968: 12-17). While the term *kacchapi* does not appear in any inscription, it is widely used in Old Javanese literature as *kacapi*, and may have referred to lutes, although it is used in West Java today to refer to board zithers with a box-like shape resonating chamber (ibid.: 11-12). These lutes are illustrated as two-, three-, or four-stringed instruments with varying shapes in these three temples. The following list is derived from the photographs published by Kunst (ibid.: 157 ff.).

lute	Borobudur O 151 left	Fig. 14
lute	Borobudur IIIB 40	Fig. 30
lute (slender type)	Borobudur Ia 1 left side	Fig. 15
lute (with plectrum)	Borobudur Ia 52	Fig. 16
lute, slender, frets	Borobudur II 128	Fig. 27
lute, two-strings	Borobudur II 122	Fig. 26
lute, two-strings w/ plectrum	Borobudur O 102	Fig. 8
lute, three strings	Borobudur II 1	Figs. 22, 23, 24
lute, three-strings	Borobudur O 125	Fig. 10
lute, three-strings	Candi Sari	Fig. 3
lute, three-strings	Prambanan, Śiva	Fig. 35
lute, four-strings	Borobudur O 151 center	Fig. 13

On walls of the Borobudur temple, all the three types of lutes are illustrated. Two- and three-string lutes are more commonly illustrated. A lone four-string lute is also illustrated in this temple. Three-stringed lutes are also illustrated in the Sari and Prambanan temples. Kunst surmised that these instruments illustrated on bas-reliefs in three central Javanese temples – Candi Sari, Candi Borobudur and Candi Prambanan – may have been brought from India during the Śailendra period (*c.* 725-850) and on to the early tenth century (ibid.: 13). These may have been called *vin* or *vina* in Old Javanese (Zoetmulder 1982). A fourteenth-century bas-relief in East Java portrays a Brahmin teaching a female student the instrument illustrated as a lute with two gourd resonators (Kunst 1968, fig. 50). Wrazen (1986) however, argued that Indian lutes were derived from polychordal zithers from Assam or Java. Three-string lutes are only found today in Kalimantan. Lutes in the Philippines, Borneo, Sumatra and Sulawesi are of the boat lute type, which are not illustrated in the Borobudur temple. Lutes illustrated on Borobudur tend to imitate Indian models. If this generalisation is correct, it may be gathered that boat lutes in Indonesia and the Philippines had long been present and were already known through their local names. When Sanskrit musical terms were introduced to this region, music communities which played lutes borrowed a new term from Sanskrit and adapted this locally.

Philippines

In the Philippines, two groups of names for two-string lutes are known. The first group uses indigenous terms generally called *kudlung*, while another group uses *kudyapi*, a term derived from Sanskrit (Maceda 1998: 43). Those found on Mindanao are usually shorter in length, while those found on Palawan Island have a length of about 6 to 7 feet (ibid.: 249). The terms *kudyapi, kutyapi, katyapi, kusyapi* or *kotapi* are known today in nine languages, on Mindoro and Palawan Islands and on the western and southern side of Mindanao. The music of two-string lutes called *kudyapiq* or *kutyapiq* of the Maguindanao uses two scales called *dinaladay*, with titles of music pieces referring to natural sounds like the chirping of birds, and the *binalig*, which evokes sentiments of sorrow and sadness, or love (Maceda 1988). Native terms not derived from Sanskrit are used for musical pieces both for *kudyapiq* and *kudlong* repertoires.

Musical Term	Language Group	Location
kudyapi	Iraya	Mindoro Island
kudyapi / kusyapi / kutyapi	Palawan	Palawan Island
kudyapi / kutyapi	Magindanao	Mindanao
kudyapi / kutyapi	Maranao	Mindanao
kudyapi	Manobo	Mindanao
kutyapi	Manobo Cotabato	Mindanao
koítapi / kutapi	Subanon	Mindanao
katyapi	Bukidnon	Mindanao

A second group of boat lutes on Mindanao from thirteen language groups use the term kudlong, with the following variations – faglong, fuglung, fegarong, hagelung, segarong. The distribution of indigenous terms for boat lutes among language groups on Mindanao is listed as follows:

Language Group	Musical Terms		
Bilaan	kudlong	faglong
		faglung
		foglong
Manobo Cotabato	kudlong	
	kudyung	fuglong
Manobo Agusan	kudlong	
	kudyung	
Ata	kudlong	
	kuglong	
Bagobo	kudlong	
Mangguangan	kudlong	
Mamanua	kudlong	
Mandaya	kudlong	
Mansaka	kudlung	
Mansaka		binalig, binarig
Mansaka		binudyaan
Tiboli		hagalong
		hagelung
Tiruray		fegarong
		segarong

Thailand

In Thailand, the *krajappi,* derived from the Pali-Sanskrit *kachapa,* is a two-string lute with a short tortoise-shaped sound box and a long neck the total length of which may reach up to 6 feet. Another instrument, the *chakhe* is a two-string zither-type of instrument that had been used since the early fourteenth century of the Ayutthaya Period. Like the Javanese *kecapi,* it is a floor zither (Morton 1976: 92).

Celebes (Sulawesi)

Kaudern's earlier survey on boat lutes showed that these were found mostly in the western and southern parts of Celebes island (now Sulawesi), and they were scarce on the eastern side (1927: 187-93). Quoting Sachs (1983 [1923]: 105), Kaudern validates that the terms used in Celebes for boat lutes – *katjapi, katjaping, katjapin, kasapi, ketjapi* – are all derived from the Sanskrit *kacchapa* or *kaccappi vina* (ibid.: 190). Kaudern observed that all the boat lutes in these areas were not bowed, but were generally plucked either with a plectrum or with the fingers. Furthermore, he noted that boat lutes in Borneo were similar to those found in the western and southern part of Celebes. There is still an absence of a distribution study of boat lutes in Indonesia as a whole, such that it is still not possible to draw a total picture.

In summary, there is a geographical division between groups that use Sanskrit derived terms and indigenous terms for lutes. Two-string lutes from eight Philippines language groups with names derived from Sanskrit are found on the western side of the archipelago. These names may have been acquired from maritime traders that originated either directly from India, Champa, or from Sumatra, Java or Borneo after the introduction of Sanskrit in this area. This also means that only groups found on the western shores of Sulawesi, and the Philippines were borrowing Sanskrit musical terms for lutes. The second group, largely to be found in thirteen language groups on eastern Mindanao, has more varied terms, indicating local preferences, as well as localisation of musical practices. The presence of significant indigenous terms for boat lutes in the eastern side of Mindanao indicate local origins of the instrument, and that those with Sanskrit derived terms may have changed the name when new musical ideas emerged as a result of the expansion of trade in the areas where lutes are known in maritime Asia from Champa, Cambodia, Thailand, Sumatra, Java, Borneo, Sulawesi (Celebes), Borneo and the Philippines.

KAṆSÁ, KAṆSYA (SANSKRIT: BELL METAL, GONG, PERCUSSION PLATE)

The terms *kaṇsá, kaṇsya* in India

According to Monier-Williams, the Sanskrit *kansá* (1899: 241) or *kansya* (1993: 266) is a type of white-copper or bell-metal or brass. It is also a kind of musical instrument, a gong or plate of bell-metal struck with a stick or rod. *Kansâsthi* is white copper, any alloy of tin and copper (ibid.: 241). *Kansá, kansya* or *kaṁsa, kāṁsya* (2008: 394) are representations of a form with nasalized vowel preceding s [kāsa], which today, in some languages, is reflected with a velar nasal pronunciation [kāṇsa]. The symbol ṁ or ṃ does not represent a bilabial nasal [m]. [Ritsuko Kikusawa and Lawrence Reid (pers. com.)]

In India, an early site attesting to the presence of gongs is a bas-relief in Amaravati, dated from at least the second century BCE and seventh century CE (Murthy 1985: 2, 76, Pl. 23). The relief itself or the picture in the book is not clear enough to indicate whether this is a flat gong or a bossed gong. The gong is hung from a bar borne on the shoulders of two men, one of which is portrayed with a stick beating the gong. A twelfth-century relief from the temples in Hoysala in India shows a thick, even-shaped gong of about 30 to 40 cm. diameter, held by a player with the left hand and struck with a mallet with the right hand. The gong appears to be flat, suspended from the left hand of the player by a rope that had been inserted through the rim of the gong. Two other musicians play double-membraned drums beaten with two hands and hanging from the neck and shoulders with a strap (Deloche 1988: Fig. 1a, nos. 2, 3, 4). This recalls many other illustrations of gongs in temples in Cambodia, Champa and Java, as well as numerous similar practices where bossed gongs and double-headed drums are carried in processions in Java (Kunst 1973) and Bali (McPhee 1968 [or 1966 ?]) and in Sulu (Maceda 1998: 142, Ill. 151, 153).

In northern India, bronze flat gongs and bronze dish plates are called *thali*. The disc has usually raised rims. Techniques of playing vary. The flat gong can be held in one hand and then beaten with a stick by the other. The other technique is to place the gong on the ground and beat it with one or two sticks or with the hands. In the two pictures in a book by Deva, the *semmankalam* is provided with a handle made up of a rope and wrapped with cloth that had been inserted into two holes on the rim of the gong. It is held by the left hand, while the right hand beats the flat surface with a wooden stick (1978: 57). In Rajasthan, the *thali* is a flat gong that has a straight rim. It accompanies a group of women presumably singing, while others clap their hands. The flat gong is laid on the ground; the proximal end rests on the left knee of a female musician and the distal end on the ground. Both hands are used in beating the gong, the right palm strikes the surface near the centre on the distal side, while the left hand strikes the edge of the surface with all the four fingers (ibid.: Fig. 5.12), a technique quite similar to that employed in the *gangsa* playing by the Kalinga, Itneg and Ifugao in northern Luzon. In southern Rajasthan, a single brass *thali* (rimmed plate) is played with two drums (*dhak*). Its face is laid down on the floor. The rim, however, is not straight as it widens a little bit outwards. The left hand of the player dampens the rim of the gong as the right hand beats the basic beat (Roche 2000: 64, Fig. 2), a technique that is also found among the Kalinga, Itneg and Tingguian in northern Luzon (Maceda 1998: Pls. 36, 37, 38, 59-64, 67).

Several terms are used to refer to flat gongs, derived from *kamsa*, and are found in Orissa and West Bengal. In Ratijana, Orissa, flat gongs are called *kansar*, while rice bowls are called *kansa* and thin plates are called *thali* (Mukherjee 1978: 349-50). In Orissa and West Bengal, *kamsar* is used for gongs and *kamsa* for rice bowls (Srinivasan 1994: 700). Srinivasan traces the etymology of these terms to the Sanskrit word *kamsya* (bell-metal). Another literary reference he cites is the Mauryan economic treatise of the *Arthashastra* (Kangle 1972: 108-9 in Srinivasan 1994: 700), indicating factories for working alloys including *kamsa-tala*, bronzes of different proportions, with *-tala* implying measure. A twelfth-century alchemical text *Rasaratnasamuccaya* mentions the term *kamsya* as an alloy (Ray 2003: 156, 185) while a Tamil classic, the *Cilappattikaram* (third to fifth centuries CE) uses *kancam* to refer to bronze (ibid.: 109). Another set of terms use *thali*, as in Uttar Pradesh and Rajasthan (Roche in *Garland Encyclopedia* 2000: 291, 292); *thali* among the Nats and the Mali in Rajasthan (Natavar in ibid.: 640, 647); *tala* in south Karnataka, described as hand held-bronze gong (Kassebraum and Klaus in ibid.: 885), *tali* in Pushkar, Rajasthan, described as a brass plate, but the picture on the cover of the book clearly shows a raised rim (Garland 1999: cover photo); and *thal* in Maharashtra, central India (Ranade in ibid.: 727). In Pakistan this is called *tal* in Balochistan (Badalkhan in ibid.: 774) and among the Soti (ibid.: 782, 783). In temples in Benares, Brahmans play a small flat gong called *tala* together with an hourglass shaped drum called *damaru*. The *tala* has two holes through which a small rope had been inserted on its rim to provide a handle for the player who beats on the flat surface of the gong using a small round wooden stick (Danielou 1978: 8-9, 44-45, Ill. 45).

Flat gongs called *cennalam* are played with cymbals called *talam* or *ilat a lam* in the *kathakali* ensemble either for time-keeping or marking out divisions of a *tala*, or to play rhythmic patterns similar to those played by drums (Powers 2006). Travelling troupes in Karnataka perform the *yakshagana*, with a musical ensemble having a strong affinity with Kerala. It is accompanied by two drums of Kerala type, and a flat gong and cymbals for time-keeping, with no melodic accompanying instrument for the singer. In Kerala, the *kathakali* dance-drama is accompanied with an ensemble consisting of two singers, *cennalam* (flat gong), *maddalam* (barrel drum), *centa* (cylindrical drum), *itekka* (hourglass drum), and *ilat a lam* (cymbals) (Qureshi 2006). The names of flat gongs or 'struck plates' vary from region to region: *chenkala* or *chennala* (Malayalam), *semmankalam* (Tamil), *jagte* or *jagante* (Kannada), *thali* (Hindi), *ghadiyal* (Rajasthani) and others.

Given the limited sources cited above, it appears that there are a variety of terms for flat gongs in India and quite a number do not show a direct derivation from the Sanskrit term. From the survey above, it appears that *thali* or *thala* are more widespread for percussion plates, as also for flat gongs. There is no data whether these are high tin bronze made of from bell-metal, but the origins of the use might be traced to the term *kamsyatala*, *kamsya* meaning bell-metal and *tala*, plates or plates that play a certain measure.

The term '*kangsa*' in Cham, Khmer, Thai and Burmese

The earliest references to *kangsa* in Khmer inscriptions date to the seventh century and in Cham inscriptions to the ninth, tenth and twelfth centuries. Cœdès dated two Khmer inscriptions to the seventh century which mention the term *kangsatala*, translated as 'gongs en bronze' (bronze gongs). He remarked that the term *kamsatala* does not appear in Sanskrit dictionaries but is more common in Pali texts (1954 II: 73, 74). Saveros Pou later classified *kangsatal* as Middle Khmer (cymbal) and this may have been derived either from *kamsyatala* (Skt.) or from *kamsatala* (Prakrit) (2004: 254). Finot's translation of the Sdok Kak Thom inscription dated 974 S / CE 1052 rendered *kangsa-tala* as 'cymbales de cuivre' (1915: 69, 86). A ninth-century Cham inscription dated 18 May 875 mentions the term *kangsa*, 'laiton' (Finot 1904: 84-99) or 'bell-metal' (Golzio 2004: 68, 72). In another Cham inscription dated 918/CE 191, the term *kamsa* is mentioned and is translated as 'bronze' (Huber 1911: 15-22) and as 'bell-metal' (Golzio 2004: 118, 119). Another inscription dated CE 1156 mentions *kangsa bhaja* as copper pitchers (Golzio 2004: 178, 179; Finot 1904: 976-77; Majumdar 1972) [Note: 'kamsa' and 'kangsa' are both read as 'kaŋsa']

Across the Bay of Bengal, the Thai *gangsadan* or *kangsadan* (field notes 1986; Penth 1970) and the Khmer *kangsatala* refer to flat gongs that are used in Buddhist temples. References to *gaza* are known for Burmese flat gongs as early as the early sixteenth century (Pires 1944: 96, n. 5) and *ganza* as copper money (Pires 1944: 99-100).

The term *'gangsa'* in Java and Bali

In Old Javanese, Zoetmulder translates *gangsa* as derived from the Sanskrit form *kangsa,* which means bell-metal (1982: 492). The term first appears in Old Javanese inscriptions from the ninth to the tenth centuries and cannot be found in Old Balinese inscriptions. In the inscriptions, *gangsa* is mentioned in two contexts. First, it refers to bronze smiths, *pandai gangsa,* in at least six Old Javanese inscriptions dating from the late ninth to the early tenth centuries. Second, *gangsa* is either mentioned alone, or more so, in combination with three other terms used for metals in Old Javanese: *tambaga* or *tamwaga* (copper), *wsi* or *wesi* (iron) and *mas* (gold). It is mentioned as a metal alloy in several inscriptions dated 862 and 915 (Kunst 1968: 91, 92) and in 862, 880, 904, 907, 909 and 915, occurring with the term *pandai* 'smith' (Damais 1970: 748, 749, 925). Christie recently published three excerpts from the tenth- and eleventh-century inscriptions from the Brantas River area. In two of these dated 929 and 1021, *gangsa* is used as a single term to refer to bronze, in association with three other metals – iron (*wsi*), copper (*tambaga*), tin (*timah*). The third is without a date, but may have been copied during the Majapahit Period from a tenth or eleventh century inscription (Christie 1998: 370-71).

There is continuity in the use of *gangsa* in inscriptions for both periods: from the central Javanese period to the beginning of the East Javanese period, the meaning of this term has not changed. The term does not show up in later inscriptions, but appears in literary texts in Old Javanese, exemplified by the *Ramayana* and *Smarradahana*. The term refers to a type of alloy or metal, as found in the references in inscriptions and from examples in the *kakawin* literature, and may not yet refer to a musical instrument. In a study of Middle Indian terms in Old Javanese, Casparis provides a list of words which, he suggests, are not directly traceable to a Sanskrit, Hindi or Tamil prototype. More significantly, he concludes that the majority of the words in the list are those which may have been used by traders and artisans. Four of these are directly related to metal craft: *gangsa* (Skt. *kamsa,* bell-metal, brass), *gusali* (blacksmith), *pandai* (smith), and *tamwaga* or *tambaga* (Skt, *tamra, tamraka,* copper) (1988: 51-52). The other terms refer to crafts, trade commodities and trader (*banyaga*) (ibid.: 68), numbering thirty-four, and are dated from CE 798 to 934, and may have been incorporated into Old Javanese well before CE 1000 (ibid.: 66). In another study, Sedyawati notes that blacksmiths and coppersmiths are frequently mentioned in inscriptions as compared to goldsmiths. The former are 'always mentioned in relation to the restriction of the number of producing smithies, which are free from taxation, within one village' (1999: 7-8). The blacksmiths and coppersmiths are makers of common utensils in daily village use, while goldsmiths can be found in larger towns and more so, in palaces.

The term *'gangsa'* in Northern Luzon

In the Philippines, the term *gangsa* refers to flat gongs and flat gong ensembles in highland northern Luzon. The term first appears in an account by Father Aduarte and several other Spanish friars, describing initial attempts at Christianization in the area, and who arrived in Nueva Segovia, now the province of Cagayan, on the first of August 1595 (Aduarte 1640). The friars reported that they could hear from afar rituals being performed by the people, during which they made 'a great noise with their voices and their *gazas* – which are their bells, though they are not formed like our bells' (Aduarte in Blair & Robertson, 30: 300). The passage gives the earliest description of flat gongs as bells (*campana*) in Spanish. In many subsequent Spanish accounts, including dictionaries, the term *campana* had been consistently used to refer to gongs, whether these are flat or bossed gongs. The term *gaza* was not described as a flat gong, but simply as a musical instrument.

An early reference to what might be a flat gong is in Morga's *Succesos de las Islas Filipinas* in 1609. In his account, Morga described the musical life of the Tagals (Tagalog) and referred to 'metal bells' shaped like 'large pans brought from China'. The sound was described as sonorous. These were used in feasts, and were also carried in boats when going to war in lieu of drums or other instruments. These were also exchanged in barter with local products (Morga 1867: 303). That flat gongs were known to the Tagals or Tagalog in the early seventeenth century is corroborated by the term *palayi* in a Tagalog dictionary published by San Buenaventura in 1613 (1994: 139). This term is quite rare in the literature. In a 1904 dictionary of the Pangasinan, the term *pala-y* is entered as 'campana de china' (Pellicer 1904). *Palayi* today is a term for flat gongs used by the Ayta in Zambales and Bataan (Maceda 1998: 8) while *pinalaiyan* is a flat gong ensemble among the Tingguian in northern Luzon (ibid.: 14).

A dictionary of the Pangasinan language compiled in the late seventeenth century by Lorenzo Cosgaya (1661-1731), listed *gansa* as 'cobre y significa tambien laton' (copper, and may mean as brass). The term 'bronce' is likewise translated as *gansa*. This is the only reference so far obtained for *gangsa* as metal on Luzon (Cosgaya 1865: 18, 165). However, another Pangasinan dictionary published later in 1904 listed the term *pala-y* as 'campana de china' (Pellicer 1904: 14, 257). Pangasinan lies on the promontory of the western coasts of central Luzon, and was known in the Chinese Ming annals in 1406. Its position is intermediary between the highland northern Luzon where a flat gong music today is cultivated, and the central Luzon region, including Manila and Laguna, where the term *pala-yi* was known as early as the seventeenth century. Thus, until the early twentieth century, flat gongs were known as *gangsa* in highland Luzon, Ilocos, Cagayan, and as *palayi* in Pangasinan, Tingguian and until the early seventeenth century, in Laguna and nearby areas.

In highland northern Luzon today, all language groups play a music of flat gongs (Maceda 1998: 17, Ill. 5). The following lists terms for flat gongs in northern Luzon that are derived from Sanskrit term *kamsya*.

Bontok	*kangsa*	*gangsa*		*cangsa*
Sagada	*kangsa*			
Ibaloi		*gangsa*		
Isneg		*gangsa*	*gansa*	*hansa*
Kalinga		*gangsa*		
Karaw		*gangsa*		
Tingguian		*gangsa*		
Ilongot			*cangsa*	
Ifugao				*gangha*

While *gangsa* is widely used as a common term for flat gongs and flat gong ensembles in northern Luzon, what appears more significant are the individual names assigned to each gong in an ensemble, which are not derived from Sanskrit. For example, the Kalinga play music of flat gongs in two different styles, the *gangsa palook* and *gangsa topayya*, with these six gongs named as *balbal, kadua, katlo, kapat, opop, anungos*. The Ifugao play three flat gongs known collectively as *gangha*, with each gong having a particular name of its own – *tobob, hibat, ahot*. Among the Bontok, the terms *changsa* and *gangsa* are known. Among the Ilongot, the term *changsa* is also used. And among the Tingguian/Itneg, the term *gansa* is utilised. In the table above, indigenous terms are significantly used to refer to individual names of gongs with specific musical functions in musical ensembles.

MUSICAL EXCHANGES IN ASIA

We have thus presented a number of evidence for the spread of two Sanskrit musical terms in Southeast Asia. The term *kacchapi*, which in Sanskrit means 'tortoise', became more widespread in Indonesia and the Philippines as a term for boat lutes. The term *kamsa*, meaning 'bell-metal' in Sanskrit, is known today in northern Luzon as flat gongs and as a term for flat gong ensembles, in Java and Bali as metallophone, as a term for musical ensemble, and as bronze.

The distribution of the term *gangsa* and its derivations or variations from Sanskrit and Indian sources provide an important link to the movement of Indian or Sanskrit musical terms into the Philippines and Indonesia beginning from the first contacts with India and the maritime areas from Vietnam, Malaysia, Sumatra, Java, Bali, Borneo and the Philippines. Though not found in the whole of Southeast Asia, such a wide area of distribution also brings into light the spread of metallurgy, and the manufacture of bronze drums, gongs and other bronze musical instruments. Bronze has been dated to Thailand in a new interpretation by Higham to 1500 BCE (Higham 1996, 2002, 2004) as well as in Vietnam around seventh century BCE (Xiaorong Han 2004: 10-16) with the appearance of bronze drums. Bronze kettledrums, both as musical instruments and archeological artefacts, can be found today in a wide area of distribution from South China and Vietnam in the northeast down to Indonesia reaching up to Kei Islands (Bernet-Kempers 1988) and more recently on Banggi Island off the coast of northeast Borneo and south-western Mindanao (Majid 2003). Associations of bell-metal with production of high tin bronze, among which are flat gongs, with a proportion of 20 to 30 per cent tin and 70 to 80 per cent copper have been made for bronzes in India (Srinivasan 1994, 1998; Srinivasan and Glover 1995) and northern Luzon (Goodway and Conklin 1987). In China, however, bronze bell chimes from the Shang and Zhou periods have lesser tin contents from 12 to 16 per cent (Falkenhausen 1993: 104-06). The centres of gong manufacture for the last two hundred years or so are confined to a few areas in Santubong, Sarawak and Brunei on Borneo and in Java and Bali. In the Philippines, *kulintang* gongs are manufactured in Cotabato among the Maguindanao and the Maranao, while flat gongs are now made in Baguio City and Kalinga in northern Luzon. According to Tran Ky Phuong, in Vietnam (pers. com.) flat gongs (*chieng* or *cing*) and bossed gongs (*rong*) are manufactured in the Dien Phoung village, Dien Ban district, Quang Nam province and are also brought to Laos.

While we find early evidence for flat gongs in temple reliefs in India, there are also parallel and perhaps older developments in China (Yuan and Mao 1986; Trasher 2000, 2001; Salmon 2003). By the tenth century until the thirteenth century, flat gongs had been circulating from China to Sumatra as evidenced by shipwrecks carrying flat gongs (Nicolas 2007, 2009). A shipwreck, dated to the tenth century, recently found in the shores off Brunei yielded 61 flat gongs inscribed with Chinese characters (Sjostrand 2006). The characters on the gongs, which are also found painted on the ceramics found on the site, refer to a person's name, Guo (Mandarin, in Hokkien – Kwek or Quek). These were marks of a merchant either on the ship or at the receiving destination (Wade, pers. com.). Contemporary practices of flat gong owners for *longsay* (dragon dances) in Manila and Singapore paint their names on either side of the gong. If such flat gongs were being transported around Borneo during the tenth century, then a flat gong culture was already

TABLE: NAMES OF FLAT GONG ENSEMBLES AND FLAT GONGS IN NORTHERN LUZON, PHILIPPINES

Bontrok	Ibaloi	Ifugao	Isneg	Kalinga	Kalingga / Tingguian	Karaw	Tingguian
a. pattong feshwat pattong papap	a. sulibaw pinsak kalsa palas	a. gangha tobob hebat ahot	a. hansa gangsa (2)	a. topayya (6) balbal kadua katlo kapat opop anungos	a. inilaud (3) patpat keb-ong sapul	a. itundak (7) salaksak maleok 1 maleok 2 banengbeng sitot 1 sitot 2 dulong	a. sinuklit gangsa (6)
b. takik gangsa (1-2)	b. sulimbat gangsa (1)			b. pallok gangsa (6)	b. pinalaiyan (4) talagutok pawwok saliksik pattong	b. tenebreb-ak (7)	b. tinalokatikan gangsa (3)
					c. pinalandok gangsa (6)		c. palook gangsa (6)

Note: Top column refers to names of language groups in northern Luzon; terms after a letter are names of musical ensembles; numbers in parentheses indicate the number of flat gongs used in one ensemble; all other terms for drums and other instruments are omitted (Maceda 1977; 1998: 17, ill. 5).

developing during this period. Such gongs could have reached Kota Cina in Sumatra and Singapore during the same period or later, where Chinese settlements had been found (McKinnon and Lukman Sinar 1974; Miksic 1985). The late Roxanna Brown, in an interview during the conference, noted that based on the *kendi* found in this site, the date might be placed around the twelfth century. Subsequently, by the thirteenth century, with the appearance of bossed gongs in shipwrecks, a new musical practice using bossed gongs had started to appear in the regions around Butuan and Palawan, Borneo, eastern Java, Sumatra, Thailand, Cambodia and Vietnam (Nicolas 2007).

In the case of flat gongs in northern Luzon, the problem at hand is to explain how flat gongs, reportedly borne by Chinese ships and/or mainly Southeast Asian ships, had eventually taken on the Sanskrit-derived term *gangsa* (see Table on p. 361). Francisco, in his translation of the Laguna Copper Plate Inscription dated CE 900, observed that the thirty-two Sanskrit terms used in this document clearly indicated that by the tenth century, Sanskrit was already known in Luzon (Francisco 1995). The term *gangsa* is also mentioned in the literary corpus in classical Malay dating to at least the seventeenth century, derived mostly from Javanese sources, and from Old Javanese and Old Balinese paleographical and literary sources, dating to as early as the ninth century. Today *gangsa* is understood in Java as a high Javanese term (*kromo*) for *gamelan*. In Bali, it refers to a metallophone (*gangsa jongkok*) and in Surakarta (*gangsa colopito*). Maceda recently suggested that the flat gongs of northern Luzon might have come from groups in central Vietnam associated with Chenla and Funan during the first millennium of the present era (2003: xxii). The term *gangsa* was known in ancient Champa, and today flat gongs are called *ching* or *cing* (Condominas 1974). Similarly, the use in Indonesia of the different terms for boat lutes derived from Sanskrit in a wide area of distribution from Sumatra to the Eastern Indonesia Islands (Kartomi 1985) may indicate such a shift in musical terminology although earlier protoforms may have used local names that are now lost.

FROM SOUTHEAST ASIA TO INDIA

The evidence of movement of two Sanskrit musical terms into Southeast Asia comes from an early period in the history of Southeast Asia in relation to India, taken from inscriptions, the bas-reliefs from temples, and from the ethnographic data on contemporary practices in courts, temples and villages. Little is known about the movement of musical ideas from Southeast Asia to India. Three aspects of this musical exchange can now be cited.

During the eleventh century, the Burmese ruler Kyanzittha sent musical instruments to Bodhgaya during the reconstruction of the temple, among which were bronze drums together with musicians, singers and dancers. The

Sri Bajras is the Vajrasana temple of Bodhgaya in India where the Buddha attained Buddhahood. Luce translates the passages as follows:

'for the Holy One of Sri Bajras Pitruk blaN (?), which had been irremediably destroyed by another king', Kyanzittha 'got together all sorts of precious things, and sent a ship with the intent to (re)build the Holy Sri Bajras: to buy (land?), dig a reservoir, make irrigated ricefields, make dams, cause candles and lamps to be lit which should never be quenched; and give drums, frog-drums, stringed and percussion instruments, and singing and dancing better than ever before. In that, too, no other king is like him' (Luce 1969, I: 62).

Wrazen (1986) proposed the possibility of origins of the *bin* and *vina* from bamboo idiochords in Assam and Java, following studies by Deva (1978) and Marcel Dubois (1941). Wrazen notes that examples of the early *bin* can be found on Java (as in those at Borobudur (early ninth century), in a bronze statuette in the Regency of Tegal, from the ninth century, and in a relief on Candi Sari, from the second half of the eighth century) (Kunst 1968: Figs. 7, 10, 12, 13, 14, 22, 30; Fig. 43; Fig. 2), and possibly the Prambanan Temple reliefs (*c.* 850).

Flat gongs had been circulating in maritime Asia in China, Vietnam, Philippines, Borneo, Sumatra, and Singapore since the tenth century. Overland routes through the mainland had certainly transported these gongs. These could have reached India around this time, and would have been then etched on the walls of Hoysala temple by the twelfth century. The medium sized, suspended gongs on walls of Angkor Wat in Cambodia are bossed rather than flat, and the circular gongs-in-a-row clearly show these were already bossed gongs, earlier than the *gulintangan* (gongs-in-a-row) fragment found in a Brunei fifteenth century site (Nicolas 2007: 117).

The mapping of the music histories of Asia is readily structured around metal instruments that have survived – the bells from the Shang and Zhou dynasty, the bronze drums in Yunnan and Dong Son, the flat gongs and bossed gongs in the region and the other metal or bronze musical instruments, and lithophones. A new music has evolved upon the introduction or the discovery of the science and art of metallurgy in Asia, which led to the invention of new musical instruments (Nicolas 2007: 278 ff; 2008b; 2009). Sanskrit terms were circulating alongside the earlier spread of Austronesian, Austroasiatic, Tai-Kadai, and Chinese musical terms. The movement of musical terms is not synchronous and congruous with the movement of musical instruments. The history of the music of the unwritten and oral traditions, of bamboo and wooden musical instruments is still largely unknown. Present research directions in music lack a wider engagement with long term processes of musical exchanges in Asia. Early contacts between South and Southeast Asia were precursors to the spread of Indic ideas to Asia (Nilakanta Sastri 1949; Hall 1985; Glover 1989; Rao 2003). New and recent archaeological research view the millennium from the later prehistoric to the early state formation as a continuum rather than an abrupt shift to accommodate Indian influence, thus reflecting mutual interplay between indigenous complexities and foreign ideas (Higham 2003: 288). The peoples of Southeast Asia were innovative farmers, metallurgists, musicians and mariners (Hall 1999: 185-86). In the Neolithic period, the Austronesians sailed thousands of miles from their home islands reaching as far as Madagascar in east Africa to the Easter Island of the Pacific (Blust 1995; Bellwood 1997). In these journeys, very little is yet known about the spread of musical ideas that may have reached India and China from the centres of Austronesian and Austroasiatic migrations before the historic period. Such musical exchanges are indeed more compelling themes for future researches on the history of music in Asia.

REFERENCES

Aduarte, Diego O.P., 1640, *Historia de la Provincia del Sancto Rosario de Orden de Predicadores*, in Emma H. Blair and James A. Robertson (eds.), *The Philippine Islands, 1493-1898*, vol. 30, pp. 115-322.

Ardika, I. Wayan, 1997, 'Early Evidence of Indian Contact with Bali', in Pierre-Yves Manguin, ed. *Southeast Asian Archaeology 1994*, pp. 139-46, Hull: University of Hull, Centre for Southeast Asian Studies.

Ardika, I. Wayan and Peter Bellwood, 1991, 'Sembiran: The Beginnings of Indian Contact with Bali', *Archaeology* 65: 221-32.

Ardika, I. Wayan, Peter Bellwood, I. Made Sutaba and Kade Citha Yuliati, 1997, 'Sembiran and the First Indian Contacts with Bali: An Update', *Antiquity* 71: 193-95.

Aymonier, E. and A. Cabaton, 1906, *Dictionnaire cam-francais*, Paris: EFEO.

Bellina, Berenice and Ian Glover. 2004, 'The Archaeology of Early Contact with India and the Mediterranean World, from the Fourth Century, BC to the Fourth Century AD', in Glover and Bellwood, pp. 68-88.

Bellwood, Peter, 1997, *Prehistory of the Indo-Malaysian Archipelago*, Honolulu: University of Hawaii Press.

Bernet Kempers, A.J., 1988, *The Bronze Kettledrums of Southeast Asia*. MORSEA 10. Rotterdam: A.A. Balkema, tr. and ed. E.H. Blair and J.A. Robertson.

——, 1905-09, *The Philippine Islands: 1493-1898*, 55 volumes, Cleveland: Arthur H. Clark.

Blust, Robert A., 1995, 'The Prehistory of the Austronesian-speaking Peoples: A View from Language', *Journal of World Prehistory* 9: 453-510.

Casparis, J.G. de, 1988, 'Some Notes on Words of Middle Indian Origin in Indonesian Languages (especially Old Javanese)', in *Papers from the III European Colloquium on Malay and Indonesian Studies, Naples, 2-4 June 1981*, ed. Luigi Santa Maria, Faizah Soenoto Rivai and Antonio Sorrentino, Naples: Dipartimento di Studi Asiatici, Instituto Universitario Orientale.

——, 1997, *Sanskrit Loan-Words In Indonesian: An Annotated Checklist of Words from Sanskrit in Indonesia and Traditional Malay*, Jakarta: Badan Penyelenggara Seri NUSA, Universitas Katolik Indonesia Atma Jaya.

Champion, Paul, 1987, 'Fabrication of Gongs or Tom-toms at Un-Chong-Lan, Near

Shanghai. Industries anciennes et modernes de L'empire chinois', Paris. [1869]. English translation in Appendix A, Goodway and Conklin, 1987, pp. 20-24.

Christie, Jan Wisseman, 1998, 'Javanese Markets and the Asian Sea Trade Boom of the Tenth to Thirteenth Centuries, AD', *JESHO* 41, 3: 344-81.

Chutiwongs, Nandana, ed., 1996, *Ancient Trades and Cultural Contacts in Southeast Asia*, Bangkok: The Office of the National Culture Commission.

Cœdès, George, 1954, *Inscriptions du Cambodge*, Paris: EFEO.

———, 1968, *The Indianized States of Southeast Asia*, ed. Walter F. Vella, tr. Sue Brown Cowing, Honolulu: University of Hawaii Press.

Collaer, Paul, ed., 1978, *Sudostasien. Musikgeschichte in Bildern*. Band I: *Musikethnologie*, Lieferung 3. Leipzig: VEB Deutscher Verlag fur Musik.

Condominas, George, 1974, *Musique Mnong Gar du Vietnam*. One 12" LP record. OCORO OCR 80, Paris: Collection du Musee de l'Homme, ORTF.

Cortesao, A. (trans.), 1944, *The Suma Oriental of Tome Pires*, 2 vols., London: Hakluyt Society. Reprinted 1980.

Cosgaya, Lorenzo Fernandez. 1865, *Diccionario Pangasinan-Español*, Manila: Establecimiento Tip. del Colegio de Santo Tomas.

Damais, Louis Charles, 1970, *Répertoire onomastique de l'épigraphie javanaise, jusqu'a pu sindok 'Sri Isanawikrama Dharmmotungadewa; étude d'epigraphie indonésienne*, Paris: École française d'Extrême-Orient.

Danielou, Alain, 1978, *Sudasien. Die indische Musik und ihre Traditionen. Musikgeschichte in Bildern*. Band I: *Musikethnologie*, Lieferung 4. Leipzig: VEB Deutscher Verlag fur Musik.

Deloche, Jean, 1988, 'Musical Instruments in Hoysala Sculpture (12th and 13th centuries)', *BEFEO* 77: 57-68.

Deva, Bigamudre Chaitanya, 1978, *Musical Instruments of India: Their History and Development*, Calcutta: Firma KLM.

Falkenhausen, Lothar von, 1993, *Suspended Music and Chime Bells in the Culture of Bronze Age China*, Berkeley: University of California Press.

Ferdinandus, Peter, 2003, 'Buddhism and Hinduism: Their Interaction and Impact on Musical Aspect during the Old Javanese Period', in *Sanskrit in Southeast Asia : The Harmonizing Factor of Cultures: Proceedings, International Sanskrit Conference, May 21-23, 2001, Bangkok, Thailand*, Bangkok: Sanskrit Studies Center, Silpakorn University, pp. 236-47.

Finot, Louis, 1904, 'Notes d'epigraphie', *BEFEO* 4, 4: 53-106, 897-977.

———, 1915, 'Notes d'epigraphie', *BEFEO* 15, 2: 1-210.

Francisco, Juan, 1960, 'Sanskrit in Philippine Languages', *Adyar Library Bulletin* 24, 3-4: 154-72.

———, 1964, *Indian Influences in the Philippines, with Special Reference to Language and Literature*, Quezon City: University of the Philippines.

———, 1972, 'Sanskrit in Philippine Language and Literature', paper presented to the International Sanskrit Conference, held in New Delhi on 27-31 March 1972.

———, 1973, *Philippine Palaeography*, Quezon City: Linguistic Society of the Philippines.

———, 1995, 'Notes on the Sanskrit Terms in the Laguna Copper Plate Inscription', in *Studies and Reflections in Asian Art, History and Archaeology. Essays in Honor of H.S.H. Prof. Subhadradis Diskul*, pp. 297-309, Bangkok: Mahawitthayalai Sinlapakon.

Garland Encyclopedia of World Music, 2000, South Asia: The Indian Subcontinent, ed. Alison Arnold, New York and London: Garland Publishing, Inc.

Glover, Ian. C., 1989, *Early Trade Between India and South-East Asia: A Link in the Development of a World Trading System*, Hull: University of Hull, Centre for South-East Asian Studies, Occasional Papers No. 16.

Glover, Ian and Peter Bellwood (eds.), 2004, *Southeast Asia: From Prehistory to History*, London and New York: Routledge Curzon.

Golzio, Karl-Heinz, 2004, *Inscriptions of Campa*. Based on the editions and translations of Abel Bergaigne, Etienne Aymonier, Louis Finot, Edouard Huber and other French scholars and of the work of R.C. Majumdar; newly presented, with minor corrections of texts and translations, together with calculations of given dates. Aachen: Shaker.

Gonda, Jan, 1973, *Sanskrit in Indonesia*, New Delhi: International Academy of Indian Culture.

Goodway, Martha and Harold C. Conklin, 1987, Quenched High-Tin Bronzes from the Philippines, *Archaeomaterials* 2: 1-27.

Grove Music Online. http://www.grovemusic.com/index.html

Hall, Kenneth R., 1985, *Maritime Trade and State Development in Early Southeast Asia*, Honolulu: University of Hawaii Press.

——, 1999, 'Economic History of Early Southeast Asia', in Nicholas Tarling, ed., *The Cambridge History of Southeast Asia*, Vol. One, Chapter 4, From Early Time to *c.* 1500, Cambridge: Cambridge University Press.

Han Xiaorong, 1998, 'The Present Echoes of the Ancient Bronze Drum: Nationalism and Archeology in Modern Vietnam and China', *Explorations in Southeast Asian Studies* 2, 2 Fall.

——, 2004, 'Who Invented the Bronze Drum? Nationalism, Politics, and a Sino-Vietnamese Archaeological Debate of the 1970s and 1980s', *Asian Perspectives* 43, 1: 7-33.

Harrisson, Tom, 1955, 'Indian Pioneers in Borneo, *c.* 500 A.D.', *Sarawak Museum Journal* 6: 511-17.

Higham, Charles, 1996, *The Bronze Age of Southeast Asia*, Cambridge World Archaeology. Cambridge: Cambridge University Press.

Huber, E. 1911, 'Etudes Indochinoises, *BEFEO* XI, 3-4: 259-311.

Jacobson, E. and J.H. van Hasselt, 1975, 'The Manufacture of Gongs in Semarang', tr. and with an introduction by Andrew Toth, *Indonesia* 19: 127-72.

Kartomi, Margaret, 1985, *Musical Instruments of Indonesia: An Introductory Handbook*, Melbourne: Indonesia Arts Society.

Kaudern, Walter, 1927, *Musical Instruments in Celebes*. Ethnographical Studies in Celebes, vol. III. Göteberg: Elanders AB.

Kern, Hendrick, 1880, 'Sanskritische woorden in het Tagala', *BKI* IV: 252-78.

——, 1881, 'Sanskritische woorden in het Bisaya', *BKI* V: 280-87.

Kulke, H., 1978, *The Dewaraja Cult*, tr. from the German by I.W. Mabbett, with an introduction by the Author and Notes on the translation of Khmer terms by J. M. Jacob. Data Paper no. 108. Ithaca: Cornell University.

——, 1990, 'Indian Colonies, Indianization or Cultural Convergence? Reflections on the Changing Image of India's Role in South-East Asia', in H. Schulte Nordholt, ed. *Onderzoek in Zuidoost-Azie: Agenda's voor de Jaren Negentig*, Leiden: Rijksuniversiteit te Leiden, Vakgroep Talen en Culturen van Zuidoost-Azie en Oceanie, pp. 8-32.

Kunst, Jaap, 1927, *Hindoe-Javaansche muziek-instrumenten: speciaal die van Oost-Java*. Met medewerking van Dr. R. Goris, Weltevreden: Druk G. Kolff & Co.

——, 1968, *Hindu-Javanese Musical Instruments*, 2nd revd and enlr. edn., The Hague: M. Nijhoff.

Lansing, J.S., A.J. Redd, T.M. Karafet, J. Watkins, I.W. Ardika, S.P.K. Surata, J.S. Schoenfelder, M. Campbell, A.M. Merriwether, M.F. Hammer, 2004, 'An Indian Trader in Ancient Bali?', *Antiquity* 78: 287-93.

Luce, Gordon H. and Bo-Hmu Ba Shin, 1969, 'Old Burma: Early Pagan', *Artibus Asiae, Supplementum* 25, Volume One: Text, pp. 2-422.

Mabbett, I.W., 1969, 'Dewaraja', *Journal of Southeast Asian History* 10: 202-23.

Maceda, Jose, 1977, 'Flat Gongs in the Philippines', in *Proceedings of the 30th International Congress of Human Sciences in Asia and North Africa*, Mexico, 1976.

——, 1988, *Kulintang and Kudyapi: Gong Ensemble and Two-Stringed Lute among the Maguindanaon in Mindanao, Philippines.* Two long playing records of field recordings with annotations. Quezon City: University of the Philippines.

——, 1998, *Gongs and Bamboo: A Panorama of Philippine Musical Instruments.* Tables, Maps, Glossary and Photo Layout by Marialita Yraola, Quezon City: University of the Philippines.

——, 2003, 'Introduction: A Search in Asia for a New Theory of Music', in Jose Buenconsejo, ed., *A Search for a New Theory of Music*, Quezon City: University of the Philippines, pp. ix-xxv.

Majid, Zuraina, 2003, *Archaeology in Malaysia. Arkeologi di Malaysia*, Bilingual Edition, Penang, Malaysia: Centre for Archaeological Research Malaysia, Universiti Sains Malaysia.

Majumdar, Ramesh, 1927, *Ancient Indian Colonies in the Far East,* Lahore: Punjab Sanskrit Book Depot.

Mckinnon, E. Edwards and T. Lukman Sinar, 1974, 'Kota China: Notes of Further Developments at Kota China', *BKI* 4, 1: 63-86.

——, 1976, *Kota Cina: An Important Early Trading Site on the East Coast of Sumatra*, Mimeographed Research Report.

McPhee, Colin, 1966, *Music in Bali: A Study in Form and Instrumental Organization in Balinese Orchestral Music*, New Haven: Yale University Press.

Miksic, John N., 1985, *Archaeological Research on the 'Forbidden Hill' of Singapore: Excavations at Fort Canning 1984*, Singapore: National Museum.

Monier-Williams, Monier, 1899, *A Sanskrit-English Dictionary and philologically arranged with special reference to cognate Indo-European languages*, Oxford: Clarendon Press [Revised 1993 and 2008].

Morga, Antonio de, 1609, 'Sucesos de las Islas Filipinas', in Blair & Robertson 16: 75-133.

Morton, David, 1976, *The Traditional Music of Thailand,* Berkeley: University of California Press.

Mukherjee, Meera, 1978, *Metalcraftsmen of India.* Anthropological Survey of India Memoir No. 44, Calcutta: Reliance Printing Works.

Murthy, K. Krishna, 1985, *Archaeology of Indian Musical Instruments*, Delhi: Sundeep Prakashan.

New Grove Dictionary of Music and Musicians, 2001, ed. Stanley Sadie, 2nd edn., 29 vols., London: Macmillan (also Grove Music Online).

Nicolas, Arsenio, 1977, *Ang mga Kulintang sa Mindanao at Sulu*, Two long playing records with notes, Quezon City: University of the Philippines.

——, 1979, *Ang Musika ng mga Kalinga.* With Felicidad Prudente, co-ed. LP record with annotations, Quezon City: University of the Philippines.

——, 1987, 'A Typology of Bamboo Musical Ensembles in Southwest Central Java', unpublished paper read at the Symposium of the International Musicological Society, 28 August-2 September, Melbourne, Australia.

——, 1993, 'Music and Temple Systems in Southeast Asia', in *Transactions of the International Conference of Orientalists in Japan* (Tokyo) 38: 176-77.

——, 1994, *Alat-Alat Muzik Melayu dan Orang Asli*, Bangi: Universitas Kebangsaan Malaysia.

——, 2007, 'Musical Exchange in Early Southeast Asia: The Philippines and Indonesia, *c.* 100 to 1600 CE', Ph. D. dissertation, Cornell University.

——, 2008a, 'Music, Southeast Asia', *Oxford Encyclopedia of the Modern World*, vol. 5, pp. 315-18.

——, 2008b, 'Bamboo, Bronze Drums, and Gongs: A Musical Exchange in Maritime Asia', Review Essay. Jose Maceda. *Gongs and Bamboo. A Panorama of Music Instruments*. Quezon City: University of the Philippines. *Musika Jornal* 4: 198-215.

——, 2009, 'Gongs, Bells and Cymbals: The Archaeological Record in Maritime Asia from the Ninth to the Seventeenth Centuries', *Yearbook for Traditional Music*, 2009, 62-93.

Nilakanta Sastri, K.A., 1949, *South Indian Influences in the Far East*, Bombay: Hind Kitabs.

Pellicer, Mariano, 1904, *Arte de la Lengua Pangasinan ó Cabolóan: Corregido, Aumentado y Llevando en sí el Mismo Compendio*, Manila: Imprenta del Colegio de Sto. Tomás.

Penth, Hans, 1970, 'Kunst in Lan Na Thai (1): Der Grosse Gong im Kloster Phrathat Haripunchai', *Artibus Asiae* 32, 4: 307-14.

Picken, Laurence, 1981-2000, *Music from the T'ang Court*. Transcribed from the original, unpublished, Sino-Japanese manuscripts, together with a survey of relevant historical sources (both Chinese and Japanese). With editorial comments by Laurence Picken, together with Rembrandt F. Wolpert et al., 7 vols., London: Oxford University Press.

Pires, Tomé and Francisco Rodrigues, 1944, *The Suma Oriental of Tomé Pires*, tr. A. Cortesao, London: The Hakluyt Society.

Po Dharma, 1999, *Quatre lexiques malais-cam anciens. Rediges au Campa*. Paris: Presses de l'Ecole francaise d'Extrême-Orient.

Powers, Harold, 2006, In Grove Music Online.

Qureshi, Regula, 2006, In Grove Music Online.

Ray, Himanshu Prabha, 1989, 'Early Maritime Contact between South and Southeast Asia', *Journal of Southeast Asian Studies*, XX: 42-54.

——, 2003, *The Archaeology of Seafaring in Ancient South Asia*, Cambridge: Cambridge University Press.

Roche, David, 2000, 'The "Dhak", Devi Amba's Hourglass Drum in Tribal Southern Rajasthan, India', *Asian Music*, 32, 1: 59-99.

Sachs, Kurt, 1940, *The History of Musical Instruments*, New York: W.W. Norton.

——, 1983, *Die Muziekinstrumentene Indiens und Indonesiens*, 2nd edn., 1923; George Olms, rpt. Hildesheim, Zurich and New York.

Salmon, Claudine, 2003, La diffusion du gong en Insulinde vue essentiellemnt a travers diverses epaves orientales (periode Song-Ming). *Mirabilia Asiatica*, vol. 2, ed. Jorge M. Dos Santos Alves, Claude Guillot, Roderich Ptak, Weisbaden: Harrassowitz Verlag, and Lisboa Fundacao Oriente, pp. 89-116.

San Buenaventura, Pedro de, 1994, *Vocabulario de Lengua Tagala. El romance Castellano presta primera. Primera y segunda parte*, Dirigido a D. Ivan de Silva. Valencia: Librerías Paris-Valencia. [1613] (Originally published: Con Licencia Impreso en la noble Villa de Pila, por Thomas Pinpin, y Domingo Loag, Tagalos, Año de 1613).

Saveros Pou, 2004, *Dictionnaire Vieux Khmer-Francais-Anglais: An Old Khmer-French-English Dictionary*, Paris: Cedoreck.

Schaefner, Andre, 1951, Une importante decouverte archaeologique: Le Lithophone de Ndut Ling Krak, Vietnam. *La Revue de Musicologie* 33: 11-19.

Sedyawati, Edi. 1999, 'Preface: Precious Metals in Early Southeast Asia', *Proceedings of the Second Seminar on Gold Studies*, ed. Wilhelmina H. Kal, Amsterdam: Royal Tropical Institute, Tropenmuseum, pp. 7-8.

Sjostrand, Sten, 2006, http://www.maritimeasia.ws/tsimpang/.

Srinivasan, Sharada, 1994, 'High-Tin Bronze Bowl Making in Kerala, South India, and its Archaeological Implications', in Asko Parpola and Petteri Koskikallio, eds., *South Asian Archaeology 1993 : Proceedings of the Twelfth International Conference of the European Association of South Asian Archeologists held in Helsinki University, 5-9 July 1993*, vol. 2: 695-706.

——, 1998, 'High Tin Bronze Working in India: The Bowl Makers of Kerala', in Vibha Tripathi, ed., *Archaeometallurgy in India*, pp. 239-50, Delhi: Sharada Publishing House.

Srinivasan, Sharada and Ian Glover. 1995, 'Wrought and Quenched, and Cast High-tin Bronzes in Kerala State, India', *The Journal of the Historical Metallurgy Society* 19, 2: 69-88.

Stargardt, Janice, 1971, 'Burma's Economic and Diplomatic Relations with India and China from Early Medieval Sources', *Journal of the Economic and Social History of the Orient*, vol. 14, 1: 38-62.

Thrasher, Alan R., 2000, *Chinese Musical Instruments*, New York: Oxford University Press

——, 2001, 'China: Musical Instruments, Gong', in: *New Grove Dictionary of Music and Musicians*, vol. 10. 134-35, London: Macmillan.

Wade, Geoffrey Philip, 1993, 'On the Possible Cham Origins of the Philippines Scripts', *JSEAS* 24, 1: 44-87.

Wrazen, Louise, 1986, 'The Early History of the Vina and Bin in South and Southeast Asia', *Asian Music* 18, 1: 35-55.

Yuan Bingchong and Mao Jizeng, eds., 1986, *Zhongguo shaosu minzu yueqi zhi* (The Musical Instruments of the Ethnic Minorities in China: A Dictionary), Beijing: Xinsjijie Chubanshe.

Zoetmulder, P. J., 1982, *Old Javanese-English Dictionary*. With the Collaboration of S.O. Robson, 2 vols., s-Gravenhage: Nijhoff.

18

Buddhism and the Circulation of Ritual in Early Peninsular Southeast Asia

Peter Skilling

The paper examines the circulation of Buddhist thought and ritual in 'early Southeast Asia' up to about CE 1000. It does not attempt a chronological narrative, but concentrates on the significance of relics and images and the circulation of ritual as seen from the mass production of clay images and *stūpas*. Although the peninsula was a crossroads or interface with mainland and insular Southeast Asia, and it shared with them certain practices and ideas, in some aspects the peninsula differed, often considerably. The conclusions proposed here for the peninsula cannot be applied in identical terms to any other region.

ORIGINS, LOCALISATION, AND
THE CIRCULATION OF IDEAS

The study of religion in Southeast Asia suffers from several problems in conceptualisation, including that of the 'very idea' of religion. The interpretation of the artefacts of Buddhism has relied on categories and theories about Indian Buddhism that were developed in the late nineteenth and early twentieth centuries in imperial Europe and in colonised Asia. Buddhism has come to be painted in broad strokes as 'Hīnayāna', 'Mahāyāna', or 'Vajrayāna', which are seen as monolithic and exclusive blocs, as 'sects', and even as 'churches'. Cultural movement is presented as unidirectional; the maps show arrows moving confidently from India and Sri Lanka to Southeast Asia, and stopping there (or moving on to the 'Far East'). Southeast Asia is portrayed as a passive recipient of Indian 'influence', which washed its shores in 'waves' over the centuries. The possibility of cross-cultural and trans-regional exchange, of dialogue, or of interaction is rarely raised.

Many of the early categories in the field of Indian (as well as Tibetan and East Asian) Buddhism have since been, refined, revised, or rejected, but the field of Southeast Asian Buddhism, with some notable exceptions, lags well behind (see Skilling 2001a). Even today, much of what is written about the introduction of Buddhism to Southeast Asia and its development is inaccurate and unnecessarily speculative. It remains under the shadow of outdated theories of 'Indianisation'. It continues to use inappropriate categories, and is skewed by misconceptions about the nature of Buddhism, its 'sectarian' identities, and its transmission and expansion.

What does it mean to say that Buddhism – or Brahmanism – 'came from India'? What is this 'India'? India was not, and is not, homogeneous, whether in terms of administration, social organisation, language, or religion. There was no monolithic Indian religion, there was no monolithic Brahmanism, and there was no monolithic 'Indian Buddhism'. In historical research we should try to determine, as far as possible, when, where, how, and why ideas or practices were transmitted. It is not sufficient simply to trace them to an ideal and atemporal textbook 'India'.

Did Buddhism become localised, and, if so, to what degree? The very spread of Buddhism in India itself was a process of continual localisation – or interlocalisation, if I may use the word. If the cradle and heartland of Buddhism was Magadha, within several centuries Buddhism spread and flourished in Mathura, Kashmir, and Gandhara, in the Deccan, and elsewhere throughout and beyond the subcontinent. There is no 'non-localised' or 'neutral' or 'original' Buddhism, as Indian Buddhists participated in and were agents of transformation in diverse societies. The relationships between this 'India' and 'Southeast Asia' were intricate and multidirectional.

One important sense in which Buddhism was localised was in terms of monastic lineage. A century or more before the beginning of the Christian Era, eighteen monastic orders or *nikāya* spread over much of India, with different centres or spheres of influence, with their own interpretations of the monastic codes and of the Buddha's teachings, their own collections of scriptures, and their own practices.[1] Each order was independent; there was no central body to control either the eighteen as a whole or the individual orders. When monastics of a particular lineage established a community (*saṃgha*), that community immediately became autonomous – it was not under the control of the parent lineage. Admittedly, the evolution of the eighteen orders is sparsely documented and poorly understood. In any case, models that compare Buddhism with Catholicism or Protestantism are unsuitable because the Buddhist orders were by definition monastic rather than lay, and also because of the lack of centralisation of the Buddhist schools.

Religion travelled as part of the circulation of ideas, practices, rituals, and technologies. Brahmanism and Buddhism were not imported as separate packages that were dropped off on the shores of Southeast Asia by brahmans, monks, or merchants. Buddhism was brought by Buddhist monastics; Brahmanism was introduced by brahmans. Ritual and interaction began immediately, as the religious masters had to establish their credibility and the relevance of their teachings and practices to new audiences and potential patrons. Monastics did not introduce Brahmanical rituals; brahmans did not introduce Buddhist rituals. Moreover, brahmans would have belonged to different lineages, and specialised in different rites – Śaiva, Vaiṣṇava, or Saura, etc., with further subdivisions. Monastics and brahmans each had their own functions and roles; each were specialists in their own rites and teachings. The notion of syncretism does not apply. The people would have participated in the activities of either, according to ritual and calendrical needs. In India, the circulation of ideas was stimulated by festivals, which were advertised, for example, by announcements draped over elephants, and were attended by people from various regions.[2] While the trans-regional flow of pilgrims to the 'seat of awakening' at Bodh Gaya in Magadha or to the footprint of the Buddha atop Śrīpāda in Sri Lanka is well known, the role of pilgrimage in the circulation of ideas in early Southeast Asia needs further study.

One of the questions that perennially intrigues historians of Buddhism is that of 'school affiliation'. We want to know which monastic orders established themselves, when and where; how they expanded or contracted, or how they eventually died out. This is certainly important, but perhaps the problem of school affiliation has been exaggerated. There is no explicit epigraphic evidence for any of the orders in the region of Southeast Asia, and all we have to go on is a general statement made by the seventh-century Chinese pilgrim-scholar Yijing, which has been cited so often that it has lost its meaning.[3] Can we not ask other questions, or approach the subject in different ways? Whether in India or elsewhere, the primary objects of worship were shared. All Buddhists – monastic and lay – paid reverence to relics or reliquaries, to *bodhi*-trees, and to images of the Buddha. All Buddhists affirmed and reaffirmed their identities through rituals like taking refuge in the 'Three Jewels' or through practices like donation and ethics, with a view to benefit in the present and future lives. Beyond this, followers of the Mahāyāna revered Buddhas other than Śākyamuni and bodhisattvas along with their images. They had their own scriptures, the Mahāyāna *sūtras*, but they did not reject the *sūtras* of the Śrāvaka schools, which they studied, recited, and respected and as the word of the Buddha, the 'Blessed One'.[4]

How does this relate to the archaeological record? Firstly, a *stūpa* or an image of Śākyamuni Buddha simply attests to the cults of relics and images. These cults do not belong to either the Śrāvaka schools or to the Mahāyāna

– they are *shared*. The same holds, in general, for images of Maitreya, the future Buddha, although here there may be qualifications (see e.g. Nandana Chutiwongs and Leidy 1994). An image of a bodhisattva is evidence for the cult of that particular bodhisattva. I prefer to limit the conclusion: I prefer to say that 'an image of Avalokiteśvara attests to a cult of that bodhisattva at that site or in that region'. It may go too far to conclude that an Avalokiteśvara proves 'the presence of Mahāyāna Buddhism', as if the latter were some kind of formal institution. All we know is that someone, or some group, worshipped Avalokiteśvara. We do not know whether they followed other practices, or to what degree they self-consciously studied Mahāyāna texts or philosophy. Devotion to Avalokiteśvara can stand in its own right within the quest for merit, blessings, and security.

ICONOGRAPHY AND THE CIRCULATION OF RITUAL

Relic- and image-worship played key roles in the spread of Buddhism, and the importance of images in the social life of Buddhism can scarcely be over-stated. Across Asia, images multiplied and played multiple roles – bringing rain, warding off disease, offering protection and victory in war, and acting as tribute in diplomatic missions.

Buddhist images around the Gulf of Siam participated in a cognate aesthetic, which was often inspired by broader ideals that were current in India. But it is not a question of a migration of art styles – rather of migrations of models of famous or potent images, the sharing of aesthetic ideals, and the transmission of rituals and ceremonies. Buddhist images are not simple 'art objects'; they are products of complex ideologies. Art historians often draw conclusions from iconography and style, but in some cases iconographic vocabulary and style may be traced to one region, while ritual or ideological inspiration may belong to another region. Some of the moulded images from central Thailand and the Malay peninsula share stylistic inspirations with Deccan or Lankan images, but they have no counterparts in those areas. Other images follow north Indian models, and are stamped with texts in the northern Siddha-mātṛkā script.

In the absence of contemporary local records, we cannot know the social or political needs that may have led to the establishment of a particular *stūpa*, image, or temple in early peninsular Southeast Asia; nor can we retrieve the specific rituals of consecration and installation. Consecration – empowerment or animation – brings an image to life. It is not just an effigy or a commemorative statue that is installed; rather it is the Buddha himself who is invited to reside. There were daily and calendrical rites, such as ceremonial bathing or image processions. In the seventh century Yijing noted both of these rituals in the 'Ten Islands of the Southern Seas'.[5] The two ceremonies are regularly celebrated today in mainland Southeast Asia, in the Thai and Tai cultural areas – can we take this as example of continuity?

Despite the lack of records, the rich iconographic heritage is evidence for ritual practices. Most of the bodhisattva images retrieved in Southeast Asia are of Avalokiteśvara. Many but not all are quite small. They attest unequivocally to a widespread veneration of Avalokiteśvara, during a period when this might be expected, given that during the second half of the first millennium the compassionate bodhisattva inspired much of Asia.[6] Even though a large number of Avalokiteśvara images have been found across mainland and peninsular Southeast Asia, his mantra *oṃ maṇipadme hūṃ* is attested only a single time in epigraphy, and that about a century after our period (Skilling 2003). In addition, particular configurations of images, such as triads made up of a central Buddha flanked by a pair of bodhisattvas, attest to more elaborate cultic and ritual systems.

RITUAL AND THE MASS-PRODUCTION OF IMAGES

One of the significant ritual practices of Buddhism was the mass-production of small clay images from seals or moulds, often stamped with the *ye dharmā* verse, a stanza on the essence of the Buddha's teaching widely used in consecration ceremonies (Skilling 1999, 2004b, 2008a, 2008b). Some of the images and moulds were conceived and produced locally. These are found only at a single site, and the moulds appear to have been produced for a single specific ceremony, after which the images were enshrined within a *stūpa* or a cave. Some moulds were regional; that is, their products are found at several sites. Certain images were widely diffused trans-regionally across Asia through the export of moulds and, in some cases, the local manufacture of copies of moulds in response to ritual fashion. It is especially these moulds and the images they produce which substantiate the long-distance diffusion of iconography with its attendant ritual or liturgical practices. The mass production of moulded images spread throughout certain parts of South and Southeast Asia starting from about the sixth century CE.[7] In Southeast Asia mass-production was prominent in the peninsula, where a wide range of miniature clay images and *stūpas*, some iconographically quite complex, were installed in *stūpa* foundations and in caves. Here I limit myself to a few examples.

The Eight Bodhisattvas

One type of stamped clay image was a hierarchical *maṇḍala* depicting eight bodhisattvas encircling a central Buddha. In India, texts, images, and rituals relating to a group of eight bodhisattvas proliferated by the Vākāṭaka and early

Pāla periods (as usual, there are divergent views about the dates of the various representations). Several versions of a text called the '*Sūtra* on the eightfold *maṇḍala*' are extant in Chinese and Tibetan translation; the Sanskrit version is not extant, or at least has not been published.[8]

The two Tibetan versions, both translated about CE 800, have different settings. One opens quite traditionally in Anāthapiṇḍada's park in Prince Jeta's grove at Śrāvastī.[9] In the second, the Blessed One 'was staying at Potala Mountain, the residence of Ārya Avalokiteśvara, together with a vast gathering of bodhisattvas'.[10] The two texts agree on the list of eight bodhisattvas:[11]

1. Avalokiteśvara
2. Maitreya
3. Ākāśagarbha
4. Sāmantabhadra
5. Vajrapāṇi/Guyhapati
6. Mañjuśrī
7. Sarvanīvaraṇaviṣkambhin
8. Kṣitigarbha.

The short texts, which do not supply any iconographic details, are literary evidence for a cult that is widely represented in various media. The eight bodhisattvas were carved in stone in the caves at Ellora (Malandra 2004: text Fig. 4.1, etc.) and Ajanta (Bautze-Picron 1997). They were ranged in a row on slabs or lintels at Nalanda (Mitra 1999) and at Bodh Gaya, as well as on lintels of unknown provenance (Mitra 1998). At Ratnagiri, Lalitagiri, and Udayagiri in Orissa the bodhisattvas appear both as large free-standing individual images or as sets on steles surrounding the seated image of the Buddha (Mitra 1996). The veneration of the eight bodhisattvas was introduced to Tibet, where large standing images flanked altars with the Buddha as presiding image (Yoritomi 1990). In China the bodhisattvas are depicted in an early ninth-century Dunhuang silk painting (Whitfield 2004: 202-03 and Cat. no. 120). They are also fashioned in bronze, for example on a bronze *stūpa* from Nalanda (Mitra 1999). Forty cm in height, it is encircled by the eight bodhisattvas as well as by the eight great sites (for which see below), and it thus conjoins two of the important cults of the period. A 40 cm high bronze icon, dated by Alam to the ninth century, was recovered at Mainamati in Bangladesh (Alam 1985: 91-92 and Fig. 28), and the eight bodhisattvas are depicted in Java at several sites. Clearly, the worship of the eight bodhisattvas was important for a period of several centuries over a wide region. The central figure is usually Śākyamuni, for example in the Tibetan '*Sūtra* on the eightfold *maṇḍala*', which invokes the 'Blessed One at the centre' of the *maṇḍala* with the 'heart' syllables *oṃ mahā hūṃ mahā bīra svāhā*. In some cases the central Buddha may be Vairocana, though the identity needs further research.[12]

Clay sealings with the eight bodhisattvas have been found in Thailand in Trang (Piriya Krairiksh 2001: 102), at Wat Khao Khrom, Surat Thani province (Pattaratorn Chirapravati 1997: 38-39; 2000: 188-91) and at Phunphin in the same province (Woodward 2003: 86-87; for further references see Woodward's n. 207). Other models are displayed in the Asian Civilisations Museum, Singapore (Asian Civilisations Museum 2003: 354-5). In 1991, baked clay tablets of the same design were excavated in the limestone cave of Gua Berhala in Upper Kelantan, Malaysia, along with others stamped from a mould of standing Avalokiteśvara (Jaafar 2003: 181). The number and diffusion of sites where sealings of the eight bodhisattva plaques were produced or installed, most frequently in caves, is impressive. It suggests that, for a period, perhaps a short period over a century, ritual practices connected with the eight bodhisattvas spread from eastern India through the peninsula, and that the practice entailed the installation of the plaques in caves – limestone caves which were usually hard to get to. This aspect of the cult of the eight bodhisattvas is distinctive, and seems unique to the peninsula. It is interesting to reflect that the hinterlands of the peninsula were the sources of many of the ingredients – aromatic woods and fragrances – used in Indian and Buddhist rituals. Can there have been any link between the trade routes and the performance of ritual in caves? Did some itinerant monks or masters seek ritual ingredients at the source?

The distribution of the clay plaques and the general absence of structural remains where they have been found raises many questions. Who performed the practices? Who presided, who participated? Were the limestone caves the residences of monastic groups, or of communities of monastic and lay practitioners, or of single practitioners? Were they sites for temporary retreats? What was the relationship between the caves and settlements, monastic or economic centres, and trade routes? What was the relationship between the practice of Buddhism and urbanisation? These questions apply, of course, for the tablets and *stūpas* discussed below.

Buddhas and Bodhisattvas

Other tablets depict Buddhas and bodhisattvas. Not all of the configurations can be identified. One of the most widely distributed clay images depicts a central Buddha seated on a throne, flanked by a pair of standing bodhisattvas. The Buddha has a halo; his right hand is raised with the palm open. Above an arch over the Buddha's head float three cross-legged Buddhas seated in meditation. This tablet has been found in lower Burma at Sri Ksetra, in the Kawgun Caves, and near Rangoon (Luce 1985: I 152, II Pl. 56 f, g). In Thailand it has been found in the provinces of Nakhon Sawan (Piriya Krairiksh 2001: Fig. 43.1), Nakhon Pathom (Pattaratorn Chirapravati 1997:

Fig. 7), Ratchaburi, and Phetchaburi, and through the peninsula at Krabi (Khao Ok Thalu) and Phatthalung at Khao Khanab Nam (Piriya Krairiksh 1980: Pl. 28; Pattaratorn Chirapravati 2000: 178, n. 31) and Tham Khuha Sawan (Jacq-Hergoualc'h 2002: Fig. 58). It is also found in western Java (on the border that frames the image are two pairs of *stūpas* with tall series of parasols), and in Champa in Vietnam (Nandana Chutiwongs 2005: 69 Fig. 4). The scene or configuration has not been identified (although Cœdès mistakenly interpreted it as the great miracle of Śrāvastī). The model seems to be Southeast Asian – no examples are known to date from India. That is – and this is important – a locally conceived Southeast Asian mould was widely diffused in the region. The images did not have to be 'Indian' to possess power or to circulate widely.

Miniature *Stūpas* and the Eight Great Sites

The mass production of small clay *stūpas* was especially popular, and such *stūpas* have been found in India, Pakistan, Afghanistan, Kashmir, Central Asia, Tibet, Bangladesh, Thailand, Malaysia, and Indonesia. In some models the main *stūpa* is encircled by four or eight lesser *stūpas*, the latter representing eight major events or prodigies in the life of the Buddha and their sites. The small *stūpas* are closely linked to – and empowered by – the *ye dharmā* verse, usually in Sanskrit, which is either stamped on the surface or printed on tiny tablets and inserted into the base. Small *stūpas* of this type have been recovered in the Malay peninsula in large numbers. Examples have been found in the south of Thailand at Phatthalung (Pattaratorn Chirapravati 2000: Fig. 8) and at Tham Khuhaphimuk in Yala province (Jaqc-Hergoualc'h 2002: Fig. 150), as well as in Malaysia. The miniature *stūpas* attest to the veneration of the eight sites, and the production of the *stūpas* would have been accompanied by specific litanies and rituals. Some of the former are preserved in Pali and Tibetan. It is conceivable that the *stūpa* encircled by eight lesser *stūpas* was formulated around the same time as figural representations of the sites (or the events that they commemorate), such as those on stone, in clay tablets, and in painting. The miniature *stūpas* belong to a complex of texts and ritual practices connected with the life of Śākyamuni. *Stūpas* of this type are still produced in the Himalayan and Tibetan regions (see Dorjee 1996).

Dhāraṇī Sealings

Some tablets derived their power from the word alone. A text was impressed or stamped on the clay without any image, beyond in some cases a *stūpa* in relief. Shortest and most common is the *ye dharmā* stanza. Longer texts are *dhāraṇī* – spells or incantations which promote well-being and security.

The miniscule letters, usually worn and abraded, are difficult to read, but several *dhāraṇīs* can be identified. One of these is an excerpt from the *Bodhimaṇḍālaṃkāra-lakṣa-dhāraṇī*.[13] Stamps of these *dhāraṇīs* have been widely found across northern India (Lawson 1982: II 357 foll.); others come from the Malay peninsula. Another popular *dhāraṇī* was the *Raśmivimala-dhāraṇī*, which was especially widespread, being inscribed in Chinese transcription throughout the Far East, in China, Korea, and Japan, where it was installed in large numbers in small *stūpas* made of clay or wood. These in turn were often placed within larger *stūpas* or foundations. *Dhāraṇī* were not *translated* into Chinese but were *transposed* from the Indian writing system into the Chinese, in an attempt to maintain the sounds of the original. The power of these *dhāraṇī* – or, rather, of those who promoted them – to inspire large-scale projects leading to technological innovations in the field of printing and involving the mobilisation of considerable resources and expenditure is an extraordinary feature of the Buddhism from about the eighth century on.

CONCLUSION

Evidence for the circulation of ritual is uneven in terms of both geography and time, and at this point it is impossible to attempt a systematic account of peninsular Southeast Asian Buddhism. Geography and demography dictate that the realisations of ritual be specific and local, and we must be cautious of over-reliance on texts originating from India. Nonetheless, certain patterns can be proposed. Jacq-Hergoualc'h has subtitled his book on the Malay peninsula 'Crossroads of the Maritime Silk Road'. Whether or not there was really a 'maritime silk road' may be debated, but the peninsula was certainly more than a series of emporia or an economic network. The peninsula was a crossroad of ideas, of culture, and of ritual in a vibrant and creative Buddhist world, participating in the great movements that swept across much of Asia. These include devotion to Avalokiteśvara and other bodhisattvas, to the eight bodhisattvas, and to Buddha-bodhisattva triads, expressed in the mass-production of clay tablets, stamped with icons or texts. Some of these small icons circulated within the region of Southeast Asia but were not known on the Indian subcontinent – that is, the practice was fully naturalised and had its own localised momentum. The ideologies of the age were codified in *dhāraṇī* like the *Bodhimaṇḍālaṃkāra-lakṣa* and the *Raśmivimala*, which enjoyed a remarkable diffusion across Buddhist Asia. Among the dynamic and diverse expressions of Buddhism, Southeast Asia stands in its own right in its production of unique iconographic forms and its use of caves as centres of production, or at least as deposits, for ritual artefacts.

What did the rituals offer? How can we explain their remarkable proliferation? In the '*Sūtra* on the eightfold *maṇḍala*' the Buddha states that the recitation of the 'heart' (*hrdaya*, the essence distilled in a mantra) of the eightfold *maṇḍala*, purifies the most heinous deeds and accomplishes all aims.[14] Further,[15]

If son of good family or a daughter of good family recites this *hrdaya* of the eight bodhisattvas together with that of the Tathāgata in front of the *maṇḍala*, his or her aims will all be accomplished, and he or she will quickly realise unsurpassed perfect and complete awakening.

The production of sealings was inspired by the ideologies of Buddhism which, remaining in a sense constant over centuries, at the same time continually found new outlets and new expressions – the quest for merit, the desire to cleanse or eradicate bad deeds, and the ultimate aspiration, that to unsurpassed awakening.

NOTES

1. The common translation of *nikāya* as 'sect' is inappropriate because a *nikāya* was a *monastic* order, and its lineage was transmitted though ordination within and observance of a shared code of rules for monks and nuns, the *Prātimokṣa*. 'Eighteen' is a conventional figure; the number was in fact higher; some remain obscure and seem to have had little influence outside of their individual centres.
2. *nānādeśī*: Schopen 2005: 304 and n. 21.
3. The exceptions are the Ratu Baka inscription from central Java, dated CE 792, which refers to an 'Abhayagiri-*vihāra* built for the Sinhalese *saṃgha*', and the extensive use of Pali in lower Burma and central Siam, both of which point to the presence of Theravādin monastic lineages (for Pali inscriptions see e.g. Skilling 1997a and b and 2001b).
4. The 'Śrāvaka schools' or the 'Śrāvakayāna' are the eighteen *nikāyas* taken together. The Mahāyāna evolved within these orders, developing new orientations and new interpretations. For relics see Strong 2004 and Skilling 2005a.
5. Takakusu [1896] 1982: 45-46; for processions see also Schopen 2005b.
6. For Avalokiteśvara in Southeast Asia see Nandana Chutiwongs 2002.
7. Such images are often called 'votive tablets', but the term is inappropriate (see Skilling 2005c). In Indian archaeological writing they are usually called 'sealings'; there is no suitable term in English, and in this paper I call them sealings, tablets, or plaques.
8. Nanjio 1883 §§ 880, 981; Lancaster 1979 § 1215 = Taishō § 1168a (vol. 20), translated by Fa-hsien, for whom see Lancaster 1979: 395-96; K 1304 = T 1167 (vol. 20), translated by Amoghavajra. The Chinese versions are discussed in Lin Li-kouang 1935; see further Kuo Li-ying 1994, p. 158.
9. *Ārya-maṇḍala-aṣṭa-nāma-mahāyāna-sūtra*: Peking Tibetan Tripiṭaka (Otani Reprint) Cat. no. 773, vol. 28, *mdo, gu,* 312a4-314a5, tr. Bhante Ye shes sde; Tohoku 105, *mdo sde, nga, 'Phags pa dkyil 'khor brgyad ces bya ba'i chos kyi rnam grangs theg pa chen po'i mdo.* Cf. Taishō § 486 (vol. 14), Lancaster 1979 § 497, Nanjio 1883 § 462. The Sanskrit *Ārya-maṇḍala-aṣṭa-nāma-mahāyāna-sūtra* looks more like a 'reconstruction' of the *Kanjur* editors than an authentic title. The Tohoku Tibetan title might be

rendered into Sanskrit as **Ārya-aṣṭamaṇḍalaka-nāma-dharmaparyāya-mahāyāna-sūtra*. The original Sanskrit title of the *sūtra* remains to be determined.

10. *Ārya-aṣṭamaṇḍalaka-nāma-mahāyānasūtra/ 'Phags pa dkyil 'khor brgyad pa zhes bya ba theg pa chen po'i mdo*, tr. the Indian Upādhyāya Jinamitra, Dānaśila, and the great editor Bhante Ye shes sde. The Tibetan text is given twice in the Tantra section of the Peking Kanjur: Tibetan Tripiṭaka (Otani Reprint) Cat. no. 507, vol. 11, *rgyud ha*, 119a2-120a2 duplicated as Peking no. 158, vol. 6, *rgyud na*, 37a1-38a1). The title of the Tibetan version was listed in Stanislas Julien, 'Concordance', *Journal Asiatique*, novembre-decembre 1849, title no. 579. The earliest description of the text that I know of was given in Csoma de Körös 1836, p. 511: 'Eight *mandalas*. The *bija-mantras* of eight *Bodhisatwas*, uttered by SHA'KYA, at the request of RATNA GARBHA, &c. at *Gru-hdsin* (Sans. *Potala*)' (cf. French version in Feer 1881, p. 312).

11. Tohoku 105, Derge Kanjur *nga* 288a6: *de nas dkyil 'khor khor yug tu, 'khor gyi dkyil 'khor rnams bya ste 'jig rten dbang dang, byams pa dang, thub pa skyes mchog nam mkha' dang, kun tu bzang po blo ldan dang, gsang ba pa yi bdag po dang 'jam dpal gzhon nur gyur pa dang, sgrib pa thams cad rnam sel dang de bzhin sa yi snying po ste, de dag gi ched du dkyil 'khor brgyad bya'o.*

12. For an early opinion that the central Buddha is Vairocana see Woodward 1988.

13. The textual history of this *dhāraṇī* is rather confused: see Schopen 1985 and Scherrer-Schaub 1994.

14. These are the five deeds of immediate retribution (*ānantarya-karma*) – killing one's mother, killing one's father, killing an arhant, causing a Tathāgata's blood to flow, and creating division in the *saṃgha*.

15. Peking Tripiṭaka no. 507 – see above, n. 10.

REFERENCES

In accordance with convention, Thai authors are listed under their first names. Japanese authors are listed family name first.

Alam, A.K.M. Shamsul, 1985, *Sculptural Art of Bangladesh: Pre-Muslim Period*, Dhaka: Department of Archaeology and Museums, 1985.

Asian Civilisations Museum, 2003, *The Asian Civilisations Museum A-Z Guide*, Singapore: Asian Civilisations Museum.

Bautze-Picron, Claudine, 1997, 'Le groupe des huit grands bodhisatva en Inde: genèse et développement', in Natasha Eilenberg et al. (eds.), *Living a Life in Accord with Dhamma: Papers in Honor of Professor Jean Boisselier on His Eightieth Birthday*, Bangkok: Silpakorn University, pp. 1–55.

Dorjee, Pema, 1996, *Stūpa and its Technology: A Tibeto-Buddhist Perspective*, New Delhi: Indira Gandhi National Centre for the Arts and Motilal Banarsidass.

Feer, Léon, 1881, 'Analyse du Kandjour recueil des livres sacrés du Tibet par Alexandre Csoma, de Körös Hongrois-Siclien, de Transylvanie, traduite de l'anglais et augmenté de diverses additions et remarques par M. Léon Feer.' Lyon: Imprimerie Pitrat Ainé (*Annales du Musée Guimet*, Tome deuxième).

Jacq-Hergoualc'h, M., 2002, *The Malay Peninsula: Crossroads of the Maritime Silk Road (100 BC–1300 AD)*. Leiden: E.J. Brill (*Handbook of Oriental Studies*, Section 3, South-East Asia, vol. 13; ed. B. Arps et al.).

Joo, Kyeongmi, 2004, 'The Significance of *Raśmivimalaviśuddhaprabhānāma-dhāraṇī-sūtra* in Korean Buddhist Reliquaries.' *Bulkyomisulsahak*, no. 2, October 2004 (English abstract, pp. 195-96).

——, 2007, 'The Sutra of the Great Dharani of Pure Light and the Relic Veneration in the Unified Silla.' Unpublished paper given at Yale University, 10 November 2007.

de Körös, Alexander Csoma, 1836, 'Analysis of the Gyut.' *Asiatic Researches*, vol. XX, Calcutta.

Kuo Li-ying, 1994, *Confession et contrition dans le bouddhisme chinois du ve au xe siècle*. Paris: École française d'Extrême-Orient (Publications de l'École française d'Extrême-Orient, monographies, no. 170).

Lancaster, Lewis R. with Sung-bae Park, 1979, *The Korean Buddhist Canon: A Descriptive Catalogue*, Berkeley: University of California Press.

Lawson, Simon D., 1982, 'A Catalogue of Indian Buddhist Clay Sealings in British Museums', Ph.D. thesis, University of Oxford, Trinity Term, 1982. 2 vols.

Lin Li-kouang, 1935, 'Puṇyodaya (Na-t'i), un propagateur du tantrisme en Chine et au Cambodge à l'époque de Hiuan-Tsang.' *Journal Asiatique*, juillet-septembre 1935, pp. 83-100.

Luce, G.H., 1985, *Phases of Pre-Pagán Burma: Languages and History*, 2 vols. Oxford: Oxford University Press.

Malandra, Geri H., 1993, *Unfolding a Mandala: The Buddhist Cave Temples at Ellora*, Albany, New York: SUNY.

Mitra, Debala, 1996, 'An Iconographic Study of the Figures of Eight Great Bodhisattvas in Lalitagiri, Udayagiri and Ratnagiri in Orissa', in Debala Mitra (ed.), *Explorations in Art and Archaeology of South Asia: Essays Dedicated to N.G. Majumdar*, Calcutta: Directorate of Archaeology and Musuems, Government of West Bengal, pp. 353-91.

——, 1998, 'Lintels with the Figures of the Eight Great Bodhisattvas', in *Facets of Indian Culture (Gustav Roth Felicitation Volume)*. Patna, 1998, pp. 276-300.

——, 1999, 'Representation of Astamahabodhisattvas from Nalanda: An Iconographic Study', in N.N. Bhattacharyya and Amartya Ghosh (eds.), *Tantric Buddhism: Centennial Tribute to Dr Benoytosh Bhattacharyya*, New Delhi: Manohar, pp. 31-53.

Nandana Chutiwongs 2002. *The Iconography of Avalokiteśvara in Mainland South-East Asia*, New Delhi: Indira Gandhi National Centre for the Arts and Aryan Books International.

——, 2005, 'Le bouddhisme du Champa', in Pierre Baptiste and Thierry Zéphir, *Trésors d'art du Vietnam: la sculpture du Champa, V-XVe siècles*, Paris: Réunion des musées nationaux/Musée des arts asiatiques Guimet, 2005, pp. 65-87.

Nandana Chutiwongs and Denise Patry Leidy, 1994, *Buddha of the Future: An Early Maitreya from Thailand*, New York: The Asia Society Galleries/ Singapore: Sun Tree Publishing.

Nanjio Bunyiu, 1883, *A Catalogue of the Chinese Translation of the Buddhist Tripiṭaka, the Sacred Canon of the Buddhists in China and Japan*, Oxford: Clarendon Press.

Pattaratorn Chirapravati, 1997, *Votive Tablets in Thailand: Origins, Styles, and Uses*, Kuala Lumpur: Oxford University Press.

——, 1999, 'Buddhist Votive Tablets and Amulets from Thailand', in R.L. Brown (ed.), *Art from Thailand*, Mumbai: Marg Publications, pp. 79-92.

——, 2000, 'Development of Buddhist Traditions in Peninsular Thailand: A Study Based on Votive Tablets (Seventh to Eleventh Centuries)', in Nora A. Taylor (ed.), *Studies in Southeast Asian Art: Essays in Honor of Stanley J. O'Connor*, Ithaca, New York: Southeast Asia Program, Cornell University, pp. 172-93.

Piriya Krairiksh, 1980, *Art in Peninsular Thailand Prior to the Fourteenth Century A.D.* Bangkok: The Fine Arts Department.

——, 2542 [1999], 'Phra phim thi phop nai phak tai kon phutthasatawat thi 20', in *Saranukrom watthanatham thai phak tai*, Bangkok: Munlanithi Saranukrom Watthanatham Thai Thanakhan Thai Phanit, vol. 10, pp. 5041-63.

——, 2544 [2001], *Arayatham thai: phuenthan tang prawatisatsilapa*, vol. 1, *Silapa kon phutthasatawat thi 19*, Bangkok: Khana Silpasat, Silpakorn University.

Scherrer-Schaub, Cristina, 1994, 'Some Dhāraṇī Written on Paper Functioning as Dharmakāya Relics: A Tentative Approach to PT 350', in Per Kvaerne (ed.), *Tibetan Studies: Proceedings of the 6th Seminar of the International Association for Tibetan Studies, Fagernes, 1992*, Oslo: The Institute for Comparative Research in Human Culture, vol. 2, 711-27.

Schopen, Gregory, 1985, 'The *Bodhigarbhālaṃkāralakṣa* and *Vimaloṣṇīṣa Dhāraṇīs* in Indian Inscriptions: Two Sources for the Practice of Buddhism in Medieval India.' *Wiener Zeitschrift für die Kunde Südostasiens* 29, 119-49. Reprinted in Schopen 2005: 314-44.

——, '*Stūpa* and *Tīrtha*: Tibetan Mortuary Practices and an Unrecognized Form of Burial *ad sanctos* at Buddhist Sites in India', in T. Skorupski and U. Pagel (eds.), *The Buddhist Forum*, vol. III, 1991-93, *Papers in Honour and Appreciation of Professor David Seyfort Ruegg's Contribution to Indological, Buddhist and Tibetan Studies*, London: School of Oriental and African Studies, University of London, pp. 273-93. Reprinted in Schopen 2005: 350-69.

——, 2005a, *Figments and Fragments of Mahāyāna Buddhism in India: More Collected Papers*. Honolulu: University of Hawaii Press.

——, 2005b, 'Taking the Bodhisattva into Town. More Texts on the Image of 'the Bodhisattva' and Image Processions in the Mūlasarvāstivāda-vinaya.' *East and West* 55.1-4, 299-311.

Skilling, Peter, 1997a, 'New Pāli Inscriptions from Southeast Asia,' *Journal of the Pali Text Society* XXIII, pp. 123-157.

——, 1997b, 'The Advent of Theravāda Buddhism to Mainland Southeast Asia', *Journal of the International Association of Buddhist Studies* 20.1, pp. 93-107.

——, 1999, 'A Buddhist Inscription from Go Xoai, Southern Vietnam and Notes Towards a Classification of *ye dharmā* Inscriptions', In *80 pi sasatrachan dr. prasert na nagara: ruam botkhwam vichakan dan charük lae ekasan boran* [80 Years: A collection of articles on epigraphy and ancient documents published on the occasion of the celebration of the 80th birthday of Prof. Dr. Prasert Na Nagara], Bangkok, 21 March 2542 [1999], pp. 171-87.

——, 2001a, 'The Place of South-East Asia in Buddhist Studies', *Buddhist Studies (Bukkyo Kenkyu)* XXX, pp. 19-43.

——, 2001b, 'Some Citation Inscriptions from South-East Asia', *Journal of the Pali Text Society* XXVII, pp. 159-75.

——, 2003, 'An *Oṃ maṇipadme hūṃ* Inscription from South-East Asia', *Aséanie* 11 (June 2003), pp. 13-20.

——, 2004a, 'Mahāyāna and Bodhisattva: An Essay Towards Historical Understanding', in Pakorn Limpanusorn, Chalermpon Iampakdee (ed.), *Phothisatawa barami kap sangkhom thai nai sahatsawat mai* [*Bodhisattvaparami and Thai Society in the New Millennium*]. Chinese Studies Centre, Institute of East Asia, Thammasat University. Bangkok: Thammasat University Press, 2547 [2004] [Proceedings of a seminar in celebration of the fourth birth cycle of Her Royal Highness Princess Maha Chakri Sirindhorn held at Thammasat University, 21 January 2546 (2003)], pp. 139-56.

——, 2004b, 'Traces of the Dharma: Preliminary Reports on Some *ye dhamma* and *ye dharma* Inscriptions from Mainland South-East Asia.' *Bulletin de l'Ecole française d'Extrême-Orient* 90-91 (2003-04), pp. 273-87.

——, 2005a, 'Cutting Across Categories: The Ideology of Relics in Buddhism', *Annual Report of The International Research Institute for Advanced Buddhology at Soka University for the Academic Year 2004*, vol. VIII. Tokyo: The International Research Institute for Advanced Buddhology, Soka University, pp. 269-322.

——, 2005c, ''Buddhist Sealings: Reflections on Terminology, Motivation, Donors' Status, School-affiliation, and Print-technology', in Catherine Jarrige and Vincent Lefèvre (eds.), *South Asian Archaeology 2001*, vol. II, *Historical Archaeology and Art History*, Paris: Éditions Recherches sur les Civilisations, pp. 677-85.

——, 2008a, 'Buddhist Sealings and the *ye dharmā* Stanza', in Gautam Sengupta and Sharmi Chakraborty (eds.), *Archaeology of Early Historic South Asia*, New Delhi: Pragati Publications: Kolkata: Centre for Archaeological Studies and Training, Eastern India, pp. 503-25.

——, 2008b, 'Buddhist Sealings in Thailand and Southeast Asia: Iconography, Function, and Ritual Context', in *Interpreting Southeast Asia's Past: Monument, Image and Text*, ed. E.A. Bacus, I.C. Glover and P.D. Sharrock (with editorial assistance of J. Guy and V.C. Pigott). Singapore: National University of Singapore Press.

Strong, John, 2004, *Relics of the Buddha*, Princeton, New Jersey: Princeton University Press.

Takakusu, J. (tr.) 1896, *A Record of the Buddhist Religion as Practised in India and the Malay Archipelago (AD 671–95) by I-Tsing* [London, 1896] New Delhi: Munshiram Manoharlal, 1982.

Whitfield, Susan 2004. *The Silk Road: Trade, Travel, War and Faith*, London: The British Library.

Woodward, Hiram W., Jr. 1988. 'Southeast Asian Traces of the Buddhist Pilgrims.' *MVSE Annual of the Museum of Art and Archaeology*, University of Missouri-Columbia, no. 22: 75-91.

——, 2003, *The Art and Architecture of Thailand from Prehistoric Times through the Thirteenth Century* (Handbook of Oriental Studies, Section Three, South-East Asia, vol. 14), Leiden and Boston: E.J. Brill.

Yoritomi M., 1990, 'An Iconographic Study of the Eight Bodhisattvas in Tibet', in Tadeusz Skorupski (ed.), *Indo-Tibetan Studies: Papers in Honour and Appreciation of Professor David L. Snellgrove's Contribution to Indo-Tibetan Studies* (*Buddhica Britannica Series Continua II*), Tring, UK: The Institute of Buddhist Studies, pp. 323-32.

Zulkifli, Jaafar, 2003, *Gua-gua Batu Kapur di Malaysia dalam Perspektif Arkeologi/Ancient Limestone Landscapes of Malaysia: An Archaeological Insight*, vol. 1. Kuala Lumpur: Jabatan Muzium dan Antikuiti/Department of Museums and Antiquities.

19

Early Buddhism in Myanmar:
Ye Dhammā Inscriptions from Arakan[1]

Kyaw Minn Htin

Arakan[2] is one of the fourteen states and divisions that composed together in the Union of Myanmar (formerly Burma). It is located on the boundary of present-day Myanmar and Bangladesh. Situated east of Vaṅga and Samataṭa of ancient India, Arakan was in olden days a thriving, independent border state beyond the Indian subcontinent. Indologists who write about the history and culture of ancient India have never mentioned this area where high standards of life, culture and art flourished. Under the cultural influence of India, city-states flourished in the first millennium of the Christian Era (CE). They are Dhaññavatī and Vesālī. The Gupta-period sculptures point the city of Dhaññavatī to the fifth century CE (Gutman 2001: 19) and art and numismatic studies place Vesālī between about sixth and tenth centuries CE (Gutman 1976; 2001: 41), although a fourteenth-century radiocarbon date from a city gatepost suggests intermittent reoccupation (Hudson 2005).

About fifty Sanskrit and Pāli inscriptions written in Gupta, Devanāgarī and proto-Bengali scripts between the period of fifth and tenth centuries CE were found in Arakan. Most of the inscriptions can be assigned to the Vesālī period. Interestingly, none of the inscriptions found in Arakan during the first millennium CE were inscribed in vernacular languages; all were written in the classical languages of Sanskrit or Pāli using Indian scripts. This is due to the cultural impact, especially the Buddhicisation, of ancient India on this region which is situated very close to the subcontinent.

Most of the inscriptions from the Vesālī period bear the *gāthā* (verse) of *ye dhammā*. According to archaeological data, the *ye dhammā* verses were first inscribed around the fifth-sixth centuries (Mya 1961b: 17). We do not know whether the custom of inscribing the *ye dhammā gāthā* appeared first among the Mahāyāna or Theravāda schools. However, most of the *ye dhammā* inscription of the fifth century CE were written in Pāli. Between sixth and seventh centuries, the *ye dhammā gāthā* were commonly in usage both in Pāli and Sanskrit languages. This custom remained among the Mahāyāna and Theravāda Buddhism until the eleventh century. After the eleventh century, the *ye dhammā* disappeared from the Theravāda artefacts while it remained in usage in the Mahāyāna context for many centuries (Ni Min Shin 2003: 30).

Ye dhammā inscriptions were widely spread in northern and southern Indian scripts by using the languages of Pāli, Sanskrit and a mixture of Pāli and Sanskrit (Mya 1961b: 17). The materials of inscriptions are gold or silver leaves, stone slabs, bricks, terracotta plaques, miniature *stūpas*, the plinths or the backs of the Buddha statues (ASB 1959-60: 2).

Ye dhammā gāthā is the abstract of the *Dhammacakka pavattana sutta,* the first sermon of the Buddha. However, this *gāthā* was not uttered by the Master himself. It was preached by Ven. Assaji, who was one of the first five followers (*pañcavaggiya bhikkhus*) of the Buddha to Upatissa, the future Ven. Sāriputtarā, the chief disciple (*agga sāvaka*) of the Buddha. It is said that after hearing this verse, Upatissa immediately reached *sotāpana,* the first stage of the path to *nibbāna.* The meaning of the *gāthā* is: 'Out of all the laws, the law of cause is the origin. Thatāgato (i.e. Buddha) has spoken of the conditions arising from a cause. He has also spoken of their cessation. This is the doctrine of the great monk (i.e. Buddha)' (San Tha Aung 1974: 103). In Sanskrit Buddhism, this *gāthā* is known as the *pratītyasamūtpāda gāthā* of the *Ārya-Pratītyasamūtpāda sūtra,* proclaimed by the Buddha in the response to Avalokiteśvara's request for the demonstration of the *Dhamma* (Gutman 1976: 76).

Although, the *ye dhammā* inscriptions widely spread between the fifth and eleventh centuries CE, the writing system of this verse slightly differs between the Theravāda and the Mahāyāna schools. The Pāli *ye dhammā gāthā* reads:

ye dhammā hetuppa bhavā
tesaṁ hetuṁ Tathāgato āha
tesañca yo nirodho
evaṁ vādi mahā samaṇo

The Mahāyāna school also inscribed the Sanskrit *ye dhammā* inscriptions. The Tibetan Mahāyānist *ye dhammā gāthā* is as follows:

ye dharmā hetuprabhavā
hetuṁ teṣāṁ Tathāgato hyavadat
teṣaṁ ca yo nirodha
evaṁ vādi mahā śramaṇa:

Ye dhammā inscriptions were also present in Sri Ksetra. Two gold-leaf inscriptions from Mhawza found at Sri Ksetra in 1897 bear the verse of *ye dhammā* in Pāli. The inscription can be assigned to be fifth-sixth centuries CE (Ray 1936: 33). *Ye dhammā* inscriptions of Sri Ksetra dating back between seventh and tenth centuries were written in Nāgarī script in Sanskrit language. Such verses were inscribed on the statues of Tārādevī and Avalokiteśvara (Mya 1961b: Pl. 16, 19, 24, 34, 40).

The Môn people of ancient Myanmar and Thailand also wrote the *ye dhammā* inscriptions. A seventh-century *ye dhammā* inscription discovered at the Bo-ta-htaung pagoda, Yangon was written in Pāli. Another terracotta votive inscription belonging to seventh-eighth centuries CE from Pra Pathom, Thailand bears the *ye dhammā gāthā* in Pāli (Mya 1961a: 6).

The votive tablets of the Pagan period (eleventh-thirteenth century CE), Myanmar, also display the *ye dhammā* inscriptions in Nāgarī scripts (Nai Pan Hla 1998).

The *ye dhammā* inscriptions from Arakan have been published by different authors. In 1879, G.E. Fryer published a *ye dhammā* inscription in 'Proceedings of the Asiatic Society of Bengal'. In his 'Report on the Antiquities of Arakan' (1891), Forchhammer published one *ye dhammā* inscription from Dhaññavatī. In 1944, E.H. Johnston wrote an article 'Some Sanskrit Inscriptions of Arakan' where he produced five epigraphs, including one *ye dhammā* inscription from Sandoway, southern Arakan. D.C. Sircar, in 1962, published three inscriptions of the Candra kings from Arakan in *Epigraphia Indica*. Among them is the *ye dhammā* inscription of the Queen of Nīti Candra of Vesālī. *Ye dhammā* inscriptions were also frequently published in the Annual Reports of the Director, Archaeological Survey of Myanmar/ Burma. In 1974, U San Tha Aung presented eleven Gupta-script inscriptions from Arakan, including seven *ye dhammā* inscriptions in *Scripts of Arakan, Sixth Century CE and Before*. In her Ph.D. thesis of 'Ancient Arakan' (1976), Pamela Gutman produced thirty Pāli and Sanskrit inscriptions from Arakan. Among them, seventeen contain the *ye dhammā gāthā*.

U San Tha Aung counted the total number of *ye dhammā* inscriptions written with Gupta characters from Arakan to be over thirty[3] (San Tha Aung 1979: 17). Ni Min Shin gives a list of twenty-two *ye dhammā* inscriptions and inscribed miniature *stūpas* with their localities (Ni Min Shin 2003: 33-34).

The present author has counted twenty-three *ye dhammā* inscriptions and eight *ye dhammā* inscribed *stūpas*; making a total number of thirty-one.

Many inscriptions have been found in Vesālī and its surroundings, but *ye dhammā* inscriptions have also been found in other parts of Arakan. This paper will focus particularly on *ye dhammā* inscriptions that were discovered in the whole area of Arakan.

THE *YE DHAMMĀ* INSCRIPTIONS

Twenty-three *ye dhammā* inscriptions have been discovered in different parts of Arakan. They are as follows.

1. Inscription of the time of Nīti Candra (Sircar 1962, *EI* XXXII, 2, pp. 103-09; *ASB*[4] 1958-59, Pl. 37; San Tha Aung 1974, Pl. 15; Gutman 1976, Pl. XVIII, San Tha Aung 1979, Pl. 15).
2. Inscription from Vesālī (*ASB* 1958-59, Pl. 39; San Tha Aung 1974, Pl. 21; Gutman 1976, Pl. XXc).
3. Inscription from Vesālī Great Buddha Image (*ASB* 1958-59, Pl. 43; San Tha Aung 1974, Pl. 22; Gutman 1976, Pl. XXIa).
4. Inscription from Vesālī Mound No. 4 (Shwe Zan 2004: 170).
5. Inscription from Thinkyittaw, Vesālī (*Arch Neg*[5] 13669 (1967-8); San Tha Aung 1974, Pl. 17; Gutman 1976, Pl. XXb).
6. Fragmentary Inscription from Thinkyittaw, Vesālī (Gutman 1976, Pl. XXa).
7. Inscribed base of a bronze Buddha image, Vesālī (Gutman 1976, Pl. XXXIVa, LXVIa).
8. Inscribed base of a Buddha image from Vesālī (Gutman 1976, Pl. XXXIVc, LXIV).
9. Inscription found near the road to Khrit village, east of Vesālī (unpublished).
10. Inscription found in the vicinity of Dhaññavatī (Forchhammer 1891, Pl. VII, 3; *ASB* 1958-59, Pl. 40; San Tha Aung 1974, Pl. 19; Gutman 1976, Pl. XVIIb).
11. Inscription from Min-tha-chaung, north of Mahāmuni (Gutman 1976, Pl. XVI).
12. Inscription on the plinth of the Buddha image from Shin-kyam village, Kyauktaw (Rakhine Thahaya 2006: 32-33).
13. Inscription from MraukU Museum (Aung Tha Oo 1966: 51).
14. Inscription from Minbya (Min Thein Zan 1997, Pl. A; Saw Tun Aung 1999: 38-41).
15. Inscription from Pa-taw, Minbya (unpublished).
16. Inscription from Shin-ywa, Pauktaw (Maung Ba Thein 1994, Pl. I).
17. Inscription from Kyaukpyu (*IB*[6] CCCLIId; *Arch Neg* 3264 (1940-41); *ASB* 1958-59, Pl. 41; San Tha Aung 1974, Pl. 18; Gutman 1976, Pl. XXVII).
18. Inscription from a statue at Let-cha-byin, Ramree (unpublished).
19. Inscription from Nga-lun-maw, Sandoway (*IB* CCCLIIe; G.E. Fryer, in *Proceedings of the Asiatic Society of Bengal,* 1879, Pl. VIIb; Johnston 1944, Pl. IV, Fig. 2; *ASB* 1958-59, Pl. 42; San Tha Aung 1974, Pl. 20; Gutman 1976, Pl. XXVIb).

20. Inscription from Lamu, Sandoway (Gutman 1976, Pl. XXVII).
21. Inscription from Pyit-wa, Sandoway (RSPC 1984).
22. Inscription from Shwe Andaw, Sandoway (Panthu Okkar 1996: 51-55).
23. Inscription from Candra Cetī, Sandoway (Panthu Okkar 1996: 51-55).

THE *YE DHAMMĀ* INSCRIBED MINIATURE *STŪPAS*

The miniature stone *stūpas* from Arakan consist of two parts. The lower portion is a square base which may be regarded as a plinth. The height of the plinth is about 20 cm. The upper portion is the *stūpa* proper, about 45 cm in height. This portion has a square platform made to fit in its base. Above this platform is a cube. In some miniature *stūpas*, the complete *ye dhammā gāthā* is inscribed on one of the faces of this cube. The term *stūpa* is found in the *ye dhammā* inscription of Lamu, Sandoway and a miniature *stūpa* from the MraukU Museum (see no. 20 and 27 inscriptions) and the Vīra Candra inscription of the sixth century. On the cube, where the inscriptions exist, there is another square platform. Above the platform are three terraces, and above the terraces is the cylindrical drum decorated with three bands. The middle band is broader and thicker than the other two. The top of the cylinder is hemispherical. It looks like an inverted bowl or a bell. On the top of the hemisphere is a ring of beads surmounted by moulding which support the *htī:* (San Tha Aung 1979: 14-15). The inscription of Vīra Candra, a king of Vesāli states that a hundred *stūpas* were constructed and dedicated by him because of his love for the true law (San Tha Aung 1974: 107). Altogether, 123 miniature stone *stūpas* have been discovered in the different parts of Arakan (Min Thein Zan 2003: 11).

The *ye dhammā* inscribed miniature *stūpas* are as follows:

24. Inscribed *stūpa* from Selāgīri, Kyauktaw (Gutman 1976, Pl. XVIIb, LXb; San Tha Aung 1979, Pls. 10, 11).
25. Inscribed *stūpa* from Thingyaing-taung, Vesāli (*Arch Neg* 2171 (1920-21); Gutman 1976, Pl. LXIa).
26. Inscribed *stūpa* from Tejarāma Monastery, MraukU (*IB* CCCLIIc; *Arch Neg* 4365 (1940-41); Gutman 1976, Pls. XXIb, LXIb).
27. Inscribed *stūpa* from MraukU Museum (unpublished).
28-29. Two inscribed *stūpas* from Mee-wa, Kyauktaw (Gutman 1976, Pls. XVII, c, d; San Tha Aung 1979, Pls. 12, 13).
30-31. Two inscribed *stūpas* from Mya-mala pagoda, An (Maung Ba Thein 1987: 59).

In this paper, I will present all the above mentioned *ye dhammā* inscriptions except the last two inscribed *stūpas*, as they were not accessible to me.

A BRIEF DESCRIPTION OF THE *YE DHAMMĀ* INSCRIPTIONS

1. Inscription of the Time of Nīti Candra

The first inscription, engraved on a slab, which dates back from the reign of Nīti Candra, was recovered from a ruined *stūpa* at Thinkyit-taung or Unhissaka hill situated to the east of Vesālī in 1956 or 1957.[7] It is situated now at MraukU Museum in Arakan. The size of the slab is 38.5 × 14 × 25 cm.[8] The first two lines of the inscription contain the *ye dhammā gāthā* and the remaining two lines describe the meritorious deed of the queen of Nīti Candra. The name of Nīti Candra can be found in the eighth-century Ānanda Candra inscription inscribed on the western face of the pillar now at Shitthaung temple at MraukU, Arakan. Sircar's chronology gives Nīti Candra's ruling period as CE 520-75 (Sircar 1962: 108). Pamela Gutman suggests that this inscription is from the first half of the sixth century.

Text[9]

(1) *ye dharmmā hetu prabhavā hetu[ṁ] teṣā[ṁ] Tathāga[ta]*
(2) *āha teṣāṁca yo nirodho evaṁ vādi mahā śramaṇa[:]*
(3) *Śrī [Nīticandra]sya candra vatpa chīnā ṣya devī sāvītaṁ*
(4) *candra śrī yā nāma pare[mo] pāsikasya*
(5) *deyyā dharmmo yaṁm sarvva satvānāṁ manuka[tta]ma*

2. Inscription from Vesālī

This inscription can be found in 'Report of the Director, Archaeological Survey for the year 1958-59', Pl. 39. The report states page 26 that it was found in 1920-21 and only rubbing is available (San Tha Aung 1974: 119). Dr. Gutman thinks that this inscription, two lines on a broken stone plaque, was presumably found at Letkhat-taung. 'In 1973, I was told that and inscription had been taken from the entrance to the original shrine, now buried in front of the monastery, and this appears to be the only published inscription whose provenance is not stated' (Gutman 1976: 91).

Text[10]

(1) *ye dharmmā hetuprabhavā hetuṁ teṣaṁ Tathāgato*
(2) *. . . datte ṣāñca yo nirodho evaṁ vādi mahā ṣa . . .*

3. Inscription from Vesālī Great Buddha Image

This inscription was discovered at Phayagyi (Great Image) shrine in Vesālī. There are four lines of inscription bearing *ye dhammā gāthā* in Pāli language. The slab is damaged at the right. Dimension of the stone is 28 × 11.5 × 6.5

cm.[11] Palaeographically, it can be dated from the first half of the sixth century CE. It is located at the MraukU Archaeological Museum in Arakan.

Text[12]

(1) *ye dhammā hetupabhavā*
(2) *hetu tesaṁ Tathāgata āha*
(3) *tesañca yo niroṭha*
(4) *evaṁ vādī mahā sama[ṇa]*

4. Inscription from Vesālī Mound no. 4

This inscription was excavated from mound no. 4 of Vesālī in 1984 (Nyunt Han 1984: 17). It was engraved on a stone slab. The dimensions are – length: 25 cm, width: 10 cm and thickness: 17 cm.[13] There are seven lines of text. At present, the inscription is deposited at the Archaeology Museum of MraukU, Arakan.

Text[14]

(1) *y[e]dha[rm]ma h[e]tu [prabhava] [. . . .] tatha [. .]*
(2) *tesāṁca [yo]nirodh[o] evaṁ vādi mahā śramaṇa:*
(3) *yadatra puṇyaṁ mātā pi[tu] [. . . . . .] pa [. .]*
(4) *cāyya prabhūti sutaṅga vatpa sarvva satvā[na] manutta [. .]*
(5) *vā vā [.] ye saṁsara pa[.]. khāṇṇaṁ cama . me [.]*
(6) *jagatvā ma . tvihatāra ye[yaṁ] avijjhā [. . .] pa . .*
(7) *. . . dhayeye varadharmma [. . . . .]*

5. Inscription from Thinkyittaw, Vesālī

It was found at Thinkyittaw hill, on a ridge southeast of the outer walls of Vesālī in May 1965. Now, it is situated at MraukU Museum. It may have been one part of a small stone pagoda. The inscription consists of four lines on a well-preserved rectangular stone slab. The dimensions are – length: 21.5 cm, width: 14 cm and thickness: 13.7 cm.[15] The date is in the third quarter of the sixth century (Gutman 1976: 90).

Text[16]

(1) *ye dharmma hetuprabhavā hetu*
(2) *tesāṁ Tathāgato hyavadat*
(3) *tesāñca yo ṇirodho evaṁ*
(4) *vādī mahā śramaṇa:*

6. Fragmentary Inscription from Thinkyittaw, Vesālī

This inscription was also discovered at Thinkyittaw. There are four lines of inscriptions on a grey sand stone, measuring 22 × 11 × 15 cm.[17] Now, it is preserved at the Archaeological Museum of MraukU. As stone has been badly damaged in various places, reading is difficult. Transliteration of the inscription by Pamela Gutman is as follows:

Text[18]

(1) *ye dharmma hetuprabhavā*
(2) *teṣaṁ [hetuṁ] dattenaṁ / Tathā*
(3) *gato [hy avadat]* . . . .
(4) . . . . *deyyo dharmmā*

7. Inscribed Base of a Bronze Buddha Image, Vesālī

This headless Buddha image is now situated at MraukU Museum. The height is 0.21 m. The seat has an inscription, almost entirely illegible. Only the first letter *ye* is certain. The sixth and seventh letter can be vaguely seen as *prabha*. So, the sentence can be part of the *ye dhammā* verse. The inscription can be palaeographically placed in the second half of the sixth century (Gutman 1976: 120).

Text[19]

(1) *ye* . . . . *pra[bha]*

8. Inscribed Base of a Buddha Image from Vesālī

The inscription appears on the portion of two lines at the front of the seat of the image. However, the statue of the Buddha is lost. Now, the seat is situated at the MraukU Museum. It measures 8 cm. The scripts are small and neatly curved. It can be assigned to the second half of the sixth century (Gutman 1976: 119).

Text[20]

(1) . . . . . . *n[i]rodha evaṁ vādi mahāśra* . .
(2) . . . . . *ye kārayati* . . .

9. Inscription found near the Road to Khrit Village, East of Vesālī

This inscription was found near the road to Khrit village, situated east of Vesālī. The dimensions are – length: 26 cm and width: 15 cm. Now, it is in the collection of U Oung Hla Thein in Sittwe, Arakan. It has never been published. In February 2005, the rubbing of this inscription was shown to the author by Venerable Ashin Paññācāra of the Mahāmuni Buddha Vihāra Monastery in Sittwe.

Text[21]

(1) *ye dharmma hetu prabhavā*
(2) *hetuṁ teṣā Tathāgato hya*
(3) *vadata te ṣāñca yo*
(4) *nirodho evaṁ vādī mahā*
(5) *śramaṇa:*

10. Inscription found in the Vicinity of Dhaññavatī

Forchhammer discovered the inscription in the ruins of Selāgīri Cetī at Kyauktaw Hill. Now the place where this inscription is situated is not known. Two lines of inscriptions were written on a block of sandstone about 30 cm long.[22] The inscription may palaeographically be assigned to around the beginning of the sixth century (Gutman 1976: 79-80).

Text[23]

(1) *ye dharmmā hetuprabhavā hetum teṣa Tathāgato [hya]vatatta ṣāñca*
(2) *yo nirodho [e]vamvādī mahā śamaṇa:*

11. Inscription from Min-tha-chaung, North of Mahāmuni

This inscription is said to have been found at Min-tha-chaung, about 6 km north of Mahāmuni, Kyauktaw. The dimensions are 21 × 30 cm. The slab could not be located in 1975 (Gutman 1976: 81). Thanks to U San Tha Aung, Pamela Gutman obtained the xerox copy of his rubbing. There are nine lines but apparently very damaged. Gutman deciphered four lines of the *ye dhammā gāthā* in her thesis.

Text[24]

(1) *ye dharmma [hetupra]bhavā*
(2) *hetum teṣā[ṁ] Tathāgato hyavoca*
(3) *t teṣāñca yo nirodha*
(4) *evaṁ vādī mahā śramaṇa:*

12. Inscription on the Plinth of the Buddha Image from Shin-kyam Village, Kyauktaw

The inscription on the plinth of the bronze Buddha image was discovered on 5 December 1996 in Wa-pyan village, Pee-chaung, Kyauktaw.[25] The height of the bronze statue is 15 cm. It is now kept at the monastery in Shin-kyam village, Kyauktaw. There is a line of inscription on the plinth (Rakhine Thahaya Athin 2006: 32).

Text[26]

(1) *ye dharmma hetuprabhavā hetu . . samāṇa*

13. Inscription from MraukU Museum

In 1966, U Aung Tha Oo published this inscription with a facsimile, without mentioning the location or further information. Now, this inscription can be observed at the MraukU Archaeological Museum in Arakan. Dimension is 15 × 10.5 cm. There are six lines of inscription in Môn/Burmese characters.

Text[27]

(1) *ye dhammā hetuppabhavā Ta*
(2) *thāgato āha te*
(3) *sañ yoniro*
(4) *dho evaṁ vādi ma*
(5) *hā sama*
(6) *ṇo*

14. Inscription from Minbya

This inscription was discovered at the bottom of Kyein-taung hill, Minbya. The rubbing of the inscription was sent to U San Tha Aung in 1980 to decipher (Saw Tun Aung 1999). As U San Tha Aung died in 1981, he did not publish this inscription. In 1997, Min Thein Zan wrote a paper on this epigraph without any transcription. In 1999, U Saw Tun Aung, son of the late U San Tha Aung, published the inscription with U San Tha Aung's transliteration. The dimensions as given are – length: 57.5 cm, width: 22.5 cm, thickness (upper part): 7.5 cm and (lower part): 10 cm[28] (Min Thein Zan 1997: 94; Saw Tun Aung 1999: 40). Now it is kept at the Rakhine State Cultural Museum in Sittwe, Arakan.

Text[29]

(1) *ye dharmmā hetupabhavāhetu*
(2) *tesaṁ Tathāgato . . . tesa*
(3) *ñca yo nirodho evaṁ vādī ma*
(4) *hā śramaṇa . . . saha*
(5) *hedurāga . . . ca . . . maṅgela*
(6) *kintri bhe*[30] *saṅkhamsa ro nahitaṁ*
(7) *tattāya satā*[31] *navindtuva . . .*
(8) *. . . anumedantūti*

15. Inscription from Pa-taw, Minbya

This inscription was recovered in 2001 from the Pa-taw Hill in Minbya township. Now, it can be seen in the local monastery of Pa-taw village. Dimensions are 42 × 22 cm. There are seven lines of inscriptions including the *ye dhammā gāthā*. It can be assigned to the sixth-seventh centuries (Gutman et al. 2007: 657). This inscription is under transliteration by the scholars.

16. Inscription from Shin-ywa, Pauktaw

This inscription was found at Shin-ywa village in Peinnè-chaung island, Pauktaw, in 1982 (Maung Ba Thein 1994, 61). The dimensions are 36.75 × 23.75 × 11.5 cm. The upper part of the inscription is erased so that reading of that portion is impossible. This inscription is now kept in the residence of U Maung Ba Thein in Sittwe, Arakan.

Text[32]

(1) *. . . hetu prabhavā hetu*
(2) *ta . . . . . . tesāñca yo niro .*
(3) *evaṁ . . . hā śramaṇa*

17. Inscription from Kyaukpyu

G.H. Luce notes that the stone slab referred to in *ASB* 1913, p. 25, and in *ASI*[33] 1930, pp. 181-82, came from Ganga-ywa-ma village, Kyaukpyu district (Gutman 1976: 92). According to *Inscriptions of Burma*, this inscription (Pl. CCCLIId) was sent from the office of deputy commissioner of Kyaukpyu and it was kept at the archaeological office in Mandalay (Gutman 1976: 92). The stone-slab is damaged at the top and upper part of the right side. The annual report of the archaeological survey (1958-59) estimates it to be eighth

century CE (Than Tun 1969, 66). But Pamela Gutman suggests that the script
is derived from Vesālī (i.e. middle of the sixth century) (Gutman 1976: 92).

Text[34]

(1) . . *dharmmā hetuprabhavā hetu*
(2) . . *Tathāgatato vādi yo nirodha*
(3) *evaṁ di mahā śava[ṇa]*
(4) . *[.?pri] bhūta . .[na?ya]*
(5) *diṭha Budddha pratima* ...

18. Inscription from the Statue at Let-cha-byin, Ramree

A line of inscription was made on the plinth of the statue. According to the
rubbing, we can make a suggestion that it could be a *ye dhammā* inscription.
It is found *in situ*.

19. Inscription from Nga-lun-maw, Sandoway

It was exhumed by Col. G.E. Fryer from a cave in a hill near Nga-lun-maw
village, Sandoway district in 1872. The dimensions as given are – length:
17.4 cm, width: 14 cm and thickness: 2.4 to 2.7 cm[35] (Johnston 1944: 359).
The inscription was sent to the Museum of Indian Institute, Oxford before
the First World War[36] (Johnston 1944: 383; Gutman 1976: 94). The language
is Sanskrit with a certain amount of Pāli influence.

Text[37]

(1) *ye dharmma hetuprabhava hetu*
(2) *teṣaṁ Tathāgata hyavocat teṣāñca yo*
(3) *nirotha evaṁ vādi mahā śraṇa*
(4) *upāsa[kā] Ma[ï]gā upāsa*
(5) *ka [Sā]ko ma[vamma] makāra*
(6) *yi mātapitā ku*
(7) *sala*

20. Inscription from Lamu, Sandoway

U San Tha Aung gives a piece of information on this inscription in his book
Scripts of Arakan, Sixth Century and Before published in 1974. Thanks to
U San Tha Aung, who sent a copy of the photo of this inscription, Pamela
Gutman reproduced it in her thesis. The language is a mixture of Pāli and
Sanskrit.

Text[38]

(1) *ye dharmmā hetupabhavā hetu[ṁ]*
(2) *Tathāgato hyavocat yo nirodha evaṁ*
(3) *vādi mahāśramaṇa:*
(4) *upāsakā Śrīyya stūpaṁ kṛtvā*

21. Inscription from Pyit-wa, Sandoway

This inscription is mentioned in the vol. 5 of the *Rakhine State Gazetteers* (1984). Its present location is unknown.

22. Inscription from Shwe Andaw, Sandoway

This inscription was discovered near the western platform of the Shwe Andaw pagoda, Sandoway, in November 1994. The dimensions are – length: 40 cm, width: 25 cm and thickness: 5 cm[39] (Panthu Okkar 1996: 52). Now, it is kept in the custody of the Venerable Ashin Kosalla of the Shwe Andaw Monastery in Sandoway. Lines 5 to 8 tell us about the meritorious gift of Devī Savītācandraśrīyā. This name has already been found in another inscription of the time of Nīti Candra and it is roughly similar to the first inscription of this article.[40]

Text[41]

(1) *ye dha[r]mma hetu prabhavā*
(2) *hetuṁ tesaṁ Tathāgato hyavo*
(3) *dattesañca yo nirodho*
(4) *evaṁ vādi mahā sāmaṇa*
(5) *devī Savītācandraśrīyā nāma*
(6) *parame pāsikasya deyya dhammo*
(7) *yamma sarvva satvā nāṁ manu*
(8) *kattama*

23. Inscription from Candra Cetī, Sandoway

This inscription on a terracotta-slab was recovered from a ruined brick mound near Candra Cetī pagoda in April 1993 when the pagoda was repaired. The dimensions are – length: 22.5 cm, width: 17.5 cm and thickness: 2.5 cm[42] (Panthu Okkar 1996: 54). The lower part of the left is broken. Now it is kept in the Shwe Andaw Monastery of Ashin Kosalla in Sandoway.

Text[43]

(1) *ye dhammā hetuprabhava*
(2) *hetuṁ teṣā Tathāgato*
(3) *hyavada tesañca yo*
(4) *nirodha evaṁ vādī mahā*
(5) *sa[ma]ṇa*

24. Inscribed *Stūpa* from Selāgīri, Kyauktaw

The inscription was found at the foot of Kyauktaw Hill aka Selāgīri when an old stone *stūpa* collapsed to reveal the miniature encased inside (San Tha Aung 1979: 14). This miniature *stūpa* consists of two parts. The lower part is a square base which may be considered as a plinth. The upper part is the *stūpa* proper. This part has a square platform. Above this is a cube. The *ye dhammā gāthā* is inscribed on one of the faces of this cube, measuring 25 × 12.5 cm. The date of the inscription can be in the first half of the sixth century (Gutman 1976: 81). Now, the *stūpa* is kept at the Mahāmuni Museum in Kyauktaw, Arakan.

Text[44]

(1) *ye dharmā hetuṁprabhavā hetuṁ tesām*
(2) *Tathāgato hyavada tesañca yo nirodho*
(3) *eva[ṁ] vadī mahā śramaṇa:*

25. Inscribed *Stūpa* from Thingyaing-taung, Vesālī

According to Pamela Gutman who visited the site in 1975, this inscription was not then *in situ*. We see from a photograph at the Archaeology Department that the *ye dhammā* verse in two lines, is inscribed on the upper square base of the *stūpa*. The scripts suggest the date to be before the middle of the sixth century (Gutman 1976: 89).

Text[45]

(1) *ye dhar[mmā] hetuprabhavā hetuṁ tesaṁ Tath[ā]gāto . . .*
(2) *. . . nirodho evaṁ vādī mahā . . .*

26. Inscribed *Stūpa* from Tejarāma Monastery, MraukU

This *stūpa* may have originally come from Vesālī, like the rest of the Tejarāma collections. The inscription comprising two lines is engraved on the lower part of the *aṇḍa*. However, a portion of the first line is readable and it is the *ye dhammā gāthā*. The date can be assigned after the middle of the sixth century (Gutman 1976: 88-89).

Text[46]

(1) *ye dharmma hetuprabhava hetu* . . . . .

27. Inscribed *Stūpa* from MraukU Museum

The *ye dhammā* inscription is inscribed on the three faces of the square platforms of the *stūpa*. The dimension of each platform is 27 × 8 cm. It is now in the Archaeological Museum of MraukU, Arakan.

Text[47]

F.1
(1) *ye dhramma hetuprabhavā Tathāgato*
(2) *hetuṁ tesañca yo nirodha*
(3) . *evaṁ [vā]di mahasamaṇa*
F.2
(1) *bhagavatā stūpaṁ karoti karita*
(2) *tathā upāsaka pañciya mātā*
(3) *pitu aṭhaṅgamaṁ kṛtvā ṣa[r]vva ṣatā*
F.3
(1) *nā anatta [ra] [.]navāṁga ye*

28-29. Two Inscribed *Stūpas* from Mee-wa, Kyauktaw

The inscriptions were engraved on the one side of the upper square bases. The square base of the first inscription measures 24 × 11.5 cm while the second one measures 30 × 7 cm. These two *stūpas* are now deposited at the Rakhine State Cultural Museum in Sittwe, Arakan.

Text of the first inscription[48]

(1) *ye dharmma hetuṁ*
(2) *prabhava hetu*

Text of the second inscription[49]

(1) *ye dharmmā hetuprabhava hetu*

EARLY BUDDHISM IN ARAKAN, MYANMAR: REFLECTIONS ON THE *YE DHAMMĀ* INSCRIPTIONS

The Earliest Buddhism in Arakan

Apart from Arakanese traditions about the Buddha's visit to Arakan during his lifetime (Leider 2005), the local Burmese chronicles traditionally said that Ven. Mahā Revata came to the region of Mahimsaka Mandala to spread the Buddhism after the third Buddhist Synod (Maha Dhamma Thingyan 1925: 21). Some consider that Mahimsaka is present-day Arakan, or that Arakan was once part of Mahimsaka (Aung Tha Oo n.d.: 6). But, scholars insist that Mahimsaka was the region of Mysore in the southern part of India (Kyaw Zan Tha 1980: 19).

Above traditions trace that Buddhism arrived in Arakan in the third century BCE by means of a Buddhist missionary. However, there is no contemporary evidence for it.

An inscription discovered at the Nāgārjunakoṇḍa in the Andhra country of southern India says that the Buddhist missions were sent to the countries of Kāśmīra, Gandhāra, Cīna, Cilāta (Kirāta), Tosali, Avaraṃta, Vaṃga, Vanavāsī, Yuvana (?), Damila (?), Palura (?) and the Isle of Taṃbapaṃni (Ray 1946: 14).

This epigraph was inscribed in the fourth regnal year of King Māḍhariputa. Scholars consider him to be identical with King Māḍhariputa Śrī Virapuriśadata of the Ikṣvāku dynasty of the third century CE (Ray 1946: 14). Niharranjan Ray attempted to identify the Cilāta (Kirāta) country with the regions of Arakan and Lower Myanmar (Ray 1946: 14-18). As Nāgārjuna-koṇḍa inscription was written in the third century, the sending of the Buddhist mission must be some time before the third century. Therefore, it would not be far too wrong to conclude that Buddhism might have already arrived in Arakan in the third century CE, if the suggestion of Ray is correct.

Evidence for Buddhism in the third century CE is also found in the Ānanda Candra inscription (*c.* CE 729) of Arakan. Sircar suggested the reign of King Candrodaya of the Ānanda Candra inscription as CE 202-29 (San Tha Aung 1979: 6). In this inscription, the kings prior to Candrodaya were described as 'zealous in doing kindness to the world', 'the able', 'eminent for stoutheartedness', 'fair of form and heroic in policy' (Johnston 1944: 379). However, starting from King Candrodaya and his successors, they were said to be 'approved by the good', 'giving countless gifts', 'eminent in religious practices' and to have gone 'to heaven' (Johnston 1944: 379). In contrast with the former kings, the kings starting with Candrodaya appear to be more religious. Based on this fact, we may assume that starting with the reign of King Candrodaya in the third century CE, some kind of religion had already been introduced in Arakan (Kyaw Zan Tha 1980: 22).

A large stone slab which lies near the Ānanda Candra pillar inscription at Shitthaung Temple is probably related to the early phase of the Buddhistic introduction to Arakan. The slab is depicted in relief, a couch, a lotus flower and a *dhammacakka* (Forchhammer 1891: 20-21). Lotus flower represents the nativity and *dhammacakka* (the wheel of the law) represents the first sermon of the Buddha. Both were widely used as the symbols of Buddhism in the pre-iconic worship in India. It may be wrong but it is likely to presume that these two symbols are the earliest evidences for the coming of Buddhism to Arakan (Kyaw Zan Tha 1980: 23). Forchhammer suggests that the symbols represent the emergence of Buddhism from Brahmanism (Forchhammer 1891: 20-21).

The first concrete evidence of the existence of Buddhism in Arakan is a line of the Sanskrit inscription written in Gupta characters discovered in the complex of the Mahāmuni Shrine in Arakan. It is also the earliest inscription discovered in Arakan (Gutman 1976: 118). The inscription reads: *Yakṣasenāpati Panāda*. The writing is similar to the scripts used by Kumāragupta I of the Gupta Empire who founded the Nālandā Buddhist University (Gutman 1976: 118; Maung Pruu 1996: 61). *Yakṣasenāpati Panāda* is one of the 28 *Yakṣa* Generals led by Kubera of the *Dīgha Nikāya* of the Buddhist literature (Tun Shwe Khine 1990: 123; San Tha Aung 1979: 92). Therefore, this inscription is the first record to prove the existence of Buddhism in Arakan before the middle of the fifth century CE. Moreover, it is likely to suggest that the Mahāmuni, the famous Buddhist Shrine in Myanmar, already existed around the fifth century in Arakan (Kyaw Zan Tha 1977: 89).

BUDDHISM IN ARAKAN AS RECONSTRUCTED FROM THE *YE DHAMMĀ* INSCRIPTIONS AND OTHER INSCRIPTIONAL EVIDENCE

Much evidence for Buddhism was found in Arakan for the period after the fifth century CE. They are miniature stone *stūpas* and the *ye dhammā* inscriptions. Miniature stone *stūpas* are mostly found in the Kaladan valley area where the cities of Dhaññavatī and Vesālī flourished. Some of the miniature *stūpas* bear the *gāthā* of *ye dhammā*. According to the scripts written on the *stūpas*, it can be suggested that the miniature *stūpas* were made around the fifth and sixth centuries (San Tha Aung 1979: 14-15).

As presented in this paper, over thirty *ye dhammā* inscriptions were discovered in the whole area of Arakan. Therefore, we can suggest that Buddhism was flourishing in the whole of Arakan in the fifth and sixth centuries. Most of the inscriptions from Arakan were written in Sanskrit. In the history of Buddhism, Theravāda school never used the Sanskrit language. The *ye dhammā gāthā* of the Thinkyittaw inscription from Vesālī is identical to the Sanskrit *ye dhammā* verse of Tibetan Mss of the *Ārya-Pratītyasamutpāda sūtra* (Gutman 1976: 77-78). Moreover, the Arakanese *ye dhammā* inscriptions resemble strongly the Sanskrit votive inscriptions from Yunnan during the period of the seventh-eighth centuries (Gutman 1976: 78). It can be suggested that Buddhist missions were travelling between the countries of Arakan, East Bengal, Assam and Yunnan between the seventh and eighth centuries (Gutman 1976: 79).

There were also connections between Arakan and the Gupta Empire of northern India. The scripts used in the *ye dhammā* inscriptions of Arakan are neither Pallava nor Kadamba scripts of southern India, but Gupta scripts of the sixth century (San Tha Aung 1974). One may therefore suggest that Buddhism arrived in Arakan from the Gupta Empire during this century. Additional evidence is provided by the discovery of Gupta-type Buddha statues in Arakan (Kyaw Zan Tha 1977: 90).

After the Gupta Period, Pāla kings ruled in Bengal and Bihar between the eighth and twelfth centuries. The Nālandā University appeared during this period in Bihar. Nālandā was a well-known centre for the distribution of Buddhist texts. There are traces of connections between Arakan and India for the Pāla period. In the verse (50) of the Ānanda Candra inscription of Arakan, it is stated that: 'also books of the Holy Law have been caused to be written by the good [king] in large numbers' (Johnston 1944, 381). Some suggest that the Mahāyāna texts were copied from the Nālandā University (Kyaw Zan Tha 1977: 90). The verse (47) of the inscription also reads: 'There have been made golden and silver caityas containing images and relics of the Buddhas and Bodhisattvas and of Cunda and others. ...'

The reference to bodhisattvas in this verse shows that Mahāyāna Buddhism existed in Arakan (Johnston 1944: 371). The religious deeds of King Ānanda Candra were related to Mahāyāna and it can be suggested that there might be a relationship between Arakan and the Pāla kings of India. Many crowned Buddha images and boddhisattva statues which underwent Pāla influence were found in Arakan. They were possibly the earliest crowned Buddha images in Southeast Asia (Gutman 1976: 187). The crowned Buddha images of Vesālī, Arakan, can probably be the statues of Mahāyānist Amitābha. The ornaments such as crowns, beads, necklaces and earrings of the statues are not described in Theravāda texts. Pamela Gutman says that the characteristics of the images from Arakan are also similar to the Amitābha statues of Tibet and China (Maung Pruu 1996: 63).

Though Māhāyāna influenced Arakan, Theravāda was present then as well. A *ye dhammā* inscription from Vesālī Great Buddha image was written in Pāli language. Many other *ye dhammā* inscriptions were also written in a mixture of Pāli and Sanskrit. Verse (61) of the Ānanda Candra inscription reads:

A pulpit, an excellent cow-elephant, and brilliant robes of silk [?] have been dispatched by the king [Ānanda Candra] to the noble congregation of friars in the land of King Śilāmegha. (Johnston 1944: 382)

Scholars suggest Śilāmegha to be the title used by Sinhalese kings (Gutman 1976: 37; Than Tun 1969: 75). There may have been religious exchange between Arakan and the Theravāda country of Sri Lanka in those days already and, as a consequence, a branch of Theravāda Buddhism may also have arrived in Arakan in the seventh century (Kyaw Zan Tha 1977: 96; Maung Pruu 1996, 64). However, evidence for Theravāda Buddhism is less than for Mahāyāna Buddhism in Arakan at this time.

In conclusion, Buddhism may probably have reached Arakan during the first millennium CE in different waves, by the following routes: (1) from East Bengal and northern India by land and sea routes, (2) from south India by sea route and, (3) from Sri Lanka by sea route.

NOTES

1. The author would like to thank Ven. Paññācāra, Ven. Jayanta Bodhi, U Maung Ba Thein and U Nyein Lwin for their invaluable help during my research in Arakan. The author also gratefully acknowledges the help and advice of Bénédicte Brac de la Perrière while preparing this English version.
2. Now officially known as Rakhine State.
3. According to Tun Shwe Khine, over seventy stone inscriptions belonging to the sixth century, bearing Gupta characters and *ye dhammā* verse in full have been found at various sites in Arakan (Tun Shwe Khine 1990, 45; 1996: 9). However, as we do not get any list of those inscriptions with their localities from his sources, his data is doubtful.
4. Report of the Superintendent, Archaeological Survey, Burma (from 1901-02 to 1904-05) Report on Archaeological work in Burma, issued annually until 1926, then incorporated into *Archaeological Survey of India Annual Report* until 1947, 1947-65, Report of the Director, Archaeological Survey of Burma.
5. *A List of Archaeological Photo-Negatives of Burma* (Delhi 1935).
6. *Inscriptions of Burma* Porfolios I-V (Plates 1-609, arranged chronologically down to CE 1364 and the founding of Ava. Published by the University of Rangoon, 1933-56).
7. San Tha Aung 1974 *Scripts of Arakan, Sixth Century and Before*, p.100, gives the date of its finding as 1957. However, 'The Buddhist Art of Ancient Arakan' by the same author gives the date of recovery as 1956 (San Tha Aung 1979: 24).
8. 14.5 × 38 cm (Gutman 1976: 84). 18 × 10 × 6 inches [45 × 25 × 15 cm] (San Tha Aung 1974: 103).
9. Deciphered by D.C. Sircar (1962, 108-09).
10. Transliterated by U San Tha Aung (1974: 119).
11. 27 × 10.5 cm (Gutman 1976: 87); 12 × 7 × 5 inches [30 × 17.5 × 12.5 cm] (San Tha Aung 1974: 120).
12. Deciphered by U San Tha Aung (1974: 120).
13. 0 × 4 × 7 inches [25 × 10 × 17.5 cm] (Shwe Zan 2004: 142b).

14. Transcribed from rubbing and stone. The author's thanks go to U Nyein Lwin, Assistant Director, Department of Archaeology, MraukU for his kind permission to examine the stone inscription at the MraukU Museum in June 2006.
15. 8 × 5.5 inches [20 × 13.75 cm] (San Tha Aung 1974: 107).
16. Deciphered by U San Tha Aung (San Tha Aung 1974: 108).
17. 22 × 11 cm (Gutman 1976: 90).
18. Transliterated by Pamela Gutman (1976: 91).
19. Deciphered from Pl. LXVI of Gutman 1976.
20. Transcribed by Pamela Gutman (1976: 119).
21. Deciphered from the rubbing at Mahāmuni Buddha Vihāra Monastery in February 2005.
22. Forchhammer said that the length of the inscription is 1 foot (Forchhammer 1891, 14).
23. Deciphered by U San Tha Aung (1974: 113).
24. Transliterated by Pamela Gutman (1976: 82).
25. Announcement of the Department of Archaeology, Ministry of Culture, the Union of Myanmar. Letter No. (5712/13) dated 5 September 2005.
26. Deciphered from photograph.
27. Deciphered from the rubbing.
28. In the articles of Min Thein Zan and Saw Tun Aung, the dimensions are given as length: 23 inches, width: 9 inches, thickness (upper part) 3 inches and (lower part): 4 inches.
29. Transcribed by the late U San Tha Aung (Saw Tun Aung 1999).
30. *or ?jo* (San Tha Aung).
31. *? sattā or ? sattā* (San Tha Aung).
32. Deciphered from the stone. The author would like to express his gratitude to U Maung Ba Thein for his permission to examine and read the stone inscription in his house in December 2006.
33. *Archaeological Survey of India Annual Report,* yearly from 1902-03 to 1936-37.
34. Deciphered from pl. 18 of San Tha Aung 1974.
35. 7 × 5.5 × 1 inches [17.5 × 13.75 × 2.5 cm] (San Tha Aung 1974: 114).
36. U San Tha Aung states that the inscription is kept in Calcutta Museum (San Tha Aung 1974: 114).
37. Deciphered by E.H. Johnston (1944: 383).
38. Transliterated by Pamela Gutman (1976: 93).
39. Panthu Okkar gives the dimensions as length: 16 inches, width: 10 inches and thickness: 2 inches.
40. Cf. the first inscription of this article.
41. Transcribed from the stone. The author is grateful to Ven. Kosalla of Shwe Andaw Monastery, Sandoway, Arakan, for his kind permission to examine and photograph this inscription and another one from Candra Cetī in April 2002.
42. Panthu Okkar gives the dimensions as length: 9 inches, width: 7 inches and thickness: 1 inch.
43. Deciphered from the terracotta-slab. The author would like to thank Ven. Kosalla of Shwe Andaw Monastery, Sandoway.
44. Deciphered by Pamela Gutman (1976: 81).
45. Transliterated by Pamela Gutman (1976: 89).
46. Deciphered from Pl. XXI of Gutman 1976.

47. Transcribed from the rubbing and stone *stūpa*. The author's thanks go to U Nyein Lwin, Assistant Director, MraukU Archaeological Museum, for his permission to read the inscription of the *stūpa* in April 2005.
48. Deciphered by Pamela Gutman (1976: 83).
49. Ibid.

REFERENCES

ASB, 1958-59, *Report of the Director, Archaeological Survey of Burma.* Rangoon: Office of the Director, Government Printing.
——, 1959-60, *Report of the Director, Archaeological Survey of Burma.* Rangoon: Office of the Director, Government Printing.
Aung Tha Oo, 1966, *Rakhuiṅ yañkye: mhu Vesālī khet.* Rangoon: Aung Yadanar Press.
——, n.d., *Buddha sāsanā nhaṅ. Rakhuiṅ Prañ* (typed manuscript).
Forchhammer, E., 1891, *Report on Antiquities of Arakan.* Rangoon: The Archaeology Department, Burma.
Fryer, G.E., 1879, *Proceedings of the Asiatic Society of Bengal.* 201-02.
Gutman, P., 1976, 'Ancient Arakan, with Special Reference to its Cultural History between the Fifth and Eleventh Centuries' (Ph.D. thesis), Canberra: Australian National University, http://thesis.anu.edu.au/public/adt-ANU20050901112732/index.html.
——, 2001, *Burma's Lost Kingdoms: Splendors of Arakan,* Hong Kong: Orchid Press.
Gutman, P., B. Hudson, Kyaw Minn Htin and Kyaw Tun Aung 2007, 'Rock Art and Artisans in the Lemro Valley, Arakan', *Antiquity* 81 (313): 655-74.
Hudson, B., 2005, *Ancient Geography and Recent Archaeology: Dhanyawadi, Vesali and Mrauk-u* (The Forgotten History of Arakan Conference), Bangkok: Chulalongkorn University.
Johnston, E.H. 1944, 'Some Sanskrit inscriptions of Arakan.' *BSOAS* 21: 357-85.
Kyaw Zan Tha, 1977, Khet-ū: Rakhuiṅ Prañ sui. Buddha sāsanā rokrhi pran.nhaṁ. puṁ. *Rakhine* 4: 88-96.
——, 1980, 'Buddhism in Arakan before Yedhamma.' *Rakhine Tazaung* 16: 20-24.
Leider, J., 2005, 'Lord Buddha comes to Arakan: Relics, Statues and Predictions.' (unpublished manuscript).
Maha Dhamma Thingyan, 1925, *Sāsanā Laṅkāra Cātam,* Rangoon: Hamsavati Press.
Maung Ba Thein, 1987, 'Mhattam: taṅkrasamhya Vesālī khet athok athā myā:.' *Rakhine Yinkyaymhu* 1: 56-59.
——, 1994, 'Pokto mrui. nay mha Vesālī khet athok athā myā:,' *Rakhine Nyuntphu* 2: 60-64.
Maung Pruu, 1996, 'Edī 5 rācu atwaṅ:ka Rakhuiṅ Prañ rok Buddha sāsanā', *Rakhine Thahaya* 2: 59-64.
Min Thein Zan, 1997, 'Man:prā: mrui. nay mha Vesālī khet athok athā myā:', *Rakhine Nyuntphu* 4: 89-107.
——, 2003, *Rakhuiṅ Catūpā kyok cetī ṅay myā:.* Yangon: Publishers of Eminent Arakanese Literature.
Mya, U., 1961a, *Rhe: hoṅ: utkhwak ruppwā: chaṅ:tu tau myā:* vol. 1, Rangoon: University of Rangoon Press.
——, 1961b, *Rhe: hoṅ: utkhwak ruppwā: chaṅ:tu tau myā:* vol. 2, Rangoon: University of Rangoon Press.
Nai Pan Hla, 1998, *Sutesana cāpe myā:,* Yangon: Mhway Sarpay.
Ni Min Shin, 2003, 'Vesālī khet ye dhammā gāthā myā:', *Rakhine* 25: 30-37.

Nyunt Han, 1984, 'Vesālī mrui.hoṅ: le.lākhyak' (Departmental Report), Rangoon: Department of Archaeology.

Panthu Okkar, 1996, 'Yaṅkye:mhu ratanā amrute', *Rakhine Tazaung* 19: 51-55.

RSPC, 1984, *Rakhine State Gazetteers*, vol. 5, Sittwe: Rakhine State Peoples' Council.

Rakhine Thahaya Athin, 2006, 'Vesālī khet abhaya mudra muni kre: chaṅ:tutau.' *Rakhine Thahaya* 7: 32-33.

Ray, N., 1936, *Sanskrit Buddhism in Burma*, Amsterdam: H.J. Paris.

——, 1946, *An Introduction to the Study of Theravāda Buddhism in Burma*. Calcutta: University of Calcutta.

San Tha Aung, 1974, *Edī khrok rācu nhan, yaṅ: matuiṅ mī Rakhuiṅ Prañ suṁ: akkharā.* Rangoon: Ohnmar Aung.

——, 1979, *The Buddhist Art of Ancient Arakan*. Rangoon: Daw Saw Saw.

Saw Tun Aung, 1999, 'Kyin: toṅ tau cetī kyokcā,' *Kyein Yeik Myay* 3: 39-40.

Shwe Zan, 2004, *The Golden Mrauk-U, An Ancient Capital of Rakhine*. Yangon: U Shwe Zan (2nd edn.).

Sircar, D.C., 1962, 'Inscriptions of Chandras of Arakan', *Epigraphia Indica* 32: 103-09.

Than Tun, 1969, *Khethoṅ: Mranmā rājawaṅ*, Rangoon: Maha Dagon.

Tun Shwe Khine, 1990, *Rakhuiṅ Vesālī khet Buddha anu paññā*. Yangon: Sitthitaw.

——, 1996, 'The Latest Discoveries of Buddhist Sculptures', *Rakhine Tazaung* 19: 8-11.

20

Hindu Deities in Southern Vietnam: Images on Small Archaeological Artefacts

Le Thi Lien

INTRODUCTION

From the end of the nineteenth century and more often in the early part of the twentieth century, remains of ancient Oc Eo culture have been discovered by French scholars in southern Vietnam. Many of these artefacts are Hindu sculptures (Malleret 1959). A number of deity images were also found from surveys and excavations conducted by the Vietnamese since then (Le Xuan Diem et al. 1995: 284-328; Dao Linh Con 1997: 673; Bui Phat Diem et al. 2001). So far, around 200 sculptures and fragments have been found from various archaeological sites in various topographical areas and datable to long chronological time periods. Despite the rich variety of types of sculpture, the Hindu pantheon is only represented by a few gods and goddesses. We mainly meet with images of Vishnu and *Shivalinga*, and fewer images of Ganesha, Surya, Brahma, or the goddesses Mahishasuramardini and Lakshmi. Only a few images of Shiva and Harihara were found, though a number of fragments make it difficult to identify the iconographical feature of gods and goddesses. We can nevertheless say that these stone sculptures are simple in character and may have played an important role in a somewhat impoverished Hindu pantheon (Le Thi Lien 2006a: 198-204, 209).

On the contrary, a large number of tiny artefacts, particularly gold plaques, appear to represent a much richer number of Hindu deities and more complex iconographic features. In order to provide a reliable source for the study of Hindu iconography and of the beliefs of the ancient people in southern Vietnam, the gold plaques found *in situ* in the architectural remains are focused on in this paper.

There are several problems that prevent us from clearly identifying and classifying the whole collection at this stage of our study. Some of the important sites have been excavated a long time ago and it is difficult to make an eye-observation of the real artefacts or to identify clearly the images from the photographs. Archaeological reports of the most recent excavations are also in process of preparation, which make it difficult to see the whole picture of one site or a group of sites. Finally, tiny gold plaques and foils, together with other related artefacts, are too numerous (more than 900) to be included in this paper. Therefore, results presented here are mainly from collections found in the sites of Go Thap (Dong Thap province) and Cat Tien (Lam Dong province), with some others from Da Noi (An Giang province).

SELECTED COLLECTIONS IN CONTEXT OF THEIR ARCHITECTURAL REMAINS

The archaeological context of the gold plaques found in southern Vietnam has been discussed here and there. Most of them have been identified as temple deposits, used in religious rituals (Le Thi Lien 2005: 145-54). The collections on which I will focus in this paper have been unearthed from three important sites in various areas of southern Vietnam (Fig. 20.1).

The Go Thap Site

The site of Go Thap (also known as Prasat Pream Loven, Chua Nam Gian or Thap Muoi) is located in Thap Muoi village, Tan Kieu commune, Thap Muoi district, Dong Thap province (11° 78'2" North and 111° 98'4" East). The role of this site in the Oc Eo Culture has been defined not only by the scale of its distribution but also by the characteristics of unearthed artefacts (Le Thi Lien 2006b: 232-44). Of these, the gold plaques found in the architectural ruins during excavations from 1984 to 1998 have exposed the earliest features of Hindu iconography (Le Thi Lien 2006a: 131-42) (Fig. 20.2).

The Da Noi Site

The site of Da Noi covers an area of 1500 × 1000 m in the low fields of Hoa Tay B hamlet, Phu Hoa Commune, Thoai Son district, An Giang province. The 1985 excavation unearthed seven structural remains that contain 331 small artefacts, including 317 gold plaques. Many of them are engraved with

FIGURE 20.1
Location of Da Noi, Go Thap and Cat Tien sites in Southern Vietnam

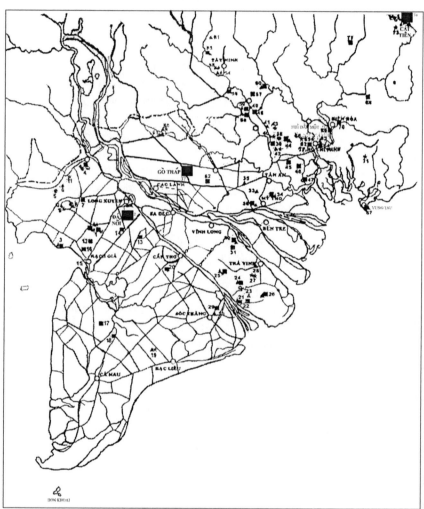

images and symbols related to Hindu beliefs (Le Xuan Diem et al. 1995: 30-33; Dao Linh Con 1995: 40-47).

The Cat Tien Site

The name has been assigned to a group of 12 architectural remains found in the Quang Ngai commune, Cat Tien district, Lam Dong province. The site was discovered in 1985. The excavations conducted in this area during 1994-97 and 2001-02 have unearthed important vestiges of Hindu temples

FIGURE 20.2
GT93.M1, Go Thap site, Architectural remain containing gold plaques
(Drawing: Bui Xuan Long)

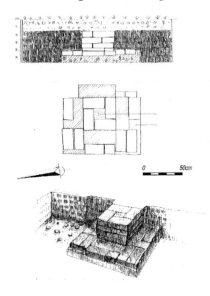

and related artefacts (Le Dinh Phung 2006; Bui chi Hoang 2004: 319-70). The gold plaques found from the foundation of these sites provide the most important source for the study of Hindu iconography in the highland area of southern Vietnam. Collections of gold plaques from several architectural remains of the mounds Go 1, Go 2 and Go 6 are analysed in this paper.

The mound **Go 1** (also called as Doi Khi – Monkey Mound) is the biggest and most important mound at Cat Tien complex site. The site G1A contains the foundation of the main collapsed temple, situated in the top northern part of the mound. A huge stone *Shivalinga* has been unearthed in this area (Fig. 20.3). The foundation of the temple has been unearthed in 1996, and has a square plan of 12 × 12 m. From the bottom of a central brick block built under the foundation, 166 artefacts have been unearthed, including mainly gold plaques. Out of these artefacts, 25 pieces have images of gods and goddesses, 5 pieces have images of the conch/*shankha*, 7 pieces have image of lotuses, 3 pieces are in lotus shape, 4 are small *lingas*, and another 25 are rings. Many other gold plaques and their fragments have no images. The way these artefacts are arranged point towards a typical Hindu temple construction ceremony (Le Dinh Phung 2006: 49-50).

Go 2A is one of four architectural remains that occupied the area of about 2000 m square on mound Go 2, which is located in the even and flat valley of the Cat Tien site complex. The foundation of the temple is square in plan, measuring 7.8 × 7.8 m, under which a brick block was constructed, in the

FIGURE 20.3
Shivalinga from G1A, Cat Tien. Photo: Le Thi Lien

central part. At the bottom of this brick block was found a hollow square that contained 109 gold plaques and 9 fragments of coloured stones. Although a smaller number of artefacts was found, in comparison with the G1A site, a larger proportion are decorated with images of god, goddess and symbols (Le Dinh Phung 2006: 88-130).

Mound Go 6 is a low hillock situated on the northern bank of the Dong Nai River. The excavation in 2003 unearthed the vestiges of three architectural remains, named Go 6A, Go 6B and Go 6C. From two rectangular foundations of these architectural remains, Go 6A and Go 6B, a number of deposited artefacts, mainly gold plaques, have been unearthed.

In the centre part of the foundation of Go 6A, a brick block was unearthed, measuring 3.3 m in height, constructed with 33 brick courses. At the bottom of the square hollow in the brick block, 90 artefacts were recovered, including gold and silver artefacts, fragments of semi-precious stone and glass. They are arranged in a typical way: in the middle of the bottom surface, there is an oval silver box. The cover of the box is decorated with the image of a lion in repose. Surrounding the box, there are small *lingas* made of silver and gold, plain round rings and gold plaques, many of which are incised with figures of gods and goddesses, and secret animals (Le Dinh Phung 2006: 177). In June 2006, 50 artefacts of Go 6A have been studied by the present writer. They include mainly gold plaques, fragments of stone and glass and several plain golden rings. Among these artefacts, there are 12 gold plaques engraved with Hindu images.

In the same mount Go 6, under the foundation of the brick temple Go 6B, at the depth of 1.5 m, 3 pottery boxes and 1 silver box, all in the forms of *Shivalingas* were unearthed; they contained smaller iron, bronze, silver, gold and possibly ivory *lingas* respectively. In addition, 3 gold rings and 20 gold plaques, 10 of which bear inscriptions, were also found (Dao Linh Con 2004).

The large number of Hindu images in the above collections provides rich and useful data for the study of Hindu deities in southern Vietnam.

THE PRESENTATION OF HINDU DEITIES ON GOLD PLAQUES

Although a large number of images and symbols were unearthed from the mentioned sites, not all Hindu gods and goddesses, mainly represented by symbols and their incarnations can be identified clearly, due to the small size of the gold pieces, the shallow lines of the drawing or the lack of iconographical indication (Dao Linh Con 1995; Le Thi Lien 2005: 145-54; 2006a: 131-44).

Shiva in Various Forms

There are almost no Shiva images in human form found from the sites in lower Mekong delta. Among his emblems and vehicle, *Shivalingas* in phallic form have been found from Go Thap site (Dong Thap province) (Le Thi Lien 2006a: 138, Fig. 125, 126). Despite the presence of several sculptures of tiny *Shivalingas* in the temple deposits found from Cat Tien, very few image of this symbol appear on the gold plaques, whereas some images of him in other aspects have been identified.

One image from Go 1A probably represents Shiva as *Maheshvara*, Supreme God of creation, protection and destruction. He has 5 heads, 6 arms and 6 legs. One of his left hands is in *varada* pose, another left hand is resting on the left thigh, and the third left hand may hold an object, which is unclear. His three right hands seem to hold objects that are unclear. His two front legs are in *yogasana* posture, the others are stretched freely. His matted hair is not clearly seen (Fig. 20.4).

Another piece in the same collection represents an image of the god flanked by two consorts. The god is seated in a *lilasana* posture, pot bellied, wearing round earrings. His left consort holds in her two hands the *akshamala* (rosary of beads) and a mirror. She has full breasts and rather big hips. This may be an image of Shiva accompanied by Parvati and Bhu (Fig. 20.5). A similar scene also appears in the north side of Dashavatara temple, Deogarh, India (Harle 1974: Fig. 104).

One piece in Go 1A represents an image of a god in a standing posture. He is holding an object that is possibly a *vina* (musical instrument). This is probably Shiva in *Vinadhara-dakshinamurti*, as a great teacher of music. The

FIGURE 20.4
Shiva as *Maheshvara*, G1A, Cat Tien (Photo: Nguyen Tien Dong)

FIGURE 20.5
Shiva (with Parvati and Bhu ?) (Photo: Nguyen Tien Dong)

presentation of this image with its details seems to be close to the description of G. Rao, following the *Kamikagama*: '. . . The *vina* should be held at the top by the left hand and by the right hand at the lower end; the resonating body of the instrument should rest on the right thigh. The lower right hand should be manipulating the strings of the instrument . . .', '. . . The face of *dakshinamurti* should be turned towards the hand held in the *sandarshana mudra* (pose); also the gaze of the god may be fixed on this hand' (Rao 1916: 290). The differences in posture, standing rather than sitting, and the form of the *vina* create some doubts regarding the meaning of this image (Fig. 20.6). In comparison with another image on a potsherd, one can also see a big difference in the form of the *vina* (Le Thi Lien 1998: 696-98).

From the temple deposit in Go 2A, several images are supposedly identified as various forms of Shiva. One piece probably describes a god sitting on a Meru mountain base. He has a heavy belly and wears a round-top hat. His left hand stretches straight in the *danda* pose, the right hand holds an object (a *gada/ akshamala* or a fire?) (Fig. 20.7). This may be the image of *Dakshinamurti Shiva* (Rao 1916: 274; Gupte 1980: Pl. XIII, 75). However, iconographical features might have been simplified.

An image of Shiva may also be recognised from other pieces. The god is seated on the ground, crossed legs to the left, the right hand rests on the ground, and the left hand holds a *vajra* (Fig. 20.8).

One piece from the same collection of Go 2A represents image of a god seated on a chariot, of which only one side and a wheel are visible. His right hand holds an unclear object (lotus?); the left hand is folded and rests on the back. Although simply represented, the god seems to be seated on a fast moving chariot (Fig. 20.9). The iconographical features of the image cannot be identified with certainty. This scene may describe the story of Shiva in *Tripurantakamurti*, removing the three castles of the *asuras*. In one of the sculptural forms, he is represented as driving a chariot. In several sculptures from the Dashavatara cave, Kailasha temple (Ellora) and Conjeevaram, the chariot is seen in motion (Rao 1916: 169, Pls. XXXVII-XXXIX). However, the dots, which seem to be emphasised around the head of the god and the

FIGURE 20.6	**FIGURE 20.7**
Shiva in *Vinadhara-dakshinamurti*	Shiva in *Vinadhara-dakshinamurti*,
(Photo: Le Thi Lien)	G2A, Cat Tien (Photo: Le Thi Lien)

FIGURE 20.8
Shiva image?, G2A, Cat Tien
(Photo: Le Thi Lien)

FIGURE 20.9
Shiva in *Tripurantakamurti*, or Surya?,
G2A, Cat Tien (Photo: Le Thi Lien)

lotus of the sample from Go 2A, probably indicate also the character of the Sun god *Surya*.

Another piece from the same collection provides a problematic image. We can see a god sitting on a plain pedestal. His two legs are crossed, two hands hold unidentified objects, which may be a sword or spear in the left hand. There are two vertical lines connected to the pedestal part. On the tops of these lines, there are several details that cannot be identified clearly (Fig. 20.10). This image may recall the scene of Shiva in *Gajasurasamharamurti* similar to that from Cave 16 (Kailasha), Ellora, Virupaksha temple, Pattadakal (Gupte 1980: 43-44, Pl. VIII).

Vishnu and his Incarnations

The incarnations of Vishnu in the forms of Matsya, Varaha and Kurma *avataras* are most frequently observed in Go Thap and Da Noi sites (Le Thi Lien 2005: 149-51, 2006a: 131-33). They are represented in very simple forms on the gold plaques found from the Go Thap site (Fig. 20.11b, c, d). The more developed and combined forms are represented on their counterparts from Da Noi site (Fig. 20.12b, c). Different mythical stories seem to have been told at Cat Tien sites. We almost meet with no image of Varaha in the posture of uplifting the Earth goddess. The presence of Kurma together with various animals and objects seems to indicate mainly the complicated ritual of the temple construction and the presence of many gods and goddesses, rather than simply the incarnation of Vishnu.

FIGURE 20.10
Shiva in *Gajasurasamharamurti*, G2A, Cat Tien (Photo: Le Thi Lien)

FIGURE 20.11
Images of Vishnu and his incarnations, Go Thap site
(Photo: Le Thi Lien, drawings: Nguyen Dang Cuong)

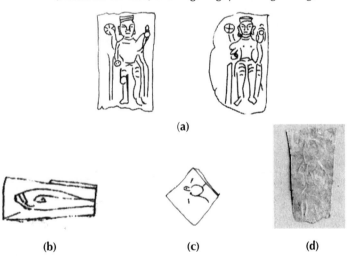

Several Vishnu images in human forms are found from Go Thap, Da Noi and Cat Tien site. Main iconographical features of his image from Go Thap and Da Noi are in standing posture and having 4 hands (Figs. 20.11a, 20.12a). They represent similar postures as seen from stone sculptures (Le Thi Lien 2006a: 131, H213, 214).

Some images found from Cat Tien are noteworthy for their iconographical features. There is only one piece from Go 6A in Cat Tien area that represents

FIGURE 20.12
Images of Vishnu and his incarnations, Da Noi site (Photos: Le Xuan Diem)

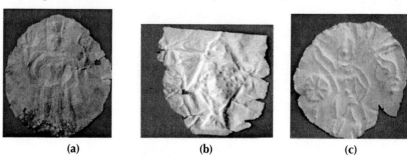

(a)　　　　　　　(b)　　　　　　　(c)

a two-handed Vishnu image in standing posture. The symbols in his hands are not clear: they may be a round disc in the right hand and a conch in the left hand. One piece from Go 1A (Fig. 20.13) represents an image of a four-handed Vishnu riding on Garuda. The upper right hand holds a *shankha* (conch); the upper left hand holds a lotus-like wheel. Two lower hands seem to hold the *danda* (staff). He is wearing a *kirita mukuta* (cylindrical crown) and round earrings. Garuda is in human form having wide-stretched wings and bird-like legs. Another piece from Go 2A represents a four-handed Vishnu riding on Garuda, the semi-god bird. Two front hands are not very clear. The back right hand holds an ornamented *chakra*, the wheel; the back left hand holds a *shankha*, the conch. He is wearing *kirita mukuta* and earrings. The garment is unclearly represented. Garuda is in human form. The third image, from the site Go 6A, although in a very simple line-engraving technique, presents the same form of Vishnu.

One image from Go 6A (Fig. 20.14) poses many difficulties. It represents a god riding on a human-like figure, holding a round object in his right hand and an unclear one in his left hand. The eyes are represented by dots. The hands and legs are without details. The head of the human figure, which is slightly turned to the left, seems not to be human. This may be an image of Vishnu, or of Nirruti, the god of the south-western direction.

Brahma

Very few images of Brahma can be clearly recognised from temple deposits. Two pieces from site Go 1A are noteworthy. The first piece represents the image of a god seated on a lotus base, holding a lotus bud in his left hands, a rosary of beads (*akshamala*) in his right hand. He wears a high *mukuta*. His three faces are visible. This image may be a representation of Brahma (Fig. 20.15). The second piece represents an image of a god holding

FIGURE 20.13
Vishnu image, G1A, Cat Tien
(Photo: Le Thi Lien)

FIGURE 20.14
Vishnu or Nirruti ?, G6A, Cat Tien
(Photo: Le Thi Lien)

unidentified objects and riding on a swan (*hamsa*). The presence of his mount indicates his status as god Brahma.

Surya

Although many symbols appeared in the deposits of various sites in the low lands of the Mekong Delta, it is difficult to identify the presence of god Surya. However, at least 3 clear images have been found in the Cat Tien sites. Two pieces from Go 1A represent the god Surya riding on his chariot, holding lotus buds in his hands. He wears a type of two-storeyed *mukuta* and round earrings. Two round objects on the two sides may be the representation of a two-wheel chariot. Only one horse pulling the chariot is visible with the front legs and head (Fig. 20.16). The image found from Go 6A represents the same icon features, but in a minimal line-engraving style.

Kubera

Due to the lack of iconographical indication, it is difficult to identify the image of Kubera. One piece from Go 2A represents a god seated in ease, pot bellied, right hand resting on the right knee, left hand resting on the ground. He is wearing a round-top crown. A node of the lower garment is visible. Although typical symbols are absent, the pot-belly of the god points to Kubera (Fig. 20.17).

FIGURE 20.15
Brahma, Go 1A, Cat Tien site
(Photo: Le Thi Lien)

FIGURE 20.16
Surya, Go 1A, Cat Tien site
(Photo: Le Thi Lien)

Ganesha

The image of Ganesha on gold plaques is almost absent in the lower Mekong Delta. From Cat Tien site, there is only one plaque from the ruins of temple Go2A that represents an image of Ganesha in a seating pose. His left hand holds an object that cannot be identified clearly (Fig. 20.18).

Karttikeya

From Go 2A, an image of Karttikeya/Subrahmanya seating on his peacock mount can be recognised. His left hand may be resting on his hip; the right hand is holding a *danda* (staff) (Fig. 20.19). This may be the third mode of sculpture representation of Karttikeya, in the *katyavalambita* pose (Rao 1916, vol. II: 425). His face and body are represented as a young man. However,

FIGURE 20.17
Kubera, Go 1A, Cat Tien site
(Photo: Le Thi Lien)

FIGURE 20.18
Ganesha, Go 2A, Cat Tien site
(Photo: Le Thi Lien)

details of the garment and colour cannot be seen here (Rao 1916: 433). His image can also be identified in another piece from Go 2A.

The Goddesses

Images of Lakshmi appear frequently, in several forms. Symbols of the goddess, such as the lotus, the kendi, or a lotus branch inserted into a vase, are often represented in gold plaques found at the Go Thap and Da Noi sites, whereas her human form appears more often in the collections of temple deposits found from the sites of Cat Tien. One piece from G1A represents an image of Lakshmi in standing posture, holding two lotus buds in her hands, wearing a pointed-top crown, and a long and broad garment. The second layer of a short garment is visible, wrapped around her hip and rolled in the front. She wears ear-rings and a necklace. On the back of her head, there is a round halo, similar to that of Vishnu, Indra and Surya (Fig. 20.20).

Using a technique of line-engraving rather than embossment, the images of Lakshmi found at Go 2A represent a very delicate female beauty. Two pieces found from this temple structure represent the same image of a goddess sitting on a *padmasana* (lotus base). Her two hands hold lotus buds. The base is in the form of a full-blown lotus, having large petals. Despite the small size, the lines of her neck and the earrings are still visible. This is certainly a representation of Mahalakshmi (Fig. 20.21). From site Go 6A, a similar image of Lakshmi is also found. The *padmasana* is seen with larger number of lotus petals.

FIGURE 20.19
Karttikeya, Go 2A, Cat Tien site
(Photo: Le Thi Lien)

FIGURE 20.20
Lakshmi, Go 1A, Cat Tien
site (Photo: Le Thi Lien)

Some other types of the goddesses are present. In the collection of Go 1A, several images of goddesses seated in different postures and holding lotuses or other objects in their hands may be representations of the consorts of the main gods in the Hindu pantheon, such as Parvati, related to Shiva, or Lakshmi, related to Vishnu (Fig. 20.22).

One example from Go 2A is noteworthy. The goddess is sitting with thighs widely opened. Among the objects in her hands, only a lotus in her left hand is identifiable. She is wearing a round-top crown and earrings. Her breasts are heavy, having two lower lines, which indicate the maturity of motherhood. The image of another goddess is presented in a beautiful sitting pose. Her two thighs turning to the right, the right hand holds a half blown lotus-like object, the left hand is resting on the ground. In addition to the usual round-top crown and earrings, her lower garment is clearly visible, having horizontal folds. The simple lines represent the slender body, full of vitality of a young woman. Although her precise name cannot be determined, she may be the consort of Vishnu. (Fig. 20.23)

An interesting image of the river goddess comes from the site Go 2A, Cat Tien. Her hands and emblems are not clear and only the upper part of her body is visible. Her character can be determined mainly by the lower part of her body, which represents a river with wavy lines (Fig. 20.24). This image recalls the scene showing the descent of the river goddess Ganga in Indian art.

Other images that do not follow the classical canons of iconography need more research to be identified.

FIGURE 20.21
Lakshmi, Go 2A, Cat Tien site
(Photo: Le Thi Lien)

FIGURE 20.22
Goddess, Go 1A, Cat Tien site
(Photo: Le Thi Lien)

FIGURE 20.23
Goddess, Go 2A, Cat Tien site
(Photo: Le Thi Lien)

FIGURE 20.24
River goddess, Go 2A, Cat Tien site
(Photo: Le Thi Lien)

The Dikpalakas

While studying the inscriptions appearing on gold plaques from the collection unearthed in the site Go 6B (Cat Tien), Michael Witzel has recognized the whole set of names of the Dikpalakas, the gods of directions. These names are written in late Brahmi script, in south Indian style. Their names and nature have been identified as:

1. Vaishravana (or Kubera) residing in the northern direction
2. Ishana residing in the north-eastern direction
3. Indra residing in the eastern direction
4. Agni residing in the south-eastern direction
5. Yama residing in the southern direction
6. Nirruti (or Surya) residing in the south-western direction
7. Varuna residing in the western direction
8. Vayu residing in the north-western direction

In addition, two other pieces with the words *Brahma* and *Vedi*, and pieces bearing the images of the tortoise, snake and bull, represent a complete Hindu *mandala*, linked to beliefs and practices in Shaiva temple architecture (Witzel and Le Thi Lien 2007).

Interestingly, various images unearthed in other collections from Go 1A, Go 2A and Go 6A in Cat Tien also bear representations of the Dikpalakas in human form (Fig. 20.25).

FIGURE 20.25
The Dikpala images, G1A, Cat Tien (Photos: Le Thi Lien)

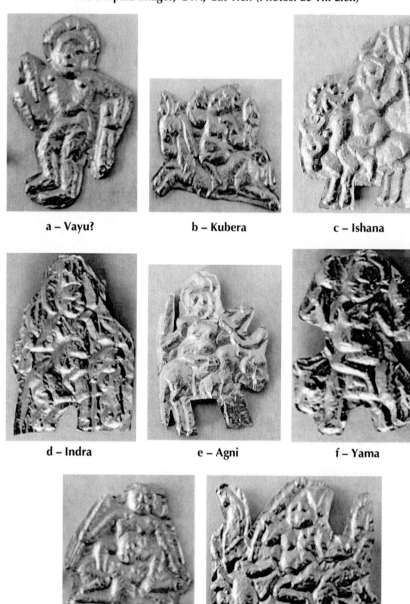

a – Vayu?   b – Kubera   c – Ishana

d – Indra   e – Agni   f – Yama

g – Nirruti   h – Varuna

Vaishravana (or Kubera)

Two images from Go 1A and Go 2A can be identified as Kubera. One piece from Go 1A represents image of a god riding on a horse. He seems to hold a lotus bud (?) in the right hand and an unidentified object in the left hand. The god is pot-bellied, wearing a *jata mukuta* and round earrings. The horse is in running posture (Fig. 20.25-b). The feature of the pot belly makes him identifiable as Kubera, one of the Dikpalakas of the north direction (Gupte 1980: 105).

Ishana

So far, there is only one piece from Go 1A identified as image of Ishana. He is holding a *vajra* and a rosary, and is riding on Nandi. In front of him, there is an object that most probably is a skull. This seems to indicate both benign and terrific aspects of the god (Fig. 20.25-c).

Indra

Three images of this god have been identified from Go 1A, Go 2A and Go 6A. One piece in Go 1A represents an image of God Indra riding on Airavata (the elephant). His right hand holds a double *vajra*. The left hand is stretching out above the head of the elephant. He wears a *kirita mukuta* with a round nimbus behind the head. He and his mount seem to be draped in fine garment and ornaments (Fig. 20.25-d).

In another piece in Go 6A, above the head of the god, there is an object resembling a coconut tree. T.G. Rao describes Indra as holding *shakti* and *ankusha*. These do not appear clearly in these gold plaques. In some cases, Indra may hold the *nilotpala* flower (Rao 1916: 519-20).

Agni

Two images of Agni seem to be present in the collections from Go 1A and Go 2A. The image from Go 1A represents Agni (?) holding a sword in his right hand; the left hand is unclear. He is riding on Nandi. In front of him, there seems to be a skull. His bulging eyes and probably two faces indicate the terrific form (Fig. 20.25-e). Images of two-headed Agni are found in the Shiva temples at Kandiyur, Travancore and Chidambaram (Rao 1916: Pl. CLII, CLIII, Fig. 20.2). The second image from Go 2A represents the image of a god sitting on an animal. The god is wearing a *jata mukuta*, and his right hand holds a trident adorned with dots. There may be another object in the same hand, which is unidentifiable. The left hand rests on the back of the animal and holds an unclear object. This may be the image of Agni riding on his ram (*mesha*).

Yama

Two images of Yama seem to be present in the collections of Go 1A and Go 2A. One image from Go 1A represents a god sitting on the buffalo. He has a pot-belly and holds two lotus buds in his hands. Such artefacts do not appear frequently appear in the iconographical descriptions of Yama (Fig. 20.25-f). The image from Go 2A represents a god sitting on the bull/buffalo (?). He holds a sword or staff in the right hand; the left hand is stretching out.

Nirruti (or Surya)

If the identification of this god is correct, the image of Nirruti appears most often, in comparison with other Dikpalakas. About six images of him have been identified from sites Go 1A, Go 2A and Go 6A. Two pieces from Go 1A represents images of Nirruti riding on a man (*nara*). He is wearing round earrings and has an ill-looking presentation: erect hair, gaping mouth, exposed teeth. . . . He holds a *danda* in the right hand, the left hand is stretched down. His vehicle, the *nara* (man), is sitting in *paryankasana* (Fig. 20.25-g). Although not all the details can be represented, the image fits rather well with the description of T.G. Rao (1916: 527-28, Pl. CLIV, Fig. 2).

From the site Go 2A, three images are found. Two of them represent images of a god sitting on a lion. The first image has a heavy belly; the left hand rests on the left thigh, the right hand holds a weapon (*shakti?*). He wears a round-top crown and a kind of *sampot*, of which only the nodes of the waist bell are visible. The other image has the right hand holding an oblong object. The left hand is resting on the waist. No objects can be observed in the hands. These may be images of Nirruti riding on a *bhadrapitha* (lion base) (Rao ibid.: 528).

The image of Nirruti from Go 6A is seen probably holding a long *danda* (staff) in his left hand, mounting his *nara* figure. The *nara* is very sketchily engraved.

Varuna

About 3 images are probably identified as Varuna from sites Go 1A and Go 6A. One piece from Go 1A represents the god riding on a sea-monster (*makara*). His right hand holds a *pasha* (noose). His left hand seems to be in the *abhaya* pose. The second piece from the same collection represents the god holding a long staff-like object in the right hand and a big lotus bud (?)

in the left hand. He is riding on a *makara*-like mount, having four legs and a long tail (Fig. 20.25-h). The animal and the pointed hat of the god remind the image of the Varuna from cave 16 (Kailasha), Ellora (Gupte ibid.: 95, Pl. XVII).

One image from Go 6A can only be identified by his vehicle, a *makara*; the hands and symbols are not clear. The god may hold a *pasha* in the right hand, as described by Rao (1916: 529).

Vayu

One piece found from Go 1A represents a standing God, wearing round ear-rings, holding a staff and a fly whisk (Fig. 20.25-a). The image seems to fit with the description of Vayu as the guardian of the north-west direction (Rao 1916: 532-33).

Groups of Gods and Goddesses

From the collection of Go 2A, six gold plaques represented the gods and/or goddesses in groups. The tiny size of the artefacts and unclear iconographical details make it difficult to identify their name and nature. However, one can see all of them are seated in a relaxed posture, the left hand resting on the ground/base; the right hand rests on the right knee. The number of images on each piece are 4, 7, 8, 9, 11, and 12 respectively. Detailed identification of these images needs further investigation; we may, however, think of these as the groups of the Saptamatrikas (the seven mother goddesses), the eight semi-god Vasus, the nine planets (Nava-grahas), the eleven Sadhyas, the semi-gods of light, the twelve Adityas, that correspond to the twelve months of the year. At this stage of my study, I have found no explanation for the first group with four images (Fig. 20.26).

Other Images

It is noteworthy that many images have not yet been identified clearly. Several unidentified images of gods in various postures have been found from the sites of Da Noi M2, Da Noi M3, Da Noi M4 (An Giang province), of whom the symbols cannot be recognised clearly (Fig. 20.27). Whereas, there are many images from the sites of Go 1A, Go 2A, Go 6A (Cat Tien), whose emblems may have been simplified or suppressed. At least twenty images seating in ease have been found in the collection of site Go 2A. The letter *ma* appears on the side of some images. Further study on these images may provide interesting information on the beliefs and practices of the followers of Hindu deities in these temples.

FIGURE 20.26
Group of gods, G1A, Cat Tien (Photo: Nguyen Tien Dong)

FIGURE 20.27
Image of god, Da Noi site (Photo: Le Xuan Diem)

ART CHARACTERISTICS AND CHRONOLOGY

From the selected collections, it is clear that each area possesses its own artistic characteristics; all, however, share strong common beliefs in Hinduism. Images on gold plaques found from architectural remains in Go Thap site are very clumsily and sketchily represented. They are mainly the symbols of Hindu deities, which seem to be the early product of Hindu art in the region. Phallic forms of Shiva, incarnations of Vishnu in the form of Varaha, Kurma and Matsya, and various images of his vehicle Garuda, are all reflections, on one hand, of the influence of early types of Hindu deities and, on the other hand, of local iconographical modes. Although it is difficult to define the exact date of their manufacturing, the style of several short inscriptions and results of C14 dating of the site provide a time bracket from fifth-fourth centuries BCE to about the fifth century CE (Le Thi Lien 2006a: 142).

More developed styles of art and inscriptions are observed on the images found at the Da Noi site. The mythical story of the Varaha incarnation of Vishnu can be observed from several images, which reflect the influence of Gupta art in the cave temples of Ellora, Aihole and Badami (Gupte 1980:

Pls. II, 11, 12; III, 13, 14; Le Thi Lien 2006a: 133, H 217, 218). As in other sites, temple structures at Da Noi were probably built over a long time span. The influence of south Indian art on several human images and the inscriptions of about the fourth-sixth centuries are also notable (Le Thi Lien 2006a: 140, 143; Sivaramamurti 1952: 117, 120, Figs. 47, 49).

The chronology of architectural remains in Cat Tien is still in controversy. All the unearthed architectural remains have been assigned to a long time bracket from fourth to eighth centuries CE, of which the sites Go 6A, Go 6B belong to early periods and the site Go 2A belongs to the latest period of construction (Bui Chi Hoang 2004). Contrary to this, Le Dinh Phung, on the basis of the characteristic of artefacts and architectural features, proposes ninth century, eighth century, and late eighth century dates for the architectural remains of Go 1A, Go 2A, and Go 6A-B respectively (Le Dinh Phung 2006: 249-54).

Stylistically, the images of Go 6A represent the simplest form of line-engraving technique. Iconographical features are so simplified that one cannot recognise the details of head, hands and legs, as well as garment of these figures. However, the body of several images is represented strongly and stiffly with very broad shoulders, slim waist and *samabhanga* posture. These features are close to the stone sculptures found in southern Vietnam, which are datable to the late seventh to early eighth century CE. Although the presence of inscriptions, which are close to the south Indian style of the sixth century CE, these images are datable to the same period as that of the sculpture. The date of early eighth century is probably assigned for the site Go 6B, on palaeographic considerations.

The images of gods and goddesses from the site Go 1A are manufactured carefully and delicately, and by the embossing technique. Not only the details of the face, the body, the symbols and the vehicle are represented but also their mien and divine nature. A different technique, line-engraving, is used to create the images from the site Go 2A. Interestingly, the same effect and even more lively images are created there. Similarity in mythical content and artistic representation seems to indicate that the same sources of influence have come from the art of Western Deccan and southern India during the Pallava and Chalukya periods, with slight differences in the chronology of temple construction. Thus, we can assume that the site Go 1A was probably built in the middle of eighth century, whereas site Go 2A was built in the late eighth century. In comparison with sculptures, terracotta and pottery found from these sites, the temples might have been in activity for a long time, with changes in the worshipping of religious representations and the rebuilding of architectural structures.

It is noteworthy that the number of gold plaques, their artistic quality and their religious content may reflect not only the time of their appearance but also the role of the temple and its donors. In spite of spatial limitation, that make it difficult to represent the religious ideas and stories told, the artists have created unique types of religious art and belief representations for the people in this area. While the similarity in mythical content can be realised from various collections, the simplification and differences in posture and iconographical details might reflect local taste of the people in their religious life.

CONCLUSION

Starting with the very early history of Hindu beliefs in southern Vietnam, by means of minuscule gold plaques, a world of Hindu deities was created to serve the beliefs of the people. These type of artefacts reflect a longer process of iconographical development and a much richer pantheon of Hindu deities than those on sculpture. The Go Thap site played an important political role during the early centuries of Christian Era, and appears as well to have been a religious centre: it mainly provides evidence for the worship of Shiva in his phallic form, of incarnations of Vishnu, and of the goddess of fertility, in combination with local beliefs. Containing more complicated images of Hindu pantheon, the architectural remains at Da Noi site also appear to have been one of the religious centres in the lower delta of the Cuu Long (Mekong) River. Religious activities of this centre might have spanned the fourth to sixth centuries CE, as testified by art styles and inscriptions. The most crowded pantheon of Hinduism has been developed in the Cat Tien area during the late seventh to eighth century. The presence of gods and goddesses and their symbols in each period of time indicates continuous contacts between southern Vietnam and various places in India. As no similar counterparts have yet been found elsewhere in Southeast Asia, this type of small artefacts provides most important information for the study of religious and art history, as well as for the history of cultural contacts between India and Southeast Asia.

ACKNOWLEDGEMENTS

The collections of gold plaques analysed in this paper are the outcome of several excavations conducted by Vietnamese archaeologists (Dr Dao Linh Con and his colleagues in Go Thap during 1984 and 1993, in Da Noi during 1985, in Cat Tien during 2001-02; Professor Hoang Xuan Chinh, Dr Le Dinh Phung and Dr Nguyen Tien Dong in Cat Tien during 1994-96). Research on inscriptions is being carried out by Professor Michael Witzel at Harvard University. The present writer wishes to sincerely thank the Museums of Dong Thap, Lam Dong, and An Giang provinces for giving me permission to work with these collections. Many thanks are also given for the encouragement

and financial support of the Institute of Archaeology (Vietnamese Academy
of Social Sciences), the Toyota Foundation (1998-2000) and the Harvard-
Yenching Institute (2006-07) for my fieldwork and research projects.

REFERENCES

Bui Chi Hoang, 2004, *Tu lieu va nhan thuc moi* (Data and new awareness), document of
    the Museum of Lam Dong Province (in Vietnamese).
Bui Chi Hoang, Dao Linh Con, 2004, 'Khai quat Cat Tien – Lam Dong' (Excavations
    at Cat Tien – Lam Dong), in *Mot so van de khao co hoc o Mien Nam Viet Nam*
    (Some Archaeological Achievements in Southern Vietnam), Hanoi: Social Sciences
    Publishing House (in Vietnamese).
Bui Phat Diem, Dao Linh Con, Vuong Thu Hong, 2001, *Khao co hoc Long An – Nhung
    the ki dau Cong Nguyen* (Archaeology in Long An – The Early Centuries A.D.), Long
    An (in Vietnamese).
Dao Linh Con, 1995, 'Mo tang trong van hoa Oc Eo' (The graves in Oc Eo culture),
    Ph.D. thesis, Ho Chi Minh City (in Vietnamese).
——, 1997, Tro lai Go Thap (Returning back to Go Thap), *New Discoveries in Archaeology
    of 1996*, Hanoi: Social Sciences Publishing House (in Vietnamese).
——, 2004, *Bao cao ket qua dieu tra, khai quat di tich Cat Tien (2002-2004)*, [Report on
    the result of the surveys and excavations at Cat Tien site (2002-2004)], document of
    the Museum of Lam Dong Province (in Vietnamese).
Gupte, R.S., 1980, *Iconography of the Hindus, Buddhists and Jains*, Bombay: D.B.
    Taraporevala Sons & Co. Private Ltd.
Harle, J.C., 1974, *Gupta Sculpture: Indian Sculpture of the Fourth to the Sixth Centuries A.D.*,
    Oxford: Clarendon Press.
Le Dinh Phung, 2006, *Di tich Cat Tien, Lam Dong – Lich su va Van hoa* (Cat Tien site,
    Lam Dong province – A History and Culture), Hanoi: Social Sciences Publishing
    House (in Vietnamese).
Le Thi Lien, 1998, 'Ve nhung hinh trang tri tren mot manh gom o Bao tang Kien Giang'
    (The decorated motifs on a potsherd in the Museum of Kien Giang Province),
    NPHMVKCH nam 1997 (New Discoveries in Archaeology of 1997), pp. 696-98,
    Hanoi: Social Sciences Publishing House (in Vietnamese).
——, 2005, 'Gold Plaques and their Archaeological Context in the Oc Eo Culture',
    Bulletin of the Indo-Pacific Prehistory Association, vol. 25, pp. 145-54, Canbera:
    Australian National University.
——, 2006a, *Nghe thuat Phat giao va Hindu giao o Dong bang Song Cuu long truoc The
    ky X* (Buddhist and Hindu Art in the Cuu Long River Delta Prior to Tenth Century
    A.D.), Hanoi: The Gioi Publishing House (in Vietnamese).
——, 2006b, 'Excavations at Minh Su Mound, Go Thap site, Dong Thap Province,
    South Vietnam', *Uncovering Southeast Asia's Past – Selected Papers from the 10th
    International Conference of the European Association of Southeast Asian Archaeologists*,
    pp. 232-44, Singapore: NUS Press.
Le Xuan Diem, Dao Linh Con, Vo Si Khai, 1995, *Van hoa Oc Eo – Nhung kham pha moi*
    (Oc Eo culture – Recent Discoveries), Hanoi: Social Sciences Publishing House (in
    Vietnamese).
Malleret, Louis, 1959, *L'archéologie du Delta du Mekong*, T.I., Paris: EFEO.
Rao, T.A. Gopinatha, 1916, *Elements of Hindu Iconography*, 2nd edn., Delhi: Motilal
    Banarsidass.

Sivaramamurti, C., 1952, *Indian Epigraphy and South Indian Scripts*, Madras Government Museum, Bulletin, G.S. III, 4.

Witzel, Michael and Le Thi Lien, 2007, 'Gop them thong tin tu cac manh vang cua Go 6B (Cat Tien, Lam Dong)' [More information from the gold plaques of Go 6B (Cat Tien site, Lam Dong province)], paper presented in the annual conference 'New Discoveries in Archaeology of 2007', Hanoi: Institute of Archaeology (in Vietnamese).

21

'The Depositing of the Embryo' – Temple Consecration Rituals in the Hindu Tradition of South and Southeast Asia: A Study of the Textual and Archaeological Evidence

Anna A. Ślączka

INTRODUCTION

Excavation and restoration works conducted on ancient sites of Southeast Asia brought to light numerous miscellaneous objects installed at different locations inside the walls or in the foundations of ancient temples. These objects include precious and semi-precious stones, figures cut out of gold leaf, fragments of metals, inscribed metal sheets, grains and seeds, often enclosed in containers, such as jars or boxes. The number of excavated containers and stray objects is very high. In the course of my research I could trace over one hundred such finds originating from the temples of Southeast Asia.[1] But their number is certainly higher as not all finds have been documented.

The excavated objects have been mentioned in a number of publications, mainly in the archaeological reports. Yet, there was, until present, no publication in which all the information about these finds could be gathered and analysed as a group. Consequently, no satisfactory explanation of the function and meaning of these finds could be given. A few scholars (see, for example O'Connor 1966 and Mitra 1981) suggested a connection between one or other specific finds and temple construction ceremonies. But no thorough study on this subject was ever conducted. The hints as to how to interpret the excavated objects cannot unfortunately be found in the very regions where the objects were discovered. In Java, Cambodia, Malaysia and Vietnam, where the majority of the objects were found, the indigenous manuals on temple architecture and temple building rituals either did not exist or did not survive. The surviving textual sources – the literary works of Java or Cambodia and the inscriptions – do not mention such objects or their installation within temples.

THE ARCHAEOLOGICAL FINDS

Among the objects unearthed from ancient monuments of Southeast Asia, at least two types can be distinguished on the basis of shared characteristics. The first type consists of cubical containers divided into a fixed number of regular compartments. Inside these compartments were found numerous small items, such as those listed above, namely semi-precious stones, figures cut out of gold leaf, grains, and so on. The second type consists of four bricks and a number of miscellaneous items. At the moment of discovery, the four bricks formed a square and the small items were lying in the middle of them.

In my paper I would like, first, to present a few examples of each of the two mentioned types of archaeological finds. And next, I would like to argue – on the basis of the correspondences between archaeological and textual data – that these and similar objects are remains of temple consecration ceremonies, which were performed according to the prescriptions given in a particular group of Sanskrit manuals on ritual and architecture, written and used in ancient India.

Jolotundo

As an example of the first type, I would like to give the stone box discovered in Jolotundo, a well-known site and a sacred bathing place near the village of Pandaan, south of Surabaya in East Java. On the site there is a terraced structure cut into a slope of a mountain. The terraced structure consists of three so-called ponds. In the middle of the central 'pond' there is a stone structure that resembles a small shrine. The site is Hindu and is dated to a year equivalent to CE 977 on the basis of an inscription.[2]

The stone box was unearthed in 1817. It was found buried in the ground, probably a few meters below the small shrine. The box is cubical and rests on a double lotus cushion. It is divided in nine compartments, which are square and arranged in three rows of three. At the moment of discovery, the compartments of the box were filled with several objects, which included a small gold casket, pieces of silver and several figures cut out of gold leaf, namely a tortoise, two snakes, a crescent and two rectangles. All the gold pieces bore inscriptions in Old Javanese script.

Containers with compartments, such as the Jolotundo box, are a common appearance among the objects excavated from ancient temples throughout Southeast Asia. They were found in Java, Bali, Thailand, Malaysia and Sri Lanka.[3] Unfortunately, in many cases the items that originally occupied the compartments were stolen in antiquity by treasure seekers. Apart from Jolotundo, compartmented boxes still containing a number of items were found in Candi Ngempon on the Dieng Plateau, in the Loro Jonggrang complex on the Prambanan Plain, in Karangrejo in East Java, in Candi Bukit Batu Pahat in Kedah, Malaysia and in several locations in Sri Lanka. In Candi Gebang near Yogyakarta, bronze and gold objects were found in the vicinity of a compartmented box.[4] Empty compartmented boxes can be seen on various archaeological sites and in museums. They are especially frequent in Java. In all the cases where the boxes still contained objects, the objects were of the same nature as those discovered in Jolotundo. They included figures cut out of gold leaf, inscribed metal sheets, semi-precious stones, and so on.

Po Nagar

As an example of the second type of the archaeological finds originating from Southeast Asian temples, I would like to present the objects discovered in Po Nagar in present-day Vietnam. Po Nagar is a group of Śaiva temples in the province of Nha Trang, in the south of the country. All the temples of the Po Nagar group have a deep shaft in the centre of their foundations, formed by the interior sides of four very thick foundation walls. The objects, which probably date to the eighth or early ninth century CE,[5] were discovered on the bottom of the shafts belonging to the so-called north-west tower and the west tower of the temple complex. The shaft of the north-west tower contained, on the bottom, four bricks, which were touching each other at the corners thus forming a square. In the small cavity between the bricks a number of gold sheets were found, apparently deposited according to a specific order. Four square gold sheets were engraved with the figure of an elephant. The remaining gold sheets were cut out in various forms, namely a crocodile, a tortoise and a trident. In the centre, there was a golden lotus. The objects discovered in the foundations of the west tower of the Po Nagar group also included four bricks forming a square and a number of gold objects.

Although bricks forming a square and housing gold objects between them were not as frequently found in the foundations of ancient temples as containers with compartments, still, a few other examples can be named. These were found in Angkor, Cambodia: in Prasat Trapeang Run and in Prasat Ak Yom (Parmentier 1936: 283-84; Trouvé 1933: 1130-31).

TEXTS

As mentioned previously, it was suggested that the objects excavated from ancient temples are remains of one or other construction ritual. Yet, partly because of the lack of indigenous textual sources and partly because the tradition of temple building, at least in some of the regions concerned, died out centuries ago, it could not be established exactly which ceremony guided the depositing of the objects in the ancient temples.

Indigenous sources would, of course, form the best basis for the study of the excavated objects. In the lack of indigenous sources, however, it is desirable to search for answers outside Southeast Asia. I specifically think here of India – the region that for centuries kept close relations, via trade and diplomatic contacts, with several countries of Southeast Asia, and where the first Hindu and Buddhist temples were built. Contrary to Southeast Asia, in India, where the tradition of constructing Hindu temples is still very much alive, ancient texts on temple building and temple building rituals survived in great abundance. These texts are written in Sanskrit and date from around the sixth to the sixteenth century CE. That these sources were thus far not used for the study of the objects excavated from Southeast Asian temples is surprising.[6]

The Indian texts that mention construction rituals are either technical manuals on temple building and iconography, the so-called *vāstu-* and *śilpa-śāstras*, or ritual treatises written by followers of distinct religious schools. Further to this, construction rituals are briefly mentioned in certain Purāṇas. For the interpretation of the archaeological finds discussed today, the most important is the fact that one of the rituals described in the ancient Indian texts involves the placing, in a temple under construction, of a cubical box with compartments, and that another ritual mentions the depositing, in the foundation or in the lower strata of a temple, of four bricks forming a square, accompanied by miscellaneous objects.

Garbhanyāsa

The ritual that involves placing a compartmented box in a temple under construction is described in a large number of Sanskrit architectural and ritual manuals.[7] The majority of the texts that describe this ritual originated in the south of India. This ritual has in the Sanskrit literature a curious name: *garbhanyāsa* (in a few texts: *garbhādhāna*), 'the depositing of the embryo', which is the same term as used to refer to one of the Hindu *saṃskāras*, the one performed to assure a conception of a child. The 'embryo' in the *garbhanyāsa* ritual is a compartmented box, especially constructed for the occasion. The number of the compartments is usually nine, arranged in three rows of three, or twenty-five, arranged in five rows of five. A few treatises also add that such a box should be in the shape of a lotus (*padmākāra*).

During the ritual the box is filled up with objects of symbolic value, which mainly include various 'riches of the earth', such as minerals, grains, metals, precious stones, herbs and earth taken from different locations as well as miniature emblems of the main deity of the temple, in which the box is installed. According to the Śaiva texts, the 'embryo-box' also receives, additionally, a series of *bīja*s and *akṣara*s (the 'seed-syllables' and letters of the Sanskrit alphabet). The placing of the objects and the letters happens under the recitation of various *mantra*s. The objects and the *akṣara*s are deposited according to a well-defined scheme: it is of great importance to put the right ingredient in the right compartment. Prior to the ceremony of placing the objects, the box is purified and receives a protective thread (*kautuka* or *pratisara*), which is tied around it. Further follows the ceremony of placing the jars (*kumbha-* or *kalaśasthāpana*), during which either the Guardians of the Directions (*lokapāla*s) or, according to the Śaiva texts, various forms of Śiva, are invoked, and the fire oblation. Finally, the purified and filled up box is placed in the base, the plinth, or in the foundation of the temple. The level on which the box is installed depends on the caste of the patron – the higher the caste, the higher the level on which the box will be installed.

The Sanskrit texts that mention the *garbhanyāsa* are mainly technical manuals and do not contain extensive information about the meaning of the rituals that they describe. Yet, it can be deduced from the few available passages that the principal function of the *garbhanyāsa* is to bring prosperity and welfare to human beings in general and to those who perform the ritual in particular. Besides, in a few texts the 'embryo-deposit' is called 'life' (*jīva*) or the 'life breath' (*prāṇa*) of the temple to be constructed.[8]

Prathameṣṭakānyāsa

The ritual involving the depositing of four bricks is described in more or less the same Sanskrit texts as the *garbhanyāsa*. It is referred to as *prathameṣṭakānyāsa*, 'the placing of the first bricks'. This ritual marks the end of the foundation works and the beginning, after the technical and ceremonial preparation of the soil, of the actual construction of the temple. It forms a part of numerous ritual activities whose aim is to 'take possession of the site', to consecrate it and make it fit to serve as a construction ground. In the texts it directly precedes the *garbhanyāsa*.

During this ritual a number of especially prepared bricks or stones are installed within the lower strata of a temple under construction. According to the majority of the texts, the number of bricks are four and they are placed in such a way that they form a square. Inside the square several small objects are deposited. They are similar to those placed into the compartments of the 'embryo-box'. The installation of the bricks is accompanied by the same activities and ceremonies that take place during the *garbhanyāsa* ritual. It must be added that the so-called bricks should, in fact, be of the same material as the building in which they are installed, namely one should use genuine bricks for a brick temple, stones for a stone temple, and so on.[9]

CORRESPONDENCES BETWEEN THE TEXTUAL AND THE ARCHAEOLOGICAL DATA

It can easily be noticed that there are significant correspondences between the objects installed in the course of these two rituals described in the Indian texts and the objects excavated from the temples of Southeast Asia. The appearance of the deposit boxes excavated in Jolotundo and many other sites corresponds very well with the prescriptions for the 'embryo-box' as given in the Indian Sanskrit manuals. Not only are the excavated boxes divided in compartments, but the prescription that an 'embryo-box' should have the shape of a lotus brings in mind several Javanese containers that have their compartments in the shape of lotus petals. Also the objects discovered inside the compartmented containers, such as pieces of metals and figures cut out of gold leaf as found in Jolotundo, Karangrejo and Candi Bukit Batu Pahat and minerals and semi-precious stones as found in Candi Ngempon, Loro Jonggrang and Candi Bukit Batu Pahat, correspond very well with the prescriptions given in the Indian textual sources. It should be added that depositing images of snakes, two of which were found inside the Jolotundo box, is especially prescribed for structures connected with water – wells and ponds – such as Jolotundo.[10]

The inscribed gold plates discovered in Jolotundo provide another link with the Indian texts. Two of the inscribed pieces bore invocations to the Guardians of the Directions, namely to Īśāna and Agni. Although the textual sources do not explicitly state that the names of the Guardians of the Directions are written down and placed into the deposit casket, as stated previously, the *lokapālas* are invoked in the jars placed during the *kumbhasthāpana* ceremony, which is a part of the *garbhanyāsa* ritual. Subsequently, by pouring water from the jars over the deposit casket, the *lokapālas* are transferred into it. This may explain the presence of the invocations to these deities inside the Jolotundo box.

As with the *garbhanyāsa* ritual and compartmented boxes, there are also significant correspondences between the ritual involving the installation of four bricks described in the Indian texts and the objects discovered in Po Nagar, Prasat Trapeang Run and Prasat Ak Yom. These correspondences are noticed both in the way the bricks were positioned and in the nature of the objects deposited along with the bricks. Also the prescription that the so-called bricks should be made of the same material as the temple in which they are installed seems to have been followed. In the stone temples of Prasat Trapeang Run and Prasat Ak Yom the 'bricks' are in fact large stones while in the brick towers of Po Nagar genuine bricks were deposited.

On the other hand, there are also a few points on which the archaeological finds of Southeast Asia do not correspond with the textual passages. The most important of them concern the material of which the 'embryo-box' should be made and the location on which the four bricks should be installed within a temple. According to the texts, the box should be made of metal while the majority of the excavated boxes are made of stone. Stone is mentioned by only one text (*Kāmikāgama* 31.13) as a suitable material for a deposit box. There are a few examples of compartmented boxes made of metal but they were found in India and in Sri Lanka, not in Southeast Asia. Concerning the location, there is a difference between the texts that originated in south India and those that originated in north India. Four bricks forming a square and housing miscellaneous items between them are prescribed by the south Indian texts only. And, according to these, the bricks should be installed to the right or to the south of the entrance to the *garbhagrha* (the expression used is *dvārasya dakṣiṇe* or *dvāradakṣiṇe*, which might be translated both as 'to the right' and 'to the south' of the door), not at the centre of the building as found in Po Nagar, Prasat Trapeang Run and Prasat Ak Yom. The north Indian texts do prescribe the bricks to be installed in the centre but then the number of the bricks is higher, namely eight or nine. The *Viṣṇudharmottara-purāṇa* seems to allow the installation of four first bricks in the centre of the foundation pit. Yet, it does not mention that any objects should be placed, without a container, in the middle of the bricks.

CONCLUSION

Although no 100 per cent correspondence between a particular object excavated in Southeast Asia and a description of a ritual in a specific text could be found, several excavated objects do correspond with the descriptions of the texts as far as many important features are concerned. The characteristic shape of the deposit box as employed in Jolotundo and other ancient sites of Java, Bali, Thailand, Malaysia and Sri Lanka – namely a cubical box with square- or lotus-shaped compartments – and the practice of installing four bricks forming a square as attested in Vietnam and Cambodia, are consistent with details given in the Sanskrit treatises. The majority of the objects placed in the compartmented boxes and deposited along with the four bricks, such as gold images of tortoises and elephants, metal sheets inscribed with 'seed letters', grains and semi-precious stones as well as the importance apparently attached to the geographical directions and their guardians, the *lokapālas*, too, agree with the prescriptions in the Indian texts.

Burying precious objects in the foundations of buildings under construction is, and was, a well-known custom that is spread far beyond the area of Indian cultural influence. Yet, it does not seem likely that certain specific features, like those mentioned above, were invented in each of the regions from India to Indonesia independently. Rather, the fact that numerous Indian texts describe comparable items points to India as a plausible source of inspiration.

Therefore, it can be assumed that the objects – at least those of the type discussed here – excavated from ancient temples of Southeast Asia are consecration deposits whose installation was directly or indirectly inspired by the Indian ritual tradition as described in the Sanskrit manuals. In the present state of knowledge, it is impossible to tell how far this inspiration of the Indian texts reached and whether it had any implications for the way these rituals were viewed by the people of Southeast Asia. In Java, for example, the presumable modification of the function and meaning of the construction rituals is reflected in the fact that the foundations of temples and even the excavated consecration deposit boxes (not the compartmented boxes though) sometimes contained animal ashes and bones.[11] And animal remains are never prescribed as a part of a consecration deposit in the Indian treatises. The presence of animal remains inside and in the vicinity of consecration deposit containers in Java therefore suggests the influence of the local tradition, which is one of the reasons the consecration deposits discovered in Southeast Asia should not, in my opinion, be referred to by the Sanskrit terms used in the Indian texts.

Nevertheless, the fact that the outer appearance of a great number of temple consecration deposits discovered in Southeast Asia show such close correspondences with the Indian textual tradition, and in many cases, for example in Jolotundo, especially with the south Indian tradition, is certainly significant and may improve our understanding of the transition and transformation of ritual forms as part of the historic process of cultural interaction between India and Southeast Asia.

NOTES

1. Similar objects are also frequently found in both Hindu and Buddhist sites of Sri Lanka. For a list of excavated objects, see Ślączka 2007: Appendix 4.
2. For the information about Jolotundo and the box discovered there, see: van Hoëvel 1851: 112, Groeneveldt 1887: 120, 216-17; Krom 1923/2: 38-39; Stutterheim 1937b; Bosch 1961; Bosch and De Haan 1965.
3. In Bali, compartmented boxes were discovered in Gunung Kawi, in Thailand in

Sukhothai, Ku Bua and Songkhla and in Malaysia in the so-called Site no. 19 in Kedah. See: Damsté 1921; Wales 1940 and 1964; and Ślączka 2007: Appendix 4.

4. For these finds, see Soekmono 1995: 10 (Candi Ngempon); Stutterheim 1939: 106-07 (Loro Jonggrang); Stutterheim 1939: 121 (Karangrejo); Wales 1940: 18-21 and Lamb 1960a, 1960b and 1961 (Candi Bukit Batu Pahat); and Stutterheim 1937a: 24 (Candi Gebang).

5. The temples of Po Nagar have been rebuilt several times and the present exteriors can be dated to the eleventh or twelfth centuries CE (Guillon 2001: 195-96). However, the construction of the temples begun at the late eighth century CE and some of the towers bear inscriptions from the early ninth century. It can therefore be assumed that the foundations of the towers were not altered and that the objects discovered there should therefore date to the late eighth or early ninth centuries at the latest (William Southworth, personal communication). For the objects discovered at Po Nagar, see: Parmentier 1906, 1918: 443.

6. Dagens (1994: 121, nn. 1 and 3) and Mitra (1981) suggested a link between a few specific objects excavated in Southeast Asian temples and Indian textual tradition but these ideas were never fully developed.

7. I was able to find and read twenty-five of them. For the complete list, see Ślączka 2007: Appendix 2.

8. See *Dīptāgama* 4.1cd-3ab and *Kāśyapaśilpa garbhanyāsa* chapter 1cd. See Ślączka 2007.

9. See, for example, *Kāraṇāgama* 4.93, *Dīptāgama* 2, *Suprabhedāgama* 27.3cd-4ab, *Pādmasamhitā* 5.43cd-44ab, *Mamayata* 12.103cd.

10. See, for example *Mayamata* 12.99.

11. It is true that many claims concerning animal remains being a part of a consecration deposit proved false. On the other hand, animal bones were indeed found in some temple shafts, for example in Loro Jonggrang and in the (Buddhist) Candi Plaosan Lor (Ijzerman 1891: 67-68).

REFERENCES

Bosch, F.D.K., 1961, Review of 'Chandi Bukti Batu Pahat: A Report on the Excavation of an Ancient Temple in Kedah' and 'Candi Bukit Batu Pahat: Three Additional Notes' by Alastair Lamb, *Bijdragen tot de Taal-, Land- en Volkenkunde* 117: 485-91.

Bosch, F.D.K. and B. de Haan, 1965, 'The Old Javanese Bathing Place Jalatunda.' *Bijdragen tot de Taal-, Land- en Volkenkunde* 121: 189-232.

Dagens, Bruno. 1994. See: *Mayamata*.

Damsté, H.T., 1921, 'Een Boeddhistisch Rotsklooster op Bali', *Oudheidkundig Verslag 1921*: 60-64.

Dīptāgama, Institut français de Pondichéry T1018, Paper transcript in Devanāgarī script.

Dīptāgama, ed. Marie-Luce Barazer-Billoret, Bruno Dagens and Vincent Lefèvre with S. Sambandha Sivacarya, vol. 1, Publications du Département d'Indologie 81.1. Pondichéry: Institut français de Pondichéry, 2004.

Groeneveldt, W.P., 1887, *Catalogus der archeologische verzameling van het Bataviaasch Genootschap van Kunsten en Wetenschappen*, Batavia: Albrecht and Co.

Guillon, Emmanuel, 2001, *Cham Art*, London: Thames and Hudson.

Hoëvell, W.R., van, 1851, *Reis over Java, Madura en Bali, in het midden van 1847, met platen en kaarten*. vol. 2, Amsterdam: P.N. van Kampen.

Ijzerman, J.W., 1891, *Beschrijving der oudheden nabij de grens der residentie's Soerakarta en Djogdjakarta*. Batavia: Bataviaasch Genootschap van Kunsten en Wetenschappen.

Kāraṇāgama, Institut français de Pondichéry T313a, paper transcript in Devanāgarī script.

Krom, N.J., 1923, *Inleiding tot Hindoe-Javaansche kunst*, 2 vols., 'sGravenhage: Nijhoff.

Lamb, A., 1960a, *Chandi Bukit Batu Pahat: A Report on the Excavation of an Ancient Temple in Kedah*, Monographs on Southeast Asian Subjects 1. Singapore: Eastern Universities Press.

——, 1960b, 'Report on the Excavation and Reconstruction of Chandi Bukit Batu Pahat, Central Kedah', *Federation Museums Journal* 5: X-108.

——, 1961, 'Chandi Bukit Batu Pahat: Some Additional Notes', *Federation Museums Journal* 6: 1-9.

Mayamata, ed. and tr. Bruno Dagens, 2 vols., New Delhi: Indira Gandhi National Centre for the Arts, 1994.

Mitra, Debala, [1981?], 'Observations on Some Carved Slabs and Deposit Boxes in Museum Pusat, Jakarta', in *Indian Studies: Essays Presented in Memory of Prof. Niharranjan Ray*, ed. Amita Ray, H. Sanyal and S.C. Ray, Delhi: Caxton Publications.

O'Connor, Stanley J., 1966a, 'Ritual Deposit Boxes in Southeast Asian Sanctuaries.' *Artibus Asiae* 28 (1): 53-60.

Pādmasaṃhitā (Pāñcarātraprāsādaprasādhanam, Chapters 1-10 of the 'kriyāpāda', Pādmasaṃhitā), ed. H. Daniel Smith. Madras: Rathnam Press, 1963.

Parmentier, H., 1906, 'Nouvelles notes sure le sanctuaire de Po-Nagar Nhatrang', *Bulletin de l'École française d'Extrême-Orient* 6: 291-300.

——, 1918, *Inventaire descriptif des monuments Chams de l'Annam*, vol. 2, *Étude de l'art cam*. Paris: Leroux.

——, 1936, 'La construction dans l'architecture khmère classique', *Bulletin de l'École française d'Extrême-Orient* 35: 242-311.

Ślączka, Anna A., 2007, *Temple Consecration Rituals in Ancient India: Text and Archaeology*. Leiden: Brill.

Soekmono, R., 1995, *The Javanese Candi: Function and Meaning*, Leiden: E.J. Brill.

Stutterheim, W.F., 1937a, 'Vondsten', *Oudheidkundig Verslag*, 1937, 22-32.

——, 1937b, 'Het zinrijke waterwerk van Djalatoenda', *Tijdschrift voor Indische Taal-, Land- en Volkenkunde* 77: 214-50.

——, 1939, 'De archaeologische verzameling, Lijst van aanwinsten', *Jaarboek van het Koninklijk Bataviaasch Genootschap van Kunsten en Wetenschappen* 6: 97-122.

Suprabhedāgama. Institut français de Pondichéry T360, paper transcript in Devanāgarī script.

Trouvé, G., 1933, '[Rapport sur le dégagement du] Prasat Ak Yom', *Bulletin de l'École française d'Extrême-Orient* 33: 1129-30.

Wales, Quaritch H.G., 1940, 'Archaeological Research on Ancient Indian Colonization in Malaya', *Journal of the Malayan Branch of the Royal Asiatic Society* 18 (1): 1-85.

——, 1964, 'A Stone Casket from Satiñpra', *Journal of the Siam Society* 52 (2): 217-21.

22

Localisation of Indian Influences as Reflected in the Laotian Versions of the *Ramayana*

Sachchidanand Sahai

The paper addresses the wider issue of regional culture and localisation of Indian influences, taking into account the *Ramayana* theme in the Mekong River basin. The Laotian *Ramayana*, its literary versions, its oral variants and fine art renderings have been used to illustrate the process in its actual operation.

How do the local Laotian writers, storytellers and painters use the legend of Rama to produce their own social space, locating all the incidents of the Indian epic in the Mekong valley from Vientiane to Phnom Penh? In what way do they transform the Indic story to express the cultural ethos of the Mekong ethnic communities? How do they resolve the Lao/Tai endemic issues of bride price, sibling rivalry, etc.? What is the pedagogical use of the *Ramayana* to teach the local geography at the innumerable Buddhist monasteries along the Mekong? How did the *Ramayana* survive in Laos after the fall of monarchy and installation of the Communist regime, leading to the establishment of the Phra Lak Phra Lam Theatre at the Royal Palace, now turned into a museum at Luang Prabang? While attempting to answer these pertinent questions in the light of written versions of the Laotian *Ramayana*, I would also present the panels of mural paintings of a Vientiane Buddhist monastery to illustrate the process of localisation.

So far four written versions of the Rama story are known in Laos. They are:

The Phra Lak Phra Lam (The August Laksmana, The August Rama)
The Khvay Thuaraphi (The Buffalo Dundubhi)
The Phommachak (Brahmacakra)
The Lanka Noi (The Little Lanka)

THE *PHRA LAK PHRA LAM*

Six parallel palm-leaf manuscripts of the *Phra Lak Phra Lam* (A-F) recovered from different parts of Laos formed the basis of a critical and collated edition of the text which I prepared and published from Vientiane. A manuscript from the village Ban Naxon Tai, 40 km from Vientiane and, consisting of forty-three sections divided into four parts, provided the basic text (MS D). Other Vientiane manuscripts, particularly that of Mr Chan Kam of the Village Ban Hom (MS D) offered readings which closely correspond to the Ban Naxon manuscript. The palm-leaf manuscripts of this text reported from Roi Et, Savannakhet and Champassak suggest that is widely known throughout central and southern Laos and north-eastern Thailand.

The *Phra Lak Phra Lam* is a popular text in Laos recited by the monks during the Buddhist lent at different monasteries along the Mekong valley.

From the date given in the colophons of manuscripts D and E, it is evident that the text continued to be copied in the nineteenth and twentieth centuries. In 1891 and 1934, two new palm-leaf manuscripts (D, E) were prepared by copying another manuscript, one for a village monastery and another for an individual in the neighbourhood of Vientiane. A final colophon at the end of the manuscript of Ban Naxon Tai (MS D) says that Phra Lamma Kumman was written (*khit khyn*) by a certain Buddhaghosacarya on Wednesday, the eleventh day of the waxing moon of the seventh month of the *Culla Sakaraja* 1212 in the year *kot set*, corresponding to the 22 May CE 1850. I have argued elsewhere that the acts of copying and composing a text are normally not distinguished by different verbs in the Lao manuscripts. It appears, however, that the first three colophons in the manuscript D indicate the names of the copyists and the date of copying while the final colophon gives the name of the author and the date of composition. It appears that the present text was developed in 1850 from a smaller nucleus, either from a written text composed in an earlier period or directly from an oral tradition. In fact, the actual Rama story occupies only a portion of the text. The description of Lao place-names, customs, and beliefs has assumed a far greater prominence. The relationship between these two distinct elements in the text obviously implies the superimposition of a mass of details concerning Lao culture on an existing Rama story core. The internal evidences analysed in the critical edition of the text suggest that the *Phra Lak Phra Lam* was most probably composed in the post-1713 period when the empire of Lan-Xang was split into three smaller kingdoms. The text was developed in this period to glorify the kingdom of Vientiane – Lan Xang and its king the Bodhisattva Phra Lam and his younger brother who was the viceroy (*chao uparat*) of the kingdom. Some historic king of Vientiane, Lan Xang, may be behind the portrayal of mythic Phra Lam.[1]

I have shown elsewhere the difficulty in identifying Buddhaghosacarya of the *Phra Lak Phra Lam* which was composed in 1850 according to the last colophone of MS D and E, and Buddhaghosacarya of Pu Son Lan, supposed to be written in the reign of Suriyavongsa (1637-94). Buddhaghosa, the scholar-monk of the fifth century CE, who compiled the commentary on the Pali canon known as the *Visuddhimagga* (*The Path of Purification*) became so popular in mainland Southeast Asia that a number of indigenous writers of the region adopted this name in different epochs. The existence of more than one author bearing the name of the famous Buddhaghosacarya in Laos is in keeping with the literary traditions of the region.

THE CORE STORY

The core story is compact. A Brahma-couple founds the city of Indraprastha (the present-day Cambodia). Their last son Tapa Paramesvara succeeds his father to the throne of Indraprastha. Tapa Paramesvara in his turn, gives his throne to his younger/last son Virulaha. Aggrieved, his elder son Dhatarattha leaves Indraprastha, travels northward along the western bank of the Mekong through the present-day north-east Thailand and reaches Ban Phan Phao. Then he crosses the Mekong, and opposite Ban Phan Phao establishes the city of Candrapuri Sri Satta Naga (Vientiane).

In Indraprastha a *maha-brahma* is reborn first as a deformed child in the house of a farmer and then as Ravana, the handsome son of Virulaha after the proper remoulding of his soul in the abode of Indra. At the age of three, Ravana travels northward, and abducts his cousin Cantha, the daughter of King Dhatarattha from Vientiane, without formally begging her hand in customary Laotian tradition.

Offended, the king prays to Indra for powerful sons to take revenge upon Ravana. Indra directs two *devaputtas* to take birth as twin sons of the aggrieved king of Vientiane: Rama, the Bodhisattva and Lak his younger brother. The god sends a flying horse Mahnikap for the new-born princes. One year ten months old Rama with his younger brother rides to Indraprastha along the eastern bank of the Mekong, recovers his elder sister from the palace of Ravana, and brings her back to Vientiane along the western bank of the Mekong.

In course of his expedition against Ravana, Rama and his younger brother contract marriage alliances with a number of princely families in the Mekong valley. But they refuse to take their wives with them without formal proposal in accordance with Laotian customs. Rama sends messengers to those princely families with bride-price for customary marriage negotiations after he returns to Vientiane and succeeds his father as king.

After his defeat at the mouth of the Bang Muk River, Ravana returns to Indraprastha and sends his messengers with bride-price to beg for the hand of Cantha. Following his messengers, Ravana reaches Vientiane, and after he fulfils all the conditions laid down by Rama, he is married formally and ritually with Cantha, the elder sister of Rama. Ravana dips his sword in water, and drinking that water, takes an oath of loyalty towards Rama.

Rama and his younger brother, Lak, have numerous progeny from their different wives. Sixteen of them are meticulously enumerated.

Aggrieved by the bad conduct of his grandson Ravana, Tapa Paramesvara leaves Indraprastha with his wife, his daughter-in-law and his son Virulaha, and travels to Vientiane where he is joined by his other daughters-in-law, and his elder son Dhatarattha. All the six travel to Mount Yugandhara.

At Mount Yugandhara, Indra consecrates Tapa Paramesvara as the lord of all the human beings and spirits and gives him the title of Isvara. Two sons are born to Isvara at Mount Yugandhara. His four sons protect the four quarters of the universe as *lokapalas*.

In brief, the conflict between the two cousins – Rama and Ravana, has been presented as a family feud between two princely houses of mainland Southeast Asia – Indraprastha (Cambodia) and Candrapuri Sri Satta Naga (Vientiane), tracing their origin from a common ancestor.[2]

THE *KHVAY THUARAPHI*

Though considerably smaller than the *Phra Lak Phra Lam*, the *Khvay Thuaraphi* or the Buffalo Dundubhi is an altogether independent version of the story of Rama. It provides a unique example of adaptation of the Indian theme to the local habits and mores.

Written in the Yuan script and dialect in two bunches of palm-leaves (*phuk*), the original manuscript was preserved in the royal palace at Luang Prabang in the 1970s. The Royal Palace manuscript is the only copy so far known of this narrative. The original Yuan manuscript does not bear any date. The narrative incorporates a lot of local elements, suggesting its prevalence in the region of Xieng-Khwang and northern Laos for many centuries as an oral text before it was finally recorded in its present form. Ayuthaya which was founded in CE 1350 and Lavo which was flourishing in the eleventh century under the Khmer occupation are mentioned in this text. In all probability this is a post-Ayuthaya text, prevalent in the region of Xieng-Mai and northern Laos.

The story of buffalo Thuaraphi corresponds to the episode of Dundubhi in the *Ramayana* of Valmiki. In Valmiki as well as in the present version this episode occupies a very small portion of the story. The fact that the entire story of Rama was known by a title representing a single episode of Kiskindhakanda, suggests the popularity of that particular episode.

In this version, the whole story is built around three princes descending from the same royal line: Raphanasuan, Rama and Phari ruling over the kingdoms of Lanka, Kururatthanagara and Kasi. The kingdom of Kasi seems to be identical with the city of the same name situated in the northern part of Laos. In fact, according to local beliefs, the bones of the buffalo Thuaraphi are still preserved in the vicinity of Kasi.

One scholar would like to identify the island kingdom of Lanka with Langkasuka in the Malay Peninsula.[3] According to another opinion, Sri Lanka corresponds to the island kingdom of Ravana, since the Buddhist writers of Laos are expected to be more familiar with this island.[4]

The narrator includes Kururatthanagara in Jambudvipa. Its location in the mainland Southeast Asia is problematic, though one of the traditional names of Cambodia is Kururatha. Another kingdom, Pattalum in the bed of ocean may be identical with Phattalung near Nakhon Si Thammarat in south Thailand.[5]

After the victory of Lanka, the founding of new settlements in Thailand by Rama is related in this version, as it is done in the *Phra Lak Phra Lam*. It is believed that after his victory of Lanka on his return journey Rama founded the cities of Lavo, Phitsanulok, Nakhonsavan and Ayuthaya in Thailand.

A number of folk legends have been introduced in the story in an effort to enhance the popular appeal of the narrative. Though the legends are quite naïve, they lend local colour to the story. Thus the art of making a new skirt with different pieces, old and new, dates from the time when the wife of Phari fought the buffalo Thuaraphi and her skirt was torn into pieces. Another attempt is to explain why the horns of the buffalo are bent backward and curved.

The process of localisation and naturalisation of the story of Rama has gone very far in this version. The whole genealogy has been recast to give a prominent position to Valin and Sugriva and to locate the important part of the story in the city of Kasi in northern Laos. The episode of Dundubhi being quite popular in Kasi, the oral tradition has tried to bring Valin and Sugriva, the principal figures in this episode at par with Rama and Ravana, the two main characters in the Indian epic. Thus the parentage of Rama has been transferred to Valin and Sugriva, and all together a new parentage has been invented for Rama in the *Khvay Thuaraphi*. The transformation of genealogy to suit the local spatial preferences could be summarised thus: In the beginning of the cosmic age, a great Brahma, Tapa Paramesvara rules over the kingdom of Kasi. Later his three sons Dhatarattha, Virulaha and Viruppakha rule respectively the kingdom of Kasi, Lanka and Kururatthanagara. Dhatarattha has two sons, Valin and Sugriva and a daughter Nang Kasirajathida. Nang

Kasirajathida is married to her elder brother Phari. Virulaha, the king of Lanka has three sons Raphanasuan (Ravana), Phikphi (Vibhisana) and Indasik (Indrajita). Viruppakha, the king of Kururatthanagara has two sons – Rama and Lakkhana.

The birth of Sita and explanation of her name are also due to the interesting local transformations: Assuming the form of Indra, Ravana seduces Nang Sujata, the chief queen of Indra. To take revenge upon him Nang Sujata reincarnates herself on the lap of Ravana. On the advice of the astrologers who predict that the child will cause his death, Ravana casts her adrift on a raft shutting her up in a golden casket. When her raft arrives at the shores of Jambudvipa a sage named Kassapa adopts her. He calls her Sita because after opening the casket he sees inside the little girl raising her hand and rubbing (*si*) her eyes (*ta*).

PHOMMACHAK (BRAHMACAKRA)

At Muang Sing in the extreme north-west of Laos, a few kilometres from the frontiers of China, two manuscripts written in Tai Leu script were noticed by P-B Lafont in 1950s. They consist of twelve and eleven sections (*phuk*) respectively. They represent a Tai Lue version of the Rama story which is narrated on 209 leaves in one version and 216 on the other.

Though the text follows the grand line of the *Ramayana* of Valmiki, there are a number of story elements which make it another interesting extra-Valmikian version. However, this version differs sensibly from the Indonesian, Malaysian and Indo-Chinese texts where Sita is presented as the daughter of Ravana. In one version of Phommachak, she is born of a tree, and in another version, one finds her amidst the flowers of a tree. Having transited through Lanka, as in many of the extra-Valmikian texts of Southeast Asia, she is adopted by the King Kannaka (Janaka) who marries her to Rama. Though Phommachak (Ravana) has ten heads and six hands, each one of his heads is exceptionally beautiful.

The narrative of *Phommachak* is placed in a context which recalls the regional environment and highlights certain beliefs and ceremonies described by the European travellers of nineteenth century.

This epic has for its setting, cities, forests and mountains implanted in a region subjected to pronounced rainy seasons, but also to the heat of dry seasons. These climatic conditions correspond to the region of upper Mekong. Though the text breathes the atmosphere of the upper Mekong valley, it does not actually describe the great river valley, differing in this respect from the *Phra Lak Phra Lam* which is an epic attempt to describe the Mekong River through the Indic theme of the Rama story. One part of the story has for the setting the island of Lanka, which could be identified with Sri Lanka or an island in insular Southeast Asia.

The cities in the *Phommachak* are the capitals of the kingdoms and designate the kingdoms themselves. They are situated in the middle of a plain, surrounded by forests. Always enclosed by a rampart with gates and sometimes by a moat, these cities are divided into two quarters: the one in which the nobility lives and the other where the rest of the population is settled. The nobles, the farmers and the slaves are mentioned in a hierarchical scheme, and the whole population is subjected to a dichotomy of 'elder and younger siblings'.

The daily life of the people and the major stages of their life – birth, marriage by negotiation or abduction, death, etc., as they are presented in this narrative recall the life of Laotian people before the imposition of the revolutionary regime in Laos.[6]

THE *LANKA NOI*

Henri Deydier reported a 120-page manuscript, *The Lanka Noi* (Little Lanka), written on paper with ink in Tai Lue character. The manuscript was in possession of Nai Kon of Ou-Neua. Written recto-verso, each page consisted of 40 lines, each line including 25 to 30 characters. The original palm-leaf manuscript of eight sections was available at Muang Hung, the capital of Sip Song Phan Na in the south-west China (Yunnan).

The narrative begins with Phraya Singha (Ravana), the king of Lanka and his two brothers Neltha and Mentha. It then relates the reincarnation of the wife of Indra as Sita, the daughter of Ravana to take revenge upon the latter for his misbehaviour to her. Prince Bhuma (Rama) and Ramchak (Laksmana), born as the sons of king of Varanasi enter the scene next. Then the usual bow contest in which Phraya Singha fails. Bhuma succeeded in the test and married Sita. The story follows the grand line of Valmiki while incorporating a number of non-Valmikian motifs, taking Lanka and Varanasi as two poles of the narrative.[7]

THE MURAL PAINTINGS OF WAT OUP MOUNG

The Wat Oup Moung, a well-known Buddhist monastery in Vientiane, was distinguished by the mural paintings illustrating the episodes from the Lao version of the story of Rama. These mural paintings depicted a related series of episodes and attracted the attention of a number of *Ramayana* scholars and visitors in general. H. Deydier counted 31 episodes. Vo Thu Tinh described 34 panels. However, no. 11 of Vo Thu Tinh is actually part of no. 10, since no inscription has been given below the supposed no. 11. In fact, the thirty-three episodes are identified by as many short descriptions in modern Laotian language.

They were executed on the interior walls of the temple, measuring 20 m long and 5.30 m wide. In 1938, a Lao artist named Thit Panh made these paintings with cheap house paints.

In recent years, the chapel that contained these murals was demolished and replaced by a new building. Efforts are being made to decorate the walls of this new building with the replica of the same mural paintings with the help of international agencies.

The opening scene of the murals represents the city of Inthapathanakhone (Indraprasthanagara). The house of the parents of Lum Lu, the deformed child is depicted next, thereby indicating that the family lived in this city. It was a *maha-brahma* who was born as the deformed child. The father takes the deformed child to the field and ploughs the land. Indra descends from the heaven and poses riddles to the child.

Indra takes the deformed child to heaven. After many futile attempts to remould him in the mould of *Thaen*, the god gets him remoulded in his own divine mould and asks him to stay in heaven. Turning himself into Indra, the remoulded Lum Lu violates Sita, the wife of Indra. After consulting Indra, she descends to be born to the chief queen of Ravana in Lanka. Ravana throws Sita into a pond and a hermit adopts her.

Thus the first nine episodes describe the early life of Ravana and the birth of Sita in the same sequence and with similar details as in the *Phra Lak Phra Lam*. The earlier life and deeds of Ravana precede those of Rama in both the sources.

Keeping in view the restricted space at his disposal, the artist appears to have condensed the story. Immediately after Lum Lu is remoulded in the heaven, the artist depicts Ravana's attempt to seduce Sita, the wife of Indra. In the *Phra Lak Phra Lam*, however, after being remoulded, Lum Lu was reborn as Ravana to the queen of Virulaha in the city of Inthapathanakhone. His activities in this city are described in detail, particularly the abduction of Rama's elder sister Nang Chantha by him. Later Ravana abandoned Inthapathanakhone and settled in Lanka. Then he visited Indra to acquire magical powers. Indra remoulded him for the second time in his own mould and Ravana became just like Indra in his physical form. Taking advantage of his resemblance with Indra, he seduced the wives of Indra. The frescoes do not illustrate the abduction of Nang Chantha by Ravana. Unlike the *Phra Lak Phra Lam*, the inscription below one panel says that Ravana changed himself into Indra to seduce the wife of the latter. After depicting Lum Lu in Inthapathanakhone, the fresco shows Ravana in Lanka suggesting thus the abandonment of the old kingdom in favour of the new one.

It may be remarked that one of the inscriptions under the mural representation describes Sita as the wife of Indra, in spite of the fact that Sujata is well known as the chief queen of Indra. This may have resulted from an effort to simplify the fact that Sujata, the wife of Indra, was reborn as Sita, the daughter of Ravana, to take revenge upon the latter.

After the above nine episodes, Rama and Laksmana entered the scene. Unlike the *Phra Lak Phra Lam* in which Rama is described as the king of Candrapuri Sri Satta Naga (Vientiane), the fresco represents him as the lord of Varanasi. Accompanied by Laksmana, Rama sets off from Varanasi to win the hand of Sita. The artist has drawn this information from a source other than *Phra Lak Phra Lam*. It is significant that Dasaratha the father of Rama is described as the king of Varanasi in the *Dasaratha Jataka*.

Before Rama's arrival at the hermitage of the sage, the 101 kings make vain efforts to win the hand of Sita. Finally, Rama succeeds by lifting the bow. In this respect, the mural painting agrees with the *Khvay Thuaraphi* and the *Phommachak*, but disagrees with the *Phra Lak Phra Lam* in which the 101 kings are not mentioned. According to this text, Ravana first tries to lift the bow, but he does not succeed. Then Rama lifts the bow and marries Sita.

The mural painting follows the *Phra Lak Phra Lam* in describing the abduction of Sita by introducing the motif of a deer, and garuda's attempt to attack Ravana and rescue Sita.

While in search of Sita, Rama turns into a monkey after eating a fruit of forest tree, and then meets Nang Pheng Si. As a result of Nang Pheng Si's union with the Monkey Rama, a monkey son Hanuman is born to her. The artist mentions at a later stage the fact that Hanuman is the son of Rama.

A couple of panels are devoted to the episodes relating to Valin and Sugriva. The mural paintings offer a version of the career of Sugriva and Valin slightly different from the written versions. Hanuman's journey to Lanka, the march of the troops of Sugriva, Rama and Hanuman to Lanka and the details of the battle of Lanka complete the visual representation of Laotian version of the story of Rama.

The mural painting terminates the story after the victory of Lanka. The post-battle episodes such as the banishment of Sita and the birth of her son are not illustrated, though the *Phra Lak Phra Lam* and the *Khvay Thuaraphi* narrate these episodes in detail.

Though the mural paintings at Wat Oup Moung did not offer an example of a masterpiece, they were a unique specimen of Lao folk-art. With the skill of a gifted folk artist, Thit Panh has depicted the story of Rama in the background of Lao culture and society. He vividly painted the Lao people, their costume and ornaments, houses, and household articles.

The opening scene illustrates the city of Indraprastha with its palace in a purely Lao style, and its streets displaying the serenity and calm of the traditional Lao life. Women are shown carrying commodities on beam-ends, a quite familiar scene in the street in Laos. Some of them are shown walking leisurely, and a man is shown pulling a handcart. Equally lively is the representation of the house of the parents of Lum Lu – a Lao house with all its simplicity and grace, displaying the uniqueness of Lao architecture and family life. The wooden thatch house stands on posts. A ladder takes us to the apartment in the upper portion. The parents are shown swinging their child. An earthen water jar is placed in the corner. As it is usual in Laos, the area under the house shelters the ox. The plough is kept nearby. In the background of this realistic scene of the Lao rural life, the artist has depicted the previous birth of Ravana as a deformed child (Lum Lu) in the family of a farming couple.[8]

THE MEKONG AXIS OF THE LAO *RAMAYANA*

Locating the events of the Indian epic in the Mekong Valley, the author of the *Phra Lak Phra Lam* offers a rich variety of legends to describe the river. The physical and human geography of the middle and lower Mekong emerges accurately from the mythic cartography that the author draws through a string of toponymic legends, connecting them fancifully with the Laotian Rama story. Till the 1970s, the Buddhist monks in Laos recited the palm-leaf manuscript of the *Phra Lak Phra Lam* every year during three months of the rainy season at their monasteries. Listening to the melodious recital of the story, the Laotians were overwhelmed by the exploits of the Bodhisattva Rama in the Mekong. Everyday they learnt about some tributaries of the Mekong, some islands or sandbars in the river or about some dangerous whirlpool or rapids. They heard about miraculous *nagas* and angry serpents and wonderful fish, which lived in the water of the Mekong. Candrapuri Sri Satta Naga (Chanthaburi Si Sattanak) is the ancient name of Vientiane, the present-day capital of Laos. Indraprastha represents both a kingdom and its capital. As the text makes it explicit it is the Khmer kingdom and its capital on the west bank of the Mekong is Phnom Penh in all probability. The dense forests, infested with ferocious elephants and enlivened by beautiful birds, beasts, and insects, the clearings and the rolling rice fields – the whole landscape of the Mekong reemerged everyday for three months of the rainy season. The Laotians refreshed every year their memories of the lived experiences through the recital of an elaborate, accurate and detailed account of the Mekong in the exploits of their Lam (Rama), Lak (Laksmana), Raphanasuana (Ravana) the magical flying horse, Nang Chantha and Nang Sita *who are all sons or daughters born along the Mekong.*[9]

This Laotian version of Rama story swings between two opposite poles, represented by the upstream city of Chanthaburi Si Sattanak and the downstream city of Inthapathanakhone. The mythic description is as accurate as the report of the Mekong Exploration by the French explorers.

Structurally the text is a virtual flow-chart of inter-related movements along the Mekong. The protagonists of the story, Rama, Ravana, their allies and their armies move along the Mekong. The story progresses through these movements, which accurately describe the Mekong, sector by sector, taking into, account both the left and right banks of the river.

In course of this representation, I would examine the local compulsions of the storyteller of Laos to fancifully double the theme of the abduction. It may be noted here that in the first part of the story, Ravana abducts Nang Chantha, the elder sister of Rama and take her as his wife. Rama fights Ravana in the Mekong valley to recover his sister. In the second part, Ravana abducts Nang Sita. Rama fights the battle of Lanka to recover his wife.

It is at the ancestral home in Inthapathanakhone that the family splits. The younger son, the father of Ravana remains in the city of origin. The elder brother, father of Rama and Laksmana quits the ancestral home, travels northward along the western bank of the Mekong through the present-day north-east Thailand and reaches Ban Phan Phao, a small hamlet opposite present-day Vientiane. On the intervention and objection of the seven-headed *naga*, the guardian deity of the area, Rama's father leaves the hamlet, crosses the Mekong and founds the city of Si Sattanak (Vientiane).

Both Ravana and Rama are born in the Mekong valley – Ravana as the prince of the family of Indraprastha and Rama and Laksmana as the princes of the family of Si Sattanak (Vientiane). Rama and Laksmana travel along the eastern bank of the Mekong to recover their elder sister abducted by Ravana. The storyteller takes this opportunity to describe various city-states along the Mekong where the royal brothers contract marriage alliances. Ravana is defeated at the mouth of Bang Muk, a tributary of the Mekong and surrenders to the royal princes from Vientiane.

In the second part of the story, the axis of the narrative expands, covering an area between Si Sattanak (Vientiane) and the island of Lanka. Indraprastha stands midway between these two points. All the movements between these two poles take place via Indraprastha. The probability of the island of Lanka being identical with an island around the mainland Southeast Asia cannot be all-together rejected. But I have argued elsewhere that the Laotian author of Theravada Buddhist persuasion was expected to be familiar with Sri Lanka as the island in question. It cannot be ruled out that the Mekong has been brought within the larger context of South and Southeast Asia and the Indian Ocean through the story of Rama. However, the author of the *Phra Lak Phra Lam* offers precious little geographical detail regarding the extended axis of the story.[10]

RAMA-RAVANA CONFLICT AS THE EXPRESSION
OF SIBLING RIVALRY

The *Phra Lak Phra Lam* models Rama-Ravana conflict as sibling rivalry, so endemic to Tai society as a whole. The expression *phi-naung* designates elder sibling-younger sibling in almost all the languages of the Tai family. In a limited biological sense, the expression signifies blood brothers and sisters or full siblings. In its widest application, the term is used for all males and females of ego's generation. Rather than specifying sex, it specifies relative age.

In the Tai society, the relations at various levels were governed by the notion of elder and younger. The younger has to respect and obey the elder. The elder has to protect the younger. This notion is crystallized in the Tai institution of marriage. The general rule, which governs the Tai marriage, stipulates that the husband must be older than his wife. To express this relative age differentiation the wife addresses the husband as *phi* (the elder brother). The husband addresses the wife as *naung* (younger sister).

In the *Phra Lak Phra Lam*, the theme of sibling rivalry is embedded to give a local colour to the story so that the Lao audience could appreciate it at a deeper level. The father of Ravana rules the kingdom of Indraprastha (Cambodia). His elder brother, the father of Rama carves out a kingdom for himself at Vientiane. Thus the younger rules the upstream kingdom of Vientiane. To enhance the dramatic effect of the narrative, the storyteller introduces the tensions of sibling rivalry in the next generation of protagonists. To achieve his goal, the author picks up a character known only in the northern Indian versions of the *Ramayana* of Valmiki – an elder sister of Rama called Shanta. In the Laotian version, she is called Nang Chantha.

Ravana abducts her and takes her to his kingdom of Indraprastha to be his wife. In the text, both are declared to be three years old. Though they are of the same age, Nang Chantha claims to be elder, as she is the daughter of Ravana's elder uncle. She warns her abductor against the reversal of status:

My younger brother! As I see, I am the daughter of your elder uncle (*lung*). People will call me your elder sister (*phi ueai*). Why do you say that you will take me as your wife? Are you not afraid of this bad action causing your death that you propose to take me to be your wife? Moreover, if you wanted me to be your wife, why did you not negotiate in accordance with the customary traditions? Instead, you abducted me to be your wife.

It is obvious that Ravana is considered younger brother, not because he is younger in age, but due to the fact that he is the son of the younger brother of Nang Chantha's father. The hierarchical position of the older uncle (*lung*) and the younger uncle decides the position of their offspring. It is not the actual age that counts. In actual age, Ravana is older than Lak and Lam. He was three years old when he abducted Nang Chantha. Only after this abduction, Lak and Lam were born to punish Ravana for violating the established norm of Lao society.

The Mekong expedition of Rama against Ravana lasts for seven years, before he could rescue his elder sister and bring her back to Vientiane from Indraprastha. On the eve of the final assault at the mouth of Bang Muk, a tributary of the Mekong, Rama reflects: 'Ravana is so stubborn that he does not stop his offensive. I must teach him a lesson so that he might realise that I am his elder brother. If I do not teach him the etiquette of the two types (governing the behaviour of the elder brother and the younger brother), he will never cease to fight.'

When Ravana is finally defeated at the mouth of Bang Muk River, he surrenders saying: 'Now I beg to be the servant to carry the water to wash the feet of Phra Lak and Phra Lam in accordance with the customary code of conduct for the elder and the younger brother.'[11]

It is evident from the genealogical setting of the story that Ravana is the first cousin of Nang Chantha. Marriage between first cousins is prohibited in the village of Ban Phran Muan in north-east Thailand, as studied by Tambiah.[12] However, the marriage between biological brothers and sisters was always authorised in the royal family of Lan-Xang. On the other hand, such marriages were forbidden for the common people.[13]

So the marriage between first cousins is not at stake in the *Phra Lak Phra Lam*. The cause of tension is Nang Chantha's claim that she is an older sibling. The universal rule accepted by Tai society that the husband should be older than the wife is set aside by Ravana. The violation of this rule is considered as very serious matter, capable of causing the death of Ravana as a divine punishment.

The Laotian version of the *Ramayana* presents a clear case of unacceptable social and linguistic asymmetry between husband and wife. Before they are ritually married, following customary process of negotiation and payment of bride-price, Nang Chantha continues to address her husband Ravana as 'younger brother'. Ravana calls her 'elder sister'. After their ritual marriage, the usual linguistic and social convention of addressing the husband as 'elder brother' and the wife as 'younger sister' is restored. Abduction of the elder cousin is termed as an act of violence (*sahasa*) by the grandfather of Ravana. The grandfather does not compromise. As a protest against the violation of customary rules governing the dichotomy of 'elder-younger' sibling relationship, he quits the city of Indraprastha and goes to live on Mount Yugandhara.

The social norm of expressing husband-wife relationship through the proper sibling terminology has been re-affirmed by the marriage of Lam with nine and Lak with seven women of the Mekong valley.

THE FIRST RAMA-RAVANA WAR FOR THE BRIDE-PRICE

The Laotian custom for marriage requires: the preliminary proposal from the side of the groom, tribute paid for the guardian deities and the Kha Dong, some sort of dowry which is paid by the future husband to his future wife or to her parents. The Kha Dong, which, from the legal point of view is optional, is compulsory in practice.

'Discuss first, then take a wife' (*kalav tan om aw*) is the time tested Lao tradition the *Phra Lak Phra Lam* elaborates at great length. This involves making a formal proposal for a girl and offering gifts termed as bride-price (*kha bua kha nang*) and wedding price (*kha keo kha dong*).

Ravana violates this tradition. Before Rama's birth, Ravana goes to Vientiane, intimidates his uncle and takes his only daughter Nang Chantha by force. In other words he does not beg for her decorously, but abducts her using his authority and supernatural powers. Nang Chantha protests: '(…) If you wanted me to be your wife, why did you not negotiate in accordance with the customary tradition?'

After their birth, less than two years old, Lak and Lam set forth to bring their abducted elder sister from Indraprastha back to Vientiane. From the palace of Ravana they take Nang Chantha back along the Mekong River. Ravana follows them, fighting many rounds of battle along the river to get his wife back. After his final defeat at the mouth of Bang Muk River, he requests Rama's permission to take Nang Chantha back as his wife.

He is advised to return alone to Indraprastha leaving Nang Chantha, and to visit Vientiane again to formally beg for her hand in the customary way. Thus to undo his act of abduction, Ravana is required to present himself at the royal court of Vientiane to formally beg for the hand of their elder sister by paying bride-price. They also impose an interesting pre-condition: Ravana should be able to build a road of earth and stone on both sides of the Mekong (Dhananadi) from Indraprastha to Vientiane to qualify for the hand of their sister. According to the narrator the road was actually built by Ravana before he could win the hand of Nang Chantha.

In the course of his expedition to Indraprastha, Rama and his younger brother married a number of local women along the Mekong. But they did not bring them to Vientiane on the grounds that they had not paid the bride-price. To contrast Rama's ideal behaviour against Ravana's violation of norms, the story-teller gives lengthy description of the six negotiation trips and presentation of the bride-price to the local chiefs of the Mekong, before taking their daughters to the court of Vientiane as the wives of Lam and his younger brother Lak.[14]

While Valmiki describes the India of his times in his *Ramayana*, the *Phra Lak Phra Lam*, the Laotian retelling of the story, portrays the landscape and life of the Mekong valley in the pre-colonial era.

Out of the four written versions of the Lao *Ramayana*, the *Phra Lak Phra Lam* and the *Phommachak* are written in the *Jataka* format. They follow a vernacular indigenous literary genre developed in mainland Southeast Asia, inspired by the previous lives of the Buddha. These literary creations in the local languages follow the style of *Jataka*, but they stand outside the 550 standard *Jatakas* of Pali literature. The *Phra Lak Phra Lam*, which is the major Laotian version of the Rama story, is presented as the *Rama Jataka*. Following the standard *Jataka* format, Buddha himself preaches the story of Rama and in the end compares the past story with the present and establishes a correlation between the past roles and the present ones. Thus Rama in the past is the Tathagata himself. Ravana is Devadatta. Twenty-six other roles of the Laotian story are reincarnated as the contemporaries of the Buddha. In a bid to expound the Buddhist thesis of antagonism between vices and virtues on the analogy of Devadatta-Buddha, the author of the *Phra Lak Phra Lam* had radically transformed the genealogy of the Indian epic. As we have seen, Rama and Ravana are represented as cousins, tracing their origin to a common ancestor. Rama, the Bodhisattva has been represented as a Buddhist antidote of human failings symbolised by Ravana. Ravana, the *maha-brahma* and Rama, the Bodhisattva are juxtaposed in the *Rama Jataka*: Ravana acts and Rama counteracts.

Notwithstanding its general adherence to the canonical pattern, the *Phra Lak Phra Lam* or the *Rama Jataka* differs considerably from the *Dasaratha Jataka* (no. 461), the earliest Rama-related birth story in the Pali literature, which presents only selected characters and events of the epic story.

While the Laotian *Rama Jataka* presents Sita as the daughter of Ravana, the *Dasaratha Jataka* takes her as the sister of Rama. In the Laotian version, Ravana is a dynamic, major character. In the Pali *Dasaratha Jataka*, he is altogether absent. The third son Bharata and banishment of Rama for twelve years or fourteen years due to the machination of Bharata's mother are completely absent from the Laotian version.

The *Dasaratha Jataka* has been structured to explain only one aspect of Theravada Buddhism: the impermanence of things. The *Rama Jataka*, on the other hand, proposes to teach the Laotian masses as many aspects of Theravada Buddhism as possible: the Buddhist cosmology, the ideal of *arhant*-ship, the goal of Bodhisattva and the basic teachings of Buddha.

The *Rama Jataka* was raised to the status of a sacred text to be preserved and heard from generation to generation for the propagation of the Buddhist faith. In this respect, *Rama Jataka* ranks next to only *Vessantara Jataka* whose reading has taken the form of a religious festival in which merit is earned from listening to a sermon.[15]

The transmission of the manuscript of the *Phra Lak Phra Lam* or the *Rama Jataka* by the act of copying is prescribed so that the text could be heard by people from generation to generation and could be treated as an object of veneration for men and gods. 'If you cannot copy the text by yourself', the author exhorts, 'then pay some honorarium to get it copied by a Royal *Pandita*, by a *Sramana* or a *Brahmana* and preserve it as an object of veneration. In case you are unable to get it copied, respectfully request a *Sramana* or *Brahmana* to recite the text. You should listen to the story from the beginning to the end and then narrate it to your children and grand children.'[16]

However, this Laotian version of the Rama story presented in the form of a *Jataka* is a compendium of the Buddhist doctrine and spirit cult. There is almost a symbiosis of the exogenous religious faith and indigenous Tai belief system. The concept of the vital forces, loosely called the soul (*khvan*), the ceremonies of calling the souls back to the physical body of its owner, the remoulding of soul in the yonder heaven to produce different human shapes, etc., have been woven into the story of Rama with such a skill that they do not appear as appendage, but as integral part of the life of various protagonists. Particularly interesting is the case of a woman spirit who had to die and reincarnate herself in the next life as a goddess (*nang tevada*) to marry the Bodhisattva Rama.

The *Phra Lak Phra Lam* is, in fact, the epic of Laotian life in the Mekong valley told through an Indic theme. No wonder that even after the abolition of kingship and expulsion of the king and his descendants from the royal palace by the revolutionary regime, the story of the *Phra Lak Phra Lam* depicted on the walls of the palace of Luang Prabang was retained and carefully preserved in the palace now turned into a museum. Within the palace precincts, one building is furthermore turned into the Phra Lak Phra Lam Theatre. Such is the abiding local compulsion created by the retelling of the *Ramayana*, known as the *Phra Lak Phra Lam*!

NOTES

1. Sachchidanand Sahai, *The Phra Lak Phra Lam or the Phra Lam Sadok*, Part I, Vientiane: Indian Council for Cultural Relations, 1973, p. xxxvi.
2. Ibid., pp. xxix-xxxviii.
3. Dhani Nivat, 'The Rama Jataka' (*Collected Articles by H.H. Prince Dhani Nivat*), Bangkok: The Siam Society, 1969, p. 88.
4. Sachchidanand Sahai, *The Ramayana in Laos: A Study in the Gvay Dvorahbi*, New Delhi: B.R. Publishing, 1976, p. 4
5. Nivat, op. cit., p. 88.
6. Pierre-Bernard Lafont (tr.), *Phommachak. Ramayana Tai Loe de Muang Sing (Haut Mekong)*, Paris: A.C.H.C.P.I., 2003
7. Henri Deydier's unpublished work.
8. Sachchidanand Sahai. *The Ramayana in Laos: A Study in the Gvay Dvorahbi*, New Delhi: B.R. Publishing, 1976, pp. 75-81.

9. Sachchidanand Sahai, *The Mekong River: Space and Social Theory,* New Delhi: B.R. Publishing, 2005, p. 63.
10. Sachchidanand Sahai, *The Rama Jataka in Laos: A Study in the Phra Lak Phra Lam,* vol. II, New Delhi: B.R. Publishing, 1996, pp. 59-71.
11. Ibid., vol. 1, pp. 33-37.
12. S.J. Tambiah, *Buddhism and Spirit Cults in North-East Thailand,* Cambridge: Cambridge University Press, 1970, p. 16.
13. P. Le Boulanger. *Histoire du Laos Francais,* p. 61, n. 1 cited by Saveng Phinith, Contribution a l'histoire du royaume de Laung Prabang, Paris: EFEO, 1987, p. 100.
14. Sahai, op. cit., vol. I, pp. 39-42.
15. Tambiah, op.cit., p. 161.
16. Sahai, op. cit., vol. 1, pp. 9-15.

23

Broken Threads: Contested Histories of Brahminism in Cambodia and Thailand and the Construction of Ritual Authority

Boreth Ly

One of the major imports to early Southeast Asia from India was religion: specifically, Buddhism and Hinduism. In particular, the Hindu religion (Brahminism) established the cosmological and political legitimisation of kingship in the courts of Southeast Asia. The 'brahmins' who preside over court rituals in contemporary Cambodia and Thailand are said to be direct descendants of Angkorian 'brahmins', but this identification is highly contested. By Indian definition and from a ritual perspective, the term brahmin generally referred to those whose caste and gotras (ritual lineage) go back to the Vedic period. Scholars of ritual and religions have questioned whether the 'brahmins' of Southeast Asia were 'brahmins' by the Indian definition, and if so, in what sense.[1] Was there a caste system in ancient Cambodia?

This paper will address the debate and ask what information about ritual and what religious criteria are needed in order to evaluate the status of these so-called 'brahmins' in ancient Cambodia. My agenda here is not to reveal the illegitimate status of these so-called 'brahmins' but to provide alternative explanations for the construction of ritual authority, and to determine who has the power to define and to legitimise the social status of 'brahmins' in local contexts.

NATIONAL NARRATIVE ACCORDING TO *NATIONAL GEOGRAPHIC MAGAZINE*

A series of narrative paintings was featured in the March 1960 issue of *National Geographic Magazine*. These paintings accompanied an article written by W.

Robert Moore, Chief, Foreign Editorial Staff, entitled, 'Angkor, Jewel of the Jungle'.[2] The paintings, by Maurice Fiévet, a French artist, provide a visual, chronological narrative of the history of ancient Cambodia from the founding of Angkor in CE 802 to the collapse of the Khmer empire in CE 1431. The most conspicuous aspect of the juxtaposition of text and image is Moore's[3] apparent efforts to present the events depicted in Fiévet's paintings as 'fact' rather than fiction. For instance, the opening statement reads:

A many-time visitor to Angkor's ruins and keen student of Khmer culture, the author links his 35 years of research with remarkable paintings by Maurice Fiévet . . . recreating the daily life of this lost civilisation. The talented artist's drawings underwent minute scrutiny for accuracy by Bernard [Philippe] Groslier and George Cœdès, French scholars who have devoted years to unraveling Angkor's riddles. The contributions of these talented men, teamed on the following pages, provide a vivid portrait of a vanished people.[4]

In sum, Moore suggests that readers will find in Fiévet's works a visual 'master narrative' of Khmer history.

One painting of specific interest to this paper is 'The Fall of Angkor', which portrays the Siamese invasion of Angkor in CE 1431 and the abduction of the Khmer 'brahmins' to Thailand.[5] In this painting, Angkor Wat serves as the backdrop for the Siamese sack of Angkor (Fig. 23.1). In the upper right-

FIGURE 23.1
Maurice Fiévet, 'The Fall of Angkor' *National Geographic Magazine*, April 1960
(Photo: author, from the Marriott Library copy, University of Utah)

hand corner we see a *naga*, the protector of treasure, who is defenseless while the Siamese soldiers loot all the gold and jewels. In the lower left-hand corner are three Khmer 'brahmins' who can be identified by the sacred threads they wear across their chests. The three 'brahmins' are like trophies, taken away by Siamese soldiers. To the Siamese invaders, these Khmer 'brahmins' were more valuable than gold because they possessed the knowledge of ritual: it was this same religious role, and the power to bestow legitimation, that made these 'brahmins' indispensable to Khmer rulers. The 'brahmins' religious and political significance is underscored by the *Sdok Kak Thom* inscription (K.235), dated to CE 1052 (Fig. 23.2):

> Then H.M. Paramesvara [Jayavarman II] went as a *kurung* on the Mahendraparvata. Then a brahmin, Hiranyadama by name, an expert on magic science, came from Janapada, because H.M. invited him to elaborate an additional ceremony so that it made impossible for this country of Kambujas any allegiance to Java, so that it made possible the existence of an absolutely unique king, who should be *Cakravartin*.[6]

We see in another one of Fiévet's paintings how the artist imagines the ceremony was carried out in the year CE 802: a 'brahmin', presumably Hiranyadama, is shown performing an *abhisheka* on a *Shivalinga*; the figure on the right is King Jayavarman II himself, paying homage to Shiva in the form of *linga* (Fig. 23.3). An additional painting depicts the victorious moment in CE 802 when King Jayavarman II stands as *cakravartin* on top of Mt. Mahendraparvata (i.e. Phnom Kulen) (Fig. 23.4). Accompanying

FIGURE 23.2
The Sdok Kak Thom Inscription (K.235), dated CE 1052

FIGURE 23.3
Maurice Fiévet, 'Hiranyadama Performing an *Abhisheka* on a *Shivalinga'*
National Geographic Magazine, April 1960
(Photo: author, from the Marriott Library copy, University of Utah)

FIGURE 23.4
Maurice Fiévet, 'King Jayavarman II Standing on Top of Mt. Mahendraparvata',
National Geographic Magazine, April 1960
(Photo: author, from the Marriott Library copy, University of Utah)

Jayavarman II are his three 'brahmins' and courtly entourage; all of them are depicted as having a panoramic view of his empire. One might view these three paintings as representing the high and low points in the development of ancient Cambodian history. The ascension of Jayavarman II marks the beginning of the Khmer 'Golden Age', and the 'Fall of Angkor' signifies its end. Perhaps unsurprisingly, the imaginary narrative of the 'Fall of Angkor' is still a topic favoured by Khmer students who are enrolled in the School of Fine Arts in Phnom Penh; its violent and nostalgic subject reflects unresolved nationalist themes.[7]

CONTESTED VOICES

I have visited the 'Brahmin' temple in Bangkok three times: in June 1998, in January 2001, and again in July 2007. The temple was presumably built in the eighteenth century, and it comprises three shrines, dedicated respectively to Vishnu, Ganesha, and Shiva. In 1998 I took the opportunity to ask one of the 'brahmins', named Pt. Pibul Nakvanich, the following questions (Fig. 23.5):

Boreth Ly: Do you trace your genealogy back to the Angkorian period?[8]
Pibul Nakvanich: No, we came from Tamil Nadu recently.
BL: Where did your ancestors settle when they first arrived from India?
PN: King Ramkhamheng brought my ancestors over from Madras to Ayuthaya, but they first settled in Nakhon Si Thammarat.[9]

FIGURE 23.5
Interior view of the Shiva temple, Brahmin temple, Bangkok (Photo: author)

BL: Where do these images come from? [I gestured towards the images on the altar of the
   Shiva temple (Fig. 23.6).]
PN: I don't know. Some say they came from Sukhothai, but others say Ayuthaya. It
   doesn't matter where they came from.

The bronze images of Shiva, Vishnu, and his two consorts housed at the
'Brahmin' temple in Bangkok are indeed dated to the Sukhothai and Ayuthaya
periods.[10] These images were once enshrined in the 'Brahmin' temples found
at these two former capitals. Interestingly, these bronze images are executed in
a style similar to south Indian Chola bronzes. For instance, if one compares
the formal appearance of Vishnu and his two consorts, Shri and Bhu Devi,
and looks at the sway of the hips, the figures are clearly similar to the sensual
rendering of the body found in bronze images from south India.[11]

   Likewise, one finds similar influence in ritual texts that have roots in
south India. Jean Filliozat, in an article titled '*Kailasaparampara*' (translated
as 'Opening the Portal of Mt. Kailasha')[12] concludes that this particular
south Indian ritual text, dated to the sixteenth century, was one of the
major ritual texts for both Cambodian and Thai 'brahmins'. The use of
the *Kailasaparampara* in both Thai and Cambodian 'brahminical' rituals
leads Filliozat to propose that these 'brahmins' came from south India in
the sixteenth century. According to Filliozat, the Thai 'brahmins' trace their
genealogy back to Mt. Kailasha, the abode of Shiva.

   Indeed, most of the ancient and contemporary 'brahmin' priests who
immigrated to mainland Southeast Asia were predominantly Shivaites,

FIGURE 23.6
Pt. Pibul Nakvanich (Photo: author)

and they repeated and sounded out *mantras* from Shivaite *agamas*. In corroboration, Fred W. Clothey describes how south Indian Shivaite texts were used by Southeast Asian 'brahmins':

Contemporary South Indian Hindu temple rituals overseas (and Singapore is no exception) are increasingly expressions of perceived 'agamization'. The term 'agamization' is used advisedly here, for it does not connote a matter of locating ritual texts and following them to the letter. In fact, many of the priests conducting these rituals overseas neither have access to the texts nor can they read them (at least not in Sanskrit). For that matter, Smarta Brahmins (even Tamil ones, for example, in Bombay) denigrate the 'agamas' and evoke the authenticating arche of Sankara, Sankaracharya, and the presumed 'Vedic' character of Sanskrit utterances.[13]

The uncertainty and flexibility apparent in these textual and ethnographic accounts entirely contradict the 'accuracy' of Fiévet's narrative, because the 'brahmins' of Thailand are evidently not direct descendants of the Angkorian *purohita*.

We must ask, then, whether the 'brahmins' of Southeast Asia were 'brahmins' in the Indian sense? More specifically, we must address what we do know about ancient Khmer 'brahmins'.

Scholars such as Jean Filliozat, A.J. Bernet-Kempers, and Dick van der Meij have expressed skepticism about the status of these so-called 'brahmins' in Southeast Asia. This skepticism is directly related to the 'brahmins' having crossed the ocean from India to Southeast Asia, an act discouraged in sacred texts such as the *Law of Manu*, the Dharmashastras, and some of the Puranas. We know that Manu, the law-giver, encouraged the higher classes (and castes) to live in the land extending to the eastern and western oceans, for this was the land of the Aryas, the place that was 'fit for the performance of sacrifice'.[14] Sea travel, however, was discouraged among brahmins for fear of intermarriage with people outside their caste and community.

As I mentioned earlier in relation to the *Sdok Kak Thom* inscription, 'brahmins' were imported by both Khmer and Thai rulers to the mainland because of their knowledge of ritual.[15] Why, then, would they have risked violating such an important prohibition? Vasudha Narayanan provides us with the following insight:

In Southern India, where the landscape is studded with temple towers and where deities are said to have manifested themselves spontaneously, it was hard to live in a town where there was not a temple. When the early Saiva Brahmins crossed the seas in the fifth and sixth centuries CE to Cambodia and Indonesia, they carried on their temple building activity. We may never know if these early emigrants ever ruminated about leaving the land that Manu, the law-giver, describes as that 'where the black antelope naturally roams'.[16]

From an art historical perspective, the invention of sacred geography in Southeast Asia suggests that the 'brahmin' priests who journeyed overseas might have considered Southeast Asia to be an 'extended' Hindu world.

would like to propose two alternative ways of looking at this issue. First, I would like to consider and to develop further an explanation put forward by Oliver Wolters in his paper, 'Khmer "Hinduism" in the Seventh Century'. He suggested that perhaps ancient Cambodian 'brahmins' did not see themselves as living overseas, but rather as inhabiting part of an extended 'Hindu' holy land.[17]

As early as the seventh century CE, Khmer 'brahmins' began to localise 'Hindu' sacred sites in Cambodia. For example, Bhavavarman's Pashupata poet left us with an account of his mystic vision of Shiva. While sleeping on a mountaintop, he dreamed that Shiva brought him to a *linga*. The *linga* that appeared in the poet's vision is comparable to the *Svayambhu linga* nestled on top of the mountain of Vat Phu. Moreover, Chinese sources referred to this natural *Shivalinga* as a *lingaparvata*, and until the eleventh century, this region of Laos – in particular the *tirtha* – was called 'Kurukshetra', the field where the battle in the *Mahabharata* was fought. The name of the *tirtha* was coined during the reign of King Devanika in the fifth century. Even though Wolters' paper focused specifically on the seventh century, this localisation of the 'Hindu' sacred sites in Cambodia continued through subsequent centuries. For example, there is another *Svayambhu linga* found at Prasat Ta Muan Thom, an eleventh-century temple located in present-day north-east Thailand.[18]

Another sacred site established in the eleventh century is the 'River of a Thousand *Lingas*', situated on top of Phnom Kulen. Phnom Kulen was mentioned in the *Sdok Kak Thom* inscription as the Mahendraparvata where Jayavarman II was crowned *cakravartin* in the year 802. The 'River of a Thousand *Lingas*' is named after the many *lingas* carved directly into the riverbed. They were probably carved in the late tenth to mid-eleventh century CE because we know from an inscription that King Udayadityavarman II, the patron king of the Baphuon, consecrated a golden *linga* in this river. Not surprisingly, this river was identified as the Ganga, flowing down to the plains of Angkor.[19] According to Vaishnavite mythology, the Ganga is supposed to flow from Vishnu's toe. *Kbal Spean*, a nearby mountain also has a similar river with *lingas* carved on the bottom of the river.[20]

While the phenomenon of inventing sacred geographies is initially 'brahminical', it also appears in Cambodia in Buddhist contexts, during the late twelfth century. For example, the sacred pool of Neak Pean is a Buddhist site modelled after Lake Anavatapta located in the Himalayas. It is probable that the four tanks situated on the four cardinal points symbolise the four sacred rivers: Ganga, Tarim, Oxus, and Indus.[21] At Neak Pean we see a story narrated in three-dimensional form. It tells the story of a group of merchants who were on the verge of drowning due to a shipwreck, but a horse, *Balaha*, an incarnation of Avalokiteshvara, transported them safely to shore. Thus, a precise geographical narrative is made local in Cambodia: Lake Anavatapta is incorporated into the sacred landscape.

A second possible explanation for the Indian brahmins being willing to travel over sea is to purify the kings of Southeast Asia. As a case in point, a ninth-century Sanskrit inscription from the temple of Phnom Bakong reads, 'A Brahmin who knows all the Vedas came here to purify the praiseworthy country of Kambu' (Kambu is the ancient name of Cambodia).[22] In exchange for the 'brahmins' ritual service and merit making on behalf of the ruler, Khmer kings granted them and their temples the modern equivalence of tax-exempt status. For example, an inscription dated CE 968 from the tenth-century temple of Banteay Srei mentions the founding of the temple by the royal *guru* and 'brahmin' priest, Yajnavaraha and his brother, Vishnukumara, who served King Harshavarman I:

> Of all the merits of these foundations, may the King, who will protect them, receive one-fourth of the merit. If any misfortune befalls the temple, may the Sivaite priest who is the chief, Rajakulamahamantrin and the good people, who shall inform the king seven times, receive half of the spiritual merits.[23]

Judging from epigraphic evidence, it is thus likely that Khmer kings imported 'brahmins' or Shivaite ascetics to Cambodia in order to legitimise their kingship. One of the earliest visual depictions of ancient Khmer kings and their 'brahmins' is found on a seventh-century lintel from Vat Eng Khna (Fig. 23.7).[24] One is inclined to identify as 'brahmins' the group of men performing an *abhisheka* (ritual ablution) on a king who seated directly below a *Shivalinga*, but the lack of sacred threads on their chests makes their status as 'brahmins' uncertain (Fig. 23.8). On top of the lintel, we also see the story of the *Lingodbhavamurti*, which narrates the triumph of Shiva over Brahma and Vishnu as the supreme deity in the form of a *linga*. It is probable that this is an early representation of the association of Shivaite religion and kingship in Cambodia. It is also possible that these men are simply Shivaite ascetics,

FIGURE 23.7
Overview of the Lintel from Vat Eng Khna
(dated seventh century CE, National Museum, Phnom Penh, Cambodia)
(Photo: author)

FIGURE 23.8
Detail showing the *'Abhisheka* of a King' (Lintel from Vat Eng Khna)
(Photo: author)

FIGURE 23.8A
Detail showing a group of 'Brahmins' holding ritual water jars
(Lintel from Vat Eng Khna) (Photo: author)

comparable to those depicted at the foot of Mt. Kailasha, as seen on a fronton from the south library at the temple of Banteay Srei.[25]

Another possible visual rendering of 'brahmins' is found in a twelfth-century bas-relief situated in the south gallery of Angkor Wat. It shows a group of men, presumably 'brahmins' or possibly Shivaite ascetics, serving food to King Suryavarman II, the patron king of Angkor Wat. These figures wear their hair in buns wrapped by pieces of cloth. There is a similar group of men in the procession accompanying the 'sacred fire' (*vrah vrlen*), a political source of power for King Suryavarman II (Figs. 23.9 and 23.10). The inscription identifies the figure seated in a hammock as *Rajahota* (royal chaplain) who is shown in the act of writing on a palm-leaf manuscript Fig. 23.11).[26] The fact that they are holding *vajra*-like bells suggests that

FIGURE 23.9
View of bas-relief showing 'Brahmins' accompanying the 'Sacred Fire'
(south gallery, Angkor Wat, twelfth century) (Photo: author)

FIGURE 23.10
Detail showing the 'Sacred Fire' procession
(south gallery, Angkor Wat, twelfth century) (Photo: author)

FIGURE 23.11
Detail showing the *purohita*
(south gallery, Angkor Wat, twelfth century) (Photo: author)

they might have practised some forms of Shivaite tantric rituals (Fig. 23.12). Moreover, Zhou Daguan, a Chinese dignitary who visited Angkor in the late thirteenth century, provides a glimpse of 'brahmanical' activities:

As for the *pan-ch'i* (*pandita*, in this passage 'brahmins'), I am unable to say what inherited creed lies back of them, as they have no school or seminary for training. It is equally difficult to find out what are their sacred books. I have only observed that they dressed like men of the people, except that all their lives they wear round the neck a white thread that marks them as men of learning. The *pan-ch'i* often rise to high positions (...). The Taoists (*pa-ssu-wei*, Chinese for *Pasupata?*) wear a white or red hood (...) they worship nothing but a block of stone (a *linga?*) (...). [They] are permitted to roof their temples with tiles. They do not share their food with others, nor do they eat in public. They allow themselves no wine.[27]

It is possible that what Zhou Daguan described as white and red hoods may correspond to the headdresses worn by the group of ascetics depicted on the relief at Angkor Wat (Fig. 23.13).[28]

Finally, I would like to turn to the question of caste in ancient Cambodia. We know that only brahmins, kshatriyas, and servants are mentioned in ancient Khmer epigraphy.[29] Ian Mabbett, moreover, in his 1977 paper 'Varnas in Angkor and the Indian Caste System' pointed out that the Sanskrit term, *varnas*, which connotes caste in India, was used rather more flexibly in ancient Cambodia. Mabbett concluded that unlike in India, *varna* in ancient

FIGURE 23.12
Detail showing Shivaite priests with bells and *vajra*
(south gallery, Angkor Wat, twelfth century) (Photo: author)

FIGURE 23.13
Detail showing Shivaite priests
(south gallery, Angkor Wat, twelfth century) (Photo: author)

Cambodia included a person's profession and social hierarchy within the court, rather than simply an inherited social structure:

> . . . the names of all the *varnas* considered [in Sanskrit inscriptions found in Cambodia] could be accommodated to the view that *varnas* were divisions of the population at large; in this view, it would be necessary to suppose that these divisions were largely professional. The names noticed can be seen as those of professions, but they are not very representative of the range of professions actually followed by the largely agricultural Khmer population. . . . They appear to be professions associated with royal service or official ceremony, and unless examples are found militating against this view, it seems more appealing to regard *varnas* as privileged orders or dignities to which favoured individuals were appointed by the king.[30]

For example, the word *varna* might be attached to the prefix *prah*, meaning sacred; and some *varna* suggest ritual functions, as in *Kotihoma varna*, of a person conducting rituals of fire, the *varna* of door guardians, or the *varna* of holders of the sacred fly whisk.[31]

Mabbett's suggestion that *varnas* described the social hierarchy within the court makes sense, especially when analysing the symbiotic connection between ritual and politics in both ancient and modern Cambodia. These so called 'brahmins' were imported to consecrate the king through ritual, and thus to legitimise his kingship. The 'brahmins' remain indispensable only as long as there is a monarchy. Consider, for example, the *Bakou*, 'brahmin' priests who preside over courtly ritual in contemporary Cambodia. A *coup d'etat* in 1970, which led to the establishment of a republican regime, not only terminated the Cambodian monarchy but also led to the expulsion of the *Bakou* from the palace. The return and the restoration of the Cambodian monarch in 1993 required the simultaneous return of the *Bakou*. Olivier de Bernon has argued that, comparable to the Thai brahmins, the *Bakou* have roots in south India and are not the descendants of the Angkorian *purohita*, or priestly families.[32] Only two *Bakou* 'brahmins' survived the Khmer Rouge genocide, but they have slowly trained and initiated more priests; they were intimately involved in the coronation of King Norodom Sihamoni on 29 October 2004.[33] The *Bakou* have now resumed their ritual duties in the shrines situated within the palace compound in Phnom Penh.

CONCLUSION

Dick van der Meij, in his paper 'Were the Brahmins of Southeast Asia Brahmins?' argues:

> . . . Buddhist Brahmins of Thailand and Cambodia crossed the sea from South India, though it happened only a few centuries ago. Like the brahmins of Bali, they lack *Vedic* mantras, *upanayana*, the sacred thread and *gotras*, not to mention more exotic *Vedic* paraphernalia. . . . It seems safe to conclude that the large majority of the so-called brahmins of Southeast Asia were not brahmins.[34]

Van de Meij outlines essential criteria to evaluate the 'authenticity' of brahmins in Southeast Asia, at the basis of which is lineage traced back to the *Veda*. This very orthodox and logocentric approach is highly problematic, especially when considering that the term *Veda* is as much a nationalist construct as Hinduism in India proper: an unbroken history of *Vedic* texts and ritual is a modern construct, directly related to colonial and nationalist narratives of South Asia.[35]

Another layer to the complexity of the situation in Southeast Asia is that most Thai and Cambodian 'brahmins' are also Buddhists. For example, when I interviewed Pibul Nakvanich, he told me that he entered the monkhood before he received his sacred thread.

As an art historian with an abiding interest in the materiality and semiotics of ritual and religion, I propose that it is most fruitful to consider Southeast Asian 'brahminism' from a political perspective. First, a sacred geography is invented through arts and architecture so that ancient Cambodia and Southeast Asia may constitute an extended 'Hindu' world. Second, the 'brahmin' priests justified their travel overseas by stating that they were there to purify the kings of Kambu. Third, both Khmer and Thai kings imported 'brahmins' for their ritual expertise; therefore, the king legitimised the brahmins' ritual authority as much as the 'brahmins' legitimised the king's power. Fourth, it is hard to define and understand the 'brahmin' caste in ancient Cambodia if all what we know of caste system is a list of titles signifying social rank within the Khmer court. Fifth, much of what we know of the contemporary history of 'brahminism' in mainland Southeast Asia coincides with the history of modernisation and the rise of nationalism.[36] In the case of the Thai court, the 'brahmins' participated fully in the staging of power for the Thai monarchs and contributed enormously to the formation of what Clifford Geertz has called the 'Theatre States of Southeast Asia'.[37]

I would like to conclude by looking at a recent wave of Hindu immigrants to Thailand. There is a thriving Hindu community in Thailand, and the Sri Maha Mariamman temple found in the Silom Road area of Bangkok is built in the style of south Indian architecture (Fig. 23.14). Moreover, the imported 'brahmin' priests all come from south India. Both local Thais and Indians living in Bangkok participate in the daily ritual of offerings to the gods. I visited the Sri Maha Mariamman temple in July 2007, and I discovered that all the 'brahmin' priests at that particular temple had arrived recently from south India. Two of the 'brahmins' priests told me that 'the locals [Thais] have *bhakti* but no sense of ritual purity'.[38] Indeed, I witnessed during my visit at the temple, Thais who made offerings to the gods insisted on touching the images housed in small shrines situated on the temple compound (Fig. 23.15). It is possible that the Thais' lack of profound understanding of the Hindu practice of ritual purity explains the need for a sign written

FIGURE 23.14
View of the Sri Maha Mariamman temple, Bangkok, Thailand
(Photo: author)

FIGURE 23.15
Thais and Indians make offerings at the
Sri Maha Mariamman temple, Bangkok, Thailand (Photo: author)

in English, 'Please don't put oil and Don't touch Statues' (Figure 23.16). The sign written in English is intended for all non-Hindus. The teaching of ritual purity (as one of the requirements in the practice of Hinduism) is a slow process, and thus a site of ritual and symbolic negotiation between Hindu priests and the local Thai Buddhists. If one projects this contemporary practice to the past, it is possible to imagine that the 'brahmin' priests married locals and were integrated and assimilated into the local culture; this lent itself to the creation of a new Hindu tradition.

Clearly, the practice of the Hindu religion worldwide is both fluid and flexible, which explains why there are so many different Hindu traditions found all over the world and among different diasporas. In brief, Hindu (or

FIGURE 23.16
View of one of the exterior shrines at the Sri Maha Mariamman temple, Bangkok, Thailand (Photo: author)

Brahminical) notions of caste and ritual authority were, and are, legitimised by local kings. Presently in Thailand, the social status of 'brahmin' priests is legitimised by the king and in some cases, the Hindus belonging to the business class, living in diasporas. There has also emerged a group of nomadic Hindu priests, whose length of stay in different Hindu temples around the world is guided by different national rules and regulations of immigration. Hindu priests in Bangkok, for example, usually stay in Thailand for three years and then return to south India. This nomadic existence is driven by economic survival and thus globalism shapes notions of ritual authority. Priests are part of exchanges of capital between different patrons around the world. Based on epigraphic and other evidence, it seems that 'brahmin' priests who journeyed to Cambodia in the early period of history were an embodiment of capital and symbolic exchange, based on mutual reinforcement of ritual authority and kingship.

NOTES

* The author would like to thank Dr Kara Olsen-Theiding for reading drafts of this paper.
1. Vasudha Narayanan, 'Vaishnava Traditions in Cambodia', in Festschrift for Dennis Hudson, *Journal of Vaishnava Studies*, 11/1 (September 2002): 153-87.
2. Moore 1960: 517-69.
3. Of course, I am assuming that it is Moore who wrote the paper and not another, unnamed editor.
4. Ibid., 517. *National Geographic* continues to exoticize and to orientalise other ancient civilisations by creating highly fictitious and imaginary paintings of past civilisations (see Lutz and Collins 1993).
5. I will refer to the term 'brahmin' in quotation marks throughout this paper because it is precisely this very term that is under investigation here.
6. Jacques 1992: 3. See also Brown 2003: 1-6 and Kulke 1993.
7. Fiévet's paintings became the *Ur*-text of history painting for Cambodian students, and has thus been integrated into a national narrative. See Muan 2005.
8. The above interview is extracted from a longer interview with Pibul Nakvanich conducted in 20 June 1998. I would like to thank Pt. Pibul Nakvanich for his patience and for sharing his perspective with me. I am grateful to him for allowing me to take a photograph of him wearing a sacred thread across his chest.
9. Indeed, a 'Brahmin' temple is located in Nakhon Si Thammarat and many Hindu images are found in the area. See O'Connor 1972.
10. Subhadradis Diskul provides a very detailed and meticulous analysis of style of these bronzes in *Hindu Gods at Sukhodaya*, Bangkok: White Lotus Co., Ltd., 1990.
11. The styles are similar but the Thai images are clearly not carbon copies of south Indian bronzes. One does, however, see formal similarity between the two traditions of bronze casting. See McGill 2006: 134-37.
12. Filliozat 1965: 241-47.
13. Clothey 1992: 129.
14. Narayanan 1992: 147.
15. Suk-Humphry 2005: 4-5.

16. *Manusmriti* 2: 22-24, see Narayanan 1992: 147.
17. Wolters 1979: 427-42.
18. A photograph of this *Svayambhu Linga* is reproduced in Moore 2001: 142. These *Svayambhu lingam* complement the already established indigenous megalithic tradition of phallic worship, *Nak Ta* in Khmer. See the following two books on this subject by Choulean 1986, 2000.
19. Jacques 1999: 357-374.
20. A similar reinvention of the Hindu sacred landscape can be found in the Hindu religion and traditions in the United States. See Narayanan 2000: 139-59.
21. See photographs of this monument reproduced in Jacques 1997: 226-29.
22. Cœdès, *Inscriptions du Cambodge* (Paris: EFEO, 1952): 42. The Bakong Inscription (K. 923) dated CE 881 says: *'Lui qui était pourtant devenu dans son illustre pays le plus célèbre de ceux qui connaissent le Veda, it est venu ici en vue de la purification des éminents pays de Kambu'* (Stanza XV). See also Briggs 1952-54: 177-85.
23. Quoted in Sahai 1977: 133.
24. I would like to thank Hab Touch for granting me permission to photograph the seventh-century lintel from Vat Eng Khna (now housed at the National Museum in Phnom Penh) in August 2009.
25. See Ly 2005: 151-86. A photograph of the above-mentioned pediment reproduced in Jacques 1997: 111.
26. Le Bonheur 1995: 21.
27. Clearly, Zhou Daguan saw the ancient Khmer 'brahmin' priests as similar to the Chinese Taoists. See Chou Ta Kuan 1993: 11.
28. See Thomas 2007 and Roveda 2007 for photographic reproductions of the bas-reliefs at Angkor Wat.
29. See Siyonn, 2006: 45.
30. Mabbett 1977: 435.
31. Ibid., 436.
32. Bernon 1997: 33-58. The *Bakou* 'brahmins' assisted in all ritualistic aspect of the coronation ceremony of King Norodom Sihamoni on 29 October 2004.
33. The coronation can be viewed on YouTube: http://www.youtube.com/watch?v=SMICHYKFuNQ&feature=related
34. Van der Meij 1995: 101. Likewise, Kamaleswar Bhattacharya came to a similar conclusion in his book (1961); see also Narayanan 1994: 72-73.
35. See Hardy 1995: 35-50.
36. See Peleggi 2002 and Wales 1931.
37. Geertz 1990.
38. I would like to thank my friend and colleague, Dr. Vasudha Narayanan for sharing her profound knowledge of the diverse Hindu religious traditions with me. Moreover, I am indebted to her for her willingness to act as my interpreter during our discussion with the priests (conducted in Tamil) at the Sri Maha Mariamman temple in Bangkok, Thailand in July 2007. We were not allowed to photograph the interior of inner shrines and thus only a few images of the outer shrines are reproduced in this paper.

REFERENCES

Bernon, Olivier de, 'A Propos du retour des bakous dans le palais royal de Phnom Penh', *Renouveaux réligieux en Asie*, ed. Catherine Clémentin-Ojha, Paris: EFEO, 1997: 33-58.

Bhattacharya, Kamaleswar, *Les religions Brahmanique dans l'ancien Cambodge*, Paris: EFEO, 1961.

Briggs, Lawrence Palmer, 'The Genealogy and Successors of Sivacharya', *BEFEO*, vol. 46 (1952-54): 177-85.

Brown, Robert L., 'A Magic Pill: The Protection of Cambodia by the Recitation of the Vinasikhatantra in AD 802', *Udaya: Journal of Khmer Studies*, vol. 4 (2003): 1-6.

Chou, Ta-Kuan, *The Customs of Cambodia*, trs. Gilman d'Arcy Paul, Bangkok: The Siam Society, 1993.

Choulean, Ang, *People and Earth*, Phnom Penh, Cambodia: Reyum Publishing and the Kasumisou Foundation, 2000.

————, *Les êtres surnaturels dans la religion populaire Khmère*. Paris: Cedoreck, 1986.

Clothey, Fred, W., 'Ritual and Reinterpretation: South Indians in Southeast Asia', in *A Sacred Thread: Modern Transmission of Hindu Traditions in India and Abroad*, ed. Raymond Brady Williams, Chambersburg, PA: Anima Publications, 1992: 127-46.

Cœdès, George, *Inscriptions du Cambodge*, Paris: EFEO, 1952.

Diskul, Subhadradis, *Hindu Gods at Sukhodaya*, Bangkok: White Lotus Co. Ltd., 1990.

Filliozat, Jean, '*Kailasaparampara*', *Felicitation Volumes of Southeast-Asian Studies Presented to His Highness Prince Dhaninivat Kromamum Bridhyakom*, Bangkok: The Siam Society, 1965: 241-47.

Geertz, Clifford, *Nagara: The Theatre State in Nineteenth-Century Bali*. Princeton, NJ: Princeton University Press, 1990.

Hardy, Friedhelm, 'A Radical Reassessment of the Vedic Heritage – The Acaryahrdayam and Its Wider Implications', in *Representing Hinduism: The Construction of Religious Traditions and National Identity*, ed. Vasudha Dalmia and Heinrich von Stietencron, New Delhi: Sage, 1995: 35-50.

Jacques, Claude, 'Les inscriptions du Phnom Kbal Span', *Bulletin de l'École française d'Extrême-Orient*, vol. 86, Paris, 1999: 357-74.

————, 'On Jayavarman II: The Founder of the Khmer Empire', in Ian Glover, ed., *Southeast Asian Archaeology 1990*, Hull: Centre for Southeast Asian Studies, 1992: 1-5.

————, *Angkor: Cities and Temples*, Bangkok: River Books, 1997.

Kulke, Herman, *Kings and Cults: State Formation and Legitimation in India and Southeast Asia*, New Delhi: Manohar, 1993.

Le Bonheur, Albert, *Of Gods, Kings, and Men: Bas-reliefs of Angkor Wat and Bayon*, London: Serindia Publications, 1995.

Lutz, Catherine A. and Jane L. Collins, *Reading National Geographic*, Chicago, IL: University of Chicago Press, 1993.

Ly, Boreth, 'Picture-Perfect Pairing: The Politics and Poetics of a Visual Narrative Program at Banteay Srei', in *Udaya: Journal of Khmer Studies*, vol. 6 (2005): 151-86.

Mabbett, Ian W., '*Varnas* in Angkor and the Indian Caste System', *The Journal of Asian Studies*, vol. 36, no. 3 (May 1977): 429-42.

McGill, Forest, ed., *The Kingdom of Siam*, San Francisco, CA: Asian Art Museum, 2006: 134-37.

Moore, Elizabeth, *Palaces of the Gods: Khmer Art and Architecture in Thailand*. Bangkok: River Books, 2001.

Moore, Robert W., 'Angkor, Jewel of the Jungle', *National Geographic Magazine*, vol. 117, no. 3 (March 1960): 517-69.

Muan, Ingrid, 'Haunted Scenes: Painting and History in Phnom Penh', *Udaya: Journal of Khmer Studies*, no. 6 (2005): 15-39.

Narayanan, Vasudha, 'Creating the South Indian "Hindu" Experience in the United States', in Raymond Bradley Williams, ed., *A Sacred Thread: Modern Transmission of Hindu Traditions in India and Abroad,* Chambersburge, PA: Anima Publications, 1992: 147-76.

——, 'Sacred Land, Sacred Service: Hindu Adaptations to the American Landscape', in *A Nation of Religions: The Politics of Pluralism in Multi-religious America,* ed. Stephen Prothero, Chapel Hill, NC: University of Carolina Press, 2000: 139-59.

——, *The Vernacular Veda: Revelation, Recitation, and Ritual,* Durham, SC: University of Southeast Carolina Press, 1994.

O'Connor, Stanley J., *Hindu Gods in Peninsula Siam,* Ascona, Switzerland: Artibus Asiae Publishers, 1972.

Peleggi, Maurizio, *Lords of Things: The Fashioning of the Siamese Monarchy Modern Image,* Honolulu, HI: University of Hawaii Press, 2002.

Roveda, Vittorio, *Sacred Angkor: The Carved Reliefs of Angkor Wat,* Bangkok: River Books, 2007.

Sahai, Sachchidananda, 'Fiscal Administration in Ancient Cambodia', *The South East Asian Review,* vol. 1, no. 2 (February 1977): 123-38.

Siyonn, Sophearith, 'The Life of the *Ramayana* in Ancient Cambodia: A Study of the Political, Religious and Ethical Roles of an Epic Tale in Real Time', *Udaya: Journal of Khmer Studies,* no. 7 (2006): 93-149.

Thomas, Maxwell, *Of Gods, Kings and Men: The Reliefs at Angkor Wat,* Chiangmai: Silkworm Books, 2007.

Van der Meij, Dick. 'Were the Brahmins of Southeast Asia Brahmins?', *Mantra Between Fire and Water,* ed. Frits Staal, Leiden: North-Holland, 1995: 101-19.

Wales, Quaritch, H.G., *Siamese State Ceremonies: Their History and Function,* London: Bernard Quaritch Ltd., 1931.

Wolters, Oliver W., 'Khmer "Hinduism" in Seventh Century', in *Early South East Asia: Essays in Archaeology, History and Historical Geography,* New York: Oxford University Press, 1979: 427-42.

Contributors
(In chapter order)

Pierre-Yves Manguin is a professor at the Ecole franxcaise d'Extrême-Orient (EFEO, French School of Asian Studies), where he heads the Southeast Asian archaeology unit. He teaches at the Ecole des Hautes Etudes en Sciences Sociales (EHESS), Paris). He has lived and worked in Indonesia for extended periods, and headed the Research Centre of the EFEO in Jakarta. His research focuses on history and archaeology of the coastal states and trade networks of Southeast Asia. He has led archaeological work in Indonesia and Vietnam and published on themes related to maritime history and archaeology of Southeast Asia, the Indian Ocean and South China Sea, and on the archaeology of Funan (Vietnam), Srivijaya (South Sumatra), and Tarumanagara (West Java).

A. Mani, Ph.D., is Vice-President, Ritsumeikan Asia Pacific University, Japan. Since April 2006, he has been an Associate Research Fellow at the Institute of Southeast Asian Studies (ISEAS), Singapore. His publications include *Indian Communities in Southeast Asia* (1993, 2006) with Kernail Singh Sandhu; *Rising India and Indian Communities in East Asia* (2008) with K. Kesavapany and P. Ramasamy. He has also published various papers on themes related to Indians in Southeast Asia as well as on education, ethnicity and migration with reference to contemporary development. He was one of the conveners, together with Professor P. Ramasamy of the 'Conference on Early Indian Influences in Southeast Asia: Reflections on Cross-cultural Movements' from 21-23 November 2007 organised by ISEAS.

Lam Thi My Dzung is Professor at the University of Social Sciences and Humanities (USSH), Vietnam National University (VNU), Hanoi. She joined the USSH in 1989 as an archaeologist and a lecturer on Vietnamese Traditional Culture and General and Vietnamese Archaeology. Since 2004 she has directed the Museum of Anthropology, USSH, VNU and from

2009 she is chairman of the Archaeology Department, USSH, VNU. Her archaeological and cultural field experience involves field-based research in several locations of Central and Northern Vietnam. From 1989 up to now she has carried out many archaeological excavations in provinces of northern and central Vietnam. Her current research focuses on studies on transformation to history and formation of early states in central Vietnam.

Ian Glover is Emeritus Reader in Southeast Asian Archaeology at the Institute of Archaeology, University College, London. He studied at the Universities of Sydney and the Australian National University where he undertook field research on the prehistory of East Timor. Subsequently he has worked in Sulawesi, Sumatra, Thailand, India and is still researching on the emergence of the Cham Civilisation in Central Vietnam. He has particular interests in the expansion of rice agriculture; in early trade networks linking South and Southeast Asia; in the emergence of Indic-influenced civilisations in Thailand and Vietnam; and in glass and metal-working technologies in the region.

Bérénice Bellina, Ph.D., is researcher at the National Center for Scientific Research (CNRS). She studied Archaeology and Art History of South and Southeast Asia at Sorbonne University and has participated in excavations in Europe, Laos, Thailand and India. After completing her doctoral dissertation in 2001 in Indian Studies, she pursued postdoctoral research at the Research Laboratory for Archaeology and the History of Art, University of Oxford. Since 2005, along Praon Silapanth, she is the co-director of a French-Thai archaeological project in the Thai-Malay peninsula. Dr Bellina's research interests are cultural exchange processes during the late prehistoric and early historical periods in Asia and especially between South and Southeast Asia, and between the South China Sea focusing on the technological transfers and material sciences, State formation and urbanisation.

Phaedra Bouvet is a Ph.D. candidate (Laboratory 'Prehistory and Technology', University of Paris X) [Direction: Dr Valentine Roux (CNRS, UMR 7055), Dr. Bérénice Bellina-Pryce (CNRS, UMR 7528)]. Her studies, based on a technological approach, focus on trade ceramics of the first exchanges between South and Southeast Asia (fourth century BCE-fourth century CE). She is the ceramicist for the French-Thai team of Khao Sam Khaeo (peninsular Thailand) and has studied ceramics from sites of north and south India, and also from Indonesia, south Vietnam and peninsular Thailand.

Boonyarit Chaisuwan graduated in Archaeology from the Silpakorn University, Bangkok, Thailand (1991). His first job as a curator was at the History and Military Museum, Armed Forces Education Department

Supreme Command Head Quarters, Ministry of Defence (1991-97). Later, he transferred to work with the Ministry of Culture as an Archaeologist at the Office of Archaeology, the Fine Arts Department in Suphanburi and Ayuthaya (1997-2001). Currently, he is with the 15th Regional Office of Fine Arts, Phuket. Due to his interest in early port and cultural exchange during the late prehistoric to early historic periods in south of Thailand, he has excavated at the ancient ports of trade on the Andaman Coast.

Agustijanto Indradjaya holds a degree in Archaeology from Gajah Mada University in Yogyakarta and is a researcher at the Pusat Penelitian dan Pengembangan Arkeologi Nasional (National Research and Development Centre of Archaeology) in Jakarta. He is the co-leader (with Pierre-Yves Manguin) of the Indonesian-French Archaeology of Tarumanagara programme in West Java. He has carried out archaeological excavations in a variety of other Indonesian classical or proto-historic sites and is now engaged in research on pre-Srivijayan sites of South Sumatra.

Edmund Edwards McKinnon, art historian and ceramicist is an independent scholar and long-time resident of Indonesia with interests in medieval inter-regional trade; Indian and Sri Lankan influences in Indonesia generally and in Sumatra in particular; activities of the Tamil trading guilds, Buddhism and the arrival of Islam. He has an M.A. and Ph.D. from Cornell University and is a Fellow of the Royal Asiatic Society, London.

Daniel Perret graduated from the EHESS Paris in 1994 with a Ph.D. thesis on the history of ethnicity in northeast Sumatra. Recruited as a researcher by the Ecole franxcaise d'Extrême-Orient the same year, he was posted as EFEO representative in Kuala Lumpur until 1999, before moving to Jakarta and then again to Kuala Lumpur as EFEO representative since 2007.

His researches are focused on ancient settlements of the Malay World, and more generally on the history of the western Malaya World (Sumatra and Peninsular Malaysia) until the nineteenth century. Since 1994, he has conducted fieldworks and published in cooperation with various local institutions on the following topics: old fortifications and tombstones in Malaysia, the history of Barus and Padang Lawas in North Sumatra, and the history of the sultanate of Patani in Thailand.

Heddy Surachman graduate from Universitas Udayana (Bali) in 1991 and was recruited as an archaeologist by the National Centre for Archaeological Research of Indonesia the following year (currently Pusat Penelitian dan Pengembangan Arkeologi Nasional). He has conducted many surveys and excavations all over the Indonesian archipelago, and has been working in cooperation with the EFEO in North Sumatra since 1997.

K. Rajan, Department of History, Pondicherry University, Pondicherry, is known for his extensive archaeological explorations discovering around 1,500 archaeological sites ranging from palaeolithic times down to early historic phase. He actively participated in archaeological excavations at Appukallu, Ramapuram, Kodumanal, Poompuhar and Dwarka. Besides, he directed excavations at Mayiladumparai, Thandikudi and Porunthal. He had twelve books and more than 75 articles to his credit and completed 15 major research projects funded by UGC, INSA, ICHR, ASI and CIIL.

V. Selvakumar is currently working as Assistant Professor in the Department of Epigraphy and Archaeology, Tamil University, Thanjavur, Tamil Nadu, India. He completed doctoral and postdoctoral research from Deccan College, Pune, India. He worked at Centre for Heritage Studies, Kerala for four years. His research interests are archaeology of south India, archaeological theory, heritage management, ethnoarchaeology and Indian Ocean studies.

Sundaresh has worked at the National Institute of Oceanography, Goa, since 1989, and has carried out extensive research in the field of Marine Archaeology. He has participated in an international expedition for the study of submerged structures in Japan waters. He has more than 70 research papers to his credit. He has also co-authored two books *Archaeology of Bet Dwarka* (2005) and *Underwater Archaeology of Dwarka and Somnath*. A large number of research papers have been published by him in reputed Scientific and Archaeological journals.

A.S. Gaur has worked at the National Institute of Oceanography, Goa since 1988, has carried out extensive research in the field of Marine Archaeology. He has authored a book *Harappan Maritime Legacies of Gujarat* (2000) and co-authored two books *Archaeology of Bet Dwarka* (2005) and *Underwater Archaeology of Dwarka and Somnath*. He has also co-edited two books. A large number of research papers have been published by him in National and International reputed Scientific and Archaeological journals.

John Guy is Curator of South and Southeast Asian Art at the Metropolitan Museum of Art, New York, and an elected Fellow of the Society of Antiquaries, London. His research focuses on Hindu-Buddhist sculpture and devotional worship in both India and early Southeast Asia. He has worked on a number of archaeological excavations, at both land and maritime sites, and served as an advisor to UNESCO on historical sites in Southeast Asia. Publications include *Indian Art and Connoisseurship* (1995), *Vietnamese Ceramics: A Separate Tradition* (1997), *Woven Cargoes: Indian Textiles in the East* (1998, 2009) and *Indian Temple Sculpture* (2007), and he has curated and contributed to many exhibitions, including Cholas Bronzes of Southern India (Royal Academy

2006), La Escultura en Los Templos Indios (Barcelona 2007) and Buddhist Manuscript Painting (Metropolitan Museum of Art 2008).

Johannes Bronkhorst is Professor of Sanskrit and Indian studies at the University of Lausanne, Switzerland, since 1987. Numerous publications on the history of Indian philosophical and scientific thought in the broadest sense; many are listed on the following site: http://www.unil.ch/orient/page5552_fr.html. Most notable recent publication: *Greater Magadha* (2007).

Daud Ali, Ph.D., is Senior Lecturer in early and medieval Indian History at the School of Oriental and African Studies (SOAS), University of London. He is author of *Courtly Culture and Political Life in Early Medieval India* (2004). He has also co-authored, with Ronald Inden and Jonathan Walters, *Querying the Medieval: Texts and the History of Practice in South Asia* (2000), and edited *Invoking the Past: the Uses of History in South Asia* (1999).

Julie Romain is currently a Ph.D. candidate in the UCLA Art History program, and is studying stylistic transitions in Indian temple sculpture between the sixth and eighth century. She received her Master's degree from University of Chicago in 2001, where she wrote her Master's thesis on 'Indianness, Art and Imperial Identity at the 1924 British Empire Exhibition'. Julie has also been a member of the South and Southeast Asian Department at the Los Angeles County Museum of Art since 2003.

Robert L. Brown is Professor of Indian and Southeast Asian Art History at the University of California, Los Angeles, and Curator of South and Southeast Asian Art at the Los Angeles County Museum of Art. His publications include a number of books and articles on Buddhist and Hindu art, on the nature of Indian artistic influence in Southeast Asia, and on the colonial and Western basis for art historical understanding of India.

Martin Polkinghorne, Ph.D., is an Honorary Associate of the Department of Asian Studies, School of Languages and Cultures, The University of Sydney. In 2009 he undertook an Australian Government Endeavour Postdoctoral fellowship based in Cambodia. His current research focuses on the artistic workshops and individual artists of medieval mainland Southeast Asia.

Arsenio Nicolas, Ph.D., is a Senior Lecturer at the College of Music, Archaeological Studies Program, Department of Anthropology and Center for International Studies, University of the Philippines. His field studies started in the Philippines (since 1972), Java (1979-84), Bali (1985-86), Thailand (1986), Sabah (1987), West Malaysia (1989-91), Japan (1991-92), and USA

(1999-2007). His current interests include music archaeology, anthropology of religion, music composition, literature, dance, music psychology and bio-musicology.

Peter Skilling is Maître de Conférences with the École française d'Extrême-Orient, Bangkok. He has been visiting professor at Harvard, Oxford, Berkeley, and Sydney. He is Special Lecturer at Chulalongkorn University and Honorary Associate, Department of Indian Subcontinental Studies, University of Sydney. His publications include *Mahasutras: Great Discourses of the Buddha* (1994, 1997), and he is the editor of *Wat Si Chum, Sukhothai* (2008), for which he was awarded the Ikuo Hirayama Prize, Académie des Inscriptions et Belle-Lettres, Paris.

Kyaw Minn Htin graduated in Metallurgical Engineering from Yangon Technological University and obtained the degrees of Master of Arts and Master of Research in Archaeology from Yangon University. He is currently working as Research Assistant at the Ecole française d'Extrême-Orient (EFEO) in Yangon, Myanmar. He participated in the excavation at Batujaya in West Java, Indonesia, under the supervision of Professor Pierre-Yves Manguin. He has presented papers on Archaeology in several international conferences on Southeast Asian Studies.

Le Thi Lien, Ph.D. in Archaeology, is Senior Researcher and Assistant in International Cooperation at the Institute of Archaeology (Vietnamese Academy of Social Sciences). Her field of interest includes the 'Archaeology of Historical period in Vietnam, Ancient Sino-Nom', 'Buddhist and Hindu Art in Vietnam and Southeast Asia', and 'Archaeology of Oc Eo culture (in Southern Vietnam)'. She has published more than 80 papers (in Vietnamese and English), including a book *Nghe thuat Phat giao va Hindu giao o Dong Bang song Cuu Long truoc the ki 10* (Buddhist and Hindu Art in the Cuu Long River Delta prior to 10th century AD) (2006).

Anna A Ślączka, Ph.D. in Indology, Leiden University, the Netherlands, was a research fellow at the Research School for Asian, African and Amerindian Studies (CNWS) and later at the International Institute for Asian Studies (IIAS) in Leiden. She lectured at Leiden University (Sanskrit and South Asian art). At present she is a curator of South Asian art at the National Museum (the Rijksmuseum) in Amsterdam.

Sachchidanand Sahai is a cultural historian of Southeast Asia, well-known for his work *Les institutions politiques et l'organisation administrative du Cambodge ancien* (1970). To his credit are thirty volumes of *Southeast Asian*

Review of which he is the founder editor, besides a number of books on Laos, Thailand and Cambodia authored by him. Currently Professor Sahai is Advisor to Apsara National Authority and Preah Vihear National Authority, Government of Cambodia.

Boreth Ly is Assistant Professor of Southeast Asian Art History and Visual Culture at the University of California, Santa Cruz. He was born in Phnom Penh, Cambodia and was educated in Paris and United States. His research interests are grounded in both ancient and contemporary arts of Southeast Asia and its diaspora. Some of the topics that he has written about are Buddhist and Hindu visual narrative arts, films, and performance as well as representations of gender, sexuality, and the body.

Index

CPSIA information can be obtained
at www.ICGtesting.com
Printed in the USA
LVOW08s1521241217
560723LV00001B/56/P